INTERNATIONAL
POLITICAL
ECONOMY

FIFTH EDITION

FIFTH EDITION

INTERNATIONAL POLITICAL ECONOMY

Perspectives on Global Power and Wealth

Jeffry A. Frieden
HARVARD UNIVERSITY

David A. Lake
UNIVERSITY OF CALIFORNIA, SAN DIEGO

J. Lawrence Broz
UNIVERSITY OF CALIFORNIA, SAN DIEGO

W. W. Norton & Company ■ New York ■ London

W. W. Norton & Company has been independent since its founding in 1923, when William Warder Norton and Mary D. Herter Norton first published lectures delivered at the People's Institute, the adult education division of New York City's Cooper Union. The firm soon expanded its program beyond the Institute, publishing books by celebrated academics from America and abroad. By midcentury, the two major pillars of Norton's publishing program—trade books and college texts—were firmly established. In the 1950s, the Norton family transferred control of the company to its employees, and today—with a staff of four hundred and a comparable number of trade, college, and professional titles published each year—W. W. Norton & Company stands as the largest and oldest publishing house owned wholly by its employees.

The text of this book is composed in New Aster
with the display set in Akzidenz Grotesk
Project supervised by the Westchester Book Group / Susan Baker.
Manufacturing by the Maple Press—York, PA.
Senior Production Manager, College: Benjamin Reynolds.

Library of Congress Cataloging-in-Publication Data

International political economy : perspectives on global power and wealth / [edited by] Jeffry A. Frieden, David A. Lake, J. Lawrence Broz. — 5th ed.
     p.   cm.
   Includes bibliographical references and index.
   ISBN 978-0-393-93505-9 (pbk.)
   1. International economic relations.   I. Frieden, Jeffry A.   II. Lake, David A., 1956–
III. Broz, J. Lawrence.
   HF1411.I51757   2009
   337—dc22   2009042585

W. W. Norton & Company, Inc., 500 Fifth Avenue, New York, N.Y. 10110-0017
www.wwnorton.com

W. W. Norton & Company Ltd., Castle House, 75/76 Wells Street, London W1T 3QT

1   2   3   4   5   6   7   8   9   0

CONTENTS

III PRODUCTION 153

IV MONEY AND FINANCE 217

V TRADE 337

VI ECONOMIES IN DEVELOPMENT 443

VII CURRENT PROBLEMS IN INTERNATIONAL POLITICAL ECONOMY 505

PREFACE

The readings in *International Political Economy: Perspectives on Global Power and Wealth* are primarily intended to introduce the study of international political economy to those with little or no prior knowledge of it. The book is designed for use in courses in international political economy, international relations, and international economics. The selections present both clear and identifiable theoretical arguments and important substantive material. Eighteen of the thirty-two articles are new to this fifth edition of our book.

Although the selections can be read in any order, they are grouped into seven parts that reflect some of the more common organizing principles used in international political economy courses. Each part begins with an introduction by the editors that provides background information and highlights issues raised in the readings. Each reading is preceded by an abstract summarizing its specific arguments and contributions. The readings have been edited to eliminate extraneous or dated information, and most footnotes were removed.

The introduction defines the study of international political economy, summarizes major analytical frameworks in the field, and identifies several current debates. To capture the most important work and current debates in the international political economy, we highlight the analytic tensions between international and domestic explanations, on the one hand, and institutionalist- and society-centered explanations, on the other. These two dimensions create four distinct views, which we refer to as the international political, international economic, domestic institutionalist, and domestic societal approaches. Part I presents examples of these different perspectives on international political economy. The readings in this part are intended to suggest the underlying logic and types of arguments used by proponents of each approach. Although they are representative of their respective schools, they do not necessarily capture the wide range of opinion within each approach.

Part II, which reviews the history of the international economy since the nineteenth century, provides the background and perspective necessary to understand the contemporary international political economy. The selections describe the major developments in the history of the modern international economy from a variety of different theoretical viewpoints.

The remainder of the book is devoted to the modern international political economy. Separate sections on production, money and finance, and trade look at the principal issue areas associated with the politics of international economic relations. Part VI focuses on the particular political and economic problems of developing economies. Finally, Part VII examines current problems in the politics of international economics.

The selections in this volume have been used successfully in our courses on international political economy at the University of California, Los Angeles; Harvard University; and the University of California, San Diego. In our own research, we approach the study of international political economy from very different perspectives. Yet, we find that this set of readings accommodates our individual approaches to the subject matter while simultaneously covering the major questions of the field.

For this edition, we thank Ann Shin, our editor at W. W. Norton & Company, for helping prepare the manuscript for publication. We also thank our respective spouses, Anabela Costa, Wendy K. Lake, and Rebecca L. Webb, for their continuing encouragement.

JEFFRY A. FRIEDEN
DAVID A. LAKE
J. LAWRENCE BROZ

ABOUT THE EDITORS

JEFFRY A. FRIEDEN (Ph.D., Columbia University) is professor of government at Harvard University. He specializes in the political economy of international monetary and financial relations. His book publications include *Global Capitalism: Its Fall and Rise in the Twentieth Century* (2006), *Debt, Development, and Democracy: Modern Political Economy and Latin America, 1965–1985* (1991), and *Banking on the World: The Politics of American International Finance* (1987).

DAVID A. LAKE (Ph.D., Cornell University) is distinguished professor of political science at the University of California, San Diego. He has published widely in the field of international relations and international political economy. His principal book publications include *Power, Protection, and Free Trade: International Sources of U.S. Commercial Strategy, 1887–1939* (1988), *Entangling Relations: American Foreign Policy in Its Century* (1999), and *Hierarchy in International Relations* (2009).

J. LAWRENCE BROZ (Ph.D., University of California, Los Angeles) is associate professor of political science and director of graduate studies at the University of California, San Diego. He studies the institutions that regulate national and international monetary and financial relations: central banks, exchange rate regimes, and international financial institutions. He is the author of *International Origins of the Federal Reserve System* (1997).

INTERNATIONAL
POLITICAL
ECONOMY

FIFTH EDITION

INTRODUCTION

International Politics and International Economics

During the past forty years, the study of international political economy has undergone a remarkable resurgence. Virtually nonexistent as a field of study before 1970, it is now a popular area of specialization for both undergraduates and graduate students, as well as the source of much innovative and influential scholarship. The revival of international political economy after nearly forty years of dormancy has enriched both social science and public debate, and promises to continue to do so.

International political economy is the study of the interplay of economics and politics in the world arena. In the most general sense, the economy can be defined as the system of producing, distributing, and using wealth; politics is the set of institutions and rules by which social and economic interactions are governed. *Political economy* has a variety of meanings. For some, it refers primarily to the study of the political basis of economic actions—the ways that government policies affect market operations. For others, the principal preoccupation is the economic basis of political action—the ways that economic forces mold government policies. The two focuses are, in a sense, complementary, for politics and markets are in a constant state of mutual interaction.

Most markets are governed by certain fundamental laws that operate more or less independently of the will of firms and individuals. Any shopkeeper knows that an attempt to raise the price of a readily available and standardized product—a pencil, for example—above that charged by nearby and competing shopkeepers will rapidly cause customers to stop buying pencils at the higher price. Unless the shopkeeper wants to be left with piles of unsold pencils, he or she will have to bring the price back into line with "what the market will bear." The shopkeeper will have learned a microcosmic lesson in what economists call *market-clearing equilibrium*, the price at which the number of goods supplied equals the number demanded—the point at which supply and demand curves intersect.

At the base of all modern economics is the general assertion that, within certain carefully specified parameters, markets operate in and of themselves to maintain balance between supply and demand. Other things being equal, if the supply of a good increases far beyond the demand for it, the good's price will be driven down until demand rises to meet supply, supply falls to

1

meet demand, and market-clearing equilibrium is restored. By the same token, if demand exceeds supply, the good's price will rise, thus causing demand to decline and supply to increase until the two are in balance.

If the international and domestic economies functioned as perfectly competitive markets, they would be relatively easy to describe and comprehend. But such markets are only highly stylized or abstract models, which are rarely reproduced in the real world. A variety of factors influence the workings of domestic and international markets in ways that a focus on perfectly competitive and unchanging market forces does not fully capture. Consumer tastes can change—how large is the American market for spats or sarsaparilla today?—as can the technology needed to make products more cheaply, or even to make entirely new goods that displace others (stick shifts for horsewhips, computers for slide rules). Producers, sellers, or buyers of goods can band together to try to raise or lower prices unilaterally, as the Organization of Petroleum Exporting Countries (OPEC) has done with petroleum since 1973. And governments can act, consciously or inadvertently, to alter patterns of consumption, supply, demand, prices, and virtually all other economic variables.

This last fact—the impact of policy and politics on economic trends—is the most visible, and probably the most important, reason to look beyond market-based, purely economic explanations of social behavior. Indeed, many market-oriented economists are continually surprised by the ability of governments or of powerful groups pressuring governments to contravene economic tendencies. When OPEC first raised oil prices in December 1973, some market-minded pundits, and even a few naive economists, predicted that such naked manipulation of the forces of supply and demand could last only a matter of months. However, what has emerged from more than forty years' experience with oil prices is the recognition that they are a function of both market forces and the ability of OPEC's member states to organize concerted intervention in the oil market.

Somewhat less dramatic are the everyday operations of local and national governments, which affect prices, production, profits, wages, and almost every other aspect of the economy. Wage, price, and rent controls; taxation; incentives and subsidies; tariffs and other barriers to trade; and government spending all serve to mold modern economies and the functioning of markets themselves. Who could understand the suburbanization of the United States after World War II without taking into account government tax incentives to home mortgage holders, government-financed highway construction, and politically driven patterns of local educational expenditures? How many American (or Japanese or European) farmers would be left if agricultural subsidies were eliminated? How many Americans would have college educations were it not for public universities, government scholarships and publicly subsidized student loans, and tax exemptions for private universities? Who could explain the proliferation of nonprofit groups in the United States without knowing the tax incentives given to charitable donations?

In these instances and many more, political pressure groups, politicians, and government bureaucrats have at least as much effect on economic outcomes as do the laws of the marketplace. Social scientists, especially political scientists, have spent decades trying to understand how these political pressures interact to produce government policy. Many of the results provide as elegant and stylized a view of politics as the economics profession has developed of markets. As in economics, however, social science models of political behavior are little more than didactic devices whose accuracy depends on a wide variety of unpredictable factors, including underlying economic trends. If an economist would be equally foolish to dismiss the possibilities of intergovernmental producers' cartels (such as OPEC) out of hand, a political scientist would be foolish not to realize that the economic realities of modern international commodity markets ensure that successful producers' cartels will be few and far between.

It is thus no surprise that political economy is far from new. Indeed, until a century ago, virtually all thinkers concerned with understanding human society wrote about political economy. For individuals as diverse as Adam Smith, John Stuart Mill, and Karl Marx, the economy was eminently political and politics was obviously tied to economic phenomena. Few scholars before 1900 would have taken seriously any attempt to describe and analyze politics and economics independently of each other.

Around the turn of the century, however, professional studies of economics and politics became increasingly divorced from one another. Economic investigation began to focus on understanding more fully the operation of specific markets and their interaction; the development of new mathematical techniques permitted the formalization of, for example, laws of supply and demand. By the time of World War I, an economics profession per se was in existence, and its attention was focused on understanding the operation of economic activities in and of themselves. At the same time, other scholars were looking increasingly at the political realm in isolation from the economy. The rise of modern representative political institutions, mass political parties, more politically informed populations, and modern bureaucracies all seemed to justify the study of politics as an activity that had a logic of its own.

With the exception of a few isolated individuals and an upsurge of interest during the politically and economically troubled Depression years, the twentieth century saw an increasing separation of the study of economics from that of politics. Economists developed ever more elaborate and sophisticated models of how economies work, and similarly, political scientists spun out ever more complex theories of political development and activity.

The resurgence of political economy after 1970 had two interrelated sources. The first was dissatisfaction among academics with the gap between abstract models of political and economic behavior, on the one hand, and the actual behavior of polities and economies, on the other. Theory had become more ethereal and seemed less realistic. Many scholars therefore questioned the intellectual justifications for a strict analytic division between politics and economics. Second, as the stability and prosperity of the first twenty-five postwar years started to disintegrate in the early 1970s, economic issues became politicized while political systems became increasingly preoccupied with economic affairs. In August 1971, President Richard Nixon ended the gold–dollar standard, which had formed the basis for postwar monetary relations; two and a half years later, OPEC, a previously little-known group, succeeded in substantially raising the price of oil. In 1974 and 1975, the industrial nations of Western Europe, North America, and Japan fell into the first worldwide economic recession since the 1930s; unemployment and inflation were soon widespread realities and explosive political issues. In the world arena, the underdeveloped countries—most of them recently independent—burst onto center stage as the third world and demanded a fairer division of global wealth and power. If, in the 1950s and 1960s, economic growth was taken for granted and politics occupied itself with other matters, in the 1970s and 1980s, economic stagnation fed political strife while political conflict exacerbated economic uncertainty.

For both intellectual and practical reasons, then, social scientists once again began seeking to understand how politics and economics interact in modern society. As interest in political economy grew, a series of fundamental questions was posed and a broad variety of contending approaches arose.

To be sure, today's political economists have not simply reproduced the studies of earlier (and perhaps neglected) generations of scholars in the discipline. The professionalization of both economics and political science led to major advances in both fields, and scholars now understand both economic and political phenomena far better than they did a generation ago. It is on this improved basis that the new political economy has been constructed, albeit with some long-standing issues in mind.

Just as in the real world, where politicians pay close attention to economic trends and economic actors keep track of political tendencies, those who would understand the political process must take the economy into account, and vice versa. A much richer picture of social processes emerges from an integrated understanding of both political and economic affairs than from the isolated study of politics and economics as separate realms. This much is, by now, hardly controversial; it is in application that disagreements arise. Government actions may influence economic trends, but these actions themselves may simply reflect the pressures of economic interest groups. Economic interest groups may be central in determining government policy, yet the political system—democratic or totalitarian, two-party or multiparty, parliamentary or presidential—may crucially color the outlooks and influence of economic interests. In the attempt to arrive at an integrated view of how politics and economics interact, we must disentangle economic and political causes from effects. In this effort, different scholars have different approaches, with different implications for the resulting views of the world.

PERSPECTIVES ON THE INTERNATIONAL POLITICAL ECONOMY

Analysts of the international political economy must understand the interaction of many disparate forces. It is possible to simplify many such factors so that they can be arrayed on two dimensions. These two dimensions also capture many of the theoretical approaches that characterize scholarship on the politics of international economic relations. While the dimensions are not necessarily mutually exclusive, they do often reflect the fact that scholars can disagree about the relative weights to be placed on explanatory factors that all agree play some role. One set of disagreements has to do with the relationship between the international and domestic political economies; another set concerns the relationship between the state and social forces.

The first dimension of interest concerns the degree to which the causes of international political and economic trends are to be found at the domestic or international level. All observers agree that in a complex world, both global and national forces are important. But different analysts place different emphases on the importance of one or the other. Some focus on how international forces tend to overpower domestic interests; others emphasize the degree to which national concerns override global considerations.

It should surprise no one that, for example, American trade policy, Japan's financial goals, and South Korean development strategies are important in the world's political economy. Scholars may differ, however, over how best to explain the sources of the foreign economic policies of individual nations, or of nation-states in general. At one end of the spectrum, some scholars believe that nations' foreign economic policies are primarily determined by the global environment. The actual room for national maneuver of even the most powerful of states, these scholars believe, is limited by characteristics inherent in the international system. At the other end of the spectrum are scholars who see foreign economic policies primarily as the outgrowth of nations' domestic-level political and economic processes. For them, the international system exists only as a jumble of independent nation-states, each with its own political and economic peculiarities.

The international–domestic distinction is at the base of many debates within international political economy, as in the world at large. While some argue, for example, that the cause of third world poverty is in the unequal global economic order, others blame domestic politics and economics in developing nations. Similarly, many scholars see multinational corporations as a powerful independent force in the world—whether working for good or for evil—while others see international firms as extensions of their home countries.

Moreover, for some analysts, global geopolitical relations among nations dominate the impulses that arise from their domestic social orders.

The difference between the two approaches can be seen quite clearly, for example, in explanations of trade policy. To take a specific instance, starting in the early 1980s, the United States and many European governments imposed restrictions on the import of Japanese automobiles. The form of the controls varied widely: The U.S. and Japanese governments negotiated "voluntary" export restraints, with which Japanese producers agreed to comply, while in some European countries, quantitative quotas were imposed unilaterally. Concerned about stiff Japanese competition, which was reducing profits and employment, European and North American automakers and the trade unions that represent their employees provided key support for these policies.

From this example, one clear analytic conclusion would be that domestic political and economic pressures—the electoral importance of the regions where auto industries are concentrated; the economic centrality of that sector to the European and North American economies; government concern about the broad, national ramifications of the auto industry; the political clout of the autoworkers' unions—led to important foreign economic measures involving the restriction of Japanese automobile imports. Indeed, many scholars saw the restrictions as confirmation of the primacy of domestic concerns in the making of foreign economic policy.

Yet, analysts who search for the causes of national foreign economic policies in the international rather than the domestic arena could also find support in the auto import restrictions. After all, the policies were responsive to the rise of Japan as a major manufacturer and exporter of automobiles, a fact that had little to do with the domestic scene in the United States or Europe. Many North American and European industries had lost competitive ground to rapidly growing overseas manufacturers, a process that is complex in origin but clearly one of worldwide proportions. Some have argued that trade policies are a function of realities inherent in the international system, such as the existence of a leading, hegemonic power and the eventual decline of that state (see Krasner, Reading 1). In this view, the decline of American power set the stage for a proliferation of barriers to trade.

The internationally minded scholar might also argue that it is important to understand why the European and American measures took the relatively mild form they did in simply limiting the Japanese to established (and, often, very appreciable) shares of the markets. If the measures had been adopted solely to respond to the distress of local auto industries, the logical step would have been to exclude foreign cars from the markets in question. Yet the positions of Europe and the United States in the global economic and political system—including everything from world finance to international military alliances—dictated that European and North American policy makers not pursue overly hostile policies toward the Japanese.

More generally, scholars have explained long-term changes in trade policy in very different ways. During the period between World Wars I and II, and especially in the 1930s, almost all European nations and the United States were highly protectionist. After World War II, on the other hand, the North American and Western European markets were opened gradually to one another and to the rest of the world, a phenomenon that eventually spread to much of the developing world as well.

Scholars whose theoretical bent is international point out that domestic politics in Europe and the United States did not change enough to explain such a radical shift. But the postwar role of the United States and Western Europe in the international political and economic system has indeed been different from what it was during the 1930s: after 1945, North American and Western European countries were united in an American-led military and economic alliance against the Soviet Union. Some internationally oriented analysts argue that the causes of postwar foreign economic policies in North America and Western Europe can be found in international geopolitical positions of these regions—the increase in American power, the decline of Europe, the Soviet challenge, and the rise of the Atlantic Alliance. Others point to broad technological and economic developments such as dramatic improvements in telecommunications and transportation that have altered governments' incentives to either protect or open their economies.

Scholars who favor domestic-level explanations take the opposite tack. For them, the postwar system was itself largely a creation of the United States and the major Western European powers. To cite the modern international political economy as a source of American or British foreign economic policy, these scholars argue, is to put the cart before the horse in that the United States and its allies had created the institutions—the Marshall Plan, the Bretton Woods agreement, the European Union—of today's international political economy. We must therefore search within these nations for the true roots of the shift in trade policy in North America and Western Europe.

The example of trade policy illustrates that serious scholars can arrive at strikingly different analytic conclusions on the basis of the same information. For some, domestic political and economic pressures caused the adoption of auto import restrictions, whereas for others, geopolitical, economic, or technological trends in the international environment explain the same action.

The second dimension along which analysts differ in their interpretation of trends in the international political economy has to do with the relative importance of politicians and political institutions, on the one hand, and private social actors, on the other. The interaction between state and society—between national governments and the social forces they, variously, represent, rule, or ignore—is indeed another dividing line within the field of international political economy. In studying the politics of the world economy, questions continually arise about the relative importance of independent government action and institutions versus a variety of societal pressures on the policy-making process.

The role of the state is at the center of all political science; international political economy is no exception. Foreign economic policy is made, of course, by foreign economic policy makers; this much is trivial. But just as scholars debate the relative importance of overseas and domestic determinants of foreign economic policies, so too they disagree over whether policy makers represent a logic of their own or instead reflect domestic socioeconomic interest groups or classes. According to one view, the state is relatively insulated or autonomous from the multitude of social, political, and economic pressures that emanate from society. The most that pluralistic interest groups can produce is a confused cacophony of complaints and demands; coherent national policy comes from the conscious actions of national leaders and those who occupy positions of political power and from the institutions in which they operate. The state, in this view, molds society, and foreign economic policy is one part of this larger mold.

The opposing school of thought asserts that policy makers are little more than the transmitters of underlying societal demands. At best, the political system can organize and regularize these demands, but the state is essentially a tool in the hands of socioeconomic and political interests. Foreign economic policy, like other state actions, evolves in response to social demands; it is society that molds the state, and not the other way around.

We can illustrate the difference in focus with the previously discussed example of trade policy in North America and Western Europe before and after World War II. Many of those who look first and foremost at state actors would emphasize the dramatic change in the overall foreign policy of these governments after World War II, starting with the Atlantic Alliance, which was formed to meet the demands of European reconstruction, and the cold war, which required that the American market be opened to foreign goods in order to stimulate the economies of the country's allies. Eventually, the European Union arose as a further effort to cement the Atlantic Alliance and bolster it against the Soviet Union.

According to this view, trade liberalization arose out of national security concerns, as understood and articulated by a very small number of individuals in the American and Western European governments, who then went about "selling" the policies to their publics. Alternatively, it might be argued that the traumas of the Great Depression taught the managers of nation-states that a descent into protectionism could lead to intolerable social tensions. In this context, political leaders may have developed a strong belief in the desirability of trade relations that are generally open. In this view of the world, explanatory precedence goes to the opinions, beliefs, and desires of national political leaders—in short, to the state.

Other scholars, for whom society is determinant, emphasize the major socioeconomic and political changes that had been gaining force within the industrial capitalist nations after World War I. Corporations became more international and thus came to fear overseas competition less. For important groups, trade protection was counterproductive because it limited access to the rest of the world economy; however, freer trade and investment opened broad and profitable new horizons for major economic actors in North America and Western Europe.

By the same token, socioeconomic trends at a global level were also pushing toward international trade liberalization. The rise of internationally integrated financial markets and global corporations, for example, created private interests that oppose interference with the free movement of goods and capital across national borders. This new group of social forces has, in the opinion of some analysts (see, for example, Frankel, Reading 4), fundamentally transformed the very nature of economic policy making in all nations.

When combined, these two dimensions give rise to four different perspectives in international political economy. An *international political* view emphasizes the constraints imposed on national states by the global geostrategic and diplomatic environment within which they operate. It focuses on the inherent conflict among states in a hostile world, within which cooperation, although often desirable and feasible, can be difficult to achieve.

The *international economic* perspective similarly emphasizes the importance of constraints external to individual nations, but it highlights global socioeconomic factors rather than political ones. Accordingly, international developments in technology, telecommunications, finance, and production fundamentally affect the setting within which national governments make policy. Indeed, these developments can matter to the point of making some choices practically impossible to implement and others so attractive as to be impossible to resist.

Domestic approaches look inside nation-states for explanations of the international political economy. The *domestic institutional* view turns its attention to states, as does the international political perspective, but it emphasizes the role and institutions of the state in a domestic setting rather than in the global system. This view, which at times is called simply *institutionalism,* tends to downplay the impact of constraints emanating both from the international system and from domestic societies. National policy makers, and the political institutions within which they operate, are thus seen as the predominant actors in determining national priorities and implementing policies to carry out these goals. Some variants of institutionalism emphasize the autonomy of states from societal actors, while others focus on how state institutions mediate and alter social forces.

The *domestic societal* perspective shares with domestic institutionalism an emphasis on developments within national borders but looks first and foremost at economic and sociopolitical actors rather than political leaders. This view, which at times is known simply as *societal,* tends to minimize international constraints and to emphasize socioeconomic pressures that originate at home. Accordingly, the determinants of national policy are the demands made by individuals, firms, and groups rather than independent action by policy makers.

These diverse perspectives can once again be illustrated by recalling their approaches to the example of trade policy tendencies. International political interpretations would rely on geopolitical trends among states at the global level to explain changing patterns of trade relations. An international economic view would emphasize trends in market forces, technologies, and the like that alter the environment in which governments make trade policy. The domestic institutional approach focuses on the goals and actions of the government within the national political system, for which foreign trade can represent ways to help politicians stay in power. Finally, a domestic societal perspective looks primarily at the pressures brought to bear on policy by various socioeconomic groups, some desirous of trade liberalization and others interested in protection from imports.

It should be noted that these simplistic categories hardly describe the nuance and complexity of actual theoretical approaches; all scholars recognize that the foreign economic policies of all countries are constrained by both international and domestic—and by both political and economic—factors. It may indeed be the case that one set of forces matters more or less in some issue areas than others, in some times than others, and in some countries than others. In particular, international geopolitical concerns will presumably have more impact on a small, weak country surrounded by enemies than a large, powerful nation far from any threat. Similarly, domestic concerns, whether institutional or societal, may have more effect on policy in times of great social and political conflict than in less turbulent times.

Nonetheless, analysts of the international political economy do differ in their interpretations. Rather than being absolute, the disagreements concern relative weights to be assigned to each set of causes. Some scholars assign primacy to social forces, others to autonomous state action; some to global factors, others to domestic ones.

These perspectives can lead to widely different explanations of specific events and general processes within the international political economy. Their differences have generated numerous debates in the field, many of which are contained in the readings in this volume.

FOUR ALTERNATIVE VIEWS OF INTERNATIONAL POLITICAL ECONOMY

In addition to the perspectives already mentioned, some scholars attempt to classify interpretations of global political and economic developments in a somewhat different manner. Many theories of international political economy can also be categorized into one of four perspectives: Liberalism, Marxism, Realism, and Constructivism. Note that in international political economy, advocates of free trade and free markets are still referred to as Liberals. In twentieth-century American domestic politics, however, the term has come to mean something different. In the United States today, whereas "conservatives" generally support free markets and less government intervention, "liberals" advocate greater governmental intervention in the market to stimulate growth and mitigate inequalities. These contradictory usages of the term *Liberal* may seem confusing, but the context will usually make an author's meaning clear.

The Liberal argument emphasizes how both the market and politics are environments in which all parties can benefit by entering into voluntary exchanges with others. If there are no impediments to trade among individuals, Liberals reason, everyone can be made as well-off as possible, given the existing stocks of goods and services. All participants in the market, in other words, will be at their highest possible level of utility. Neoclassical economists, who are generally Liberals, believe firmly in the superiority of the market as a mechanism for allocating scarce resources. Liberals therefore reason that the economic role of government should be quite limited. Many forms of government intervention in the economy, they argue, intentionally or unintentionally restrict the market and thereby prevent potentially rewarding trades from occurring.

Liberals do generally support the provision by government of certain "public goods"—goods and services that benefit society and that would not be provided by private markets.[1] The government, for example, plays an important role in supplying the conditions necessary for the maintenance of a free and competitive market. Governments must provide for the defense of the country, protect property rights, and prevent any unfair collusion or concentration of power within the market. The government should also, according to most Liberals, educate its citizens, build infrastructure, and provide and regulate a common currency. The proper role of government, in other words, is to provide the necessary foundation for the market.

At the level of the international economy, Liberals assert that a fundamental harmony of interests exists between, as well as within, countries. They argue that all countries are best off when goods and services move freely across national borders in mutually rewarding exchanges. If universal free trade were to exist, all countries would enjoy the highest level of utility and there would be no economic basis for international conflict or war. Liberals also believe that governments should manage the international economy in much the same way as they manage their domestic economies. They should establish rules and regulations, often referred to as "international regimes," to govern exchanges between different national currencies and ensure that no country or domestic group is damaged by "unfair" international competition.

Marxism originated with the writings of Karl Marx, a nineteenth-century political economist and perhaps the severest critic of capitalism and its Liberal supporters. Marx saw capitalism and the market as creating extremes of wealth for capitalists and poverty for workers. While the entire populace may have been better-off than before, the capitalists were clearly expanding their wealth more rapidly than everyone else. Marx rejected the assertion that exchange between individuals necessarily maximizes the welfare of the whole society. Accordingly, he perceived capitalism as an inherently conflictual system that both should, and will, be inevitably overthrown and replaced by socialism.

Marxists believe that classes are the dominant actors in the political economy. Specifically, they identify as central two economically determined aggregations of individuals or classes: capital, or the owners of the means of production, and labor, or the workers. Marxists assume that classes act in their economic interests, that is, to maximize the economic well-being of the class as a whole. Accordingly, the basis of the capitalist economy is the exploitation of labor by capital: capitalism, by its very nature, denies labor the full return for its efforts.

Marxists see the political economy as necessarily conflictual, since the relationship between capitalists and workers is essentially antagonistic. Because the means of production are controlled by a minority within society—the capitalists—labor does not receive its full return; conflict between the classes is inevitably caused by this exploitation. Marxists also believe that capitalism is inherently prone to periodic economic crises, which will, they believe, ultimately lead to the overthrow of capitalism by labor and the erection of a socialist society in which the means of production will be owned jointly by all members of society and exploitation will cease.

V. I. Lenin, the Russian revolutionary who founded the Soviet Union, extended Marx's ideas to the international political economy to explain imperialism and war. Imperialism, Lenin argued, was endemic to modern capitalism. As capitalism decayed in the most developed nations, capitalists would attempt to solve their problems by exporting capital abroad. As this capital required protection from both local and foreign challengers, governments would colonize regions to safeguard the interests of their foreign investors. Eventually, capitalist countries would compete for control over these areas and intracapitalist wars would follow.

Today, Marxists who study the international political economy are primarily concerned with two issues. The first is the fate of labor in a world of increasingly internationalized capital. The growth of multinational corporations and the rise of globally integrated financial markets appear to have weakened labor's economic and political power. If workers in a particular country demand higher wages or improved health and safety measures, for example, the multinational capitalist can simply shift production to another country where labor is more compliant. As a result, many Marxists fear that labor's ability to negotiate with capital for a more equitable division of wealth has been significantly undermined.

Second, Marxists are concerned with the poverty and continued underdevelopment of the third world. Some Marxists argue that development is blocked by domestic ruling classes, which pursue their own narrow interests at the expense of national economic progress. Others, known as "dependency" theorists, extend class analysis to the level of the international economy. According to these Marxists, the global system is stratified into a wealthy area (the "core," or first world) and a region of oppression and poverty (the "periphery," or third world). International capitalism, in this view, exploits the periphery and benefits the core, just as capitalists exploit workers within a single country. The principal questions here focus on the mechanisms of exploitation—whether they be multinational corporations, international financial markets and organizations, or trade—and the appropriate strategies for stimulating autonomous growth and development in the periphery.

Realism traces its intellectual roots back to Thucydides' writings in 400 B.C.E., as well as those of Niccolò Machiavelli, Thomas Hobbes, and the mercantilists Jean-Baptiste Colbert and Friedrich List. Realists believe that nation-states pursue power and shape the economy to this end. Moreover, they are the dominant actors within the international political economy. According to Realists, the international system is anarchical, a condition under which nation-states are sovereign, the sole judges of their own behaviors, and subject to no higher authority. If no authority is higher than the nation-state, Realists believe, then all actors must be subordinate to it. While private citizens can interact with their counterparts in other countries, Realists assert that the basis for this interaction is legislated by the nation-state. Thus, where Liberals focus on individuals and Marxists on classes, Realists concentrate on nation-states.

Realists also argue that nation-states are fundamentally concerned about international power relations. Because the international system is based on anarchy, the use of force or coercion by other nation-states is always a possibility and no higher authority is obligated to come to the aid of a nation-state under attack. Nation-states are thus ultimately dependent on their own resources for protection. For Realists, then, each nation-state must always be prepared to defend itself to the best of its ability. For Realists, politics is largely a zero-sum game and by necessity conflictual. In other words, if one nation-state is to win, another must lose.

Realists also believe that nation-states can be thought of as rational actors in the same sense that other theorists assume individuals to be rational. Nation-states are assumed to operate according to cost-benefit analyses and choose the option that yields the greatest value, especially regarding the nation's international geopolitical and power positions.

The emphasis on power is what gives Realism its distinctive approach to international political economy. While economic considerations may often complement power concerns, the former are, in the Realist view, subordinate to the latter. Realists allow for circumstances in which nation-states sacrifice economic gain to weaken their opponents or strengthen themselves in military or diplomatic terms. Thus, trade protection, which might reduce a country's overall income by restricting the market, may nonetheless be adopted for reasons of national political power.

Realist political economy is primarily concerned with how changes in the distribution of international power affect the form and type of international economy. The best known Realist approach to this question is the *theory of hegemonic stability,* which holds that an open international economy—that is, one characterized by the free exchange of goods, capital, and services—is most likely to exist when a single dominant or hegemonic power is present to stabilize the system and construct a strong regime (see Krasner, Reading 1, and Lake, Reading 8). For Realists, then, the pursuit of power by nation-states shapes the international economy.

Each of these first three perspectives features different assumptions and assertions. Liberals assume that individuals are the proper unit of analysis, while Marxists and Realists make similar assumptions for classes and nation-states, respectively. The three perspectives also differ on the inevitability of conflict within the political economy. Liberals believe economics and politics are largely autonomous spheres, Marxists maintain that economics determines politics, and Realists argue that politics determines economics.

Constructivism, a fourth and relatively new approach to international political economy, has roots in critical theory and sociology. Unlike the first three approaches, Constructivism is more of a method of analysis than a set of alternative assumptions and assertions. Constructivists believe that actors in the international political economy and their interests are not innate but are produced or constructed through social interactions. Sectors, factors of production, classes, and especially nation-states are not fixed and immutable in this view, but are themselves produced by their social environments. Rather than pursuing wealth over power, or vice versa, individuals, classes, and states vary in their interests and contain the potential for both conflict and cooperation in different social settings.

Constructivists also believe that norms play an important role in international political economy. The other approaches all assume implicitly that actors are purposive and select among possible courses of action by their anticipated effects. This is sometimes referred to as a "logic of consequences." Constructivists assume that actors select roles and actions by what is right, just, or socially expected. In other words, actors choose according to a "logic of appropriateness." In this view, countries may open themselves to trade or international investment not because, as Liberals assert, this improves their welfare in any instrumental sense, but because this is what responsible or "developed" states understand as appropriate in the modern international political economy.

In addition, Constructivists assert that actors and their interactions can be transformed through the introduction of new norms or understandings of their interests or identities. The rough-and-tumble international political economy described by Realists, for example, is not, according to Constructivists, foreordained by the condition of anarchy. If actors come to understand the world differently, the conception of appropriate behavior could also change dramatically. As the "Washington Consensus" took hold internationally during the 1990s, for instance, countries liberalized their economies and held to this policy long after its promised effects failed to materialize.

This fourfold division of international political economy is useful in many ways, especially as it highlights differing evaluations of the importance of economic efficiency, class conflict, and geostrategic and normative considerations. However, the lines between these views are easily blurred. Some Marxists agree with the Realist focus on interstate conflict, while others concur with the Liberal emphasis on economic interests, while still others agree with Constructivists on the role of norms. Likewise, there are many Liberals who use neoclassical tools to analyze interstate strategic interaction in much the same way Realists do or to investigate the clash of classes as do the Marxists. Nearly all Liberals, Marxists, and Realists have come to a deeper understanding of the role of norms, emphasized by Constructivists. Such substantial overlap, in our view, helps clarify the two-dimensional categorization outlined above. We also believe that these two dimensions—international–domestic and state–society—most accurately characterize analytical differences among scholars and observers of the international political economy.

THE CONTEMPORARY INTERNATIONAL POLITICAL ECONOMY: AN OVERVIEW

Following initial sections on theoretical perspectives and historical background, the remainder of this book of readings concerns the politics of international economic relations since World War II. Developments since 1945 have, indeed, raised a wide variety of theoretical, practical, and policy issues.

The contemporary international political economy is characterized by unprecedented levels of multinational production, cross-border financial flows, and international trade. It is also plagued by increasing political conflict as individuals, groups, classes, and countries clash over the meaning and implications of these economic transactions. The contradiction between increasing economic integration and the wealth it produces, on the one hand, and the desire for political control and national autonomy, on the other, defines much of what happens in the global political economy.

For the first thirty years after World War II, the general pattern of relations among noncommunist nations was set by American leadership, and this pattern continues to influence the international political economy today. In the political arena, formal and informal alliances tied virtually every major noncommunist nation into an American-led network of mutual support and defense. In the economic arena, a wide-ranging set of international economic organizations—including the International Monetary Fund (IMF), the General Agreement on Tariffs and Trade (GATT), and the International Bank for Reconstruction and Development (World Bank)—grew up under a protective American "umbrella," and often as a direct American initiative. The world economy itself was heavily influenced by the rise of modern multinational corporations and banks, whose contemporary form is largely of U.S. origin.

American plans for a reordered world economy go back to the mid-1930s. After World War I, the United States retreated into relative economic insularity, for reasons explored in Part II, "Historical Perspectives." When the Great Depression hit, American political leaders virtually ignored the possibility of international economic cooperation in their attempts to stabilize the domestic economy. Yet, even as the Franklin Roosevelt administration looked inward for recovery, by 1934 new American initiatives were signaling a shift in America's traditional isolation. Roosevelt's secretary of state, Cordell Hull, was a militant free trader, and in 1934 he convinced Congress to pass the Reciprocal Trade Agreements Act, which allowed the executive to negotiate tariff reductions with foreign nations. This important step toward trade liberalization and international economic cooperation was deepened as war threatened in Europe and the United States drew closer to Great Britain and France.

The seeds of the new international order, which had been planted in the 1930s, began to grow even as World War II came to an end. The Bretton Woods agreement, reached among the Allied powers in 1944, established a new series of international economic organizations that became the foundation for the postwar American-led system. As the wartime American–Soviet alliance began to shatter, a new economic order emerged in the noncommunist world. At its center were the three pillars of the Bretton Woods system: international monetary cooperation under the auspices of the IMF, international trade liberalization negotiated within the GATT, and investment in the developing countries stimulated by the World Bank. All three pillars were essentially designed by the United States and dependent on its support.

As it developed, the postwar capitalist world reflected American foreign policy in many of its details. One principal concern of the United States was to build a bulwark of anti-Soviet allies; this was done with a massive inflow of American aid under the Marshall Plan and the encouragement of Western European cooperation within a new Common Market. At the same time, the United States dramatically lowered its barriers to foreign goods and American corporations began to invest heavily in foreign nations. Of course, the United States was not acting altruistically: European recovery, trade liberalization, and booming international investment helped ensure great prosperity within its own borders as well.

American policies, whatever their motivation, had an undeniable impact on the international political economy. Trade liberalization opened the huge American market to foreign producers. American overseas investment provided capital, technology, and expertise for both Europe and the developing world. American governmental economic aid, whether direct or channeled through such institutions as the World Bank, helped finance economic growth abroad. In addition, the American military umbrella allowed anti-Soviet governments in Europe, Japan, and the developing world to rely on the United States for security and to turn their attentions to encouraging economic growth.

All in all, the noncommunist world's unprecedented access to American markets and American capital provided a major stimulus to world economic growth, not to mention the profits of American businesses and general prosperity within the United States. For more than twenty-five years after World War II, the capitalist world experienced impressive levels of economic growth and development, all within a general context of international cooperation under American political, economic, and military tutelage.

This period is often referred to as the *Pax Americana* because of its broad similarity to the British-led international economic system that operated from about 1820 until World War I, which was known as the Pax Britannica. In both instances, general political and economic peace prevailed under the leadership of an overwhelming world power—the United Kingdom in one case, the United States in the other. There were, nonetheless, major differences between the two eras (see Lake, Reading 8).

Just as the Pax Britannica eventually ended, however, the Pax Americana gradually eroded. By the early 1970s, strains were developing in the postwar system. Between 1971 and 1975, the postwar international monetary system, which had been based on a gold-backed U.S. dollar, fell apart and was replaced by a new, improvised pattern of floating exchange rates in which the dollar's role was still strong but no longer quite so central. At the same time, pressures for trade protection from uncompetitive industries in North America and Western Europe began to mount; and although tariff levels remained low, a variety of nontariff barriers to world trade, such as import quotas, soon proliferated. In the political arena, détente between the United States and the Soviet Union seemed to make the American security umbrella less relevant for the Japanese and Western Europeans; in the less-developed countries, North–South conflict appeared more important than East–West strife. In short, during the 1970s, as American economic strength declined, the Bretton Woods institutions weakened, and the cold war thawed, the Pax Americana drew to a close.

The quickening pace of change in the Soviet Union and its allies eventually culminated in the collapse of former Soviet bloc nations in the late 1980s and early 1990s, and ultimately in the disintegration of the former Soviet Union. The end of the cold war did not, of course, mean an end to international conflict, but it did put an end to the East–West divide that had dominated global politics for so long.

As the cold war wound down, international economic issues grew in importance, along with a greater willingness on the part of many nations to integrate with the rest of the world economy. Over the course of the 1980s, a wave of trade liberalization and privatization swept many countries in the developing world, so that by the early 1990s they were clearly committed to global economic integration. Then came the most striking development, the collapse of the centrally planned economies and their startling change in direction toward domestic and world markets. The process started in China and Vietnam, but when the Soviet Union disintegrated and the countries of Eastern and Central Europe joined the European Union, the resurgence of an integrated global economy seemed complete.

Since the mid-1990s, the world economy has continued on the general path of globalization. All of the indicators of integration have trended upward— some of them, such as international financial flows, at a very rapid pace. Yet, concern has grown about globalization in many quarters, and the generalized enthusiasm of the early 1990s is now less general, and less enthusiastic.

The principal issue facing analysts of the international political economy today has to do with the future of this era of globalization. Despite continued conflict over the international economy, most people—especially in the industrialized nations—appear to accept that an international system in which goods and capital can move quite freely among countries has become the normal state of affairs, and is likely to continue for the foreseeable future. Nonetheless, there is widespread unease about the current state of international economic relations. Activists worry that footloose corporations may undermine attempts to protect the environment, labor, and human rights. Beleaguered businesses are troubled by foreign competitors. Nationalists and religious traditionalists fear that globalization will undermine cultural and other norms.

All of these apprehensions were heightened by the global economic crisis that began in 2008. Difficulties in the American financial system were quickly transmitted around the world, and within months the entire international economy was in recession. There were even fears that the recession might deepen into depression. The economic downturn raised the spectre of economic conflicts among the world's major powers, as each nation focused its efforts on defending itself and its citizens from the fallout of the economic collapse. National governments and international economic institutions were confronted with problems of unprecedented breadth and scope. In this uncertain and rapidly changing environment, the United States remains the most important country within the international political economy, but it is no longer dominant. The era of American hegemony has been replaced by a new, multilateral order based on the joint leadership of Western Europe, Japan, and the United States. So far, these countries have successfully managed—or, some would say, muddled through—the "oil shocks" of the 1970s, the debt crisis of the early 1980s, the transition to the market of the former centrally planned economies after 1989, the currency crises and other financial volatility of the 1990s, and the macroeconomic imbalances of the new millennium.

Despite greater success than many thought possible, multilateral leadership and the liberal international order remain fragile. Conflicts of interest and economic tensions remain muted, but they could erupt at any time. The politics of international economic relations are made more complex by the new involvement of such countries as China, India, and Russia. These nations played virtually no role in international economic affairs for fifty years after World War II, but they are now actors to be reckoned with on the world economic scene. It is unclear whether, and how, the developed nations will work together with these newly resurgent developing countries in confronting the economic and political problems of the twenty-first century.

The remainder of this book is devoted to understanding the contemporary international political economy and its likely future. In the sections that follow, a variety of thematic issues are addressed; in each cluster of issues, alternative theoretical and analytical perspectives compete. The selections in this reader serve both to provide information on broad trends in the politics of international economic relations and to give an overview of the contending approaches to be found within the discipline.

NOTE

1. More specifically, a public good is one that, in its purest form, is *nonrival in consumption* and *nonexcludable*. The first characteristic means that consumption of the good by one person does not reduce the opportunities for others to consume that good; for example, clean air can be breathed by one individual without reducing its availability to others. The second characteristic means that nobody can be prevented from consuming the good: Those who do not contribute to pollution control are still able to breathe clean air. These two conditions are fully met only rarely, but goods whose characteristics come close to meeting them are generally considered public goods.

I

CONTENDING PERSPECTIVES ON INTERNATIONAL POLITICAL ECONOMY

As outlined in the Introduction, two principal theoretical dimensions can be used to organize debates within international political economy. The first addresses the relative importance of international and domestic variables in accounting for trends in the international political economy; the second, the significance of institutional and societal factors. Part I contains four selections, one representing each approach as applied to a specific issue. In a classic example of an international political approach, Stephen D. Krasner (Reading 1) examines patterns of trade openness within the international economy over the nineteenth and twentieth centuries. Barry Eichengreen (Reading 2) uses a domestic society–centered theory to account for the Smoot-Hawley Tariff, which contained some of the highest duties in history. Kenneth L. Sokoloff and Stanley L. Engerman (Reading 3) emphasize the effect of domestic institutions on economic growth. Finally, Jeffrey A. Frankel (Reading 4) explores how international economic factors such as the reduction in transportation and communication costs have contributed to global economic integration. As exemplars of their respective approaches, these essays are intended only to illustrate basic themes and arguments; all four approaches contain a rich diversity of styles and conclusions, and the essays selected here are only a sample. Nonetheless, they serve to highlight key analytic debates and provide a useful empirical introduction to critical trends and cases in international political economy.

1

State Power and the Structure of International Trade

STEPHEN D. KRASNER

In this essay, Stephen D. Krasner addresses the relationship between the inter-ests and power of major states and the trade openness of the international econ-omy. In his international political analysis, he identifies four principal goals of state action: political power, aggregate national income, economic growth, and social stability. He then combines these goals with different national abilities to pursue them, relating the international distribution of potential economic power to alternative trade regimes. Krasner maintains, most significantly, that the hegemony of a leading power is necessary for the creation and continuance of free trade. He applies his model to six periods. Krasner's analysis in this 1976 article is a well-known attempt to use international political theory, and Real-ism more generally, to explain international economic affairs. The theory he propounds, which has been dubbed the "theory of hegemonic stability," has influenced many subsequent analyses.

INTRODUCTION

In recent years, students of international relations have multinationalized, transnationalized, bureaucratized, and transgovernmentalized the state until it has virtually ceased to exist as an analytic construct. Nowhere is that trend more apparent than in the study of the politics of international economic relations. The basic conventional assumptions have been undermined by asser-tions that the state is trapped by a transnational society created not by sover-eigns, but by nonstate actors. Interdependence is not seen as a reflection of state policies and state choices (the perspective of balance-of-power theory), but as the result of elements beyond the control of any state or a system cre-ated by states.

This perspective is at best profoundly misleading. It may explain develop-ments within a particular international economic structure, but it cannot explain the structure itself. That structure has many institutional and behav-ioral manifestations. The central continuum along which it can be described is openness. International economic structures may range from complete autarky (if all states prevent movements across their borders), to complete openness (if no restrictions exist). In this paper I will present an analysis of one aspect of the international economy—the structure of international trade; that is, the degree of openness for the movement of goods as opposed to capital, labor, technology, or other factors of production. Since the beginning of the nineteenth century, this structure has gone through several changes. These can be explained, albeit imperfectly, by a state-power theory: an approach that begins with the assumption that the structure of international trade is determined by the interests and power of states acting to maximize national goals. The first step in this argument is to relate four basic state interests— aggregate national income, social stability, political power, and economic growth—to the degree of openness for the movement of goods. The relationship between these interests and openness depends upon the potential economic power of any given state. Potential economic power is operationalized in terms of the relative size and level of economic development of the state. The second step in the argument is to relate different distributions of potential power, such as multipolar and hegemonic, to different international trading structures. The most important conclusion of this theoretical analysis is that a hegemonic distribution of potential economic power is likely to result in an open trading structure. That argument is largely, although not completely, substantiated by empirical data. For a fully adequate analysis it is necessary to amend a state-power argument to take account of the impact of past state decisions on domestic social structures as well as on international economic ones. The two major organizers of the structure of trade since the beginning of the nineteenth century, Great Britain and the United States, have both been prevented from making policy amendments in line with state interests by particular societal groups whose power had been enhanced by earlier state policies.

THE CAUSAL ARGUMENT: STATE INTERESTS, STATE POWER, AND INTERNATIONAL TRADING STRUCTURES

Neoclassical trade theory is based upon the assumption that states act to maximize their aggregate economic utility. This leads to the conclusion that maximum global welfare and Pareto optimality are achieved under free trade. While particular countries might better their situations through protectionism, economic theory has generally looked askance at such policies. . . . Neoclassical theory recognizes that trade regulations can . . . be used to correct domestic distortions and to promote infant industries, but these are exceptions or temporary departures from policy conclusions that lead logically to the support of free trade.

State Preferences

Historical experience suggests that policy makers are dense, or that the assumptions of the conventional argument are wrong. Free trade has hardly been the norm. Stupidity is not a very interesting analytic category. An alternative approach to explaining international trading structures is to assume that states seek a broad range of goals. At least four major state interests affected by the structure of international trade can be identified. They are: political power, aggregate national income, economic growth, and social stability. The way in which each of these goals is affected by the degree of openness depends upon the potential economic power of the state as defined by its relative size and level of development.

Let us begin with aggregate national income because it is most straightforward. Given the exceptions noted above, conventional neoclassical theory demonstrates that the greater the degree of openness in the international trading system, the greater the level of aggregate economic income. This conclusion applies to all states regardless of their size or relative level of development. The static economic benefits of openness are, however, generally inversely related to size. Trade gives small states relatively more welfare benefits than it gives large ones. Empirically, small states have higher ratios of trade to national product. They do not have the generous factor endowments or potential for national economies of scale that are enjoyed by larger—particularly continental—states.

The impact of openness on social stability runs in the opposite direction. Greater openness exposes the domestic economy to the exigencies of the world market. That implies a higher level of factor movements than in a closed economy, because domestic production patterns must adjust to changes in international prices. Social instability is thereby increased, since there is friction in moving factors, particularly labor, from one sector to another. The impact will be stronger in small states than in large, and in relatively less developed than in more developed ones. Large states are less involved in the international economy: a smaller percentage of their total factor endowment is affected by the international market at any given level of openness. More developed states are better able to adjust factors: skilled workers can more easily be moved from one kind of production to another than can unskilled laborers or peasants. Hence social stability is, *ceteris paribus*, inversely related to openness, but the deleterious consequences of exposure to the international trading system are mitigated by larger size and greater economic development.

The relationship between political power and the international trading structure can be analyzed in terms of the relative opportunity costs of closure for trading partners. The higher the relative cost of closure, the weaker the political position of the state. Hirschman has argued that this cost can be measured in terms of direct income losses and the adjustment costs of reallocating factors. These will be smaller for large states and for relatively more developed states. Other things being equal, utility costs will be less for large states because they generally have a smaller proportion of their economy engaged in the international economic system. Reallocation costs will be less for more advanced states because their factors are more mobile. Hence a state that is relatively large and more developed will find its political power enhanced by an open system because its opportunity costs of closure are less. The large state can use the threat to alter the system to secure economic or noneconomic objectives. Historically, there is one important exception to this generalization—the oil-exporting states. The level of reserves for some of these states, particularly Saudi Arabia, has reduced the economic opportunity costs of closure to a very low level despite their lack of development.

The relationship between international economic structure and economic growth is elusive. For small states, economic growth has generally been empirically associated with openness. Exposure to the international system makes possible a much more efficient allocation of resources. Openness also probably furthers the rate of growth of large countries with relatively advanced technologies because they do not need to protect infant industries and can take advantage of expanded world markets. In the long term, however, openness for capital and technology, as well as goods, may hamper the growth of large, developed countries by diverting resources from the domestic economy, and by providing potential competitors with the knowledge needed to develop their own industries. Only by maintaining its technological lead and continually developing new industries can even a very large state escape the undesired consequences of an entirely open economic system. For medium-size states, the relationship between international trading structure and growth is impossible to specify definitively, either theoretically or empirically. On the one hand, writers from the mercantilists through the American protectionists and the German historical school, and more recently analysts of *dependencia*, have argued that an entirely open system can undermine a state's effort to develop, and even lead to underdevelopment. On the other hand, adherents of more conventional neoclassical positions have maintained that exposure to international competition spurs economic transformation. The evidence is not yet in. All that can confidently be said is that openness furthers the economic growth of small states and of large ones so long as they maintain their technological edge.

From State Preferences to International Trading Structures

The next step in this argument is to relate particular distributions of potential economic power, defined by the size and level of development of individual states, to the structure of the international trading system, defined in terms of openness.

Let us consider a system composed of a large number of small, highly developed states. Such a system is likely to lead to an open international trading structure. The aggregate income and economic growth of each state are increased by an open system. The social instability produced by exposure to international competition is mitigated by the factor mobility made possible by higher levels of development. There is no loss of political power from openness because the costs of closure are symmetrical for all members of the system.

EU vs. NAFTA

Now let us consider a system composed of a few very large, but unequally developed states. Such a distribution of potential economic power is likely to lead to a closed structure. Each state could increase its income through a more open system, but the gains would be modest. Openness would create more social instability in the less developed countries. The rate of growth for more backward areas might be frustrated, while that of the more advanced ones would be enhanced. A more open structure would leave the less developed states in a politically more vulnerable position, because their greater factor rigidity would mean a higher relative cost of closure. Because of these disadvantages, large but relatively less developed states are unlikely to accept an open trading structure. More advanced states cannot, unless they are militarily much more powerful, force large backward countries to accept openness.

Finally, let us consider a hegemonic system—one in which there is a single state that is much larger and relatively more advanced than its trading partners. The costs and benefits of openness are not symmetrical for all members of the system. The hegemonic state will have a preference for an open structure. Such a structure increases its aggregate national income. It also increases its rate of growth during its ascendency—that is, when its relative size and technological lead are increasing. Further, an open structure increases its political power, since the opportunity costs of closure are least for a large and developed state. The social instability resulting from exposure to the international system is mitigated by the hegemonic power's relatively low level of involvement in the international economy, and the mobility of its factors.

What of the other members of a hegemonic system? Small states are likely to opt for openness because the advantages in terms of aggregate income and growth are so great, and their political power is bound to be restricted regardless of what they do. The reaction of medium-size states is hard to predict; it depends at least in part on the way in which the hegemonic power utilizes its resources. The potentially dominant state has symbolic, economic, and military capabilities that can be used to entice or compel others to accept an open trading structure.

At the symbolic level, the hegemonic state stands as an example of how economic development can be achieved. Its policies may be emulated, even if they are inappropriate for other states. Where there are very dramatic asymmetries, military power can be used to coerce weaker states into an open structure. Force is not, however, a very efficient means for changing economic policies, and it is unlikely to be employed against medium-size states.

Most importantly, the hegemonic state can use its economic resources to create an open structure. In terms of positive incentives, it can offer access to its large domestic market and to its relatively cheap exports. In terms of negative ones, it can withhold foreign grants and engage in competition, potentially ruinous for the weaker state, in third-country markets. The size and

CHART 1 Probability of an Open Trading Structure with Different Distributions of Potential Economic Power

Level of Development of States	Size of States		
	Relatively Equal		Very Unequal
	Small	Large	
Equal	Moderate-High	Low-Moderate	High
Unequal	Moderate	Low	Moderate-High

economic robustness of the hegemonic state also enable it to provide the confidence necessary for a stable international monetary system, and its currency can offer the liquidity needed for an increasingly open system.

In sum, openness is most likely to occur during periods when a hegemonic state is in its ascendency. Such a state has the interest and the resources to create a structure characterized by lower tariffs, rising trade proportions, and less regionalism. There are other distributions of potential power where openness is likely, such as a system composed of many small, highly developed states. But even here, that potential might not be realized because of the problems of creating confidence in a monetary system where adequate liquidity would have to be provided by a negotiated international reserve asset or a group of national currencies. Finally, it is unlikely that very large states, particularly at unequal levels of development, would accept open trading relations.

These arguments, and the implications of other ideal typical configurations of potential economic power for the openness of trading structures, are summarized in [Chart 1].

THE DEPENDENT VARIABLE: DESCRIBING THE STRUCTURE OF THE INTERNATIONAL TRADING SYSTEM

The structure of international trade has both behavioral and institutional attributes. The degree of openness can be described both by the *flow* of goods and by the *policies* that are followed by states with respect to trade barriers and international payments. The two are not unrelated, but they do not coincide perfectly.

In common usage, the focus of attention has been upon institutions. Openness is associated with those historical periods in which tariffs were substantially lowered: the third quarter of the nineteenth century and the period since the Second World War.

Tariffs alone, however, are not an adequate indicator of structure. They are hard to operationalize quantitatively. Tariffs do not have to be high to be effective. If cost functions are nearly identical, even low tariffs can prevent trade. Effective tariff rates may be much higher than nominal ones. Non-tariff barriers to trade, which are not easily compared across states, can sub-stitute for duties. An undervalued exchange rate can protect domestic markets from foreign competition. Tariff levels alone cannot describe the structure of international trade.

A second indicator, and one which is behavioral rather than institutional, is trade proportions—the ratios of trade to national income for different states. Like tariff levels, these involve describing the system in terms of an agglomeration of national tendencies. A period in which these ratios are increasing across time for most states can be described as one of increasing openness.

A third indicator is the concentration of trade within regions composed of states at different levels of development. The degree of such regional encap-sulation is determined not so much by comparative advantage (because rela-tive factor endowments would allow almost any backward area to trade with almost any developed one), but by political choices or dictates. Large states, attempting to protect themselves from the vagaries of a global system, seek to maximize their interests by creating regional blocs. Openness in the global economic system has in effect meant greater trade among the leading indus-trial states. Periods of closure are associated with the encapsulation of certain advanced states within regional systems shared with certain less developed areas.

A description of the international trading system involves, then, an exercise that is comparative rather than absolute. A period when tariffs are falling, trade proportions are rising, and regional trading patterns are becoming less extreme will be defined as one in which the structure is becoming more open.

Tariff Levels

The period from the 1820's to 1879 was basically one of decreasing tariff lev-els in Europe. The trend began in Great Britain in the 1820's, with reductions of duties and other barriers to trade. In 1846 the abolition of the Corn Laws ended agricultural protectionism. France reduced duties on some interme-diate goods in the 1830's, and on coal, iron, and steel in 1852. The *Zollverein* established fairly low tariffs in 1834. Belgium, Portugal, Spain, Piedmont, Nor-way, Switzerland, and Sweden lowered imposts in the 1850's. The golden age of free trade began in 1860, when Britain and France signed the Cobden-Chevalier Treaty, which virtually eliminated trade barriers. This was followed by a series of bilateral trade agreements between virtually all European states. It is impor-tant to note, however, that the United States took little part in the general move-ment toward lower trade barriers.

The movement toward greater liberality was reversed in the late 1870's. Austria-Hungary increased duties in 1876 and 1878, and Italy also in 1878; but the main breach came in Germany in 1879. France increased tariffs modestly in 1881, sharply in 1892, and raised them still further in 1910. Other countries followed a similar pattern. Only Great Britain, Belgium, the Netherlands, and Switzerland continued to follow free-trade policies through the 1880's. Although Britain did not herself impose duties, she began establishing a system of preferential markets in her overseas Empire in 1898. The United States was basically protectionist throughout the nineteenth century. The high tariffs imposed during the Civil War continued with the exception of a brief period in the 1890's. There were no major duty reductions before 1914.

During the 1920's, tariff levels increased further. Western European states protected their agrarian sectors against imports from the Danube region, Australia, Canada, and the United States, where the war had stimulated increased output. Great Britain adopted some colonial preferences in 1919, imposed a small number of tariffs in 1921, and extended some wartime duties. The successor states of the Austro-Hungarian Empire imposed duties to achieve some national self-sufficiency. The British dominions and Latin America protected industries nurtured by wartime demands. In the United States the Fordney-McCumber Tariff Act of 1922 increased protectionism. The October Revolution removed Russia from the Western trading system.

Dramatic closure in terms of tariff levels began with the passage of the Smoot-Hawley Tariff Act in the United States in 1930. Britain raised tariffs in 1931 and definitively abandoned free trade at the Ottawa Conference of 1932, which introduced extensive imperial preferences. Germany and Japan established trading blocs within their own spheres of influence. All other major countries followed protectionist policies.

Significant reductions in protection began after the Second World War; the United States had foreshadowed the movement toward greater liberality with the passage of the Reciprocal Trade Agreements Act in 1934. Since 1945 there have been seven rounds of multilateral tariff reductions. The first, held in 1947 at Geneva, and the Kennedy Round, held during the 1960's, have been the most significant. They have substantially reduced the level of protection.

The present situation is ambiguous. There have recently been some new trade controls. In the United States these include a voluntary import agreement for steel, the imposition of a 10 percent import surcharge during four months of 1971, and export controls on agricultural products in 1973 and 1974. Italy imposed a deposit requirement on imports during parts of 1974 and 1975. Britain and Japan have engaged in export subsidization. Non-tariff barriers have become more important. On balance, there has been movement toward greater protectionism since the end of the Kennedy Round, but it is not decisive. The outcome of the multilateral negotiations that began in 1975 remains to be seen.

In sum, after 1820 there was a general trend toward lower tariffs (with the notable exception of the United States), which culminated between 1860 and 1879; higher tariffs from 1879 through the interwar years, with dramatic increases in the 1930's; and less protectionism from 1945 through the conclusion of the Kennedy Round in 1967.

Trade Proportions

With the exception of one period, ratios of trade to aggregate economic activity followed the same general pattern as tariff levels. Trade proportions increased from the early part of the nineteenth century to about 1880. Between 1880 and 1900 there was a decrease, sharper if measured in current prices than constant ones, but apparent in both statistical series for most countries. Between 1900 and 1913—and here is the exception from the tariff pattern—there was a marked increase in the ratio of trade to aggregate economic activity. This trend brought trade proportions to levels that have generally not been reattained. During the 1920's and 1930's the importance of trade in national economic activity declined. After the Second World War it increased.

. . . There are considerable differences in the movement of trade proportions among states. They hold more or less constant for the United States; Japan, Denmark, and Norway . . . are unaffected by the general decrease in the ratio of trade to aggregate economic activity that takes place after 1880. The pattern described in the previous paragraph does, however, hold for Great Britain, France, Sweden, Germany, and Italy.

. . . Because of the boom in commodity prices that occurred in the early 1950's, the ratio of trade to gross domestic product was relatively high for larger states during these years, at least in current prices. It then faltered or remained constant until about 1960. From the early 1960's through 1972, trade proportions rose for all major states except Japan. Data for 1973 and 1974 show further increases. For smaller countries the trend was more erratic, with Belgium showing a more or less steady increase, Norway vacillating between 82 and 90 percent, and Denmark and the Netherlands showing higher figures for the late 1950's than for more recent years. There is then, in current prices, a generally upward trend in trade proportions since 1960, particularly for larger states. This movement is more pronounced if constant prices are used.

Regional Trading Patterns

The final indicator of the degree of openness of the global trading system is regional bloc concentration. There is a natural affinity for some states to trade with others because of geographical propinquity or comparative advantage. In general, however, a system in which there are fewer manifestations of trading within given blocs, particularly among specific groups of more and less developed states, is a more open one. Over time there have been extensive changes in trading patterns between particular areas of the world whose relative factor endowments have remained largely the same.

Richard Chadwick and Karl Deutsch have collected extensive information on international trading patterns since 1890. Their basic datum is the relative acceptance indicator (RA), which measures deviations from a null hypothesis in which trade between a pair of states, or a state and a region, is precisely what would be predicted on the basis of their total share of international trade. When the null hypothesis holds, the RA indicator is equal to zero. Values less than zero indicate less trade than expected, greater than zero more trade than expected. For our purposes the critical issue is whether, over time, trade tends to become more concentrated as shown by movements away from zero, or less as shown by movements toward zero. . . .

There is a general pattern. In three of the four cases, the RA value closest to zero—that is the least regional encapsulation—occurred in 1890, 1913, or 1928; in the fourth case (France and French West Africa), the 1928 value was not bettered until 1964. In every case there was an increase in the RA indicator between 1928 and 1938, reflecting the breakdown of international commerce that is associated with the depression. Surprisingly, the RA indicator was higher for each of the four pairs in 1954 than in 1938, an indication that regional patterns persisted and even became more intense in the postwar period. With the exception of the Soviet Union and Eastern Europe, there was a general trend toward decreasing RAs for the period after 1954. They still, however, show fairly high values even in the late 1960's.

If we put all three indicators—tariff levels, trade proportions, and trade patterns—together, they suggest the following periodization.

> Period I (1820–1879): Increasing openness—tariffs are generally lowered; trade proportions increase. Data are not available for trade patterns. However, it is important to note that this is not a universal pattern. The United States is largely unaffected: its tariff levels remain high (and are in fact increased during the early 1860's) and American trade proportions remain almost constant.
>
> Period II (1879–1900): Modest closure—tariffs are increased; trade proportions decline modestly for most states. Data are not available for trade patterns.
>
> Period III (1900–1913): Greater openness—tariff levels remain generally unchanged; trade proportions increase for all major trading states except the United States. Trading patterns become less regional in three out of the four cases for which data are available.
>
> Period IV (1918–1939): Closure—tariff levels are increased in the 1920's and again in the 1930's; trade proportions decline. Trade becomes more regionally encapsulated.
>
> Period V (1945–c. 1970): Great openness—tariffs are lowered; trade proportions increase, particularly after 1960. Regional concentration decreases after 1960. However, these developments are limited to non-Communist areas of the world.

THE INDEPENDENT VARIABLE: DESCRIBING THE DISTRIBUTION OF POTENTIAL ECONOMIC POWER AMONG STATES

Analysts of international relations have an almost pro forma set of variables designed to show the distribution of potential power in the international *political* system. It includes such factors as gross national product, per capita income, geographical position, and size of armed forces. A similar set of indicators can be presented for the international economic system.

Statistics are available over a long time period for per capita income, aggregate size, share of world trade, and share of world investment. They demonstrate that, since the beginning of the nineteenth century, there have been two first-rank economic powers in the world economy—Britain and the United States. The United States passed Britain in aggregate size sometime in the middle of the nineteenth century and, in the 1880's, became the largest producer of manufactures. America's lead was particularly marked in technologically advanced industries turning out sewing machines, harvesters, cash registers, locomotives, steam pumps, telephones, and petroleum. Until the First World War, however, Great Britain had a higher per capita income, a greater share of world trade, and a greater share of world investment than any other state. The peak of British ascendance occurred around 1880, when Britain's relative per capita income, share of world trade, and share of investment flows reached their highest levels. Britain's potential dominance in 1880 and 1900 was particularly striking in the international economic system, where her share of trade and foreign investment was about twice as large as that of any other state.

It was only after the First World War that the United States became relatively larger and more developed in terms of all four indicators. This potential dominance reached new and dramatic heights between 1945 and 1960. Since then, the relative position of the United States has declined, bringing it quite close to West Germany, its nearest rival, in terms of per capita income and share of world trade. The devaluations of the dollar that have taken place since 1972 are reflected in a continuation of this downward trend for income and aggregate size.

The relative potential economic power of Britain and the United States is shown in [Tables 1 and 2].

In sum, Britain was the world's most important trading state from the period after the Napoleonic Wars until 1913. Her relative position rose until about 1880 and fell thereafter. The United States became the largest and most advanced state in economic terms after the First World War, but did not equal the relative share of world trade and investment achieved by Britain in the 1880's until after the Second World War.

TABLE 1 Indicators of British Potential Power (ratio of British value to next highest)

	Per capita income	Aggregate size	Share of world trade	Share of world investment*
1860	.91(US)	.74(US)	2.01(FR)	n.a.
1880	1.30(US)	.79(1874–83 US)	2.22(FR)	1.93(FR)
1900	1.05(1899 US)	.58(1899 US)	2.17(1890 GERM)	2.08(FR)
1913	.92(US)	.43(US)	1.20(US)	2.18(1914 FR)
1928	.66(US)	.25(1929 US)	.79(US)	.64(1921–29 US)
1937	.79(US)	.29(US)	.88(US)	.18(1930–38 US)
1950	.56(US)	.19(US)	.69(US)	.13(1951–55 US)
1960	.49(US)	.14(US)	.46(1958 US)	.15(1956–61 US)
1972	.46(US)	.13(US)	.47(1973 US)	n.a.

*Stock 1870–1913; Flow 1928–1950.

NOTE: Years are in parentheses when different from those in first column.

Countries in parentheses are those with the largest values for the particular indicator other than Great Britain. n.a. = not available.

TABLE 2 Indicators of U.S. Potential Power (ratio of U.S. value to next highest)

	Per capita income	Aggregate size	Share of world trade	Share of world investment flows
1860	1.10(GB)	1.41(GB)	.36(GB)	Net debtor
1880	.77(GB)	1.23(1883 GB)	.37(GB)	Net debtor
1900	.95(1899 GB)	1.73(1899 GB)	.43(1890 GB)	n.a.
1913	1.09(GB)	2.15(RUS)	.83(GB)	Net debtor
1928	1.51(GB)	3.22(USSR)	1.26(GB)	1.55(1921–20 UK)
1937	1.26(GB)	2.67(USSR)	1.13(GB)	5.53(1930–38 UK)
1950	1.78(GB)	3.15(USSR)	1.44(GB)	7.42(1951–55 UK)
1960	2.05(GB)	2.81(USSR)	2.15(1958 GB)	6.60(1956–61 UK)
1972	1.31(GERM)	n.a.	1.18(1973 GERM)	n.a.

NOTE: Years are in parentheses when different from those in first column.

Countries in parentheses are those with the largest values for the particular indicator other than the United States. n.a. = not available.

TESTING THE ARGUMENT

The contention that hegemony leads to a more open trading structure is fairly well, but not perfectly, confirmed by the empirical evidence presented in the preceding sections. The argument explains the periods 1820 to 1879, 1880 to 1900, and 1945 to 1960. It does not fully explain those from 1900 to 1913, 1919 to 1939, or 1960 to the present.

1820–1879

The period from 1820 to 1879 was one of increasing openness in the structure of international trade. It was also one of rising hegemony. Great Britain was the instigator and supporter of the new structure. She began lowering her trade barriers in the 1820's, before any other state. The signing of the Cobden-Chevalier Tariff Treaty with France in 1860 initiated a series of bilateral tariff reductions. It is, however, important to note that the United States was hardly involved in these developments, and that America's ratio of trade to aggregate economic activity did not increase during the nineteenth century.

Britain put to use her internal flexibility and external power in securing a more open structure. At the domestic level, openness was favored by the rising industrialists. The opposition of the agrarian sector was mitigated by its capacity for adjustment: the rate of capital investment and technological innovation was high enough to prevent British agricultural incomes from falling until some thirty years after the abolition of the Corn Laws. Symbolically, the Manchester School led by Cobden and Bright provided the ideological justification for free trade. Its influence was felt throughout Europe where Britain stood as an example to at least some members of the elite.

Britain used her military strength to open many backward areas: British interventions were frequent in Latin America during the nineteenth century, and formal and informal colonial expansion opened the interior of Africa. Most importantly, Britain forced India into the international economic system. British military power was also a factor in concluding the Cobden-Chevalier Treaty, for Louis Napoleon was more concerned with cementing his relations with Britain than he was in the economic consequences of greater openness. Once this pact was signed, however, it became a catalyst for the many other treaties that followed.

Britain also put economic instruments to good use in creating an open system. The abolition of the Corn Laws offered continental grain producers the incentive of continued access to the growing British market. Britain was at the heart of the nineteenth-century international monetary system which functioned exceptionally well, at least for the core of the more developed states and the areas closely associated with them. Exchange rates were stable, and countries did not have to impose trade barriers to rectify cyclical payments difficulties. Both confidence and liquidity were, to a critical degree, provided by Britain. The use of sterling balances as opposed to specie became increasingly widespread, alleviating the liquidity problems presented by the erratic production of gold and silver. Foreign private and central banks increasingly placed their cash reserves in London, and accounts were cleared through changing bank balances rather than gold flows. Great Britain's extremely sophisticated financial institutions, centered in the City of London, provided the short-term financing necessary to facilitate the international flow of goods. Her early and somewhat fortuitous adherence to the gold—as opposed to the silver or bimetallic—standard proved to be an important source of confidence as all countries adopted at least a *de facto* gold standard after 1870 because of the declining relative value of silver. In times of monetary emergency, the confidence placed in the pound because of the strength of the British economy allowed the Bank of England to be a lender of last resort.

Hence, for the first three-quarters of the nineteenth century, British policy favored an open international trading structure, and British power helped to create it. But this was not a global regime. British resources were not sufficient to entice or compel the United States (a country whose economy was larger than Britain's by 1860 and whose technology was developing very rapidly) to abandon its protectionist commercial policy. As a state-power argument suggests, openness was only established within the geographical area where the rising economic hegemony was able to exercise its influence.

1880–1900

The last two decades of the nineteenth century were a period of modest closure which corresponds to a relative decline in British per capita income, size, and share of world trade. The event that precipitated higher tariff levels was the availability of inexpensive grain from the American Midwest, made possible by the construction of continental railways. National responses varied. Britain let her agricultural sector decline, a not unexpected development given her still dominant economic position. Denmark, a small and relatively well-developed state, also refrained from imposing tariffs and transformed its farming sector from agriculture to animal husbandry. Several other small states also followed open policies. Germany, France, Russia, and Italy imposed higher tariffs, however. Britain did not have the military or economic power to forestall these policies. Still, the institutional structure of the international monetary system, with the city of London at its center, did not crumble. The decline in trade proportions was modest despite higher tariffs.

1945–1960

The third period that is neatly explained by the argument that hegemony leads to an open trading structure is the decade and a half after the Second World War, characterized by the ascendancy of the United States. During these years the structure of the international trading system became increasingly open. Tariffs were lowered; trade proportions were restored well above interwar levels. Asymmetrical regional trading patterns did begin to decline, although not until the late 1950's. America's bilateral rival, the Soviet Union, remained—as the theory would predict—encapsulated within its own regional sphere of influence.

Unlike Britain in the nineteenth century, the United States after the Second World War operated in a bipolar political structure. Free trade was preferred, but departures such as the Common Market and Japanese import restrictions were accepted to make sure that these areas remained within the general American sphere of influence. Domestically the Reciprocal Trade Agreements

Act, first passed in 1934, was extended several times after the war. Internationally the United States supported the framework for tariff reductions provided by the General Agreement on Tariffs and Trade. American policy makers used their economic leverage over Great Britain to force an end to the imperial preference system. The monetary system established at Bretton Woods was basically an American creation. In practice, liquidity was provided by the American deficit; confidence by the size of the American economy. Behind the economic veil stood American military protection for other industrialized market economies—an overwhelming incentive for them to accept an open system, particularly one which was in fact relatively beneficial.

The argument about the relationship between hegemony and openness is not as satisfactory for the years 1900 to 1913, 1919 to 1939, and 1960 to the present.

1900–1913

During the years immediately preceding the First World War, the structure of international trade became more open in terms of trade proportions and regional patterns. Britain remained the largest international economic entity, but her relative position continued a decline that had begun two decades earlier. Still, Britain maintained her commitment to free trade and to the financial institutions of the city of London. A state-power argument would suggest some reconsideration of these policies.

Perhaps the simplest explanation for the increase in trade proportions was the burst of loans that flowed out of Europe in the years before the First World War, loans that financed the increasing sale of goods. Germany and France as well as Britain participated in this development. Despite the higher tariff levels imposed after 1879, institutional structures—particularly the monetary system—allowed these capital flows to generate increasing trade flows. Had Britain reconsidered her policies, this might not have been the case.

1919–1939

The United States emerged from the First World War as the world's most powerful economic state. Whether America was large enough to have put an open system in place is a moot question. As Table 2 indicates, America's share of world trade and investment was [respectively] only 26 and 55 percent greater than that of any other state, while comparable figures for Great Britain during the last part of the nineteenth century are 100 percent. What is apparent, though, is that American policy makers made little effort to open the structure of international trade. The call for an open door was a shibboleth, not a policy. It was really the British who attempted to continue a hegemonic role.

In the area of trade, the U.S. Fordney-McCumber Tariff of 1922 increased protection. That tendency was greatly reinforced by the Smoot-Hawley Tariff of 1930 which touched off a wave of protective legislation. Instead of leading the way to openness, the United States led the way to closure.

In the monetary area, the American government made little effort to alter a situation that was confused and often chaotic. During the first half of the 1920's, exchange rates fluctuated widely among major currencies as countries were forced, by the inflationary pressures of the war, to abandon the gold standard. Convertibility was restored in the mid-twenties at values incompatible with long-term equilibrium. The British pound was overvalued, and the French franc undervalued. Britain was forced off the gold standard in September 1931, accelerating a trend that had begun with Uruguay in April 1929. The United States went off gold in 1933. France's decision to end convertibility in 1936 completed the pattern. During the 1930's the monetary system collapsed.

Constructing a stable monetary order would have been no easy task in the political environment of the 1920's and 1930's. The United States made no effort. It refused to recognize a connection between war debts and reparations, although much of the postwar flow of funds took the form of American loans to Germany, German reparations payments to France and Britain, and French and British war-debt payments to the United States. The Great Depression was in no small measure touched off by the contraction of American credit in the late 1920's. In the deflationary collapse that followed, the British were too weak to act as a lender of last resort, and the Americans actually undercut efforts to reconstruct the Western economy when, before the London Monetary Conference of 1933, President Roosevelt changed the basic assumptions of the meeting by taking the United States off gold. American concern was wholly with restoring the domestic economy.

That is not to say that American behavior was entirely obstreperous; but cooperation was erratic and often private. The Federal Reserve Bank of New York did try, during the late 1920's, to maintain New York interest rates below those in London to protect the value of the pound. Two Americans, Dawes and Young, lent their names to the renegotiations of German reparations payments, but most of the actual work was carried out by British experts. At the official level, the first manifestation of American leadership was President Hoover's call for a moratorium on war debts and reparations in June 1931; but in 1932 the United States refused to participate in the Lausanne Conference that in effect ended reparations.

It was not until the mid-thirties that the United States asserted any real leadership. The Reciprocal Trade Agreements Act of 1934 led to bilateral treaties with twenty-seven countries before 1945. American concessions covered 64 percent of dutiable items, and reduced rates by an average of 44 percent. However, tariffs were so high to begin with that the actual impact of these agreements was limited. There were also some modest steps toward tariff liberalization in Britain and France. In the monetary field, the United States, Britain, and France pledged to maintain exchange-rate stability in the Tripartite Declaration of September 1936. These actions were not adequate to create an open international economic structure. American policy during the interwar period, and particularly before the mid-thirties, fails to accord with the predictions made by a state-power explanation of the behavior of a rising hegemonic power.

1960–Present

The final period not adequately dealt with by a state-power explanation is the last decade or so. In recent years, the relative size and level of development of the U.S. economy has fallen. This decline has not, however, been accompanied by a clear turn toward protectionism. The Trade Expansion Act of 1962 was extremely liberal and led to the very successful Kennedy Round of multilateral tariff cuts during the mid-sixties. The protectionist Burke-Hartke Bill did not pass. The 1974 Trade Act does include new protectionist aspects, particularly in its requirements for review of the removal of non-tariff barriers by Congress and for stiffer requirements for the imposition of countervailing duties, but it still maintains the mechanism of presidential discretion on tariff cuts that has been the keystone of postwar reductions. While the Voluntary Steel Agreement, the August 1971 economic policy, and restrictions on agricultural exports all show a tendency toward protectionism, there is as yet no evidence of a basic turn away from a commitment to openness.

In terms of behavior in the international trading system, the decade of the 1960's was clearly one of greater openness. Trade proportions increased, and traditional regional trade patterns became weaker. A state-power argument would predict a downturn or at least a faltering in these indicators as American power declined.

In sum, although the general pattern of the structure of international trade conforms with the predictions of a state-power argument—two periods of openness separated by one of closure—corresponding to periods of rising British and American hegemony and an interregnum, the whole pattern is out of phase. British commitment to openness continued long after Britain's position had declined. American commitment to openness did not begin until well after the United States had become the world's leading economic power and has continued during a period of relative American decline. The state-power argument needs to be amended to take these delayed reactions into account.

AMENDING THE ARGUMENT

The structure of the international trading system does not move in lockstep with changes in the distribution of potential power among states. Systems are initiated and ended, not as a state-power theory would predict, by close assessments of the interests of the state at every given moment, but by external events—usually cataclysmic ones. The closure that began in 1879 coincided with the Great Depression of the last part of the nineteenth century. The final dismantling of the nineteenth-century international economic system was not precipitated by a change in British trade or monetary policy, but by the First World War and the Depression. The potato famine of the 1840's prompted abolition of the Corn Laws; and the United States did not assume the mantle of world leadership until the world had been laid bare by six years of total war. Some catalytic external event seems necessary to move states to dramatic policy initiatives in line with state interests.

Once policies have been adopted, they are pursued until a new crisis demonstrates that they are no longer feasible. States become locked in by the impact of prior choices on their domestic political structures. The British decision to opt for openness in 1846 corresponded with state interests. It also strengthened the position of industrial and financial groups over time, because they had the opportunity to operate in an international system that furthered their objectives. That system eventually undermined the position of British farmers, a group that would have supported protectionism if it had survived. Once entrenched, Britain's export industries, and more importantly the City of London, resisted policies of closure. In the interwar years, the British rentier class insisted on restoring the prewar parity of the pound—a decision that placed enormous deflationary pressures on the domestic economy—because they wanted to protect the value of their investments.

Institutions created during periods of rising ascendancy remained in operation when they were no longer appropriate. For instance, the organization of British banking in the nineteenth century separated domestic and foreign operations. The Court of Directors of the Bank of England was dominated by international banking houses. Their decisions about British monetary policy were geared toward the international economy. Under a different institutional arrangement more attention might have been given after 1900 to the need to revitalize the domestic economy. The British state was unable to free itself from the domestic structures that its earlier policy decisions had created, and continued to follow policies appropriate for a rising hegemony long after Britain's star had begun to fall.

Similarly, earlier policies in the United States begat social structures and institutional arrangements that trammeled state policy. After protecting import-competing industries for a century, the United States was unable in the 1920's to opt for more open policies, even though state interests would have been furthered thereby. Institutionally, decisions about tariff reductions were taken primarily in congressional committees, giving virtually any group seeking protection easy access to the decision-making process. When there were conflicts among groups, they were resolved by raising the levels of protection for everyone. It was only after the cataclysm of the Depression that the decision-making processes for trade policy were changed. The presidency, far more insulated from the entreaties of particular societal groups than congressional committees, was then given more power. Furthermore, the American commercial banking system was unable to assume the burden of regulating the international economy during the 1920's. American institutions were geared toward the domestic economy. Only after the Second World War, and in fact not until the late 1950's, did American banks fully develop the complex institutional structures commensurate with the dollar's role in the international monetary system.

Having taken the critical decisions that created an open system after 1945, the American government is unlikely to change its policy until it confronts some external event that it cannot control, such as a worldwide deflation, drought in the great plains, or the malicious use of petrodollars. In America perhaps more than in any other country "new policies," as E. E. Schattschneider wrote in his brilliant study of the Smoot-Hawley Tariff in 1935, "create new politics,"[1] for in America the state is weak and the society strong. State decisions taken because of state interests reinforce private societal groups that the state is unable to resist in later periods. Multinational corporations have grown and prospered since 1950. International economic policy making has passed from the Congress to the Executive. Groups favoring closure, such as organized labor, are unlikely to carry the day until some external event demonstrates that existing policies can no longer be implemented.

The structure of international trade changes in fits and starts; it does not flow smoothly with the redistribution of potential state power. Nevertheless, it is the power and the policies of states that create order where there would otherwise be chaos or at best a Lockean state of nature. The existence of various transnational, multinational, transgovernmental, and other nonstate actors that have riveted scholarly attention in recent years can only be understood within the context of a broader structure that ultimately rests upon the power and interests of states, shackled though they may be by the societal consequences of their own past decisions.

NOTE

1. E. E. Schattschneider, *Politics, Pressures and the Tariff: A Study of Free Enterprise in Pressure Politics as Shown in the 1929–1930 Revision of the Tariff* (New York: Prentice-Hall 1935).

2

The Political Economy of the Smoot-Hawley Tariff

BARRY EICHENGREEN

Barry Eichengreen presents a domestic societal explanation of the passage of the Smoot-Hawley Tariff Act of 1930, which set historically high tariffs on thousands of items in the United States and likely contributed to the problems of the Great Depression. Eichengreen argues that economic interest groups were the key actors underlying the passage of the act. Specifically, he asserts that certain sectors of agriculture and industry supported each other's desire for protection and together pressured the U.S. government to pass the highly restrictive Smoot-Hawley Tariff. He shows both how the actions of self-interested groups in national societies affect the making of foreign economic policy and how international political and market forces can influence the interests of societal actors.

The intimate connection between the Great Depression and the Smoot-Hawley Tariff of 1930 was recognized by contemporaries and continues to be emphasized by historical scholars. But just as contemporaries, while agreeing on its importance, nonetheless viewed the tariff in a variety of different ways, historians of the era have achieved no consensus on the tariff's origins and effects. The definitive study of the Smoot-Hawley's origins, by Schattschneider [1935], portrays the tariff as a classic example of pork-barrel politics, with each member of Congress after his particular piece of pork. Revisionist treatments characterize it instead as a classic instance of party politics; protectionism being the household remedy of the Republican Party, the tariff's adoption is ascribed to the outcome of the 1928 election. Yet proponents of neither interpretation provide an adequate analysis of the relationship of Smoot-Hawley to the Depression. . . .

POLITICS, PRESSURES AND THE TARIFF

The debate surrounding the passage of the Tariff Act of 1930 remains a classic study in the political economy of protection. A number of theories have been developed to explain Smoot-Hawley's adoption, starting with that advanced in Schattschneider's [1935] classic monograph whose title this section bears.

Schattschneider's influential study "set the tone for a whole generation of political writing on pressure groups. . . ." and "cut the lens through which

Americans have since visualized the making of U.S. foreign trade policy. . . ."[1] Schattschneider focused on the influence of special interest groups. In his account, the actions of lobbyists and special interests were responsible for both the tariff's adoption and its form.

Schattschneider dubbed the principal around which the tariff coalition organized "reciprocal noninterference." The coalition was assembled by offering limited protection to everyone involved. Since only moderate protection was provided and no single import-competing sector reaped extraordinary benefits at the expense of others, they could combine in support of tariff legislation. In addition, under provisions of the original House and Senate bills, credits (or "debentures") were to be made available to exporters, extending the coalition beyond the import-competing to the export-producing sector. Not just the number of duties raised but the very process by which the bill was passed is invoked in support of the log-rolling interpretation. Passage required 14 months from when Hoover called a special session of Congress to when the final bill was signed. The record of public hearings in which the bill was discussed ran to 20,000 pages, while the final bill provided tariff schedules for more than 20,000 items. Since insurgency was easier under Senate than House rules, log-rolling was more conspicuous there: the Senate amended the House bill over 1,200 times, most of them on the Senate floor. Still other changes were engineered in conference committee.

If the distinguishing feature of the Tariff Act of 1930 was the dominance of special interests, one must ask why they had grown so much more powerful. Schattschneider provides no explicit answer, although he indicts Hoover for failing to guide the legislation through Congress. But the systematic explanation implicit in his analysis is the rise of the "new lobby." Although fraternal, religious, social, and economic groups had always been part of the American scene, they had never been so well organized or visible in the Capitol as in the 1920s. . . .

A number of influences prompted the rise of the new lobby. First, the activities of the "muckrakers" in the first decade of the twentieth century had intensified public scrutiny of political affairs. Second, whereas businessmen had traditionally dealt with government in "a spasmodic and haphazard fashion," the panic of 1907 spurred them to cultivate more systematic representation. Simultaneously, the U.S. Chamber of Commerce took a more prominent role in representing the interests of business. . . . Finally, much as the Chamber of Commerce represented business's general interests, trade associations filled this role for more specialized groups. A Department of Commerce publication listed some 1,500 organizations classified as trade associations, nearly double the number known to exist in 1914. Some were organized by products produced, others by materials used, still others by markets in which sales took place. Like the other three influences, the growth of trade associations was a distinctively twentieth-century development, but in contrast to other trends, which had been under way in the early years of the century, the sudden rise to prominence of trade associations was attributable to World War I. The war effort required closer ties between government and industry, but upon attempting to establish them the authorities found it difficult to deal with individual enterprises and requested that associations be formed. If the war occasioned the formation and growth of trade associations, the armistice by no means signalled their demise. Once formed into an association the process of marshalling a constituency was no longer so difficult. Improvements in communication, notably the telephone, reinforced these advantages, and associations quickly learned to use pamphlets and other media to publicize their case. The adoption of new Congressional rules made it more difficult for powerful individuals to dictate policy, opening the legislative process to competing interests.

The same forces tending to promote effective representation of industrial interests in Washington encouraged the formation of effective organizations representing farmers and labor. The American farm movement had long been distinguished by its inability to organize effectively and represent its interests before Congress. The ad hoc methods of agricultural organizations, such as sending a representative to Washington in response to specific developments, had proven ineffectual. For agriculture as for industry, World War I and the impetus it provided for the formation of the War Trade Board and the Food Administration permitted farmers' organizations to assume new importance. In 1918 the National Grange opened a permanent legislative office in Washington, and the militant American Farm Bureau Federation, founded in 1919, lobbied actively for farm legislation. In 1921 a bipartisan Farm Bloc of senators and congressmen from the South and West was formed, and it acquired a pivotal position in the balance of power in the 66th and 67th Congresses. Although it had at best mixed success in passing farm legislation before falling into disarray, the prominence of the Farm Bloc did much to alert agricultural interests to the advantages of effective congressional representation.

By encouraging the development of direct government-labor relations, the war had a similar impact on the American Federation of Labor. While maintaining its distance from party politics, by the 1920s the AFL was commonly acknowledged as the most formidable group in the United States other than the political parties. Thus, in the 1920s the three principal American interest groups—business, agriculture, and labor—were for the first time ably represented in Washington.

The rise of the new lobby is consistent with Schattschneider's characterization of Smoot-Hawley as an instance of pork-barrel politics. But his theory of reciprocal noninterference—that the Smoot-Hawley bill by offering something for everyone garnered widespread support—fails to confront the question of why the vote on the final bill so closely followed party lines, with only 5 Democratic Senators voting in favor and 11 Republicans against. Neither does it explain why tariff-rate increases differed so widely by schedule.

An alternative explanation, recently advanced by Pastor [1980], is that Smoot-Hawley is simply an instance of party politics. Protection in general and for industry in particular was regularly advocated by the Republican Party. With the White House occupied by a Republican President and the Senate in Republican hands, there were few obstacles to revising upward existing tariff schedules. It is curious that this straightforward explanation has attracted so little attention. It may be that partisan aspects of the debate were disguised by the absence of a change in party in 1928 like that following the 1920 election which preceded the 1922 Fordney-McCumber Tariff Act. Moreover, the issue of protection had not been hotly disputed in the 1928 campaign. Although the Democrats had traditionally campaigned on the basis of staunch opposition to protectionist measures, in 1928 they moderated their position and joined the Republicans in endorsing protection, albeit in vague and reserved terms. . . . Given the extent of consensus, there was little debate in the subsequent Congress over principles of free trade and protection. Hence even Free Traders among the Democrats were ill positioned to mount effective opposition to tariff increases.

The problem with this partisan interpretation is that it provides no explanation for Smoot-Hawley's timing or its form. It is suggested that Congress was simply accustomed to engaging in tariff revision every seven years (the average life of a tariff law between the Acts of 1883 and 1930), and that by 1929 Congress and the public had recovered from the exhausting Fordney-McCumber deliberations of 1920–22. But this mechanical explanation neither recognizes links between protectionist pressure and economic events nor provides an explanation for the observed variation in import duty levels.

The explanation coming closest to satisfying these requirements is the view of Smoot-Hawley as a response to the problems of American agriculture. The explanation runs as follows. While the 1920s were boom years for the country as a whole, prosperity was unevenly distributed. After benefiting from high prices from 1917 to 1920, American agriculture failed to recover from the recession of 1920–21. For much of the decade, farm gate prices declined relative to the prices of nonagricultural goods. . . . In 1926, a relatively favorable year for farmers when average wholesale prices were 51 percent above their 1913 levels, the prices of farm products were only 42 percent above those levels. The explanation for lagging prices was that World War I had prompted the expansion of agricultural production outside Europe. While European sugar production, for example, fell by 50 percent during the war, the shortfall was offset by expanding output in Cuba, Java, and South America. Once European production recovered, often under cover of import duties or production subsidies, world prices were depressed. Similarly, wartime disruptions of the global wheat market greatly stimulated production in Argentina, Australia, Canada, and the United States. The consequent decline in prices was magnified in the second half of the 1920s by the imposition of import duties on wheat by Germany, Italy, and France.

Agrarian distress in the United States took various forms, notably farm foreclosures which, after averaging 3.2 per thousand farms between 1913 and 1920, rose to 10.7 per thousand in 1921–25 and 17.0 per thousand in 1926–29. Foreclosure reflected not just the declining relative price of agricultural products but overall price level trends; since much agricultural land had turned over between 1917 and 1920 when prices were high, the subsequent deflation greatly augmented the burden of mortgage debt. The value of total farm mortgage debt rose by 45 percent between 1917 and 1920 and by a further 28 percent between 1920 and 1923 despite the deflation that set in after the beginning of the decade. The foreclosures of the second half of the 1920s were most heavily concentrated in Idaho, Montana, North and South Dakota, Colorado, and Arizona, the sources of strongest pressure for agrarian relief.

In the 1928 presidential campaign Hoover laid stress on tariff protection for agriculture. Previously, agriculture had been the recipient of only modest tariffs, in part because duties on farm imports would have been ineffective given U.S. status as a net exporter of most agricultural goods (sugar, wool and hides being the principal exceptions). In 1922, for reasons detailed above, the U.S. balance of trade in farm products turned negative, where it remained except in 1925 for the duration of the decade. Hence an expanding segment of American agriculture grew to appreciate the relevance of tariff protection.

By this interpretation, Smoot-Hawley was predominantly a form of agricultural relief. . . . Farm interests were well positioned to press their case. Although the United States had grown increasingly urbanized over preceding decades, Congress had not been reapportioned following the 1920 Census. Consequently, farm interests were overrepresented in the House, just as, on the two senator per state rule, they were overrepresented in the Senate.

This characterization of Smoot-Hawley as an agricultural measure won by the West over the opposition of the East is consistent not only with the partisan interpretation, given the regional concentration of Democratic and Republican voters, but it explains a number of defections from party ranks. To the extent that agricultural distress intensified with the onset of the Depression, it links the tariff to macroeconomic conditions. Where it falls short is in explaining why tariffs on manufactured imports were raised as part of an agrarian relief measure, or why the tariff was supported not only by representatives of agricultural districts but by those of industrial regions as well. Many accounts emphasize the extent of discord between agriculture and industry. . . . What explains the pattern of voting and the tariff schedule that emerged from Congressional debate?

A MODEL OF THE TARIFF-MAKING PROCESS

The framework I use to analyze the adoption of Smoot-Hawley is a variant of Gerschenkron's [1943] model of the political economy of protection. This is a member of the class of "interest-group models" of tariff formation. . . . I first review Gerschenkron's application of his model to Bismarckian Germany before adapting it to analysis of the Smoot-Hawley Tariff.

In Gerschenkron's model, a tariff is adopted when narrow yet well-placed interest groups combine in its support. Gerschenkron divides German society not merely along sectoral lines but into heavy industry (producers of basic products such as coal, iron and steel), light industry (manufacturers of consumer goods, along with whom might be included artisans and shopkeepers), large agriculture (the Junkers, or estate owners of the east), and small agriculture (commercial producers located primarily west of the Elbe). He explains the Bismarckian tariff as a coalition of iron and rye, allying large agriculture and heavy industry.

In the 1870s as in the 1920s, the impetus for agrarian protection was the fall in grain prices. The position of traditional German agriculture, which specialized in grain, was seriously undermined. The alternative to continued grain production behind tariff walls was to shift into the production of high quality foodstuffs such as dairy products and meat for rapidly expanding urban markets. Cheap imported grain could serve as an input into such production. But, crucially, large and small agriculture differed in their capacity to adjust. Variations in soil quality and proximity to urban markets provided greater scope for the production of dairy products and meat west of the Elbe. In addition, dairy products, meats and vegetables were most efficiently produced on small owner-managed farms. Hence costs of adjustment were lowest where long-term leaseholders and small owner-managed farms predominated—west of the Elbe—and highest where landless laborers worked large estates. The model predicts that small agriculture should have opposed agricultural protection due to its impact on costs, while large agriculture should have favored it.

Neither light nor heavy industry, with the possible exception of yarn spinning, desperately required protection from import competition. Under competitive conditions, Germany probably would have imported grain and exported both light manufactures and the products of the basic industries. While it is not clear that import duties on industrial goods would have succeeded in raising the prices of domestically produced goods, given competition at home but the net export position of German manufacturers, heavy industry in fact supported the imposition of a tariff on manufactured goods. One interpretation is that, with high levels of fixed capital, heavy industry was exceptionally susceptible to cyclical fluctuations. Tariffs may have reduced the risk of falling prices, thereby encouraging the fixed investments which permitted scale economies to be reaped. A more compelling interpretation is that barriers to cheap imports were a necessary condition for firms producing basic goods to combine and extract monopoly profits from domestic users. Consistent with this interpretation, producers of final goods like stoves, pots and pans, shovels and rakes opposed tariffs on the products of basic industries because of their impact on production costs.

What is relevant for our purposes is that no group favored the final out-come: high tariffs on both agricultural and industrial goods. But because of the dispersion of interests, action required compromise. The two likely outcomes were a coalition of large industrialists and landowners obtaining general protection, and a coalition of small manufacturers and farmers successfully defending free trade. Gerschenkron ascribes the victory of the protectionist coalition to institutional factors. The Junkers, as members of the squirearchy, occupied a privileged position in the political system. Not only did they staff the bureaucracy and judiciary but, like the wealthy industrialists, they benefitted from the structure of the electoral system. Heavy industry, aided by smaller numbers, organized more effectively than small manufacturing. Managers of large enterprises formed new associations and worked to convert existing ones to protectionism. Their cause was not hurt by the fact that the Chancellor found protection a useful tool for achieving his political goals and played an active role in forging the alliance of iron and rye.

Gerschenkron's model can be applied to the case of the Smoot-Hawley Tariff by again distinguishing industry by size and agriculture by region. Naturally, the interests of the groups and the coalitions are entirely different from those observed in Bismarckian Germany. So is the role of national leadership. Nonetheless, distinctions of region and scale shed considerable light on the American case.

In the case of Smoot-Hawley, it is useful to distinguish sheltered from unsheltered agriculture and, as in Germany, light from heavy industry, where it is light industry and unsheltered agriculture that combined to support protection. As noted previously, critics of the Smoot-Hawley Tariff argued that duties on agricultural products would not be "effective" in raising prices because the United States was a net exporter of these goods. . . . The problem with this contention is that net trade may not be the appropriate indicator of the effectiveness of a tariff. It may mislead either if there existed segmented regional markets or if products were heterogeneous. For goods such as wheat with a high ratio of value to volume, there existed not merely a national but an international market. But wheat was not a homogenous product, and the United States both imported and exported different grades of what was often regarded in policy debate as a single commodity. Since, for example, little if any exportable surplus of high grade milling wheat was produced in the United States, it was argued that a tariff would therefore be effective in raising the Minneapolis price relative to that prevailing in Winnipeg. Even if the product was homogenous, for perishable products the United States was sufficiently large geographically that transport costs might impede the equalization of prices across regions. . . . Northern states like Minnesota and Eastern Seaboard states like Massachusetts might find their markets flooded by cheap Canadian potatoes, milk, cream, butter and eggs. Since these goods could not penetrate further into the interior because of their high ratio of volume to value or due to the danger of spoilage, inland producers remained insulated from imports. Moreover, Southern farmers who engaged in the production of cotton (other than the long staple variety, which was imported and received a generous increase in tariff protection under the 1930 Act) were oriented toward the export market. Northern farmers close to the Canadian border had reason to favor protection to a much greater extent than their counterparts in the Interior or the South.

There existed equally sharp divisions within manufacturing. The pressure for protection was greatest in light industry concentrating in the batch production of goods tailored to market. Heavy industry and manufacturers of standardized products had mechanized their operations and largely held their own against foreign competition. But labor-intensive industries dominated by small-scale firms experienced growing competition from abroad. In the bottle-making industry, producers of "fancy ware" such as perfume and toilet water bottles suffered from an increasing volume of French imports. Manufacturers of watches faced Swiss competition and producers of jewelry complained of German imports. Eastern glove manufacturers experienced difficulty in matching the prices of foreign goods. The New England shoe industry experienced competition from Czechoslovak producers. Some producers were sheltered by relatively generous Fordney-McCumber duties. But, for most, foreign trends such as the desperate attempts of English mills to hold onto market share exacerbated their woes. Still, only a minority of American industries were seriously injured by competition from foreign goods.

In opposition stood heavy industries producing standardized products, particularly segments which relied on the assembly line, mass production, the latest technology and the multi-divisional form. By the turn of the century, the United States had gained a competitive advantage in many of the industries of the Second Industrial Revolution, automobiles being a prime example. In 1929 motor cars and parts comprised 10 percent of total U.S. merchandise exports, while imports were negligible due only partially to a modicum of tariff protection. Given the importance of export sales and the anticipated impact of a tariff on production costs, the automobile producers, led by Henry Ford, made clear their opposition to the tariff bill. The same was true of producers of farm machinery, iron and steel bars, sheet, rails and metal manufactures.

The banking community had traditionally supported the protectionist system. Bankers doing business in industrial regions where firms depended on the tariff favored the maintenance of protection. But in the 1920s their support was tempered by events. World War I had transformed the United States from a debtor to a creditor nation and reoriented America's banking business abroad. Already in 1923 spokesmen for the financial community acknowledged that Europe's continued ability to service its dollar debt hinged upon foreign industries' access to American markets.

The opposite shift was evident in the attitudes of organized labor. Traditionally, labor had opposed protection for its impact on the cost of living. Those groups of workers injured by import competition were incapable of changing this policy. For half a century the AFL's position on the tariff had been one of carefully cultivated neutrality. Although individual unions might lobby for protection against imported goods or for lower duties on raw materials, the Federation's policy was to take no position on the issue. In 1930 it went only so far as to accede to individual unions' requests for legislative assistance. However, at the November 1928 AFL convention the first official caucus of pro-tariff unions was formed. This "Wage Earners Protective Conference" represented 8 or 9 percent of the Federation's membership, the leading participants including the photo-engravers, wallpaper craftsmen, glass bottle blowers and potters. Clearly, labor's traditional opposition to protection was attenuated by the success of pro-tariff unions in organizing to lobby for a change in policy.

In sum, the situation in 1930 appeared as follows. Farmers along the Canadian border and Eastern seaboard desired higher protection but, comprising only a minority of American agriculture, found it difficult to obtain alone. Light industries producing goods tailored to market also desired protection but similarly comprised only a portion of American manufacturing. In principle, neither group favored protection for the other, but each was willing to support the claims of its counterpart in return for participation in the coalition. While agriculture received generous protection under the final Smoot-Hawley bill, so did light industry producing goods tailored to market. . . .

This interpretation has advantages over the view of Smoot-Hawley that divides the American economy into monolithic agricultural and industrial blocs. It explains why sections of the industrial Midwest and East should have complained about the height of agricultural tariffs, and why certain agrarian interests, notably in the South, should have complained of industrial protection. It is consistent also with the observed alliance of industrial and agricultural protectionists and explains why the Smoot-Hawley Tariff, originally conceived as agricultural relief, evolved into a bill extending protection to portions of both industry and agriculture. It is consistent with Schattschneider's emphasis on log-rolling aspects of the legislative process, but rather than characterizing log-rolling as entirely general suggests that "reciprocal noninterference" should have favored border agriculture and light industry. It is consistent with the notion that Hoover lost control of the legislative process by permitting the debate to extend beyond the question of agricultural relief and with the inference that Hoover failed to take forceful action on the grounds that he saw the small businesses which dominated light industry as his constituency, but not necessarily with the opinion of Senator Borah that a narrowly agricultural tariff could have passed in 1929 had Hoover taken the bit in his teeth. National leadership, while important in both Gerschenkron's and this paper's application of the model, plays opposite roles in the two instances, since Bismarck favored widespread protection and played a prominent role in obtaining it, while Hoover personally opposed blanket protection but failed to effectively guide the legislative process. Finally, by invoking the rise of the trade association, the model can be used to explain how diverse agricultural and industrial interests succeeded in influencing the legislative process.

The model can be elaborated in various directions. One extension would introduce the long history of protectionism in the United States and the country's habit of neglecting the impact of its economic policies on the rest of the world. Another would build on the tendency of the Depression to undermine confidence in the self-equilibrating nature of the market. In many countries, the depth of the Depression provided a rationale for the extension of economic planning. In Britain, for example, Keynes went so far for a time as to argue for central planning along Soviet lines. In the United States this desire for intervention and control was most clearly manifest in the New Deal, but the same tendencies contributed to the pressure for tariff protection in 1930. . . .

CONCLUSION

. . . Economic histories view the Great Depression and the Smoot-Hawley Tariff as inextricably bound up with one another. They assign a central role to the Depression in explaining the passage of the 1930 Tariff Act and at the same time emphasize the role of the tariff in the singular depth and long duration of the slump. This paper has reexamined the historical evidence on both points. It is not hard to identify relationships linking the tariff to the Depression and vice versa. But the evidence examined here suggests that previous accounts have conveyed what is at best an incomplete and at worst a misleading impression of the mechanisms at work. It is clear that the severity of the initial business cycle downturn lent additional impetus to the campaign for protection. But it is equally clear that the impact of the downturn on the movement for protection worked through different channels than typically posited. Rather than simply strengthening the hand of a Republican Executive predisposed toward protection, or increasing the burden borne by a depressed agricultural sector which had long been agitating for tariff protection, the uneven impact of the Depression occasioned the birth of a protectionist coalition comprised of producers particularly hard hit by import competition: border agriculture and small-scale industry engaged in the production of specialty goods. That coalition was able to obtain for its members substantial increases in levels of tariff protection because of an unusual conjuncture of distinct if related developments including reforms of Congressional procedure, the rise of trade associations and the growth of interventionist sentiment. The experience of Smoot-Hawley documents how macroeconomic distress accompanied by import penetration gives rise to protectionist pressure, but does so only once the analysis transcends the model of monolithic agricultural and industrial blocs. . . .

NOTE

1. The first quote is from Bauer et al. [1972: 25], the second from Pastor [1980: 70].

REFERENCES

Bauer, de Sola Pool, and Dexter [1972]. Raymond Bauer, Ithiel de Sola Pool, and L.A. Dexter. *American Business and Public Policy.* Chicago: Aldine-Atherton, 1972.

Gerschenkron [1943]. Alexander Gerschenkron. *Bread and Democracy in Germany.* University of California Press, 1943.

Pastor [1980]. Robert A. Pastor. *Congress and the Politics of U.S. Foreign Economic Policy, 1929–1976.* University of California Press, 1980.

Schattschneider [1935]. E.E. Schattschneider. *Politics, Pressures and the Tariff.* Prentice-Hall, 1935.

3

History Lessons: Institutions, Factor Endowments, and Paths of Development in the New World

KENNETH L. SOKOLOFF AND STANLEY L. ENGERMAN

In this essay, Kenneth L. Sokoloff and Stanley L. Engerman argue for the importance of domestic political institutions as determinants of economic growth. Their objective is to understand why some former colonies in the Americas have grown so much more than others, producing the wide disparity in economic development seen in the Western Hemisphere today. The authors begin by showing that English colonies in the Caribbean (such as Barbados) and many Spanish colonies (such as Mexico and Peru) were initially just as well-off, or even richer, than northern colonies like the present-day United States or Canada. To explain the subsequent differences in development, Sokoloff and Engerman develop an argument that runs from initial factor endowments (in soil and climatic conditions, as well as land, labor, and capital) to the development of domestic institutions, to long-term growth rates. In areas like the Caribbean and Brazil, soils and climate were suited to valuable plantation crops, such as sugar, which stimulated the importation of slaves. This created a large, poor, and disenfranchised segment of the population. In other places, like Peru, large indigenous populations and ample silver ore deposits combined with inequitable land tenure systems to produce a similar outcome: highly unequal societies. Sugar and silver made these colonies wealthy in their early histories, but economic and political inequality impeded the development of domestic institutions necessary for modern economic growth. By contrast, colonies in the northeastern United States and eastern Canada had soils suited for wheat and other grains that required smallholder production. The authors contend that this led to settlement by European immigrants working relatively small farms. These colonies developed more egalitarian societies and political institutions, which provided better protection of property rights and thereby generated more investment and growth.

INTRODUCTION

As Europeans established colonies in the New World of North and South America during the sixteenth, seventeenth, and eighteenth centuries, most knowledgeable observers regarded the North American mainland to be of relatively marginal economic interest, when compared with the extraordinary opportunities available in the Caribbean and Latin America. Voltaire, for example, considered the conflict in North America between the French and the British during the Seven Years' War (1756–63) to be madness and characterized the two countries as "fighting over a few acres of snow." The victorious British were later to engage in a lively public debate over which territory should be taken from the French as reparations—the Caribbean island of Guadeloupe (with a land area of 563 square miles) or Canada. Several centuries later, however, we know that the U.S. and Canadian economies ultimately proved far more successful than the other economies of the hemisphere. The puzzle, therefore, is how and why the areas that were favored by the forecasters of that era, and the destinations of the vast majority of migrants to the Americas through 1800, fell behind economically. . . .

These differentials in paths of development have long been of central concern to scholars of Latin America and have recently attracted more attention from economic historians and economists more generally (North, 1988; Coatsworth, 1998; Acemoglu, Johnson and Robinson, 2000). Although conventional economic factors have certainly not been ignored, the explanations offered for the contrasting records in growth have most often focused on institutions and highlighted the variation across societies in conditions relevant to growth such as the security of property rights, prevalence of corruption, structures of the financial sector, investment in public infrastructure and social capital, and the inclination to work hard or be entrepreneurial. But ascribing differences in development to differences in institutions raises the challenge of explaining where the differences in institutions come from. Those who have addressed this formidable problem have typically emphasized the importance of presumed exogenous differences in religion or national heritage. Douglass North (1988), for example, is one of many who have attributed the relative success of the United States and Canada to British institutions being more conducive to growth than those of Spain and other European colonizers. Others, like John Coatsworth (1998), are skeptical of such generalizations, and suggest that they may obscure the insight that can be gained by examining the extreme diversity of experiences observed across the Americas, even across societies with the same national heritage.

Indeed, . . . the relationship between national heritage and economic performance is weaker than popularly thought. During the colonial period, the economies with the highest per capita incomes were those in the Caribbean, and it made little difference whether they were of Spanish, British, or French origin. The case for the superiority of British institutions is usually based on the records of the United States and Canada, but the majority of the New World societies established by the British—including Barbados, Jamaica, Belize, Guyana, and the lesser-known Puritan colony on Providence Island—were like their other neighbors in not beginning to industrialize until much later. Having been part of the British Empire was far from a guarantee of economic growth. Likewise, there was considerable diversity across the economies of Spanish America. This is most evident in the contrasts between the experiences of the nations of the southern cone and those with large populations of Native American descent, such as Mexico or Peru. It is the former class of countries, including Argentina, that of all the other economies of the New World most closely resemble the United States and Canada in experience over time.

With the evidence of wide disparities even among economies of the same European heritage, scholars have begun to reexamine alternative sources of differences. Though not denying the significance of national heritage, nor of idiosyncratic conditions that are unique to individual countries, they have begun to explore the possibility that initial conditions, or factor endowments broadly conceived, could have had profound and enduring impacts on long-run paths of institutional and economic development in the New World. Economists traditionally emphasize the pervasive influence of factor endowment, so the qualitative thrust of this approach may not be entirely novel. What is new, however, is the specific focus on how the extremely different environments in which the Europeans established their colonies may have led to societies with very different degrees of inequality, and on how these differences might have persisted over time and affected the course of development through their impact on the institutions that evolved. In particular, while essentially all the economies established in the New World began with an abundance of land and natural resources relative to labor, and thus high living standards on average, other aspects of their factor endowments varied in ways that meant that the great majority were characterized virtually from the outset by extreme inequality in wealth, human capital, and political power. From this perspective, the colonies that came to compose the United States and Canada stand out as somewhat deviant cases.

FROM FACTOR ENDOWMENTS TO INEQUALITY

The "discovery" and exploration of the Americas by Europeans was part of a grand, long-term effort to exploit the economic opportunities in underpopulated or underdefended territories around the world. European nations competed for claims and set about extracting material and other advantages through the pursuit of transitory enterprises like expeditions as well as by the establishment of more permanent settlements. At both the levels of national governments and private agents, adaptation or innovation of institutional forms was stimulated by formidable problems of organization raised by the radically novel environments, as well as by the difficulties of effecting the massive and historically unprecedented intercontinental flows of labor and capital. Common to all of the colonies was a high marginal product of labor, as evidenced by the historically unprecedented numbers of migrants who traversed the Atlantic from Europe and Africa despite high costs of transportation.

Well over 60 percent of the more than 6 million individuals who migrated to the New World from 1500 through the end of the eighteenth century were Africans brought over involuntarily as slaves. With their prices set in competitive international markets, slaves ultimately flowed to those locations where they were most productive. There were no serious national or cultural barriers to owning or using them; slaves were welcomed in the colonies of all the major European powers. The fraction of migrants who were slaves grew continuously, from roughly 20 percent prior to 1580 to nearly 75 percent between 1700 and 1760. The prominence of slaves, as well as the increase over time in the proportion of migrants going to the colonies of Portugal, France, and the Netherlands, and the continued quantitative dominance in the destinations of migrants to British America of colonies in the West Indies and on the southern mainland, reflects the increasing specialization by the New World over the colonial period in the production of sugar, coffee, and other staple crops for world markets. These colonies attracted heavy inflows of labor (especially slaves) because their soils and climates made them extraordinarily well-suited for growing these lucrative commodities, and because of the substantial economies of scale in producing such crops on large slave plantations (Fogel, 1989). Indeed, there are few examples of significant colonies which were not so specialized: only the Spanish settlements on the mainlands of North and South America (some of which had concentrations of labor in silver or other mines) and the New England, Middle Atlantic, and Canadian settlements of Britain and France. It was not coincidental that these were also the colonies that relied least on slaves for their labor force.

The economies that specialized in the production of sugar and other highly valued crops associated with extensive use of slaves had the highest per capita (including slaves) incomes in the New World. Most, including Barbados, Cuba, and Jamaica, were in the West Indies, but some (mainly Brazil) were in South America. They specialized in these crops early in their histories, and through the persistent working of technological advantage and international markets in slaves, their economies came to be dominated by large slave plantations and their populations by slaves of African descent. The greater efficiency of the very large plantations, and the overwhelming fraction of the populations that came to be black and slave, made the distributions of wealth and human capital extremely unequal. Even among the free population, there was greater inequality in such economies than in those on the North American mainland.

Although the basis for the predominance of an elite class in such colonies may have been the enormous advantages in sugar production available to those able to assemble a large company of slaves, as well as the extreme disparities in human capital between blacks and whites (both before and after emancipation), the long-run success and stability of the members of this elite were also facilitated by their disproportionate political influence. Together with the legally codified inequality intrinsic to slavery, the greater inequality in wealth contributed to the evolution of institutions that protected the privileges of the elites and restricted opportunities for the broad mass of the population to participate fully in the commercial economy even after the abolition of slavery.

The importance of factor endowments is also evident in a second category of New World colonies that can be thought of as Spanish America, although it also included some islands in the Caribbean. Spain focused its attention on, and designed their New World policies around conditions in, colonies such as Mexico and Peru, whose factor endowments were characterized by rich mineral resources and by substantial numbers of natives surviving contact with the European colonizers. Building on preconquest social organizations, whereby Indian elites extracted tribute from the general population, the Spanish authorities adopted the approach of distributing enormous grants of land, often including claims to a stream of income from the native labor residing in the vicinity, and of mineral resources among a privileged few. The resulting large-scale estates and mines, established early in the histories of these colonies, endured even where the principal production activities were lacking in economies of scale. Although small-scale production was typical of grain agriculture during this era, their essentially non-tradeable property rights to tribute from rather sedentary groups of natives (tied to locations by community property rights in land) gave large landholders the means and the motive to operate at a large scale.

Although the processes are not well understood, it is evident that large-scale agriculture remained dominant in Spanish America . . . and that the distribution of wealth remained highly unequal over time. Elite families generally acted as local representatives of the Spanish government in the countryside during the colonial period and maintained their status long after independence. The persistence and stability of elites, as well as of inequality generally, were also certainly aided by the restrictive immigration policies applied by Spain to her colonies, and by laws throughout Spanish America requiring that a citizen (a status entailing the right to vote and other privileges) own a substantial amount of land (qualifications that were modified in post-independence constitutions to require literacy and a specified economic standing). For different reasons, therefore, Spanish America was like the colonies specializing in the production of crops like sugar in generating an economic structure in which wealth, human capital, and political power were distributed very unequally, and where the elites were drawn from a relatively small group that was of European descent and racially distinct from the bulk of the population.

As in the colonial sugar economies, the economic structures that evolved in this second class of colonies were greatly influenced by the factor endowments, viewed in broad terms. The fabulously valuable mineral resources and abundance of labor with low amounts of human capital were certainly major contributors to the extremely unequal distributions of wealth and income that came to prevail in these economies. Moreover, without the extensive supply of native labor, it is unlikely that Spain could have maintained its policies of tight restrictions on European migration to its colonies and of generous awards of property and tribute to the earliest settlers. The colonists in Spanish America endorsed formidable requirements for obtaining permission to go to the New World—a policy that limited the flow of migrants and helped to preserve the political and economic advantages enjoyed by those of European descent who had already made the move. In 1800, less than 20 percent of the population in Spanish colonies such as Mexico, Peru, and Chile was composed of whites; it would not be until the major new inflows from Europe late in the nineteenth century that Latin American countries such as Argentina and Chile would attain the predominantly European character they have today.

The final category of New World colonies were those located in the northern part of the North American mainland—chiefly those that became the United States, but including Canada as well. These economies were not endowed with substantial populations of natives able to provide labor, nor with climates and soils that gave them a comparative advantage in the production of crops characterized by major economies of using slave labor. For these reasons, their development, especially north of the Chesapeake, was based on laborers of European descent who had relatively high and similar levels of human capital. Compared to either of the other two categories of New World colonies, this class had rather homogenous populations. Correspondingly equal distributions of wealth were also encouraged by the limited advantages to large producers in the production of grains and hays predominant in regions such as the Middle Atlantic and New England. With abundant land and low capital requirements, the great majority of adult men were able to operate as independent proprietors. Conditions were somewhat different in the southern colonies, where crops such as tobacco and rice did exhibit some limited scale economies; cotton, which was grown predominantly on large slave plantations, was not a quantitatively important crop until the nineteenth century. But even here, the size of the slave plantations, as well as the degree of inequality in these colonies, were quite modest by the standards of Brazil or the sugar islands of the Caribbean.

THE ROLE OF INSTITUTIONS IN THE PERSISTENCE OF INEQUALITY

There is strong evidence that various features of the factor endowments of these three categories of New World economies—including soils, climates, and the size or density of the native population—predisposed them toward paths of development associated with different degrees of inequality in wealth, human capital, and political power. Although these conditions might reasonably be treated as exogenous at the beginning of European colonization, it is clear that such an assumption becomes increasingly tenuous as one moves later in time after settlement. Particularly given that both Latin America and many of the economies of the first category, such as Haiti and Jamaica, are known today as generally the most unequal in the world, we suggest that the initial conditions had lingering effects, not only because certain fundamental characteristics of New World economies were difficult to change, but also because government policies and other institutions tended to reproduce them. Specifically, in those societies that began with extreme inequality, elites were better able to establish a legal framework that insured them disproportionate shares of political power, and to use that greater influence to establish rules, laws, and other government policies that advantaged members of the elite relative to nonmembers—contributing to persistence over time of the high degree of inequality. In societies that began with greater equality or homogeneity among the population, however, efforts by elites to institutionalize an unequal distribution of political power were relatively unsuccessful, and the rules, laws, and other government policies that came to be adopted, therefore, tended to provide more equal treatment and opportunities to members of the population.

Land policy provides an illustration of how institutions may have fostered persistence in the extent of inequality in New World economies over time. Since the governments of each colony or nation were regarded as the owners of the public lands, they set those policies which influenced the pace of settlement as well as the distribution of wealth, by controlling its availability, setting prices, establishing minimum or maximum acreages, and designing tax systems. We have already mentioned the highly concentrated pattern of landownership produced and perpetuated by land policies in most of Spanish America. In the United States, where there were never major obstacles to acquiring land, the terms of land acquisition became even easier over the course of [the] nineteenth century. Similar changes were sought around the mid-nineteenth century in both Argentina and Brazil, as a means to encourage immigration, but these steps were less successful than in the United States and Canada in getting land to smallholders. The major crops produced in the expansion of the United States and Canada were grains, which permitted relatively small farms given the technology of the times and may help explain why such a policy of smallholding was implemented and was effective. But as the example of Argentina indicates, small-scale production of wheat was possible even with ownership of land in large units, maintaining a greater degree of overall inequality in wealth and political power.

The contrast between the United States and Canada, with their practices of offering small units of land for disposal and maintaining open immigration, and the rest of the Americas, where land and labor policies led to large landholdings and great inequality, seems to extend across a wide spectrum of institutions and other government interventions. In the areas of law and administration pertaining to the establishment of corporations, the regulation of financial institutions, the granting of property rights in intellectual capital (patents), industrial policies, as well as the provision of access to minerals and other natural resources on government-owned land, New World societies with greater inequality tended to adopt policies that were more selective in the offering of opportunities. Of course, members of wealthy elites almost always enjoy privileged positions, but these societies were relatively extreme in the degree to which their institutions advantaged elites. Moreover, this contrast across New World societies with respect to the differences in the breadth of the respective populations having effective access to opportunities for economic and social advancement seems much more systematic than has been generally recognized.

Perhaps the most straightforward way of subjecting to an empirical test our hypothesis that elites in societies which began with greater inequality evolved more power to influence the choice of legal and economic institutions is to look at how broadly the franchise was extended and what fractions of respective populations actually voted in elections. Since most societies in the Americas were nominally democracies by the middle of the nineteenth century, this sort of information has a direct bearing on the extent to which elites—based largely on wealth, human capital, and gender—held disproportionate political power in their respective countries. . . . Although it was common in all countries to reserve the right to vote to adult males until the twentieth century, the United States and Canada were the clear leaders in doing away with restrictions based on wealth or literacy, and in attaining secrecy in balloting. . . .

. . . But meaningful extension of the franchise occurred much later in Latin America. Although a number of Latin countries relaxed restrictions based on landholding or wealth during the nineteenth century, they almost always chose to rely on a literacy qualification; as late as 1900, none had a secret ballot and only Argentina was without a wealth or literacy requirement. As a result, through 1940 the United States and Canada routinely had proportions voting that were 50 to 100 percent higher than their most progressive neighbors to the South (Argentina, Uruguay, and Costa Rica—countries notable as well for their relative equality and small shares of the population that were not of European descent), three times higher than in Mexico, and up to five to ten times higher than in countries such as Brazil, Bolivia, Ecuador, and Chile. . . .

Our conjecture is that these differences across societies in the distribution of political power may have contributed to persistence in the relative degrees of inequality through the effects on institutional development. The institution of public primary schools, which was the principal vehicle for high rates of literacy attainment and an important contributor to human capital formation, is interesting to examine in this regard. Nearly all of the New World economies were sufficiently prosperous by the beginning of the nineteenth century to establish a widespread network of primary schools. However, although many countries (through their national governments) expressed support for such efforts, few actually made investments on a scale sufficient to serve the general population before the twentieth century. The exceptional societies in terms of leadership were the United States and Canada. Virtually from the time of settlement, these North Americans seem generally to have been convinced of the value of mobilizing the resources to provide their children with a basic education. Especially in New England, schools were frequently organized and funded at the village or town level. It is likely that the United States already had the most literate population in the world by 1800, but the "common school movement" that got under way in the 1820s (following closely after the movement for the extension of the franchise) put the country on an accelerated path of investment in education institutions. Between 1825 and 1850, nearly every state in the American west or north that had not already done so enacted a law strongly encouraging localities to establish "free schools" open to all children and supported by general taxes. Although the movement made slower progress in the south, which had greater inequality and population heterogeneity than the north, schooling had spread sufficiently by the middle of the nineteenth century that over 40 percent of the school-age population was enrolled, and more than 90 percent of white adults were literate. . . . Schools were also widespread in early nineteenth-century Canada, and even though it lagged the United States by several decades in establishing tax-supported schools with universal access, its literacy rates were nearly as high.

The rest of the hemisphere trailed far behind the United States and Canada in primary schooling and in attaining literacy. Despite enormous wealth, the British colonies (with the exception of Barbados) were very slow to organize schooling institutions that served broad segments of the population. Indeed, it was evidently not until the British Colonial Office took an interest in the promotion of schooling late in the nineteenth century that significant steps were taken in this direction. Similarly, even the most progressive Latin American countries—like Argentina, Uruguay and Costa Rica—were more than 75 years behind the United States and Canada. Major investments in primary schooling did not generally occur in any Latin American country until the national governments provided the funds; in contrast to the pattern in North America, local and state governments in Latin America were generally not willing or able to fund them on their own. As a consequence, most of these societies did not achieve high levels of literacy until well into the twentieth century.

CONCLUSIONS

Many scholars have been concerned with why the United States and Canada have developed so differently and were so much more successful than other economies of the Americas. All of the New World societies enjoyed high levels of product per capita early in their histories. The divergence in paths can be traced back to the achievement of sustained economic growth by the United States and Canada during the late eighteenth and early nineteenth centuries, while the others did not manage to attain this goal until late in the nineteenth or in the twentieth century. Although many explanations have been proposed, the substantial differences in the degree of inequality in wealth, human capital, and political power, which were initially rooted in the factor endowments of the respective colonies but persisted over time, seem highly relevant.

These early differences in the extent of inequality across New World economies may have been preserved by the types of economic institutions that evolved and by the effects of those institutions on how broadly access to economic opportunities was shared. This path of institutional development may in turn have affected growth. Where there was extreme inequality, and institutions advantaged elites and limited the access of much of the population to economic opportunities, members of elites were better able to maintain their elite status over time, but at the cost of society not realizing the full economic potential of disadvantaged groups. Although the examples we have discussed— landownership, the extension of the franchise and investment in public schools—do not prove the general point, they are suggestive of a pattern whereby institutions in New World societies with greater inequality advantaged members of the elite through many other types of government policies as well, including those concerned with access to public lands and natural resources, the establishment and use of financial institutions, and property rights in technological information. Overall, where there existed elites who were sharply differentiated from the rest of the population on the basis of wealth, human capital, and political influence, they seem to have used their standing to restrict competition. Although one could imagine that extreme inequality could take generations to dissipate in even a free and even-handed society, such biases in the paths of institutional development likely go far in explaining the persistence of inequality over the long run in Latin America and elsewhere in the New World.

REFERENCES

Acemoglu, Daron, Simon Johnson and James A. Robinson. 2000. "The Colonial Origins of Comparative Development: An Empirical Investigation." Working paper, Massachusetts Institute of Technology and University of California, Berkeley.

Coatsworth, John H. 1998. "Economic and Institutional Trajectories in Nineteenth-Century Latin America," in *Latin America and the World Economy Since 1800.* John H. Coatsworth and Alan M. Taylor, eds. Cambridge, MA: Harvard University Press.

Fogel, Robert William. 1989. *Without Consent or Contract.* New York: Norton.

North, Douglass C. 1988. "Institutions, Economic Growth and Freedom: An Historical Introduction," in *Freedom, Democracy and Economic Welfare.* Michael A. Walker, ed., Vancouver: Fraser Institute.

4

Globalization of the Economy

JEFFREY A. FRANKEL

The globalization of trade and finance has come a long way over the past half century, but it is not as complete as many people think. In this chapter, econo-mist Jeffrey Frankel documents the extent of globalization and the barriers that remain from an international economic perspective. Judged either by the stan-dard of one hundred years ago or by the hypothetical standard of perfect interna-tional integration, Frankel contends that globalization is neither new nor very extensive. While recent technological advances in transportation and communi-cations have greatly lowered the costs of economic integration, significant barri-ers still remain. Differences in language, culture, legal traditions, and currencies pose significant hurdles to foreign trade and investment. Moreover, distance itself remains a major deterrent to integration. Given such limits to globalization, Fran-kel considers the implications for economic growth, equality, and the environ-ment. His conclusion is that globalization is not the primary obstacle to efforts to address such concerns.

Economic globalization is one of the most powerful forces to have shaped the postwar world. In particular, international trade in goods and services has become increasingly important over the past fifty years, and interna-tional financial flows over the past thirty years. This chapter documents quantitatively the process of globalization for trade and finance. It then briefly goes beyond the causes of international economic integration to con-sider its effects, concluding that globalization is overall a good thing, not just for economic growth but also when noneconomic goals are taken into account.

The two major drivers of economic globalization are reduced costs to transportation and communication in the private sector and reduced policy barriers to trade and investment on the part of the public sector. Technologi-cal progress and innovation have long been driving the costs of transporta-tion and communication steadily lower. In the postwar period we have seen major further cost-saving advances, even within ocean shipping: supertank-ers, roll-on-roll-off ships, and containerized cargo. Between 1920 and 1990 the average ocean freight and port charges per short ton of U.S. import and export cargo fell from $95.00 to $29.00 (in 1990 dollars). An increasing share of cargo goes by air. Between 1930 and 1990, average air transport revenue per passenger mile fell from $0.68 to $0.11. Jet air shipping and refrigeration have changed the status of goods that had previously been classified altogether as not tradable internationally. Now fresh-cut flowers, perishable broccoli and strawberries, live lobsters, and even ice cream are sent between continents. Communications costs have fallen even more rapidly. Over this period the cost of a three-minute telephone call from New York to London fell from $244.65 to $3.32. Recent inventions such as faxes and the Internet require no touting.

It is easy to exaggerate the extent of globalization. Much excited discussion of the topic makes it sound as though the rapid increase in economic integration across national borders is unprecedented. Some commentators imply that it has now gone so far that it is complete; one hears that distance and national borders no longer matter, that the nation-state and geography are themselves no longer relevant for economic purposes, and that it is now as easy to do business with a customer across the globe as across town. After all, has not the World Wide Web reduced cross-border barriers to zero?

It would be a mistake for policy makers or private citizens to base decisions on the notion that globalization is so new that the experience of the past is not relevant, or that the phenomenon is now irreversible, or that national monetary authorities are now powerless in the face of the global marketplace, or that the quality of life of Americans—either economic or noneconomic aspects—is determined more by developments abroad than by American actions at home.

It is best to recognize that at any point in history many powerful forces are working to drive countries apart, at the same time as other powerful forces are working to shrink the world. In the 1990s, for example, at the same time that forces such as the Internet and dollarization have led some to proclaim the decline of the nation-state, more new nations have been created (out of the ruins of the former Soviet bloc) than in any decade other than the decolonizing 1960s, each with its own currencies and trade policies. The forces of shrinkage have dominated in recent decades, but the centrifugal forces are important as well.

TWO BENCHMARKS FOR MEASURING ECONOMIC INTEGRATION

The overall post–World War II record of economic integration across national borders, powerful as it has been, is, in two respects, not as striking as widely believed. The first perspective is to judge by the standard of 100 years ago. The second is to judge by the standard of what it would mean to have truly perfect global integration.

Judging Globalization 2000 by the Standard of 1900

The globalization that took place in the nineteenth century was at least as impressive as the current episode. The most revolutionary breakthroughs in transportation and communication had already happened by 1900—for example, the railroad, steamship, telegraph, and refrigeration. Freight rates had fallen sharply throughout the century. An environment of political stability was provided by the Pax Britannica, and an environment of monetary stability was provided by the gold standard. . . . As a result of rapidly growing trade, international differences in commodity prices narrowed dramatically.

It is inescapable to invoke a particularly famous quote from John Maynard Keynes: "What an extraordinary episode in the progress of man that age was which came to an end in August 1914! . . . The inhabitant of London could order by telephone, sipping his morning tea in bed, the various products of the whole earth . . . he could at the same time and by the same means adventure his wealth in the natural resources and new enterprise of any quarter of the world."[1]

The world took a giant step back from economic globalization during the period 1914–1944. Some of the causes of this retrogression were isolationist sentiments in the West that followed World War I, the monetary instability and economic depression that plagued the interwar period, increases in tariffs and other trade barriers including most saliently the adoption by the U.S. Congress of the Smoot-Hawley tariff of 1930, the rise of the fascist bloc in the 1930s, and the rise of the communist bloc in the 1940s. All of these factors pertain to barriers that were created by governments, in contrast to the forces of technology and the private marketplace, which tend to reduce barriers. As a result, the world that emerged in 1945 was far more fragmented economically than the world that had turned to war in 1914.

The victors, however, were determined not to repeat the mistakes they had made at the time of the first world war. This time, they would work to promote economic integration in large part to advance long-term political goals. To govern international money, investment, and trade, they established multilateral institutions—the International Monetary Fund, World Bank, and General Agreement on Tariffs and Trade. The United States initially led the way by reducing trade barriers and making available gold-convertible dollars.

By one basic measure of trade, exports or imports of merchandise as a fraction of total output, it took more than twenty-five years after the end of World War II before the United States around 1970 reached the same level of globalization that it had experienced on the eve of World War I. This fraction continued to increase rapidly between 1971 and 1997—reaching about 9 percent today, still far lower than that in Britain throughout the late and early twentieth centuries. By other measures, some pertaining to the freedom of factor movements, the world even by the turn of the millennium was no more integrated than that of the preceding turn of the century.

Most people find it surprising that trade did not reattain its pre–World War I importance until the early 1970s. The significance of the comparison with 100 years ago goes well beyond factoids that economic historians enjoy springing on the uninitiated. Because technological know-how is irreversible—or was irreversible over the second millennium, if not entirely over the first— there is a tendency to see globalization as irreversible. But the political forces that fragmented the world for thirty years (1914–44) were evidently far more powerful than the accretion of technological progress in transport that went on during that period. The lesson is that nothing is inevitable about the process of globalization. For it to continue, world leaders must make choices of the sort made in the aftermath of World War II, instead of those made in the aftermath of World War I.

Judging by the Globalization 2000 Standard of Perfect International Integration

Perhaps perfect economic integration across national borders is a straw man. (The reader is likely to think so by the end of this chapter, even if he or she did not at the beginning.) But straw men have their purposes, and in this case ample rhetoric exists to justify the interest. A good straw man needs to be substantial enough to impress the crows and yet not so substantial that he can't be knocked flat. On both scores the proposition of complete international integration qualifies admirably.

Consider again the basic statistics of trade integration—a country's total exports of goods and services, or total imports, as a fraction of GDP. With the rapid increase in services included, these ratios now average 12 percent for the United States. The current level of trade likely represents a doubling from 100 years ago. As remarkable as is this evidence of declining transportation costs, tariffs, and other barriers to trade, it is still very far from the condition that would prevail if these costs and barriers were zero. More sophisticated statistics below will document this claim. But a very simple calculation is sufficient to make the point. U.S. output is about one-fourth of gross world product. The output of producers in other countries is thus about three-fourths of gross world product. If Americans were prone to buy goods and services from foreign producers as easily as from domestic producers, then foreign products would constitute a share of U.S. spending equal to that of the spending of the average resident of the planet. The U.S. import-GDP ratio would equal .75. The same would be true of the U.S. export-GDP ratio. And yet these ratios are only about one-sixth of this hypothetical level (12 percent / 75 percent = one-sixth). In other words, globalization would have to increase another sixfold, as measured by the trade ratio, before it would literally be true that Americans did business as easily across the globe as across the country.

Other countries are also a long way from perfect openness in this sense. The overall ratio of merchandise trade to output worldwide is about twice the U.S. ratio. This is to be expected, as other countries are smaller. For the other two large economies—Japan and the European Union considered as a whole—the ratio is closer to the U.S. level. In almost all cases, the ratio falls far short of the level that would prevail in a perfectly integrated world. . . . Other countries have a higher ratio of trade to GDP than the United States as a result of being smaller and less self-sufficient. Nonetheless, they are similarly far from perfect openness.

Why is globalization still so far from complete? To get an idea of the combination of transportation costs, trade barriers, and other frictions that remains yet to be dismantled, we must delve more deeply into the statistics.

STATISTICAL MEASURES OF ECONOMIC INTEGRATION

It can be instructive to look at direct measures of how some of the barriers to transborder integration have changed during the twentieth century—the level of tariffs on manufactures as an illustration of trade policy, or the price of a trans-Atlantic telephone call as an illustration of technological change in communications and transportation. Nevertheless, the political and physical determinants are too numerous and varied to be aggregated into a few key statistics that are capable of measuring the overall extent of integration in trade or finance. Tariff rates, for example, differ tremendously across commodities, and there is no single sensible way to aggregate them. The situation is even worse for nontariff barriers. Alternative possible measures of the importance of tariffs and other trade barriers have very low correlation with each other. . . .

It is more rewarding to look at summary measures of the *effects* of cross-border barriers on the patterns of trade and investment than to look at measures of the barriers themselves. Two sorts of measures are in use: those pertaining to quantities and those pertaining to prices.

Measures of quantities might appear more direct: "just how big are international flows?" But economists often prefer to look at price measures. In the first place, the quality of the data is often higher for prices than quantities. (This is particularly true of data on international financial markets—the data on the prices of foreign securities are extremely good, the data on aggregate international trade in securities are extremely bad.) In the second place, even at a conceptual level, international differentials in the prices of specific goods or specific assets, which measure the ability of international arbitrage to hold these prices in line, are more useful indicators of the extent of integration in a causal sense. Consider the example of U.S. trade in petroleum products. It is not especially large as a percentage of total U.S. output or consumption of petroleum products. And yet arbitrage ties the price of oil within the

United States closely to the price in the world market. Even a pair of countries that records no bilateral oil trade whatsoever will find that their prices move closely together. It is the absence of barriers and the *potential* for large-scale trade that keeps prices in line and makes the markets integrated in the most meaningful sense, not the magnitude of trade that takes place.

The Ability of Arbitrage to Eliminate International Differentials in Goods Prices

According to basic economic theory, arbitrage, defined as the activity of buying an item in a place where it is cheap and simultaneously selling the same item where it is expensive, should drive prices into equality. Its failure to do so perfectly is a source of repeated surprise to economists (though perhaps to nobody else). Often the explanation is that the commodities in question are not in fact identical. Brand names matter, if for no other reason than matters of retailing, warranty, and customer service. A BMW is certainly not the same automobile as a Lexus, and even a BMW sold in Germany is not the same as a BMW sold in the United States (different air pollution control equipment, for example). When the comparison across countries uses aggregate price indexes, as in standard tests of "purchasing power parity," it is no surprise to find only weak evidence of arbitrage. The finding of international price differentials is more surprising in the case of nondifferentiated non-brand-name commodities such as standardized ball bearings. Tests find that price differentials for specific goods are far larger across national borders than they are within countries. Exchange rate variability is a likely culprit.

Even more surprising is the paucity of evidence of a tendency for price differentials to diminish over the long sweep of history. Kenneth Froot, Michael Kim, and Kenneth Rogoff have obtained data on prices in England and Holland since the year 1273 for eight commodities (barley, butter, cheese, eggs, oats, peas, silver, and wheat).[2] Deviations from the so-called Law of One Price across the English Channel are no smaller or less persistent now than they were in the past, even though technological progress has certainly reduced the cost of shipping these products dramatically. Evidently other forces have counteracted the fall in transport costs; candidates are trade barriers under Europe's Common Agricultural Policy and volatility in the exchange rate between the guilder and the pound.

Factors Contributing to Home-Country Bias in Trade

Geography in general—and distance in particular—remain far more important inhibitions to trade than widely believed.

DISTANCE. Distance is still an important barrier to trade and not solely because of physical shipping costs. The effects of informational barriers are observed to decrease with proximity and with linguistic, cultural, historical, and political links. We might call it social distance. . . .

Among many possible proofs that distance is still important, one of the simplest is the observed tendency toward geographical agglomeration of industries. The tendency for industry to concentrate regionally is evidence both of costs to transportation and communication and of increasing returns to scale in production.

The agglomeration occurs even in sectors where physical transport costs are negligible, as in financial services or computer software. Financial firms concentrate in Manhattan and information technology firms concentrate in Silicon Valley. The reason they choose to locate near each other is not because they are trading physical commodities with each other and wish to save on shipping costs. Rather, face-to-face contact is important for exchanging information and negotiating deals.

The importance of distance is also revealed by analysis of data on prices of goods in different locations. If transport costs and other costs of doing business at a distance are important, then arbitrage should do a better job of keeping prices of similar goods in line when they are sold at locations close together rather than far apart. Charles Engel and John Rogers study prices in fourteen consumption categories for twenty-three Canadian and U.S. cities.[3] They find that the distance between two North American cities significantly affects the variability of their relative prices.

Similar results emerge by looking at trade quantities rather than prices. The gravity model says that trade between a pair of countries is inversely related to the distance between them, and proportional to the product of their sizes, by analogy with Newton's law of gravitational attraction. It fits the data remarkably well and is well founded in the theory of trade in goods that are imperfect substitutes. In part because data are so abundant (a set of 100 countries offers $100 \times 99 = 9,900$ pairs of export observations), standard errors tend to be small.

Statistical estimates find highly significant effects of distance on bilateral trade. When the distance between two countries is increased by 1 percent, trade between them falls by 0.7 to 1.0 percent. This statistic, like the others that follow, pertains to the effect in isolation, holding constant other effects on trade, such as the size of the trading partners. The wonderful property of ordinary least squares regression analysis is that it is capable of examining the independent effect of one factor at a time.

OTHER GEOGRAPHICAL VARIABLES.   Other physical attributes of location also have statistically significant effects. Landlocked countries engage in less trade by a factor of about one-third, holding other factors equal. Two countries that are adjacent to each other trade about 80 percent more than two otherwise similar countries.

LINGUISTIC AND COLONIAL FACTORS.   Linguistic barriers remain an impediment to trade. Two countries that speak the same language trade about 50 percent more than two otherwise similar countries. The multitude of languages is one of the reasons why economic integration remains far from complete in the European Union.

Colonial links have also been important historically. In 1960, the year when the breakup of the largest colonial empires began in earnest, trade between colonies and the colonial power was on average two to four times greater than for otherwise similar pairs of countries. This effect, already reduced from an earlier peak in the colonial era, has continued to decline in the 1970s and 1980s. But it has not disappeared. Indeed, if small dependencies are included in the sample, then two units that share the same colonizer still trade on average an estimated 80 percent more with each other than two otherwise similar countries (as recently as 1990). In addition, if one of the pair is the colonial mother country, trade is five to nine times greater than it would otherwise be.

MILITARY FACTORS. The effects on bilateral trade of politico-military alliances, wars, have also been examined. Theoretically and empirically (in the gravity framework) trade is generally higher among countries that are allies and lower among countries that are actual or potential adversaries. Understandably, if two countries are currently at war, there is usually a negative effect on trade. It runs as high as a 99 percent reduction in 1965. More typical is an 82 percent reduction in 1990.

FREE TRADE AREAS. Regional trading arrangements reduce tariffs and other trade barriers within a group of countries, though there is a range from mild preferential trading arrangements to full-fledged economic unions. Often the members of such groups are already tightly linked through proximity, common language, or other ties. But even holding constant for such factors, in the gravity model, the formation of a free trade area is estimated on average to raise trade by 70 to 170 percent. A serious common market, such as the European Union, can have a bigger effect. Nevertheless, in each of the EU member countries, a large bias toward trade within that country remains.

POLITICAL LINKS. A naive economist's view would be that once tariffs and other explicit trade barriers between countries are removed, and geographic determinants of transportation costs are held constant, trade should move as easily across national boundaries as within them. But this is far from the case in reality. If two geographic units belong to the same sovereign nation, such as France and its overseas departments, trade is roughly tripled. Thus political relationships among geographic units have larger effects on trade than such factors as explicit trade policies or linguistic barriers.

COMMON COUNTRY. Even after adjusting for distance (including non-contiguity) and linguistic barriers, all countries still exhibit a substantial bias toward buying domestic goods rather than foreign. Shang-Jin Wei estimates this bias for countries in the Organization for Economic Cooperation and

Development; it has declined only very slowly over time and is still statistically significant (though the United States has the smallest bias of all).[4]

There would be some great advantages of having data at the level of states or provinces within countries. We would be able to ascertain how trade between two geographical entities is affected by their common membership in a political union. We have learned that when two geographical units share such links as speaking a common language, their bilateral trade is clearly boosted. It stands to reason that when two units share a common cultural heritage or legal system, their trade will be enhanced by even more. Data are not generally available on trade among U.S. states, Japanese prefectures, German länder, British counties, or French departments. But there do exist data on trade undertaken by Canadian provinces, among one another and with major American states. They show a strong intranational bias to trade. Ontario exports three times as much to British Columbia as to California, even though the latter has ten times as many people. . . .

John McCallum has applied the gravity model to trade among the provinces and states. The usual effects of size and distance show up.[5] The fascinating result is the effect of a dummy variable to represent when two states or provinces lie in the same country. Two such provinces trade twenty-two times as much with each other as would a province and a state that are otherwise similar but lie on opposite sides of the border. . . .

The result is reminiscent of the striking finding in "How Wide Is the Border?" by Engel and Rogers, that crossing the Canadian-U.S. border adds as much to the relative price variability between two cities as does traversing a physical distance of 2,500 to 10,000 miles within either country.[6] This tendency for Canadian provinces to trade with one another is all the more surprising because they tend to maintain trade barriers against one another, never having had the advantage of a Constitution like the one in the United States that reserves trade policy exclusively for the federal level. Reasons for the intra-Canadian bias in trade include the ease of doing business within the same legal system, an integrated media and advertising sector, nationwide store chains, and an East-West railroad network. John Helliwell and John McCallum "suspect that the answers lie in a whole host of educational and geographic ties based on migration and family ties and supported by networks of transportation, communication and education, along with portability of health care and pension rights—if not completely of beer."[7] Presumably the sources of intranational bias are even stronger for other countries that do not share the cultural proximity and liberalized trade relations of Canada and the United States.

CURRENCIES. There has long been reason to suspect that the existence of different currencies, and especially the large fluctuation in the exchange rates between currencies since the breakup of the Bretton Woods monetary system in 1971, has been a barrier to international trade and investment. Exchange rate fluctuations are clearly related to the failures of the law of one price observed in goods markets. When it is observed that, for example, Canadians and Americans trade far more with their countrymen than with each other, in a context where trade barriers, geography, and linguistic barriers have been eliminated, the currency difference is one of the prime suspects. Until recently, however, it has been difficult to find strong evidence that currency factors discourage trade and investment. The gravity model has now been used for this purpose. It turns out that eliminating one standard deviation in exchange rate variability—for example, from its mean of 7 percent to zero—raises trade between a pair of countries by an estimated 13 percent. Furthermore, Rose has found that going all the way and literally adopting a common currency has a much bigger effect; it multiplies trade by an additional 3.5 times.[8]

Promoting trade and finance is one of several motivations for the recent adoption of common currencies or currency boards by roughly twenty countries over the past decade (including the eleven members of the European Economic and Monetary Union in 1999). At the same time, however, approximately the same number of new currencies have come into existence, as a result of the breakup of the former Soviet bloc.

Measures of Financial Market Integration

The delegates who met at Bretton Woods in 1944 had a design for the world monetary system that explicitly did not accord financial markets the presumption that was accorded trade in goods, the presumption that international integration was unambiguously good and that barriers should be liberalized as rapidly as possible. Although economic theory can make as elegant a case in favor of free trade in assets as for free trade in goods and services, the delegates had been persuaded by the experience of the 1930s that some degree of controls on international capital movements was desirable. It was not until the final 1973 breakdown of the system of fixed exchange rates that Germany and the United States removed their capital controls. Japan and the United Kingdom kept theirs until the end of the 1970s, and most other European countries did not liberalize until the end of the 1980s. Many emerging-market countries also opened up to large-scale international capital movements in the 1990s (though the subsequent crises have convinced some observers that those delegates at Bretton Woods might have had it right in the first place).

Tests regarding financial markets show international integration that has increased tremendously over the past thirty years but that is less complete than often supposed. This generalization applies to quantity-based tests as well as to price-based tests.

It is true that the gross volume of cross-border capital flows has grown very large. Perhaps the most impressive and widely cited statistic is the gross volume of turnover in foreign exchange markets: $1.5 trillion per day worldwide, by April 1998, which is on the order of a hundred times greater than the volume of trade in goods and services. *Net* capital flows are for most purposes more interesting than gross flows, however. Net capital flows today are far smaller as a share of GDP than were pre–World War I net flows out of Great Britain and into such land-abundant countries as Argentina, Australia, and Canada. Furthermore, Martin Feldstein and Charles Horioka argued in a very influential paper that net capital flows are far smaller than one would expect them to be in a world of perfect international capital mobility: a country that suffers a shortfall in national saving tends to experience an almost commensurate fall in investment, rather than making up the difference by borrowing from abroad.[9] Similarly, investors in every country hold far lower proportions of their portfolios in the form of other countries' securities than they would in a well-diversified portfolio, a puzzle known as home country bias. Evidently, imperfect information and transactions costs are still important barriers to cross-country investment.

The ability of arbitrage to equate asset prices or rates of return across countries has been widely tested. One would expect that in the absence of barriers to cross-border financial flows, arbitrage would bring interest rates into equality. But the answer depends on the precise condition tested. Interest rates that have had the element of exchange risk removed by forward market cover are indeed virtually equated across national borders among industrialized countries, showing that they have few controls on international capital movements. But interest rates seem not to be equalized across countries when they are adjusted for expectations of exchange rate changes rather than for forward exchange rates, and interest rates are definitely not equalized when adjusted for expected inflation rates. Evidently, currency differences are important enough to drive a wedge between expected rates of return. Furthermore, residual transactions costs or imperfect information apparently affects cross-border investment in equities. They discourage investors altogether from investing in some information-intensive assets, such as mortgages, across national borders. Furthermore, country risk still adds a substantial penalty wedge to all investments in developing countries.

In short, though international financial markets, much like goods markets, have become far more integrated in recent decades, they have traversed less of the distance to perfect integration than is widely believed. Globalization is neither new, nor complete, nor irreversible.

The Impact of Economic Globalization

What are the effects of globalization and its merits? We must acknowledge a lower degree of certainty in our answers. It becomes harder to isolate cause and effect. Moreover, once we extend the list of objectives beyond maximizing national incomes, value judgments come into play. Nevertheless, economic theory and empirical research still have much to contribute.

The Effect of Trade on the Level and Growth of Real Income

Why do economists consider economic integration so important? What are the benefits of free trade for the economy?

THE THEORETICAL CASE FOR TRADE. Classical economic theory tells us that there are national gains from trade, associated with the phrase "comparative advantage." Over the past two decades, scholars have developed a "new trade theory." It suggests the existence of additional benefits from trade, which are termed dynamic. We consider each theory in turn.

The classical theory goes back to Adam Smith and David Ricardo. Adam Smith argued that specialization—the division of labor—enhances productivity. David Ricardo extended this concept to trade between countries. The notion is that trade allows each country to specialize in what it does best, thus maximizing the value of its output. If a government restricts trade, resources are wasted in the production of goods that could be imported more cheaply than they can be produced domestically.

What if one country is better than anyone else at producing *every* good? The argument in favor of free trade still carries the day. All that is required is for a country to be *relatively* less skilled than another in the production of some good in order for it to benefit from trade. This is the doctrine of comparative advantage—the fundamental (if perhaps counterintuitive) principle that underlies the theory of international trade. It makes sense for Michael Jordan to pay someone else to mow his lawn, even if Jordan could do it better himself, because he has a comparative advantage at basketball over lawn mowing. Similarly, it makes sense for the United States to pay to import certain goods that can be produced more efficiently abroad (apparel, shoes, tropical agriculture, consumer electronics), because the United States has a comparative advantage in other goods (aircraft, financial services, wheat, and computer software).

This is the classical view of the benefits of free trade in a nutshell. Two key attributes of the classical theory are worth flagging. First, it assumes perfect competition, constant returns to scale, and fixed technology, assumptions that are not very realistic. Second, the gains from trade are primarily static in nature—that is, they affect the *level* of real income. The elimination of trade barriers raises income, but this is more along the lines of a one-time increase.

What of the "new trade theory"? It is more realistic than the classical theory, in that it takes into account imperfect competition, increasing returns to scale, and changing technology. It can be viewed as providing equally strong, or stronger, support for the sort of free trade policies that the United States has followed throughout the postwar period, that is, multilateral and bilateral negotiations to reduce trade barriers, than did the classical theory.

To be sure, these theories say that, under certain very special conditions, one country can get ahead by interventions (for example, subsidies to strategic sectors), provided the government gets it exactly right and provided the actions of other countries are taken as given. But these theories also tend to have the property that a world in which everyone is subsidizing at once is a world in which everyone is worse off, and that we are all better off if we can agree to limit subsidies or other interventions.

Bilateral or multilateral agreements where other sides make concessions to U.S. products, in return for whatever concessions the United States makes, are virtually the only sorts of trade agreements the United States has made. Indeed, most recent trade agreements (like the North American Free Trade Agreement and China's accession to the WTO) have required much larger reductions in import barriers by U.S. trading partners than by the United States. The reason is that their barriers were higher than those of the United States to start with. But the natural implication is that such agreements raise foreign demand for U.S. products by more than they raise U.S. demand for imports. Hence the United States is likely to benefit from a positive "terms of trade effect." This just adds to the usual benefits of increased efficiency of production and gains to consumers from international trade.

Furthermore, even when a government does not fear retaliation from abroad for trade barriers, intervention in practice is usually based on inadequate knowledge and is corrupted by interest groups. Seeking to rule out all sector-specific intervention is the most effective way of discouraging rent-seeking behavior. Globalization increases the number of competitors operating in the economy. Not only does this work to reduce distortionary monopoly power in the marketplace (which is otherwise exercised by raising prices), it can also reduce distortionary corporate power in the political arena (which is exercised by lobbying).

Most important, new trade theory offers reason to believe that openness can have a permanent effect on a country's rate of growth, not just the level of real GDP. A high rate of economic interaction with the rest of the world speeds the absorption of frontier technologies and global management best practices, spurs innovation and cost-cutting, and competes away monopoly.

These dynamic gains come from a number of sources. They include the benefits of greater market size and enhanced competition. Other sources include technological improvements through increased contact with foreigners and their alternative production styles. Such contact can come, for example, from direct investment by foreign firms with proprietary knowledge or by the exposure to imported goods that embody technologies developed abroad. Each of these elements of international trade and interactions has the effect of promoting growth in the domestic economy. When combined with the static effects, there is no question that the efforts to open markets, when successful, can yield significant dividends.

THE EMPIRICAL CASE FOR TRADE. Citing theory is not a complete answer to the question, "how do we know that trade is good?" We need empirical evidence. Economists have undertaken statistical tests of the determinants of countries' growth rates. Investment in physical capital and investment in human capital are the two factors that emerge the most strongly. But other factors matter. Estimates of growth equations have found a role for openness, measured, for example, as the sum of exports and imports as a share of GDP. . . .

The estimate of the effect of openness on income per capita ranges from 0.3 to 3.0. Consider a round middle number such as 1.0. The increase in U.S. openness since the 1950s is 0.12. Multiplying the two numbers together implies that the increased integration has had an effect of 12 percent on U.S. income. More dramatically, compare a stylized Burma, with a ratio close to zero, versus a stylized Singapore, with a ratio close to 100 percent. Our ballpark estimate, the coefficient of 1.0, implies that Singapore's income is 100 percent higher than Burma's as a result of its openness. The fact that trade can affect a country's growth rate—as opposed to affecting the level of its GDP in a "one-shot" fashion—makes the case for trade liberalization even more compelling.

One possible response is that this approach demonstrates only the growth benefits from geographically induced trade and need not necessarily extend to the effects of policy-induced trade. But popular critics of globalization seem to think that increased international trade and finance is the problem, regardless of whether it comes from technological progress or government liberalization. As the critics make their arguments against government dismantling of policy barriers, they seldom specify that cross-border interactions attributable to geography or to technological innovations in transport are economically beneficial.

MACROECONOMIC INTERDEPENDENCE. Trade and financial integration generally increase the transmission of business cycle fluctuations among countries. Floating exchange rates give countries some insulation against one another's fluctuations. When capital markets are highly integrated, floating rates do not give complete insulation, as the post-1973 correlation among major industrialized economies shows. But international transmission can be good for a country as easily as bad, as happens when adverse domestic developments are in part passed off to the rest of the world. The trade balance can act as an important automatic stabilizer for output and employment, improving in recessions and worsening in booms.

Contagion of financial crises is more worrying. The decade of the 1990s alone abounds with examples: the 1992–93 crises in the European exchange rate mechanism, the "tequila crisis" that began with the December 1994 devaluation of the Mexican peso, and the crises in East Asia and emerging markets worldwide from July 1997 to January 1999. Evidently when one country has a crisis it affects others. There is now a greater consensus among economists than before that not all of the observed volatility, or its cross-country correlation, can be attributed to efficient capital markets punishing or rewarding countries based on a rational evaluation of the economic fundamentals. It is difficult to do justice in one paragraph to a discussion that is as voluminous and vigorous as the debate over the welfare implications of the swelling international capital flows. Still, the majority view remains that countries are overall better off with modern globalized financial markets than without them.

The Effect of Trade on Other Social Goals

Many who fear globalization concede that trade has a positive effect on aggregate national income but suspect that it has adverse effects on other highly valued goals such as labor rights, food safety, culture, and so forth. Here we consider only two major values—equality and the environment—and briefly at that.

INCOME DISTRIBUTION. International trade and investment can be a powerful source of growth in poor countries, helping them catch up with those who are ahead in endowments of capital and technology. This was an important component of the spectacular growth of East Asian countries between the 1960s and the 1990s, which remains a miracle even in the aftermath of the 1997–98 currency crises. By promoting convergence, trade can help reduce the enormous worldwide inequality in income. Most of those who are concerned about income distribution, however, seem more motivated by within-country equality than global equality.

A standard textbook theory of international trade, the Heckscher-Ohlin-Samuelson model, has a striking prediction to make regarding within-country income distribution. It is that the scarce factors of production will lose from trade, and the abundant factors will benefit. This means that in rich countries, those who have capital and skills will benefit at the expense of unskilled labor, whereas in poor countries it will be the other way around. The same prediction holds for international capital mobility (or, for that matter, for international labor mobility). It has been very difficult, however, to find substantial direct evidence of the predictions of the model during the postwar period, including distribution effects within either rich or poor countries. Most likely the phenomena of changing technology, intraindustry trade, and worker ties to specific industries are more important today than the factor endowments at the heart of the Heckscher-Ohlin-Samuelson model.

In the United States, the gap between wages paid to skilled workers and wages paid to unskilled workers rose by 18 percentage points between 1973 and 1995 and then leveled off. The fear is that trade is responsible for some of the gap, by benefiting skilled workers more than unskilled workers. Common statistical estimates—which typically impose the theoretical framework rather than testing it—are that between 5 and 30 percent of the increase is attributable to trade. Technology, raising the demand for skilled workers faster than the supply, is the major factor responsible for the rest. One of the higher estimates is that trade contributes one-third of the net increase in the wage gap. . . .

Clearly, income distribution is determined by many factors beyond trade. One is redistribution policies undertaken by the government. In some cases such policies are initiated in an effort to compensate or "buy off" groups thought to be adversely affected by trade. But a far more important phenomenon is the tendency for countries to implement greater redistribution as they grow richer.

A long-established empirical regularity is the tendency for income inequality to worsen at early stages of growth and then to improve at later stages. The original explanation for this phenomenon, known as the Kuznets curve, had to do with rural-urban migration. But a common modern interpretation is that income redistribution is a "superior good"—something that societies choose to purchase more of, even though at some cost to aggregate income, as they grow rich enough to be able to afford to do so. If this is right, then trade can be expected eventually to raise equality, by raising aggregate income.

ENVIRONMENT.   Similar logic holds that trade and growth can also be good for the environment, once the country gets past a certain level of per capita income. Gene Grossman and Alan Krueger found what is called the environmental Kuznets curve: growth is bad for air and water pollution at the initial stages of industrialization but later on reduces pollution as countries become rich enough to pay to clean up their environments.[10] A substantial literature has followed. A key point is that popular desires need not translate automatically into environmental quality; rather government intervention is usually required to address externalities.

The idea that trade can be good for environment is surprising to many. The pollution-haven hypothesis instead holds that trade encourages firms to locate production of highly polluting sectors in low-regulation countries in order to stay competitive. But economists' research suggests that environmental regulation is not a major determinant of firms' ability to compete internationally. Furthermore, running counter to fears of a "race to the bottom," is the Pareto-improvement point: trade allows countries to attain more of whatever their goals are, including higher market-measured income for a given level of environmental quality or a better environment for a given level of income. . . . If openness raises GDP by 1 percent, then it reduces sulphur dioxide concentrations by 1 percent. The implication is that, because trade is good for growth, it is also good for the environment.

The econometric studies of the effects of trade and growth on the environment get different results depending on what specific measures of pollution they use. There is a need to look at other environmental criteria as well. It is difficult to imagine, for example, that trade is anything but bad for the survival of tropical hardwood forests or endangered species, without substantial efforts by governments to protect them.

The argument that richer countries will take steps to clean up their environments holds only for issues when the effects are felt domestically—where the primary "bads," such as smog or water pollution, are external to the firm or household but internal to the country. Some environmental externalities that have received increased attention in recent decades, however, are global. Biodiversity, overfishing, ozone depletion, and greenhouse gas emissions are four good examples. A ton of carbon dioxide has the same global warming effect regardless of where in the world it is emitted. In these cases, individual nations can do little to improve the environment on their own, no matter how concerned their populations or how effective their governments. For each of the four examples, governments have negotiated international treaties in an attempt to deal with the problem. But only the attempt to address ozone depletion, the Montreal Protocol, can be said as yet to have met with much success.

Is the popular impression then correct, that international trade and finance exacerbates these global environmental externalities? Yes, but only in the sense that trade and finance promote economic growth. Clearly if mankind were still a population of a few million people living in preindustrial poverty, greenhouse gas emissions would not be a big issue. Industrialization leads to environmental degradation, and trade is part of industrialization. But virtually everyone wants industrialization, at least for themselves. Deliberate self-impoverishment is not a promising option. Once this point is recognized, there is nothing special about trade compared with the other sources of economic growth: capital accumulation, rural-urban migration, and technological progress.

U.S. congressional opponents of the Kyoto Protocol fear that if the industrialized countries agreed to limit emissions of carbon dioxide and other greenhouse gases, there would be an adverse effect on American economic competitiveness vis-à-vis the developing countries, who are not yet covered by the treaty. This is partially true: those U.S. sectors that are highly carbon intensive, such as aluminum smelting, would indeed suffer adversely. But other U.S. sectors would be *favorably* affected by trade with nonparticipating countries. The real issue—the true reason why we need the developing countries to participate in a global climate change agreement—is that the industrialized countries would otherwise have very little effect on aggregate global emissions over the coming decades, even if they were willing to cooperate and to bear moderately high costs involved in restructuring their energy economies. But this point has nothing to do with trade. It would be the same in a world without economic globalization.

SUMMARY OF CONCLUSIONS

This chapter gives confident answers to questions about the extent and sources of economic globalization and moderately confident answers to some questions about its effects.

The world has become increasingly integrated with respect to trade and finance since the end of World War II, owing to declining costs to transportation and communication and declining government barriers. The phenomenon is neither new nor complete, however. Globalization was more dramatic in the half-century preceding World War I, and much of the progress during the last half-century has merely reversed the closing off that came in between. In the second regard, globalization is far from complete. Contrary to popular impressions, national borders and geography still impede trade and investment substantially. A simple calculation suggests that the ratio of trade to output would have to increase at least another six-fold before it would be true that Americans trade across the globe as readily as across the country. Such barriers as differences in currencies, languages, and political systems each have their own statistically estimated trade-impeding influences, besides the remaining significant effects of distance, borders, and other geographical and trade policy variables.

The chapter's discussion of the impacts of economic globalization has necessarily been exceedingly brief. Both theory and evidence are read as clearly supportive of the proposition that trade has a positive effect on real incomes. This is why economists believe it is important that the process of international integration be allowed to continue, especially for the sake of those countries that are still poor.

Effects on social values other than aggregate incomes can be positive or negative, depending on the details, and the statistical evidence does not always give clear-cut answers about the bottom line. In the two most studied cases, income distribution and environmental pollution, there seems to be a pattern whereby things get worse in the early stages of industrialization but then start to get better at higher levels of income. Societies that become rich in terms of market-measured output choose to improve their quality of life in other ways as well. It is possible that the same principle extends to noneconomic values such as safety, human rights, and democracy. In short, there is reason to hope that, aside from the various more direct effects of trade on noneconomic values, there is a general indirect beneficial effect that comes through the positive effect of trade on income.

. . . I will conclude with an observation on the subject of labor and environmental standards, which inspired fervent demonstrations at the November 1999 World Trade Organization meeting in Seattle. An international "trilemma" composed of sovereignty, regulation, and integration has been noted: countries can have any two of these three desirable goals, but they cannot have all three at once. Does this mean that globalization impedes sovereign countries from choosing their own labor and environmental regulations? Perhaps. But such cross-border concerns as child labor, endangerment of species, and emissions of greenhouse gases do not arise from international trade and investment. These problems would exist even without trade. The concerns arise from a noneconomic kind of globalization having more to do with the transmission of information and ideas. . . . Presumably the demonstrators do not favor shutting off this transmission. But in that case shutting off economic globalization would not help either.

Neither international trade nor global institutions such as the WTO are obstacles to addressing those concerns. To the contrary, the obstacle to multilateral efforts to protect the global environment, such as ratification of the Kyoto Protocol on Climate Change, *is precisely national sovereignty*, along with a failure of citizens of each country to agree among themselves on the priority that their society should place on environmental benefits. These two obstacles— obsession with national sovereignty and internal disagreements—are, ironically, as bad or worse in the United States as in other countries. The obstacle to international action on the environment is not, as most of the Seattle demonstrators appeared to believe, the *infringement* of sovereignty by multilateral institutions such as the WTO.

NOTES

1. John Maynard Keynes, *The Economic Consequences of the Peace* (Harcourt, Brace, and Howe, 1920).

2. Kenneth Froot, Michael Kim, and Kenneth Rogoff, "The Law of One Price over 700 Years," Working Paper 5132 (Cambridge, Mass.: National Bureau of Economic Research, May 1995).

3. Charles Engel and John Rogers, "How Wide Is the Border?" *American Economic Review*, vol. 86 (December 1996), pp. 1112–25.

4. Shang-Jin Wei, "How Stubborn Are Nation States in Globalization?" Working Paper 5331 (Cambridge, Mass.: National Bureau of Economic Research, April 1996).

5. John McCallum, "National Borders Matter: Canada-U.S. Regional Trade Patterns," *American Economic Review*, vol. 85 (June 1995), pp. 615–23.

6. Engel and Rogers, "How Wide Is the Border?"

7. John Helliwell and John McCallum, "National Borders Still Matter for Trade," *Policy Options/Options Politiques*, vol. 16 (July–August 1995), pp. 44–48.

8. Andrew Rose, "One Money, One Market: Estimating the Effect of Common Currencies on Trade," *Economic Policy*, vol. 30 (April 2000), pp. 7–46.

9. Martin Feldstein and Charles Horioka, "Domestic Saving and International Capital Flows," *Economic Journal*, vol. 90 (1980): 314–29.

10. Gene Grossman and Alan Krueger, "Economic Growth and the Environment," *Quarterly Journal of Economics*, vol. 110 (1995), pp. 353–77.

II

HISTORICAL
PERSPECTIVES

A truly international economy first emerged during the "long sixteenth century," the period from approximately 1480 to 1650. In its earliest form, the modern international economy was organized on the basis of mercantilism, a doctrine asserting that power and wealth were closely interrelated and were legitimate goals of national policy. Thus, wealth was necessary for power, and power could be used to obtain wealth. Power is a relative concept because one country can gain it only at the expense of another; thus, mercantilist nations perceived themselves to be locked in a zero-sum conflict in the international economy.

During this period, countries pursued a variety of policies intended to expand production and wealth at home while denying similar capabilities to others. Six policies were of nearly universal importance. First, countries sought to prevent gold and silver, common mercantilist measures of wealth, from being exported. At the beginning of the sixteenth century, Spain declared the export of gold or silver punishable by death. Similarly, France declared the export of coined gold and silver illegal in 1506, 1540, 1548, and 1574, thereby demonstrating the difficulties of enforcing such laws. Second, regulations (typically, high tariffs) were adopted to limit imports to necessary raw materials. Importing raw materials was desirable because it lowered prices at home and thereby reduced costs for manufacturers. By limiting imports of manufactured and luxury items, countries sought to stimulate production at home while reducing it abroad. Third, exports of manufactured goods were encouraged for similar reasons. Fourth, just as they sought to encourage imports of raw materials, countries aimed to limit the export of these goods so as to both lower prices at home and limit the ability of others to develop a manufacturing capability of their own. Fifth, exports of technology—including both machinery and skilled artisans—were restricted in order to inhibit potential foreign competitors. Finally, many countries adopted navigation

laws mandating that a certain percentage of their foreign trade had to be carried in native ships. This last trade regulation was intended to stimulate the
domestic shipping and shipbuilding industries—both of which were necessary resources for successful war making.

By the early nineteenth century, mercantilist trade restrictions were coming under widespread attack, particularly in Great Britain. Drawing on the
Liberal writings of Adam Smith and David Ricardo, Richard Cobden and
other Manchester industrialists led the fight for free trade, which culminated
in 1846 in the abolition of the "Corn Laws" (restrictions on grain imports), the
last major mercantilist impediment to free trade in Britain (see Schonhardt-
Bailey, Reading 5). Other countries soon followed England's example. Indeed,
under Britain's leadership, Europe entered a period of free trade that lasted
from 1860 to 1879. However, this trend toward freer trade was reversed in the
last quarter of the nineteenth century. The purported causes of this reversal
are many, including the decline of British hegemony, the onset of the first
Great Depression (of 1873–1896), and the new wave of industrialization on the
Continent, which led to protection for domestic manufacturers from British
competition (see Gourevitch, Reading 6). For whatever reason—and the debate
continues even today—by 1890, nearly all the major industrialized countries
except Great Britain had once again imposed substantial restrictions on
imports.

Coupled with this trend toward increased protection was a new wave of
international investment and formal colonialism (see Frieden, Reading 7).
Britain had already begun to expand its holdings of foreign territory during
the period of free trade, and after 1880, it was joined by Germany and France.
In 1860, Great Britain possessed 2.5 million square miles of colonial territory, and France, only .2 million square miles; Germany had not yet entered
the colonial race. By 1899, Britain's holdings had expanded to 9.3 million
square miles, France's to 3.7 million, and Germany's to 1.0 million, an expansion that occurred primarily in Africa and the Pacific. In 1876, slightly less
than 11 percent of Africa and nearly 57 percent of Polynesia were colonized,
yet by 1900, more than 90 percent of Africa and almost 99 percent of Polynesia were controlled by European colonial powers and the United States.

World War I, which many analysts believe to have been stimulated by the
race for colonies, and in particular by Germany's aggressive attempt to catch
up with Great Britain, destroyed the remaining elements of the Pax Britannica. The mantle of leadership, which had previously been borne by Britain,
was now divided between Britain and the United States. Yet neither country
could—or desired to—play the leadership role previously performed by Britain (see Lake, Reading 8).

World War I was indeed a watershed in American international involvement. The terrible devastation caused by the war in Europe served to weaken
the traditional world powers, while it brought the United States a period of
unexpected prosperity. The Allies, which were short of food and weapons,

bought furiously from American suppliers. To finance their purchases, they borrowed heavily from American banks and, once the United States entered the war, from the U.S. government. As a result, American factories and farms hummed as the war dragged on; industrial production nearly doubled during the war years. Moreover, because the war forced the European powers to neglect many of their overseas economic activities, American exporters and investors were also able to move into areas they had never before influenced. When the war began, the United States was a net debtor of the major European nations; by the time it ended, however, it was the world's principal lender and all the Allies were deeply in debt to American banks and the U.S. government.

Despite the position of political and economic leadership that the United States shared with Great Britain after World War I, Washington rapidly retreated into its traditional inward orientation. To be sure, many American banks and corporations continued to expand abroad very rapidly in the 1920s and the country remained an important world power, but the United States refused to join the League of Nations or any of the other international organizations created in the period. American tariff levels, which had been reduced on the eve of World War I, were once again raised. The reasons for the country's post–World War I *isolationism,* as it is often called, are many and controversial. Chief among them were the continued insularity of major segments of the American public, which were traditionally inward-looking in political and economic matters; the resistance to American power of such European nations as Great Britain and France; and widespread revulsion at the apparently futile deaths that had resulted from involvement in the internecine strife of the Old World.

Whatever the reasons for the isolationism of the 1920s, these tendencies were heightened as the world spiraled downward into depression after 1929. In the Smoot-Hawley Act of 1930, the United States dramatically increased its tariffs, and by 1933 the world was engulfed in bitter trade and currency conflicts. In 1933, desperate to encourage domestic economic recovery, U.S. president Franklin Roosevelt significantly devalued the dollar, thus effectively sounding the death knell of what remained of the nineteenth-century international economic order.

During the nearly four centuries summarized here, the international economy underwent several dramatic transformations. From a closed and highly regulated mercantilist system, the international economy evolved toward free trade in the middle of the nineteenth century. However, after a relatively brief period of openness, the international economy reversed direction and, starting with the resurgence of formal imperialism and accelerating after World War I, once again drifted toward closure. This historical survey highlights the uniqueness of the contemporary international political economy, which is the focus of the rest of this reader; David A. Lake compares the central characteristics of the international economy in the nineteenth and twentieth centuries. This survey also raises a host of analytic questions, many of which appear elsewhere in the book as well. Particularly important here is the question of what drives change in the international economy. In the readings that follow, Cheryl Schonhardt-Bailey, in a domestic society–centered approach, highlights the role of interest group lobbying and electoral politics; Peter Alexis Gourevitch examines interest groups and domestic institutions; Jeffry A. Frieden focuses on the evolving nature of international investment and its impact on the need for direct, colonial control over peripheral regions; and Lake emphasizes changes in the international political and economic systems.

5

Free Trade: The Repeal of the Corn Laws

CHERYL SCHONHARDT-BAILEY

In 1846, England unilaterally dismantled its mercantilist trade restrictions (known as the "Corn Laws") and adopted free trade in what is broadly recognized as the single most important economic liberalization in modern world history. Cheryl Schonhardt-Bailey presents a domestic society–centered argument to explain the repeal of the Corn Laws by the world's first industrial nation. She documents a struggle for political power between a rising manufacturing and export industry and a declining agricultural sector controlled by the landed aristocracy. Industrialists wanted to repeal the Corn Laws to increase foreign consumption of British manufactured products; if foreigners were allowed to sell grain to Great Britain, they could earn the foreign exchange to buy British manufactured goods. Agricultural elites, by contrast, saw repeal of the Corn Laws as a direct threat to their interests because the trade barriers kept the price of the grain they produced artificially high. With each side cloaking its interests in terms of national welfare and national security, it took a gifted leader, Prime Minister William Peel, to craft a political compromise.

150 YEARS ON, WHY REPEAL REMAINS RELEVANT

At four o'clock in the morning of Saturday, 16 May 1846, Members of the British House of Commons voted 327 to 229 to abolish tariff protection for agriculture. Economists, political scientists, historians and sociologists have spilled much ink attempting to explain this historic decision. That the repeal of the protectionist Corn Laws was a crucially significant event in British history is undisputed, but exactly *why* repeal was significant is a question that produces a variety of responses. Britain's unilateral move to free trade is said to have signified the triumph of Manchester School liberal thinking; marked the birth of its international economic hegemony; launched a new form of British imperialism; paved the way for the disintegration of the Conservative party for a generation; been the catalyst for class conflict between the rising industrial middle class and the politically dominant landed aristocracy; given testimony to the organization, political astuteness and tenacity of the pro-repeal lobby, the Anti-Corn Law League; been an inevitable outcome of changes in the financial system and industrial structure; and illustrated the dramatic and abrupt change of mind of one absolutely pivotal individual—Prime

Minister Sir Robert Peel. Researchers will undoubtedly continue to debate the significance of repeal, as well as its causes and consequences. Indeed, over the past twenty years researchers have applied a number of new methods and new theories to explain Britain's move to free trade, and this renewed interest shows no sign of abating. At its core, the question that continues to puzzle and intrigue us is, why did Britain unilaterally open its domestic market to free trade—and particularly free trade in agriculture? . . .

THE CORN LAWS, IN BRIEF

Government regulation of exports and imports of corn was well-established long before the nineteenth century. The Corn Laws of the seventeenth and eighteenth centuries had a dual purpose—they sought to prevent "grain from being at any time, either so dear that the poor cannot subsist, or so cheap that the farmer cannot live by growing of it."[1] The Napoleonic Wars brought a fundamental change in the history of the Corn Laws. During the war years, agriculturists had enjoyed high grain prices, but with the peace, prices fell dramatically. In response, Parliament enacted the Corn Law of 1815, which allowed free entry when the price of corn was above 80s. per quarter, and prohibited entry when the price fell below 80s. Some argue that this new legislation, unlike that of the earlier Corn Laws, was "defiantly protective." 'It sought to fasten on a country at peace the protection furnished by a generation of war."[2] However, others maintain that fear of scarcity drove government policy. Rapid population growth and a dependence upon foreign corn are said to have justified a policy of self-sufficiency based on concerns for national security. Evidence for both interpretations may be found, . . . as we shall see below. . . .

In brief, 1815, 1828 and 1842 were the years of significant changes in the Corn Laws, although numerous other minor (and often temporary) modifications were also made in the regulation of corn during the early nineteenth century. Paralleling the history of Corn Law legislation were major demographic and economic changes that cut against the fabric of protection for food. From 1811 to 1841 the population of Great Britain increased from 12.6 million to 18 million and British farmers were becoming less able to provide sufficient supplies for the home market. This said, while Britain had not been self-sufficient in corn since the early 1760s, British agriculturists "still managed to feed every year on the average all except about 700,000 and as

---

1. C. Smith, *Tracts on the Corn Trade and Corn Laws*, II.72, as quoted in C.R. Fay, *The Corn Laws and Social England* (Cambridge University Press, 1932), p. 34.

2. Fay, p. 35.

late as 1831–40, all except about 1,050,000 of the population."[3] A second factor proved more fatal to the Corn Laws—the growth of British manufacturing industry and export trade, particularly in textiles. More particularly, as the industrial prosperity and export boom of the early 1830s began to crack, industrialists became increasingly vocal about "unfair" protection enjoyed by the agriculturists. Beginning in 1836, an economic downturn together with a series of poor harvests, sparked the industrialists into action. High food prices and unemployment gave impetus both to the middle and working classes, the former organized as the Anti-Corn Law League and the latter as the Chartist movement.

THE LEAGUE MACHINE

The Anti-Corn Law League was the first modern and national-level political pressure group to emerge in Britain. It began in London in 1836 as the Anti-Corn Law Association, but by 1838 had found its natural base in Manchester. The leaders of the League were manufacturers and professionals engaged in export trade, most of whom were concentrated in the county of Lancashire. Foremost among its leaders were two cotton textile manufacturers—Richard Cobden and John Bright. In the course of the struggle against the Corn Laws, both were to become Members of Parliament, Cobden for Stockport and Bright for Rochdale. Another key MP in the Corn Law struggle was Charles Villiers, Member for Wolverhampton. It was Villiers who became famous for his annual motions for repeal of the Corn Laws, which began in 1838 and continued through 1846.

Historians refer to the League as "the most impressive of nineteenth-century pressure groups, which exercised a distinct influence on the repeal of the Corn Laws in 1846."[4] It was called the *league machine*, whose organization "presents one of the first examples of a recurring feature of modern political life, the highly organized political pressure group with its centralized administration and its formidable propaganda apparatus."[5] . . . The two key features of the League's operational strategy were its nation-wide propaganda and electoral registration campaigns. The League raised substantial subscriptions to finance its propaganda campaign. It maintained a small army of workers and speakers, who toured the country distributing numerous tracts (most notably, the famous *Anti-Corn Law Circular*) and giving thousands of speeches on the virtues of free trade and the evils of protection.

3. W. H. Chaloner, "Introduction to the Second Edition," in Archibald Prentice, *History of the Anti-Corn Law League*, vols. I & II (London: Frank Cass & Co. [1853], 1968). p. x.

4. Anthony Howe, *The Cotton Masters, 1830–1860* (Oxford University Press, 1984).

5. Norman McCord, *The Anti-Corn Law League 1838–1846* (London: George Allen & Unwin, 1958), p. 187.

The registration campaign was, however, the League's tool for replacing protectionist landowners in Parliament with free trade supporters. After electoral losses in 1841–2, the League focused its energy and resources on returning a free trade majority in the anticipated general parliamentary election of 1848. Its leaders' tactical strategy included manipulating the voter registers and employing propaganda devices on existing voters. Looking toward the 1848 election, the League sought to add as many free traders and delete as many protectionists from these registers as possible. The latter they accomplished by making objections against thousands of protectionists at the annual revisions of the registers. The former required a different tactic— exploiting a loophole in the 1832 Electoral Reform Act (which effectively enfranchised the middle class). This loophole was the forty-shilling county property qualification, which Bright referred to as "the great constitutional weapon which we intend to wield."[6] . . . While the 40s. qualification had been a feature of the system since 1430, the increase in county seats from 188 to 253 (an increase from roughly 29% to 38% of the total seats) magnified the importance of this overlooked loophole in the 1832 Reform Act. The League used the 40s. qualification to create several thousand new free trade voters in county constituencies with large urban electorates, constituencies whose representation was increased by the Reform Act. Leaguers went so far as to urge parents, wanting to create a nest egg for a son, to make him a freeholder: in Cobden's words, "it is an act of duty, for you make him thereby an independent freeman, and put it in his power to defend himself and his children from political oppression." . . . In spite of the Appeal Court ruling in February 1845 and January 1846 that votes created by the 40s. freehold qualification were valid, protectionists continued to challenge the constitutionality of the League's registration campaign, . . . and Leaguers continued to defend their activities. . . .

The propaganda and registration campaigns, moreover, were brought together to further the political success of the League. As its agents distributed propaganda tracts to every elector in 24 county divisions and 187 boroughs, they submitted to the League headquarters consistent and complete reports on the electorate in their districts. These reports provided the League with a comprehensive picture of the electoral scene throughout England, thereby allowing it much greater knowledge of, and control over, electoral districts than either the Conservatives or Liberals possessed. . . . The earlier distribution of propaganda tracts thus provided the League with an extensive database from which they could inflict political pressure on Members of

---

6. Unless otherwise noted, all quotes are from writings and statements reprinted in Cheryl Schonhardt-Bailey, ed., *Free Trade: The Repeal of the Corn Laws* (London: Thoemmes Continuum, 1995).

Parliament, who were concerned with their bids for re-election in the anticipated 1848 election.

In 1844, as the League's success—particularly that of its registration campaign in the counties—became more conspicuous, a defensive Anti-League
(or, Agricultural Protection Society) emerged. . . . This group of protectionist
landowners and farmers did not, however, ever obtain the momentum or
backing of the League. . . . In financial terms, while the League grew from a
£5,000 annual fund in 1839 to one of £250,000 in 1845, the latter year saw the
core of the Anti-League (the Essex Agricultural Protection Society) scraping
together the paltry sum of £2,000 to fund its campaign. . . .

THE ISSUES AT STAKE

From today's perspective, the high drama and intense conflict that surrounded the question of protection for grain seems a bit exaggerated. One
must bear in mind, however, that during the early nineteenth century the
working and middle classes spent a large percentage of their income on food,
and central to their food consumption was bread. The price of bread was
therefore key to the cost of living. Yet the importance of the price of bread, in
itself, does not reveal why the Corn Laws created such fury in British political
life. Underlying the cry for a "cheap loaf" was the economic tension between
a rising manufacturing and export industry and a declining agricultural sector, which translated into a struggle for political power between the industrial middle class and the landed aristocracy. The language of the debates,
not surprisingly, focused predominantly on the economic issues and the "interests" who gained or lost from protection—although, ample evidence exists of
middle class resentment towards the landed aristocracy for their "political
oppression." To the industrialists, the Corn Laws were a form of pilfering by
the landed aristocracy. They argued that high food prices, the direct consequence of restrictions on food imports, resulted in near-famine conditions
among the poor. Manufacturing districts were particularly hard hit since
foreigners, limited in their capacity to export grain to Britain, were unable to
import British manufactured goods. Free traders provided widely varying
estimates of the cost of protection for agriculture—in 1838, Villiers estimated
the annual cost at £15.6 million . . . and in 1839, James Deacon Hume (Secretary to the Board of Trade) estimated the annual cost at £36 million . . . G. R.
Porter's estimate for 1840 (including duties for silk) was £53.6 million, . . .
while an Anti-Corn Law League circular calculated the total cost of the Corn
Laws from 1815 to 1841 as £1,365 million. . . . It was argued that landowners,
as rentiers, were the primary if not sole beneficiaries of this legislated protection. Defenders of the Corn Laws retorted that cheap bread (the effect of
repeal) would result in lower wages for workers, thus revealing that the "true"
motive of the industrialists was to obtain cheaper labour. Additionally, they

argued that agriculture was a unique and ultimately essential industry and therefore deserved to be protected from destruction. Overlaying this clash of interests were arguments concerning aggregate national welfare, such as the effect of repeal on government revenue and the nation's security.

One way to lend order to the arguments for and against repeal is to group them into two broad categories—those relating to aggregate national welfare, and those associated with the interests of groups or classes.

The Corn Laws and National Welfare

The debate over the nation's welfare highlighted four main issues: (1) unilateralism versus reciprocity; (2) the threat of foreign competition in manufactures; (3) self-sufficiency as a national security concern; and (4) the effect of repeal on government revenue.

The theory of free trade in the 1840s was, it should be emphasized, just that—*theory*. No hard evidence existed as to its effects, particularly on its trading partners. While Britain had, after Peel's 1842 tariff reforms, liberalized most of its trade in manufactures, it had not endorsed a universal policy of free trade. One critical question of repeal, then, was—would other countries follow Britain's lead and open their home markets to British manufacturing exports? That is, what would be the effect of unilateral free trade, with no demands for reciprocal tariff reductions? Free traders such as Hume maintained that others would indeed follow Britain's lead: "I feel the strongest confidence that if we were to give up our protective system altogether, it would be impossible for other countries to retain theirs much longer." Protectionists challenged this claim, arguing that because foreign countries saw infant industry protection as the road to industrialization, reciprocal free trade would never emerge. . . .

Some historians have imputed a more sinister motive to Britain's move to free trade—that of staving off the competition in manufactures from other countries. Statements from contemporaries lend some weight to this hypothesis. For instance, Nassau Senior wrote that free trade would "increase the productiveness of our labour" and "diminish, or perhaps destroy, the rivalry of many of our competitors in third markets," . . . and Hume noted that "(al) together, I conceive that the reduction in the price of food, and particularly the admission of it from abroad, must tend to prevent other countries from being able to surpass us in manufactures."

Because free trade meant relying on foreigners for Britain's food supply, the nation's security became a topic of concern. National security remains to this day one of the more compelling arguments for protection for agriculture, since many countries (island nations perhaps more than most) strongly resist forfeiting food self-sufficiency. Anti-Leaguers argued that international specialization of production—with Britain producing manufactures and other countries producing food—was too risky. . . . If export markets were to dry up or agricultural exporters were to withhold supplies (such as during time of war), how would Britain obtain its food? Free traders responded by labelling this a bogus argument for protection: a League spokesman retorted that "(i)n 1810, when we were engaged in war with almost every European power, we imported 1,491,000 quarters of wheat, nearly half a million of which were obtained from France alone" . . . and Porter wrote that "(t)he dread of dependence upon foreigners for food is, indeed, a childish dread; and we act like children in our choice of a remedy for the evil." . . .

The final argument which related to the nation as a whole centres on the contribution of duties to the government's revenue. Although Peel instituted the first peace time income tax in 1842, the government still relied on customs for 38% of its revenue in 1846. The question then became, to what extent would the repeal of duties on corn harm the public purse? Some protectionists pointed to the £800 million national debt, claiming that free trade would put Britain at risk of failing to meet the interest payments on its debt. . . . J. R. McCulloch and Senior, both defenders of free trade, were sensitive to the reliance of the government on customs revenue. . . . Senior advocated levying duties only for the purposes of revenue, while McCulloch argued for the replacement of the sliding scale with a moderate, fixed duty. A fixed duty would prevent speculation and would protect agriculture as a "business," but it would also bolster the government's revenue. Villiers, a strong advocate of repeal, argued that the Corn Laws actually operated to reduce revenue from customs by increasing the cost of production (presumably by increasing wage costs) and thereby limiting foreign trade. The Corn Laws therefore reduced excise duties by limiting consumption through higher prices. Insofar as customs and excise provided 75% of government revenue, Villiers maintained that savings would be had by repeal. Free traders also tended to link the revenue issue to the importance of bolstering British exports, and thereby ensuring the future prosperity of the country—a topic to be discussed below.

In Whose Interests?

Both the industrialists and the landowners claimed to be defending the interests of the workers and farmers. Both sought to present their case in terms of the common man and concern for public welfare. Morality and ethics were often woven into their economic arguments in an effort to pitch the battle in terms of good versus evil. Free traders were particularly adept at this form of argumentation, while the protectionists found the morality of protection a difficult case to defend, except by treating agriculture as a "unique" industry (see below). Villiers set the tone in 1838 by speaking of the principle of freedom in trade: "For what is this freedom, but liberty for persons to provide, and the community to enjoy, that which is needful and desired at the lowest cost and at the greatest advantage?" Some free traders carried the morality of free trade further, arguing that free trade constituted (1) a "civil liberty," as it insured the right to buy in the cheapest market and sell in the dearest, (2) "political justice," or a justice which shows no favouritism or partisanship,

(3) "peace" in bringing peace between nations and peace between classes, and (4) "civilization," or the bringing of man near man, for mutual help and solace. . . . The League, moreover, sought and obtained the backing of the religious community. . . . In an effort to regain the moral high ground, protectionists lamely argued that the League denied "the liberty . . . of expressing publicly a difference of opinion," endangered the peace of society, and failed to tell the "truth." . . .

Yet, however persuaded the common man may have been by these appeals to a higher order, economic interests lay at the heart of the arguments for and against repeal. These arguments centred on six distinct issues: (1) the relationship between bread prices and wages; (2) class conflict; (3) the taxation of landowners relative to other groups; (4) the extent to which farmers, as opposed to landowners, benefited from protection; (5) agriculture as a "unique" industry deserving of protection; and (6) the effect of the Corn Laws on the export trade.

If one topic could be labelled as central to the debates between free traders and protectionists, it was the relationship between bread prices and wages. Chartists suspected that the true motive of the industrialists was to obtain lower wages through repeal, and the protectionists were happy to feed this suspicion. League circulars and Anti-League pamphlets were filled with claims and counter-claims about the effect of bread prices on workers wages. . . . Villiers, in a House of Commons speech in 1845, remarked that he had looked "over all the publications of the Protection Society, and he found that the leading topic, from beginning to end, was that if you made food cheap you would reduce the wages of the people, and that if you made it dear you would increase their wages. Was he to understand, then, that there were still some persons in that house who maintained this doctrine?" The writings of the political economists were more informative on the price/wage issue. According to Torrens, . . . the Corn Laws prevented workers from obtaining higher wages, which would reflect their higher productivity relative to foreign labour, thereby dismissing the claim of the protectionists. On the same lines, Porter argued that high food prices did not yield high wages, but just the reverse. . . . High prices for food were said to have lessened the demand for labour and therefore lessened wages (which rests on the argument that demand for food is price inelastic, and that the demand for other goods—notably manufactured goods—is more elastic with respect to food prices). James Pennington rejected the hoopla associated with this issue, arguing that free traders and protectionists alike exaggerated the effects of repeal on corn prices (and on domestic agriculture more generally). . . . He doubted that the quantity of foreign grain available to Britain would be great enough to bring about any significant fall in prices. In defence of the protectionist case, Alison argued that repeal would not lower food prices, but rather food prices would initially fall but subsequently rise when foreigners became monopoly suppliers of grain to Britain. . . . Moreover, labourers would not benefit from lower grain prices because the increased labour supply (resulting from agricultural decline) would release labour into industry and thereby force wages down.

A second issue—indeed, for some historians, the *key* issue—was class conflict between the industrial middle class and the landed aristocracy. While Chartism raised the pitch of class conflict . . . , further Parliamentary reform was so remote at this time as to place working class conflict in the shadow of the main struggle. Perhaps one of the clearest statements of the class conflict between the industrialists and the aristocracy was in a speech by Bright in Covent Garden. . . . According to the *Times*, the theatre was filled to overflowing and the popular speaker was received "with deafening cheers." Bright's incendiary speech spoke of the free trade struggle as "a struggle between the numbers, wealth, comforts, the all in fact, of the middle and industrious classes, and the wealth, the union, and the sordidness of a large section of the aristocracy of this empire." The League presented itself as a defender not only of the middle class but also the working class, and even tenant farmers, against the landed interest. Landowners, in turn, maintained that the manufacturing class constituted only a small percentage of the population, and it was only by enjoying an innate skill at organization that this class had acquired influence beyond their share. Free traders vehemently rejected that the battle for repeal was for the sole benefit of industry. . . . A more sophisticated variant of the landowners' counter-attack is seen in E. S. Cayley's address in 1844. . . . Cayley called upon Adam Smith to argue that because land is (internationally) immobile and capital is (internationally) mobile, landowners had an "abiding interest in the country in which they live" since they could not pack up their land and move it to another country. Thus, the landowners were able to turn on its head the industrialists' implicit threat of capital flight to the continent if repeal was not forthcoming. . . .

A third issue is closely related to class conflict—namely, the supposed heavy tax burden incurred by the landowners. Defenders of the Corn Laws suggested that because landowners paid disproportionately large taxes, they were entitled to protection as compensation for their tax burden. . . . Free traders challenged landowners to demonstrate this "excessive tax burden," and claimed instead that landowners paid less than their fair share of taxes. League circulars repeatedly pointed out that the land tax had not increased since 1692, while land values (and therefore, rents) had increased seven-fold. . . .

As mentioned earlier, the League endeavoured to present itself as a national movement, one that included the interests not only of industrialists but also of farmers and farm labourers. To this end, Cobden shifted the focus of the League away from the theme of urban distress (with Peel shouldering "individual responsibility" for the present distress of the country) to an attack on the rental income of landowners. . . . Cobden asserted that "if the corn law operates to cause a profit at all, it also operates to put that profit into the pockets of the landlord." The argument put to tenant farmers was that it was the landlord, not the farmer, who benefited from high food prices. As food prices rose, so too would the value of land. Thus, while in the short term farmers may enjoy the benefits of higher prices for their produce, in the longer term, as they renewed their leases, these benefits would evaporate with higher rental charges. . . . One protectionist attempted to use the League's own data (presented to manufacturers to illustrate the high prices they were forced to pay because of the Corn Laws) to demonstrate the inconsistency in its argument. Ignoring the question of rents, George Game Day argued that the League could not, on the one hand, tell manufacturers about the high prices they paid as a result of food tariffs, and on the other hand persuade farmers that they did not benefit from the high prices associated with the Corn Laws. . . . Other landowners challenged the rent argument directly, claiming that landowners received only three-percent return (rent) while capitalists received from 20% to 50% interest on their investments. . . .

A fifth argument was often used as a fallback position by the agriculturists. Not unlike farmers in present day Japan, Europe and the United States, British farmers and landowners wholly believed that agriculture was a unique industry, and thereby entitled to special privileges. Its status as producer of the nation's food supply meant that it could not be allowed to decline, since this would create a dangerous reliance on untrustworthy foreigners for food (thus relating back to the earlier national security argument). Protectionists argued that agriculture provided employment for a large share of the workforce, in addition to providing a constant and reliable food supply. They defended their stance by quoting Adam Smith: "The land is the greatest, most important, and most durable part of the wealth of every extensive country," whereas "capital . . . is . . . a very precarious and uncertain possession, till some part of it has been secured and realised in the cultivation . . . of its lands." . . . Free traders decried the basis of this claim, maintaining that agriculture was no more and no less than any other business, which, if unprofitable, closes up shop and reallocates its resources elsewhere. . . . Responding to the question of whether free trade ought to apply equally to food as it does to manufactures, Hume responded bluntly, "I conceive myself, if I were compelled to choose, that food is the last thing upon which I would attempt to place any protection."

A final issue of interests touches on the core feature of industrialization—a rising industrial sector and a declining agricultural sector. The middle classes, and eventually many MPs, recognized that the present and future of the country's wealth depended on industry, and not on agriculture. When asked, "Do you consider the wealth of England to be caused and maintained by her commercial and manufacturing industry?" Hume replied, "Certainly: if meant as in contradistinction from the produce of the soil. . . . (H)aving always had the land, but not the trade, I must conceive that the increase of our riches arises from the trade and not from the land." Landowners were, however, undeterred. They argued that home trade was more important than export trade. Because foreign trade was often the victim of other countries' tariffs on British goods, it could not be relied upon for the future welfare of the country. In the meantime, since the export industry employed only a fraction of the workforce, the merits of a policy which served predominantly the interests of this fraction would be unfair to the rest of the population. . . .

CONCLUSION

. . . Peel argued that the principle of free trade was welfare-enhancing because it would: (1) allow Britain to retain its pre-eminence in world trade (thereby staving off foreign competition); (2) be a winning strategy, regardless of whether or not other countries reciprocated with lower duties; and (3) not result in a loss to public revenue, as the trade and industrial prosperity combined with the new income tax would offset the lost income from duties. Quoting League sources, Peel explained why he believed that the prosperity following the 1842 reduction of duties could not continue without further liberalization.

At the heart of Peel's speech was a plea to the opposing manufacturing and agricultural interests to accept a policy of mutual concessions. He urged manufacturers to forfeit their remaining protective duties on woollens, linen, silks, and other manufactured goods, in order to adhere to the general rule that no duty should exceed 10% (15% for silks). He introduced a further simplification of the tariff code and reduced tariffs on a number of other items (shoes, spirits, sugar). His greatest hurdle, however, was to gain the support of the agriculturists. Duties on certain foods (butter, cheese, hops and fish) would be reduced while those on others (meat, beef, port, potatoes, vegetables, bacon, and other non-grains) would be abolished. And, of course, grain protection would be abolished as of 1849. After discounting the link between bread prices and wages, Peel sought to address two issues associated with the clash of interests. First, in regard to class conflict, Peel argued that agitation had grown to such an extent that the government had no option but to act to appease the industrial and working classes. Second, the "heavy" financial burden of the landowning classes was lessened by a number of incentives to agriculturists—a consolidation of the highways system, relief to rural districts from pauperism, a number of expenses shifted from the counties to the consolidated fund, and finally loans for agricultural improvements at moderate interest rates.

If one were to view each of the issues associated with national welfare and economic interests as potentially competing explanations for repeal, one would find evidence to support almost every one of them in Peel's speech. It is therefore not surprising that modern interpretations of repeal show no signs of converging on a single explanation.

6

International Trade, Domestic Coalitions, and Liberty: Comparative Responses to the Crisis of 1873–1896

PETER ALEXIS GOUREVITCH

Peter Alexis Gourevitch examines the impact upon the trade policies and political coalitions of four countries of the Great Depression of 1873–1896, during which Germany and France adopted high tariffs on both agricultural and industrial products, Great Britain maintained its historic policy of free trade, and the United States protected industry but not agriculture. In attempting to explain this pattern of response, Gourevitch compares four alternative hypotheses: economic explanations, emphasizing domestic societal interests; political system explanations, focusing on domestic institutional variables; international system explanations, combining international political and economic factors; and economic ideology explanations. He concludes that domestic societal interests supplemented by a concern with domestic institutions provide the most persuasive account of these four cases. Gourevitch not only gives a detailed and informative history of the trade policies of the four great economic powers of the late nineteenth century, he also provides a useful test of several of the main approaches in international political economy.

For social scientists who enjoy comparisons, happiness is finding a force or event which affects a number of societies at the same time. Like test-tube solutions that respond differently to the same reagent, these societies reveal their characters in divergent responses to the same stimulus. One such phenomenon is the present worldwide inflation/depression. An earlier one was the Great Depression of 1873–1896. Technological breakthroughs in agriculture (the reaper, sower, fertilizers, drainage tiles, and new forms of wheat) and in transportation (continental rail networks, refrigeration, and motorized shipping) transformed international markets for food, causing world prices to fall. Since conditions favored extensive grain growing, the plains nations of the world (the United States, Canada, Australia, Argentina, and Russia) became the low cost producers. The agricultural populations of Western and Central Europe found themselves abruptly uncompetitive.

In industry as well, 1873 marks a break. At first the sharp slump of that year looked like an ordinary business-cycle downturn, like the one in 1857. Instead, prices continued to drop for over two decades, while output continued to rise. New industries—steel, chemicals, electrical equipment, and shipbuilding—sprang up, but the return on capital declined. As in agriculture, international competition became intense. Businessmen everywhere felt the crisis, and most of them wanted remedies.

The clamour for action was universal. The responses differed: vertical integration, cartels, government contracts, and economic protection. The most visible response was tariffs. . . .

Although the economic stimuli were uniform, the political systems forced to cope with them differed considerably. Some systems were new or relatively precarious: Republican France, Imperial Germany, Monarchical Italy, Reconstruction America, Newly Formed Canada, Recently Autonomous Australia. Only Britain could be called stable. Thirty years later when most of these political systems had grown stronger, most of the countries had high tariffs. The importance of the relation between the nature of the political system and protection has been most forcefully argued by Gershenkron in *Bread and Democracy in Germany*. The coalition of iron and rye built around high tariffs contributed to a belligerent foreign policy and helped to shore up the authoritarian Imperial Constitution of 1871. High tariffs, then, contributed to both world wars and to fascism, not a minor consequence. It was once a commonly held notion that free trade and democracy, protection and authoritarianism, went together. . . .

These basic facts about tariff levels and political forms have been discussed by many authors. What is less clear, and not thoroughly explored in the literature, is the best way to understand these outcomes. As with most complex problems, there is no shortage of possible explanations: interest groups, class conflict, institutions, foreign policy, ideology. Are these explanations all necessary though, or equally important? This essay seeks to probe these alternative explanations. It is speculative; it does not offer new information or definitive answers to old questions. Rather, it takes a type of debate about which social scientists are increasingly conscious (the comparison of different explanations of a given phenomenon) and extends it to an old problem that has significant bearing on current issues in political economy—the interaction of international trade and domestic politics. The paper examines closely the formation of tariff policy in late nineteenth-century Germany, France, Britain, and the United States, and then considers the impact of the tariff policy quarrel on the character of each political system.

EXPLAINING TARIFF LEVELS

Explanations for late nineteenth-century tariff levels may be classified under four headings, according to the type of variable to which primacy is given.

1. *Economic Explanations*. Tariff levels derive from the interests of economic groups able to translate calculations of economic benefit into public policy. Types of economic explanations differ in their conceptualization of groups (classes vs. sectors vs. companies) and of the

strategies groups pursue (maximizing income, satisficing, stability, and class hegemony).

2. *Political System Explanations.* The "statement of the groups" does not state everything. The ability of economic actors to realize policy goals is affected by political structures and the individuals who staff them. Groups differ in their access to power, the costs they must bear in influencing decisions, prestige, and other elements of political power.

3. *International System Explanations.* Tariff levels derive from a country's position in the international state system. Considerations of military security, independence, stability, or glory shape trade policy. Agriculture may be protected, for example, in order to guarantee supplies of food and soldiers, rather than to provide profit to farmers (as explanation 1 would suggest).

4. *Economic Ideology Explanations.* Tariff levels derive from intellectual orientations about proper economic and trade policies. National traditions may favor autarchy or market principles; faddishness or emulation may induce policy makers to follow the lead given by successful countries. Such intellectual orientations may have originated in calculations of self-interest (explanation 1), or in broader political concerns (explanation 2) or in understandings of international politics (explanation 3), but they may outlive the conditions that spawned them.

These explanations are by no means mutually exclusive. The German case could be construed as compatible with all four: Junkers and heavy industry fought falling prices, competition, and political reformism; Bismarck helped organize the iron and rye coalition; foreign policy concerns over supply sources and hostile great powers helped to create it; and the nationalist school of German economic thought provided fertile ground for protectionist arguments. But were all four factors really essential to produce high tariffs in Germany? Given the principle that a simple explanation is better than a complex one, we may legitimately try to determine at what point we have said enough to explain the result. Other points may be interesting, perhaps crucial for other outcomes, but redundant for this one. It would also be useful to find explanations that fit the largest possible number of cases.

Economic explanation offers us a good port of entry. It requires that we investigate the impact of high and low tariffs, both for agricultural and industrial products, on the economic situation of each major group in each country. We can then turn to the types of evidence—structures, interstate relations, and ideas—required by the other modes of reasoning. Having worked these out for each country, it will then be possible to attempt an evaluation of all four arguments.

GERMANY

Economic Explanations

What attitude toward industrial and agricultural tariffs would we predict for each of the major economic groups in German society, if each acted according to its economic interests? A simple model of German society contains the following groups: small peasants; Junkers (or estate owners); manufacturers in heavy, basic industries (iron, coal, steel); manufacturers of finished goods; workers in each type of industry; shopkeepers and artisans; shippers; bankers; and professionals (lawyers, doctors). What were the interests of each in relation to the new market conditions after 1873?

Agriculture, notes Gerschenkron, could respond to the sharp drop in grain prices in two ways: modernization or protection. Modernization meant applying the logic of comparative advantage to agriculture. Domestic grain production would be abandoned. Cheap foreign grain would become an input for the domestic production of higher quality foodstuffs such as dairy products and meat. With rising incomes, the urban and industrial sectors would provide the market for this type of produce. Protection, conversely, meant maintaining domestic grain production. This would retard modernization, maintain a large agricultural population, and prolong national self-sufficiency in food.

Each policy implied a different organization for farming. Under late nineteenth-century conditions, dairy products, meats, and vegetables were best produced by high quality labor, working in small units, managed by owners, or long-term leaseholders. They were produced least well on estates by landless laborers working for a squirearchy. Thus, modernization would be easier where small units of production already predominated, as in Denmark, which is Gerschenkron's model of a modernizing response to the crisis of 1873. The Danish state helped by organizing cooperatives, providing technology, and loaning capital.

In Germany, however, landholding patterns varied considerably. In the region of vast estates east of the Elbe, modernization would have required drastic restructuring of the Junkers' control of the land. It would have eroded their hold over the laborers, their dominance of local life, and their position in German society. The poor quality of Prussian soil hindered modernization of any kind; in any case it would have cost money. Conversely, western and southern Germany contained primarily small- and medium-sized farms more suited to modernization.

Gerschenkron thinks that the Danish solution would have been best for everyone, but especially for these smaller farmers. Following his reasoning, we can impute divergent interests to these two groups. For the Junkers, protection of agriculture was a dire necessity. For the small farmers, modernization optimized their welfare in the long run, but in the short run protection would keep them going; their interests, therefore, can be construed as ambivalent.

What were the interests of agriculture concerning industrial tariffs? Presumably the agricultural population sought to pay the lowest possible prices for the industrial goods that it consumed, and would be opposed to high industrial tariffs. Farmers selling high quality produce to the industrial sector prospered, however, when that sector prospered, since additional income was spent disproportionately on meat and eggs. Modernizing producers might therefore be receptive to tariff and other economic policies which helped industry. For grain, conversely, demand was less elastic. Whatever the state of the industrial economy, the Junkers would be able to sell their output provided that foreign sources were prevented from undercutting them. Thus, we would expect the Junkers to be the most resolutely against high industrial tariffs, while the smaller farmers would again have a less clear-cut interest.

Neither were the interests of the industrial sector homogenous. Makers of basic materials such as iron and steel wanted the producers of manufactured products such as stoves, pots and pans, shovels, rakes, to buy supplies at home rather than from cheaper sources abroad. Conversely the finished goods manufacturers wanted cheap materials; their ideal policy would have been low tariffs on all goods except the ones that they made.

In theory, both types of industries were already well past the "infant industry" stage and would have benefited from low tariffs and international specialization. Indeed, German industry competed very effectively against British and American products during this period, penetrating Latin America, Africa, Asia, and even the United States and United Kingdom home markets. Low tariffs might not have meant lower incomes for industry, but rather a shift among companies and a change in the mix of items produced.

Nevertheless, tariffs still offered certain advantages even to the strong. They reduced risk in industries requiring massive investments, like steel; they assured economies of scale, which supported price wars or dumping in foreign markets; and to the extent that cartels and mergers suppressed domestic production, they allowed monopoly profits. Finally, iron and steel manufacturers everywhere faced softening demand due to the declining rate of railroad building, not wholly offset by shipbuilding. As we shall see, steelmen were in the vanguard of protectionist movements everywhere, including Britain (their only failure).

All industrialists (except those who sold farm equipment) had an interest in low agricultural tariffs. Cheap food helped to keep wages down and to conserve purchasing power for manufactured goods.

The interests of the industrial work force were pulled in conflicting directions by the divergent claims of consumer preoccupations and producer concerns. As consumers, workers found any duties onerous, especially those on food. But as producers, they shared an interest with their employers in having

TABLE 1 Interests of Different Groups in Relation to Industrial and Agricultural Tariffs (Germany)

AGRICULTURAL TARIFFS

		HIGH	LOW
INDUSTRIAL TARIFFS	HIGH	The Outcome: High Tariffs Small|Farmers	Heavy Industry Workers in Heavy Industry
	LOW	Junkers	Workers in FM Finished Manufacturers

their particular products protected, or in advancing the interests of the industrial sector as a whole.

Shippers and their employees had an interest in high levels of imports and exports and hence in low tariffs of all kinds. Bankers and those employed in finance had varied interests according to the ties each had with particular sectors of the economy. As consumers, professionals and shopkeepers, along with labor, had a general interest in keeping cost down, although special links (counsel to a steel company or greengrocer in a steel town) might align them to a high-tariff industry.

This pattern of group interests may be represented diagrammatically. Table 1 shows each group's position in relation to four policy combinations, pairing high and low tariffs for industry and agriculture. The group's intensity of interest can be conveyed by its placement in relation to the axis: closeness to the origin suggests ambiguity in the group's interest; distance from the intersection suggests clarity and intensity of interest.

Notice that no group wanted the actual policy outcome in Germany—high tariffs in both sectors. To become policy, the law of 1879 and its successors required trade-offs among members of different sectors. This is not really surprising. Logrolling is expected of interest groups. Explanation 1 would therefore find the coalition of iron and rye quite normal.

Nevertheless, a different outcome—low tariffs on both types of goods— also would have been compatible with an economic interest group explanation. Logrolling could also have linked up those parts of industry and agriculture that had a plausible interest in low tariffs: finished goods manufacturers, shippers and dockworkers, labor, professionals, shopkeepers, consumers, and farmers of the West and South. This coalition may even have been a majority of electorate, and at certain moments managed to impose its policy preferences. Under Chancellor Georg von Caprivi (1890–1894), reciprocal trade treaties were negotiated and tariffs lowered. Why did this coalition lose over the long run? Clearly because it was weaker, but of what did this weakness consist?

Political Explanations

One answer looks to aspects of the political system which favored protectionist forces at the expense of free traders: institutions (weighted voting, bureaucracy); personalities who intervened on one side or another; the press of other issues (socialism, taxation, constitutional reform, democratization); and interest group organization.

In all these domains, the protectionists had real advantages. The Junkers especially enjoyed a privileged position in the German system. They staffed or influenced the army, the bureaucracy, the judiciary, the educational system, and the Court. The three-class voting system in Prussia, and the allocation of seats, helped overrepresent them and propertied interests in general.

In the late 1870s, Bismarck and the emperor switched to the protectionists' side. Their motives were primarily political. They sought to strengthen the basic foundations of the conservative system (autonomy of the military and the executive from parliamentary pressure; a conservative foreign policy; dominance of conservative social forces at home; and preservation of the Junkers). For a long time, industry and bourgeois elements had fought over many of these issues. Unification had helped to reconcile the army and the middle classes, but many among the latter still demanded a more liberal constitution and economic reforms opposed by the Junkers. In the 1870s Bismarck used the Kulturkampf to prevent a revisionist alliance of Liberals, Catholics, and Federalists. In the long run, this was an unsatisfactory arrangement because it made the government dependent on unreliable political liberals and alienated the essentially conservative Catholics.

Tariffs offered a way to overcome these contradictions and forge a new, conservative alliance. Industrialists gave up their antagonism toward the Junkers, and any lingering constitutionalist demands, in exchange for tariffs, anti-Socialist laws, and incorporation into the governing majority. Catholics gave way on constitutional revision in exchange for tariffs and the end of the Kulterkampf (expendable because protection would now carry out its political function). The Junkers accepted industry and paid higher prices for industrial goods, but maintained a variety of privileges, and their estates. Peasants obtained a solution to their immediate distress, less desirable over the long run than modernization credits, but effective nonetheless. Tariff revenues eased conflicts over tax reform. The military obtained armaments for which the iron and steel manufacturers received the contracts. The coalition excluded everyone who challenged the economic order and/or the constitutional settlement of 1871. The passage of the first broad protectionist measure in 1879 has aptly been called the "second founding" of the Empire.

Control of the Executive allowed Bismarck to orchestrate these complex trade-offs. Each of the coalition partners had to be persuaded to pay the price, especially that of high tariffs on the goods of the other sector. Control of foreign policy offered instruments for maintaining the bargain once it had been struck. . . . The Chancellor used imperialism, nationalism, and overseas crises to obscure internal divisions, and particularly, to blunt middle-class criticism. Nationalism and the vision of Germany surrounded by enemies, or at least harsh competitors, reinforced arguments on behalf of the need for self-sufficiency in food and industrial production, and for a powerful military machine. . . .

The protectionists also appear to have organized more effectively than the free traders. In the aftermath of 1848, industry had been a junior partner, concerned with the elimination of obstacles to a domestic German free market (such as guild regulations and internal tariffs). Its demands for protection against British imports were ignored. . . . The boom of the 1860s greatly increased the relative importance of the industrialists. After 1873, managers of heavy industry, mines and some of the banks formed new associations and worked to convert old ones: in 1874 the Association of German Steel Producers was founded; in 1876, the majority of the Chambers of Commerce swung away from free trade, and other associations began to fall apart over the issue. These protectionist producers' groups were clear in purpose, small in number, and intense in interest. Such groups generally have an easier time working out means of common action than do more general and diffuse ones. Banks and the state provided coordination among firms and access to other powerful groups in German society.

The most significant of these powerful groups—the Junkers—became available as coalition allies after the sharp drop in wheat prices which began in 1875. Traditionally staunch defenders of free trade, the Junkers switched very quickly to protection. They organized rapidly, adapting with remarkable ease, as Gerschenkron notes, to the *ère des foules*. Associations such as the Union of Agriculturalists and the Conservative Party sought to define and represent the collective interest of the whole agricultural sector, large and small, east and west. Exploiting their great prestige and superior resources, the Junkers imposed their definition of that interest—protection as a means of preserving the status quo—on the land. To legitimate this program, the Junker-led movements developed many of the themes later contained in Nazi propaganda: moral superiority of agriculture; organic unity of those who work the land; anti-Semitism; and distrust of cities, factories, workers, and capitalists. . . .

The alternative (Low/Low) coalition operated under several political handicaps. It comprised heterogeneous components, hence a diffuse range of interests. In economic terms, the coalition embraced producers and consumers, manufacturers and shippers, owners and workers, and city dwellers and peasants. Little in day to day life brought these elements together, or otherwise facilitated the awareness and pursuit of common goals; much kept them apart—property rights, working conditions, credit, and taxation. The low tariff groups also differed on other issues such as religion, federalism, democratization of the Constitution, and constitutional control of the Army and Executive. Unlike the High/High alliance, the low tariff coalition had to overcome its diversity without help from the Executive. Only during the four years of Caprivi was the chancellor's office sympathetic to low tariff politics, and Caprivi was very isolated from the court, the kaiser, the army, and the bureaucracy.

Despite these weaknesses, the low tariff alliance was not without its successes. It did well in the first elections after the "re-founding" (1881), a defeat for Bismarck which . . . drove him further toward social imperialism. From 1890, Caprivi directed a series of reciprocal trade negotiations leading to tariff reductions. Caprivi's ministry suggests the character of the programmatic glue needed to keep a low-tariff coalition together: at home, a little more egalitarianism and constitutionalism (the end of the antisocialist laws); in foreign policy, a little more internationalism—no lack of interest in empire or prestige, but a greater willingness to insert Germany into an international division of labor.

International System Explanations

A third type of explanation for tariff levels looks at each country's position in the international system. Tariff policy has consequences not only for profit and loss for the economy as a whole or for particular industries, but for other national concerns, such as security, independence, and glory. International specialization means interdependence. Food supplies, raw materials, manufactured products, markets become vulnerable. Britain, according to this argument, could rely on imports because of her navy. If Germany did the same, would she not expose her lifeline to that navy? If the German agricultural sector shrank, would she not lose a supply of soldiers with which to protect herself from foreign threats? On the other hand, were there such threats? Was the danger of the Franco-British-Russian alliance an immutable constituent fact of the international order, or a response to German aggressiveness? This brings us back to the Kehr-Wehler emphasis on the importance of domestic interests in shaping foreign policy. There were different ways to interpret the implications of the international system for German interests: one view, seeing the world as hostile, justified protection; the other, seeing the world as benevolent, led to free trade. To the extent that the international system was ambiguous, we cannot explain the choice between these competing foreign policies by reference to the international system alone.

A variant of international system explanations focuses on the structure of bargaining among many actors in the network of reciprocal trade negotiations. Maintenance of low tariffs by one country required a similar willingness by others. One could argue that Germany was driven to high tariffs by the protectionist behavior of other countries. A careful study of the timing of reciprocal trade treaties in this period is required to demonstrate this point, a type of study I have been unable to find. The evidence suggests that at least in Germany, the shift from Caprivi's low tariff policy to Bernhard Bülow's solidarity bloc (protection, naval-building, nationalism, antisocialism) did not come about because of changes in the behavior of foreign governments. Rather, the old Bismarckian coalition of heavy industry, army, Junkers, nationalists, and conservatives mobilized itself to prevent further erosion of its domestic position.

Economic Ideology

A fourth explanation for the success of the protectionist alliance looks to economic ideology. The German nationalist school, associated with Friedrich List, favored state intervention in economic matters to promote national power and welfare. Free trade and laissez-faire doctrines were less entrenched than they were in Britain. According to this explanation, when faced with sharp competition from other countries, German interests found it easier to switch positions toward protection than did their British counterparts. This interpretation is plausible. The free trade policies of the 1850s and 1860s were doubtless more shallowly rooted in Germany and the tradition of state interventionism was stronger.

All four explanations, indeed, are compatible with the German experience: economic circumstances provided powerful inducements for major groups to support high tariffs; political structures and key politicians favored the protectionist coalition; international forces seemed to make its success a matter of national security; and German economic traditions helped justify it. Are all these factors really necessary to explain the protectionist victory, or is this causal overkill? I shall reserve judgement until we have looked at more examples.

FRANCE

The French case offers us a very different political system producing a very similar policy result. As with Germany, the causes may explain more than necessary. The High/High outcome (Table 1) is certainly what we would expect to find looking at the interests of key economic actors. French industry, despite striking gains under the Second Empire and the Cobden-Chevalier Treaty, was certainly less efficient than that of other "late starters" (Germany and the United States). Hence manufacturers in heavy industry, in highly capitalized ones, or in particularly vulnerable ones like textiles had an intense interest in protection. Shippers and successful exporters opposed it.

Agriculture, as in Germany, had diverse interests. France had no precise equivalent to the Junkers; even on the biggest farms the soil was better, the labor force freer, and the owners less likely to be exclusively dependent on the land for income. Nonetheless, whether large or small, all producing units heavily involved in the market were hard hit by the drop in prices. The large proportion of quasi-subsistence farmers, hardly in the market economy, were less affected. The prevalence of small holdings made modernization easier than in Prussia, but still costly. For most of the agricultural sector, the path of least resistance was to maintain past practice behind high tariff walls.

As we would expect, most French producer groups became increasingly protectionist as prices dropped. In the early 1870s Adolphe Thiers tried to raise tariffs, largely for revenue purposes, but failed. New associations demanded tariff revision. In 1881, the National Assembly passed the first general tariff measure, which protected industry more than agriculture. In the same year American meat products were barred as unhealthy. Sugar received help in 1884, grains and meats in the tariffs of 1885 and 1887. Finally, broad coverage was given to both agriculture and industry in the famous Méline Tariff of 1892. Thereafter, tariffs drifted upwards, culminating in the very high tariff of 1910.

This policy response fits the logic of the political system explanation as well. Universal suffrage in a society of small property owners favored the protection of units of production rather than consumer interests. Conflict over nontariff issues, although severe, did not prevent protectionists from finding each other. Republican, Royalist, Clerical, and anti-Clerical protectionists broke away from their free trade homologues to vote the Méline Tariff. Méline and others even hoped to reform the party system by using economic and social questions to drive out the religious and constitutional ones. This effort failed but cross-party majorities continued to coalesce every time the question of protection arose and high tariffs helped reconcile many conservatives to the Republic.

In France, protection is the result we would expect from the international system explanation: international political rivalries imposed concern for a domestic food supply and a rural reservoir of soldiers. As for the economic ideology explanation, ideological traditions abound with arguments in favor of state intervention. The Cobden-Chevalier Treaty had been negotiated at the top. The process of approving it generated no mass commitment to free trade as had the lengthy public battle over the repeal of the Corn Laws in Britain. The tariffs of the 1880s restored the *status quo ante*.

Two things stand out in the comparison of France with Germany. First, France had no equivalent to Bismarck, or to the state mechanism which supported him. The compromise between industry and agriculture was organized without any help from the top. Interest groups and politicians operating through elections and the party system came together and worked things out. Neither the party system, nor the constitution, nor outstanding personalities can be shown to have favored one coalition over another.

Second, it is mildly surprising that this alliance took so long to come about—perhaps the consequence of having no Bismarck. It appears that industry took the lead in fighting for protection, and scored the first success. Why was agriculture left out of the Tariff of 1881 (while in Germany it was an integral part of the Tariff of 1879), when it represented such a large number of people? Why did it take another eleven years to get a general bill? Part of the answer may lie in the proportion of people outside the market economy; the rest may lie in the absence of leaders with a commanding structural position working to effect a particular policy. In any case, the Republic eventually secured a general bill, at about the same time that the United States was also raising tariffs.

GREAT BRITAIN

Britain is the only highly industrialized country which failed to raise tariffs on either industrial or agricultural products in this period. Explanation 1 appears to deal with this result quite easily. British industry, having developed first, enjoyed a great competitive advantage over its rivals and did not need tariffs. International specialization worked to Britain's advantage. The world provided her with cheap food; she supplied industrial products in exchange and made additional money financing and organizing the exchange. Farmers could make a living by modernizing and integrating their units into this industrial order. Such had been the logic behind the repeal in the Corn Laws in 1846.

Upon closer inspection, British policy during the Great Depression seems less sensible from a materialist viewpoint. Conditions had changed since 1846. After 1873, industry started to suffer at the hands of its new competitors, especially American and German ones. Other countries began to substitute their own products for British goods, compete with Britain in overseas markets, penetrate the British domestic market, and erect tariff barriers against British goods, Britain was beginning that languorous industrial decline which has continued uninterrupted to the present day.

In other countries, industrial producers, especially in heavy industry, led agitation for protection in response to the dilemma of the price slump. Although some British counterparts did organize a Fair Trade league which sought protection within the context of the Empire (the policy adopted after World War I), most industrialists stayed with free trade.

If this outcome is to be consistent with explanation 1, it is necessary to look for forces which blunted the apparent thrust of international market forces. British producers' acceptance of low tariffs was not irrational if other ways of sustaining income existed. In industry, there were several. Despite Canadian and Australian tariff barriers, the rest of the Empire sustained a stable demand for British goods; so did British overseas investment, commercial ties, and prestige. International banking and shipping provided important sources of revenue which helped to conceal the decline in sales. Bankers and shippers also constituted a massive lobby in favor of an open international economy.

To some degree, then, British industry was shielded from perceiving the full extent of the deterioration of her competitive position.

In agriculture, the demand for protection was also weak. This cannot be explained simply by reference to 1846. Initially the repeal of the Corn Laws affected farming rather little. Although repeal helped prevent sharp price increases following bad harvests, there was simply not enough grain produced in the world (nor enough shipping capacity to bring it to Europe) to provoke a major agricultural crisis. The real turning point came in the 1870s, when falling prices were compounded by bad weather. Why, at this moment, did the English landowning aristocracy fail to join its Junker or French counterpart in demanding protection? The aristocrats, after all, held a privileged position in the political system; they remained significantly overrepresented in the composition of the political class, especially in the leadership of Parliament; they had wealth and great prestige.

As with industry, certain characteristics of British agriculture served to shield landowners from the full impact of low grain prices. First, the advanced state of British industrial development had already altered the structure of incentives in agriculture. Many landowners had made the change from growing grain to selling high quality foodstuffs. These farmers, especially dairymen and meat producers, identified their interests with the health of the industrial sector, and were unresponsive to grain growers' efforts to organize agriculture for protection.

Second, since British landowners derived their income from a much wider range of sources than did the Junkers, the decline of farming did not imply as profound a social or economic disaster for them. They had invested in mining, manufacturing, and trading, and had intermarried with the rising industrial bourgeoisie. Interpenetration of wealth provided the material basis for their identification with industry. This might explain some Tories' willingness to abandon protection in 1846, and accept that verdict even in the 1870s.

If repeal of the Corn Laws did not immediately affect the British economy, it did profoundly influence politics and British economic thought in ways, following the logic of explanations 2 and 4, that are relevant for explaining policy in the 1870s. The attack on the Corn Laws mobilized the Anti-Corn Law League (which received some help from another mass movement, the Chartists). Over a twenty-year period, the League linked the demand for cheap food to a broader critique of landed interest and privilege. Its victory, and the defection of Peel and the Tory leadership, had great symbolic meaning. Repeal affirmed that the British future would be an industrial one, in which the two forms of wealth would fuse on terms laid down for agriculture by industry. By the mid-1850s even the backwoods Tory rump led by Disraeli had accepted this; a decade later he made it the basis for the Conservative revival. To most of the ever larger electorate, free trade, cheap food, and the reformed political system were inextricably linked. Protection implied an attack on all the gains realized since 1832. Free trade meant freedom and prosperity. These identifications inhibited the realization that British economic health might no longer be served by keeping her economy open to international economic forces.

Finally, British policy fits what one would expect from analysis of the international system (explanation 3). Empire and navy certainly made it easier to contemplate dependence on overseas sources of food. It is significant that protection could be legitimated in the long run only as part of empire. People would do for imperialism what they would not do to help one industry or another. Chamberlain's passage from free trade to protection via empire foreshadows the entire country's actions after World War I.

UNITED STATES

Of the four countries examined here, only the United States combined low-cost agriculture and dynamic industry within the same political system. The policy outcome of high industrial tariffs and low agricultural ones fits the logic of explanation 1. Endowed with efficient agriculture, the United States had no need to protect it; given the long shadow of the British giant, industry did need protection. But despite its efficiency (or rather because of it) American agriculture did have severe problems in this period. On a number of points, it came into intense conflict with industry. By and large, industry had its way.

> *Monetary policy* The increasing value of money appreciated the value of debt owed to Eastern bankers. Expanding farm production constantly drove prices downward, so that a larger amount of produce was needed to pay off an ever increasing debt. Cheap money schemes were repeatedly defeated.
>
> *Transportation* Where no competition among alternative modes of transport or companies existed, farmers were highly vulnerable to rate manipulation. Regulation eventually was introduced, but whether because of the farmers' efforts or the desire of railroad men and other industrialists to prevent ruinous competition—as part of their "search for order"—is not clear. Insurance and fees also helped redistribute income from one sector to the other.
>
> *Tariffs* The protection of industrial goods required farmers to sell in a free world market and buy in a protected one.
>
> *Taxation* Before income and corporate taxes, the revenue burden was most severe for the landowner. Industry blocked an income tax until 1913.
>
> *Market instability* Highly variable crop yields contributed to erratic prices, which could have been controlled by storage facilities, government price stabilization boards, and price supports. This did not happen until after World War I.
>
> *Monopoly pricing practices* Differential pricing (such as Pittsburgh Plus, whereby goods were priced according to the location of the head office rather than the factory) worked like an internal tariff, pumping money

from the country into the Northeast. The antitrust acts addressed some of these problems, but left many untouched.

Patronage and pork-barrel Some agrarian areas, especially the South, fared badly in the distribution of Federal largesse.

In the process of political and industrial development, defeat of the agricultural sector appears inevitable. Whatever the indicator (share of GNP, percentage of the work force, control of the land) farmers decline; whether peasants, landless laborers, family farmers, kulaks, or estate owners, they fuel industrialization by providing foreign exchange, food, and manpower. In the end they disappear.

This can happen, however, at varying rates: very slowly, as appears to be the case in China today, slowly as in France, quickly as in Britain. In the United States, I would argue, the defeat of agriculture as a *sector* was swift and thorough. This may sound strange in light of the stupendous agricultural output today. Some landowners were successful. They shifted from broad attacks on the system to interest group lobbying for certain types of members. The mass of the agricultural population, however, lost most of its policy battles and left the land.

One might have expected America to develop not like Germany, . . . but like France: with controlled, slower industrial growth, speed sacrificed to balance, and the preservation of a large rural population. For it to have happened, the mass of small farmers would have to have found allies willing to battle the Eastern banking and industrial combine which dominated American policy-making. To understand their failure it is useful to analyze the structure of incentives among potential alliance partners as was done for the European countries. If we take farmers' grievances on the policy issues noted above (such as money and rates) as the functional equivalent of tariffs, the politics of coalition formation in the United States become comparable to the equivalent process in Europe.

Again two alliances were competing for the allegiance of the same groups. The protectionist core consisted of heavy industry, banks, and textiles. These employers persuaded workers that their interests derived from their roles as producers in the industrial sector, not as consumers. To farmers selling in urban markets, the protectionists made the familiar case for keeping industry strong.

The alternative coalition, constructed around hostility toward heavy industry and banks, appealed to workers and farmers as consumers, to farmers as debtors and victims of industrial manipulation, to the immigrant poor and factory hands against the tribulations of the industrial system . . . and to shippers and manufacturers of finished products on behalf of lower costs. Broadly this was a Jackson-type coalition confronting the Whig interest—the little man versus the man of property. Lower tariffs and more industrial regulation (of hours, rates, and working conditions) were its policies.

The progressive, low tariff alliance was not weak. Agriculture employed by far the largest percentage of the workforce. Federalism should have given it considerable leverage: the whole South, the Midwest, and the trans-Mississippi West. True, parts of the Midwest were industrializing, but then much of the Northeast remained agricultural. Nonetheless the alliance failed: the explanation turns on an understanding of the critical realignment election of 1896. The defeat of Populism marked the end of two decades of intense party competition, the beginning of forty years of Republican hegemony and the turning point for agriculture as a sector. It will be heuristically useful to work backwards from the conjuncture of 1896 to the broader forces which produced that contest.

The battle of 1896 was shaped by the character and strategy of William Jennings Bryan, the standard bearer of the low-tariff alliance. Bryan has had a bad historical press because his Populism had overtones of bigotry, anti-intellectualism, archaicism, and religious fundamentalism. Politically these attributes were flaws because they made it harder to attract badly needed allies to the farmers' cause. Bryan's style, symbols, and program were meaningful to the trans-Mississippi and Southern farmers who fueled Populism, but incomprehensible to city dwellers, immigrants, and Catholics, to say nothing of free-trade oriented businessmen. In the drive for the Democratic nomination and during the subsequent campaign, Bryan put silver in the forefront. Yet free coinage was but a piece of the Populist economic analysis and not the part with the strongest appeal for nonfarmers (nor even the most important element to farmers themselves). The city dweller's grievances against the industrial economy were more complex. Deflation actually improved his real wages, while cheap money threatened to raise prices. In the search for allies other criticisms of the industrial order could have been developed, but Bryan failed to prevent silver from overwhelming them.

Even within the agrarian sector, the concentration on silver and the fervid quality of the campaign worried the more prosperous farmers. By the 1890s, American agriculture was considerably differentiated. In the trans-Mississippi region, conditions were primitive; farmers were vulnerable, marginal producers: they grew a single crop for the market, had little capital, and no reserves. For different reasons, Southern agriculture was also marginal. In the Northeast and the Midwest farming had become much more diversified; it was less dependent on grain, more highly capitalized, and benefited from greater competition among railroads, alternative shipping routes, and direct access to urban markets. These farmers related to the industrial sector, rather like the dairymen in Britain, or the Danes. Bryan frightened these farmers as he frightened workers and immigrants. The qualities which made him attractive to one group antagonized others. Like Sen. Barry Goldwater and Sen. George McGovern, he was able to win the nomination, but in a manner which guaranteed defeat. Bryan's campaign caused potential allies to define their interests in ways which seemed incompatible with those of the agricultural sector. It drove farmers away rather than attracting them. Workers saw Bryan not as an ally against their bosses but as a threat to the industrial sector of the economy of which they were a part. To immigrants, he was a nativist xenophobe. Well-to-do Midwestern farmers, Southern Whigs, and Northeast shippers all saw him as a threat to property.

The Republicans, on the other hand, were very shrewd. Not only did they have large campaign funds, but, as Williams argues, James G. Blaine, Benjamin Harrison, and William McKinley understood that industrial interests required allies the support of which they must actively recruit. Like Bismarck, these Republican leaders worked to make minimal concessions in order to split the opposition. In the German coalition the terms of trade were social security for the workers, tariffs for the farmers and the manufacturers, guns and boats for the military. In America, McKinley, et al., outmaneuvred President Grover Cleveland and the Gold Democrats on the money issue; when Cleveland repealed the Silver Purchase Act, some of the Republicans helped pass the Sherman Silver Purchase Act. The Republican leaders then went after the farmers. Minimizing the importance of monetary issues, they proposed an alternative solution in the form of overseas markets: selling surpluses to the Chinese or the Latin Americans, negotiating the lowering of tariff levels, and policing the meat industry to meet the health regulations Europeans had imposed in order to keep out American imports. To the working class, the Republicans argued that Bryan and the agrarians would cost them jobs and boost prices. Social security was never mentioned—McKinley paid less than Bismarck.

In 1896, the Republican candidate was tactically shrewd and the Democratic one was not. It might have been the other way around. Imagine a charismatic Democrat from Ohio, with a Catholic mother, traditionally friendly to workers, known for his understanding of farmers' problems, the historical equivalent of Senator Robert Kennedy in the latter's ability to appeal simultaneously to urban ethnics, machine politicians, blacks, and suburban liberals. Unlikely but not impossible: had he existed, such a candidate would still have labored under severe handicaps. The difference between Bryan and McKinley was more than a matter of personality or accident. The forces which made Bryan the standard bearer were built into the structure of American politics. First, McKinley's success in constructing a coalition derives from features inherent in industrial society. As in Germany, producers' groups had a structural advantage. Bringing the farmers, workers, and consumers together was difficult everywhere in the industrial world during that period. In America, ethnic, geographic, and religious differences made it even harder.

Second, the industrialists controlled both political parties. Whatever happened at the local level, the national Democratic party lay in the firm grip of Southern conservatives and Northern businessmen. Prior to 1896, they wrote their ideas into the party platforms and nominated their man at every convention. The Gold Democrats were not a choice but an echo. . . . A Bryan-type crusade was structurally necessary. Action out of the ordinary was required to wrest the electoral machine away from the Gold Democrats. But the requirements of that success also sowed seeds for the failure of November, 1896.

Why, in turn, did the Industrialists control the parties? The Civil War is crucial. At its inception, the Republican party was an amalgam of entrepreneurs, farmers, lawyers, and professionals who believed in opportunity, hard work, and self-help; these were people from medium-sized towns, medium-sized enterprises, medium-sized farms. These people disliked the South not because they wished to help the black race or even eliminate slavery, but because the South and slavery symbolized the very opposite of "Free Soil, Free Labor, Free Men." By accelerating the pace of industrialization, the Civil War altered the internal balance of the Party, tipping control to the industrialists. By mobilizing national emotions against the South, the Civil War fused North and West together, locking the voter into the Republican Party. Men who had been antibusiness and Jacksonian prior to 1860 were now members of a coalition dominated by business.

In the South, the Old Whigs, in desperate need of capital, fearful of social change, and contemptuous of the old Jacksonians, looked to the northern industrialists for help in rebuilding their lands and restoring conservative rule. What would have been more natural then to have joined their northern allies in the Republican Party? In the end, the hostility of the Radical Republicans made this impossible, and instead the Old Whigs went into the Democratic Party where they eventually helped sustain the Gold Democrats and battled with the Populists for control of the Democratic organization in the South.

There were, then, in the American system certain structural obstacles to a low-tariff coalition. What of economic ideology (explanation 4) and the international system (explanation 3)? Free trade in the United States never had the ideological force it had in the United Kingdom. Infant industries and competition with the major industrial power provided the base for a protectionist tradition, as farming and distrust of the state provided a base for free trade. Tariffs had always been an important source of revenue for the Federal government. It is interesting that the "Free Soil, Labor and Men" coalition did not add Free Trade to its program.

Trade bore some relation to foreign policy. . . . Nonetheless, it is hard to see that the international political system determined tariff policy. The United States had no need to worry about foreign control of resources or food supply. In any case the foreign policy of the low-tariff coalition was not very different from the foreign policy of the high-tariff coalition.

In conclusion, four countries have been subjected to a set of questions in an attempt to find evidence relevant to differing explanations of tariff levels in the late nineteenth century. In each country, we find a large bloc of economic interest groups gaining significant economic advantages from the policy decision adopted concerning tariffs. Hence, the economic explanation has both simplicity and power. But is it enough? It does have two weaknesses. First, it presupposes a certain obviousness about the direction of economic pressures upon groups. Yet, as the argumentation above has sought to show, other economic calculations would also have been rational for those groups. Had farmers supported protection in Britain or opposed it in Germany and France, we could also offer a plausible economic interpretation for their behavior. The same is true for industrialists: had they accepted the opposite policy, we could find ways in which they benefited from doing so. We require an explanation, therefore, for the choice between two economic logics. One possibility is to look at the urgency of economic need. For protectionists, the incentive for high tariffs was intense and obvious. For free traders, the advantages of their policy preference, and the costs of their opponents' victory, were more ambiguous. Those who wanted their goals the most, won.

Second, the economic explanation fails to flesh out the political steps involved in translating a potential alliance of interest into policy. Logrolling does take some organization, especially in arranging side payments among the partners. The iron-rye bargain seems so natural that we forget the depth of animosity between the partners in the period preceding it. To get their way, economic groups had to translate their economic power into political currency.

The political structures explanation appears to take care of this problem. Certain institutions and particular individuals helped to organize the winning coalition and facilitate its victory. Looking at each victory separately, these structures and personalities bulk large in the story. Yet viewed comparatively, their importance washes out. Bismarck, the Junkers, the authoritarian constitution, the character of the German civil service, the special connections among the state, banking, and industry—these conspicuous features of the German case have no equivalents elsewhere. Méline was no Bismarck and the system gave him no particular leverage. Mobilization against socialism did not occur in the United States, or even in Britain and France. Yet the pattern of policy outcomes in these countries was the same, suggesting that those aspects of the political system which were *idiosyncratic* to each country (such as Bismarck and regime type) are not crucial in explaining the result. In this sense the political explanation does not add to the economic one.

Nonetheless, some aspects of the relation between economic groups and the political system are *uniform* among the countries examined here and do help explain the outcome. There is a striking similarity in the identity of victors and losers from country to country: producers over consumers, heavy industrialists over finished manufacturers, big farmers over small, and property owners over laborers. In each case, a coalition of producers' interests defined by large-scale basic industry and substantial landowners defeated its opponent. It is probable, therefore, that different types of groups from country to country are systematically not equal in political resources. Rather, heavy industrialists and landowners are stronger than peasants, workers, shopkeepers, and consumers. They have superior resources, access to power, and compactness. They would have had these advantages even if the regimes had differed considerably from their historical profiles. Thus a republicanized or democratized Germany would doubtless have had high tariffs (although it might have taken longer for this to come about, as it did in France). A monarchist France (Bourbon, Orleanist, or Bonapartist) would certainly have had the same high tariffs as Republican France. An authoritarian Britain could only have come about through repression of the industrialists by landowners, so it is possible a shift in regime might have meant higher tariffs; more likely, the industrialists would have broken through as they did in Germany. Certainly Republican Britain would have had the same tariff policy. In the United States, it is possible (although doubtful) that without the critical election of 1896, or with a different party system altogether, the alternation between protectionist Republicans and low-tariff Democrats might have continued.

Two coalitions faced each other. Each contained a variety of groups. Compared to the losers, the winners comprised: (1) groups for which the benefits of their policy goal were intense and urgent, rather than diffuse; (2) groups occupying strategic positions in the economy; and (3) groups with structurally superior positions in each political system. The uniformity of the winners' economic characteristics, regardless of regime type, suggests that to the extent that the political advantages derive from economic ones, the political explanation is not needed. The translation of economic advantage into policy does require action, organization, and politics; to that extent, and to varying degrees, the economic explanation by itself is insufficient. It is strongest in Germany, where the rapidity of the switch from free trade to protection is breathtaking, and in France where economic slowness made the nation especially vulnerable to competition. It works least well for Britain where the policy's advantages to the industrialists seem the least clear, and for the United States, where the weakness of agriculture is not explicable without the Civil War. Note that nowhere do industrialists fail to obtain their preferences.

In this discussion, we have called the actors groups, not classes, for two reasons. First, the language of class often makes it difficult to clarify the conflicts of interest (e.g., heavy industry vs. manufacture) which exist within classes, and to explain which conception of class interest prevails. Second, class analysis is complex. Since interest group reasoning claims less, and works, there is no point in going further.

The international system and economic ideology explanations appear the least useful. Each is certainly compatible with the various outcomes, but has drawbacks. First, adding them violates the principle of parsimony. If one accepts the power of the particular economic-political explanation stated above, the other two explanations become redundant. Second, even if one is not attracted by parsimony, reference to the international system does not escape the difficulty inherent in any "unitary actor" mode of reasoning: why does a particular conception of the national interest predominate? In the German case, the low tariff coalition did not share Bismarck's and Bülow's conception of how Germany should relate to the world. Thus the international system explanation must revert to some investigation of domestic politics.

Finally, the economic ideology explanation seems the weakest. Whatever its strength in accounting for the Free Trade Movement of the 1850s and 1860s, this explanation cannot deal with the rapid switch to protection in the 1870s. A national culture argument cannot really explain why two different policies are followed within a very short span of time. The flight away from Free Trade by Junkers, manufacturers, farmers, and so on was clearly provoked by the price drop. For the United Kingdom, conversely, the continuity of policy makes the cultural argument more appropriate. Belief in free trade may have blunted the receptivity of British interest groups toward a protectionist solution of their problems. The need for the economic ideology explanation here depends on one's evaluation of the structure of economic incentives facing industry: to whatever extent empire, and other advantages of having been first, eased the full impact of the depression, ideology was superfluous. To whatever extent industry suffered but avoided protection, ideology was significant.

7

International Investment and Colonial Control:
A New Interpretation

JEFFRY A. FRIEDEN

The origins of colonial imperialism have long been a topic of intense debate. In this reading, Jeffry Frieden examines the relationship between different forms of international investment and varying political ties among developed and developing countries. Frieden argues that direct colonial control was likely when international investments were particularly easy to seize or protect unilaterally, as was the case with raw materials or agricultural investments. Where investments were more difficult to seize or protect, as with multinational manufacturing affiliates, colonialism was less likely to take hold. Frieden does not claim that international investment caused imperialism. Rather, he argues only that colonialism and site-specific international investments coincided historically and were mutually reinforcing. In the twentieth century, as imperialism came under challenge and as manufacturing superseded extractive investments, colonialism gradually became obsolete.

. . . This article recasts the relationship between international investment and colonialism in a more general context. Putative ties between metropolitan investment and colonial control are one subset of a problem associated with the monitoring and enforcement of property rights across national jurisdictions. Cross-border investment involves an implicit or explicit contract between the host country and the investor. The arrangements developed to monitor and enforce these contracts—from gunboat diplomacy to private negotiations—are varied institutional forms responding to different characteristics of the investments and the environment. Colonialism is a particular, perhaps particularly noxious, form that the "resolution" of these quasi-contractual issues can take: the use of force by a home government to annex the host region and so eliminate the interjurisdictional nature of the dispute.

This approach leads to two principal dimensions of variation in overseas investments expected to be associated with different levels of interstate conflict and the propensity for such investments to have been involved in colonialism. The first is the ease with which rents accruing to investments can be appropriated by the host country, or protected by the home country, by coercive means. Everything else being equal, the more easily rents are seized, the more likely the use of force by home countries. The second dimension is the difference between the net expected benefits of cooperation among home countries as compared with unilateral action by a single home country. This is a function both of the degree to which interinvestor cooperation facilitates monitoring and enforcing property rights to the investment and of the cost of organizing and sustaining such concerted action by home countries. All else being equal, the lower the net expected benefits of cooperation, the more likely are home countries to engage in unilateral action, including colonialism.

Certain types of investments appear to have lent themselves more easily than others to protection by the unilateral use of force by home governments. This is especially true for investments with site-specific and easily appropriated rents, such as raw materials extraction and agriculture. For such investments, colonial control resolved inherent property rights problems that arose in its absence. This is not to say that these investments caused colonialism, for the reverse might have been the case—the greater security colonialism offered might have attracted disproportionate amounts of certain kinds of investments; it is, however, to argue for an affinity between certain cross-border investments and colonialism. I do not claim that these factors exhaust all explanation. Clearly geopolitical, technological, ideological, and other forces were important; but the sorts of differentiated economic variables discussed here often have been neglected in studies of colonialism. Further, their importance appears confirmed by historical evidence. . . .

COLONIALISM AND INTERNATIONAL INVESTMENT: THE ISSUES

. . . Most controversy over colonialism and foreign investment has to do with the so-called economic theory of imperialism. The debate seems peculiar to the student of political economy, for it revolves around the simple question of whether economic considerations were important to colonial imperialism or not. As such it is not about an economic theory as normally understood but rather about the relative importance of the totality of economic concerns and the "contending" totality of noneconomic concerns, even though all scholars agree that both were present. This confusion is compounded by all sides in the debate. Supporters of the "economic approach" point to instances in which nationals of a colonial power made money as a result of colonialism, while opponents call upon examples of colonial possessions devoid of economic significance. If the question were whether colonialism was solely and entirely motivated by expectations of direct and measurable economic profits, this might be appropriate; inasmuch as this is manifestly not the question scholars ask, it is not.

In general, an economic theory of political behavior tries to correlate different kinds of economic activity with different kinds of policy or political outcomes. For example, some common economic theories of politics hypothesize a relationship between firm and industry characteristics on the one hand and levels of support for trade protection, regulatory outcomes, or other government actions on the other. Typically, an economic explanation is not about the relationship between the economy and politics in general but rather about the relationship of a specific economic independent variable to a specific political or policy dependent variable. It is variation in the economic variable that is purported to explain corresponding variation in the political or policy outcome. If so desired, confrontation with noneconomic theories can then be made by seeing whether noneconomic variables outperform economic variables in explaining outcomes; more commonly, scholars accept that economic and noneconomic factors are not mutually exclusive. In any case, the appropriate test of a typical economic theory is not whether or not economic considerations matter, but whether they matter in the ways hypothesized by the theory in question. An economic theory of colonialism, in this context, would correlate particular kinds of economic activities with the likelihood of colonial rule.

It is also useful to get a clearer sense than is usually provided in the debate over colonialism of what is being explained by contending theories. Colonial rule is but one possible outcome of relations between and among countries— one value that the dependent variable can take. Its uniqueness is twofold. First, it involves the explicit or implicit use of force by the colonial power over the annexed region. Second, the relationship is exclusive; that is, the colonial power acts unilaterally and not in concert with other powers (and often explicitly to exclude them).

To express the thing to be explained more generally, colonialism is simply one example of interstate interaction occurring along two dimensions. [For ease of exposition, I refer to potential colonial powers as "home countries" (that is, sources of foreign investment) and to potential colonized regions as "host countries" (that is, sites of foreign investment).] The first dimension of variation is the extent to which a home country engages in the use or threat of military force in its relations with the host country. Variation along this dimension runs from military intervention at one limit to the absence of government involvement at the other. The second dimension is the degree to which home countries act in concert toward a host country. Variation along this dimension runs from unilateral and exclusionary action by a home country at one limit to cooperative multilateral action by many home countries at the other. . . . In this context, colonialism (the unilateral use of force) is one possible outcome. Other potential outcomes include multilateral use of force, bilateral arms-length, negotiations, or multilateral negotiations—and gradations in between. . . .

INTERNATIONAL INVESTMENT, PROPERTY RIGHTS, AND INTERNATIONAL CONFLICT

The international politics of international investment are largely organized around two broad problems. The first is the desire of investors to monitor and enforce the host country's respect for cross-border property rights. The second is the degree to which different foreign investors engage in collective action to carry out these monitoring and enforcement activities.

The security of property across borders is in essence a contractual problem. Overseas investment involves an implicit or explicit contract between the investor and the host state. This contract may commit a host government to repay a loan, to allow a firm to mine copper, or to permit the establishment of a local branch factory of a multinational corporation. If the host government breaks the contract—by not servicing the loan, expropriating the mine, or closing down the factory—foreign investors have no direct recourse. This requires investors to devise some mechanism to monitor and enforce their property rights. In this sense home-country military force is one choice among a number of devices to protect overseas assets. . . .

. . . Regarding the security of property across borders as a problem in relational contracting directs attention to characteristics of the assets, product markets, and informational environment that affect the ability of the parties to monitor and enforce their contract. Variation in such contractual problems in turn gives rise to different organizational or political responses.

In addition to underlying contractual questions, the need for investors to monitor and enforce host-country compliance can lead to problems of collective action. In many cases, of course, property rights can be secured on a purely individual basis so that there is no incentive for investor collaboration. All investors may have a common interest in ensuring stable rights to private property, but this does not mean that such stable rights must necessarily be provided to all investors. Each investor is first concerned about the investor's own property rights, and an investor can, in fact, benefit by receiving exclusive property rights. Where secure property rights can be supplied on a specific basis to specific investors, there is little reason for cooperation among investors.

On the other hand, the protection of foreign property may be made substantially more effective if investors cooperate. Whenever the combined action of many investors reduces the cost of protecting their property to each investor, cooperation would be desirable to them. This might be the case, for example, when evaluating the host government's compliance with contractual commitments can be costly—such as when it is difficult to separate the impact of exogenous events from straightforward cheating. In this case, crucially important accurate information about the host government's actions and intentions serve all interested investors, and it is in the interest of all to cooperate in obtaining the information. . . .

However, the circumstances that can make cooperation attractive to investors can also make it difficult. If the benefits of joint action accrue to larger groups of (or all) foreign investors, such protection may come to take on the characteristics of a public good. Under these circumstances, a host government's commitment to respect the property of foreign investors (or a class of foreign investors) is indivisible, inherently available to all investors (or all members of a class of investors). When monitoring and enforcing compliance with quasi-contractual commitments to property rights serves a large class of (or even all) investors, there may be collective action problems associated with the provision of this public good. Because the public good would benefit a large group of actors, actors have an incentive to cooperate to help provide it; cooperation is hindered by the fact that noncooperators cannot be excluded from benefiting from the provision of the public good.

The more the protection of property requires joint action to accomplish, the greater the potential gains from cooperation; but the more difficult collective action, the less likely such cooperation is to succeed. Where joint action by international investors to monitor and enforce property rights improves their welfare, the probability of successful cooperation is a function of free-rider problems. To summarize: cooperation among investors becomes more likely as the potential return to investor collaboration increases (i.e., the more monitoring and enforcement are public goods). And as collaboration among investors becomes more likely, the easier it is to organize collective contribution to monitoring and enforcement. Emphasizing these considerations is not to downplay the importance of other, noneconomic, elements; it is to argue for the anticipated political implications of these economic factors, all else being equal.

Thus the two dimensions of variation in the characteristics of international investment that I expect will affect the probability that such investment will be associated with colonial rule may be summarized as follows: the first is the ability of the investment to be protected by force; the second is the degree to which monitoring and enforcing a host government's respect for foreign property has the character of a public good, and (if it does) the difficulties in overcoming collective action problems to supply the public good.

INTERNATIONAL INVESTMENT AND CONFLICT: ANALYTICAL EXPECTATIONS

The preceding discussion is only useful inasmuch as it leads to otherwise nonobvious analytical expectations. In what follows, I summarize features of cross-border investments and of the markets in which those investments operate, both of which I expect will affect the character of the monitoring and enforcement of international property rights and the degree of collaboration among international investors in pursuit of this monitoring and enforcement. In other words, variation in these factors should be associated with (1) variation in home-state use of force against a host state and (2) the degree of home-state cooperation over investments of this type. Once again, these should be taken as potentially contributory rather than necessarily competing variables in a complex explanation that includes a wide variety of economic, political, military, cultural, and other considerations. For my more limited purposes, the factors relevant to this evaluation of the use of force by and cooperation among investing countries can be grouped into the two categories described above and then can be applied to particular classes of investments.

Site Specificity and the Costs of Physical Protection

Some assets can be more easily protected, and some contracts more easily enforced, by the use or threat of force than others. Put another way, the rents accruing to some assets can be more easily appropriated or protected by force than the rents accruing to other assets. To some extent, the appropriability of the asset and its income stream is related to the asset's specificity to a particular site or corporate network. For example, the income stream created by a copper mine is specific to the place where the copper is located. The mine, and the resource rents associated with it, can be seized by a host country with relative ease. On the other hand, the income stream accruing to a branch plant of a manufacturing multinational corporation typically is specific to its participation in a global enterprise—it relies on managerial, marketing, or technological inputs available only within the firm. While the host government can seize the factory, it cannot appropriate the rents.

By the same token, site-specific assets can be protected by force on the part of investors or their home countries. A mine or plantation can be retaken from a host government by force, and it can continue to earn income once retaken, especially if it is producing for export. While a branch factory can be retaken by force, inasmuch as it is integrated into the local economy— perhaps with networks of suppliers and customers—it would be unlikely to continue to earn income in such circumstances.

This leads me to expect that investing country governments will tend to use or threaten force more the easier it is for the income accruing to the asset in question to be physically seized or protected. The more the rents earned by an asset are site-specific, the more the use of force will serve to protect them, and hence the more likely it is to be used.

Net Expected Benefits of Investor Cooperation

Leaving aside whether or not investors and their home countries use force, we want to understand the circumstances under which investors cooperate with one another instead of pursuing unilateral solutions (including colonialism). I assume the goal of cooperation would be to monitor and enforce the host country's compliance with explicit or implicit contractual commitments. I expect cooperation among investors to be more common when the net expected benefits of collaborative action compare favorably with those of private enforcement by a single investor.

As discussed above, one important determinant of the benefits of collective action is the degree to which monitoring and enforcement become easier for each investor as more investors participate. At one extreme, the cost of monitoring an agreement can be the same for each investor no matter how many there are. This might be the case when each firm must observe aspects of the contract specific to itself; no matter how many firms are in similar situations, no one firm's efforts affect those of any other firm. At the other extreme, there may be significant economies of scale in monitoring and enforcing an agreement, such that the cost per firm declines steeply with the number of investors.

This continuum applies to monitoring and enforcement costs. If a debtor threatens default on foreign loans, information about the government's solvency, macroeconomic conditions, and other contingencies may be valuable to all creditors. This information is essentially the same for all creditors, and if they each contribute a small amount toward a common effort to obtain the information, they will be better off than if each goes about trying to gather the data on its own. By the same token, in some instances each investor has effective ways of punishing a host government that violates a contract. The owner of a mine that is nationalized might withhold technological information without which the mine cannot run and which is not available elsewhere. In other instances, however, cooperation among investors may be necessary to ensure effective enforcement. Perhaps the technology in question is available to a dozen foreign mining firms; all would need to participate in withholding this technology for the sanctions to bind.

Monitoring and enforcement both may be characterized by diminishing costs (increasing returns) for many reasons. For my purposes, it is enough to observe that the incentives for investors to cooperate in monitoring and enforcing contractual compliance by host governments increase the more such efforts are characterized by diminishing costs (increasing returns); the specifics of each case can be examined separately.

Nevertheless, it is also necessary to look at the costs of organizing such beneficial cooperation. As the number of investors rises, if the increased benefits of monitoring are outweighed by the increased costs of holding an ever more fractious group of investors together, then cooperation will not be stable.

The costs of obtaining and sustaining cooperation are a function of well-known collective action considerations. As mentioned above, the cooperative monitoring and enforcement of cross-border contractual commitments by a host country can have characteristics of a public (or at least a club) good. Using the earlier example of creditors who agree to cooperate to monitor a troubled debtor, if all the creditors expect the information to be gathered by others and shared with them, no single creditor has an incentive to contribute toward its gathering. Similarly, creditors who agree to impose sanctions on a recalcitrant debtor face the problem that while all benefit from successful sanctions, no one creditor alone has an incentive to impose the sanction.

Many circumstances conduce toward reducing free riding. These include relatively small numbers, so that all members of the group can observe which members are not contributing and try to design effective sanctions; selective incentives, by which those who contribute can be rewarded; and long time horizons, which increase incentives to cooperate by increasing the expected benefits of cooperation. All of these conditions vary from international investment to international investment; collective action will be easier among some investors than among others. The greater the ability to control free riding, the more I expect cooperation among investors. . . .

PRIMARY PRODUCTION FOR EXPORT. Overseas investments in primary production for export include both extractive industries and agriculture: for example, the mining of precious metals, copper, and oil, and the raising of sugar, cotton, and tea. Such assets are quite specific as to site and can be protected (or attacked) by force relatively easily. I expect force to be linked to them more than to other investments.

Monitoring and enforcing property rights to extractive and agricultural investments are not, in most instances, characterized by increasing returns. One mine or plantation owner seldom benefits from efforts by other owners to protect their own investments. There may be gains from cooperation when investors can boycott the output of a seized facility. If copper mining corporations control the world copper market, they can collude to make it impossible for a host government that nationalizes a mine to sell its product. Among other things, this will depend on how differentiated the product is (the more differentiated, the easier the embargo), how large spot markets are (the larger, the easier for the host government to evade the embargo), and other conditions. However, collective action among overseas investors in primary production cannot be assumed. It will depend on how many producers there are; on whether they are linked on some other dimension (such as marketing the product); and on other such collective action considerations.

The prediction, then, is that overseas investments in primary production for export will be more likely to be associated with the use of force. Except where an embargo of the product is technically feasible and free riding can be readily combatted, these investments also will be more likely to be associated with unilateral action by home countries. In addition to the use of force, such investment will be correlated with other unilateral action, such as intervention or colonial annexation.

AFFILIATES OF MANUFACTURING MULTINATIONAL CORPORATIONS. Modern theories emphasize that foreign direct investment, especially in manufacturing, is but a special case of the internalization of economic activities within one corporate entity. In this sense, a local affiliate is an integral part of a corporate network, and if separated from this network it loses most of its value. The assets of the local affiliate are specific to their use within a broader international enterprise, generally for technological, managerial, or marketing reasons. Most of the value of an overseas Ford affiliate, for example, is inseparable from the affiliate's connection with Ford. This may be because the affiliate makes parts (or requires inputs) which are used (or supplied) only by the parent company, or because the affiliate depends on the reputation and managerial expertise of the international firm. The host government could not appropriate most of the rents that accrue to these assets; once the assets are separated from the integrated corporation, they lose much of their value.

Host governments have little incentive to take assets whose value disappears with the takeover. For this reason, affiliates of integrated multinational corporations have relatively secure property rights. The more specific the assets to a corporate network, the less likely is the host government to threaten the asset, and the less likely is the firm to require home country involvement.

The limited incentive to take such affiliates is paralleled by the difficulties a home country would have in defending a manufacturing affiliate. Unlike the typical mine, the typical branch plant is integrated into the local economy; it cannot function in protected isolation, ringed by a protective force. Similarly, because the assets of affiliates are quite specific to the global firms, there are few externalities created by the defense of one such affiliate—thus the incentive to cooperate is limited. For all these reasons, I expect very little home country political involvement in foreign direct investment in manufacturing and hence little cooperation among home countries.

PUBLIC UTILITIES. International investment in public utilities was especially important during the century before World War II. Foreign-owned railroads, water and power plants, and urban transportation were common throughout the developing world. Such facilities are in a sense intermediate between primary production for export and manufacturing affiliates. On the one hand, like manufacturing affiliates, utilities are often fully integrated into the local economy, so that physical protection by a home government would not assure the investment's earning power: for a railroad to pay off, it has to be used by local customers. In addition, some utilities are technically sophisticated enough that local operators in developing economies might have difficulty running them. However, in many instances, utilities are site-specific and can be seized by force: this might be true of a railroad line or power plant. Force might be useful in some cases—where, for example, the railroad line serves only to transport bananas from foreign-owned plantations to the coast—but in many others it is less likely to be practical.

Scale economies are rare in monitoring and enforcing contracts involving utilities. Each facility is likely to face specific conditions, such as rates for a power company, that in themselves have little impact on other investors in the sector. Even when different utilities face similar problems, such as foreign railroads, the returns from cooperation appear relatively low. For example, railroad companies have little with which to threaten a boycott and similarly little on which to collaborate. Information sharing might be useful, but it is likely to be limited by the different conditions faced by different firms.

For all these reasons, I expect that utilities may be seized by host countries but are unlikely to cause a use of force by home countries. I also expect little cooperation among the home countries of utilities investors. The expected pattern, then, is one of voluntary contracts and negotiations between host countries and individual owners of utilities.

LOANS TO GOVERNMENTS.   The practice of lending to foreign sovereigns is probably as old as the nation-state, and problems in monitoring and enforcing sovereign compliance with such loan contracts are just as old. They remain important today, although their economic form has changed over the years. The loan contract comprises a government's promise to pay and is easy for the host government to violate. Since the asset is an intangible contract, it is difficult to protect by force. An exception might arise when the lender or its home government are able to seize the income stream accruing to a debtor's asset (such as a government-owned airplane or, in earlier days, a customs house); but these are strictly limited: governments with large external assets are unlikely to need to borrow heavily.

On the other hand, the returns from cooperation are enormous. Financial markets, especially international financial markets, rely on debtor fears that default will impede future borrowing. For this threat of future borrowing difficulty to be credible, financial markets must cooperate in refusing to lend to a debtor in default. The more potential lenders are expected to boycott an errant debtor, the greater the debtor's incentive to maintain debt service. In this sense, cooperation among financial institutions to monitor and enforce foreign debt contracts is crucial, and the benefits of such sanctions to each creditor rise dramatically with the scale of the cooperative effort.

There are many obstacles to collective action among creditors. Their numbers are often large and credit is undifferentiated, to name but two. However, financial institutions tend to have many connections among themselves, from correspondent banking to joint ventures, so that their reputations with each other may be important. This will conduce to cooperation.

In the case of foreign lending, then, I expect the use of force by home countries against debtors in default to be relatively rare. However, I expect to find a great deal of cooperation among creditors, for the benefits of creditor unity are large. Collaboration also will depend on circumstances that affect the costs of collective action, such as how close the ties among the creditors are along other dimensions.

To summarize, I expect foreign investment in primary production for export to be most closely associated with the unilateral use of force by the home country. I expect public utilities to be less tied to the use of force, although characterized by home-country unilateralism. Foreign loans should seldom be linked to military intervention, and I expect home governments to be relatively cooperative. Multinational manufacturing affiliates are unlikely to be seized by force and are therefore unlikely to become the focus of violent disputes and unlikely to lead to home-country cooperation. . . .

These analytical expectations do . . . lead to some straightforward predictions about the relationship between colonialism and different forms of foreign investment. I expect colonial rule to be most commonly found in association with foreign investment whose problems can be resolved most easily by unilateral intervention, for colonialism is unilateral and interventionist. Thus, I expect colonialism to be especially strongly associated, not with foreign investments in general, but rather with foreign investments in primary production. . . .

COLONIALISM AND INVESTMENT

Evidence from the British Empire

The analytical considerations presented above lead, most concretely, to hypotheses correlating colonialism with foreign investment in primary production. Although it is theoretically possible to evaluate the other hypotheses presented above, such as the likelihood that foreign lending is associated with private lender cooperation but not military intervention, colonialism is the most easily measured outcome. It is to an evaluation of this claim that I now turn. . . .

The most straightforward way to weigh my approach is to see whether colonial control is correlated with the investments I anticipate will be associated with the use of force and home country unilateralism. Some data along these lines are available for the United Kingdom. However, almost no analogous data are available for other European colonial experiences. Hence, my statistical analysis is confined to the British case.

It is worth starting with some consideration of evidence that colonialism could and did affect the composition of foreign investment in the colonial area. Although this is a controversial topic, one study shows that investors from the colonial powers systematically were overrepresented in foreign direct investments in their colonies—in 1938 by a factor of 2.2 for British colonies and 11.9 for French colonies. That is, there was 2.2 times as much investment by British investors in British colonies as would have been predicted given Britain's share of total global investment and 11.9 times as much French investment in French colonies. Another study by the same scholar indicates that British direct investment in British colonies earned higher rates of return than British investment in non-British developing regions. This dovetails with the general revival among historians of the view that economic motives played a role in colonial expansion, albeit not in the simple way posited by earlier critics.

Recently compiled quantitative evidence can be used more directly to assess my argument about the political implications of different sorts of foreign investments. . . . By looking at British overseas investments inside and outside the British Empire from 1865 to 1914, it becomes clear that investment in transport, manufacturing, and public utilities was overrepresented outside the empire, while investment in primary production was overrepresented inside the empire. Overrepresentation in this context means that a larger proportion of British investment in the region was of this particular type compared with overall British foreign investment; or, stated another way, that more of this type of investment was made in the region than would be expected given the region's overall share of total British foreign investment. For example, . . . primary investment made up 16.5 percent of British investment inside the empire but only 11.9 percent of British investment outside the empire. By this criterion, colonial areas had proportionally greater shares of investment in primary production, while independent areas had greater shares of investment in utilities (including railroads) and manufacturing. Data on government loans run counter to my expectations, which are discussed below. (British gross national product in the 1890s was approximately £1.7 billion, so the amounts involved were very substantial by contemporary standards.)

. . . [It is important] to avoid comparing areas at strikingly different stages of growth, for it could easily be argued that the differences between foreign investment in Kenya and the United States, say, are more easily attributed to level of development than to form of rule. . . . [Looking at the sectoral breakdown of British investment in different types of less developed areas (LDAs), government] lending is disproportionately concentrated in the developing empire, which is a problem for my approach. However, for the less developed empire as a whole, the relative preponderance of primary investments is clear: 46.9 percent of private-sector British investment (i.e., excluding loans to governments) in the empire went to primary activities, while 23.7 percent of British investment in the private sector in nonempire developing areas went to such agricultural and extractive investments. By the same token, transport (overwhelmingly railroads) comprised 42.0 percent of all British private-sector investment in the developing empire but 68.2 percent outside it. Again, in the terms used above, there is a clear overrepresentation of (that is, bias toward) primary investment, and a clear underrepresentation of (that is, bias against) transport investment, inside the empire. . . .

The dependent developing areas, that is the developing empire without India and South Africa, tend to confirm my expectations even more strongly. Loans to governments comprise only 27 percent of British investment in these regions. Of private-sector investment in the dependent colonies, primary production accounted for an enormous 74 percent of the total. This is a very substantial overrepresentation of (that is, bias toward) primary investment in the dependent empire. Public utilities are slightly overrepresented, while manufacturing and transport are underrepresented. In fact, taken as a whole and expressed slightly differently . . . , government loans, railroads, manufacturing, and utilities combined made up 45 percent of British investment in the dependent colonies, compared with 86 percent in noncolonial LDAs.

. . . [Looking at the empire's share of each sector's investment] shows the heavy concentration of primary investment in the empire and especially in the dependent colonies. In other words, while the dependent colonies accounted for just 11.3 percent of all British private investment in the developing world, they took 27.2 percent of all primary investment. . . .

The overrepresentation of extractive and agricultural investments in the dependent colonial areas is striking and tends to confirm my hypothesis about the correlation between colonialism and primary investment. . . .

. . . [Data on the sectoral breakdown of British investment in Latin America in 1913 indicate,] again as expected and in many ways contrary to received wisdom, that in these independent countries raw materials investments were quite insignificant, while British investments were concentrated in government loans, railroads, and utilities.

. . . During . . . [the interwar] period colonial governments . . . borrowed substantially more than independent states; the proximate reason was that the British government restricted borrowing by nonsterling areas in order to defend the pound. Looking at private investment alone, we continue to see a substantial colonial preference for primary production and a foreign preference for utilities and railroads. Oil is treated separately here, since much British oil investment was in areas under semiformal British control (such as League of Nations mandates).

Although there are many problems with the statistical data at our disposal, they do indicate the systematic bias expected by my analysis. That is, colonialism was strongly associated with foreign investment in primary production. It is not possible to determine from these data which way the causal arrow may have run, for time series are sorely inadequate. Only qualitative evidence, if that, can help clarify the direction of causation in particular cases. Nonetheless, it does appear that British overseas investment in manufacturing and utilities was correlated with independent status and investment in primary production, with colonial rule.

Other Evidence

Quantitative evidence on the British case, which is suggestive but hardly conclusive, can be supplemented with other evidence, especially that based on historical case or country studies. It is useful to discuss this by sector, to parallel the analytical predictions presented above. Of course, this information is at best impressionistic.

PRIMARY PRODUCTION FOR EXPORT.   The approach described herein leads to an expectation that primary investment will be correlated with the use of force by home countries and with a relative lack of cooperation among investors. In many historical episodes, indeed, primary investors were at the forefront of interventionist agitation; additionally, primary investment is substantially overrepresented in virtually every colonial setting. The role of mining in sub-Saharan Africa, from the Congo to the cape, is frequently remarked upon. So, too, are the colonialist proclivities of those involved in plantation agriculture in East Africa, the Indian subcontinent, and Southeast Asia. Again, whether the prior existence of primary investments gave rise to demands for annexation or prior colonial control made the area attractive to primary investors is immaterial for the theory presented here—my argument is about the affinity of a form of investment for a form of political governance.

The interventionist tendencies of the oil industry in the decades before the Organization of Petroleum Exporting Countries (OPEC) was formed are well-known. Evidence about the degree of cooperation among oil investors is less clear-cut. In some instances, oil companies procured and secured exclusive access to particular territories: especially within the colonial empires, rights to mine oil often were reserved explicitly or implicitly for metropolitan firms. However, in other instances, oil firms cooperated in the joint exploitation of the resource and presented a united front to local rulers. This was true in parts of the Middle East: the Red Line Agreement of 1928, for example, reserved much of the former Ottoman Empire for a few Anglo-Dutch, British, French, and U.S. firms. Cooperation was repeated elsewhere, as in conflict between oil producers and a nationalist Iranian regime in the early 1950s. Cooperation among oil investors—rare among other primary investors— was a function of the very small number of global oil companies and their dense and long-standing networks of economic and other linkages. As more independent producers arose, cooperation among oil investors gradually eroded, although the private cartel was largely replaced by OPEC's cartel of governments.

The overrepresentation of British primary investment in the colonies was noted above. Although similarly well-developed statistics are not available for other colonial powers, what evidence there is reinforces the impression of the British data. Some 42 percent of investment in French West Africa was in primary production; most of the rest (39 percent) was in commercial services, an important category that we ignore here. Over three-quarters of the Belgian investment in the Congo apparently was in mines and the railways connected directly to them. Japan's overseas investment before World War II was concentrated in China and its colonies. Assets in Japan's possessions— Korea, Kwantung, Taiwan, and the South Pacific—were concentrated almost exclusively in agriculture and raw materials production. It also may not be coincidental that Japanese investment in Manchuria, where Japanese political influence (later direct rule) was strongest, was concentrated in primary production, while investments in other parts of China were more diversified and included many manufacturing firms.

A particularly interesting and a difficult case to explain is that of American overseas investors. Elsewhere I have attempted to show that those most prone to demand U.S. government intervention in Latin America were primary investors. Indeed, many U.S. overseas lenders and manufacturing multinational corporations opposed gunboat diplomacy, and as U.S. investment in the region diversified toward government lending and manufacturing, demands for intervention subsided, as did intervention itself.

AFFILIATES OF MULTINATIONAL MANUFACTURING CORPORATIONS. I expect that manufacturing investment will not be strongly associated with the use of force (i.e., with colonial control); nor will it see much cooperation among investors. On the use of force, recent nationalist ambivalence about manufacturing multinational corporations has obscured prior historical experience. Indeed, in interwar South America it was common to distinguish between "bad" foreign direct investments in primary production and railroads (which were mostly British) and "good" foreign investments in manufacturing (which were mostly American). Parallel phenomena have been noted in many societies in the process of decolonization: the end of colonial rule is associated with a relative decline in foreign investment in primary production and a significant rise in the share of foreign investment going into manufacturing industries. . . .

The Indian experience is interesting in this regard. After World War I the colonial government secured substantial economic policy autonomy, and as this took place foreign investment in manufacturing rose continually (in part, due to increased Indian tariffs). The leading scholar of the economics of Indian decolonization draws a direct connection between the increasing likelihood of independence and the growth of foreign interest in local manufacturing (and the relative decline of primary investments). It should be recalled that for my purposes the chronology is not important: I argue simply that foreign investment in manufacturing is less dependent upon colonial ties than is investment in primary production, and the Indian experience appears to confirm this. . . .

. . . Rarely have manufacturing multinational corporations attempted to bring their home governments into conflict with host countries (such spectacular cases as ITT in Chile are clearly exceptions). Nor have manufacturing investors commonly cooperated with each other in their dealings with host countries. The general rule, as expected, is direct firm-to-host-government bargaining and sometimes private or quasi-public insurance schemes.

PUBLIC UTILITIES. My approach leads to the expectation that, although host governments might appropriate a utility, home governments are not likely to use force to defend it and cooperation among utility investors will be difficult (because the benefits are limited and the costs, high). By far the most historically important type of utility in which foreign investment was significant is the railroad. . . . British railroad and utilities investment was heavily biased toward independent states, and historical evidence does not provide any obvious case of military intervention in defense of either a utility or a railroad.

Cooperation among utilities investors, especially railroad investors, was also very fragile. The spectacular divisions among Western nations over railroad development in Africa and the Near East—the Berlin to Baghdad, cape to Cairo, and trans-Saharan routes all became real or potential sources of conflict—are well-known. Strife was not due to lack of attempts to cooperate. Joint railroad ventures, typically to finance the development of new lines with loans from several national financial centers, were tried in China and the Ottoman Empire but with little success. Even where investors all were British, with similar interests—as in negotiations with the Argentine government over railroad guarantees in the 1890s—cooperation was almost impossible to sustain.

PRIVATE LOANS TO GOVERNMENTS. The argument presented here, namely, that foreign loans to governments will tend not to be associated with home-country use of force and will tend to be associated with cooperation among home countries, is perhaps the most divergent from traditional impressions and received wisdom. The logic, nonetheless, is clear. A loan is a promise, and if unmet it cannot be seized by force. The principal penalty available to creditors against an errant debtor is to deny it the ability to borrow again; in this case, enforcement depends almost entirely upon cooperation among potential international lenders.

None of this is pure and simple. The use of force can help lenders, as it can help almost anyone. Although a home country might seize assets of a country in default, as mentioned above, such overseas assets of debtor nations are typically vastly outweighed by their liabilities. Creditors or their governments might seize income-earning property (such as a customs house) without the debtor government's consent, but this historically has been both extremely costly to accomplish and often useless. Nor is cooperation the only way of ensuring a return on foreign lending. Creditors use various mechanisms to cover default risk and can demand some sort of recoverable collateral from the debtor. However, my general argument still holds: relative to other investments, for international lenders the utility of military force is low and the gains from investor cooperation, high.

The myriad examples of creditor cooperation in dealings with debtors throughout history include the private creditor committees formed to monitor the finances of shaky LDA debtors during the century before World War I. Private financiers, generally with the support of their home governments, established such committees in Egypt, Greece, Morocco, Persia, Serbia, Tunisia, and elsewhere.

The Ottoman Public Debt Administration exemplifies this financial cooperation. In 1875, after fifteen years of borrowing, the Ottoman Empire began to default on its obligations. Six years later, after laborious negotiations among the empire, private bondholders' groups, and the European powers, the Decree of Mouharrem established a Public Debt Administration to be run by a Council of the Public Debt. The council had seven members: one representative of the British and Dutch bondholders, one representative apiece of the French, German, and Austro-Hungarian bank syndicates, an appointee of the Rome Chamber of Commerce, a representative of the Priority Bondholders appointed by the Anglo-French Ottoman Imperial Bank, and one representative of the Ottoman bondholders.

By 1898 the Public Debt Administration controlled about one-quarter of all Ottoman government revenues; its mandate gradually had expanded to include responsibility for new bank loans and railroad guarantees. Certainly the administration's establishment and success owed much to the empire's importance in the prewar balance of power. However, it is striking that financial cooperation was achieved with relative ease, even as the great powers were engaged in bitter rivalry within the same empire over raw materials, railroads, and other concessions. And this curious combination of financial cooperation and conflict on other economic dimensions recurred throughout the decades before World War I. More generally, the historical literature indicates quite clearly that the norm in cases of sovereign debt problems was market-based renegotiation in which creditors typically cooperated among themselves with little difficulty.

Roughly the same pattern held in the interwar period, during which the primary lending institutions were based in New York and London. Many of the postwar financial stabilization loans in Europe were arranged by committees made up of representatives of the governments and financial communities of Britain, France, and the United States, often under the aegis of the Financial Committee of the League of Nations. The Dawes and Young plans each represented collaborative international financial efforts, and the Young Plan included the formation of the Bank for International Settlements (BIS) as a supranational agency to supervise German reparations payments and, more generally, help manage intra-European capital movements. . . .

Fledgling attempts at regularizing creditor unity before World War II pale in comparison to the extraordinarily important (if generally indirect) role the International Monetary Fund has played in the complex process of monitoring and enforcing international loan agreements since the 1950s. Creditor cooperation also has been solid as regards government or government-guaranteed lending, and private financial institutions generally have cooperated among themselves in their interaction with troubled debtors.

If it is not hard to show that creditor cooperation has been common, it is more difficult to demonstrate that force has been used rarely, for the nonexistence of something is hard to document. Nonetheless, most studies that address the issue find few instances of military intervention on behalf of bondholders. Indeed, some of the cases commonly used to support the charge of debt-related gunboat diplomacy are mischaracterized. The United States had few or no financial interests in the Caribbean nations in which it intervened before 1930, while primary investments were quite substantial. The 1902 joint European blockade of Venezuela was prompted by threats to resident foreigners and their property by a capricious dictator; the debt issue was insignificant.

Two well-known historical cases do present something of a problem for my analysis: Egypt and India. As noted above, India and the Dominions were frequent borrowers, a fact that contradicts my argument that colonial control not be associated with disproportionately high levels of borrowing. In the case of the Dominions, it is likely that the effects of colonial rule on investment decisions were swamped by two factors. First, by most calculations the governments of Australia, Canada, and New Zealand were independent, and Dominion status meant little from the standpoint of property rights. Second, these areas were not typical of other capital-importing regions: they were high-income and politically very stable. These factors, and several others of a related nature, could easily explain the preference of British investors for Dominion government bonds. Investment in India and Egypt is less clearly explicable.

The analytical problem is different for the two countries. India was a heavy borrower despite its underdeveloped and colonial status: according to one set of figures, 55 percent of British investment in India between 1865 and 1914 was in government bonds. Two obvious explanations suggest themselves. First, the British government implicitly subsidized Indian bond issues (primarily by allowing them to be used for trust accounts), which increased their attractiveness. Second, India's strategic importance to the British Empire required a massive railroad network, most of which was publicly owned and much of which the British government encouraged to be financed in London. Accurate as these explanations may be, they do not represent support for my approach in this instance; at best, they reflect the potential importance of other factors, which is indubitable.

The relationship between foreign economic interests (including bondholders) and the extension of British control to Egypt is a complex and hotly contested issue. It is clear enough that Egypt's foreign debt (largely to British and French bondholders) was an important irritant in the country's relations with the European powers and that Egyptian finances were regularized, to the benefit of foreign bondholders, after the British occupation in 1882. Several considerations, however, mitigate the quick conclusion that the country's foreign debt was the sole or principal cause of the British intervention. The first is the obvious importance of other economic interests in the area—cotton cultivation and exports, the large community of resident investors, and the Suez Canal—all of which contributed to British concern. Indeed, it might well be argued that the Suez Canal was the ultimate example of an overseas asset whose value was site-specific and whose protection by the use of force was particularly feasible. The second consideration is that the Egyptian saga began, like that of the Ottoman Empire, with a joint creditors' committee, in this case an Anglo-French dual control commission. British occupation came as the French left the field, and British unilateralism may have been spurred by the gradual failure of cooperation. In any event, more work needs to be done before all the case's analytical implications are clear. It is, in fact, striking that, while loans represented roughly half of all foreign investment in the developing world before World War I, there are few cases in which even the boldest historians argue for a connection between lending and intervention.

Despite gaps, then, it does appear that sovereign lending was seldom associated with the use of force by home governments. It also appears that such lending typically involved multilateral cooperation among private creditors or their governments.

CONCLUSION

By putting forth a relatively simple set of hypotheses such as those discussed here, I do not mean to imply that these variables are the sole or even the most important explanations of colonialism or North-South relations more generally. Everything from relative military capabilities, through geostrategic considerations, to norms of sovereignty would need to be included in a full discussion of the determinants of variation in colonial policy over time and across regions. I do nonetheless argue (1) that economic characteristics of cross-border investments had certain systematic effects on the use of force against host countries and on cooperation among home countries, and vice versa and (2) that the evidence tends to support the validity of this first assertion.

The most direct purpose of this article has been to bring new analytical and empirical evidence to bear on an old debate about the relationship between foreign investment and colonialism. In the interests of analytical clarity, I reframed both the questions and the proposed answers. In so doing, I pointed out that the relevant question is not whether "the economy mattered" but under what circumstances economic considerations had predictable effects on political outcomes. I believe that the hypotheses put forth help clarify the analytical issues, and the evidence adduced provides at least some indication of the plausibility of my arguments.

Apart from its relevance to explaining the relationship between colonialism and foreign investment, one potential implication of my argument has to do with change over time. It may indeed not be coincidental that the movement away from colonialism has been correlated with a continual decline in the importance of primary investment in the Third World and an increase in sovereign lending and foreign direct investment in manufacturing. The causal arrows may go in either direction, or their direction may vary from case to case. Nonetheless, there appears to be a strong historical association between colonial rule and foreign investment in primary production for export and between independence and foreign borrowing and foreign investment in manufacturing.

8

British and American Hegemony Compared:
Lessons for the Current Era of Decline

DAVID A. LAKE

Analysts often look to the precedent of British decline, which is said to have contributed to international political and economic unrest, in attempting to understand the impact of America's relative decline. In this essay, David A. Lake points out that the analogy is deeply flawed. International political and economic structures were fundamentally different in the two hegemonic eras, as were the specific processes associated with the relative decline of Britain and of the United States. Lake summarizes the salient characteristics of the two periods and on this basis projects a continuation of past international economic openness even as American hegemony wanes.

America's decline has gained new prominence in the current political debate. There is little doubt that the country's economic competitiveness has, in fact, waned since its hegemonic zenith in the 1950s. The immediate post–Second World War era was anomalous; with Europe and Japan devastated by the war, the United States enjoyed a period of unchallenged economic supremacy. As other countries rebuilt their economies, this lead had to diminish. Yet, even in the 1970s and 1980s, long after the period of "catch up" had ended, America's economy continued to weaken relative to its principal trading partners.

Popular attention has focused on the appropriate policy response to this self-evident decline. One critical issue, which cuts across the traditional liberal–conservative spectrum, is America's relations with its allies. Should the United States maintain a policy of free trade premised on broad reciprocity as in the General Agreement on Tariffs and Trade (GATT), or must it "get tough" with its trading partners, demand equal access industry-by-industry to foreign markets, balance trade between specific countries, and retaliate if others fail to abide by America's understanding of the international trade regime? This is a question which all present and future American governments will have to address—and the answer is by no means ideologically predetermined or, for that matter, clear.

The issue of American decline is not new, despite the recent attention devoted to it. It has been a topic of lively academic debate for almost twenty years—a debate which, while not directly focused on such issues, can shed considerable light on the question of America's relations with its trading partners. The so-called theory of hegemonic stability was developed in the early 1970s to explain the rise and fall of the *Pax Britannica* and *Pax Americana*, periods of relative international economic openness in the mid-nineteenth and mid-twentieth centuries, respectively. In its early form, the theory posited that hegemony, or the existence of a single dominant economic power, was both a necessary and sufficient condition for the construction and mainte-nance of a liberal international economy. It followed that once the hegemon began to decline, the international economy would move toward greater con-flict and closure. The theory has since been refined and extended, with nearly all revisions concluding that a greater potential exists for non-hegemonic international economic cooperation than was allowed for in the original for-mulation. All variants of the theory of hegemonic stability suggest, nonethe-less, that Britain's relative decline after 1870 is the closest historical analogy to the present era and a fruitful source of lessons for American policy. Many have drawn pessimistic predictions about the future of the liberal interna-tional economy on the basis of this comparison, with the implication that a more nationalist foreign economic policy is necessary to halt the breakdown of the open international economy into a series of regional trading blocs. To understand and judge this, one must recognize and begin with the parallels between the *Pax Americana* and the *Pax Britannica* and their subsequent peri-ods of decline. Yet, one must also recognize that the differences between these two cycles of hegemony are just as important as the similarities. The two periods of declining hegemony are similar, but not identical—and the differences have tremendous import for the future of the liberal international economic order and the nature of American policy.

THE HISTORICAL ANALOGY

From the sixteenth to the eighteenth centuries, the international economy was dominated by mercantilism—a pervasive set of state regulations govern-ing the import and export of goods, services, capital, and people. Britain was no exception to this general trend and, in fact, was one of its leading propo-nents. While restrictions on trade may have been adopted largely as a result of rent-seeking by domestic groups, they also stimulated home production and innovation and allowed Britain to build an industrial base from which to challenge Dutch hegemony.

With the industrial revolution, and the resulting economic take-off, Britain slowly began dismantling its mercantilist system. Various restraints were removed, and by the 1830s few industrial tariffs and trade restrictions remained. Agricultural protection persisted, however, until industry finally triumphed over landed interests in the repeal of the Corn Laws in 1846. Brit-ain's shift to free trade ushered in a period of international economic liberal-ization. For reasons discussed below, the repeal of the Corn Laws facilitated the rise of free trade coalitions in both the emerging Germany and the United

States. Moreover, Britain finally induced France to join in the emerging free trade order in 1860, trading its acquiescence in France's military excursions into Northern Italy for lower tariffs in a bargain which underlay the important Cobden–Chevalier Treaty. Interlocking trade treaties premised on the unconditional most-favored-nation principle then served to spread these reductions throughout Europe.

British hegemony peaked in approximately 1870, after which its national product, trade and labor productivity—while continuing to grow in absolute terms—began to shrink relative to its principal economic rivals. With Britain's decline, the free trade order began to unravel. The United States returned to a policy of high protection after the Civil War. Germany adopted high tariffs in its coalition of Iron and Rye in 1879. France followed suit in the Meline Tariff of 1892.

Just as Britain had used mercantilism as a weapon against Dutch hegemony, the United States and Germany used protection to build up their infant industries, which were then able to challenge and defeat British industry in global competition. Despite a large measure of protectionist rent-seeking by various uncompetitive groups in both countries, this strategy of industrial stimulation was successful. By the late 1890s, the United States surpassed Britain in relative labor productivity and other key indicators of industrial production. Germany also emerged as a major threat to British economic supremacy, particularly in the race for colonies in the developing world.

Despite these threats, Britain continued to dominate and manage the international economy until the outbreak of the First World War. With its industrial base slipping, Britain moved into services—relying on shipping, insurance and international finance to offset its increasing trade deficits. The British pound remained the international currency and the City of London the core of the international financial system.

British weakness, however, was revealed and exacerbated by the First World War. Britain sold off many of its overseas assets to pay for the necessary wartime supplies. As a result, repatriated profits were no longer sufficient to offset its trade deficit. Moreover, the war generated several deep and insidious sources of international economic instability—war debts, German reparations, America's new status as a net creditor nation, and, at least partly through Britain's own mistakes, an overvalued pound.

Eventually, the international economy collapsed under the weight of its own contradictions, despite futile efforts at joint Anglo–American international economic leadership in the 1920s. American capital, previously channeled to Germany, which in turn used its international borrowings to pay reparations to Britain and France, was diverted to the stock market after 1927, feeding the speculative fever and precipitating a wave of bank closures in Austria and Germany. As the banking panic spread across Europe and eventually across the Atlantic, the stock market became its own victim. While the crash of 1929 did not cause the Great Depression, it certainly exacerbated the underlying instabilities in international commodity markets. As the depression worsened, each country turned inward upon itself, adopting beggar-thy-neighbor policies in a vain attempt to export the pain to other states.

The roots of American hegemony lie in the period following the Civil War. With the defeat of the South, government policy shifted in favor of the North and industrialization. By the First World War, the United States had emerged as Britain's equal. The two competed for international economic leadership (and occasionally for the abdication of leadership) throughout the inter-war period.

The United States began the process of liberalization in 1913 with the passage of the Underwood Tariff Act. While pressure for freer trade had been building for over a decade, this was the first concrete manifestation of reform. This nascent liberalism, however, was aborted by the war and the international economic instability it engendered; tariffs were raised in 1922 and again in 1930. The United States returned to international liberalism in the Reciprocal Trade Agreements Act of 1934. While free trade remained politically tenuous throughout the 1930s and early 1940s, it was locked securely in place as the centerpiece of American foreign economic policy by the end of the Second World War.

Like Britain, the United States was the principal impetus behind international economic liberalization. It led the international economy to greater economic openness through the GATT, the International Monetary Fund (IMF), the World Bank, and a host of United Nations–related organizations. The United States also made disproportionately large reductions in its tariffs and encouraged discrimination against its exports as a means of facilitating economic reconstruction. Real trade liberalization was delayed until the 1960s, when the Kennedy Round of the GATT substantially reduced tariffs in all industrialized countries. This success was soon followed by the equally important Tokyo Round, which further reduced tariffs and rendered them essentially unimportant impediments to trade.

Despite these successes, and in part because of them, challenges to international liberalism began to emerge in the late 1960s. As America's economic supremacy receded, the exercise of international power became more overt and coercive. This was especially true in the international monetary arena, where the series of stop-gap measures adopted during the 1960s to cope with the dollar overhang were abandoned in favor of a more unilateral approach in the appropriately named "Nixon Shocks" of August 1971. More importantly, as tariffs were reduced and previously sheltered industries were exposed to international competition, new pressures were placed on governments for trade restrictions. These pressures have been satisfied, at least in part, by the proliferation of non-tariff barriers to trade, the most important of which take the form of voluntary export restraints by foreign producers. While the net effect of reduced tariffs and increased non-tariff barriers to trade is difficult to discern, it is clear that domestic political support for free trade in the United States and other advanced industrialized countries has eroded.

In summary, during their hegemonic ascendancies, both Britain and the United States played leading roles in opening the international economy. And in both cases, brief successes were soon followed by increasing challenges to global liberalism. The parallels are clear. The historical analogy suggests a period of increasing economic conflict, a slide down the "slippery slope of protection," and a return to the beggar-thy-neighbor policies of the inter-war period.

THE HISTORICAL REALITY

Despite the plausibility and attractiveness of this historical analogy, it is deeply flawed. The similarities between the *Pax Britannica* and *Pax Americana* have over-shadowed the differences, but those differences may in the end prove to be more important. The points of contrast between the two periods of hegemony can be grouped into four categories.

I. International Political Structures

In the nineteenth century, and throughout the period of British hegemony, the United Kingdom, France, and then Germany all pursued empire as a partial substitute for trade within an open international economy. No country relied entirely on intra-empire trade, but as the international economy became more competitive in the late nineteenth century all three countries turned toward their colonies. This stimulated a general breakdown of the international economy into regional trading blocs and substituted government legislation and regulations for international market forces.

At the height of its hegemony, for instance, Britain pursued an open door policy within its colonies. Parliament repealed the mercantilist Navigation Laws in 1828 and soon thereafter opened the trade of the colonies to all countries on equal terms. Despite the absence of formal trade restrictions in the colonies, however, Britain continued to dominate their trade through informal means, counting on the ties between colonial administrators and the home state to channel trade in the appropriate directions.

Beginning in the late 1890s, however, Britain began to accept and, later, actively to promote preferential trade measures within the empire. While the earliest preferences took the form of unilateral reductions in colonial tariffs on British exports, by the First World War, Britain, under pressure from the colonies, began to reciprocate. The McKenna Duties, passed in 1915, and the Safeguarding of Industry Duties, enacted after the war, all discriminated against non-empire trade. In 1932, Britain returned to protection and adopted a complete system of Imperial Preference. In short, as its economic strength deteriorated in the late nineteenth century, even Britain, the paragon of international liberalism, turned inward to its empire.

Since 1945, on the other hand, formal imperialism has all but disappeared. Instead of a system of geographically dispersed empires, there now exists a system of sovereign states. As the American-dominated "Dollar bloc" of the

1930s attests, a formal empire is not necessary for the creation of a regional trade bloc. Yet the present international system is less likely to break down into regional economic blocs for two reasons.

As Hobson, Lenin and other theorists of late nineteenth-century imperialism correctly pointed out, imperialism is a finite process, the end point of which is determined by the quantity of available land. Once the hinterland is exhausted, countries can expand only through the redistribution of existing colonies. Thus, the quest for imperial trading blocs transforms exchange, at least in part, from a positive into a zero-sum game and increases the level of economic conflict endemic in the international system. Despite the decline of American hegemony, the gains from trade today are both more visible and less exclusive, helping to make the liberal international economy more durable than in the past.

In addition, colonies are not fully sovereign and have, at best, abridged decision-making powers. As a result, intra-imperial trade and trade agreements are not subject to the same possibilities for opportunism as are trade arrangements between independent states. Today, even if two countries undertake a bilateral trade treaty, as in the case of the United States and Canada, each remains fully sovereign and capable of cheating and exploiting the other. Indeed, as regional specialization expands, the quasi-rents potentially appropriable by either party will also increase, thereby raising the gains from opportunism. The higher the gains and, therefore, the risk of opportunism, the less likely it is that two countries will enter into binding bilateral relationships. As a result, trade blocs between sovereign states will always be more fragile, less beneficial and, it follows, less prevalent than those based upon imperial preference.

II. International Economic Structures

A. THE BASES OF BRITISH AND AMERICAN HEGEMONY.   While both Britain and the United States enjoyed a position of international economic dominance, the bases of their economic hegemony differed in important ways. Britain's share of world *trade* was substantially larger than that obtained by the United States, while America's share of world *product* was far larger than Britain's.

In 1870, Britain controlled approximately 24 percent of world trade, declining to less than 15 percent by the outbreak of the First World War. The United States, however, accounted for only 18.4 percent of world trade in 1950, and its share fell to less than 15 percent by the mid 1960s. Collective goods theory suggests that Britain had a stronger interest in acting as a benevolent hegemon and, specifically, in regulating and maintaining an open international economy. This interest in providing the international economic infrastructure, furthermore, was reinforced by Britain's higher dependence on trade, which reached 49 percent of national product in 1877–85 and 52 percent in 1909–13. For the United States, trade accounted for only 17 percent of national product in the 1960s, although this ratio has risen in recent years. These figures indicate that Britain also faced a considerably higher opportunity costs of international economic closure.

While British hegemony was based upon control of international trade, the United States—still the largest trader of its era—relied on the relatively greater size of its domestic economy. Throughout its hegemonic rise and decline, the British economy (measured in terms of national product) was relatively small compared to its trading rivals, and to that of the United States at a similar stage in its hegemonic cycle. In 1860, Britain's economy was only three-quarters the size of America's. Conversely, in 1950, the domestic economy of the United States was over three times larger than the Soviet Union's, its next largest rival. This difference between British and American hegemony, while highlighting variations in the opportunity costs of closure, also have important implications for the international political processes discussed below.

B. THE TRAJECTORIES OF DECLINE. Not only were the economic bases of British and American hegemony different, but their respective declines have also followed alternative trajectories. In the late nineteenth century, Britain was confronted by two dynamic, vibrant and rapidly growing rivals: the United States and Germany. Perhaps because of its latecomer status or its geographical position in Europe, Germany was singled out as Britain's principal challenger for hegemony. With the eventual assistance of the United States, . . . [Britain defeated Germany] in war and [Germany was] eliminated as an important economic actor.

The waning of British hegemony thus found the United States and the United Kingdom in roughly equal international economic positions. In the years immediately before the First World War, an economic *modus vivendi*, grounded in substantial tariff reductions in the United States, appeared possible between these two powers. Yet, Anglo–American cooperation and the potential for joint leadership of the international economy were cut short by the war and its aftermath. The breakdown of the international economy during the war created difficult problems of reconstruction and generated high international economic instability, which shortened time horizons in both the United States and Britain and rendered post-war cooperation substantially more difficult. In the absence of such cooperation, the conflicts over reconstruction were insoluble, and the international economy eventually collapsed in the Great Depression.

The decline of American hegemony has occurred primarily through a general levelling of international economic capabilities among the Western powers. Today, the international economy is dominated by the United States, the Federal Republic of Germany, France, and Japan, all substantial traders with a strong interest in free trade, even if they desire some protection for their own industries. The greatest structural threat to continued cooperation is not the absence of partners capable of joint management, but too many partners and the corresponding potential for free riding that this creates.

Despite the instability generated by the oil shocks of the 1970s, moreover, these four economic powers have successfully managed the international economy—or at least muddled through. They have coped with a major change in the international monetary regime, the rise of the Euromarkets, and the Third World debt crisis. The most immediate threats to continued cooperation are the large and, apparently, endless budget and trade deficits of the United States. Barring any further increase in international economic instability, however, even these problems may be manageable.

III. International Political Processes

A. THE THREE FACES OF HEGEMONY. Elsewhere, Scott James and I have distinguished three "faces" or strategies of hegemonic leadership.[1] The first face of hegemony, as we define it, is characterized by the use of positive and negative sanctions aimed directly at foreign governments in an attempt to influence their choice of policies. Through inducements or threats, the hegemon seeks to alter the international costs and benefits of particular state actions. Economic sanctions, foreign aid and military support (or lack thereof) exemplify the strategic use of direct and overt international power central to this first face.

In the second face, the hegemon uses its international market power, or the ability to influence the price of specific goods, to alter the incentives and political influence of societal actors in foreign countries. These individuals, firms, sectors, or regions then exert pressure upon their governments for alternative policies, which—if the hegemon has used its market power correctly—will be more consistent with the interests of the dominant international power. This is a "Trojan Horse" strategy in which the hegemon changes the constellation of interests and political power within other countries in ways more favorable to its own interests.

The third face focuses on the hegemon's use of ideas and ideology to structure public opinion and the political agenda in other countries so as to determine what are legitimate and illegitimate policies and forms of political behavior. In other words, the hegemon uses propaganda, in the broadest sense of the word, to influence the climate of opinion in foreign countries.

In the mid-nineteenth century, Britain used its dominance of world trade to pursue an essentially second face strategy of hegemonic leadership. By repealing its Corn Laws, and allowing unfettered access to its markets, Britain effectively restructured the economic incentives facing producers of raw materials and foodstuffs. Over the long term, by altering factor and sector profit rates, and hence investment patterns, Britain augmented and mobilized the political influence of the interests within non-hegemonic countries most amenable to an international division of labor. All this was premised on complementary production and the free exchange of primary goods for British manufactures. Thus, in the United States, repeal of the Corn Laws facilitated the rise of a free trade coalition between Southern cotton growers, the traditional force for international economic openness in the American politics, and Western grain producers who had previously allied themselves with the more protectionist northeastern industrialists. This South—West coalition was reflected in almost two decades of freer trade in the United States, begun with the passage of the Walker Tariff in 1846. A similar process can be identified in Prussia, where the repeal of the Corn Laws reinforced the political power and free trade tendencies of the Junkers. This is not to argue, of course, that Britain relied exclusively on the second face of hegemony, only that it was an important theme in British trade policy and international leadership.

The United States, as noted above, has never dominated international trade to the same extent as Britain, but instead bases its leadership and influence upon its large domestic market. American strategy follows from this difference. Where Britain used its trade dominance to pursue a second face strategy, the United States relies to a larger extent on a first face strategy, trading access to its own market for reciprocal tariff reductions abroad. Accordingly, the United States did not unilaterally reduce tariffs, except for the period immediately after the Second World War, but instead linked reductions in, at first, bilateral treaties under the Reciprocal Trade Agreements Act and, later, in the GATT.

The explicitly reciprocal nature of American trade policy facilitates greater multilateral openness. British liberalization was spread throughout Europe by the unconditional most-favored-nation principle, but free trade remained fragile. As soon as alternative political coalitions obtained power, as in the United States in the aftermath of the Civil War and in Germany in the coalition of Iron and Rye, liberal trade policies were quickly jettisoned in favor of protection. Committed to free trade, Britain made clear its reluctance to retaliate against new protectionism by its trading partners. As a result, it allowed countries like the United States and Germany to free ride on its leadership—specifically, to protect their domestic industries while continuing to take advantage of British openness. The reciprocal trade policy adopted by the United States has brought more countries into the fold, so to speak, by linking access to American markets to participation in the GATT system. This system of generalized reciprocity, as well as the increasing willingness of the United States to retaliate against unfair foreign trade practices, acts to restrain protectionism in foreign countries. Paradoxically, a trade strategy based upon the first face of hegemony, despite its more overt use of international power, may prove more resilient.

B. INTERNATIONAL REGIMES.   A second and related difference in the international political processes of British and American hegemony is the latter's greater reliance upon international institutions and international economic regimes. Britain led the international economy in the nineteenth century without recourse to any formal international institutions and with few international rules governing exchange relations between countries. The nineteenth century, in other words, was a period of weak or, at best, implicit international economic regimes.

In the present period, on the other hand, international economic regimes are highly prevalent, even pervasive. The GATT, the IMF, the World Bank, and many United Nations organizations all give concrete—and lasting—substance to America's global economic leadership. As a result, international liberalism has been institutionalized in international relations.

As Robert Keohane has persuasively argued, international regimes are instruments of statecraft and are created to facilitate cooperation, specifically, by (a) providing a legal liability framework, (b) reducing transactions costs, and (c) reducing uncertainty by providing information and constraining moral hazard and irresponsibility. States comply with their dictates, Keohane continues, because of reputational considerations, because regimes provide a service which is of value, and because they are easier to maintain than to create[2] For these same reasons, Keohane suggests, international regimes are likely to persist even though the interests which brought them into being change. International regimes are thus important because they create more consistent, routinized and enduring international behavior.

To the extent that this argument is correct, the greater reliance of American hegemony on international regimes can be expected to preserve the liberal international economic order for some unspecifiable period, not only in the United States but throughout the international economy as well. America's hegemonic "afterglow" may well be longer than Britain's.

C. ISSUE LINKAGE.   The "low" politics of trade have always been linked with the "high" politics of national security—the views of certain liberal economists notwithstanding. Military issues have been linked with trade treaties, as in the Cobden–Chevalier treaty between Britain and France in 1860. Trade policy also impinges upon economic growth and the basis for long-term military strength.

The free trade order constructed under British leadership bridged the political divide by including both allies and antagonists, friends and foes. In this system, not only was British influence over its military competitors limited, but the free trade order benefited all participants, often stimulating growth in antagonists and undermining the long-term strength of the United Kingdom. As Robert Gilpin noted, perhaps the most important contradiction of a free trade order, and international capitalism more generally, is that it develops rather than exploits potential competitors for international leadership.[3]

The liberal international economic regimes of American hegemony, on the other hand, have been built exclusively on one side of a bipolar political divide. All of America's important trading partners are also its allies. This provides great potential leverage for the United States in trade issues. America's contributions to the public good of common defense can be diplomatically and tactically linked to liberal trade policies. In addition, the greater benefits derived from specialization and the international division of labor are confined to allies of the United States. All economic benefits, in other words, reinforce America's security needs. As a result, challengers to American hegemony are less likely to emerge. And the United States, in turn, may be willing to make greater economic sacrifices to maintain the long-term strength and stability of the Western alliance.

IV. International Economic Processes

A. THE PATTERN OF SPECIALIZATION. The nineteenth-century international economy was built upon a pattern of complementary trade. Britain, and later a handful of other industrialized countries, exported manufactured goods and imported raw materials and foodstuffs. To the extent that complementary products were not available within any particular economy, or available only at a substantially higher cost, this system of North–South trade created conditions of mutual dependence between core and peripheral states and, in turn, high opportunity costs of closure. As the Great Depression of the early 1930s clearly demonstrated, the economic costs of international closure were considerable.

The largest and most rapidly growing area of international trade after 1945, on the other hand, has been intra-industry trade—or the exchange of similar commodities between similarly endowed countries. Accordingly, the United States is both a major importer and exporter of chemicals, machine tools and numerous other products. Similar patterns can be found in Europe and, to a lesser extent, for Japan.

This pattern of intra-industry trade creates two important but offsetting pressures, the net impact of which is unclear. First, intra-industry trade has a lower opportunity cost of closure than does complementary trade. The welfare loss of trade restraints on automobiles in the United States, for instance, is considerably less than it would be in the absence of a significant domestic car industry. In short, countries can more easily do without intra-industry trade. Second, the primary stimulus for intra-industry trade is economies of scale in production. To the extent that these economies are larger than the domestic market, and can be satisfied only by exporting to foreign countries, they create important domestic political interest in favor of free trade and international openness. This restraint on protection, of course, will vary across countries, weighing more heavily in, say, Switzerland, than in the United States.

B. INTERNATIONAL CAPITAL FLOWS. In both the mid-nineteenth and mid-twentieth centuries, Britain and the United States, respectively, were the centers of the international financial system and the primary source of foreign investment. Both hegemons invested considerable sums abroad, perhaps at the expense of their own domestic economies. Nonetheless, an important difference exists between the two cases. Britain engaged almost exclusively in portfolio investment; the United States relied to a greater extent upon foreign direct investment.

During the period of British decline, a deep conflict emerged between the City of London, the primary source of international capital, and British manufacturers. As the latter found themselves less competitive within the international economy, they began to demand and lobby for a return to protection. The protectionists, or so-called tariff reformers, had grown strong enough to split the Conservative Party by 1903, costing it the parliamentary election of January 1906. By 1912, the tariff reformers dominated the party and, before the trade issue was displaced on the political agenda by Irish home rule, appeared likely to win the next legislative battle. The City, on the other hand, remained solidly liberal. Increasingly, financial profits depended upon new capital outflows and prompt repayment of loans made to developing countries. With an international horizon stretched before it, the City would bear the costs of protection in the form of higher domestic prices and, more importantly, in the reduced ability of exporting countries to repay their loans, but would receive few if any benefits. Where the manufacturers desired to return to an industrially based economy and a trade surplus, the City was content with the reliance on services and recognized the need for Britain to run a trade deficit for the foreseeable future. This conflict lasted throughout the inter-war period, with the City emerging triumphant with the return of pre-war parity in 1925, only to be defeated on the question of protection in 1932.

Until the 1970s, on the other hand, the United States engaged primarily in foreign direct investment. The export of both capital and ownership alters the nature of America's political cleavages, creating intra-industry and capital-labor conflicts rather than an industry–finance division. The overseas manufacturing assets, globally integrated production facilities, and enhanced trade dependence of multinational corporations reduce the demands for protection by firms engaged in foreign investment, but not by labor employed in those sectors. In this sense, the trade interests of multinational corporations are more similar to those of the international financial community than they are to domestic or non-internationalized firms. While nationally oriented firms and labor may still seek rents through domestic protection, the presence of a large multinational sector creates offsetting trade policy pressures within manufacturing and, indeed, often within the same sector, thereby strengthening the free trade lobby in the United States.

WHITHER THE *PAX AMERICANA*?

The differences between British and American hegemony are considerable, and serve to call into question the appropriateness of the historical analogy. The decline of the *Pax Americana* will not follow the same path blazed by the decline of the *Pax Britannica*. Simplistic historical analogies fully deserve the skepticism with which they are greeted. What then is the likely future of the international economic order? Will openness endure, or is closure imminent?

The international constraints discussed above point in different directions. The absence of formal imperialism, the emerging structure of the post-hegemonic international economy, the moderate (so far) level of international economic instability, greater American reliance on a first face strategy of explicit reciprocity, the institutionalization of liberal international economic regimes, the overlap between the security and economic issue areas, and the importance of foreign direct investment, all suggest that international liberalism is robust and likely to endure. The potential for free riding among the great economic powers, the pattern of economic specialization, and the growing importance of intra-industry trade, are the most important challenges to the liberal international economy—and are a source of caution about the future.

While certainly more fragile than in, say, the 1960s, the open international economy has several underlying sources of resiliency. Even though America's economic competitiveness has declined, relatively free and unrestricted commerce is likely to remain the international norm. The international economy is not being held open simply through inertia; there are real interests supporting international liberalism.

This relatively optimistic view of the future of the international trading order supports continued commitment by the United States to free trade and generalized reciprocity as found in the GATT. Japan- or Korea-bashing is unnecessary; other countries share America's interest in maintaining free trade within the international economy. The United States does not carry the burden of maintaining international openness alone.

Narrow policies of reciprocity, which seek equal access industry-by-industry or balanced trade between specific countries, may prove counterproductive, encouraging a decline into bilateralism that will redound to everyone's disadvantage and create the result which pessimists fear. As recent work on iterated prisoners' dilemma shows, cooperation can be sustained best by reciprocating cooperation. To the extent that the United States is perceived as defecting from the open international economy, it encourages similar behavior in others. Economic instability enhanced this problem in the 1920s, but it is inherent in the current system as well.

On the other hand, the United States cannot benefit by being the "sucker" in international trade. It must make clear that the continued openness of the American market is contingent upon similar degrees of openness in other countries. A broad or generalized policy of reciprocity is sufficient for this task, and promises to calm rather than exacerbate international economic tensions.

CONCLUSION

Statesmen and stateswomen undoubtedly base their decisions on theories of international politics, even if such theories are so implicit and amorphous as to resemble nothing more than "world views." No policy is made in a theoretical vacuum. Rather, beginning from selected assumptions or principles of human action, all policy-makers rely upon means–ends relationships and estimates of costs and benefits either derived from or validated by historical experience. These theories can be quite wrong or poorly understood, in which case the policy is likely to fail. Good theories, well employed, lead to more positive outcomes—or at least one hopes they do.

Scholars are an important source of the theories upon which decision makers base their policies. This is especially true of the theory of hegemonic stability. Developed just as the first signs of American decline were becoming apparent and long before the pattern and its implications were recognized in diplomatic circles, the theory of hegemonic stability has slowly crept out of the ivory tower and into the public consciousness. It has helped spark a debate on the limits of American power in the late twentieth century. It has also led to demands for more aggressive trade policies under the generally accepted but nonetheless dangerous standard of "specific reciprocity."

No theory is widely accepted unless it has some empirical support and intuitive plausibility. The danger is, however, that even theories that meet these criteria may be underdeveloped and inadequately specified by their scholarly progenitors or oversimplified by those who translate academic jargon and subtlety into the language of public debate. The theory of hegemonic stability has been poorly served on both counts, leading to overly pessimistic predications on the future of the international economy and to far too aggressive trade policies which threaten to bring about the results they are supposedly designed to prevent.

NOTES

1. See Scott C. James and David A. Lake, "The Second Face of Hegemony: Britain's Repeal of the Corn Laws and the American Walker Tariff of 1846," *International Organization* 43, 1 (1989):1–29.

2. See Robert O. Keohane, *After Hegemony: Cooperation and Discord in the World Political Economy* (Princeton: Princeton University Press, 1984).

3. Robert Gilpin, *US Power and the Multinational Corporation: The Political Economy of Foreign Direct Investment* (New York: Basic Books, 1975).

III

PRODUCTION

Productive activity is at the center of any economy. Agriculture, mining, and manufacturing are the bases on which domestic and international commerce, finance, and other services rest. No society can survive without producing. Thus, production is crucial to both the domestic and international political economies.

In the international arena, production abroad by large corporations gained enormously in importance after World War I. The establishment of productive facilities in foreign lands was nothing new, however. The planters who settled the southern portion of the thirteen colonies under contract to, and financed by, British merchant companies were engaging in foreign direct investment in plantation agriculture. Indeed, before the twentieth century, foreign investment in primary production—mining and agriculture—was quite common. In particular, European and North American investors financed copper mines in Chile and Mexico, tea and rubber plantations in India and Indochina, and gold mines in South Africa and Australia, among other endeavors.

Around the turn of the century, and especially after World War I, a relatively novel form of foreign direct investment arose: the establishment of overseas branch factories of manufacturing corporations. In its origin the phenomenon was largely North American, and it remained so until the 1960s, when European, and then Japanese, manufacturers also began investing in productive facilities abroad. These internationalized industrial firms were called multinational or transnational corporations or enterprises (MNCs/TNCs or MNEs/TNEs), usually defined as firms with productive facilities in three or more countries. Such corporations have been extraordinarily controversial for both scholars and politicians.

By 2007, there were some 79,000 MNCs in the world, with 790,000 foreign affiliates.[1] Most are relatively small, but the top several hundred are so huge and so globe-straddling as to dominate major portions of the world economy. MNCs' foreign affiliates are worth about $15 trillion, and they produce goods and services worth about $31 trillion every year. These foreign affiliates account for one-third of world exports and a very substantial proportion of world output. Indeed, the largest MNCs have annual sales larger than the gross national product (GNP) of all but a few of the world's nations.

One major analytic task is to explain the very existence of multinational manufacturing corporations. It is, of course, simple to understand why English investors would finance tea plantations in Ceylon—they could hardly have grown tea in Manchester. Yet, in the abstract, there is little logic in Bayer producing aspirin in the United States. If the German aspirin industry were more efficient than the American, Bayer could simply produce the pills in its factories at home and export them to the United States. Why, then, does Ford make cars in England, Volkswagen make cars in the United States, and both companies make cars in Mexico instead of simply shipping them, respectively, across the Atlantic or the Rio Grande?

For the answer, students of the MNC have examined both economic and political factors. The political spurs to overseas direct investment are straightforward. Many countries maintain trade barriers in order to protect local industry; this makes exporting to these nations difficult, and MNCs choose to "jump trade barriers" and produce inside protected markets. Similar considerations apply where the local government uses such policies as "Buy American" regulations, which favor domestic products in government purchases, or where, as in the case of Japanese auto investment in the United States, overseas producers fear the onset of protectionist measures.

Economic factors in the spread of MNCs are many and complex. The simplest explanation is that foreign direct investment moves capital from more-developed regions, where it is abundant and cheap, to less-developed nations, where it is scarce and expensive. This captures some of the story, but it also leaves much unexplained. Why, for example, does this transfer of capital not take the form of foreign lending rather than the (much more complex) form of foreign direct investment? Furthermore, why is most foreign direct investment among developed countries with similar endowments of capital rather than between developed and developing nations?

Economists have often explained foreign direct investment by pointing to certain size-related characteristics of multinational corporations. Because MNCs are very large in comparison to local firms in most countries, they can mobilize large amounts of capital more easily than local enterprises. Foreign corporations may then, simply by virtue of their vast wealth, buy up local firms in order to eliminate competitors. In some lines of business, such as large-scale production of appliances or automobiles, the initial investment necessary to begin production may be prohibitive for local firms, giving MNCs a decisive advantage. Similarly, MNC access to many different currencies from the many markets in which they operate may give them a competitive advantage over firms doing business in only one nation and currency. Moreover, the widespread popularity of consumption patterns formed in North

America and Western Europe and then transplanted to other nations—a process that often leads to charges of "cultural imperialism"—may lead local consumers to prefer foreign brand names to local ones: for example, much of the third world population brushes their teeth with Colgate and drinks Coke, American brands popularized by literature, cinema, television, and advertising. However, though these points may be accurate, they do not amount to a systematic explanation of foreign direct investment.

The first step in the search for a more rigorous explanation of foreign direct investment was the "product cycle theory," developed by Raymond Vernon.[2] Vernon pointed out that products manufactured by MNCs typically follow similar patterns or cycles. A firm begins by introducing a new product that it manufactures and sells at home; over time, it expands exports to foreign markets; as the product becomes more widely known, it eventually engages in foreign investment; and finally, as production of the good is standardized, the firm begins exporting back to the home market. This jibes with observations that MNCs tend to operate in oligopolistic markets (those dominated by a few firms); that their products often are produced with new technologies; and that they tend to have important previous exporting experience.

The product cycle theory did not answer all the economic questions, however. There was still no explanation of why firms would invest abroad instead of simply exporting from their (presumably more congenial) home base or licensing the production technology, trademark, or other distinguishing market advantage to local producers. In the past thirty-five years, most economists have come to regard the multinational corporation as a special case of the vertically or horizontally integrated corporation. In this view, large companies come to organize certain activities inside the firm rather than through the marketplace because some transactions are difficult to carry out by normal market means—especially in cases where prices are hard to calculate or contracts hard to enforce. When applied to MNCs, this approach suggests that foreign direct investment takes place because these firms have access to unique technologies, managerial skills, or marketing expertise that is more profitable when maintained within the corporate network than when sold on the open market. In Reading 9, economist Richard E. Caves surveys the modern economic theories of MNCs.

If the origins of MNCs are analytically controversial, their effects are debated with even more ferocity. In the 1950s and 1960s, as American-based corporations expanded rapidly into Western Europe, protests about foreigners buying up the European economies were common. At the time, most Americans regarded these protests as signs of retrograde nationalism, as they had traditionally taken MNCs for granted—few even realized that such firms as Shell, Universal Studios, Bayer, Saks Fifth Avenue, Nestle, and Firestone tires were foreign-owned. However, as investment in the United States by firms from the rest of the world grew, some critics began to argue that this represented a threat to American control over the U.S. economy. Thus, even in the United States, the most important home base of MNCs, the role of foreign direct investment is hotly debated. American MNCs employ six million people around the world, while foreign firms employ five million Americans, which means that foreign direct investment is, directly or indirectly, relevant to many people at home and abroad.

While foreign direct investment is controversial in the developed countries, it is far more contentious in the third world. Developed nations, after all, have technically advanced regulatory agencies and relatively large economies. However, most of the less-developed countries (LDCs) have economies smaller than the largest MNCs, with governmental regulatory bureaucracies that are no match for MNC executives. In many LDCs, then, the very presence of MNCs is viewed with suspicion. MNCs have been known to interfere in local politics, and local businesspeople often resent the competition created by huge foreign enterprises. Over the years, many LDCs have imposed stringent regulations on foreign direct investors, although most of them continue to believe that on balance, MNCs have a beneficial impact on national economic and political development. In the section that follows, the article by Shah M. Tarzi (Reading 10) evaluates the arguments in favor of, and opposed to, multinational corporations in the third world.

Since the 1990s, the growth of foreign direct investment (FDI) by multinational corporations has outpaced the growth of international trade. FDI is now the largest type of capital inflow for many developing countries. But unlike international trade, virtually no multilateral rules exist to govern and promote FDI. In Reading 11, Zachary Elkins, Andrew T. Guzman, and Beth A. Simmons examine the recent spread of Bilateral Investment Treaties—the primary legal mechanisms by which host and home governments regulate the investments of multinationals. The authors argue that international political factors are driving the widespread adoption of MNC-friendly bilateral treaties via competition between potential host countries for investment.

International competition may also have a dark side if it results in a regulatory "race to the bottom" wherein nations lower their environmental and labor standards in order to entice multinational corporations to invest. Daniel W. Drezner (Reading 12) examines the arguments and evidence about how FDI and other aspects of globalization affect the convergence—and alleged weakening—of national regulatory policies.

NOTES

1. United Nations Conference on Trade and Development, *World Investment Report 2008: Transnational Corporations and the Infrastructure Challenge* (New York and Geneva: United Nations, 2008), p. xvi.

2. Raymond Vernon, "International Investment and International Trade in the Product Cycle," *Quarterly Journal of Economics* 80, 2 (1966): 190–207.

9

The Multinational Enterprise as an Economic Organization

RICHARD E. CAVES

Richard E. Caves, an economist, provides a survey of economic explanations of the multinational enterprise (MNE). He focuses on how certain circumstances can make it difficult to carry out transactions in the marketplace. For example, it is hard to measure or establish a "fair" price for assets such as new technologies or managerial expertise. In these cases, firms, including MNEs, can overcome the problems of market transactions involving such hard-to-price assets by carrying out transactions internally, within the corporation. This reading presents the predominant economic explanation for the rise and existence of MNEs.

The multinational enterprise (MNE) is defined here as an enterprise that controls and manages production establishments—plants—located in at least two countries. It is simply one subspecies of multiplant firm. We use the term "enterprise" rather than "company" to direct attention to the top level of coordination in the hierarchy of business decisions; a company, itself multinational, may be the controlled subsidiary of another firm. The minimum "plant" abroad needed to make an enterprise multinational is, as we shall see, judgmental. The transition from a foreign sales subsidiary or a technology licensee to a producing subsidiary is not always a discrete jump, for good economic reasons. What constitutes "control" over a foreign establishment is another judgmental issue. Not infrequently a MNE will choose to hold only a minor fraction of the equity of a foreign affiliate. Countries differ in regard to the minimum percentage of equity ownership that they count as a "direct investment" abroad, as distinguished from a "portfolio investment," in their international-payments statistics.

. . . The definition does identify the MNE as essentially a multiplant firm. We are back to Coase's (1937) classic question of why the boundary between the administrative allocation of resources within the firm and the market allocation of resources between firms falls where it does. In a market economy, entrepreneurs are free to try their hands at displacing market transactions by increasing the scope of allocations made administratively within their firms. The Darwinian tradition holds that the most profitable pattern of enterprise organization should ultimately prevail: Where more profit results from placing plants under a common administrative control, multiplant enterprises will predominate, and single-plant firms will merge or go out of business. In order to explain the existence and prevalence of MNEs, we require models that predict where the multiplant firm enjoys advantages from displacing the arm's-length market and where it does not. In fact, the prevalence of multiplant (multinational) enterprises varies greatly from sector to sector and from country to country, affording a ready opportunity to test models of the MNE.

The models of the multiplant firm potentially relevant to explaining the presence of MNEs are quite numerous and rather diverse in their concerns. It proves convenient to divide them into three groups: (1) One type of multiplant firm turns out broadly the same line of goods from its plants in each geographic market. Such firms are common in domestic industries with fragmented local markets such as metal containers, bakeries, and brewing. Similarly, the many MNEs that establish plants in different countries to make the same or similar goods can be called horizontally integrated. (2) Another type of multiplant enterprise produces outputs in some of its plants that serve as inputs to its other activities. Actual physical transfer of intermediate products from one of the firm's plants to another is not required by the definition; it needs only to produce at adjacent stages of a vertically related set of production processes. (3) The third type of multiplant firm is the diversified company whose plants' outputs are neither vertically nor horizontally related to one another. As an international firm it is designated a diversified MNE.

1. HORIZONTAL MULTIPLANT ENTERPRISES AND THE MNE

We start by equating the horizontal MNE to a multiplant firm with plants in several countries. Its existence requires, first, that *locational forces* justify dispersing the world's production so that plants are found in different national markets. Given this dispersion of production, there must be some *governance* or *transaction-cost advantage* to placing the plants (some plants, at least) under common administrative control. This abstract, static approach provides the most general and satisfying avenue to explaining the multinational company. . . . We assume at first that plant A was located in southeast England because that was the lowest-cost way to serve the market it in fact serves. We also assume that this locational choice was not essentially influenced by whether the plant was built by an MNE, bought by an MNE, or not owned by an MNE at all. The static approach also puts aside the vital question of why a company grows into MNE status—something more readily explained after the static model is in hand.

The transaction-cost approach asserts, quite simply, that horizontal MNEs will exist only if the plants they control and operate attain lower costs or higher revenue productivity than the same plants under separate managements. Why should this net-revenue advantage arise? Some of the reasons have to do with minimizing costs of production and associated logistical activities of the firm. The more analytically interesting reasons—and, we shall see, the more important ones empirically—concern the complementary nonproduction activities of the firm.

Proprietary Assets

The most fruitful concept for explaining the nonproduction bases for the MNE is that of assets having these properties: The firm owns or can appropriate the assets or their services; they can differ in productivity from comparable assets possessed by competing firms; the assets or their productivity effects are mobile between national markets; they may be depreciable (or subject to augmentation), but their lifespans are not short relative to the horizon of the firm's investment decision. Successful firms in most industries possess one or more types of such assets. An asset might represent knowledge about how to produce a cheaper or better product at given input prices, or how to produce a given product at a lower cost than competing firms. The firm could possess special skills in styling or promoting its product that make it such that the buyer differentiates it from those of competitors. Such an asset has a revenue productivity for the firm because it signifies the willingness of some buyers to pay more for that firm's product than for a rival firm's comparable variety. Assets of this type are closely akin to product differentiation a market condition in which the distinctive features of various sellers' outputs cause each competing firm to face its own downward-sloping demand curve. The proprietary asset might take the form of a specific property—a registered trademark or brand—or it might rest in marketing and selling skills shared among the firm's employees. Finally, the distinctiveness of the firm's marketing-oriented assets might rest with the firm's ability to come up with frequent innovations; its proprietary asset then might be a patented novelty, or simply some new combination of attributes that its rivals cannot quickly or effectively imitate. This asset might vary greatly in tangibility and specificity. It could take the specific form of a patented process or design, or it might simply rest on know-how shared among employees of the firm. It is important that the proprietary asset, however it creates value, might rest on a set of skills or repertory of routines possessed by the firm's team of human (and other) inputs. . . .

The proprietary assets described by these examples evidently share the necessary conditions to support foreign investment. They are things that the firm can use but not necessarily sell or contract upon. Either the firm can hold legal title (patents, trademarks) or the assets are shared among the firm's employees and cannot be easily copied or appropriated (by other firms or by the employees themselves). They possess either the limitless capacities of public goods (the strict intangibles) or the flexible capacities of the firm's repertory of routines. Especially important for the MNE, while the productive use of these assets is not tightly tied to single physical sites or even nations, arm's-length transfers of them between firms are prone to market failures. These failures deter a successful one-plant firm from selling or renting its proprietary assets to other single-plant firms and thereby foster the existence of multiplant (and multinational) firms. Proprietary assets are subject to a daunting list of infirmities for being detached and transferred by sale or lease:

1. They are, at least to some degree, *public goods*. Once a piece of knowledge has been developed and applied at a certain location, it can be put to work elsewhere at little extra cost and without reducing the capacity available at the original site. From society's point of view, the marginal conditions for efficient allocation of resources then require that the price of the intangible asset be equal to its marginal cost, zero or approximately zero. But no one gets rich selling bright ideas for zero. Therefore, intangible assets tend to be underprovided or to be priced inefficiently (at a net price exceeding their marginal cost) or both.

2. Transactions in intangibles suffer from *impactedness* combined with *opportunism*. This problem is best explained by examples: I have a piece of knowledge that I know will be valuable to you. I try to convince you of this value by describing its general nature and character. But I do not reveal the details, because then the cat would be out of the bag, and you could use the knowledge without paying for it unless I have a well-established property right. But you therefore decline to pay me as much as the knowledge would in fact be worth to you, because you suspect that I am opportunistic and overstate my claims.

3. A proprietary asset might be diffuse and therefore incapable of an enforceable lease or sale contract. The owning firm might readily contract with a customer to achieve a specific result using some competence that it possesses, but be unable to contract to install that competence within another firm. Even with well-defined intangibles, various sources of uncertainty can render contractual transfers infeasible or distort the terms of viable deals.

This application of modern transaction-cost analysis underlies a framework widely used in research on the MNE. It asserts the existence of three necessary conditions for the appearance of horizontal foreign investments: (1) The firm can appropriate some value-creating proprietary asset ("ownership"); (2) production processes that employ or apply the value-creating asset are efficiently dispersed among several national markets ("location"); and (3) the decentralized application of the proprietary asset is more efficiently managed within the owning firm than by renting it at arm's length to another firm ("internalization"). . . .

Empirical Evidence: Prevalence of Horizontal Foreign Investment

Hypotheses about horizontal MNEs have received many statistical tests. The usual strategy of research involves relating the prevalence of MNEs in an industry to structural traits of that industry: If attribute x promotes the formation of MNEs, and successful firms in industry A have a lot of x, then MNEs should be prevalent in industry A. These tests have been performed on two dependent variables: foreign operations of firms in a source country's industries normalized by their total activity level in those industries (hereafter "outbound" foreign investment), and foreign subsidiaries' share of activity in a host country's markets normalized by total transactions in those markets (hereafter "inbound" foreign investment). The exogenous variables are chosen to represent features of industries' structures that should either promote or deter foreign direct investment. . . .

. . . There is considerable agreement on the major results among studies of both outbound and inbound investment, among studies of a given type for each country, and among studies based on different countries. Therefore we offer here some generalizations about the principal conclusions without referring extensively to the conclusions reached in individual studies or about particular countries. . . .

. . . [Research] results confirm, first and foremost, the role of proprietary assets inferred from the outlays that firms make to create and maintain these assets. Research and development intensity (R&D sales ratio) is a thoroughly robust predictor. Advertising intensity has proved nearly as robust, even though most studies have lacked an appropriately comprehensive measure of firms' sales-promotion outlays. The literature also consistently finds a significant positive influence for an industry's intensive use of skilled managerial labor; this variable seems to confirm the "repertory of routines" basis for foreign investment, independent of the strictly intangible proprietary assets. . . . A third result that also supports a role for the firm's general coordinating capacity is the positive influence of multiplant operation within large countries such as the United States. . . .

Multinationals in Service Industries

Horizontal MNEs in banking and other services have received increased attention from researchers. The proprietary-assets hypothesis again makes a good showing—especially when extended to the transaction-specific assets of an ongoing semicontractual relationship between the service enterprise and its customer. A bank, advertising agency, or accounting firm acquires a good deal of specific knowledge about its client's business, and the parties' sustained relationship based on trust lowers the cost of contracting and the risks of opportunistic behavior. The service firm enjoying such a quasi-contractual relation with a parent MNE holds a transaction-cost advantage for supplying the same service to the MNE's foreign subsidiaries. If the service must be supplied locally, the service firm goes multinational to follow its customer.

Much casual evidence reveals this transaction-specific asset behind service industries' foreign investments . . . , especially in the banking sector. . . . Some banks acquire particular product-differentiating skills analogous to those found in some goods-producing industries; they can explain banks' foreign investments in less-developed countries . . . and in countries with large populations of migrants from the source country. Also, national banking markets commonly appear somewhat noncompetitive because of cartelization or regulation or both, and foreign banks are well-equipped potential entrants. The Eurocurrency markets' rise can be largely explained on this basis. The traits of foreign banks' operations in the United States affirm these propositions. . . .

The prominence of transaction-specific assets as a factor driving foreign investment is apparently matched in other service industries such as advertising agencies, accounting, and consulting firms. . . . Studies of other multinational service industries, however, bring out different factors. . . .

2. VERTICALLY INTEGRATED MNES

The vertically integrated MNE is readily regarded as a vertically integrated firm whose production units lie in different nations. Theoretical models that explain vertical integration should therefore be directly applicable. Again, we assume that production units are dispersed in different countries due to conventional locational pressures—the bauxite mine where the bauxite is, bauxite converted to alumina at the mine because the process is strongly weight-losing, and the smelter that converts alumina into aluminum near a source of low-cost electric power. The question is, why do they come under common administrative control? The proprietary-assets model is not necessary, because neither upstream nor downstream production unit need bring any distinctive qualification to the parties' vertical consolidation. Some proprietary advantage of course *could* explain which producer operating at one stage undertakes an international forward or backward vertical integration.

Models of Vertical Integration

Until the rise of transaction-cost economics the economic theory of vertical integration contained a large but unsatisfying inventory of special-case models. Some dealt with the physical integration of production processes: If you make structural shapes out of the metal ingot before it cools, you need not incur the cost of reheating it. Such gains from physical integration explain why sequential processes are grouped in a single plant, but they neither preclude two firms sharing that plant nor explain the common ownership of far-flung plants. Another group of traditional models regard vertical integration as preferable to a stalemate between a monopolistic seller and a monopsonistic buyer, or to an arm's-length relation between a monopolistic seller and competitive buyers whose activities are distorted due to paying the monopolist's marked-up price for their input. Some models explain vertical integration as a way around monopolistic distortions, while others explain it as a way to profit by fostering such distortions.

The theory of vertical integration has been much enriched by the same transaction-cost approach that serves to explain horizontal MNEs. Vertical integration occurs, the argument goes, because the parties prefer it to the ex ante contracting costs and ex post monitoring and haggling costs that would mar the alternative state of arm's-length transactions. The vertically integrated firm internalizes a market for an intermediate product, just as the horizontal MNE internalizes markets for proprietary assets. Suppose that there were pure competition in each intermediate-product market, with large numbers of buyers and sellers, the product homogeneous (or its qualities costlessly evaluated by the parties), information about prices and availability in easy access to all parties in the market. Neither seller nor buyer would then have reason to transact repeatedly with any particular party on the other side of the market. When these assumptions do not hold, however, both buyers and sellers acquire motives to make long-term alliances. The two can benefit mutually from investments that each makes suited to special attributes of the other party. Each then incurs a substantial fixed cost upon shifting from one transaction partner to another. Each seller's product could be somewhat different, and the buyer incurs significant costs of testing or adapting to new varieties, or merely learning the requirements and organizational routines of new partners. The buyer and seller gain an incentive to enter into some kind of long-term arrangement.

If transaction-specific assets deter anonymous spot-market transactions, they leave open the choice between long-term contracts and vertical integration. Contracts, however, encounter the costs of negotiation and of monitoring and haggling previously mentioned. These ex ante and ex post costs trade off against one another—a comprehensive contract can reduce subsequent haggling—but the overall cost remains. The problem is compounded because, even in a market with many participants, unattached alternative transaction partners tend to be few *at any particular time* when a party might wish to recontract. Fewness compounds the problems of governance in arm's-length vertical relationships.

One special case of the transaction-cost theory of vertical integration holds promise for explaining MNEs involved in processing natural resources. Vertical integration can occur because of failings in markets for information, as analyzed earlier in the context of proprietary assets. A processing firm must plan its capacity on some assumption about the future price and availability of its key raw material. The producers of that raw material have the cheapest access (perhaps exclusive) to that information. But they have an incentive to overstate availability to the prospective customer: The more capacity customers build, the higher they are likely to bid in the future for any given quantity of the raw material. Therefore, vertical integration could occur in order to evade problems of impacted information. . . .

To summarize, intermediate-product markets can be organized in a spectrum of ways stretching from anonymous spot-market transactions through a variety of long-term contractual arrangements at arm's length to vertical integration. Switching costs and durable, specialized assets discourage spot transactions and favor one of the other modes. If, in addition, the costs of negotiating and monitoring arm's-length contracts are high, the choice falls on vertical integration. These empirical predictions address both where vertical MNEs will appear and how they will trade off against contractual relationships.

Empirical Evidence

Far fewer statistical studies address these hypotheses than the ones concerned with horizontal MNEs. . . .

A great deal of information exists on individual extractive industries in which MNEs operate on a worldwide basis, and this case-study evidence merits a glance in lieu of more systematic findings. For example, Stuckey . . . found the international aluminum industry to contain not only MNEs integrated from the mining of bauxite through the fabrication of aluminum projects but also a network of long-term contracts and joint ventures. Market participants are particularly unwilling to settle for spot transactions in bauxite (the raw ore) and alumina (output of the first processing stage). The problem is not so much the small number of market participants worldwide as the extremely high switching costs. Alumina refining facilities need to be located physically close to bauxite mines (to minimize transportation costs), and they are constructed to deal with the properties of specific ores. Likewise, for technical and transportation-cost reasons, aluminum smelters are somewhat tied to particular sources of alumina. Therefore, arm's-length markets tend to be poisoned by the problems of small numbers and switching costs. And the very large specific and durable investments in facilities also invoke the problems of long-term contracts that were identified earlier. Finally, Stuckey gave some weight to Arrow's model of vertical integration as a route to securing information: Nobody knows more about future bauxite supplies and exploration than an existing bauxite producer.

A good deal of evidence also appears on vertical integration in the oil industry. The ambitious investigations have addressed the U.S. segment of the industry, but there appears to be no strong difference between the forces traditionally affecting vertical integration in national and international oil companies. These studies give considerable emphasis to the costs of supply disruption faced by any nonintegrated firm in petroleum extraction or refining. Refineries normally operate at capacity and require a constant flow of crude-oil inputs. Storing large inventories of input is quite costly, and so backward integration that reduces uncertainty about crude supplies can save the refiner a large investment in storage capacity. It also reduces risks in times of "shortages" and "rationing," when constraints somewhere in the integrated system (crude-oil supplies are only the most familiar constraint) can leave the unintegrated firm out in the cold. The hazard of disrupted flows translates into a financial risk, as vertically integrated firms have been found to be able to borrow long-term funds more cheaply than those with exposure to risk. . . .

Country-based studies of the foreign-investment process have also underlined vertical MNEs as the outcome of failed arm's-length market transactions. Japanese companies became involved with extractive foreign investments only after the experience of having arm's-length suppliers renege on long-term contracts; and they also experimented with low-interest loans to independent foreign suppliers as a way to establish commitment. . . .

Vertical Integration: Other Manifestations

The identification of vertically integrated foreign investment with extractive activities is traditional and no doubt faithful to the pattern accounting for the bulk of MNE assets. However, it gives too narrow an impression of the role of vertically subdivided transactions in MNEs.

First of all, it neglects a form of backward integration that depends not on natural resources but on subdividing production processes and placing abroad those that are both labor-intensive and footloose. For example, semiconductors are produced by capital-intensive processes and assembled into electronic equipment by similarly mechanized processes, both undertaken in the industrial countries. But, in between, wires must be soldered to the semiconductors by means of a labor-intensive technology. Because shipping costs for the devices are low relative to their value, it pays to carry out the labor-intensive stage in a low-wage country. The relationship of the enterprises performing these functions in the United States and abroad must obviously be a close one, involving either detailed contractual arrangements or common ownership. This subdivision of production processes should occur through foreign investment to an extent that depends again on the transactional bases for vertical integration.

Writers on offshore procurement and the associated international trade always refer to the role of foreign investment in transplanting the necessary know-how and managerial coordination. . . . [Scholars have] explored statistically both the structural determinants of this type of trade and the role of MNEs in carrying it out. . . . [The] data pertain to imports under a provision of the U.S. tariff whereby components exported from the United States for additional fabrication abroad can be reimported with duty paid only on the value added abroad. . . . [S]tatistical analysis explains how these activities vary both among U.S. industries and among countries taking part in this trade. . . . [The] results confirm the expected properties of the industries that make use of vertically disintegrated production: Their outputs have high value per unit of weight, possess reasonably mature technology (so are out of the experimental stage), are produced in the United States under conditions giving rise to high labor costs, and are easily subject to decentralized production. Among overseas countries, U.S. offshore procurement favors those not too far distant (transportation costs) and with low wages and favorable working conditions. With these factors controlled, the component flows increase with the extent of U.S. foreign investment, both among industries and among foreign countries.

A considerable amount of vertical integration is also involved in the "horizontal" foreign investments described earlier in this chapter, and the behavior of horizontal MNEs cannot be fully understood without recognizing the complementary vertical aspects of their domestic and foreign operations. Many foreign subsidiaries do not just produce their parents' goods for the local market; they process semifinished units of that good, or package or assemble them according to local specifications. Pharmaceuticals, for example, are prepared in the locally desired formulations using basic preparations imported from the parent. The subsidiary organizes a distribution system in the host-country market, distributing partly its own production, but with its line of goods filled out with imports from its parent or other affiliates. Or the subsidiary integrates forward to provide local servicing facilities. These activities are bound up with the development and maintenance of the enterprise's goodwill asset, as described earlier, through a commitment of resources to the local market. The firm can thereby assure local customers, who are likely to incur fixed investments of their own in shifting their purchases to the MNE, that the company's presence is not transitory. This consideration helps explain foreign investment in some producer-goods industries for which the proprietary-assets hypothesis otherwise seems rather dubious. . . . All of these activities represent types of forward integration by the MNE, whether into final-stage processing of its goods or into ancillary services.

The evidence of this confluence of vertical and horizontal foreign investments mainly takes the form of case studies rather than systematic data. . . . It is implied by the extent of intracorporate trade among MNE affiliates—flows that would be incompatible with purely horizontal forms of intracorporate relationships. Imports of finished goods by Dutch subsidiaries from their U.S. parents . . . are high (as percentages of the affiliates' total sales) in just those sectors where imports might complement local production for filling out a sales line—chemicals (24.9 percent), electrical equipment (35.4 percent), and transportation equipment (65.5 percent). The prevalence of intracorporate trade in engineering industries also suggests the importance of components shipments. . . .

Statistical evidence on U.S. exports and imports passing between corporate affiliates sheds light on this mixture of vertical and horizontal foreign investment. Lall . . . analyzed the factors determining the extent of U.S. MNEs' exports to their affiliates (normalized either by their total exports or by their affiliates' total production). He could not discriminate between two hypotheses that together have significant force: (1) That trade is internalized where highly innovative and specialized goods are involved, and (2) that trade is internalized where the ultimate sales to final buyers must be attended by extensive customer engineering and after-sales services. Jarrett . . . confirmed these hypotheses with respect to the importance in U.S. imports of interaffiliate trade, which in his data includes exports by foreign MNEs to their manufacturing and marketing subsidiaries in the United States as well as imports by U.S. MNEs from their overseas affiliates. Jarrett also found evidence that interaffiliate trade in manufactures reflects several conventional forms of vertical integration: More of it occurs in industries populated (in the United States) by large plants and companies, capable of meeting the scale-economy problems that arise in the international disintegration of production, and in industries that carry out extensive multiplant operations in the United States. . . .

3. PORTFOLIO DIVERSIFICATION AND THE DIVERSIFIED MNE

This section completes the roster of international multiplant firms by accounting for those whose international plants have no evident horizontal or vertical relationship. An obvious explanation of this type of MNE (though not the only one, it turns out) lies in the spreading of business risks. Going multinational in any form brings some diversification gains to the enterprise, and these reach their maximum when the firm diversifies across "product space" as well as geographical space. . . .

Now we consider empirical evidence on diversification as a motive for the MNE. Within a national economy, many shocks affect all firms rather similarly—recessions, major changes in macroeconomic policy. Between countries, such disturbances are more nearly uncorrelated. Also, changes in exchange rates and terms of trade tend to favor business profits in one country while worsening them elsewhere. Statistical evidence confirms that MNEs enjoy gains from diversification: The larger the share of foreign operations in total sales, the lower the variability of the firm's rate of return on equity capital. . . . MNEs also enjoy lower levels of risk in the sense relevant to the stock market—financial risk (beta). . . . In general, this evidence supports the hypothesis that the MNE attains appreciable international diversification. However, the diversification might result from investments that were propelled by other motives. . . .

4. SUMMARY

The existence of the MNE is best explained by identifying it as a multiplant firm that sprawls across national boundaries, then applying the transaction-cost approach to explain why dispersed plants should fall under common ownership and control rather than simply trade with each other (and with other agents) on the open market. This approach is readily applied to the horizontal MNE (its national branches produce largely the same products), because the economies of multiplant operation can be identified with use of the firm's proprietary assets, which suffer many infirmities for trade at arm's length. This hypothesis receives strong support in statistical studies, with regard both to intangible assets and to capabilities possessed by the firm.

A second major type of MNE is the vertically integrated firm, and several economic models of vertical integration stand ready to explain its existence. Once again, the transaction-cost approach holds a good deal of power, because vertical MNEs in the natural-resources sector seem to respond to the difficulties of working out arm's-length contracts in small-numbers situations where each party has a transaction-specific investment at stake. Evading problems of impacted information also seems to explain some vertical foreign investment. The approach also works well to explain the rapid growth of offshore procurement by firms in industrial countries, which involves carrying out labor-intensive stages of production at foreign locations with low labor costs. Although procurement occurs through arm's-length contracts as well as foreign investment, the role of foreign investment is clearly large. Finally, numerous vertical transactions flow between the units of apparently horizontal MNEs as the foreign subsidiary undertakes final fabrication, fills out its line with imports from its corporate affiliates, or provides ancillary services that complement these imports.

Diversified foreign investments, which have grown rapidly in recent decades, suggest that foreign investment serves as a means of spreading risks to the firm. Foreign investment, whether diversified from the parent's domestic product line or not, apparently does offer some diversification value. Diversified foreign investments can be explained in part by the parent's efforts to utilize its diverse R&D discoveries, and certain other influences as well. However, other diversified investments appear specifically aimed at spreading risks through international diversification, especially among geographic markets.

10

Third World Governments and Multinational Corporations: Dynamics of Host's Bargaining Power

SHAH M. TARZI

Shah M. Tarzi examines the bargaining relationship between third world host governments and multinational corporations (MNCs). While host governments seek to encourage firms to locate within their countries on the best terms possible, MNCs want to minimize the conditions and restrictions the host government is able to impose on their operations. Tarzi identifies several factors that affect the bargaining power of the host government. He distinguishes between factors that influence the potential power of the state, such as its managerial skills, and those that affect the ability of the state to exercise its bargaining power. Actual power, as he terms it, is determined by societal pressures the host government faces, the strategy of the MNC, and the international pressures from the MNC's home government.

INTRODUCTION

In their economic relationships with multinational corporations, Third World countries would seem to have the critical advantage, inasmuch as they control access to their own territory. That access includes internal markets, the local labour supplies, investment opportunities, sources of raw materials, and other resources that multinational firms need or desire. In practical terms, however, this apparent bargaining advantage on the part of the host nation, in most instances, is greatly surpassed by the superior advantages of the multinationals. Multinational corporations possess the required capital, technology, managerial skills, access to world markets, and other resources that governments in the Third World need or wish to obtain for purposes of economic development.

In addition to firm-specific assets—technology, managerial skills, capital and access to markets—the economic power of the multinationals grows out of a combination of additional factors. First, foreign investment accounts for large percentages of the total stock of local investment, local production and sales. Secondly, multinationals tend to dominate key sectors of the economy that are critical to the host states' economic development. Thirdly, multinationals usually prevail in the highly concentrated industries in the Third World—petroleum, aluminium, chemicals, transportation, food products and machinery. This economic concentration in single industries gives the multinational firms oligopoly power, allowing them to monopolize and control supply and price in a way that does not occur in more competitive industries.

In the first decade and a half after World War II, the multinational corporations were so powerful that they could essentially prevent any challenges to their dominance from host governments. The unique position they held as the sole source of capital, technology and managerial expertise for the Third World states gave them special negotiating advantages. Third World governments in their developing state could not easily duplicate the skills of the corporations, and when they did attempt to bypass the assistance of the multinationals, the cost to them in reduced efficiency was extremely high. Furthermore, the exposure of individual corporations was low, except for corporations in natural resources, plantations and utilities. In Latin America and the Middle East, where most of direct foreign investment in raw materials was concentrated, long-term concession contracts protected companies from immediate risk exposure. Host countries could neither remove nor replace them without sustaining enormous costs to their economies. Thus, the multinationals were usually able to exercise de facto sovereign power over the pricing and marketing of output.

Nevertheless, despite the colossal power of the multinational corporations, the historic trend has been one of increasing ascendance of Third World host states. By the 1960s the multinationals were facing pressure from the host states to make substantial contributions to the long-term goals of economic development. Regarding foreign investment in natural resources, for example, ownership and control over raw material production was transferred to OPEC members. In the process, the Seven Sisters (the major oil companies) were relegated from their positions of independence and dominance to the role of junior partners of host governments in the Middle East. Similarly, in manufacturing there is a visible trend toward a sharing of ownership and control in foreign manufacturing ventures.

Several factors help to explain the relative ascendancy or improved position of some Third World host states with respect to their relationships with multinationals. A number of changes have increased the bargaining power of the Third World countries. And in addition to favourable changes in their bargaining power, other constraining factors in both domestic and international environments of the host countries have been eased, improving the ability of the hosts to exact better terms from the multinational corporations.

THIRD WORLD GOVERNMENTS: DYNAMICS OF POTENTIAL BARGAINING POWER

In order to examine the extent to which host states in the Third World can influence the behaviour of multinational corporations, we call attention to the distinction between potential power and actual power (the power to exercise or implement).

Potential power connotes the relative bargaining power of the host state which is dependent upon: (1) the level of the host government's expertise, (2) the degree of competition among multinationals, (3) the type of direct foreign investment, and (4) the degree or extent of prevailing economic uncertainty.

Actual power, on the other hand, may be defined as the ability and willingness of host governments to exercise their bargaining power in order to extract more favorable terms from foreign firms. Domestic factors, including host country politics, along with international factors, such as foreign political and economic coercion, constrain Third World host states in their efforts to translate potential bargaining power into power that engenders favourable outcomes with foreign investors. These domestic and international factors act as a wedge between potential and actual power. The dynamics of potential bargaining power for the Third World governments is examined below.

Level of Host's Expertise

Most host states have antiquated government structures and inadequate laws for collecting taxes and controlling foreign business. These institutional weaknesses impair the ability of host states in their negotiations with multinational corporations. Shortages of competent, trained and independent administrators exacerbate these institutional problems and make it difficult for host states to manage multinationals and monitor their behaviour. . . .

The trend, however, has been toward tougher laws in the host countries. Frequently, the host countries become dependent upon the revenue generated by foreign investors in order to finance government services and meet domestic requirements for employment. In turn, the desire for economic growth produces certain incentives within host states to strengthen their administrative expertise in international tax law, corporate accounting and industrial analysis. Thus, the development of economic and financial skills in host states is facilitated by the need to monitor multinational corporations and negotiate with them more effectively. Over time, therefore, host countries have developed or acquired many of the managerial skills which had long been employed by the multinationals as bargaining tools. By improving their expertise and capacity to monitor the corporations more closely, some host states were able to renegotiate terms when conditions permitted. The development of producer cartels also created a strong impetus for improving expertise within host countries to manage multinationals better. . . . Multinational corporations can be expected to regain their bargaining advantage vis-à-vis a Third World government, however, when certain conditions arise: (1) the rate of change in technological complexity of the foreign investment regime grows faster relative to the host country's capabilities and rate of innovations; and/or (2) if the optimum scale of the investment regime expands so as to make it extremely difficult for the host government to manage it, in spite of initial strides in managerial expertise.

Both technological and managerial complexity for developing products or extracting resources correlate positively with bargaining power for the multinational corporations. Nevertheless, during the last two decades, the cumulative effect of improvement in the host countries' expertise has resulted in a relative tightening of terms with respect to direct foreign investment. This phenomenon has resulted in a relative improvement in Third World governments' bargaining positions.

Level of Competition for Investment Opportunities

Competition among multinational corporations for investment opportunities in a Third World country also affects the bargaining power of host countries. Essentially, a lack of competition among multinationals predicts a weak bargaining position for the host country. Conversely, increased competition is likely to improve the bargaining power of the host government. Competition among multinationals is likely to be greater where a host country provides a cheap source of needed labour and also functions as an 'export platform' when the purpose of the investment project is to serve external markets. Competition for investment projects is likely to be limited, however, when projects are both capital intensive and designed to serve only local markets.

During the 1950s and 1960s, the absence of competition for investment opportunities served to diminish the bargaining power of host states in the Third World. The availability of alternative sources of raw materials and the existence of cheap labour elsewhere also work together to weaken the bargaining power of any individual country. In the last two decades, the spread of multinational corporations of diverse national origins (American, Japanese, European) has provided host countries with alternatives. In the international oil industry, for example, host countries have successfully used competition among multinationals to increase revenues from oil production. As a case in point, J. Paul Getty's Pacific Western Oil Company upset the stability of other corporations' agreements when it acquired an oil concession in Saudi Arabia by offering larger tax payments than the established oil companies were then willing to pay.

The option of choice from several willing foreign investors is extremely important to a host country. The ability to choose allows a host state to avoid the concentration of investment from one traditionally dominant Western country. Thus, for instance, Japanese multinationals have emerged as an alternative to US firms in Latin America, and American firms have, in turn, emerged as an alternative to French firms in Africa.

If competition were to intensify among the multinational corporations for the resources of Third World countries and host governments' ability to manage and monitor multinationals were to improve, it is likely that host nations would pay less than before for services provided by the corporations.

Economic Uncertainty and the Obsolescing Bargain

Uncertainty about the success of a particular foreign investment project, its final cost, and the desire of a host country to attract investment create a marked asymmetry of power favouring the multinational corporations. During this initial phase, the host country must pursue permissive investment policies with the corporations. But as uncertainty decreases and the investment projects become successful, the multinational's initial bargaining advantage begins to erode. Invested fixed capital becomes "sunk," a hostage to and a source of the host country's bargaining strength as it acquires jurisdiction over valuable foreign assets. The foreign firm's financial commitment to assets located in host nations weakens the bargaining advantage it enjoyed at the beginning of the investment cycle. Consequently, when the bargaining advantage begins to shift to the host state, the initial agreements that favoured the multinationals are renegotiated.

In manufacturing, high technology, and services ventures, the probability of obsolescence is extremely low. Multinational corporations in natural resources, on the other hand, are most vulnerable. . . .

This paradigm interprets the interaction between multinational corporations and host countries as a dynamic process. Furthermore, given the level of economic uncertainty for both parties, the interests of host countries and foreign investors are likely to diverge. The two parties then become antagonists. Gradually, a change in the bargaining advantages on the side of the multinational shift to that of the host country. The developments that follow may result in the renegotiation by the government of the initial concession agreement.

Characteristics of the Foreign Investment Project

As noted earlier, the probability of obsolescence is, to a large extent, a function of the foreign investment assets. Thus, the bargaining power or negotiating ability of a host country substantially depends on the type of direct foreign investment that is involved. Characteristics of the foreign investment project affecting the outcome of the bargaining process are: (1) absolute size of fixed investment; (2) ratio of fixed to variable costs; (3) the level of technological complexity of the foreign investment regime; and (4) the degree of marketing complexity.

Those foreign investment projects which do not require high fixed investments have a low fixed-to-relative cost ratio. Based on changeable technology and marketing complexity, they are less vulnerable to the dynamics of obsolescing bargaining than are foreign investment projects having high fixed costs, slowly changing technology and undifferentiated project lines. Investment projects in natural resources, plantation agriculture and utilities fall into this group. Once the investment is sunk and the project becomes profitable, foreign firms may be exposed to the threat of nationalization or, more likely, the renegotiation of the original terms of investment.

Knowing these economic and political risks, multinational corporations would not commit large sums of money unless they were likely to get extremely generous terms. These "over-generous" terms to which the host country initially agrees often become a major source of national discontent and resentment against the foreign firm.

In manufacturing, where marketing skills are complex and products differentiated, foreign corporations have considerable flexibility in their response to the host country's demands. In order to counter the demands of the host government, these firms can diversify product lines, move to a new activity such as export, incorporate additional technology, or threaten to withdraw their operation altogether.

Corporations in the vanguard of scientific and technological development such as computers or electronics have only recently begun to penetrate Third World economies. This group is especially immune to the obsolescing bargain. The pace and complexity of research and development (R&D) in computers and electronics is, for the most part, beyond the capability and geographic reach of any of the host governments in the Third World.

Constraints on the Exercise of Power: Implementation

The literature on bargaining provides a prevailing conceptual framework of bilateral monopoly to describe Third World-multinational corporation interaction. According to this model, the distribution of benefits between multinationals and Third World countries is a function of relative power. It is assumed that power is a function of the demand of each party for resources that the other possesses. This model is essentially static, however, because it does not deal with political and economic constraints on the exercise of power arising from the international environment. Similarly, it fails to account for constraints that are posed by the multinational's economic power. More importantly, it ignores the constraints posed by the host country's domestic politics. Specifically, the bilateral monopoly model does not distinguish between potential bargaining power and its implementation. Domestic politics within a host country, as well as international political and economic pressures from multinationals (or their home governments), may hinder host countries in their efforts to exploit the bargaining advantage once gained from the relative demand for its resources.

In order to fill this theoretical gap in the literature, we identify and analyse various constraining factors in both the domestic and international environments. The objective is to illuminate the extent to which a host government is able or willing to translate its bargaining advantage into actual power, to exercise this power in order to extract favourable terms from foreign investors. These relationships are presented below.

Domestic Constraints on the Exercise of Power

Key determinants in translating potential power into actual power are the attitudes and beliefs of the ruling elite regarding foreign investment, and their willingness and ability to discount international economic and political pressure in their confrontation with multinational corporations. During the 1950s and 1960s, Third World governments provided stability to foreign investments by working to preserve the status quo, despite changes that improved their bargaining power. At least two reasons can be given for the leadership of these countries to favour the status quo. One possibility is that their ideological predisposition was such that they saw multinationals as a benevolent force for economic development. Another possibility is that they may have feared that the international political and economic costs of seeking change would outweigh the benefits. There were also, of course, those instances where individual leaders in host countries were known to accept private payments in exchange for their efforts to preserve the status quo. In other instances, changes in the host country's leadership led to classic confrontations. The new elite, having divergent ideological and policy priorities, attempted to persuade the foreign investment regimes to become more responsive to domestic economic priorities. When Mossadeq became the prime minister of Iran in the early 1950s, for example, in efforts to finance Iran's First Development Plan he attempted to nationalize the British-owned Anglo-Iranian Oil Company. Similarly, the Kinshasa government's struggle to use earnings from the copper mines of Katanga to pay for post-independence development of the Congo led to a major confrontation. The ultimate result was the nationalization of foreign assets.

Since the mid-1960s there has been a change in attitude among most Third World leaders with respect to foreign investment. Exposés of political intervention by multinational corporations in the domestic politics of host states, the IT&T scandal in Chile in particular, contributed to this change. Unlike IT&T's interference in Chilean politics, most multinationals do not pursue such ruthless politics of intervention. Nevertheless, the degree to which multinationals can influence, by legal or illegal means, the domestic political process can reduce the host country's ability to change corporate behaviour and to make it cater to domestic needs.

A major force for change has been the emergence of new diverse groups which have become involved in the host country's political processes. Students, labour, business, intelligentsia, middle echelon government technocrats and even farmers' associations have greater political clout than ever before. Mobilized by the processes of industrialization and urbanization, and facilitated by global technology, these groups came to place intense pressure on their governments for improving the domestic economy, providing welfare, housing, transportation, and creating jobs. The extractive sector in particular, dominated by foreign firms, became a focus for nationalistic demands of an intensity that could not be ignored by the leadership of Third World states. Among the above groups, business and labour are especially noteworthy. The lack of a strong labour movement, however, remains a major source of institutional weakness in underdeveloped countries. . . .

In a similar vein, the lack of competition from local businesses creates another source of institutional weakness. Too often local businesses, for whom multinational corporations might mean intense competition, are unable to compete with the giant corporations because the latter have access to cheaper sources of capital, better terms from suppliers, and marketing and distribution advantages. The absence of countervailing power via a competitive indigenous business sector helps to explain why the global corporations are able to continue to exert dominant power in underdeveloped countries. A similar and more prevalent situation is one wherein local business owners find that by cooperating with global firms, they too can benefit.

There often exists a strong alliance between the foreign corporation and various powerful home state groups such as landowners, or other pro-business conservative groups. All these groups tend to share the multinationals' distaste for radical social change. This alliance serves as a major constraint on the ability of host countries to translate their bargaining power into favourable outcomes. The effect is the perpetuation of the status quo.

International Constraints: Non-State Actors

We can distinguish between two types of constraints in the international environment. First, there are constraints posed by non-state actors. Second, constraints often emerge as a result of home governmental actions on behalf of the multinational corporations. Constraints posed by non-state actors include the level of global integration of multinationals, local political risk and transnational risk management strategies.

Global integration includes the flow of raw materials, components and final products as well as flows of technology, capital and managerial expertise between the units and subsidiaries of a global corporation. In essence, it is a complex system of a globally integrated production network, at the disposal of the corporation. This complex transnational system is augmented by global logistical and information networks, global advertising and sometimes global product differentiation. The host government's desire to acquire access to this global network and the dependence of host states on the foreign firms who created it produce a constraint on the former's bargaining power.

Global integration, therefore, is an important determinant of multinational strategy. Increasingly, multinational corporations have developed globally based systems of integrated production, marketing and distribution networks in order to reduce costs and enhance their global outreach. A host country that engages in joint ventures with highly integrated and sophisticated foreign firms invariably becomes dependent on the multinationals' controlled globally integrated networks.

Global integration is usually found in companies having very complex technology. There is little that the host country can do to influence integration, and consequently the host country may be severely constrained in its bargaining position. The majority of research and development is undertaken by highly integrated firms and is located in the industrialized home countries. As a result technological developments are beyond the reach or control of developing host countries. Royalties charged by highly integrated firms on the use of their technologies further increase the relative vulnerability of host states. International Business Machines, for instance, continues to maintain an unconditional 10 percent royalty for the use of its technology despite the efforts of host countries to reduce it.

Another constraint on a host government's ability to exercise power arises from the use of political risk management strategies by multinational corporations. In order to diminish or control better their political risks, multinationals often establish transnational alliances that dramatically increase the cost to the host state of changing the foreign investment regime in their favour. The experience of Third World governments with the pharmaceutical and automobile industries demonstrates how a web of alliances built by the global corporations can seriously impair their exercise of governmental power.

One tactic used by the multinationals is to spread the equity in the foreign investment project over a number of companies from other developed countries. This strategy increases the legal, political and economic obstacles to unilateral alterations in contracts with host states. Another tactic is to raise debt capital for the foreign investment project from banks of different countries (United States, Japan, Germany). Multinationals structure the financing in such a way that banks are paid only if the project is profitable. Host governments' retaliatory actions against the corporations could, therefore, alienate these powerful global banks which have bankrolled the investment project. In view of the significant role of some of the largest global banks involved in the Third World debt problem, this particular risk management strategy may act as a powerful constraint on the host state's ability to turn its potential bargaining power into actual power. Another tactic that multinationals use for protection is to involve the World Bank, IMF and Inter-American Development Banks. The formidable power and prestige of these institutions and their ability to deny financing to host governments' development projects can also deter the host governments from taking actions against multinational corporations.

These and other transnational risk management strategies tend to support the general proposition that multinationals can structure the international economic system and respond to their own financial needs to the detriment of host states in the Third World.

International Constraint: Home Government
of Multinational Corporations

The extent to which multinational corporations can mobilize the support of their home government, and the ability (or inability) of the Third World government to withstand retaliation from the powerful governments of the United States and Western Europe on behalf of multinationals can also affect the bargaining equation. For example, between 1945 and 1960 the bargaining power of the multinationals was strengthened by the actions of the United States, which was home to most of the corporations. The American government prevented the emergence of multilateral lending institutions that might have provided alternative capital sources to multinationals. It promoted instead direct foreign investment in the Third World as a major aspect of its foreign assistance program. It also provided diplomatic support to protect the assets of American multinationals. In a few instances, the American government used covert operations and force to protect economic and strategic interests and, in the process, promoted corporate interests.

The home government may support multinational corporations for a variety of national security reasons, to maintain access to cheap sources of foreign raw materials, to improve its balance of payments position or to use the corporations to transfer aid to pro-Western governments in the Third World. In addition, global corporations are powerful domestic political actors in their own right. They can (and do) take advantage of the fragmentation and decentralization of the democratic political process in Western countries in order to influence government policy. Since business groups are likely to be the best organized and best financed groups, with a persistent interest in the outcome of US policy, they could bias the "pluralism" of the political process in the Western countries. For example, in the United States, the Hickenlooper Amendment and the Gonzalez Amendment were the result of corporate lobbying, and both tied American foreign economic interests to the preservation of corporate interests in the Third World.

To be sure, there is no systematic relationship between the home government's interests and corporate interests that might automatically trigger home government support for multinational corporations vis-à-vis Third World governments. In the first place, if there is a conflict between the strategic interests of the nation and narrow corporate interests, the former is likely to prevail. An example of this is American support for Israel in the Arab-Israeli conflict. Secondly, there often exist sharp divisions among multinationals so that they cannot articulate a unified view of their interests. Finally, the result of American extraterritorial diplomatic support on behalf of established corporations—Alcoa, Reynolds, Anaconda, Exxon—in Latin America did not result in favourable outcomes for the corporations. As a result, corporations are becoming more reluctant to seek the support of their home government.

In spite of the above reasons, the potential for conflict with the US government weighs heavily in Third World governments' decisions to confront foreign firms. Since investment in the Third World tends to be highly concentrated according to the interests of the multinationals' home country, (often raw materials are key to national security), and because multinationals are highly influential political actors in the politics of their home country, Third World governments' fears of the US superpower are well-founded. Thus, the host government's willingness (or lack of it) to discount the corporation's home government's potential retaliation (in the form of economic, political or military pressure) may crucially alter both decision-making processes and potential bargaining advantages.

SUMMARY AND CONCLUSION

. . . The model presented in this paper predicts that multinational corporation/Third World country interaction will tend to be unstable over time and that the interests of the two actors are likely to diverge increasingly as the relative bargaining position of the host country improves.

In order to model the bargaining power of Third World countries with respect to multinational corporations, we have made a distinction between potential and actual power. The former is the capability, as yet unrealized, of a host Third World country to alter or influence the behaviour of multinationals. The latter connotes the ability or willingness of the host government to exercise this power in order to extract favourable terms from foreign firms. Potential power is a function of four variables: (1) the level of the host country's expertise, (2) the degree of competition among multinationals, (3) economic uncertainty, and (4) the type of direct foreign investment.

This discussion leads to policy implications for host governments. Obviously, they need to build national capabilities that would help them to regulate better the multinationals. More importantly, in order for them to be effective, national policies need to be revised to conform more closely to the stage of foreign investment cycle. This article's principal thesis is that, despite their apparent bargaining advantage, the dependence of Third World countries which are host to multinational corporations on the international economic system, severely limits the ability of host countries to exercise their potential power.

11

Competing for Capital: The Diffusion of Bilateral Investment Treaties

ZACHARY ELKINS, ANDREW T. GUZMAN, AND BETH A. SIMMONS

Bilateral Investment Treaties (BITs) are the most important international legal mechanism for the encouragement and regulation of foreign direct investment (FDI) and multinational corporations (MNCs). BITs are treaty agreements between two countries: a host to MNCs (typically a developing country) and a home to MNCs (typically a developed country). BITs grant extensive contractual rights and legal protections to MNCs and thereby facilitate foreign direct investment. BITs have been around for many years, but have proliferated since the 1980s. In this article, Zachary Elkins, Andrew T. Guzman, and Beth A. Simmons claim that international political factors explain the widespread adoption of BITs. The authors argue that the spread of BITs is driven by international competition among potential host countries, each seeking to capture a larger share of global foreign direct investment. They propose a set of hypotheses that derive from this international approach and develop a set of empirical tests that measure competitive pressures on host governments to sign BITs. Their evidence shows that potential hosts are more likely to sign BITs when the nations they compete with for FDI have already done so.

The global market for productive capital is more integrated than ever before. The growth of foreign direct investment (FDI) is a clear example. According to World Bank data, gross FDI as a percentage of total world production increased sevenfold from 1.2 percent to 8.9 percent between 1970 and 2000. Though such investments tend to be highly skewed across jurisdictions— developed countries account for more than 93 percent of outflows and 68 percent of inflows—foreign capital has come to play a much more visible role in many more countries worldwide.

It is widely recognized that economic globalization requires market-supporting institutions to flourish. But unlike trade and monetary relations, virtually no multilateral rules for FDI exist. Direct investments in developing countries are overwhelmingly governed by bilateral investment treaties (BITs). BITs are agreements establishing the terms and conditions for private investment by nationals and companies of one country in the jurisdiction of another. Virtually all BITs cover four substantive areas: FDI admission, treatment, expropriation, and the settlement of disputes. These bilateral arrangements have proliferated over the past forty-five years, and especially in the past two decades, even as political controversies have plagued efforts to establish a multilateral regime for FDI.

Why the profusion of bilateral agreements? The popularity of BITs contrasts sharply with the collective resistance developing countries have shown toward pro-investment principles under customary international law and the failure of the international community to make progress on a multilateral investment agreement. On its face, this seems to suggest that BITs do not simply reflect the ready acceptance of dominant international property rights norms. Our theory and findings support . . . competitive economic explanations: the proliferation of BITs—and the liberal property rights regime they embody—is propelled in good part by the competition among potential host countries for credible property rights protections that direct investors require.

The article is organized as follows. The first section describes the spread of BITs in some detail. The second section presents a model of competition for investment that could lead to diffusion among competitors. The third section discusses the methods we use to test our propositions (and a range of alternatives), and the fourth section discusses our findings. Our data are consistent with competitive pressures for BIT proliferation: governments are influenced by competitors' policies and by the mobility of FDI in manufactures, which tends to intensify competition among hosts. We interpret our findings as evidence of pressure for certain governments to adopt capital-friendly policies in highly competitive global capital markets.

SECURING INVESTORS' LEGAL RIGHTS

From Customary Law to Bilateral Investment Treaties

FDI has always been subject to contractual and political hazards that raise the expected costs of investing. Before the use of BITs, few mechanisms existed to make state promises about the treatment of foreign investment credible. Customary international law, expressed succinctly in the "Hull Rule," held that "no government is entitled to expropriate private property, for whatever purpose, without provision for prompt, adequate, and effective payment therefore."[1] Apart from the obvious problem of enforcement, this approach did not allow potential hosts to voluntarily signal their intent to contract in good faith.

Both customary international law and its practice were under attack by developing country hosts by the 1950s. The nationalization of British oil assets by Iran in 1951, the expropriation of Liamco's concessions in Libya in

---

1. See Cordell Hull's note to the Mexican Minister of Foreign Affairs during a 1938 dispute over land expropriations, reprinted in Green H. Hackworth, *Digest of International Law* v. 3, § 228 (1942).

1955, and the nationalization of the Suez Canal by Egypt a year later served notice of a new militancy on the part of investment hosts. The nationalization of sugar interests by Cuba in the 1960s further undercut assumptions about the security of international investments. Meanwhile, collective resistance to the Hull Rule in the United Nations was on the rise. In 1962, the UN General Assembly adopted the "Resolution on Permanent Sovereignty over Natural Resources" that provided for merely "appropriate" compensation in the event of expropriation. Several more UN resolutions followed in the 1970s, along with a string of undercompensated expropriations around the world.

Bilateral treaties made their debut in the late 1950s, just as consensus on customary rules began to erode. BITs were innovative in a number of respects. They require an explicit commitment on the part of the potential host government and involve direct negotiations with the government of potential investors. In this way, BITs up the political ante for the host government and raise expectations of performance. The typical BIT offers a wider array of substantive protections than did the customary rule. For example, BITs typically require national treatment and most-favored-nation treatment of foreign investments in the host country, protect contractual rights, guarantee the right to transfer profits in hard currency to the home country, and prohibit or restrict the use of performance requirements. Finally, and perhaps most importantly, BITs provide for international arbitration of disputes between the investor and the host country, typically through the International Center for Settlement of Investment Disputes (ICSID) or the UN Commission on International Trade Law (UNCITRAL).

The Spread of BITs

Despite the aggressive campaign waged by some developing countries against the relevant customary international law, BITs were embraced by many potential host governments. Figure 1 documents the geometric growth of both investment treaties and mean inflows of FDI as a percentage of GDP from 1960 to 2000. . . . The negotiation of BITs proceeded at a moderate pace until the mid-1980s, rarely exceeding twenty new treaties per year. Late in the decade, however, the rate of signings accelerated dramatically, with an average of more than one hundred new treaties a year throughout the 1990s.

The United States embraced BITs later than did its West European counterparts. Between 1962 and 1972, during which time West Germany entered into forty-six BITs and Switzerland entered into twenty-seven, the United States eschewed such treaties and signed only two Friendship Commerce and Navigation Treaties—with Togo and Thailand. One reason for the delayed U.S. participation in bilateral arrangements may have been the hope of retaining a multilateral approach. The United States was one of the most aggressive proponents of the Hull Rule and may have feared that BITs represented a threat to its claim that investment was already protected under customary interna-

FIGURE 1 Number of Bilateral Investment Treaties Signed and Mean Global Foreign Direct Investment as a Proportion of GDP, by Year, 1959–1999

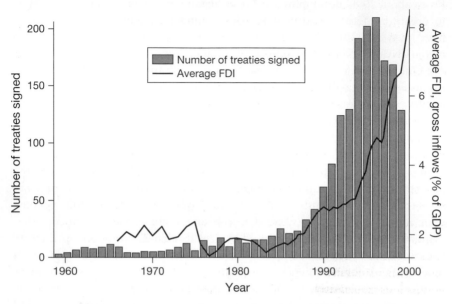

tional law. Moreover, potential hosts may have had incentives to resist the relatively onerous provisions the U.S. government typically tried to secure. One of the prime differences between the terms typically offered by the Europeans and the United States at this time was the former's emphasis on investment protection and the latter's additional insistence on liberalization.

It was not until 1981 that the United States changed its view on BITs. There is evidence that some officials in the administration of U.S. President Ronald Reagan viewed BITs as an alternative way to protect the principles contained in the embattled Hull Rule. Secretary of State George Shultz argued that BITs were designed "to protect investment not only by treaty but also by reinforcing traditional international legal principles and practice regarding foreign direct private investment."[2] By the mid-1980s, the United States pursued investor protection in the same fashion as did the Europeans.

. . . Over time, new BIT partners have become more similar, evidence that the institution is spreading to a population of dyads of similar political and economic structure and, presumably, with less reason to sign such agreements.

---

2. George P. Shultz, transmission letter to the president recommending transmission of the U.S.-Turkey Bilateral Investment Treaty, 1985. Available at http://www.state.gov/documents/organization/43615.pdf.

By the late 1990s, there emerged a few twists to the basic theme of wealthy countries picking off potentially lucrative but risky venues one at a time. From about 1999, developing countries began a rather more proactive effort to create bilateral investment treaties among themselves. These activities have been coordinated through the UN Conference on Trade and Development (UNCTAD), and sometimes with the assistance of a major capital exporting country, such as Germany or France. . . . France financed a round of discussions primarily among the Francophone countries in 2001 that attracted twenty participants and yielded forty-two BITs, many of which involved noncontiguous, poor, highly indebted African countries for which it is difficult to imagine much benefit. (What are the chances that capital from Burkina Faso would flow to Chad, or investors from Benin would soon demand entrée to Mali?) More understandable, from an economic point of view, was the German-funded and supported meeting in October 2001 that drew together seven capital-poor countries (five of which were officially "highly indebted poor countries") and four wealthy European countries, yielding both understandable (Belgium-Cambodia) and bizarre (Sudan-Zambia) bilateral treaty combinations. This recent turn toward BITs between developing states is more difficult for our theory to explain. It does seem to suggest that more political or sociological explanations may be increasingly relevant quite recently in some regions. However, these cases are still relatively few and of such recent vintage that they do not affect the broader relationships we report below.

Leaders and Followers in BIT Agreements

BITs present potential benefits for both capital-exporting and capital-importing countries. But which group of countries initiates and drives the signing of such agreements? Our theory, to anticipate the following section, assumes that potential host countries have an important (although not exclusive) role in initiating or nurturing BIT negotiations. Is this a plausible assumption? After all, power-based theories—or "coercive" theories . . . — suggest that dominant capital-exporting countries such as Germany or the United States control the agenda and begin BIT negotiations according to their schedule and needs. Indeed, the chronology described above suggests that some home countries establish BIT "programs" and sign agreements with a slate of developing countries in concentrated periods of time. . . .

. . . Rather, it appears that potential hosts are more likely to sign in clusters—suggesting that while the major capital exporters stand ready with model treaties in hand, the decision whether and when to sign is left to a large extent to the host.

The notion that home countries make take-it-or-leave-it offers to potential hosts and that hosts eventually decide to sign BITs is also consistent with the observed content of BITs. These treaties tend to provide consistent terms, even across different home countries. In particular, the core terms of the

treaties are almost always present: mandatory dispute resolution before an international arbitration body, a private right of action for investors, monetary compensation in the event of a violation, national treatment, and most-favored-nation treatment. This uniformity suggests that host countries are "price-takers" with respect to the terms of these treaties, consistent with our assumptions. In essence, each home country has market power over the terms that will govern investment by its locals. Host countries, on the other hand, realize that they must compete with other potential hosts and, therefore, cannot demand changes to the core provisions of the treaties.

A COMPETITIVE THEORY OF BIT DIFFUSION

Our theory of BIT diffusion has a simple structure. BITs are viewed by host governments and by investors as devices that raise the expected return on investments. The treaties do this by assisting governments in making credible commitments to treat foreign investors "fairly"—as described in the previous section. BITs give host governments a competitive edge in attracting capital if there are otherwise doubts about their willingness to enforce contracts fairly. Accordingly, governments with little inherent credibility are more likely to sign BITs than are governments known for their fair treatment of foreign capital. The result is a competitive dynamic among potential hosts to reduce the risks and enhance the profitability of investing.

BITs as a Credible Commitment

Governments may have many motives to sign a BIT, but the most significant is to make a credible commitment to treat foreign investors fairly. BITs allow governments to make credible commitments because they raise the *ex post* costs of noncompliance above those that might be incurred in the absence of the treaty. They do this by (1) clarifying the commitment, (2) explicitly involving the home country's government, and (3) enhancing enforcement.

BITs raise *ex post* costs of reneging on contracts by reducing the ambiguity of the host government's obligations. BITs are much more precise than customary international law in this area. They also provide a broader legal framework in which to interpret specific contractual obligations. Precision removes potential avenues of plausible deniability, making it clearer to a broader range of audiences (domestic audiences, other foreign investors, other governments), that an obligation has been disregarded. Clear violations imply a much greater reputational cost than do actions not clearly barred by law.

The second way BITs raise *ex post* costs of reneging is by involving the investor's government as a treaty party. BITs are negotiated between sovereign states. State-to-state legal arrangements implicate the interests of the home government more directly than do simple investment contracts between private parties and host governments. The home government has an interest in broader principles of good-faith treaty observance. Treatment that violates a BIT qualifies as a breach of the fundamental principle of international law: *pacta sunt servanda* (treaties are to be observed). Reneging on a contract governed by a treaty arrangement can damage important foreign policy interests.

Finally, BITs raise *ex post* costs by significantly enhancing contract enforcement. These agreements contain mandatory dispute settlement provisions that investors are entitled to use when they feel the host state has violated the relevant BIT. Significantly, investors can begin arbitration proceedings without the approval or support of their home government. Moreover, the host can neither prevent the legal proceeding from going forward, nor control the final decision of the international arbitration tribunal. The international tribunal can require a host found to be in violation of its obligations to pay monetary damages. The sovereign host state could, of course, refuse to pay, but that decision could have even more profound reputational consequences: when a government spurns the decision of a neutral authoritative third party with which it has voluntarily precommitted to comply, a range of important actors—public and private—are likely to infer that that government is an unreliable economic partner. By giving private parties a right to pursue and receive a legal remedy, BITs boost the credibility of the host government's commitment. As a result, we would expect some violations to be deterred by a BIT commitment and expected returns to investments to increase accordingly. . . .

In short, BITs represent a credible commitment because of the range of *ex post* costs—diplomatic costs, sovereignty costs, arbitration costs, and reputational costs—involved in both their observance and their violation. We argue below that some governments have incentives to increase these costs in order to attract FDI.

Competitive BIT Signings: Logic and Implications

In the previous section we argued that BITs allow governments to credibly commit themselves to protect investors' property rights. The ability to do so lowers risks and increases expected returns to investment. If this is the case, BITs can be a mechanism—such as favorable tax treatment, lower wages, and efficient infrastructure—for making a jurisdiction a more attractive place in which to invest. As with these other mechanisms, committing to a BIT involves costs for the host government. We characterize these as "sovereignty costs." They are the costs any government pays when it negotiates, ratifies, and complies with an investment treaty. We would include here the political costs of assembling a coalition in support of foreign investors' rights, as well as the costs associated with giving up a broad range of policy instruments relevant to domestic social or developmental purposes (taxation, regulation, performance requirements, property seizure, and currency and capital restrictions). Most striking are the sovereignty costs associated with the delegation of adjudicative authority: virtually any legal change or rule that affects foreign investors is potentially subject to review by a foreign tribunal. The decision to sign a BIT always involves an assessment by the host of whether the expected benefit of attracting an additional increment of foreign capital outweighs these costs. In many cases, the answer is no. In this section, we discuss the conditions under which the expected benefits for a particular government might outweigh these sovereignty costs.

BITs can attract capital from two broad resource pools. First, they can shift resources from consumption or domestic investment, effectively stimulating new international capital investments that would not have been made absent the treaty. Second, and more importantly for our theory, BITs can redirect international capital flows from one venue to another. A BIT gives the host signatory a "reputational advantage" over otherwise comparable rivals in the competition for (re) distribution of an existing investment pool. The possibility of investment diversion means that governments may have competitive reasons to implement BITs. It is the ability of a BIT—or at a minimum, its perceived ability—to give one country an advantage over other similarly situated countries in the competition for capital that we hypothesize as provoking many BIT signings.

The strategic structure we are describing creates serious collective-action problems among potential host countries. Collectively, they might be better off resisting the demands of investors (avoiding the sovereignty costs described above), but individually it is rational to sign in hopes of stimulating capital inflows. In recognition of this dynamic, one finds cases of regional attempts to coordinate host resistance. In the Caribbean, for example, collective efforts have been made to reduce BIT concessions, though predictably the "cartel" has been difficult to maintain. The breakdown of such efforts is consistent with the competitive context we believe accounts for the proliferation of BITs over the past several years.

A competitive theory of BITs has at least four observable implications. First, BITs should diffuse among host country competitors—countries that, from an investor's point of view, are closely substitutable venues for investment. It is precisely these countries that should display the clearest evidence of interdependent decision making. This is a unique prediction of competitive theory. No other diffusion mechanism—whether hegemonic, cognitive, or ideational—makes this specific prediction.

Second, BITs should spread most readily to countries where the competition for capital is the most intense. Competition intensifies where the number of plausible hosts for a particular investment project is greatest. For this reason, host competition for investment in extractive goods is far less intense than in light manufactures: while the number of countries in which bauxite mining is profitable is quite limited, almost any jurisdiction can host a Nike plant. If our competition hypothesis is correct, these treaties should be more prevalent where host competition is most fierce: in light manufactures rather than in primary production or extractive industries. This prediction is the exact opposite of what one might expect were BITs propelled in a "hegemonic" fashion, by the home country. From a home government's point of view, theories of obsolescing bargaining should predict the need for enforceable investment protections precisely in those industries that involve large upfront difficult-to-relocate investments. Obsolescing bargaining suggests that investors are more likely to demand treaties to protect their extractive and primary production investments, at least relative to easier-to-relocate light manufactures.

Third, BITs should spread as the pool of available capital grows. As the pool of global capital grows, any competitive advantage (such as that conferred by a BIT) should yield a larger marginal increase in FDI inflows. Thus, the expected return per BIT should increase with the size of the investment pool, which encourages hosts to scramble to improve access to a share of the bigger "pie." . . . Our theory suggests a possible feedback loop: the expectation of greater payoffs may stimulate more treaties. This relationship is not predicted by more sociological explanations, which might expect BITs to proliferate as a function of the density of BITs themselves, rather than the growing volume of investment. Nor is it predicted by learning theories, which would presumably require a demonstration that BITs actually "work" in attracting capital.

Finally, while all countries should be subject to some degree to the competitive pressures we have theorized above, BITs should diffuse somewhat more readily among host governments that lack credibility. For these countries, a BIT can be expected to make a real difference to investors, other factors held constant. In countries that already have institutions and practices that are favorable to investors, transparent, and predictable, a costly BIT adds relatively little value. These states may be able to compete for capital on the basis of their "inherent" credibility. This relationship is in principle consistent with power-based explanations (powerful home governments may be more likely to demand BITs from unreliable hosts than inherently reliable ones), but it is much less consistent with more sociological accounts. . . . If governments have been "socialized" to accept the dominant paradigm for investor protection, there would be no reason for the more credible host governments to largely exempt themselves.

A competitive theory of BITs predicts that the host countries most likely to sign treaties will be those whose competitors have signed, those who depend on manufacturing over extractive production, and those with a credibility gap. More generally, a competitive theory predicts increased treaties as the pool of available capital grows. In the following section, we develop an empirical strategy for testing these hypotheses against alternative explanations.

EMPIRICAL METHODS AND DATA

Analytical Design

We use an event history framework to estimate the duration of time before two countries sign a BIT. Our analysis begins in 1958, the year before the first BIT, and includes those BITs concluded up to 1 January 2000, the last year for which we have accurate data. Since the focus of the analysis is a bilateral agreement between governments in a given year, the appropriate unit of analysis is the country dyad–year. In each dyad, we identify the potential "home" and the potential "host" country based on their relative level of development, as measured by GDP per capita. Of course, such designations become less meaningful the closer the members of the dyad are in their level of development. But treaties among countries of a similar level of development—especially at the higher end—are considerably less likely. In the reported analyses we exclude "developed dyads" from the sample in order to minimize the bias from estimates derived from "irrelevant dyads." . . .

. . . We estimate the following equation:

$$y_{ij,t} = \alpha X_{i,t} + \beta Z_{j,t} + \delta V_{ij,t} + \rho W y_{t-1}^* + \varepsilon_{ij}$$

where y_{ij} is the number of years without a BIT between countries i (host) and j (home), X is a vector of conditions that affect country i's calculations, Z is a vector of conditions that affect country j's calculations, V is a vector of characteristics of the relationship between countries i and j, and Wy^* is a vector of spatial lag terms in which a count of BITs among other host countries in the previous year (y^*) is weighted by various measures of their distance (W) to country i (see our discussion of spatial lags below). We estimate this equation with a Cox proportional hazard model, a useful estimator when one does not have strong assumptions about the effect of time on the baseline hazard.

Data and Measures

Our dependent variable is the number of years a dyad goes without a treaty, marked by the year of a treaty's signing, rather than the year in which it enters into force. We reason that the signing not only approximates the moment during which a government deliberates over the treaty but is also the more important event for purposes of sending a proinvestment signal to international markets. . . . Our independent variables take on one of four analytic forms: (1) independent factors associated with the "home" country; (2) independent factors associated with the "host" country; (3) factors associated with the relationship between host and home countries; and (4) spatial lags of the dependent variable. . . .

Our theory predicts interdependent decision making among host countries that compete for the same sources of global capital. Thus we need to determine the "competitive distance" between hosts. We create spatial weights that capture this distance in three ways. The first measures the degree to which host governments compete in the same foreign markets; that is, whether they have the same export trade relationships. . . . This is a useful indicator because trade competitors are also likely to be competitors for FDI and empirical studies show that the two are strongly correlated. We reason that countries that compete for export markets are structurally positioned to compete for the same sources of FDI as well. The second measure records the degree to which nations export the same basket of goods. This measure captures the idea that investors choose between alternative locations for direct investment that they consider close substitutes with respect to the countries' traditional export products. For example, an automobile manufacturer might consider investing in countries that produce steel but will be unlikely to consider those whose leading export is cocoa. Our third measure captures the degree to which countries have similar educational and infrastructural resources. Assuming that potential foreign direct investors are concerned with a country's human assets as well as its technological and communications infrastructure, we reason that countries with similar educational and infrastructural profiles will compete for the same pool of capital. For all three competition measures, we compute a spatial lag by anchoring the distances (measured as correlations) at zero by adding 1 to each score and then using these distances to calculate a weighted sum of BITs in force in all other host countries in the previous year. . . .

We also use spatial lags in a similar way to measure the influence of an important alternative explanation [. . .]—that of cultural peers. We use three measures of "cultural distance": predominant religion, colonial heritage, and predominant language. The spatial lag for these "distances" is calculated in the same weighted-average manner as for the competitive distances. Unlike the competition measures, the cultural distances are binary; a country either shares a common language with another, or it does not. The cultural spatial lags, therefore, are equivalent to the mean number of BITs in force among those host countries with the same cultural identity (religion, language, or colonial heritage). These measures capture an important possibility: that BITs result more from socially constructed emulation of policies of important reference groups than from hard-nosed economic competition. Note that this measure does not capture whether BITs are more likely between cultural peers, an effect we test with the cultural distance variables themselves (see below).

ALTERNATIVE DIFFUSION MECHANISMS: LEARNING AND COERCION. Finally, we seek to capture the effects of policy learning and coercion. Our notion of learning . . . implies that policymakers from host countries are motivated to sign BITs based on the treaties' demonstrated benefits (specifically, increased FDI). Our model does not assume that policymakers have Herculean powers of observation or analysis; nor does it treat them as remedial statisticians. We assume simply that policymakers assess the success of countries in attracting investment over recent years given the countries' level of development and their number of treaties in force during this time. We replicate this cognitive process by regressing, each year, the average FDI inflows as a percentage of GDP for the previous five years on the average number of treaties in force for that country during that period as well as its average GDP per capita. The standardized regression coefficient for the BITs variable in each of these yearly equations is our indicator of a policymaker's estimate of the payoff of these treaties in terms of increased investment. Thus, we assume that each year decision makers observe and draw conclusions about the effects of BITs on investment, controlling for a country's level of development, and that all actors observe the same signal.

We consider one final interdependent mechanism, coercion. It may be that potential hosts are coerced or at least strongly encouraged to enter into BITs. If so, a likely juncture for the application of such pressure is at the time a country seeks International Monetary Fund (IMF) credits. We incorporate a dichotomous measure of whether or not a country has drawn on IMF resources in a given year. Though we do not believe the pursuit of or entry into BITs is explicitly stipulated in formal loan conditions, there may be more subtle pressures on a state in balance-of-payments difficulties to use these treaties to attract foreign capital.

HOME COUNTRY CONSIDERATIONS. The proliferation of BITs could be explained by two home country considerations: the desire to protect existing overseas capital, and the desire for additional investments. These considerations could significantly influence the pool of BITs that is potentially available, independently of any competitive dynamic among potential hosts. In the analysis that follows, we control for the total FDI "exposure" of the home country; that is, the degree to which a country's capital is actually invested abroad. For this we use a measure of net FDI outflows as a proportion of GDP (scored positively when outflows outweigh inflows and negatively when inflows outweigh outflows). On average, we expect high outflows to produce a greater willingness to supply BITs on the part of investors' governments.

HOST COUNTRY CONSIDERATIONS. Our competitive story of the proliferation of BITs suggests that competitive reputation building, through BITs, can set off a sequence of treaty signings among countries that compete with one another. Although all countries may be subject to such competitive pressures to some degree, we expect governments with greater indigenous credibility to be less willing to pay the sovereignty and other political costs associated with concluding BITs. We capture this idea by using an indicator of investors' perceptions of corruption in the host country. The more corrupt a state is perceived to be, the more necessary it becomes to lure investors with an explicit promise to delegate adjudication to an authoritative third party. We complement this measure with one of the nature of the legal system itself. If civil law systems are less oriented toward credible rules of capital protection, governments in those systems should more frequently reach for an external commitment mechanism, such as a BIT. Finally, we would like to use a measure of the extent to which the host's legal system is perceived by foreign investors as strong and impartial. Unfortunately, the measure that appears to be most appropriate for tapping legal strength and impartiality ("law and order") is confounded by the inclusion of investors' assessment of popular observance of the law, which likely has little to do with the judiciary's attitude toward foreign investors. Nonetheless, our argument implies that a reputation for "law and order" should reduce a host's need to sign a BIT.

Another important factor, and one with implications for our competition story, has to do with a country's exposure to competition. If BITs are driven by competition for capital, they should be most prevalent where that competition is most fierce. We have argued that competition for capital is most cutthroat in manufacturing; by comparison, there are limited sites worldwide that produce copper or other extractive commodities. The fewer the alternative investment sites, the more protected the host is from international competition, and the less likely a host is to sign a BIT. To capture this idea, we construct a measure of extractive industry dependence by summing the share of each country's exports of both fuel and "ores and metals," as recorded in the World Bank's World Development Indicators (WDI). Approaches emphasizing the coercive role of dominant powers would anticipate a positive coefficient for extractive industries, since these are most subject to obsolescing bargaining and hence intensified political risks. Our expectation, however, is that this effect will be swamped by competition among hosts for manufacturing FDI, and we anticipate a negative effect. The outcome on the extractive industry variable thus provides a fairly crisp test of the importance of competition among hosts in explaining the proliferation of BITs.

Quite aside from indicators of the need for a credible commitment discussed above, a number of economic conditions make particular hosts especially attractive BIT partners. We control for the economic desirability of the investment site by controlling for market size of the host country (log of the host's GDP), the host's level of development (GDP per capita), the quality of the host's workforce (rate of illiteracy), and the host's growth (GDP growth rate). We also include a rather direct measure of the host's attractiveness for capital: FDI net inflows in the previous year, as a percentage of GDP.

Finally, we control for other political and policy conditions in the host country. Since investors may see democracies as less capricious, we control for the host's level of democracy. It is possible that the pattern of BITs is driven by a few countries' aggressive privatization programs, and so we control for the value of privatized assets in a given year. Finally, we recognize that to sign BITs requires a certain degree of diplomatic capacity. We account for the diplomatic and legal capacity to enter into BITs by controlling for the total number of embassies a country hosts and has established in foreign countries. A host with extensive diplomatic representation is more likely to have the international political and legal capacity to conclude a larger volume of treaties.

CHARACTERISTICS OF COUNTRY PAIRS.   In this analytic category we identify the relational variables that might be associated with the likelihood of an agreement between the two nations. We focus on three kinds of relationships: business, security, and cultural relationships. Since firms are likely to want to invest in or near their export markets and to otherwise take advantage of vertical downstream linkages, we control for the intensity of business transactions, proxied by the extent of trade between the two countries. Investment agreements may also have a foreign policy or even a security rationale as well. To address this possibility, we include a measure of the intensity of the alliance relationship for each pair. We also consider the possibility that BITs reflect cultural relationships, although this variable could have opposing effects. On the one hand, it may be easier for states with cultural similarities to negotiate successfully. On the other hand, if cultural similarities also reduce the perceived risks of investment, a common culture might operate in the opposite direction, reducing the need for a BIT. We test the relationship between cultural characteristics and BIT signing by coding country pairs with shared language and colonial traditions. Note that these variables should not be confused with the cultural spatial lags, which are measures of a host's peers' treaty activity.

FINDINGS

We present estimates (as hazard ratios) from three specifications of our model (Table 1). A hazard ratio of more than 1 represents a positive effect on the odds of a BIT; less than 1, a negative effect. The first regression includes the export partner lag together with the full set of covariates described above. The last two regressions include one of the remaining two competitive spatial lags (export product similarity and infrastructure/workforce similarity) in a reduced form of the model. Several clear empirical patterns begin to emerge. There is fairly consistent and convincing evidence of the importance of competition for capital among developing countries in explaining the proliferation of BITs over the past four decades. In all cases, higher rates of BIT signing among competitors (however measured) appear to have increased the rate at which a given country itself enters into a BIT at statistically significant levels. . . .

The evidence also suggests that as global FDI has increased, potential hosts have been more willing to sign BITs. One interpretation of this finding is that as the pool of FDI has increased, the competitive stakes for a share have grown. The pattern with respect to countries with predominantly extractive industries also provides corroboratory evidence for the competition theory. The results show that higher extractive production by the potential host reduces the propensity to negotiate a BIT (contrary to expectations based on

TABLE 1 A Model of BIT Signings: Cox Proportional Hazard Model

Explanatory variables	Model 1	Model 2	Model 3
Competitive theory			
BITS AMONG EXPORT MARKET COMPETITORS	1.05***		
	(0.01)		
BITS AMONG EXPORT PRODUCT COMPETITORS		1.11***	
		(0.04)	
BITS AMONG INFRASTRUCTURE COMPETITORS			1.04
			(0.02)***
AVERAGE ANNUAL GLOBAL FDI FLOWS	1.32***	1.53***	1.46***
	(0.12)	(0.14)	(0.13)
HOST EXTRACTIVE INDUSTRIES/EXPORTS	0.73**	0.73**	0.72***
	(0.09)	(0.09)	(0.09)
PERCEPTIONS OF HOST CORRUPTION	1.03	1.01	1.01
	(0.04)	(0.04)	(0.04)
HOST LEGAL TRADITION (COMMON LAW)	0.66***	0.65***	0.66***
	(0.05)	(0.05)	(0.05)
Alternative diffusion explanations			
BITS AMONG THOSE WITH SAME RELIGION	0.99	0.98	0.99
	(0.01)	(0.01)	(0.01)
BITS AMONG THOSE WITH SAME LANGUAGE	1.01		
	(0.06)		
BITS AMONG THOSE WITH SAME COLONIZER	0.99		
	(0.04)		
LEARNING FROM SUCCESS	1.85**	1.83*	2.13*
	(0.42)	(0.61)	(0.94)
COERCION: HOST USE OF IMF CREDITS	1.44***	1.39***	1.43***
	(0.12)	(0.11)	(0.12)
Host control variables			
HOST GDP (LN)	1.07*	1.03	1.04
	(0.04)	(0.04)	(0.04)
HOST GDP/CAPITA	1.00	1.00	0.99
	(0.03)	(0.03)	(0.03)
HOST GDP GROWTH	0.97***	0.97***	0.97***
	(0.01)	(0.01)	(0.01)
HOST NET FDI INFLOWS (% OF GDP), $T-1$	1.01	1.01	1.01
	(0.01)	(0.01)	(0.01)
HOST ILLITERACY RATE	0.34***	0.30***	0.30***
	(0.06)	(0.05)	(0.06)
HOST CAPITAL ACCOUNT/GDP	1.01	1.01**	1.01**
	(0.01)	(0.01)	(0.01)
HOST LAW AND ORDER	1.34***	1.39***	1.38***
	(0.05)	(0.05)	(0.05)

TABLE 1 (*continued*)

Explanatory variables	Model 1	Model 2	Model 3
HOST DEMOCRACY	0.99	0.99	0.99
	(0.01)	(0.01)	(0.01)
HOST DIPLOMATIC REPRESENTATION	1.01***	1.01***	1.01***
	(0.00)	(0.00)	(0.00)
HOST PRIVATIZATION RECORD	1.05***	1.06***	1.06***
	(0.02)	(0.02)	(0.02)
Home control variables			
HOME NET FDI OUTFLOWS (% OF GDP)	1.13***	1.14***	1.14***
	(0.02)	(0.02)	(0.02)
Dyadic control variables			
DYADIC TRADE (% OF HOST'S GDP)	1.59*	1.61	1.64
	(0.35)	(0.56)	(0.57)
COMMON COLONIAL HERITAGE	0.41***	0.40***	0.41***
	(0.09)	(0.09)	(0.09)
COMMON LANGUAGE	1.57***	1.55***	1.54***
	(0.19)	(0.19)	(0.19)
ALLIANCE	1.18*	1.20*	1.18
	(0.10)	(0.11)	(0.14)
Common "shocks"			
COLD WAR	0.37***	0.31***	0.32***
	(0.08)	(0.06)	(0.06)
NUMBER OF BITS GLOBALLY, BY YEAR	1.03	1.00	1.01
	(0.03)	(0.03)	(0.03)
Observations	206,766	208,610	201,073
Number of country pairs analyzed	6,781	6,831	6,828
Number of BITs	1,125	1,140	1,137
Log likelihood	−8723.114	−8858.474	−8823.590

NOTES: Standard errors are in parentheses.
*** Significant at 1%; ** significant at 5%; * significant at 10%.

investors' demands to address obsolescing bargains endemic to primary and extractive production). . . . Both the magnitude and stability of this effect across models suggests that it is a fairly robust finding.

We found inconsistent evidence, however, to support our expectation that host countries with a credibility gap are most likely to sign a BIT. Contrary to expectation, BITs were more likely to be signed by countries with better reputations for "law and order." We have already noted that this indicator only partially reflects our argument, as it conflates perceptions of the strength of the court system with perceptions of popular willingness to obey the law. Even so, the strong positive result is surprising. One possibility is that this measure is picking up the relatively favorable orientation of some countries toward legal solutions to conflicts generally. As we expected, perceptions of corruption were in the correct direction, although the hazard ratio is not statistically significant in any specification that also contains "law and order." We should note that corruption is a significant determinant of signing a BIT whenever the LAW AND ORDER variable is not included. The common law variable did work as anticipated, but in light of the above findings, we think the prudent conclusion is that common law countries also refrain from entering into these agreements for reasons other than the reputational concerns developed here.

In addition to the competition variables, our coercion variable (use of IMF credits) is significant in each of the models. This may mean that states seeking assistance from the IMF are encouraged to enter into BITs. Alternatively, it may be that the conditionality of IMF loans overlaps with the obligations of the BIT, reducing the costs of the latter. Interestingly, there is some evidence of learning from BIT outcomes. BITs are significantly more likely to be signed during years in which signatory states appear to be benefiting (in terms of FDI) from the treaties than when they are not. Such a pattern, of course, is consistent with our general theory of competition over shares of FDI. We found no evidence, however, that countries sign agreements in response to signings in their cultural networks. None of the spatial lags along religion, language, or colonial heritage had consequential effects.

Many of the variables that would predict home country interest in offering a BIT to a developing country had somewhat unpredictable, and muted, effects. The size of the host economy and previous FDI inflows (as a percentage of host GDP) showed effects in the predicted direction, although rarely statistically significant across the models we tested. Meanwhile GDP per capita and economic growth had, if anything, the opposite effects of what we would expect, although only the economic growth coefficients were significant. On the other hand, we did find evidence that countries with a high quality workforce, as measured by literacy rates, and with an export orientation (current accounts tending toward surplus), were more likely to sign BITs (illiteracy is associated with a reduced likelihood of a BIT). Our prediction that privatization programs in a host country would coincide with BIT agreements was borne out as well. Similarly, host countries with a larger diplomatic presence were also more likely to enter into BITs. Finally, host's degree of democracy had practically no effect.

Certain control variables describing the relationships between home and host countries were important predictors of BITs. While the direction of dyadic trade is as hypothesized, the effect is statistically insignificant in two of the three models. Political and cultural relationships seem to be more important. In accordance with expectations, BITs are more likely among allies, which could suggest a somewhat coercive element to their conclusion. A common language within the dyad makes it much more likely that a pair of countries will negotiate a BIT, but a colonial link reduces by about two-thirds the likelihood that a country pair will do so. Perhaps investors in home countries perceive the risk in their colonial "families" to be lower than in other states. After all, colonies' legal institutions are likely to be similar to, if not partially overlap with, legal institutions in the mother country and fellow former colonies. This fits with our conception of BITs as being created to establish a credible legal framework for investment that is otherwise lacking. . . .

CONCLUSION

The use of bilateral investment treaties has grown significantly since the early 1960s. Their growth is especially remarkable given the outright rebellion many hosts have staged against customary law understandings and multilateral codifications of investors' rights that are quite similar to those contained in these proliferating bilateral accords. Why the disjuncture? How can we understand the spread of these pro-market agreements across time and space?

The diffusion mechanisms . . . suggest a broad range of empirically verifiable hypotheses about movement towards BITs. Both theoretically and empirically, the competition model seems most apt in this case. These treaties are meant to improve conditions under which global capital relocates, prospers, and repatriates. They are also meant to raise the reputational stakes for governments of capital-poor economies by committing them to respect property and contractual rights of foreign investors and to agree to arbitration—effectively clipping their sovereignty—in the event of any disagreement over subsequent investment contracts. There are clearly possibilities here for mutual gain for hosts and investors, though we are agnostic about the global welfare effects of these treaties, given their potential redistributive consequences. We admit that some of the more recent treaties between very poor countries do not square with our straightforward competitive model; nonetheless, the strongest case can be made for a competitive diffusion dynamic in this case.

Let us begin with the project's null hypothesis: that country characteristics or commonly experienced shocks explain the pattern of BIT signings. There was plenty of support in the data for traditional economic explanations. Some of the most important drivers of the spread of BITs are likely factors that drive investment decisions more generally. The pattern of BITs shows that home governments want to secure investments in developing markets that are large, somewhat open, and with high quality labor. On the other hand, BITs are most valuable where political risk is endemic. China, which has concluded a large number of BITs with both rich and poor partners, would be the quintessential BIT partner, according to our model.

We also found strong evidence that dyadic characteristics explain BITs. BITs are much more likely to be negotiated among country pairs of the same culture (at least as measured by shared language) and among country pairs with strong security commitments. But if cultural linkages explain home-host pairs, cultural emulation is much less in evidence among potential hosts. Not one indicator of cultural emulation among hosts had any purchase at all on the adoption of BITs. These cultural arguments may in the end be a more satisfying account available for the growing category of "strange BITs" between highly indebted, capital-poor, noncontiguous country pairs. We know anecdotally that third parties (France, UNCTAD) facilitated many of these agreements, indicating that in many cases external political or cultural forces may be crucial. The strong positive effect of IMF borrowing and alliance relationships on the propensity to sign a BIT also reminds us that a certain degree of coercion may be at play in some cases.

We do not doubt that multiple motives exist for the spread of this form of protection for foreign investors. But the competitive explanation has strong theoretical foundations and is the most consistently supported by the data. First, it was well supported by three different measures of "competitive space": by export market, export product, and workforce/infrastructural quality. When more of a host's closest competitors have signed BITs, that country is much more likely to do so itself. The remarkable consistency across these three highly nuanced measures of competitive space provides strong initial evidence of a tendency to match the policy choices of competitors.

Second, the size and character of markets for FDI have fed the competitive atmosphere in predictable ways. The sheer size of the available pool of investment has greatly raised countries' stakes in securing a share. More BITs are signed when the global capital pool increases. This finding is of course consistent with home countries' concern to protect their investors as well as hosts' desire to increase their access. But a second finding much more clearly indicates that the impetus for signing is host-country driven. Our theory of competition among hosts predicts more BITs where the market for FDI is most competitive—the manufacturing sector. We found, in contrast to what theories of obsolescing bargaining would predict, that dependence on extractive industries reduced the probability that a host would make such a commitment.

Finally, a theory of host-driven competition was supported by some of our findings about the qualities associated with those hosts most likely to sign. We expected BITs to be pursued most assiduously by host governments whose domestic institutions render them least able to make credible commitments to protect property rights. When we excluded the possibly confounded "law and order" variable from our analysis, hosts were much more likely to sign if their regime was perceived as corrupt by foreign investors. They were also more likely to sign depending on the nature of their legal institutions. Common law countries—legal systems that some well-documented empirical work has shown to be associated with better legal protection for property rights—are much less likely to sign than are civil law countries. We recognize there are other reasons for common law countries to be reluctant to enter into international treaty obligations generally, but it remains possible that the differential ability of various legal traditions indigenously to protect property rights is at work as well. In this context, our finding on "law and order" is somewhat puzzling. But we are far less convinced that this indicator captures the domestic institutional guarantees of protection and fairness that foreign direct investors seek.

The diffusion of norms that protect investment has been further advanced by host governments' desire to attract a share of the global capital pool. We have doubts that this phenomenon can be explained by the appeal of liberal ideas alone, for we have witnessed the proliferation of BITs just as multilateral and customary law approaches have foundered. Most governments would prefer to avoid the explicit commitments contained in these treaties; there continue to be few concluded between the wealthiest countries of the world. In some regions, developing countries have tried to coordinate their responses to BITs in hopes of gaining more favorable terms, with notably limited success. In short, we base our conclusions on the importance of competition for capital not just on statistical relationships that show up in the quantitative analysis, but also on the broader context in which our analysis is nested.

BITs are part of a larger process of globalization that has been furthered by the dynamics of competition. This competition is driven by the desire of developing countries to participate in the global capitalist system. But has this uncoordinated strategy of signing away the sovereign right to regulate a growing segment of national economic activity yielded the results developing countries have hoped for? The evidence as to whether BITs actually succeed in attracting capital is unclear on this point. Our research suggests why this may be the case. Competition for capital has important redistributive consequences. The result of the BIT competition may be only minimally improved access to capital at a high cost to national sovereignty.

12

Globalization and Policy Convergence

DANIEL W. DREZNER

In this essay, Daniel W. Drezner examines the arguments and evidence about how "globalization" affects national policies regulating the environment, labor markets, and health and safety conditions. The concern is that economic integration is forcing nations to converge at the lowest level of regulation, due to an alleged "race to the bottom" in which nations compete to attract and retain foreign investment. Drezner's assessment of regulatory convergence emphasizes international economic factors and explicitly omits attention to domestic politics. While his survey follows the traditional "Realist-Liberal-Marxist" framework outlined in the introduction of this book, the international aspect of his discussion is reflected in the "neo" prefix attached to each perspective (as in "neoliberal"). Drezner finds little support for theories that predict policy convergence and no evidence of a "race to the bottom" in environmental, labor, and health and safety regulations. Instead, he concludes that nation-states have been able to cooperate and agree on norms of governance that determine the extent of regulatory convergence.

Globalization is the cluster of technological, economic, and political innovations that have drastically reduced the barriers to economic, political, and cultural exchange. Although its salience is self-evident to policy makers and the public, the vocal protests at the 1999 World Trade Organization (WTO) ministerial meeting in Seattle and elsewhere since highlight the growing interest in it. Protestors were convinced that the WTO was accelerating market integration at the expense of environmental standards, consumer safety, and labor rights. Such clashes are largely about the anticipated but uncertain effects of globalization and the question of whether it will lead to the elimination of state regulation or to a new form of global governance.

An implicit assumption of most policy analysts and some academics is that globalization leads to a convergence of traditionally national policies governing environmental regulation, consumer health and safety, the regulation of labor, and the ability to tax capital. Convergence is the tendency of policies to grow more alike, in the form of increasing similarity in structures, processes, and performances. Some claim that the reduction of transnational barriers to economic exchange forces states to revoke long-standing social contracts that protect their citizens from the ruthlessness of the free market. Globalization leads to a race to the bottom, where concerns about the environment, the treatment of labor, and the health of consumers are sacrificed on the altar of commerce. Others argue that the growth of transnational governance structures leads to a negotiated convergence of ample regulation but also a potential democratic deficit. Does globalization lead to policy convergence in these areas? More generally, does globalization lead to the rollback of regulation or its increase?

These questions are more than intrinsically important. The question of national policy autonomy has triggered the most public anxiety about globalization. Polling data reveal that U.S. citizens believe that the integration of the United States with the rest of the world has greatly constrained U.S. policy autonomy, creating ambivalence about further international integration. This anxiety is even greater in other countries since they are far more dependent on the global economy than the United States. . . . The battle in Seattle and the now ubiquitous protests at meetings of international organizations are only the most noteworthy manifestations of the anxiety about globalization.

The scholarly work on this subject is spread across multiple disciplines, including law, economics, political science, and sociology. This problem leads to a certain redundancy in theory building, as disciplinary boundaries prevent ideas from spreading across fields. This hinders accumulating knowledge. In the long run, the lack of cumulation is dangerous; without rigorous reviews of such arguments, policymakers are prone to accept misperceptions of globalization that are politically expedient.

International relations scholars are debating the claim that globalization represents a structural change in the international system that must be addressed by new theories. Much of the discourse on globalization shows an attempt to move away from the existing paradigms of international relations theory, arguing that the changes wrought on world politics in the past twenty years overwhelm the assumptions about the state made in traditional theories. If globalization causes an inexorable policy convergence, then this discourse would be substantiated, fusing together the study of international and comparative political economy. If the effects of globalization have been exaggerated, then it should become common knowledge before discourse overwhelms praxis and wastes time and resources.

This reflection and reappraisal will examine the arguments and evidence about how globalization affects the convergence of regulatory policies, in particular the setting of labor and environmental standards. Two conclusions follow. First, theories of policy convergence diverge on whether the driving force is economic or ideational, and whether states retain agency in the face of globalization or are dominated by structural determinants. These divergences mirror the divisions among international relations paradigms. Globalization therefore has not led to the development of new theories of international relations, but merely transported existing theories to new issue areas of the global political economy. Second, the evidence on policy convergence across multiple issue areas suggests that the structurally based theories lack support. Globalization cannot be reduced to a set of deterministic forces. This suggests that the transnational economic and ideational forces commonly cited are not as powerful as previously suggested. . . .

The following discussion is divided into three main sections. The first reviews the various theoretical explanations of how globalization could affect the ability of states to regulate their own economies. The following section reviews the empirical literature on globalization and its effects on labor and environmental standards and examines the performance of the various theories. The concluding section offers some suggestions about future avenues for research.

HOW CAN CONVERGENCE OCCUR?

Not surprisingly, scholars studied policy convergence long before the recent wave of globalization came about. In this earlier literature, convergence was postulated to occur through the homogenization of societies via industrialization and modernization. The recent trend toward globalization reinforces the effects claimed by convergence theorists. The ability of ideas to permeate across borders has existed for centuries, but advances in telecommunications and computers have made this process much easier. Similarly, the erosion of capital controls has reinforced the claims about the effect of transnational economic forces on national policy autonomy.

The different theories that connect globalization to policy convergence fit into a simple 2×2 schema. The first dimension is whether the theory emphasizes the primacy of structural forces or the power of autonomous agents. Structural approaches stress the environmental conditions affecting political units. The pressures for convergence are external to states, determining their course of action by tightly constraining national policy responses. Agent-centered approaches do not dismiss the power of transnational structures but argue that states can at least choose from among multiple policies that are sustainable outcomes over time.

A clear distinction between structural and agent-based theories is the language used to describe international regulatory regimes. Structure-based theories deal with convergence as the dependent variable and imply that different national policies are homogenized into one global policy. Agent-based theories prefer the term coordination, which is more expansive than convergence. Policy coordination implies some agreement on the acceptable bounds of regulatory policies, but it does *not* mean that all states implement identical rules or regulations.

The second dimension that separates different theoretical approaches is the source of the convergence pressures. One view is that the primary pressure for convergence is economic; the pressure to modify regulatory policies comes from the threat of mobile capital to exit, causing nonconverging states to lose their competitiveness in the global economy. The other possibility is that the pressure is ideational; states alter institutions and regulations because a set of beliefs has developed sufficient normative power that leaders fear looking like laggards if they do not adopt similar policies.

The most prominent of these convergence theories is the "race-to-the-bottom" (RTB) hypothesis, an approach that combines a positive theory of regulation with strong normative disapproval of the predicted outcome. This theory assumes that the pressure for convergence comes from the mobility of trade and capital flows, and that the size of these flows overwhelms the ability of the state to act contrary to market forces. In the past thirty years, capital has become increasingly footloose, to the point where states cannot halt capital mobility, even if they tried. In such a world, capital will seek the location where it can earn the highest rate of return. High rates of corporate taxation, strict labor laws, or rigorous environmental protection lower profit rates by raising the costs of production. Capital will therefore engage in regulatory arbitrage, moving to (or importing from) countries with the lowest regulatory standards. States, fearing a loss of their tax base, have no choice but to lower regulatory standards to avoid capital flight.

The RTB hypothesis makes several strong assumptions about the political economy of the nation-state beyond the mobility of capital. First, it assumes that the state responds exclusively to the preferences of capital and not to other constituencies, such as voters, bureaucracies, or interest groups. Second, it assumes that no state has an economy large enough to endow it with market power vis-à-vis global capital. If it did, such a state would be able to set regulatory standards that raise the costs of investment above the market rate, yet still lure capital because of the potential profits from investing in a large market. Finally and most controversially, it presumes that state regulations impose enough of a cost on producers to affect location, regardless of differences in labor productivity. If state regulation of the environment, labor, consumer safety, or taxation do not have an appreciable negative impact on firms, the logic of the RTB hypothesis comes into question. . . .

The predictions of the RTB hypothesis are clear and concise. First, the more exposed a state is to global markets, such as reduced barriers to trade and controls on capital, the more likely its tax and regulatory policies will converge to other states with international exposure. Second, there should be a strong negative correlation between inward capital flows and a country's regulatory standards. Third, this policy convergence will be at the lowest common denominator; in any given regulatory arena, states will gravitate toward the policies of the most laissez-faire country.

RTB predictions about the welfare state more generally are mixed. Scholars . . . point out that increased exposure to global markets should generate more demands on the welfare apparatus because of the distributional effects of globalization. This implies that welfare expenditures should be positively correlated with globalization. . . . Yet RTB theorists point out that states are constrained from raising the revenue to finance these demands due to a race to the bottom in the taxation of mobile factors of production and the reluctance of capital markets to extend credit to countries that run persistent budget deficits. This makes point predictions difficult since at different stages of this argument state expenditures are increasing, then budget deficits are increasing, and then welfare expenditures are declining.

Neoliberal institutionalism differs from the RTB hypothesis by downplaying the magnitude of structural economic factors. States are assumed to have some market power in their relationship with capital. Even if the state imposes regulatory burdens that raise the cost of production, firms will still have an incentive to comply with those rules because of the potential profits of servicing a large market. The neoliberal hypothesis also factors in the costs of changing regulatory standards. National regulation is embedded within a historical framework that constrains political actors. Acting to change this framework incurs costs in social and institutional disruption. In altering these assumptions, the neoliberal approach presents a more conventional picture of the global political economy. States must cope with the externalities of the internationalization of production and need to cooperate to create global public goods (or reduce "public bads"). As a result, the range of possible equilibrium outcomes is greater than a race to the bottom.

Neoliberals argue that convergence is the result of the conscious policy coordination of nation-states, predicting several factors that contribute to cooperative outcomes. Neoliberals predict coordination if there are relatively few actors that are bargaining, if monitoring is easy, and if there are international institutions to enforce the outcome. Therefore, coordination is more likely to occur under the rubric of international organizations than without, and under international organizations with enforcement capabilities than without. Consistent with theories of collective action, an asymmetry of size and power should also contribute to more cooperation. Furthermore, neoliberals would also predict convergence to be stronger among regional institutions than global ones because of the reduced number of actors.

Because of the possibility of multiple equilibria, neoliberal institutionalism is fuzzier about the location of the convergent policies. Neoliberals accept the neorealist assumption that more powerful actors are more likely to have their preferences realized. Unlike neorealists, a liberal approach would predict some accommodation by hegemonic powers to other states' concerns to foster cooperation. Therefore, neoliberals would predict an outcome that varies somewhat from great power preferences. Generally, the predicted outcome is a compromise between laissez-faire and interventionist states, with a strong tilt toward the preferences of the more powerful states. Given that the Organization for Economic Cooperation and Development (OECD) countries are the most powerful in the international system and given that societal preferences in these countries are for strict regulatory standards, this implies a more interventionist bent.

The world society approach eschews the material aspects of globalization, focusing instead on the spread of models and ideas through global cultural and associational processes. In this approach, policy convergence is driven not by capital mobility but rather the development and spread of abstract concepts and the need for nation-states to conform to an ideal of the rationalized bureaucratic state. Once a dominant idea emerges, alternative models and policies lose their legitimacy. This leads to a strong degree of institutional isomorphism. Laggard states emulate the practices of global leaders, causing a convergence of regulatory policies in the process. As with the RTB hypothesis, structure dominates agency. In this case, the structure is global culture rather than the global economy.

The world society model predicts policy convergence, but convergence to which point? The answer here appears to be in favor of more regulation. This permits the "expansive structuration" of the state and the development of new bureaucracies to regulate both society and economy. The structuration process has an implied feedback mechanism; as the state expands, the number of transnational interstate interactions increases, leading to a greater demand for world society integration. . . . It would be hard to reconcile the structuration phenomenon with a convergence toward antistatist policies.

This school of thought is vague on the processes through which convergence occurs, making falsification tests difficult. The literature discusses multiple processes through which states agree on desired policy outcomes. The first is the growth of a global scientific discourse. Once a particular issue area acquires the mantle of scientific inquiry, metanorms governing the discourse are established. This makes it far easier for common models to be developed and emerge.

Second, the establishment of international governmental organizations (IGOs) facilitates the teaching of new policy models and helps less developed countries modify their governance structures to these policies. According to the world society approach, diffusion will be most rapid between like units. IGOs create the image of all states as homogenous units, accelerating the spread of common practices between them. Globalization thus accelerates policy convergence through the proliferation of international organizations, in particular the expansion of the UN system.

Third, states act mimetically to copy the forms and policies of successful nation-states. In the current context, this implies the adaptation by other countries to policies that have been instituted in the United States. It also implies that states on the periphery (i.e., non-OECD countries) will be as willing, if not more so, to adopt convergent policies. Other core states may also converge toward a particular policy, but since these states have a better track record of success, they are likely to resist policies that contravene domestic norms.

The elite consensus approach to policy convergence shares with the world society paradigm the importance of ideational factors in determining convergence but gives a greater role for the agency of states and individuals. This approach . . . emphasizes the role of epistemic communities in bringing about policy convergence. An epistemic community is defined as a network of policy experts who share common principled beliefs over ends, causal beliefs over means, and common standards of accruing and testing new knowledge. These actors play an important role in issue areas where state leaders are uncertain about the consequences of different policy options and where interdependence demands coordination. Under those circumstances, transnational epistemic communities can mold state preferences over various regulatory options, making negotiations easier and more likely to lead to a harmonization of policies.

The causal processes of the elite consensus approach are similar to those of the world society approach. As with the world society view, the development of expert communities in and out of government is a key pathway to elite consensus. . . . Also similar to the world society and neoliberal paradigms, the elite consensus model emphasizes the role of international institutions in forging and promulgating an epistemic community.

There are a few key differences. The elite consensus approach has a relational rather than structural story of convergence. Interdependence is a necessary antecedent to policy coordination. The world society paradigm presumes that states will converge to particular policies regardless of material factors. The elite consensus model argues that before there can be policy coordination, states must at least recognize the existence of policy externalities. Only at this stage can the normative consensus of an epistemic community guide states toward convergence to a particular point. In this way, this approach shares more with the neoliberal paradigm than the world society model. Epistemic communities might contribute to policy convergence, but they are not a sufficient condition.

The two approaches also disagree on the convergence point. The preferred point of convergence depends on the normative bias of the epistemic community; it is not automatically in favor of stricter regulation. It is possible, for example, for there to be an epistemic community of economists that argues for reduced state regulation. . . .

Comparing and contrasting the theories of regulatory policy reveal familiar parallels. Each of these approaches uses ontological givens, limiting assumptions, and causal mechanisms derived from preexisting paradigms of international relations. The RTB hypothesis resembles Marxism in modeling a world of economic determinism. The neoliberal approach is merely an extension of the neoliberal institutionalist paradigm. . . . World society theory borrows from the constructivist and English school of international relations. These approaches posit a world where an ideational structure dominates individual agency. . . .

Another interesting factor is the emphasis placed on international organizations as a means of ensuring policy convergence. Except for the RTB hypothesis, they play an important role in the policy convergence models. In the neoliberal model, international institutions reduce the transaction costs of bargaining and enforcement. The elite consensus and world society approaches proffer a different role for regimes—the provision of norms and discourse that govern international behavior. Again, these functions correspond to those discussed in the broader literature on international institutions.

A comparison of these theories shows that the structural models (RTB and world society) have the comparative advantage of elegance, in that the causal mechanisms and predicted outcomes are clear. This makes these approaches more conceptually elegant and easier to falsify. The structural approaches are also more parsimonious because the key variables are hypothesized to overwhelm all other explanatory factors. The agent-oriented models (neoliberal institutionalism and elite consensus) permit multiple possible outcomes. This makes these approaches potentially more realistic but more difficult to falsify.

THE EMPIRICAL EVIDENCE ON POLICY CONVERGENCE

Beyond its paucity, the empirical literature on policy convergence has several flaws. One problem that carries over from the theories is the difficulty in separating normative agendas from an analytic appraisal of the evidence. These normative biases can be crude, such as nongovernmental organization (NGO) publications intent on painting globalization as an unmitigated bad or an unmitigated good. They can also be subtler, such as scholarly work designed to support corporatist governing structures or particular social movements.

Another difficulty is that few empirical studies genuinely compare the different convergence hypotheses. The lack of empirical work on structural approaches usually limits data to surveys of the advanced industrial states of the OECD. This empirical limitation is unfortunate since the world society approach predicts more dramatic effects in the developing world. Those empirical studies focusing on agent-oriented approaches to policy coordination have frequently used comparative or case-study approaches. Such a dichotomy of empirical work is not surprising. It is significantly easier to develop statistical measures for the structural factors used in the RTB and world society hypotheses. Agent-oriented approaches necessarily allow more contingency in their predictions, and their independent variables are tougher to code across issue areas.

The incommensurate nature of the empirical work makes it difficult to evaluate competing hypotheses, which raises troubling questions. How can the different theories of policy convergence be evaluated against each other? Is it possible to control for omitted variable bias? The answers largely rest on the power of the theories. Omitted variable bias is less problematic with more accurate and complete theories of policy convergence. The empirical work can therefore be judged on whether the hypotheses tested receive any support. If an argument receives weak empirical support *without* controlling for alternatives, it suggests at best that other theories have significant explanatory power, and at worst it suggests the argument being tested is false.

Another potential problem is that much empirical work on globalization and policy formulation focuses more on the direction of policy trajectories and less on whether policies across countries are actually converging. . . . This is a surmountable roadblock because the paradigms discussed above make additional predictions about the direction and location of policy convergence under globalization. These predictions are useful for evaluating the explanatory power of the different theories.

The policies that have been discussed most frequently in terms of convergence include labor standards, environmental regulation, taxation, antitrust issues, consumer health and safety, and the protection of intellectual property rights. Space constraints prevent an exhaustive review of all of these areas; the following sections focus on labor standards and environmental protection.

Labor Standards

Labor standards are broadly defined as the humane treatment of workers by firms and governments. What this means in practice varies. There is a general distinction between "core" labor standards and additional provisions to protect workers' rights. Core standards consist of protections against forced labor, slavery, and child labor; nondiscrimination in employment practices; the right to unionize; and the right to engage in collective bargaining. Additional worker standards include health and safety conditions in the workplace, minimum wages, government provision of unemployment insurance, old age and survivor benefits, and health care.

Policy journals are replete with claims that globalization causes downward pressure on wages and a race to the bottom in labor standards. If this hypothesis were true, one would expect to find worsening labor standards in those countries most exposed to trade and foreign investment. The effect should be especially pronounced in export processing zones (EPZs). These are geographically bounded areas established in less developed countries to attract foreign investment. To invest in these areas, governments offer inducements such as duty-free imports and exports, infrastructure investment, and reduced regulatory interference. This could include exempting the EPZ from any labor legislation. If there is a race to the bottom, it should be most pronounced in EPZs.

There is little empirical evidence to support the RTB hypothesis, but there are anecdotal examples of corporations moving production to countries because of cheap labor and, implicitly, lax labor standards. Yet a 1996 OECD report reviewing the issue concluded: "There is no evidence that freedom-of-association rights worsened in any of the countries that liberalized trade. . . . The strongest finding shows a positive correlation between successfully sustained trade reforms and improvements in core standards." Statistical tests support this assertion. . . . Later studies have also demonstrated a weak to nonexistent correlation between labor standards and export patterns. The relationship between foreign direct investment (FDI) and labor standards is strongly positive, given that in the past decade more than 90 percent of FDI took place in OECD countries, which have the highest labor standards.

The data on EPZs also fail to support the image of a race to the bottom. Some countries—Pakistan, Bangladesh, Panama, and Zimbabwe—exempt their EPZs from regulation covering core labor standards. Contrary to the RTB hypothesis, this has failed to put pressure on other countries to relax labor standards in their EPZs. Several countries, including the Dominican Republic and the Philippines, reversed course in the mid-1990s, introducing labor standards in their EPZs where none previously existed. An International Labour Organization (ILO) report reveals no evidence that countries with strong trade union presence have suffered any investment loss in their EPZs. A World Bank survey notes a strong positive correlation between higher occupational safety and health conditions and foreign investment in EPZs. Furthermore, a comparison of wages in EPZs relative to the rest of the host country reveals that wages are on average higher in the EPZ.

Similarly, the world society approach also finds limited support. As noted, there has been a secular increase in government commitment to labor standards, which supports the structuration hypothesis. In contrast to the world society approach, the effect has been more pronounced in core countries than in those on the periphery. David Strang and Patricia Mei Yin Chang examine whether states adopting ILO conventions increase welfare expenditures that are included in the expanded category of labor standards. They find that ILO ratification has a positive and significant effect on eighteen OECD countries, even when trade exposure is included as a control for external exposure. This result suggests the power of ideational factors relative to the material effects of globalization. Yet there is no effect of ILO ratification on welfare expenditures in less developed countries, which is where the world society paradigm would predict the greatest effects. The limited area of policy convergence on labor standards supports an elite consensus explanation more than a world society view.

Neoliberalism has only limited success in explaining the pattern of convergence. If Strang and Chang are correct, then the source of convergence among OECD countries is the ILO, an organization that has no sanctioning power. A variant of neoliberalism would argue that the ILO's extensive monitoring abilities suffice to ensure compliance. The neoliberal paradigm can explain the U.S. inability to convert its preferences into global policy convergence by connecting labor standards to trade issues. From the Eisenhower administration onward, the United States has been unsuccessful in its attempts to add labor issues onto the international trade agenda. Less developed countries resist this attempt because they prefer that the issue be handled by the ILO and not impair access to First World markets. The U.S. effort to move the monitoring of labor standards from the ILO to the WTO, with its more powerful enforcement mechanisms, is consistent with neoliberal theory. Yet the United States has also been willing to circumvent the ILO, applying unilateral economic sanctions to force developing states to tighten their labor standards. This behavior is harder to square with neoliberal institutionalism.

Evidence from regional institutions is also mixed. The mere existence of supranational labor standards in the European Union and North American Free Trade Association (NAFTA) suggests international organizations can foster the harmonization of labor standards. Whether these standards have any effect is another question. A comparison of social insurance policies in Europe shows a secular increase in these policies across the board, but it also shows greater convergence among countries not in the European Union than those within it. This study's data ended in 1985, before Maastricht, but they still cast significant doubt on the neoliberal hypothesis.

In the aggregate, the picture of labor standards is one where there has been a convergence in the OECD countries toward strict standards, while among developing countries there is a slow drift toward the enforcement of core labor standards. This pattern is inconsistent with either structural approach and fits uneasily with the neoliberal hypothesis. The elite consensus model would predict this outcome, given the extent of ideational interaction among the OECD nations. To date, there has been no study to see if epistemic communities play a causal role in determining labor standards. Another interesting test for the future would be whether new OECD members that are still developing, such as Mexico, Poland, or South Korea, start to converge toward the OECD norm.

Environmental Protection

Issues that fall under the environmental umbrella range from the protection of endangered species to the prevention of global warming. As with the literature on labor standards, the structural explanations are more commonly tested using statistical evidence while agent-based paradigms rely more on case studies.

There are examples of countries, such as Ireland, purposefully lowering environmental standards in order to attract dirty industries. This example appears to be anomalous because there is no evidence that other countries have adopted this strategy in response to Ireland's success. . . .

Statistically, two categories of tests have been tried. The first type seeks to determine if environmental regulations adversely affect trade patterns. If this is true, it would support one leg of the RTB hypothesis—i.e., that strict environmental standards weaken the competitiveness of industry. The second type tests whether firms choose their investment locations based upon environmental regulations. . . . This would suggest the potential for strict regulations to affect investment decisions. Yet tests of investment decisions suggest otherwise. . . . Increases in regulation by one standard deviation leads to at most a 1.8 percent decline in investment. Investigations at the country level confirm the absence of an RTB dynamic in explaining firm decisions. . . . The conclusions of both the international and domestic studies of industry location are that environmental regulations do not deter investment to any statistically or economically significant degree.

The world society approach receives greater support in this arena than for labor standards. . . . The results show a consistent growth in the number of environmental associations, treaties, and organizations, to the point where the structuration of the global environmental regime reduces the need for new organizations.

The evidence is compelling but . . . incomplete. First, it is an open question whether these results demonstrate correlation or causation. It is not shocking that the growth of scientific unions is correlated with the growth of environmental associations, but it is unclear which causes which. Second, the dependent variable of international agreements masks the fact that these agreements often impose different regulatory standards on different countries. The Montreal Protocol on stratospheric ozone, or the Kyoto Protocol on global warming, imposes far more rigorous regulatory limits on the developed countries. Even if there is policy coordination, there is not necessarily convergence. Third, far less care is taken . . . to test the theory against alternative hypotheses. Variables consistent with alternative explanations—growth in global GDP, the rate of urbanization, the growth of international trade, the distribution of power, changes in communication technologies—are not included in the regressions.

The elite consensus argument also tests its hypotheses on the forces behind multinational agreements to regulate the environment. Instead of statistical evidence, the empirical works focuses on case studies of regimes governing environmental issues such as deforestation or stratospheric ozone. . . .

There remain significant criticisms of this narrative. A review of most of the international treaties negotiated since the 1972 Stockholm conference shows that scientific evidence has played a surprisingly small role in issue definition, fact-finding, bargaining, and regime strengthening. . . .

Another problem is the potential marginalization of the epistemic community over time. Analysis of the various UN conferences reveals that over time states have become adept at excluding various NGO groups from key bargaining sessions. The inclusion of other professional groups, including economists and corporate officers, also undercuts the power of the environmental epistemic community. Finally, this approach overlooks the role that domestic politics plays in implementing environmental accords. Case studies suggest that countries adhere to environmental accords as much as their domestic political institutions permit.

The neoliberal approach argues that policy coordination is determined by the number of actors, the power of international organizations, the amount of available information, and how much convergence has distributional consequences. For environmental issues, the neoliberal hypothesis holds up well. Policy convergence on stratospheric ozone depletion has been assisted by the power of the Montreal Protocol to permit the sanctioning of noncompliant states, as well as the ability of the Global Environment Facility to proffer carrots to reluctant states. Observations show a similar process to explain the degree of environmental cooperation in the European Union and NAFTA. The uneven pattern of success in deforestation prevention correlates directly with the extent of World Bank leverage over recipient countries. The lack of progress on global warming is also consistent with the neoliberal hypothesis. Objections in the United States about the Kyoto Protocol's costs of implementation, the distribution of costs, and the lack of enforcement measures have made implementation unlikely.

The neoliberal paradigm also receives support from the effect of the WTO on environmental policy. The WTO represents a classic case of a cooperation outcome, in which each party sacrifices a little to obtain the larger benefits of cooperation. The benefit for the WTO was freer trade. The developed world has paid for this by having to curtail environmental regulations that are deemed as restricting trade. Examples include WTO rulings against U.S. environmental laws such as the Marine Mammal Protection Act, the Clean Air Act, and the Endangered Species Act. The WTO has also been used to alter EU policy on leghold traps. This has drawn considerable ire from antiglobalization activists who claim that the WTO will force a reduction of environmental standards. Although this claim is exaggerated, the reaction supports the neoliberal hypothesis that strong international organizations can drive policy convergence.

The pattern in environmental regulation mirrors that of labor standards. There is an upward convergence among OECD countries and a slow and erratic upswing toward more protection in the developing world. The key difference from the story about labor standards is that the divergent trends in environmental regulation are codified by international regimes. This suggests that the neoliberal paradigm may have more explanatory power for environmental issues than the elite consensus model.

CONCLUSIONS

Most discussions of globalization stress two facets. The first is the magnitude of private economic forces such as capital flows and traded goods. The second is the deterministic quality of the phenomena; once states decide to lower their barriers to exchange, a Pandora's box is unleashed that cannot be reversed. A review of the policy convergence literature suggests both claims have been exaggerated. Although globalization has increased the size of transnational economic flows, it has not forced a race to the bottom in regulatory standards. Ideational forces have played an equally significant role in determining the rate and location of policy convergence on labor and environmental standards. Where harmonization has occurred, it has been a conscious choice of states made under the aegis of an international organization.

The lack of support for the RTB argument is striking. This absence of supporting evidence continues if one looks at other issue areas. Most econometric studies show that increased capital mobility has not constrained the ability of states to tax capital. One comes to a similar conclusion with regard to the regulation of consumer health and safety. Even in macroeconomic policy, an area commonly thought to provide the strongest support for the RTB hypothesis, the empirical evidence is debatable. Repeated studies show that domestic institutions, interests, and political parties have a significant effect on fiscal and monetary policies. This sort of variation is inconsistent with a race to the bottom.

This result is not particularly surprising when put in historical perspective. The current era shows a pattern similar to the previous era of globalization. In the late nineteenth century, there was an enormous increase in the flows of capital, goods, and labor among countries in the Atlantic basin. . . . Despite the magnitude of these flows, states responded to the trend toward globalization by increasing tariff and immigration barriers; initiating regulatory standards for consumer safety, labor, and the environment; and developing regional institutions (including a predecessor to the European Central Bank) to cope with the vicissitudes of financial markets.[1] The process of globalization did not constrain states from making autonomous policy choices.

Economic determinism can be rejected as an explanation for international regulatory regimes; where does that leave us? Most immediate is the need for more refined theories and better empirical work because good theories can be easily falsified. If the structural approaches have less empirical support, it is partly because their predictions are more precise and thus easier to falsify. The agent-based approaches to policy convergence must be able to predict the location of policy convergence better. Empirically, tests need to be developed that compare multiple theories of policy convergence against each other.

One theoretical possibility is the elimination of the agent-structure ontology as a way of crafting new theories about the state. . . . The debate about globalization has been misdirected because of squabbles about whether the

---

1. Kevin O'Rourke and Jeffrey Williamson, *Globalization and History* (Cambridge, Mass.: MIT Press, 1999); Karl Polanyi, *The Great Transformation* (Boston: Beacon Press, 1944).

primacy of the state has been threatened.[2] Instead, globalization must be understood as a phenomenon that simultaneously affects states directly and international relations through reconstitution of the state. Such an approach mirrors the repeated calls from international relations scholars to move past the agent–structure debate to a more integrative approach.[3] Given the ambiguous empirical support for existing theories of convergence, this is a promising way of improving causal inferences. To date, this call for changing the ontology of international relations theory has produced some trenchant criticism but little in the way of positive theorizing. The failure of the discourse on globalization to propose a genuinely new set of ontological givens suggests that these divisions are more difficult to overcome than previously thought.

Another possible research avenue comes from the recognition that globalization does not eliminate international political economy theories as much as find new issue areas for their application. . . . The elimination of capital controls forced a deeper level of policy coordination. The reduction of tariffs and quotas has similarly led to a change from negotiating over tariffs to negotiating over regulatory policies that can act as trade barriers. Globalization has altered the international political economy through the generation of a new set of contentious global issues that were previously purely national. This has led to new arenas of bargaining, not a new global politics.

Looked at in this way, an approach with its foundations in realism might prove to be useful. A realist theory of policy convergence would assume that states retain policy autonomy and that they can use their market power and access as a tool for negotiating and coercing. Bargaining occurs when regulatory convergence increases the size of the economic pie but also redistributes benefits toward states with domestic regulations close to the agreed-upon standard. Regional trading agreements are a strategy for expanding the domain of a state's regulatory standards and increasing leverage in global negotiations. Such an approach would also highlight something missing from existing empirical work: the use of economic coercion by the great powers to force other states to accept their regulatory standards. To date, realists have either ignored the globalization phenomenon or minimized its importance. An approach that concedes the significance of globalization but asks how states try to maximize their relative advantage in such a world might be fruitful.

The absence of a race to the bottom also suggests more research on the question of why the power of capital is constrained. The absence of private firms influencing the pace and location of policy convergence suggests that something has been overlooked in the firm–state dynamic. Firms might be

2. Ian Clark, *Globalization and International Relations Theory* (Oxford, U.K.: Oxford University Press, 1999).

3. Alexander Wendt, "The Agent-Structure Problem in International Relations Theory," *International Organization* 41, No. 3 (1987), pp. 335–370; Ian Clark, *Globalization and International Relations Theory*.

more constrained in their economic decision making than previously supposed. This could be due to the market power of states, or the dependence of multinational firms upon the institutions developed in their home countries. Another possibility is that the economic effects of globalization vary sectorally. In industries where asset specificity is minimal and labor costs are an important component of production, races to the bottom may be more likely to exist.

Finally, the study of globalization needs to be rescued from the pop commentators. As noted in the introduction, one reason the globalization phenomenon is important is the perception by many scholars and policymakers that it transforms international politics. The evidence to date rejects this perception. Globalization is not deterministic; there is no single predicted location for policy convergence. The ability of states to cooperate and their ability to agree on norms of governance determines the extent of policy convergence. These factors are at the core of the principal theories of international political economy. Globalization has led to the emergence of new issues to be analyzed by international relations scholars; it does not imply that new paradigms are needed to explain these issues.

IV

MONEY AND FINANCE

The international economy, like domestic economies, requires a common monetary standard to function smoothly. For individuals and firms to buy and sell and to save and invest, they need some generally acceptable and predictable unit of account against which other goods can be measured, a medium of exchange with which transactions can be carried out, and a store of value in which wealth can be held. National currencies serve this purpose within countries: for example, Americans buy, sell, save, and invest in dollars. In international trade and payments, a variety of possible common measures can be imagined; in practice, however, the two pure cases are a commodity standard and an international currency standard. Economic actors could use a widely traded commodity, such as gold or pork bellies, against which to measure other goods; or they might arrive at some fictitious unit in which goods could be priced. The former approximates the classical gold standard; the latter, present-day special drawing rights, which are a sort of "paper gold" issued by the International Monetary Fund and equal to a mix of national currencies. Because reaching agreement on a fictitious international currency is difficult, such national currencies as the dollar or the pound sterling have often been used as the basis for international payments.

If the international monetary system provides the measures needed to conduct world trade and payments, the international financial system provides the means to carry out trade and payments. For many hundreds of years, financial institutions—especially banks—have financed trade among clients in different nations, sold and bought foreign currencies, transferred money from one country to another, and lent capital for overseas investment. If, as is often averred, the international monetary system is the "Great Wheel" that enables goods to move in international trade, the international financial system is the grease that allows the wheel itself to turn.

In the modern era (since 1820 or so), there have been, essentially, four well-functioning international monetary systems; each has had corresponding international financial characteristics. From about 1820 until World War I, the world was on or near the classical gold standard, in which many major national currencies were tied to gold at a legally fixed rate. In principle, as J. Lawrence Broz and Barry Eichengreen explain (in Readings 13 and 14, respectively) the gold standard was self-regulating; should any national currency (and economy) move out of balance, it would be forced back into equilibrium by the very operation of the system. In practice, the pre–World War I system was actually a gold-sterling standard; the British pound sterling, backed by a strong government and the world's leading financial center, was "as good as gold," and most international trade and payments were carried out in sterling.

The world financial system in the century before World War I was indeed dominated by British banks, which financed much of world trade and channeled enormous amounts of investment capital to such rapidly developing countries as the United States, Australia, Argentina, and South Africa. As time wore on, the financial institutions of other European powers, especially France and Germany, also began to expand abroad. The result was a highly integrated system of international monetary and financial interactions under the Pax Britannica. In Reading 13, J. Lawrence Broz argues that this relatively smoothly functioning system was due largely to the concerns of the dominant private interests in the world's monetary and financial leaders.

Even before World War I, however, strains and rivalries were beginning to test the system. Once the war started, in 1914, international trade and payments collapsed: of all the world's major financial markets, only New York stayed open for the duration of the conflict. Indeed, by the time World War I ended, the center of international finance had shifted from London to New York, and Wall Street remained the world's principal lender until the Great Depression of the 1930s.

As might be expected, given the reduced economic might of Great Britain, the prewar gold-sterling standard could not be rebuilt. Yet neither was the United States, which was beset by the isolationist-internationalist conflict at home, willing to simply replace Great Britain at the apex of the world monetary system. What emerged was the so-called gold exchange standard, whereby most countries went back to tying their currencies to gold but no single national currency came to dominate the others. Dollars, sterling, and French francs were all widely used in world trade and payments, yet, given the lack of lasting international monetary cooperation in the period, the arrangement was quite unstable and short-lived. Normal international economic conditions were not restored until 1924, and within a few years, the Depression had brought the system crashing down. With the collapse of the gold exchange standard and the onset of the Depression and World War II, the international monetary and financial systems remained in disarray until after 1945.

As World War II came to an end, the Allied powers, led by the United States, began reconstructing an international monetary system under the Bretton Woods agreement. This system was based, in the monetary sphere, on an American dollar tied to gold at the rate of thirty-five dollars an ounce;

other Western currencies were, in turn, tied to the dollar. This was a modified version of the pre-1914 gold standard, with the dollar at its center rather than sterling. As in the Pax Britannica, massive flows of capital from the leading nation—Great Britain, in the first instance; the United States, in the second—were crucial to the proper functioning of the mechanism. Whereas in the British case these capital flows were primarily private loans, from 1945 to 1965 they were essentially government or multilateral loans and foreign direct investment. After 1965, private international finance once again become significant, rapidly reaching historically unprecedented proportions and developing new characteristics.

Even as the new international financial system, generally known as the Euromarket, was gathering steam, the Bretton Woods monetary system was beginning to weaken. In particular, it was becoming more and more difficult to maintain the dollar's price of thirty-five dollars an ounce. As pressure built on the dollar and attempts at reform stagnated, the Richard Nixon administration finally decided that the system was unsustainable. In August 1971, President Nixon "closed the gold window," ending the dollar's free convertibility into gold. The dollar was soon devalued, and by 1975, the gold-dollar standard had been replaced by the current floating-rate system. In Reading 14, Barry Eichengreen evaluates the ability of an international political explanation—the so-called theory of hegemonic stability—to explain the evolution of international monetary relations across these historical systems.

Under the current system of floating exchange rates, the value of most currencies is set, more or less freely, by private traders in world currency markets. Thus, the values of the dollar, the yen, the pound, and so on fluctuate on international currency markets. This has led to frequent and rapid changes in the relative prices of major currencies, as well as to frequent complaints about the unplanned nature of the new system. Because of the central role of the U.S. dollar, even in today's floating-rate system, changes in American economic policy can drive the dollar up and down dramatically, in ways that have important effects on the economy of the United States and of the rest of the world.

The "unholy trinity" of a fixed exchange rate, capital mobility, and autonomous monetary policy—and the necessary trade-offs engendered by the pursuit of these three goals—is central to understanding the current floating-rate system and the potential for cooperation among the world's leading nations in international monetary affairs. This problem is examined by Benjamin J. Cohen (Reading 15). In Reading 16, Jeffry A. Frieden discusses the domestic societal implications of the trade-offs involved, arguing that interest groups and voters will vary in their views on the desirability of one exchange rate policy or another.

In the 1970s, as American inflation rates rose, the dollar's value dropped relative to other major currencies. From 1979 to 1985, American monetary policy concentrated on fighting inflation while fiscal policy was expansionary, leading to a dramatic rise in the dollar's value. Although inflation was brought down, the strong dollar wreaked havoc with the ability of many American industries to compete internationally. In the mid-1980s, the dollar dropped back down to its lowest levels in nearly forty years, and, since the 1990s, it has gone up and down continually.

Through all these fluctuations, there was dissatisfaction in many quarters about the underlying uncertainty concerning international monetary and financial trends. Today, currencies fluctuate widely, many of the world's major nations are experiencing unprecedented trade surpluses or deficits, and capital flows across borders in enormous quantities.

Monetary uncertainty has led some nations to seek security in a variety of alternative institutions. Some countries and observers support the development of a new international money, of which special drawing rights might be a precursor. Others desire a return to the gold standard and the monetary discipline that this system implied. The principal strategy has been to seek stability through cooperative regional agreements.

The most important of these regional monetary agreements is Europe's Economic and Monetary Union (EMU). In 1999 the members of the EMU introduced a single currency, the euro, which has quickly gained a place as one of the world's three leading currencies. Matthew Gabel, in Reading 17, describes and analyzes citizen attitudes toward EMU in Europe. His results suggest that self-interest shapes attitudes toward monetary union in a manner consistent with Jeffry Frieden's (Reading 16) interest-based theory of exchange rate policy.

In international finance, the period since 1965 has been extraordinarily eventful. The Euromarket has grown to several trillion dollars, and international banking has become one of the great growth industries in the world economy. The recent explosion of international finance is unprecedented. Net international bond and bank lending amounted to $865 billion in 1997, having risen from just $245 billion five years earlier. Capital outflows from the advanced economies were $4,148 billion in 2007, in contrast to $52 billion in the late 1970s; moreover, almost two-thirds of such outflows currently consist of portfolio investment while only one-third is foreign direct investment, the reverse of forty years ago. Indeed, in the late 1970s, total global outflows of portfolio capital averaged $15 billion a year, whereas between 2004 and 2007, they averaged $2,509 billion a year, a nearly 170-fold increase.

To put these annual flows in perspective, capital outflows were equivalent to 7 percent of world merchandise trade in the late 1970s but averaged 15 percent in the 1990s and 19 percent between 2000 and 2007. Likewise, in 1980, cross-border transactions in stocks and bonds were equal to less than 10 percent of the gross domestic product (GDP) of all major industrial countries, whereas today they are equivalent to more than twice the GDP of the United States and Germany, and to three times the GDP of France and Canada.

In addition, recent changes in regulations and technology have made it possible for money to move across borders almost instantly, giving rise to massive, short-term international financial transactions. By 1997, for instance, the total amount outstanding of such short-financial "derivatives," including those traded both over the counter and on exchanges, was more than $40 trillion. Today, foreign exchange trading in the world's financial centers averaged more than $3.2 trillion a day, equivalent to $2.2 billion per minute and to a hundred times the amount of world trade each day.[1]

For developing countries, financial globalization has been a mixed blessing. On the one hand, improved access to burgeoning international financial markets has meant that more capital is available for development. On the other hand, financial crises in East Asia, Latin America, and Russia in the late 1990s and early 2000s revealed a number of costly problems and imperfections in international finance that threaten to reduce or eliminate the gains for developing countries. The most notable problems involve volatility in capital flows driven by herding behavior among investors and speculative currency attacks. Sergio L. Schmukler (Reading 18) examines the benefits and costs of financial globalization and recommends more international cooperation to address its downsides. His observations are all the more relevant in the wake of the global financial crisis of 2008–2009, which began in the United States but spread quickly to developing countries.

Among scholars, the nature of international monetary and financial relations raises important analytical issues. As in other arenas, the very rapid development of globe-straddling international financial markets has led some to believe that the rise of supranational financial actors has eroded the power of national states. In this view, international monetary relations essentially serve increasingly to enrich global international investors and their allies in such international institutions as the International Monetary Fund (IMF). Other analysts believe that national governments are still the primary determinants of international monetary and financial trends. The specific policies of major states toward their own banks and currencies are, in this view, set in line with national interests; banks and currency movements are instruments of national policy, and not the other way around. The tension between a monetary and financial system that is, in a sense, beyond the reach of individual states and currencies and banks that clearly have home countries gives rise to a fundamental tension in world politics and in the study of the international political economy.

NOTE

1. These figures are from the International Monetary Fund's *Balance of Payments Yearbook and International Financial Statistics;* from the Bank for International Settlements, *Annual Report* (Basel: Bank for International Settlements [BIS], various years, and from Jeffry A. Frieden, "Invested Interests: The Politics of National Economic Policies in a World of Global Finance," *International Organization* 45, 4 (1991): 428.

13

The Domestic Politics of International Monetary Order: The Gold Standard

J. LAWRENCE BROZ

In the late nineteenth and early twentieth centuries, the world's principal econo-
mies were tied together by the classical gold standard. The stability of this inter-
national monetary system depended on the accommodating policies of the major
financial powers. J. Lawrence Broz argues that these policies, in turn, rested on
domestic societal foundations. He surveys the British, French, and German
experiences, showing the domestic coalitional bases of support for their contri-
butions to the operation of the gold standard.

An international monetary regime is a set of clearly defined principles, rules, and conventions that regulate and harmonize the economic policies of member nations. From the perspective of international political economy, such a regime is something of an international public good. When a sufficient number of governments commit credibly to a set of international monetary rules, the result is that goods, services, and capital can flow across borders relatively unimpeded by currency concerns, creating joint-welfare gains and promoting technical efficiency. From a perspective of comparative politics, however, a smoothly functioning monetary regime is far from a natural state of affairs. Adherence to a common set of monetary rules and conventions requires a certain degree of macroeconomic-policy cooperation among member governments, despite potentially vast differences in the domestic constraints confronting policy makers. The overriding political obstacle in the way of establishing and maintaining a multilateral commitment to a common set of exchange-rate rules is that national politicians face heterogeneous *domestic* electorates and organized constituencies, not homogenous global ones. According to this view, the paradox is not the difficulty of designing a stable international monetary regime in a world of opportunistic but like-minded national governments, but that such systems, composed of an extremely diverse group of nation-states, have ever existed, let alone operated relatively smoothly for extended periods of time.

The literature on international political economy offers several solutions. One focuses on the existence of a dominant economic power in the world economy, a "hegemon," that either unilaterally provides the international public good or leads the coordination effort that produces adherence to the rules of the game. The internal logic of the argument is simple: only a state large enough to appropriate a significant share of the benefits of producing a public good like international monetary stability would have the incentive to perform the functions necessary to assure such stability. Empirical work, however, finds this hegemonic-stability thesis a weak predictor of the level of international monetary cooperation: hegemony is associated with elements of both stability and extreme instability. Logical flaws have also been uncovered. Most problematic is the supposition that the strongest incentives and constraints that states face originate at the international level, which trivializes the role of domestic political conditions in shaping the macroeconomic choices of states. Likewise, functional theories of international regimes, which predict cooperation in the absence of hegemony, also give analytical primacy to problems of international-level collective action. Here, cooperation leading to greatly expanded joint welfare gains (assuming shared preferences) can occur in the presence of international institutions because such institutions reduce information, communication, and enforcement costs.

A final possibility . . . is that, at both the international and domestic levels, a stable regime has dynamic effects that create a kind of "virtuous circle" in support of the system. At the international level, the increased trade and investment the regime engenders encourages nations to commit to the regime by offering improvements in national economic welfare. At the domestic level, the existence of exchange-rate predictability in one part of the world economy gives internationally oriented interest groups (for instance, international banks, multinational investors and corporations, and major exporters) in as yet unaffiliated areas a stronger incentive to encourage their governments to associate with the regime. . . .

Despite obvious differences, these approaches see the essential problem as one of coordinating the behavior of national governments who have, in one way or another, come to regard a certain exchange-rate regime as a common national objective. That is, regardless of the processes by which international monetary regimes are created and maintained, these perspectives treat all members of a regime as having homogenous preferences in regard to currency issues. As a result, the analytical problem becomes how a group of like-minded national governments resolve the international collective-action problems (for instance, free-riding, ex-post opportunism) that normally constrain the production of international public goods to suboptimal levels.

The approach of this chapter turns the public-goods puzzle "outside-in." The underlying premise that all parties to an exchange-rate regime share the same objectives in the same order of priority is treated as problematic. This supposition is grounded in the logic of comparative political economy: that the preferences and constraints influencing policy formation diverge markedly across countries. Nations differ in their political, economic, and institutional characteristics, and these differences make it highly improbable that national policy preferences will converge sufficiently to make international agreements on currency values simply a matter of establishing credible commitments and effective enforcement mechanisms to prevent defections of the "beggar-thy-neighbor" sort.

The argument advanced in this chapter allows for the possibility of stable international monetary regimes in conjunction with *heterogeneous* national policy preferences. Participants of a regime can have different—even conflicting—national preferences on exchange-rate policy if regime stability entails a *specialization of tasks* among members of the system, whereby members of different preference and power perform different regime-stabilizing functions. The analytical point of departure is still . . . [the] extension of public-goods theory to the international arena. However, there is no theoretical reason requiring any one nation-state to provide all of these functions. Instead, a division of responsibility may arise due to *asymmetries of interest* among states (which is a function of domestic politics) regarding the importance of these goods, and due to *asymmetries of power* among states (which is a function of the relative international positions of nation-states) in the global system.

The place to begin is with comparative politics. Nations differ with respect to their social, economic, and political characteristics; so we can expect that they will attach different values to the fundamental trade-offs entailed in adhering to alternative international monetary regimes. The primary efficiency advantage of stable exchange rates is that international trade and investment can be conducted with minimal risk of capital losses due to currency fluctuations. The well-known trade-off is that stable (fixed) exchange rates require the subordination of domestic monetary policy to currency and balance-of-payments considerations. . . . [A]ctors deeply involved in international trade and payments (export-oriented producers of tradable goods, international merchants, global investors) favor stability in exchange rates, while actors whose economic activity is confined primarily to the domestic economy (import-competing producers of tradable goods, producers of non-tradables) favor the domestic-monetary flexibility that comes with variable exchange rates. From this base it is a relatively small step to move to the comparative level: the dissimilar composition of nations in terms of their "production profiles" suggests the likelihood of *uncommon* national objectives with respect to the issue of exchange-rate variability.

The fundamental point is that national governments pursue international monetary policies for domestic political reasons having to do with the policy interests of important social groups and coalitions. But the processes of policy formation cannot be considered in a national vacuum. Exchange rates are, after all, relational. More importantly, the actions of at least the major states in the system inevitably affect the international monetary system, and thus their own domestic economies. As a result, analysis must also consider how the policy choices of major states affect the operation and stability of the international monetary system and, in so doing, feed back upon the domestic processes of exchange rate policy making.

Domestic groups and coalitions lobby government because they know that policy has direct effects on their welfare through its national impact. Domestic groups and coalitions in major "price-maker" countries, however, are also aware that government policy has indirect effects on their welfare by way of its impact on the international monetary order. Awareness of this second-order international impact suggests that groups and coalitions at least partially internalize the international externalities of their governments' actions. Full internalization does not occur because groups in other countries absorb some of the benefits or bear some of the costs of the externalities as well. And because *the international spillovers of domestic policy choices may be positive as well as negative*, a stable international monetary regime can exist even when the preferences of major states vary widely.

In essence, this is the "joint product" model applied to the workings of international monetary systems. States produce and consume two goods: a private good (happiness of the domestic dominant coalition) and a public good (international monetary stability). As long as the production of joint products involves a supply technology in which the private outputs cannot feasibly be separated from the associated collective outputs, then a convergence can arise between the private (national) and social (international) costs of public goods provision. Hence, for states large enough in economic terms to produce systemic effects, there can be incentives to absorb the overall costs of producing systemic benefits, if the private goods they seek cannot be produced without generating the associated public goods. Nevertheless, it is the excludable private benefits that drive the micro-processes of international monetary order: domestic politics are primary, while the international consequences of domestic policy choices are viewed largely as by-products. . . .

Consider the following example. There are two major nation-states in the world, state A and state B. State A prefers stable currency while state B is inclined toward domestic monetary independence. These heterogeneous preferences reflect differences in domestic political situations: the dominant political coalition in state A prefers that its government maintain stable currency over competing macroeconomic goals; the dominant coalition in state B prefers domestic macroeconomic policy flexibility over stable currency values. If we assume that state A is a large state in global economic terms, its preference for stable currency can be expected to have important and beneficial global spillovers: its strong commitment to sound money means, for example, that its national currency is well positioned to serve internationally as a medium of exchange and a reliable store of value. State B, however, can also be expected to take on a system-sustaining role—if only as a means of advancing its preference for domestic macroeconomic autonomy. Because disruptions to the flow of capital in the international economy can threaten state B's domestically oriented macroeconomic agenda (including, for instance, stable interest rates, a steady rate of economic growth, low unemployment), state B may find it advantageous to play a stabilizing role alongside state A—by acting as the system's emergency source of liquidity, for example. Since its dominant preference is to remain as free as possible to run the domestic macroeconomic policies it chooses, undertaking the role of systemic lender of last resort can serve this end by forestalling sudden and destabilizing capital flows. A *division of labor* results in the provision of the regime's sustaining functions: state A provides the international system with a key currency while state B serves as the system's lender of last resort. In both cases these are the positive international externalities of disunited, domestically determined preferences. They are externalities because the governments that actually run system-sustaining policies have no special desire to help stabilize the international system. Instead, governments are driven by domestic imperatives, to satisfy the dominant coalition. The result is a state of international relations in which unilateral actions taken for domestic reasons generate positive spillover effects for other nations.

This argument suggests that a stable international monetary order need not require implicit or explicit agreement among member states about the characteristics and requirements of membership; policy divergence and systemic stability are not logically incompatible. Nor is it necessary that a hegemon exist to provide the requisite stabilizing functions. While stability does seem to require the existence of the equilibrating functions identified by Kindleberger, member states can have divergent objectives if the international externalities of their national-policy choices are strongly positive. International stability does not mean that all states adopt identical policies, but policies that through their external effects largely complement or offset one another.

This chapter, in short, addresses the paradox of how international public goods are provided when countries are allowed to have different or conflicting policy preferences. Just as a true application of collective-goods theory undermines the hegemonic-stability thesis—privileged groups need not be limited to a single state—so, too, does the logic of the positive-externalities framework. The logic that says international economic stability results when countries with homogenous preferences solve the free-rider problem is undone when heterogeneity of preferences is allowed to enhance the probability of stability. In its place comes the logic of international stability derived from the sum of the (positive) externalities produced by major states advancing their *uncommon*, national interests. . . . [T]he systemic characteristic of stability can be the consequence of the individual actions of major states, taken for domestic political reasons. Thus international stability can arise even if national preferences vary significantly and even if no dominant stabilizer sets out to produce this result, if the externalities of individual state behavior are allowed to be positive as well as negative.

The following section applies this logic to the archetypal case of international monetary order: the era of the classical gold standard. The evidence supports two main predictions. First, the degree to which individual nations accepted the principles of the gold standard varied dramatically. These differences, in turn, are shown to have resulted from the fact that members did not share the same political and economic objectives—a function of distinct domestic socioeconomic conditions. The comparative portion of this chapter is devoted to identifying the monetary preferences of major states in the system—Great Britain, France, Germany after unification—and linking these policy preferences to each nation's unique social, economic, and political structures. Second, the evidence conforms to the expectation that the pursuit of national interests can have beneficial global spillovers; that nations pushing their self interests can have strongly positive externalities that facilitate the production of international public goods. Here, the focus is on the global effects of each nation's policy choices. Overall the evidence supports the dual claims that national (individual) as opposed to international (collective) interests motivated state behavior during the era of the gold standard and that the global result was a fixed exchange-rate regime that operated smoothly for several decades. This chapter's conclusion summarizes the findings and briefly extends the argument to the Bretton Woods system and the European Monetary System.

THE CLASSICAL GOLD STANDARD

Like other international monetary orders, an international gold standard is supposed to consist of a group of sovereign countries bound together by a common commitment to certain fundamental *principles* of monetary organization and *rules* of monetary behavior. In a true gold standard, there are two basic principles. First, a country must commit its monetary authorities to freely exchange (buy and sell) the domestic currency for gold at a fixed rate without limitation or condition. Second, monetary officials must pledge to allow residents and nonresidents the absolute freedom to export and import gold in whatever quantities they desire. When a group of countries bind themselves to the first principle, fixed exchange rates are established; when they commit to respect the free flow of gold, a pure fixed-exchange-rate mechanism of balance-of-payments adjustment comes into being. Thus a stylized international gold standard is a system of states linked together by two general monetary principles (to uphold the gold convertibility of their national currencies at par; to allow gold to cross national borders unimpeded) and two basic rules of behavior governing international monetary policy (to deflate in the event of a gold drain; to inflate in the event of an inflow). As an economic model, this describes an efficient, self-sustaining system for reducing the transactions costs of international exchange and investment and providing a nearly automatic mechanism for reconciling international imbalances. As an approximation of late nineteenth- and early twentieth-century reality, however, the model is quite inappropriate.

As the following comparison will illustrate, there were sharp national differences in the degree to which countries maintained a commitment to the underlying principles and operational rules of the gold standard.

Among the European countries, England stayed most consistently on the gold standard, meaning both that the pound sterling was convertible into gold on demand at the legally defined rate and that individuals had complete freedom to export or import gold. On the continent, in contrast, free and unlimited convertibility was by no means guaranteed, especially if gold was sought for export purposes, and monetary officials often placed administrative barriers on the free flow of gold. As for the rules of the game, the received wisdom today is that all gold-standard countries engaged at times in practices that were in "violation" of the regime's rules. Although this conclusion is certainly valid in general, it masks significant national differences.

Great Britain paid only occasional attention to internal conditions while on the continent internal targets loomed much larger. In England, discount-rate policy was the main instrument of international monetary policy, and the Bank of England looked to the size of its gold reserve in setting its discount rate. Because its reserve ratio was affected primarily by movements of gold, the Bank's operating principle was that a reduction in its reserve due to a foreign drain was to be met with a hike in "Bank Rate"—a policy that implied acceptance to at least half of the gold standard's rules. At no time did the Bank of England hold its discount rate steady in the face of a serious foreign drain. The same cannot be said of the continental central banks, which relied far less extensively on discount-rate policy as the basis for their international monetary policies. To avoid the internal consequences of gold losses or frequent variations in interest rates, the central banks developed other techniques for dealing with gold drains. Although no country perfectly subordinated considerations of internal balance to external balance, England came the closest to this principle.

Yet in spite of such national differences, the international gold standard functioned smoothly for several decades. This paradox is explained by the positive systemic externalities that the major countries' policies produced. On the one hand, England's stronger commitment to gold-standard orthodoxy gave the world a medium of exchange and a store of value of unquestioned credibility. No other currency could match sterling's supremacy as a medium for reserves and transactions, so long as gold convertibility and free gold movements were conditional elsewhere. As a result the world was provided with a currency eminently suitable for international transaction and reserve purposes—one of the necessary system-sustaining functions identified by Kindleberger. On the other hand, France (and to a lesser extent Germany) came to provide the system with lender-of-last-resort facilities for balance-of-payments financing by reason of the dominant sociopolitical interest the French had in limiting the extent to which external economic forces restricted domestic macroeconomic flexibility. In order to maintain domestic macroeconomic flexibility, France built up a very large gold reserve and made it a point of policy to lend abroad from this fund to stem speculative pressures against the franc. The goal was to prevent large and sudden movements of reserves and gold from undermining domestic macroeconomic goals. Together, the nationally based and self-interested policies of Great Britain and France meshed compatibly to provide the public goods . . . the international monetary system needed for smooth operation. England alone did not manage the gold standard. Instead, management was a collective endeavor that derived from differences in national preferences. These differences in turn were rooted in the domestic political economies of the major states.

DOMESTIC SOURCES OF ENGLAND'S GOLD STANDARD POLICIES

It was during the first decades of the nineteenth century that a powerful circle of societal interests—land, the City's merchant banks and acceptance houses, and creditors of the government—congealed in England around the internationalist and deflationary monetary framework of the gold standard. The coalition demonstrated its political power by institutionalizing the gold standard first in Peel's Act of 1819 and then more strongly in the Bank Charter Act of 1844. In the second half of the century, the financial sector reaped the international advantages of the country's domestic monetary arrangements. On the strength of the commitment to gold, London flourished as a worldwide financial center, and sterling became the premier international currency. This commitment ensured sterling's place in the international financial system and thereby generated rents for the banking sector; it also brought to the international system a medium of reserve and payment of unquestioned reliability—a systemic public good.

The Napoleonic Wars set the stage for the formal institutionalization of the gold standard in England, which was suspended due to the war effort from 1797 to 1821. Suspension brought inflation and the depreciation of sterling against other currencies, which had distinct and predictable effects: a redistribution of wealth from *all* creditors and producers of nontradable goods to *all* debtors and producers of tradables. By violating the contract to redeem notes on demand for a fixed weight of gold, suspension usurped the property rights of all persons whose wealth consisted of money (creditors). In addition, depreciation worked to the advantage of tradables producers by raising the prices of traded goods relative to nontradables. This redistribution set the stage for a broad, intersectoral battle over the terms of the postwar monetary settlement.

The key beneficiaries of suspension—and hence the advocates of "soft money" rules—were farmers and manufacturers. Tenant farmers in particular found strong incentives to support the existing state of monetary affairs. . . . The price of wheat, for example, jumped from 6s. 9d. per bushel in 1797 to 16s. in 1800, while rents on agricultural land remained fixed at pre-inflation levels by long-term leases. . . . Debtors of all classes gained by the long period of suspension as they made interest and principal payments in a currency worth about 17 percent less in gold than when their debts were contracted.

In addition, the monetary attitude of manufacturers and industrial labor tended to correspond with that of the farmer, as industrial demand, prices, and wages all rose as a result of the depreciation of sterling and the general stimulus of war. The expansion, however, brought habits attuned to price, profit, and wage levels that were difficult to sustain after the final defeat of Napoleon. With war's end, demand dropped off, import competition increased (as blockades were lifted), and prices dropped dramatically. Domestic manufacturers, represented most vocally by organized Birmingham industrialists, sided with farmers in seeking monetary relief from the deflation/appreciation. . . . The coalition's anti-gold-standard platform alternatively called for the continuation of suspension, or a return to gold convertibility at a rate substantially lower than the prewar level. . . .

In contrast to the views of farmers and manufacturers, depreciation was injurious to England's powerful creditor, rentier, and saver groups, who coalesced around the gold standard. . . .

The position of the landed aristocracy is instructive. From the late seventeenth century on, this group built larger and larger estates and rented their acres to tenant farmers in larger units on long leases. . . . During the inflationary war years, landlords found that they were receiving only about two-thirds of their rent in real terms. Unable to raise rents in line with the upward trend in commodity prices, rentier lords became strong supporters of deflation and an early return to the gold standard. In this they found ready allies in the rapidly internationalizing financial sector.

London emerged from the Napoleonic Wars as the greatest financial center in the world. Just as World War I helped shift the locus of world finance from London to New York, the years of war from 1793 to 1815 helped cement London's position by disrupting established patterns of continental finance, especially those based in Amsterdam. Émigré financiers, fleeing the tide of Napoleon's invasions and attracted by England's political stability and the prospect of financing the country's burgeoning worldwide trading relations, played a key role in this transition. Nathan Rothschild, for example, arrived in London in 1798 and the Dutch banking house of Hope and Company set up shop in the City and strengthened its ties to Baring Brothers during the war period.

The wars acted as a major stimulus to the international lending activities of these bankers. In the area of short-term foreign lending, the wars displaced Dutch participation in not only British trade credits but also in the financial arrangements behind a large and growing body of trade transactions between other countries. As a result, foreign traders, already familiar with the names and reputations of the international banking houses that had recently settled in London, began to look to these institutions for facilities to effect the international transmission of remittances.

The internationalization of the London money market was paralleled by similar developments in the London capital market. In fact, several of the same private banks that financed bilateral and multilateral trade became the channel through which foreign governments and other large borrowers approached the British capital market. By virtue of their extensive foreign connections and their knowledge of the mercantile world gained in the course of financing trade, these firms were well placed for the handling of loans to foreign governments and corporations.

The depreciation and general instability of sterling during the period of suspended gold payments constrained the foreign expansion of British finance. The City's international short-term lending business in its nascent form was harmed in two ways. First, and most obviously, instability in the exchange rate posed the risk of exchange losses to bankers long accustomed to fixed exchange rates. With the prospect of debt repayment in depreciated currency, the banks and acceptance houses involved in financing trade had strong reasons for advocating a return to the gold standard before they extended their external activities. Second, foreigners who received payment for their goods in sterling bills or held sterling assets as working balances had to be confident in the stability of the pound because they too could suffer losses from exchange instability. Indeed, for sterling to gain usage internationally as a secure means of financing trade and making payments, and for the London financial community to earn the "denomination rents" that accrue specifically to the banking sector of nations whose currency serves as international currency, foreigners had to have complete confidence in sterling's gold value. If nonresidents were to utilize sterling as an international medium of exchange and as a reserve asset, England had to produce a protracted record of low inflation and inflation variability, which in turn depended upon stable and consistent government policies, particularly monetary policy. For Britain's international banking firms, the key to sterling's status as a global currency, and the key to London's position at the hub of short-term international finance, was gold convertibility.

International investment banking operations also depended, but to a lesser degree, upon the restoration of monetary predictability. Since the fall in the value of sterling meant losses for holders of long-term foreign securities that bore a fixed rate of interest, private bankers supported the return to the gold standard. Their objective was to distribute foreign securities to English savers; the reduction of exchange risk would facilitate the sale of issues contracted in sterling.

The international segment of the financial sector was joined in its quest for sound currency by a powerful new economic group that emerged as a result of the wars. This group was composed of the owners of British government bonds (Consols) that had been issued in vast quantities to finance the wars at a time of high prices and interest rates. There were roughly 17,000 of these "fundholders." . . . Depreciation was decidedly costly to the fundholders because it reduced the purchasing power of the Consols' dividends and, through the rise in interest rates, reduced their capital value as well. If the inflationary trend could be reversed, the fundholders—who had bought into the national debt with depreciated currency—would receive repayment in a currency with much greater purchasing power. In effect, deflation—the requisite of the return to gold payments—would produce a large bonus for fundholders as the real value of the war loans and interest payments rose. Indeed, interest on the war debt came to absorb over half the government's total revenue by 1827, redistributing wealth from taxpayers to investors.

The gold standard thus had a formidable political constituency behind it. It was supported by the established center of wealth and power in England (the landed aristocracy) and the economy's most dynamic advancing sectors (international banking and finance). With the addition of the country's "first investing public" (the fundholders) it is not surprising that England returned to gold at the prewar parity as soon as the war emergency permitted. . . .

INTERNATIONAL EFFECTS OF ENGLAND'S MONETARY PRIORITIES

An important international consequence of England's early and unfaltering commitment to the principles of the gold standard was the full globalization of the London money market. The immutable commitment to pay in gold and to let market forces determine gold flows meant that sterling was as "good as gold" for all international purposes. Systemic factors, in turn, provided the demand for sterling facilities. England's position as the world greatest trading nation meant that foreigners were continually earning incomes in Britain or in countries making payments there, and also continually making payments to Britain or to countries earning incomes there. Sterling was thus attractive both as a unit of account and as a medium of international exchange, and London was positioned to serve as the world's great settling center for commercial contracts—huge sterling balances were built up in a system committed to the gold convertibility of sterling. In addition, England's head start in industrialization combined with the policy of free trade to generate a huge stock of wealth and savings available for loan and investment abroad. With the gold standard firmly in place English bankers, financiers, and investors were no longer deterred by the possibility that unfavorable exchange rate movements might cut deeply into profits. The great expansion in foreign short- and long-term lending that followed further internationalized the London money market. With London operating both as the "clearinghouse" for the world's commodity and product markets and as its primary source of capital, foreigners were obliged to keep working balances in London to meet their short-term obligations and to service British overseas portfolio investments. Finally, Britain's pledge of convertibility at a fixed rate and on unqualified terms meant that sterling was also a secure store of value. This led not just foreign individuals and banks to make short-term investments in London but foreign governments and central banks themselves to hold reserves in sterling assets and bank deposits. In short, the English commitment to the gold standard served as the primary institutional underpinning of sterling's central position in the world economy. . . .

England thus provided the world with a currency eminently suitable for international purposes—an international public good. However, to attribute other system-sustaining functions to Britain, as the international political economy literature frequently does, misinterprets the facts. First, the Bank of England definitely did not serve as the classical gold standard's lender of last resort. . . . The real "hegemon" in regard to this function was the Bank of France, as discussed below. Second, there is scant evidence confirming the view that England consciously managed the international monetary system in non-crises times, with an eye toward coordinating national macroeconomic policies so as to mitigate global inflation and business cycles. . . .

. . . [W]hile other aspects of British "hegemony" remain in doubt, the international public good that English policy *unambiguously* provided was a currency appropriate for international use. Sterling was acceptable as a private and official international money because it was convertible into gold upon demand. British authorities attached clear priority to the defense of gold convertibility and demonstrated this commitment repeatedly in the face of adverse domestic conditions. The London financial market, in turn, possessed the necessary characteristics of breadth, depth, and resilience that ensured nonresidents of the liquidity of the working balances they held there. This commitment to gold reflected the enduring dominance of the gold standard coalition: the alliance of the City of London, landlords, bondholders, and international-competitive industry. When gold flowed out or in, the Bank of England took actions on interest rates consistent with the coalition members' interest in maintaining the gold value of the currency, whether or not these actions accorded with the needs of the domestic economy. Domestic economic activity—and all those interests that were tied to it—were thus subject to frequent variations in interest rates. To internationalists and creditors, it was simply more essential that the value of the currency remain constant in terms of foreign currencies than that the Bank rate and general interest rates remain stationary and/or low.

The victory of gold at home produced a monetary orientation that was beneficial to the functioning of the international gold standard. But this public good of a key currency was not provided by Britain out of conscious concern for sustaining the international economic order. Instead, it was a spillover—a positive externality—of Britain's individual preference for monetary orthodoxy in a world in which Britain was the most powerful financial and trading nation. The externality was partially internalized, however. As City bankers and acceptance houses earned rents from the increasing internationalization of sterling, the intensity of their preference for orthodoxy increased. Nevertheless, the English preference for monetary orthodoxy reflected the hierarchy of social interests *within* Britain. That the Bank of England's policies had beneficial global effects was a by-product of this structure and of the central position of London in the global system.

The political conditions that produced this spillover were for the most part evident only in England. In other countries, deflationist and internationalist groups were generally weaker than their domestically oriented rivals, and this was reflected in monetary institutions and practices. The commitment to the gold standard's principles and rules was far more conditional and uncertain on the continent than in England. In France, our next case, the tendency to insulate the domestic economy from external influences resulted primarily from the inward orientation of land, industry, and banking but came at the expense of Paris's role as an international financial center. Yet ironically, by reason of its predominant interest in domestic objectives, France came to act globally as the system's lender of last resort during the relatively infrequent emergencies that arose, thus providing the gold-standard regime with another of its stabilizing functions.

FRENCH DOMESTIC AND INTERNATIONAL MONETARY POLICY

Nominally, France maintained a bimetallic standard throughout the nineteenth century, but silver constituted the greater part of the coinage before 1850. The Bank of France usually cashed its notes in silver; when gold coin was wanted for export in bulk, it generally commanded a premium. In the early 1870s, when a glut of silver on world markets threatened to drive gold entirely from circulation, France and the other bimetallic countries of the Latin Monetary Union responded by suspending the free coinage of silver. The French, however, did not adopt a full gold standard. Instead, from 1878 until 1914, they operated a "limping gold standard," which gave monetary authorities greater flexibility in accommodating external pressures to domestic macroeconomic priorities. The convertibility of banknotes into gold was not guaranteed by law but was left to the central bank's discretion: in effect, capital controls were imposed in order to maintain monetary sovereignty.

Under the limping standard the Bank of France could legally redeem its notes in either French gold coin or in five-franc silver pieces at its own discretion. Having the right to make any payments in silver rather than in gold, the Bank could protect its gold reserve from the pressure of foreign drains. In practice, whenever the Bank wished to limit gold exports, it refused to redeem its notes in gold at the mint par rate of exchange and developed the policy of making gold payments at a premium. In other words, instead of refusing to maintain the gold convertibility of the franc, the Bank elected to charge a premium for gold—a mini-devaluation—to check external drains. . . .

. . . While the policy had the effect of discouraging gold exports, its main disadvantage was that it impaired the credibility of the French gold standard and thereby limited the expansion of French international banking and the development of the franc as an international currency.

Indeed, the Bank of France's occasional insistence on attaching a premium to redemption of its notes in gold meant a virtual abandonment of the gold standard. The uncertainty surrounding redemption of the currency in gold at the legal parity made foreigners less eager to utilize franc exchange for international purposes or to buy bills of exchange or securities issued in francs. As long as the policy was in practice, therefore, Paris could never challenge London's position. . . .

The policy also affected the reserve-currency role of the franc. The Reichsbank and the Austro-Hungarian Bank, for example, both held large portfolios of foreign bills yet had few bills drawn on Paris because of the uncertainty of obtaining gold there. Only Russia held substantial franc assets. These holdings, however, were not based on the calculation that the franc was absolutely secure. Instead, they were closely linked to Russian access to the French capital market: the Russian State Bank, in order to insure continued access to long-term loans, kept large sums on deposit in the French banks that distributed Russian bonds to French investors. Without the connection between the deposits and long-term loans—and the special economic and political relationships between France and Russia—it is unlikely that the Russian central bank would have preferred francs as the basis of its foreign currency reserves.

After 1900, the Bank of France began to lessen its dependence on the gold premium policy. To do so, it began to accumulate and hold a much larger gold reserve so that even a substantial drain could be accommodated without threatening gold convertibility. By 1900, the Bank had amassed a gold reserve of $409 million. By 1908 the figure had increased to $593 million, well over three times the reserve held by the Bank of England. The Bank of England could maintain convertibility on such a "thin film of gold" by the adroit manipulation of interest rates; the French preference was to keep interest rates low and stable by amassing a reserve large enough to accommodate even severe foreign drains. . . .

The result of this policy (and the occasional use of the gold premium policy) was that the Bank of France was able to keep its discount rate extraordinarily stable, in line with the nation's preference for domestic monetary independence. While the Bank of England changed its discount rate about six times per year on average between 1880 and 1913, it was not uncommon for the Bank of France to go for stretches of five years or more without a change from its traditional 3 percent rate. . . .

INTERNATIONAL EFFECTS OF FRENCH MONETARY PRIORITIES

The Bank of France also had another weapon in its arsenal to defend against the contractionary effects of gold outflows and discount-rate hikes. The policy was to come to the aid of foreign countries—especially England—experiencing financial distress in order to prevent the crises from reverberating back upon France. In effect, the Bank of France used its huge gold reserves as an instrument of international stabilization. When some major disturbance caused the Bank of England to contemplate imposing an especially high rate of discount, the Bank of France released gold to England, typically by discounting sterling bills. By lending the Bank of England a portion of its gold reserves, the Bank of France helped alleviate the pressures that threatened to force the Bank of England to raise its discount rate to higher levels. Because a crisis in London necessarily produced a backlash in France in the form of gold outflows, coming to the assistance of the Bank of England allowed the Bank of France to maintain a more stable structure of domestic interest rates.

France's role as lender of last resort to England can be credited with relieving the most severe crises of the era (the Barings Crisis of 1890; the American crises of 1906 and 1907). The picture of the classical gold standard as managed by the Bank of England alone is thus far from complete. In fact, it was Bank of France officials who thought of themselves as the "monetary physicians of the world," and allocating a portion of the Bank's immense gold holdings anywhere it was needed became an explicit component of French monetary policy. It is important to stress that there was nothing cosmopolitan about this policy. The goal was always to prevent foreign crises from destabilizing the French economy and forcing an upward adjustment in interest rates. . . .

The Bank of England, often regaled as the "manager" of the classical gold standard, never made such bold statements of its international role nor consciously acted in ways consistent with the role. In fact, the Bank of England was so dependent on the French bank in times of crisis that the latter became known as the Bank of England's "second gold reserve." It is therefore difficult to substantiate the view that attributes the durability of the classical gold standard to management by a single financial center. If the Bank of England served to protect the value of sterling so essential to its role as international money, in periods of extraordinary stress, France was the international lender of last resort.

The French commitment to protect the domestic market from foreign influences was also reflected in its longer and more avid use of "gold devices." Before 1900, the Bank of France frequently charged more for gold bars or foreign gold coins to discourage the export of gold in these forms. It was also quite common for the Bank to induce gold imports by raising its purchase price for gold bullion above the mint rate. In later years the same policy of buying gold at a loss was pursued from time to time with the essential purpose of imposing upon the Bank the costs of protecting convertibility instead of imposing them upon the business community by an advance in the rate of discount. Lastly, the Bank also regularly granted interest-free advances to gold importers and on occasion bought gold at its border branches to reduce shipping and insurance fees.

Taken as a whole, French monetary institutions and policies were far less consistent with the principles and operational rules of the gold standard than England's. Indeed, even considering France a gold-standard country stretches the definition of the concept because the central bank's commitment to redeem its notes in gold was always conditional and discretionary, and the market for gold was in no sense free. Moreover, since the Bank used an array of methods to avoid adjusting domestic macroeconomic conditions in line with gold flows—which, of course, eliminated any positive equilibrating role for monetary policy—it avoided playing by the rules of the game. In contrast to England, the French monetary system was designed and operated to insulate the domestic economy as much as possible from external pressures. Domestic targets took precedence over international ones, and one important consequence of this was that Paris could not develop as an international money market. However, regarding the stability of the international gold standard, the French practice of assisting Britain in time of crisis certainly played a role. These actions as lender of last resort were not based on the desire to provide the system with this public good but to insulate the French economy from the untoward effects of British policies, to which it was vulnerable.

DOMESTIC POLITICS OF FRENCH MONETARY POLICY

The political sources of French monetary institutions and policies were deeply ingrained in the structure of French society. Unlike England, France did not develop an alliance of land, finance and bondholder in favor of gold-standard orthodoxy. Although these groups played a crucial role in the formation of the country's monetary institutions and policies, their specific situations vis-à-vis the domestic and international economies produced monetary outlooks that were quite different from those of their English counterparts. The French landed sector is a case in point.

In terms of land tenure, one of the consequences of the revolutionary period in France was that there was no precise equivalent of the English landed aristocracy. In contrast to the British landlord, who made his living by renting his land on long leases to tenant farmers, land was widely distributed in France and worked in small, inefficient units by owner-operators for subsistence needs or for the domestic market. This fundamental difference in land-tenure systems was of considerable importance to national monetary preferences. Whereas the small group of well-placed English landlords sought stable or falling prices to preserve the purchasing power of their rental incomes, the multitudes of small farmers in France preferred rising prices for their crops. For this reason, land was consistently in the nationalist camp in France, seeking a policy to insulate the domestic economy from the deflationary aspects of the gold standard. Moreover, the landed sector was politically powerful in France but for a reason different from that in England. While English lords could obtain a favorable hearing by virtue of their positions in Parliament, the rural constituencies in France were empowered by revolutionary era political structures that gave effective voice to their numbers.

The structure of French industry also tended to mitigate against the development of a strong pro-gold lobby among manufacturers. Staple French exports (other than wines and spirits) were mainly the manufactured textile specialties of silk, wool, or cotton usually produced in traditional small workshops and sold in the high-income urban areas of the world. These were not the inexpensive, standardized goods produced for mass foreign markets, such as those in which the British excelled. Even the most modern sectors of French industry (iron and steel, for example) were not competitive on world markets. Overall, exports played a much smaller role in industrial activity than in England. As a consequence, France did not possess a strong segment of the manufacturing class that stood behind a gold standard and fixed-exchange-rate regime. . . .

Without a powerful rentier landed elite and an externally oriented manufacturing segment to support it, the fate of the gold standard rested upon the position and influence of the French financial community. French finance, however, developed along lines quite distinct from the trajectory in Britain and, consequently, there were few enthusiasts among its ranks for committing to a full gold standard. . . .

. . . French finance was primarily a domestic business until the final third of the nineteenth century, when foreign-portfolio lending blossomed under the encouragement and political guidance of the state. Other than its role in distributing foreign bonds to small investors—who were protected from the vagaries of the limping standard by gold clauses in the loan contracts— French finance was decidedly parochial. The market for foreign short loans was limited, the international significance of the Paris money market small, and the use of the franc as a reserve currency largely confined to Russia for political reasons. In short, there was little internationalization to give money-market participants an interest in encouraging a stronger commitment to the gold standard. Without a key-currency position comparable to sterling and lacking an overwhelming stake in international finance, the banking sector realized no significant benefit in striving for gold-standard orthodoxy. Their business consisted in discounting domestic bills for French firms and merchants, a business that benefited from the French bank's low and non-fluctuating interest rate. For this reason, there were few calls from the financial sector for altering the existing state of affairs along British lines.

In summary, political conditions within France precluded the development of solid gold standard institutions. The prevalence of small holding gave agriculture a decidedly "easy money" orientation. The relative underdevelopment of industry left few manufacturing firms competitive enough to encourage or endure the harshness of British-style adjustment mechanisms. Finance, despite its substantial involvement in distributing foreign bonds, remained domestically bound in terms of the money market and showed little interest in pursuing the short-term international business dominated by English firms. Instead, all three sectors preferred to devote their political energies to keeping the structure of domestic interest rates stable and low, even if that put at risk confidence in the franc. Nevertheless, France came to play a crucial role in stabilizing the gold standard. Its lender-of-last-resort policies, however, were first and foremost attempts to advance national as opposed to international objectives. Though Germany did not share the obsession with interest rate stability, monetary authorities there were nearly as reticent to allow a free market in gold and to maintain gold convertibility under all conditions. As with Paris, Berlin's international standing suffered, but Germany also stood in as lender of last resort for the global economy in times of distress.

GERMAN DOMESTIC AND INTERNATIONAL MONETARY POLICY

Although the German case differs from the French in terms of monetary institutions and policy choices, there was one important similarity: at no time after the formal adoption of the gold standard in 1873 did German monetary authorities fully adhere to the principles of the gold standard. As in France, the monetary standard was jeopardized for domestic political reasons.

In 1871, one of the most pressing issues facing the newly established German Empire was monetary reform. The nascent political union needed a common coinage sufficient for national circulation. The silver standard was no longer considered advantageous as Germany's major trading partners in Eastern Europe (Russia and Austria-Hungary) had been forced by inflation off silver onto inconvertible paper. With the help of the large gold indemnity paid by France for losing the Franco-Prussian War, Germany was able to adopt the gold standard in 1873. The gold mark became the new monetary unit, and the free and unlimited coinage of silver was discontinued.

Formally, the new German standard was not a limping standard of the French variety but a full gold standard along textbook lines. In practice, however, the gold convertibility of the mark was not automatic but discretionary, and the German gold market was frequently subject to official manipulation. As in France, monetary policy was geared to restrict convertibility and gold flows whenever the well-being of the domestic economy was threatened.

Although Reichsbank officials claimed that discount-rate policy was their primary tool for increasing or protecting the gold reserve, they employed several other techniques that were outside the norms of the gold standard. Several of these were of the "gold device" variety. For example, when the Reichsbank wanted to draw gold to Germany, it often paid a premium or granted interest-free loans to importers, a policy that was given unqualified praise by German bankers and economists. To discourage gold drains, the Reichsbank also offered foreign coin for export that was as light as legally possible.

The Reichsbank also added some new twists to the manipulation of the gold market. For example, it sometimes made use of the option to redeem its notes only at its head office in Berlin rather than at its branches near the borders, with the effect that the gold export point could be raised minutely. That is, by forcing the exporter to pay the added freight and insurance costs of sending gold from Berlin to the port, the Bank initiated a small advance in the gold export point. Though small, the action could influence the foreign exchanges in Germany's favor. In addition, the Reichsbank developed what was perhaps its most powerful weapon to restrict convertibility and undesirable gold movements—a policy of quiet, yet effective, "moral suasion."

To prevent bankers from exporting gold at times when it was profitable to do so, the Reichsbank let it be known that it would look with disfavor upon gold taken for export. . . . German monetary authorities never codified or openly admitted this subtle policy; yet money-market participants understood the policy very well. It was effective in stemming foreign drains because bankers dared not risk the vengeance of the Reichsbank; to do so could mean years of discrimination or worse—the outright loss of privileges with the central bank. . . .

As a consequence of its reluctance to allow a free market in gold, international bills of exchange drawn in the German market did not have the same definite gold value as those drawn in London, and this uncertainty limited Berlin's role as an international center. . . .

What political forces steered Germany away from monetary orthodoxy? On the surface, this is a perplexing question because major segments of German industry and finance, lifted by their stunning successes in international markets after 1890, would have benefited from currency stability and ready gold convertibility. Yet German monetary policy remained focused on internal targets. The paradox is explained by the opposition and political power of Prussian landowners, the Junkers.

Banking and industry developed in Germany quite differently from how they developed in Britain. British banks had few connections with industry (which tended to be self-financed) and thus developed a completely different orientation to the international economy. Rising to prominence financing international trade, foreign governments, and overseas infrastructure, British banks championed monetary internationalism in opposition to the nationalism of the fading manufacturing sector. In Germany, however, the interests of industry and finance tended to move together because there were strong and durable links between the two sectors. German joint-stock banks were originally established to provide manufacturing with the large amounts of long-term capital it needed to initiate and sustain "late" development. Indeed, the four "D-Banks" (Deutsche Bank, Disconto-Gesellschaft, Dresdener Bank, and Darmsteder Bank) provided much of the capital, entrepreneurship, and management of the German industrial revolution. The relevant point is that these interrelations made the banks vitally concerned with the well-being of their industrial progeny. As German industry sought export markets, German banks aggressively established branches abroad to provide foreign purchasers of German goods with short-term financing and floated foreign bonds in Germany that stood to improve the market position of German businesses. Yet despite the growing internationalism of German industry, banking, and finance, monetary policy remained geared toward the needs of the domestic economy.

Part of the explanation is that the Berlin money market, like the Paris market, was still far less dependent on the confidence of foreigners than the London market. The bread and butter of German banking was channeling funds to industry, not issuing, accepting, and discounting international bills of exchange. The interests of German bankers were, thus, not as tied up with the willingness of foreign bankers, traders, and investors to deal in the home currency and in the national money market as they were in London. Since maintaining international confidence in the currency could require restrictive monetary policy inimical to industry, German banks were at best tepid supporters of gold-standard orthodoxy. The political consequence was that the financial sector's support for a full gold standard was weaker than in England.

Yet to understand fully the sources of Germany's "conditional" gold standard requires a look at the preferences and enduring political power of the German landed elite. After unification, Germany was by and large a country of free land-holding peasants and power-cultivating squires—the Junkers. The Junkers, like the British landed elite, were powerful beyond their numbers in the German political system. Their monetary interests, however, tended to be more in line with tenant and small holding farmers than with the British aristocracy. This was because Junkers were not primarily rentiers. Instead, they managed great agricultural estates organized along the lines of the Spanish system of latifundia. As agricultural producers, the Junkers preferred a monetary system capable of enhancing the price of the low-quality grains they raised, not a system that put protecting the value of the currency above all else.

Without the support of the powerful Junkers, represented at the pinnacle of the German political system by Bismark himself, it is understandable why Germany did not adhere strictly to the principles of the gold standard. That Germany also lacked an equivalent of the City of London's internationally focused money market to champion orthodoxy was another constraint on the development of the German gold standard. The result was a distinct bias in monetary policy toward domestic objectives, as revealed by the Reichsbank's frequent resort to moral pressure and gold devices when external pressures were strong.

INTERNATIONAL EFFECTS OF GERMAN MONETARY PRIORITIES

Like France, Germany also recognized how domestic priorities could be advanced by releasing gold abroad in times of international stress. This policy as lender of last resort resulted from the fact that the effectiveness of Reichsbank attempts to moderate external pressures, through the techniques outlined above, had obvious limits. If, for example, the Bank of England chose to raise Bank rate to whatever height was necessary attract capital and gold flows from the Continent, German macroeconomic independence would be threatened. Hence, Germany had a *domestic* interest in joining France in providing the gold standard system with the services of the lender of last resort. The Reichsbank was willing to open its reserves to the Bank of England because the policy offered the possibility of smaller, and certainly more predictable, gold outflows. . . .

Germany was thus more like France than England in terms of the way it resolved the age-old dilemma between the internal and external objectives of monetary policy. Neither country subordinated domestic credit conditions and economic growth to the international objective of maintaining confidence in the strength of the national currency so thoroughly or for so long as did England. Yet Germany came to share with France the role of international lender of last resort, smoothing out shocks to the payments systems that threatened the independence of domestic macroeconomic policy making. Both the source of the national concern for internal targets and the Reichsbank's regime stabilizing policies at the international level were rooted in German domestic politics. Unable to perfectly insulate the German financial system from external pressures in line with the interests of Germany's dominant coalition, monetary authorities found it advantageous to release gold to the source of the shock, via the Bank of England. The action, however, was not based on any cosmopolitan commitment to stabilizing the international gold standard on the part of German monetary authorities. Instead, the German element of "central bank cooperation" can be interpreted as an international spillover of German national preferences, which again were far from orthodox.

CONCLUSION

Although international monetary stability may require the provision of Kindleberger's equilibrating mechanisms, states can have different objectives and divergent policy preferences if the international spillovers of their national policy choices are solidly positive. Thus, agreement among member states about the rules and requirements of membership is not a necessary condition for global monetary stability. Nor is it necessary that a hegemon exist to provide the requisite stabilizing functions. An international "social order," like the classical gold standard, can be maintained when states advance their internally determined private national interests in ways that generate nonexcludable systemic benefits, according to the logic of the joint-products model.

Historical evidence tends to support these claims. Not only did major gold standard countries have different (private) preferences regarding the basic trade-offs implicit in adhering to a fixed exchange-rate regime but the aggregate (public) result of their individual national choices was a modicum of international stability. The British leaned more consistently toward gold-standard orthodoxy—monetary authorities advanced external priorities over internal concerns. This was a function of the political dominance of those economic groups that found advantages in the internationalist and deflationary agenda of the gold standard: the bankers of the City of London, rentier landlords, and bondholders. For these groups, maintaining the purchasing power of the currency took precedent over domestic targets when these objectives clashed.

In conjunction with London's central position in world trade and payments, this commitment spilled over into the international arena in the form of the elevation of sterling to the status of international currency. The commitment to gold, meant that the pound sterling became almost universally accepted as a transaction and reserve currency, and England therefore became the main source of liquidity for international payments. The two continental powers, in contrast, did not welcome their loss of independence in forming monetary policy that the gold standard required. They preferred instead to give monetary policy a decidedly domestic slant. They did so by artificially restricting the free flow of gold and restricting the gold convertibility of their currencies when necessary. Yet France and Germany came to share the position of international lender of last resort. Their concern for internal targets and for their policies of international lender of last resort had a common source—domestic politics and priorities. Unable to perfectly insulate their domestic economics from external pressures in line with the interests of their dominant coalitions, monetary authorities in France and Germany found it necessary to release gold from their reserves to the Bank of England, which then channeled it abroad to the source of the shock. The French and Germans, however, did not provide this stabilizing function for the international gold-standard system out of a commitment to global welfare or regime stability. Instead, the central bank's support operations under the gold standard were a means by which weaker members of the regime—members who were not fully committed to gold—sought to drive a wedge between gold standard discipline and domestic macroeconomic policy making. Paradoxically, it was because France and Germany did *not* share England's commitment to the gold standard that the regime was able to accommodate the handful of shocks that it experienced.

The international externalities of heterogeneous national preferences can, of course, be negative as well as positive. The collapse of the gold standard in the interwar period, the breakup of the Bretton Woods system in the early 1970s, and the 1992 crisis in the EMS can all be interpreted as the result of large negative externalities produced by the policy choices of the major states, in response to domestic political forces. Although we still lack general propositions about the conditions in which national interests sustain (or fail to sustain) an international regime, the research presented here is a necessary first step toward understanding international monetary relations. The value of the framework, and the measure against which it should be judged, is primarily empirical. The quality of the externalities produced by national policy choices determines the stability of the international monetary system. The facts of the nineteenth-century case of the gold standard are more consistent with this view than with models derived from existing international relations theory— hegemonic stability theory and regime theory. Although future theoretical work must specify the precise conditions under which heterogeneous national social orders will or will not generate the systemic public goods by which international social orders are maintained, this chapter has demonstrated the benefit of shifting the focus from international to domestic social order.

14

Hegemonic Stability Theories of the International Monetary System

BARRY EICHENGREEN

Barry Eichengreen evaluates the applicability of hegemonic stability theory (see Krasner, Reading 1, and Lake, Reading 8) to international monetary relations. He examines the argument that the existence of a single dominant power in the international arena is necessary for the establishment and maintenance of stable monetary systems. Eichengreen examines three monetary systems—the classical gold standard, the interwar gold exchange system, and the Bretton Woods system—to see whether the presence or absence of a hegemon was the primary cause of their development and maintenance. He finds that while hegemons may contribute to the smooth operation of international monetary regimes, international cooperation has been equally important to their design and functioning.

An international monetary system is a set of rules or conventions governing the economic policies of nations. From a narrowly national perspective, it is an unnatural state of affairs. Adherence to a common set of rules or conventions requires a certain harmonization of monetary and fiscal policies, even though the preferences and constraints influencing policy formulation diverge markedly across countries. Governments are expected to forswear policies that redistribute economic welfare from foreigners to domestic residents and to contribute voluntarily to providing the international public good of global monetary stability. In effect, they are expected to solve the defection problem that plagues cartels and—equivalently in this context—the free-rider problem hindering public good provision. Since they are likely to succeed incompletely, the public good of international monetary stability tends to be underproduced. From this perspective, the paradox of international monetary affairs is not the difficulty of designing a stable international monetary system, but the fact that such systems have actually persisted for decades.

Specialists in international relations have offered the notion that dominance by one country—a hegemonic power—is needed to ensure the smooth functioning of an international regime. The concentration of economic power is seen as a way of internalizing the externalities associated with systemic stability and of ensuring its adequate provision. The application of this "theory of hegemonic stability" to international monetary affairs is straightforward. The maintenance of the Bretton Woods System for a quarter century is ascribed to the singular power of the United States in the postwar world, much as the persistence of the classical gold standard is ascribed to Britain's dominance of international financial affairs in the second half of the nineteenth century. . . . By contrast, the instability of the interwar gold exchange standard is attributed to the absence of a hegemonic power, due to Britain's inability to play the dominant role and America's unwillingness to accept it.

The appeal of this notion lies in its resonance with the public good and cartel analogies for international monetary affairs, through what might be called the carrot and stick variants of hegemonic stability theory. In the carrot variant, the hegemon, like a dominant firm in an oligopolistic market, maintains the cohesion of the cartel by making the equivalent of side payments to members of the fringe. In the stick variant, the hegemon, like a dominant firm, deters defection from the international monetary cartel by using its economic policies to threaten retaliation against renegades. In strong versions of the theory . . . all participants are rendered better off by the intervention of the dominant power. In weak versions . . . either because systemic stability is not a purely public good or because its costs are shunted onto smaller states, the benefits of stability accrue disproportionately or even exclusively to the hegemon.

Three problems bedevil attempts to apply hegemonic stability theory to international monetary affairs. First is the ambiguity surrounding three concepts central to the theory; *hegemony*, the *power* the hegemon is assumed to possess, and the *regime* whose stability is ostensibly enhanced by the exercise of hegemonic power. Rather than adopting general definitions offered previously and devoting this paper to their criticism, I adopt specialized definitions tailored to my concern with the international monetary system. I employ the economist's definition of economic—or market—power: sufficient size in the relevent market to influence prices and quantities. I define a hegemon analogously to a dominant firm: as a country whose market power, understood in this sense, significantly exceeds that of all rivals. Finally, I avoid defining the concept of regime around which much debate has revolved by posing the question narrowly: whether hegemony is conducive to the stability of the international monetary system (where the system is defined as those explicit rules and procedures governing international monetary affairs), rather than whether it is conducive to the stability of the international regime, however defined.

The second problem plaguing attempts to apply hegemonic stability theory to international monetary affairs is ambiguity about the instruments with which the hegemon makes its influence felt. This is the distinction between what are characterized above as the carrot and stick variants of the theory. Does the hegemon alter its monetary, fiscal, or commercial policies to discipline countries that refuse to play by its rules, as "basic force" models of international relations would suggest? Does it link international economic policy to other issue areas and impose military or diplomatic sanctions on uncooperative nations? Or does it stabilize the system through the use of "positive sanctions," financing the public good of international monetary stability by acting as lender of last resort even when the probability of repayment is slim and forsaking beggar-thy-neighbor policies even when used to advantage by other countries?

The third problem is ambiguity about the scope of hegemonic stability theories. In principle, such theories could be applied equally to the design, the operation, or the decline of the international monetary system. Yet in practice, hegemonic stability theories may shed light on the success of efforts to design or reform the international monetary system but not on its day-to-day operation or eventual decline. Other combinations are equally plausible a priori. Only analysis of individual cases can throw light on the theory's range of applicability.

In this paper, I structure an analysis of hegemonic stability theories of the international monetary system around the dual problems of range of applicability and mode of implementation. I consider separately the genesis of international monetary systems, their operation in normal periods and times of crisis, and their disintegration. In each context, I draw evidence from three modern incarnations of the international monetary system: the classical gold standard, the interwar gold exchange standard, and Bretton Woods. These three episodes in the history of the international monetary system are typically thought to offer two examples of hegemonic stability—Britain before 1914, the United States after 1944—and one episode—the interwar years—destabilized by the absence of hegemony. I do not attempt to document Britain's dominance of international markets before 1914 or the dominance of the United States after 1944; I simply ask whether the market power they possessed was causally connected to the stability of the international monetary system.

The historical analysis indicates that the relationship between the market power of the leading economy and the stability of the international monetary system is considerably more complex than suggested by simple variants of hegemonic stability theory. While one cannot simply reject the hypothesis that on more than one occasion the stabilizing capacity of a dominant economic power has contributed to the smooth functioning of the international monetary system, neither can one reconcile much of the evidence, notably on the central role of international negotiation and collaboration even in periods of hegemonic dominance, with simple versions of the theory. Although both the appeal and limitations of hegemonic stability theories are apparent when one takes a static view of the international monetary system, those limitations are most evident when one considers the evolution of an international monetary system over time. An international monetary system whose smooth operation at one point is predicated on the dominance of one powerful country may in fact be dynamically unstable. Historical experience suggests that the hegemon's willingness to act in a stabilizing capacity at a single point tends to undermine its continued capacity to do so over time. . . .

THE GENESIS OF MONETARY SYSTEMS AND THE THEORY OF HEGEMONIC STABILITY

My analysis begins with an examination of the genesis of three different monetary systems: the classical gold standard, the interwar gold exchange standard, and the Bretton Woods system.

The Classical Gold Standard

Of the three episodes considered here, the origins of the classical gold standard are the most difficult to assess, for in the nineteenth century there were no centralized discussions, like those in Genoa in 1922 or Bretton Woods in 1944, concerned with the design of the international monetary system. There was general agreement that currencies should have a metallic basis and that payments imbalances should be settled by international shipments of specie. But there was no consensus about which precious metals should serve as the basis for money supplies or how free international specie movements should be.

Only Britain maintained a full-fledged gold standard for anything approaching the century preceding 1913. Although gold coins had circulated alongside silver since the fourteenth century, Britain had been on a de facto gold standard since 1717, when Sir Isaac Newton, as master of the mint, set too high a silver price of gold and drove full-bodied silver coins from circulation. In 1798 silver coinage was suspended, and after 1819 silver was no longer accepted to redeem paper currency. But for half a century following its official adoption of the gold standard in 1821, Britain essentially remained alone. Other countries that retained bimetallic standards were buffeted by alternating gold and silver discoveries. The United States and France, for example, were officially bimetallic, but their internal circulations were placed on a silver basis by growing Mexican and South American silver production in the early decades of the nineteenth century. The market price of silver was thus depressed relative to the mint price, which encouraged silver to be imported for coinage and gold to be shipped abroad where its price was higher. Then, starting in 1848, gold discoveries in Russia, Australia, and California depressed the market price of gold below the mint price, all but driving silver from circulation and placing bimetallic currencies on a gold basis. Finally, silver discoveries in Nevada and other mining territories starting in the 1870s dramatically inflated the silver price of gold and forced the bimetallic currencies back onto a silver basis.

The last of these disturbances led nearly all bimetallic countries to adopt the gold standard, starting with Germany in 1871. Why, after taking no comparable action in response to previous disturbances, did countries respond to post-1870 fluctuations in the price of silver by abandoning bimetallism and adopting gold? What role, if any, did Britain, the hegemonic financial power, play in their decisions?

One reason for the decision to adopt gold was the desire to prevent the inflation that would result from continued silver convertibility and coinage. Hence the plausible explanation for the contrast between the 1870s and earlier years is the danger of exceptionally rapid inflation due to the magnitude of post-1870 silver discoveries. Between 1814 and 1870, the sterling price of silver, of which so much was written, remained within 2 percentage points of its 1814 value, alternatively driving gold or silver from circulation in bimetallic countries but fluctuating insufficiently to raise the specter of significant price level changes. Then between 1871 and 1881 the London price of silver fell by 15 percent, and by 1891 the cumulative fall had reached 25 percent. Gold convertibility was the only alternative to continued silver coinage that was judged both respectable and viable. The only significant resistance to the adoption of gold convertibility emanated from silver-mining regions and from agricultural areas like the American West, populated by proprietors of encumbered land who might benefit from inflation.

Seen from this perspective, the impetus for adopting the gold standard existed independently of Britain's rapid industrialization, dominance of international finance, and preeminence in trade. Still, the British example surely provided encouragement to follow the path ultimately chosen. The experience of the Latin Monetary Union impressed upon contemporaries the advantages of a common monetary standard in minimizing transactions costs. The scope of that common standard would be greatest for countries that linked their currencies to sterling. The gold standard was also attractive to domestic interests concerned with promoting economic growth. Industrialization required foreign capital, and attracting foreign capital required monetary stability. For Britain, the principal source of foreign capital, monetary stability was measured in terms of sterling and best ensured by joining Britain on gold. Moreover, London's near monopoly of trade credit was of concern to other governments, which hoped that they might reduce their dependence on the London discount market by establishing gold parities and central banks. Aware that Britain monopolized trade in newly mined gold and was the home of the world's largest organized commodity markets, other governments hoped that by emulating Britain's gold standard and financial system they might secure a share of this business.

Britain's prominence in foreign commerce, overseas investment, and trade credit forcefully conditioned the evolution of the gold standard system mainly through central banks' practice of holding key currency balances abroad, especially in London. This practice probably would not have developed so quickly if foreign countries had not grown accustomed to transacting in the London market. It would probably not have become so widespread if there had not been such strong confidence in the stability and liquidity of sterling deposits. And such a large share of foreign deposits would not have gravitated to a single center if Britain had not possessed such a highly articulated set of financial markets.

But neither Britain's dominance of international transactions nor the desire to emulate Bank of England practice prevented countries from tailoring the gold standard to their own needs. Germany and France continued to allow large internal gold circulation, while other nations limited gold coin circulation to low levels. The central banks of France, Belgium, and Switzerland retained the right to redeem their notes in silver, and the French did not hesitate to charge a premium for gold. The Reichsbank could at its option issue fiduciary notes upon the payment of a tax. In no sense did British example or suggestion dictate the form of the monetary system.

The Interwar Gold Exchange Standard

The interwar gold exchange standard offers a radically different picture: on the one hand, there was no single dominant power like nineteenth century Britain or mid-twentieth century America; on the other, there were conscious efforts by rivals to shape the international monetary order to their national advantage.

Contemporary views of the design of the interwar monetary system were aired at a series of international meetings, the most important of which was the Genoa Economic and Financial Conference convened in April 1922. Although the United States declined to send an official delegation to Genoa, proceedings there reflected the differing economic objectives of Britain and the United States. British officials were aware that the war had burdened domestic industry with adjustment problems, had disrupted trade, and had accentuated financial rivalry between London and New York. Their objectives were to prevent worldwide deflation (which was sure to exacerbate the problems of structural adjustment), to promote the expansion of international trade (to which the nation's prosperity was inextricably linked), and to recapture the financial business diverted to New York as a result of the war. To prevent deflation, they advocated that countries economize on the use of gold by adopting the gold exchange standard along lines practiced by members of the British Empire. Presuming London to be a reserve center, British officials hoped that these measures would restore the City to its traditional prominence in international finance. Stable exchange rates would stimulate international trade, particularly if the United States forgave its war debt claims, which would permit reparations to be reduced and encourage creditor countries to extend loans to Central Europe.

The United States, in contrast, was less dependent for its prosperity on the rapid expansion of trade. It was less reliant on income from financial and insurance services and perceived as less urgent the need to encourage the deposit of foreign balances in New York. Influential American officials, notably Benjamin Strong of the Federal Reserve Bank of New York, opposed any extension of the gold exchange standard. Above all, American officials were hesitant to participate in a conference whose success appeared to hinge on unilateral concessions regarding war debts.

In the absence of an American delegation, Britain's proposals formed the basis for the resolutions of the Financial Committee of the Genoa Conference. . . . Participating countries would fix their exchange rates against one another, and any that failed to do so would lose the right to hold the reserve balances of the others. The principal creditor nations were encouraged to take immediate steps to restore convertibility in order to become "gold centers" where the bulk of foreign exchange reserves would be held. Following earlier recommendations by the Cunliffe committee, governments were urged to economize on gold by eliminating gold coin from circulation and concentrating reserves at central banks. Countries with significantly depreciated currencies were urged to stabilize at current exchange rates rather than attempting to restore prewar parities through drastic deflation, which would only delay stabilization.

To implement this convention, the Bank of England was instructed to call an early meeting of central banks, including the Federal Reserve. But efforts to arrange this meeting, which bogged down in the dispute over war debts and reparations, proved unavailing. Still, if the official convention advocated by the Financial Committee failed to materialize, the Genoa resolutions were not without influence. Many of the innovations suggested there were adopted by individual countries on a unilateral basis and comprised the distinguishing features differentiating the prewar and interwar monetary standards.

The first effect of Genoa was to encourage the adoption of statutes permitting central banks to back notes and sight deposits with foreign exchange as well as gold. New regulations broadening the definition of eligible assets and specifying minimum proportions of total reserves to be held in gold were widely implemented in succeeding years. The second effect was to encourage the adoption of gold economy measures, including the withdrawal of gold coin from circulation and provision of bullion for export only by the authorities. The third effect was to provide subtle encouragement to countries experiencing ongoing inflation to stabilize at depreciated rates. Thus Genoa deserves partial credit for transforming the international monetary system from a gold to a gold exchange standard, from a gold coin to a gold bullion standard, and from a fixed-rate system to one in which central banks were vested with some discretion over the choice of parities.

Given its dominance of the proceedings at Genoa, Britain's imprint on the interwar gold exchange standard was as apparent as its influence over the structure of the prewar system. That British policymakers achieved this despite a pronounced decline in Britain's position in the world economy and the opposition of influential American officials suggests that planning and effort were substitutes, to some extent, for economic power.

The Bretton Woods System

Of the three cases considered here, U.S. dominance of the Bretton Woods negotiations is most clearly supportive of hegemonic stability theories about the genesis of the international monetary system. U.S. dominance of the postwar world economy is unmistakable. Yet despite the trappings of hegemony and American dominance of the proceedings at Bretton Woods, a less influential power—Great Britain—was able to secure surprisingly extensive concessions in the design of the international monetary system.

American and British officials offered different plans for postwar monetary reconstruction both because they had different views of the problem of international economic adjustment and because they represented economies with different strengths and weaknesses. British officials were preoccupied by two weaknesses of their economic position. First was the specter of widespread unemployment. Between 1920 and 1938, unemployment in Britain had scarcely dipped below double-digit levels, and British policymakers feared its recurrence. Second was the problem of sterling balances. Britain had concentrated its wartime purchases within the sterling bloc and, because they were allies and sterling was a reserve currency, members of the bloc had accepted settlement in sterling, now held in London. Since these sterling balances were large relative to Britain's hard currency reserves, the mere possibility that they might be presented for conversion threatened plans for the restoration of convertibility.

U.S. officials, in contrast, were confident that the competitive position of American industry was strong and were little concerned about the threat of unemployment. The concentration of gold reserves in the United States, combined with the economy's international creditor position, freed them from worry that speculative capital flows or foreign government policies might undermine the dollar's stability. U.S. concerns centered on the growth of preferential trading systems from which its exports were excluded, notably the sterling bloc.

The British view of international economic adjustment was dominated by concern about inadequate liquidity and asymmetrical adjustment. A central lesson drawn by British policymakers from the experience of the 1920s was the difficulty of operating an international monetary system in which liquidity or reserves were scarce. Given how slowly the global supply of monetary gold responded to fluctuations in its relative price and how sensitive its international distribution had proven to be to the economic policies of individual states, they considered it foolhardy to base the international monetary system on a reserve base composed exclusively of gold. Given the perceived inelasticity of global gold supplies, a gold-based system threatened to impart a deflationary bias to the world economy and to worsen unemployment. This preoccupation with unemployment due to external constraints was reinforced by another lesson drawn from the 1920s: the costs of asymmetries in the operation of the adjustment mechanism. If the experience of the 1920s was repeated, surplus countries, in response to external imbalances, would need only to sterilize reserve inflows, while deficit countries would be forced to initiate monetary contraction to prevent the depletion of reserves. Monetary contraction, according to Keynes, whose views heavily influenced those of the British delegation, facilitated adjustment by causing unemployment. To prevent unemployment, symmetry had to be restored to the adjustment mechanism through the incorporation of sanctions compelling surplus countries to revalue their currencies or stimulate demand.

From the American perspective, the principal lessons of interwar experience were not the costs of asymmetries and inadequate liquidity, but the instability of floating rates and the disruptive effects of exchange rate and trade protection. U.S. officials were concerned about ensuring order and stability in the foreign exchange market and preventing the development of preferential trading systems cultivated through expedients such as exchange control.

The Keynes and White plans, which formed each side's basis for negotiations, require only a brief summary. Exchange control and the centralized provision of liquidity ("bancor") were two central elements of Keynes's plan for an international clearing union. . . . Exchange control would insulate pegged exchange rates from the sudden liquidation of short-term balances. Symmetry would be ensured by a charge on creditor balances held with the clearing bank.

The White plan acknowledged the validity of the British concern with liquidity, but was intended to prevent both inflation and deflation rather than to exert an expansionary influence. It limited the Stabilization Fund's total resources to $5 billion, compared with $26 billion under the Keynes plan. It was patterned on the principles of American bank lending, under which decisionmaking power rested ultimately with the bank; the Keynes plan resembled the British overdraft system, in which the overdraft was at the borrower's discretion. The fundamental difference, however, was that the White plan limited the total U.S. obligation to its $2 billion contribution, while the Keynes plan limited the value of unrequited U.S. exports that might be financed by bancor to the total drawing rights of other countries ($23 billion).

It is typically argued that the Bretton Woods agreement reflected America's dominant position, presumably on the grounds that the International Monetary Fund charter specified quotas of $8.8 billion (closer to the White plan's $5 billion than to the Keynes plan's $26 billion) and a maximum U.S. obligation of $2.75 billion (much closer to $2 billion under the White plan than to $23 billion under the Keynes plan). Yet, relative to the implications of simple versions of hegemonic stability theory, a surprising number of British priorities were incorporated. One was the priority Britain attached to exchange rate flexibility. The United States initially had wished to invest the IMF with veto power over a country's decision to change its exchange rate. Subsequently it proposed that 80 percent of IMF members be required to approve any change in parity. But the Articles of Agreement permitted devaluation without fund objection when needed to eliminate fundamental disequilibrium. Lacking any definition of this term, there was scope for devaluation by countries other than the United States to reconcile internal and external balance. Only once did the fund treat an exchange rate change as unauthorized. If countries hesitated to devalue, they did so as much for domestic reasons as for reasons related to the structure of the international monetary system.

Another British priority incorporated into the agreement was tolerance of exchange control. Originally, the White plan obliged members to abandon all exchange restrictions within six months of ceasing hostilities or joining the IMF, whichever came first. A subsequent U.S. proposal would have required a country to eliminate all exchange controls within a year of joining the fund. But Britain succeeded in incorporating into the Articles of Agreement a distinction between controls for capital transactions, which were permitted, from controls on current transactions, which were not. In practice, even nondiscriminatory exchange controls on current transactions were sometimes authorized under IMF Article VIII. As a result of this compromise, the United States protected itself from efforts to divert sterling bloc trade toward the British market, while Britain protected itself from destabilization by overseas sterling balances.

In comparison with these concessions, British efforts to restore symmetry to the international adjustment mechanism proved unavailing. With abandonment of the overdraft principle, the British embraced White's "scarce currency" proposal, under which the fund was empowered to ration its supply of a scarce currency and members were authorized to impose limitations on freedom of exchange operations in that currency. Thus a country running payments surpluses sufficiently large to threaten the fund's ability to supply its currency might face restrictions on foreign customers' ability to purchase its exports. But the scarce currency clause had been drafted by the United States not with the principle of symmetry in mind, but in order to deal with problems of immediate postwar adjustment—specifically, the prospective dollar shortage. With the development of the Marshall Plan, the dollar shortage never achieved the severity anticipated by the authors of the scarce currency clause, and the provision was never invoked.

If the "Joint Statement by Experts on the Establishment of an International Monetary Fund," made public in April 1944, bore the imprint of the U.S. delegation to Bretton Woods, to a surprising extent it also embodied important elements of the British negotiating position. It is curious from the perspective of hegemonic stability theory that a war-battered economy—Britain—heavily dependent on the dominant economic power—America—for capital goods, financial capital, and export markets was able to extract significant concessions in the design of the international monetary system. Britain was ably represented in the negotiations. But even more important, the United States also required an international agreement and wished to secure it even while hostilities in Europe prevented enemy nations from taking part in negotiations and minimized the involvement of the allies on whose territory the war was fought. The United States therefore had little opportunity to play off countries against one another or to brand as renegades any that disputed the advisability of its design. As the Western world's second largest economy, Britain symbolized, if it did not actually represent, the other nations of the world and was able to advance their case more effectively than if they had attempted more actively to do so themselves.

What conclusions regarding the applicability of hegemonic stability theory to the genesis of international monetary systems follow from the evidence of these three cases? In the two clearest instances of hegemony—the United Kingdom in the second half of the nineteenth century and the United States following World War II—the leading economic power significantly influenced the form of the international monetary system, by example in the first instance and by negotiation in the second. But the evidence also underscores the fact that the hegemon has been incapable of dictating the form of the monetary system. In the first instance, British example did nothing to prevent significant modifications in the form of the gold standard adopted abroad. In the second, the exceptional dominance of the U.S. economy was unable to eliminate the need to compromise with other countries in the design of the monetary system.

THE OPERATION OF MONETARY SYSTEMS AND THE THEORY OF HEGEMONIC STABILITY

It is necessary to consider not only the genesis of monetary systems but also how the theory of hegemonic stability applies to the operation of such systems. I consider adjustment, liquidity, and the lender-of-last-resort function in turn.

Adjustment

Adjustment under the classical gold standard has frequently been characterized in terms compatible with hegemonic stability theory. The gold standard is portrayed as a managed system whose preservation and smooth operation were ensured through its regulation by a hegemonic power, Great Britain, and its agent, the Bank of England. . . .

Before 1914, London was indisputably the world's leading financial center. A large proportion of world trade—60 percent by one estimate—was settled through payment in sterling bills, with London functioning as a clearinghouse for importers and exporters of other nations. British discount houses bought bills from abroad, either directly or through the London agencies of foreign banks. Foreigners maintained balances in London to meet commitments on bills outstanding and to service British portfolio investments overseas. Foreign governments and central banks held deposits in London as interest-earning alternatives to gold reserves. Although the pound was not the only reserve currency of the pre-1914 era, sterling reserves matched the combined value of reserves denominated in other currencies. At the same time, Britain possessed perhaps £350 million of short-term capital overseas. Though it is unclear whether Britain was a net short-term debtor or creditor before the war, it is certain that a large volume of short-term funds was responsive to changes in domestic interest rates.

Such changes in interest rates might be instigated by the Bank of England. By altering the rates at which it discounted for its customers and redis-counted for the discount houses, the bank could affect rates prevailing in the discount market. But the effect of Bank rate was not limited to the bill market. While in part this reflected the exceptional integration characteristic of British financial markets, it was reinforced by institutionalization. In London, banks automatically fixed their deposit rates half a percentage point above Bank rate. Loan rates were similarly indexed to Bank rate but at a higher level. Though there were exceptions to these rules, changes in Bank rate were immediately reflected in a broad range of British interest rates.

An increase in Bank rate, by raising the general level of British interest rates, induced foreign investors to accumulate additional funds in London and to delay the repatriation or transfer of existing balances to other centers. British balances abroad were repatriated to earn the higher rate of return. Drawings of finance bills, which represented half of total bills in 1913, were similarly sensitive to changes in interest rates. Higher interest rates spread to the security market and delayed the flotation of new issues for overseas borrowers. In this way the Bank of England was able to insulate its gold reserve from disturbances in the external accounts. . . .

But why did the Bank of England's exceptional leverage not threaten convertibility abroad? The answer commonly offered is that Britain's unrivaled market power led to a de facto harmonization of national policies. . . . As Keynes wrote in the *Treatise on Money,* "During the latter half of the nineteenth century the influence of London on credit conditions throughout the world was so predominant that the Bank of England could almost have claimed to be the conductor of the international orchestra."

Since fiscal harmonization requires no discussion in an era of balanced budgets, the stability of the classical gold standard can be explained by the desire and ability of central banks to harmonize their monetary policies in the interest of external balance. External balance, or maintaining gold reserves adequate to defend the established gold parity, was the foremost target of monetary policy in the period preceding World War I. In the absence of a coherent theory of unemployment, much less a consensus on its relation to monetary policy, there was relatively little pressure for central banks to accommodate domestic needs. External balance was not the sole target of policy, but when internal and external balance came into conflict, the latter took precedence. Viewed from an international perspective, British leadership played a role in this process of harmonization insofar as the market power and prominence of the Bank of England served as a focal point for policy coordination.

But if the Bank of England could be sure of defeating its European counterparts when they engaged in a tug of war over short-term capital, mere harmonization of central bank policies, in the face of external disturbances, would have been insufficient to prevent convertibility crises on the Continent. The explanation for the absence of such crises would appear to be the greater market power of European countries compared with their non-European counterparts. Some observers have distinguished the market power of capital-exporting countries from the inability of capital importers to influence the direction of financial flows. Others have suggested the existence of a hierarchical structure of financial markets: below the London market were the less active markets of Berlin, Paris, Vienna, Amsterdam, Brussels, Zurich, and New York, followed by the still less active markets of the Scandinavian countries, and finally the nascent markets of Latin America and other parts of the non-European world. When Bank rate was raised in London, thus redistributing reserves to Britain from other regions, compensatory discount rate increases on the Continent drew funds from the non-European world or curtailed capital outflows. Developing countries, due to either the thinness of markets or the absence of relevant institutions, were unable to prevent these events. In times of crisis, therefore, convertibility was threatened primarily outside Europe and North America. . . .

Thus, insofar as hegemony played some role in the efficiency of the adjustment mechanism, it was not the British hegemony of which so much has been written but the collective hegemony of the European center relative to the non-European periphery. Not only does this case challenge the conception of the hegemon, therefore, but because the stability of the classical gold standard was enjoyed exclusively by the countries of the center, it supports only the weak form of hegemonic stability theory—that the benefits of stability accrued exclusively to the powerful.

The relation between hegemonic power and the need for policy harmonization is equally relevant to the case of the interwar gold exchange standard. One interpretation . . . is that in the absence of a hegemon there was no focal point for policy, which interfered with efforts at coordination. But more important than a declining ability to harmonize policies may have been a diminished desire to do so. Although the advent of explicit stabilization policy was not to occur until the 1930s and 1940s, during the 1920s central banks placed increasing weight on internal conditions when formulating monetary policy. The rise of socialism and the example of the Bolshevik revolution in particular provided a counterweight to central bankers' instinctive wish to base policy solely on external conditions. External adjustment was rendered difficult by policymakers' increasing hesitancy to sacrifice other objectives on the altar of external balance. Britain's balance-of-payments problems, for example, cannot be attributed to "the existence of more than one policy" in the world economy without considering also a domestic unemployment problem that placed pressure on the Bank of England to resist restrictive measures that might strengthen the external accounts at the expense of industry and trade.

Under Bretton Woods, the problem of adjustment was exacerbated by the difficulty of using exchange rate changes to restore external balance. Hesitancy to change their exchange rates posed few problems for countries in surplus. However, those in deficit had to choose between aggravating unemployment and tolerating external deficits; the latter was infeasible in the long run and promoted an increase in the volume of short-term capital that moved in response to anticipations of devaluation. Although the IMF charter did not encourage devaluation, the hesitancy of deficit countries to employ this option is easier to ascribe to the governments' tendency to attach their prestige to the stability of established exchange rates than to U.S. hegemony, however defined. Where the singular role of the United States was important was in precluding a dollar devaluation. A possible solution to the problem of U.S. deficits, one that would not have threatened other countries' ability to accumulate reserves, was an increase in the dollar price of gold, that is, a dollar devaluation. It is sometimes argued that the United States was incapable of adjusting through exchange rate changes since other countries would have devalued in response to prevent any change in bilateral rates against the dollar. However, raising the dollar price of gold would have increased the dollar value of monetary gold, reducing the global excess demand for reserves and encouraging other countries to increase domestic demand and cut back on their balance-of-payments surpluses. But while a rise in the price of gold might have alleviated central banks' immediate dependence on dollars, it would have done nothing to prevent the problem from recurring. It would also have promoted skepticism about the U.S. government's commitment to the new gold price, thereby encouraging other countries to increase their demands for gold and advancing the date of future difficulties.

Does this evidence on adjustment support hegemonic theories of international monetary stability? The contrast between the apparently smooth adjustment under the classical gold standard and Bretton Woods and the adjustment difficulties of the interwar years suggests that a dominant power's policies served as a fixed target that was easier to hit than a moving one. . . . [W]hat mattered was not so much the particular stance of monetary policy but that the leading players settled on the same stance. The argument . . . is that a dominant player is best placed to signal the other players the nature of the most probable stance. The effectiveness of the adjustment mechanism under the two regimes reflected not just British and American market power but also the existence of an international consensus on the objectives and formulation of monetary policy that permitted central bank policies to be harmonized. The essential role of Britain before 1914 and the United States after

1944 was not so much to force other countries to alter their policies as to provide a focal point for policy harmonization.

Liquidity

Under the classical gold standard, the principal source of liquidity was newly mined gold. It is hard to see how British dominance of international markets could have much influenced the changes in the world price level and mining technology upon which these supplies depended. As argued above, where Britain's prominence mattered was in facilitating the provision of supplementary liquidity in the form of sterling reserves, which grew at an accelerating rate starting in the 1890s. It is conceivable, therefore, that in the absence of British hegemony a reserve shortage would have developed and the classical gold standard would have exhibited a deflationary bias.

Liquidity was an issue of more concern under the interwar gold exchange standard. Between 1915 and 1925, prices rose worldwide due to the inflation associated with wartime finance and postwar reconstruction; these rising prices combined with economic growth to increase the transactions demand for money. Yet under a system of convertible currencies, world money supply was constrained by the availability of reserves. Statutory restrictions required central banks to back their money supplies with eligible reserves, while recent experience with inflation deterred politicians from liberalizing the statutes. The output of newly mined gold had been depressed since the beginning of World War I, and experts offered pessimistic forecasts of future supplies. Increasing the real value of world gold reserves by forcing a reduction in the world price level would only add to the difficulties of an already troubled world economy. Countries were encouraged, therefore, to stabilize on a gold exchange basis to prevent the development of a gold shortage.

There are difficulties with this explanation of interwar liquidity problems, which emphasizes a shortage of gold. For one, the danger of a gold shortage's constraining the volume of transactions was alleviated by the all but complete withdrawal of gold coin from circulation during the war. As a result, the percentage of short-term liabilities of all central banks backed by gold was little different in 1928 from its level in 1913, while the volume of the liabilities backed by that gold stock was considerably increased. It is hard to see why a gold shortage, after having exhibited only weak effects in previous years, should have had such a dramatic impact starting in 1929. It is even less clear how the absence of a hegemon contributed to the purported gold shortage. The obvious linkages between hegemony and the provision of liquidity work in the wrong direction. The straightforward way of increasing the monetary value of reserves was a round of currency devaluation, which would revalue gold reserves and, by raising the real price of gold, increase the output of the mining industry. As demonstrated in 1931, when the pound's depreciation set off a round of competitive devaluations, sterling remained the linchpin of the international currency system; the only way a round of currency devaluation could have taken place, therefore, was if Britain had stabilized in 1925 at a lower level. But had her dominance of the international economy not eroded over the first quarter of the twentieth century, the political pressure on Britain to return to gold at the prewar parity would have increased rather than being reduced. It seems unlikely, therefore, that a more successful maintenance of British hegemony, ceteris paribus, would have alleviated any gold shortage.

An alternative and more appealing explanation for interwar liquidity problems emphasizes mismanagement of gold reserves rather than their overall insufficiency. It blames France and the United States for absorbing disproportionate shares of global gold supplies and for imposing deflation on the rest of the world. Between 1928 and 1932, French gold reserves rose from $1.25 billion to $3.26 billion of constant gold content, or from 13 to 28 percent of the world total. Meanwhile, the United States, which had released gold between 1924 and 1928, facilitating the reestablishment of convertibility in other countries, reversed its position and imported $1.49 billion of gold between 1928 and 1930. By the end of 1932 the United States and France together possessed nearly 63 percent of the world's central monetary gold. . . .

The maldistribution of reserves can be understood by focusing on the systematic interaction of central banks. This approach builds on the literature that characterizes the interwar gold standard as a competitive struggle for gold between countries that viewed the size of their gold reserve as a measure of national prestige and as insurance against financial instability. France and the United States in particular, but gold standard countries generally, repeatedly raised their discount rates relative to one another in efforts to attract gold from abroad. By leading to the accumulation of excess reserves, these restrictive policies exacerbated the problem of inadequate liquidity, but by offsetting one another they also failed to achieve their objective of attracting gold from abroad. . . .

The origins of this competitive struggle for gold are popularly attributed to the absence of a hegemon. The competing financial centers—London, Paris, and New York—worked at cross-purposes because, in contrast to the preceding period, no one central bank was sufficiently powerful to call the tune. Before the war, the Bank of England had been sufficiently dominant to act as a leader, setting its discount rate with the reaction of other central banks in mind, while other central banks responded in the manner of a competitive fringe. By using this power to defend the gold parity of sterling despite the maintenance of slender reserves, the bank prevented the development of a competitive scramble for gold. But after World War I, with the United States unwilling to accept responsibility for leadership, no one central bank formulated its monetary policy with foreign reactions and global conditions in mind, and the noncooperative struggle for gold was the result. In this interpretation of the interwar liquidity problem, hegemony—or, more precisely, its absence—plays a critical role.

In discussing the provision of liquidity under Bretton Woods, it is critical to distinguish the decade ending in 1958—when the convertibility of European currencies was restored and before U.S. dominance of international trade, foreign lending, and industrial production was unrivaled—from the decade that followed. In the first period, the most important source of incremental liquidity was dollar reserves. Between 1949 and 1958, when global reserves rose by 29 percent, less than one-third of the increment took the form of gold and one-fifteenth was in quotas at the IMF. The role of sterling as a reserve currency was limited almost exclusively to Commonwealth members and former British colonies that had traditionally held reserves in London and traded heavily with Britain. Consequently, the accumulation of dollar balances accounted for roughly half of incremental liquidity in the first decade of Bretton Woods.

In one sense, U.S. dominance of international markets facilitated the provision of liquidity. At the end of World War II, the United States had amassed 60 percent of the world's gold stock; at $35 an ounce, this was worth six times the value of the official dollar claims accumulated by foreign governments by 1949. There was little immediate question, given U.S. dominance of global gold reserves, of the stability of the gold price of the dollar and hence little hesitation to accumulate incremental liquidity in the form of dollar claims. But in another sense, U.S. international economic power in the immediate postwar years impeded the supply of liquidity to the world economy. Wartime destruction of industry in Europe and Japan left U.S. manufactured exports highly competitive in world markets and rendered Europe dependent on U.S. capital goods for industrial reconstruction. The persistent excess demand for U.S. goods tended to push the U.S. balance of payments into surplus, creating the famous "dollar shortage" of the immediate postwar years. While U.S. hegemony left other countries willing to hold dollar claims, it rendered them extremely difficult to obtain.

Various policies were initiated in response to the dollar shortage, including discrimination against dollar area exports, special incentives for European and Japanese exports to the United States, and a round of European currency devaluations starting in September 1949. Ultimately the solution took the form of two sharply contrasting actions by the hegemon: Marshall Plan grants of $11.6 billion between mid-1948 and mid-1952, and Korean War expenditures. Largely as a result of these two factors, U.S. trade surpluses shrank from $10.1 billion in 1947 to $2.6 billion in 1952; more important, U.S. government grants and private capital outflows exceeded the surplus on current account. By 1950 the U.S. balance of payments was in deficit and, after moving back into surplus in 1951–52, deficits returned to stay. Insofar as its singular economic power encouraged the United States to undertake both the Marshall Plan and the Korean War, hegemony played a significant role in both the form and adequacy of the liquidity provided in the first decade of Bretton Woods.

Between 1958 and 1969, global reserves grew more rapidly, by 51 percent, than they had in the first decade of Bretton Woods. Again, gold was a minor share of the increment, about one-twentieth, and IMF quotas were one-eighth. While foreign exchange reserves again provided roughly half, Eurodollars and other foreign currencies grew in importance: their contribution actually exceeded that of official claims on the United States. In part these trends reflected rapid growth in Europe and Japan. More important, they reflected the fact that starting in 1965 the value of foreign government claims on the United States exceeded U.S. gold reserves. Prudence dictated that foreign governments diversify their reserve positions out of dollars.

The role of U.S. hegemony in the provision of liquidity during this second decade has been much debated. The growth of liquidity reflected both supply and demand pressures: both demands by other countries for additional reserves, which translated into balance-of-payments surpluses, and the capacity of the United States to consume more than it produced by running balance-of-payments deficits financed by the willingness of other countries to accumulate dollar reserves. The United States was criticized sharply, mainly by the French, for exporting inflation and for financing purchases of foreign companies and pursuit of the Vietnam War through the balance of payments. Although these complaints cannot be dismissed, it is incorrect to conclude that the dollar's singular position in the Bretton Woods system permitted the United States to run whatever balance-of-payments deficit it wished. Moreover, it is difficult to envisage an alternative scenario in which the U.S. balance of payments was zero but the world was not starved of liquidity. Owing to the sheer size of the American economy, new claims on the United States continued to exceed vastly the contribution of new claims on any other nation. Moreover, U.S. economic, military, and diplomatic influence did much to encourage if not compel other countries to maintain their holdings of dollar claims. Thus U.S. dominance of international markets played a critical role in resolving the liquidity crisis of the 1960s.

The distinguishing feature of Bretton Woods is not that other countries continued to hold dollar reserves in the face of exchange rate uncertainty and economic growth abroad, for neither development has deterred them from holding dollars under the flexible exchange rate regime of the 1970s and 1980s. Rather, it is that they continued to hold dollar reserves in the face of a one-way bet resulting from dollar convertibility at a fixed price when the dollar price of gold seemed poised to rise. In part, the importance of American foreign investments and the size of the U.S. market for European exports caused other countries to hesitate before cashing in their chips. Yet foreign governments also saw dollar convertibility as essential to the defense of the gold-dollar system and viewed the fixed exchange rates of that system as an international public good worthy of defense. Not until 1965 did the French government decide to convert into gold some $300 million of its dollar holdings and subsequently to step up its monthly gold purchases from the United

States. But when pressure on U.S. gold reserves mounted following the 1967 devaluation of sterling, other countries, including France, sold gold instead of capitalizing on the one-way bet. They joined the United States in the formation of a gold pool whose purpose was to sell a sufficient quantity of gold to defend the official price. Between sterling's devaluation in 1967 and closure of the gold market on March 15, 1968, the pool sold $3 billion of gold, of which U.S. sales were $2.2 billion. France purchased no gold in 1967 or 1968, presumably due in part to foreign pressure. U.S. leverage undoubtedly contributed to their decisions. But a plausible interpretation of these events is that foreign governments, rather than simply being coerced into support of the dollar by U.S. economic power, were willing to take limited steps to defend the international public good of a fixed exchange rate system defined in terms of the dollar price of gold.

What does this discussion imply for the role of hegemony in the provision of international liquidity? The strongest evidence for the importance of a hegemon is negative evidence from the interwar years, when the absence of a hegemon and the failure of competing financial centers to coordinate their policies effectively contributed greatly to the liquidity shortage. In other periods, when a dominant economic power was present, it is difficult to credit that power with sole responsibility for ensuring the adequate provision of liquidity. Under the gold standard, the principal source of incremental liquidity was newly mined gold; Britain contributed to the provision of liquidity only insofar as its financial stature encouraged other countries to augment their specie holdings with sterling reserves. After World War II, U.S. economic power similarly rendered dollars a desirable form in which to acquire liquid reserves, but the same factors that made dollars desirable also rendered them difficult to obtain.

The Lender of Last Resort

If adjustment were always accomplished smoothly and liquidity were consistently adequate, there would be no need for an international lender of last resort to stabilize the international monetary system. Yet countries' capacity to adjust and the system's ability to provide liquidity may be inadequate to accommodate disturbances to confidence. Like domestic banking systems, an international financial system based on convertibility is vulnerable to problems of confidence that threaten to ignite speculative runs. Like depositors who rush to close their accounts upon receiving the news of a neighboring bank failure, exchange market participants, upon hearing of a convertibility crisis abroad, may rush to liquidate their foreign exchange balances because of incomplete information about the liabilities and intentions of particular governments. This analogy leads Charles Kindleberger, for example, to adopt from the domestic central banking literature the notion that a lender of last resort is needed to discount in times of crisis, provide countercyclical long-term lending, and maintain an open market for distress goods, and to suggest that, in the absence of a supranational institution, only a hegemonic power can carry out this international lender-of-last-resort function on the requisite scale.

Of the episodes considered here, the early Bretton Woods era provides the clearest illustration of the benefits of an international lender of last resort. The large amount of credit provided Europe in the form of grants and long-term loans and the willingness of the United States to accept European and Japanese exports even when these had been promoted by the extension of special incentives illustrate two of the lender-of-last-resort functions identi-fied by Kindleberger: counter-cyclical lending and provision of an open mar-ket for distress goods. Many histories of the Marshall Plan characterize it in terms consistent with the benevolent strand of hegemonic stability theory: the United States was mainly interested in European prosperity and stood to benefit only insofar as that prosperity promoted geopolitical stability. Revi-sionist histories have more in common with the coercive strand of hegemonic stability theory: they suggest that the United States used Marshall aid to exact concessions from Europe in the form of most-favored-nation status for Ger-many, IMF exchange rate oversight, and Swiss links with the Organization for European Economic Cooperation. While it is certain that the European countries could not have moved so quickly to relax capital controls and quan-titative trade restrictions without these forms of U.S. assistance, it is not clear how far the argument can be generalized. The Marshall Plan coincided with a very special era in the history of the international monetary system, in which convertibility outside the United States had not yet been restored. Hence there was little role for the central function of the lender of last resort: discounting freely when a convertibility crisis threatens. When convertibility was threatened in the 1960s, rescue operations were mounted not by the United States but cooperatively by the Group of Ten.

Kindleberger has argued that the 1929–31 financial crisis might have been avoided by the intervention of an international lender of last resort. The unwillingness of Britain and the United States to engage in countercyclical long-term lending and to provide an open market for distress goods surely exacerbated convertibility crises in the non-European world. Both the cur-tailment of overseas lending and the imposition of restrictive trade policies contributed greatly to the balance-of-payments difficulties that led to the sus-pension of convertibility by primary producers as early as 1929. Gold move-ments from the periphery to London and New York in 1930 heightened the problem and hastened its spread to Central Europe.

But it is not obvious that additional U.S. loans to Britain and other Euro-pean countries attempting to fend off threats to convertibility would have suc-ceeded in altering significantly the course of the 1931 financial crisis. Heading off the crisis would have required a successful defense of the pound sterling, whose depreciation was followed almost immediately by purposeful devaluation in some two dozen other countries. Britain did succeed in obtaining a substantial amount of short-term credit abroad in support of the pound, raising $650 million in New York and Paris after only minimal delay. Total short-term lending to countries under pressure amounted to approximately $1 billion, or roughly 10 percent of total international short-term indebtedness and 5 percent of world imports (more than the ratio of total IMF quotas to world imports in the mid-1970s). It is noteworthy that these credits were obtained not from a dominant power but from a coalition of creditor countries.

Could additional short-term credits from an international lender of last resort have prevented Britain's suspension of convertibility? If the run on sterling reflected merely a temporary loss of confidence in the stability of fixed parities, then additional loans from an international lender of last resort—like central bank loans to temporarily illiquid banks—might have permitted the crisis to be surmounted. But if the loss of confidence had a basis in economic fundamentals, no amount of short-term lending would have done more than delay the crisis in the absence of measures to eliminate the underlying imbalance. The existence of an international lender of last resort could have affected the timing but not the fact of collapse.

The fundamental disequilibrium that undermined confidence in sterling is typically sought in the government budget. The argument is that by stimulating absorption, Britain's budget deficit, in conjunction with the collapse of foreign demand for British exports, weakened the balance of trade. Although the second Labour government fell in 1931 precisely because of its failure to agree on measures to reduce the size of the budget deficit, historians disagree over whether the budget contributed significantly to the balance-of-payments deficit. The trade balance, after all, was only one component of the balance of payments. The effect on the balance of payments of shocks to the trade balance appears to have been small compared with the Bank of England's capacity to attract short-term capital. If this is correct and the 1931 financial crisis in Britain reflected mainly a temporary loss of confidence in sterling rather than a fundamental disequilibrium, then additional short-term loans from the United States or a group of creditor countries might have succeeded in tiding Britain over the crisis. But the loans required would have been extremely large by the standards of either the pre-1914 period of British hegemony or the post-1944 period of U.S. dominance.

The international lender-of-last-resort argument is more difficult to apply to the classical gold standard. . . . [I]n 1873, as in 1890 and 1907, the hegemonic monetary authority, the Bank of England, would have been the "borrower of last resort" rather than the lender. [This fact] might be reconciled with the theory of hegemonic stability if the lender, Paris, is elevated to the status of a hegemonic financial center—a possibility to which Kindleberger is led by his analysis of late nineteenth century financial crises. But elevating

Paris to parity with London would do much to undermine the view of the classical gold standard that attributes its durability to management by a single financial center.

What does this historical analysis of the lender-of-last-resort function imply for the validity of hegemonic theories of international monetary stability? It confirms that there have been instances, notably the aftermath of World War II, when the economic power of the leading country so greatly surpassed that of all rivals that it succeeded in ensuring the system's stability in times of crisis by discounting freely, providing countercyclical lending, and maintaining an open market. It suggests, at the same time, that such instances are rare. For a leading economic power to effectively act as lender of last resort, not only must its market power exceed that of all rivals, but it must do so by a very substantial margin. British economic power in the 1870s and U.S. economic power in the 1960s were inadequate in this regard, and other economic powers—France in the first instance, the Group of Ten in the second—were needed to cooperate in providing lender-of-last-resort facilities.

THE DYNAMICS OF HEGEMONIC DECLINE

Might an international monetary system that depends for its smooth operation on the dominance of a hegemonic power be dynamically unstable? There are two channels through which dynamic instability might operate: the system itself might evolve in directions that attenuate the hegemon's stabilizing capacity; or the system might remain the same, but its operation might influence relative rates of economic growth in such a way as to progressively reduce the economic power and, by implication, the stabilizing capacity of the hegemon.

The hypothesis that the Bretton Woods System was dynamically unstable was mooted by Robert Triffin as early as 1947. Triffin focused on what he saw as inevitable changes in the composition of reserves, arguing that the system's viability hinged on the willingness of foreign governments to accumulate dollars, which depended in turn on confidence in the maintenance of dollar convertibility. Although gold dominated the dollar as a source of international liquidity (in 1958 the value of gold reserves was four times the value of dollar reserves when all countries were considered, two times when the United States was excluded), dollars were the main source of liquidity on the margin. Yet the willingness of foreign governments to accumulate dollars at the required pace and hence the stability of the gold-dollar system were predicated on America's commitment and capacity to maintain the convertibility of dollars into gold at $35 an ounce. The threat to its ability to do so was that, under a system in which reserves could take the form of either dollars or gold (a scarce natural resource whose supply was insufficiently elastic to keep pace with the demand for liquidity), the share of dollars in total reserves could only increase. An ever-growing volume of foreign dollar liabilities was based on a fixed or even shrinking U.S. gold reserve. Thus the very structure of Bretton Woods—specifically, the monetary role for gold—progressively undermined the hegemon's capacity to ensure the system's smooth operation through the provision of adequate liquidity.

Dynamic instability also could have operated through the effect of the international monetary system on the relative rates of growth of the U.S. and foreign economies. If the dollar was systematically overvalued for a significant portion of the Bretton Woods era, this could have reduced the competitiveness of U.S. exports and stimulated foreign penetration of U.S. markets. If the dollar was overvalued due to some combination of European devaluations at the beginning of the 1950s, subsequent devaluations by developing countries, and the inability of the United States to respond to competitive difficulties by altering its exchange rate, how might this have depressed the relative rate of growth of the U.S. economy, leading to hegemonic decline? One can think of two arguments: one that proceeds along Heckscher-Ohlin lines, another that draws on dynamic theories of international trade.

The Heckscher-Ohlin hypothesis builds on the observation that the United States was relatively abundant in human and physical capital. Since, under Heckscher-Ohlin assumptions, U.S. exports were capital intensive, any measure that depressed exports would have reduced its rate of return. Reducing the rate of return would have discouraged investment, depressing the rate of economic growth and accelerating the U.S. economy's relative decline.

The dynamic trade theory hypothesis builds on the existence of learning curves in the production of traded goods. If production costs fall with cumulative output and the benefits of learning are external to the firm but internal to domestic industry, then exchange rate overvaluation, by depressing the competitiveness of exports, will inhibit their production and reduce the benefits of learning. If overvaluation is sufficiently large and persistent, it will shift comparative advantage in production to foreign competitors. The weakness of this hypothesis is that it is predicated on the unsubstantiated assumption that learning effects are more important in the production of traded goods than non-traded goods. Its strength lies in the extent to which it conforms with informal characterizations of recent trends.

Precisely the same arguments have been applied to the downfall of the interwar gold exchange standard. The interwar system, which depended for liquidity on gold, dollars, and sterling, was if anything even more susceptible than its post–World War II analog to destabilization by the operation of Gresham's law. As noted above, the legacy of the Genoa conference encouraged central banks to accumulate foreign exchange. Promoting the use of exchange reserves while attempting to maintain gold convertibility threatened the system's stability for the same reasons as under Bretton Woods. But because foreign exchange reserves were not then concentrated in a single currency to the same extent as after World War II, it was even easier under the interwar system for central banks to liquidate foreign balances in response to any event that undermined confidence in sterling or the dollar. Instead of initiating the relatively costly and complex process of acquiring gold from foreign monetary authorities in the face of at least moral suasion to refrain, central banks needed only to swap one reserve currency for the other on the open market. Gresham's law operated even more powerfully when gold coexisted with two reserve currencies than with one.

This instability manifested itself when the 1931 financial crisis, by undermining faith in sterling convertibility, induced a large-scale shift out of London balances. Once Britain was forced to devalue, faith in the stability of the other major reserve currency was shaken, and speculative pressure shifted to the dollar. The National Bank of Belgium, which had lost 25 percent of the value of its sterling reserve as a result of Britain's devaluation, moved to liquidate its dollar balances. The Eastern European countries, including Poland, Czechoslovakia, and Bulgaria, then liquidated their deposits in New York. Between the end of 1930 and the end of 1931, the share of foreign exchange in the reserve portfolios of twenty-three European countries fell from 35 to 19 percent, signaling the demise of the exchange portion of the gold exchange standard.

The argument that structuring the international monetary system around a reserve asset provided by the leading economic power led eventually to that country's loss of preeminence has been applied even more frequently to Britain after World War I than to the United States after World War II. Because the gold exchange standard created a foreign demand for sterling balances, Britain was able to run larger trade balance deficits than would have been permitted otherwise. In a sense, Britain's reserve currency status was one of the factors that facilitated the restoration of sterling's prewar parity. Despite an enormous literature predicated on the view that the pound was overvalued at $4.86, there remains skepticism that the extent of overvaluation was great or the effect on the macroeconomy was significant. While it is not possible to resolve this debate here, the point relevant to the theory of hegemonic stability is that evidence of reserve currency overvaluation is as substantial in the earlier period, when hegemony was threatened, as in the later period, when it was triumphant.

Of the three monetary systems considered here, the classical gold standard is the most difficult to analyze in terms of the dynamics of hegemonic decline. It might be argued that the pound was overvalued for at least a decade before 1913 and that Britain's failure to devalue resulted in sluggish growth, which accelerated the economy's hegemonic decline. The competitive difficulties of older British industries, notably iron and steel, and the decelerating rate of economic growth in the first decade of the twentieth century are consistent with this view. The deceleration in the rate of British economic growth has been ascribed to both a decline in productivity growth and a fall in the rate of domestic capital formation. This fall in the rate of domestic capital formation, especially after 1900, reflected not a decline in British savings rates but a surge of foreign investment. Thus, if Britain's hegemonic position in the international economy is to have caused its relative decline, this hegemony would have had to be responsible for the country's exceptionally high propensity to export capital. The volume of British capital exports in the decades preceding World War I has been attributed, alternatively, to the spread of industrialization and associated investment opportunities to other countries and continents and to imperfections in the structure of British capital markets that resulted in a bias toward investment overseas. It is impossible to resolve this debate here. But the version of the market imperfections argument that attributes the London capital market's lack of interest in domestic investment to Britain's relatively early and labor-intensive form of industrialization implies that the same factors responsible for Britain's mid-nineteenth century hegemony (the industrial revolution occurred there first) may also have been responsible for the capital market biases that accelerated its hegemonic decline.

Although the classical gold standard experienced a number of serious disruptions, such as the 1907 panic when a financial crisis threatened to undermine its European core, the prewar system survived these disturbances intact. Eventually, however, the same forces that led to the downfall of the interwar gold exchange standard would have undermined the stability of the prewar system. As the rate of economic growth continued to outstrip the rate of growth of gold (the supply of which was limited by the availability of ore), countries would have grown increasingly dependent on foreign exchange reserves as a source of incremental liquidity. As in the 1960s, growing reliance on exchange reserves in the face of relatively inelastic gold supplies would have eventually proven incompatible with the reserve center's ability to maintain gold convertibility.

De Cecco argues that the situation was already beginning to unravel in the first decade of the twentieth century—that the Boer War signaled the end of the long peace of the nineteenth century, thereby undermining the willingness of potential belligerents to hold their reserves as deposits in foreign countries. . . . More important for our purposes, he suggests that the system was destabilized by the growth of U.S. economic power relative to that of Great Britain. Given the experimental nature of U.S. Treasury efforts to accommodate seasonal variations in money demand, the United States relied heavily on' gold imports whenever economic conditions required an increase in money supply, notably during harvest and planting seasons. When the demand for money increased, the United States imported gold, mainly from the Bank of England, which was charged with pegging the sterling price of gold on the London market with a gold reserve of only £30 million. As the American economy grew, both its average demand for gold from London and that demand's seasonal fluctuation increased relative to the Bank of England's primary reserve and its capacity to attract supplementary funds from other centers. To rephrase de Cecco's argument in terms of hegemonic stability theory, the growth of the United States relative to that of Britain undermined Britain's capacity to stabilize international financial markets: specifically, its ability to serve simultaneously as the world's only free gold market, providing however much gold was required by other countries, and to maintain the stability of sterling, the reference point for the global system of fixed exchange rates. In a sense, de Cecco sees indications of the interwar stalemate—a Britain incapable of stabilizing the international system and a United States unwilling to do so—emerging in the first decade of the twentieth century. From this perspective, the process of hegemonic decline that culminated in the international monetary difficulties of the interwar years was at most accelerated by World War I. Even before the war, the processes that led to the downfall of established monetary arrangements were already under way.

CONCLUSION

Much of the international relations literature concerned with prospects for international monetary reform can be read as a search for an alternative to hegemony as a basis for international monetary stability. Great play is given to the contrast between earlier periods of hegemonic dominance, notably 1890–1914 and 1945–71, and the nature of the task presently confronting aspiring architects of international monetary institutions in an increasingly multipolar world. In this paper I suggest that hegemonic stability theories are helpful for understanding the relatively smooth operation of the classical gold standard and the early Bretton Woods system, as well as some of the difficulties of the interwar years. At the same time, much of the evidence is difficult to reconcile with the hegemonic stability view. Even when individual countries occupied positions of exceptional prominence in the world economy and that prominence was reflected in the form and functioning of the international monetary system, that system was still fundamentally predicated on international collaboration. Keohane's notion of "hegemonic cooperation"— that cooperation is required for systemic stability even in periods of hegemonic dominance, although the presence of a hegemon may encourage cooperative behavior—seems directly applicable to international monetary relations. The importance of collaboration is equally apparent in the design of the international monetary system, its operation under normal circumstances, and the management of crises. Despite the usefulness of hegemonic stability theory when applied to short periods and well-defined aspects of international monetary relations, the international monetary system has always been "after hegemony" in the sense that more than a dominant economic power was required to ensure the provision and maintenance of international monetary stability. Moreover, it was precisely when important economic power most forcefully conditioned the form of the international system that the potential for instability, in a dynamic sense, was greatest. Above all, historical experience demonstrates the speed and pervasiveness of changes in national economic power; since hegemony is transitory, so must be any international monetary system that takes hegemony as its basis. Given the costs of international monetary reform, it would seem unwise to predicate a new system on such a transient basis.

15

The Triad and the Unholy Trinity: Problems of International Monetary Cooperation

BENJAMIN J. COHEN

In this essay, Benjamin J. Cohen explores the attractions and difficulties of cooperation among nations concerning international monetary matters and emphasizes how international political realities constrain interactions among independent nation-states. Monetary policy coordination has some potential benefits, but there are many uncertainties that countries face in engaging in cooperative behavior. The primary dilemma is that governments cannot simultaneously achieve the objectives of exchange rate stability, capital mobility, and monetary policy autonomy. As governments are forced to make trade-offs among these goals, they will abandon the goal of exchange rate stability—and thus monetary cooperation—if it is too costly relative to the other policy objectives. The cyclical and episodic qualities of monetary cooperation are linked to governments' changing incentives to pursue stable exchange rates. Cohen's argument highlights the difficulty of sustaining cooperative arrangements when states' national interests diverge.

. . . Among the G-7 countries (the United States, Britain, Canada, France, Germany, Italy, and Japan), procedures for monetary cooperation have been gradually intensified since the celebrated Plaza Agreement of September 1985, which formally pledged participants to a coordinated realignment of exchange rates. Ostensibly the aim of these evolving procedures is to jointly manage currency relations and macroeconomic conditions across Europe, North America and Japan—the area referred to by many simply as the Triad. Finance ministers from the G-7 countries now meet regularly to discuss the current and prospective performance of their economies; policy objectives and instruments are evaluated for possible linkages and repercussions; the principle of mutual adjustment in the common interest is repeatedly reaffirmed in official communiqués. . . . Yet for all their promises to curb unilateralist impulses, the governments involved frequently honour the process more in word than deed. In fact, if there has been one constant in the collaborative efforts of the Triad, it has been their lack of constancy. Commitments in practice have tended to ebb and flow cyclically like the tides. In its essence, G-7 monetary cooperation has had a distinctly episodic quality to it.

The main premise of this chapter is that international monetary cooperation, like passionate love, is a good thing but difficult to sustain. The reason,

I argue, is systematic and has to do with the intrinsic incompatibility of three key desiderata of governments: exchange-rate stability, capital mobility, and national policy autonomy. Together these three values form a kind of "Unholy Trinity" that operates regularly to erode collective commitments to monetary collaboration. The impact of the Unholy Trinity has been evident in the experience of the G-7. The principal implication . . . is that the conditions necessary for a serious and sustained commitment to monetary cooperation are not easy to satisfy and, without major effort, appear unlikely to be attained any time soon. The irony is that even without such a commitment most . . . governments will find their policy autonomy increasingly eroded in the coming decade—in a manner, moreover, that may seem even less appealing to them than formal cooperation.

The organisation of this chapter is as follows. Following a brief evaluation in Part 1 of the basic case for monetary cooperation, Part 2 reviews the experience of the G-7 countries since 1985 noting, in particular, a distinctly cyclical pattern in the Triad's collective commitment to policy coordination. Reasons for the episodic quality of monetary cooperation with emphasis on the central role of the Unholy Trinity are explored in Part 3, and the question of what might be done about the resulting inconstancy of policy commitments is addressed in Part 4. . . .

1. THE CASE FOR POLICY COOPERATION

Conceptually, international cooperation may take many forms, ranging from simple consultation among governments, or occasional crisis management, to partial or even full collaboration in the formulation and implementation of policy. In this chapter, following the lead of standard scholarship on international political economy, cooperation will be identified with a mutual adjustment of national-policy behaviour in a particular issue-area, achieved through an implicit or explicit process of inter-state bargaining. Related terms such as "coordination" and "joint" or "collective decision-making" will, for our purposes, be treated as essentially synonymous in meaning.

In the issue-area of international monetary relations, the theoretical case for policy cooperation is quite straightforward. It begins with the undeniable fact of intensified interdependence across much of the world economy. In recent decades, states have become increasingly linked through the integration of markets for goods, services and capital. Structurally, the greater openness of economies tends to erode each country's insulation from commercial or financial developments elsewhere. In policy terms it means that any one government's actions will generate a variety of "spillover" effects—foreign repercussions and feedbacks—that can significantly influence its own ability, as well as the ability of others, to achieve preferred macro-economic or exchange-rate objectives. (Technically the size, and possibly even the sign, of policy multipliers is altered both at home and abroad.) Such "externalities" imply that policies chosen unilaterally, even if seemingly optimal from an individual country's point of view, will almost certainly turn out to be sub-optimal in a global context. The basic rationale for monetary cooperation is that it can *internalise* these externalities by giving each government partial control over the actions of others, thus relieving the shortage of instruments that prevents each one separately from reaching its chosen targets on its own.

At least two sets of goals may be pursued through policy coordination. At one level, cooperation may be treated simply as a vehicle by which countries together move closer to their individual policy targets. (In the formal language of game theory favoured by many analysts, utility or welfare-seeking governments bargain their way from the sub-optimality of a so-called Nash equilibrium to something closer to a Pareto optimum.) Peter Kenen calls this the *policy-optimising* approach to cooperation. At a second level, mutual adjustments can also be made in pursuit of broader collective goals, such as defence of existing international arrangements or institutions against the threat of economic or political shocks. Kenen calls this the *regime-preserving* or *public-goods* approach to cooperation. Both approaches derive from the same facts of structural and policy interdependence. Few scholars question the basic logic of either one.

What is accepted in theory, of course, need not be favoured in practice—however persuasive the logic. . . .

. . . In recent years there has been a virtual avalanche of formal literature citing various qualifications to the basic case for monetary cooperation and casting doubt on its practical benefits. The irony is evident: even as policy coordination since the mid-1980s has ostensibly become fashionable again among governments, it seems to have gone out of style with many analysts. At least five major issues have been raised for discussion by economists working in this area.

First is the question of the *magnitude of the gains* to be expected. Although in theory the move from a Nash equilibrium to Pareto optimality may seem dramatic, in practice much depends on the size of the spillovers involved. If externalities are small, so too will be the potential benefits of cooperation.

Many analysts cite a pioneering study by Oudiz and Sachs designed to measure the effects of monetary and fiscal policy coordination by Germany, Japan and the United States, using data from the mid-1970s. Estimated gains were disappointingly meagre, amounting to no more than half of one per cent of GNP in each country as compared with the best noncooperative outcomes. Although some subsequent studies have detected moderately greater income increases from coordination, most tend to confirm the impression that on balance very large gains should not be expected.

Second is the other side of the ledger: the question of the *magnitude of the costs* to be expected. Theoretical models typically abstract from the costs of coordination. In reality, however, considerable time and effort are needed to evaluate performance, negotiate agreements, and monitor compliance among sovereign governments. Moreover, the greater the number of countries or issues involved, the more complex are the policy adjustments that are likely to be required of each. All this demands expenditure of resources that may loom large when compared with the possibly meagre scale of anticipated benefits. For some analysts, this suggests that the game may simply not be worth the candle. For others, it implies the need for a more explicit framework for cooperation—some formally agreed set of rules—that could substitute for repeated negotiations over individual issues. . . . The advantage of an articulated rule-based regime is that it would presumably be more cost-effective than endless *ad hoc* bargaining. The disadvantage is that it would require a greater surrender of policy autonomy than many governments now seem prepared to tolerate (a point to which I shall return below).

Third is the so-called *time-inconsistency* problem: the risk that agreements, once negotiated, will later be violated by maverick governments tempted to renege on policy commitments that turn out to be inconvenient. The risk, in principle, is a real one. In relations between sovereign states, where enforcement mechanisms are weak or nonexistent, there is always a threat that bargains may be at some point broken. But whether the possibility of unilateral defection constitutes much of a threat in practice is hotly debated among specialists, many of whom stress the role of reputation and credibility as deterrents to cheating by individual governments. In the language of game theory, much depends on the details of how the strategic interactions are structured, for example, the number of players in the game, whether and how often the game is iterated, and how many other related games are being played simultaneously. Much depends as well on the historical and institutional context, and how the preferences of decision-makers are formed—matters about which it is inherently difficult to generalise. In the absence of more general specifications, few definitive judgements seem possible *a priori*.

Fourth is the possible *distortion of incentives* that might be generated by efforts at policy coordination. In an early and influential article, Kenneth Rogoff argued that international cooperation could actually prove to be counterproductive—welfare-decreasing rather than Pareto-improving—if the coordination process were to encourage governments collectively to choose policies that are more politically convenient than economically sound. Formal coordination of monetary policies, for example, could simply lead to higher global inflation if governments were all to agree to expand their money supplies together, thus evading the balance-of-payments constraint that would discipline any country attempting to inflate on its own. More generally, there is always the chance that ruling élites might exploit the process to promote particularist or even personal interests at the expense of broader collective goals. This risk too is widely regarded as realistic in principle and is hotly debated for its possible importance in practice. And here too few definitive judgements seem possible *a priori* in the absence of more general specifications.

Finally, there is the issue of *model uncertainty*: the risks that policy-makers simply are badly informed and do not really understand how their economies operate and interact. Frankel and Rockett in a widely cited study demonstrated that when governments do differ in their analytical views of policy impacts, coordination could well cause welfare losses rather than gains for at least some of the countries involved. For some analysts, this is more than enough reason to prefer a return to uncoordinated pursuit of national self-interest. For others, however, it suggests instead the value of consultation and exchanges of information to avoid misunderstandings about transmission mechanisms and the size and sign of relevant policy multipliers. . . .

Where, then, does all this discussion come out? None of the five issues that have been so thoroughly aired in the literature is unimportant; sceptics have been right to raise and emphasise them. But neither do any of these qualifications appear to deal a decisive blow to the underlying case for cooperation, which retains its essential appeal. For this reason most analysts, myself among them, still remain disposed to view policy cooperation for all its imperfections in much the same light as virtue or motherhood—an inherently good thing. Net gains may be small; motivations may get distorted; outcomes may not always fulfil expectations. Nonetheless, despite all the risks the effort does seem justified. . . .

2. THE EBB AND FLOW OF POLICY COMMITMENTS

A problem remains, however. To be effective, the collective commitment to cooperation must appear credible; and to be credible, that commitment must above all be *sustained*. Individual governments may play the maverick on occasion (the time–inconsistency problem); a little cheating at the margins is after all hardly unexpected, or even unusual, in international relations. But the commitment of the collectivity must be seen to be enduring: there can be no room for doubt about the continuing relevance, the *seriousness*, of the process as such. Otherwise incentives will indeed be distorted for state and non-state actors alike, and outcomes could well turn out to be every bit as counterproductive as many analysts fear. As Peter Kenen has warned, "Sporadic management may be worse than no management at all." Yet, as noted at the outset, that is precisely the pattern that policy coordination has tended to display in practice. The history of international monetary cooperation is one long lesson in the fickleness of policy fashion.

During the early inter-war period, for example, the central banks of the major industrial nations publicly committed themselves to a cooperative attempt to restore something like the pre-World War I gold standard, only to end up in the 1930s energetically battling one another through futile rounds of competitive devaluations and escalating capital controls. And similarly during the Bretton Woods era, early efforts at cooperative institution-building and joint consultations ultimately terminated in mutual recriminations and the demise of the par-value system. In the middle 1970s, endeavours to revive some kind of rule-based exchange-rate regime were overwhelmed by policy disagreements between the Carter administration in the United States and its counterparts in Europe and Japan, leading to a record depreciation of the US dollar. At the turn of the decade renewed attempts at joint stabilization were cut short by the go-it-alone policies of the new Reagan administration, leading to the record appreciation of the dollar which, in turn, set the stage for the Plaza Agreement of 1985. The broad picture of monetary relations in the twentieth century is clearly one of considerable ebbs and flows in the collective commitment to policy cooperation.

Moreover, the big picture—much in the manner of Mandelbrot fractals—tends broadly to be replicated in the small. (A fractal is an object or phenomenon that is self-similar across different scales.) Often superimposed on longer waves of enthusiasm or disillusionment with policy cooperation have been briefer "stop-go" cycles of commitment and retreat, such as the short-lived attempts of the London Monetary Conference and later Tripartite Agreement to restore some measure of monetary stability in the 1930s. In the 1960s and early 1970s, even as the Bretton Woods system was heading for breakdown, the major financial powers cooperated at one point to create a new international reserve asset, the Special Drawing Right (SDR), and then at another to temporarily realign and stabilise exchange rates in the Smithsonian Agreement of December 1971. And even before the Plaza Agreement in 1985 there were already regular meetings of finance ministers and central bankers to discuss mutual policy linkages, as well as of lower-level officials in such settings as the Organisation for Economic Cooperation and Development (OECD) and the Bank for International Settlements (BIS). The now-fashionable process of multilateral surveillance was, in fact, first mandated by the leaders of the G-7 countries at the Versailles summit in 1982.

Most significantly, the same cyclical pattern has been evident even during the brief period since the announcement of the Plaza Agreement. The appetite for mutual accommodation in the Triad continues to wax and wane episodically; inconstancy remains the rule. Formally the G-7 governments are now fully committed to the multilateral-surveillance process. In actual practice, despite regular meetings and repeated reaffirmations of principle, policy behaviour continues to betray a certain degree of recurrent recidivism. . . .

. . . This is not to suggest that the multilateral-surveillance process has been utterly without redeeming social value. On the contrary, one can reasonably argue that for all its episodic quality the effort has on balance been beneficial, both in terms of what has in fact been accomplished and in terms of what has been avoided. Anecdotal evidence seems to suggest that policy-makers have had their consciousness genuinely raised regarding the foreign externalities of their domestic actions; in any event, the regularity of the schedule of ministerial meetings now clearly compels officials to integrate the international dimension much more fully than ever before into their own national decision processes. At the same time potentially severe challenges to regime stability have been successfully averted, including in particular the rising wave of US protectionism in 1985 and the stockmarket crash of 1987.

Collective initiatives have been designed cautiously to avoid the pitfalls of model uncertainty and have not typically been chosen simply for their political convenience. Overall, gains do appear to have outweighed costs.

The gains might have been larger, however. One can also reasonably argue that the positive impact of the process might have been considerably greater than it was had there been less inconstancy of behaviour. That is perhaps the chief lesson to be learned from this brief recitation of recent monetary history. Governmental credibility has undoubtedly been strained by the cyclical ebb and flow of commitments since 1985. With each retreat to unilateralism market scepticism grows, requiring ever more dramatic *démarches* when, once again, joint initiatives seem warranted. *Net* benefits, as a result, tend to be diminished over time. Multilateral surveillance may have redeeming social value, but its stop–go pattern makes it more costly than it might otherwise be. In a real sense we all pay for the fickleness of policy fashion.

3. THE INFLUENCE OF THE UNHOLY TRINITY

Why is international monetary cooperation so episodic? To answer that question it is necessary to go back to first principles. Blame cannot be fobbed off on "karma," accidental exogenous "shocks," or even that vague epithet "politics." Consideration of the underlying political economy of the issue suggests that the dilemma is, in fact, systematic—endogenous to the policy process— and not easily avoided in relations between sovereign national governments.

The central analytical issue, which has been well understood at least since the pioneering theoretical work of economist Robert Mundell, is the intrinsic incompatibility of three key desiderata of governments: exchange-rate stability, private-capital mobility, and monetary-policy autonomy. As I wrote in the introduction to this chapter, my own label for this is the "Unholy Trinity." The problem of the Unholy Trinity, simply stated, is that in an environment of formally or informally pegged rates and effective integration of financial markets, any attempt to pursue independent monetary objectives is almost certain, sooner or later, to result in significant balance-of-payments disequilibrium, and hence provoke potentially destabilising flows of speculative capital. To preserve exchange-rate stability, governments will then be compelled to limit either the movement of capital (via restrictions or taxes) or their own policy autonomy (via some form of multilateral surveillance or joint decision making). If they are unwilling or unable to sacrifice either one, then the objective of exchange-rate stability itself may eventually have to be compromised. Over time, except by chance, the three goals cannot be attained simultaneously.

In the real world, of course, governments might be quite willing to limit the movement of capital in such circumstances—if they could. Policy-makers may say they value the efficiency gains of free and integrated financial markets. If polled "off the record" for their private preferences, however, most would probably admit to prizing exchange-rate stability and policy autonomy even more. The problem, from their point of view, is that capital mobility is notoriously difficult to control. Restrictions merely invite more and more sophisticated forms of evasion, as governments from Europe to South Asia to Latin America have learned to their regret. . . .

In practice, therefore, this means that in most instances the Unholy Trinity reduces to a direct trade-off between exchange-rate stability and policy autonomy. Conceptually, choices can be visualised along a continuum representing varying degrees of monetary-policy cooperation. At one extreme lies the polar alternative of a common currency or its equivalent—full monetary integration—where individual governments sacrifice policy autonomy completely for the presumed benefits of a permanent stabilisation of exchange rates. Most importantly, these benefits include the possible improvement in the usefulness of money in each of its principal functions: as a medium of exchange (owing to a reduction of transaction costs as the number of required currency conversions is decreased), store of value (owing to a reduced element of exchange risk as the number of currencies is decreased), and unit of account (owing to an information saving as the number of required price quotations is decreased). Additional gains may also accrue from the possibility of economies of scale in monetary and exchange-rate management as well as a potential saving of international reserves due to an internalisation through credit of what would otherwise be external trade and payments. Any saving of reserves through pooling in effect amounts to a form of seigniorage for each participating country.

At the other extreme lies the polar alternative of absolute monetary independence, where individual governments sacrifice any hope of long-term exchange-rate stability for the presumed benefits of policy autonomy. Most importantly, as Mundell demonstrated as early as 1961, these benefits include the possible improvement in the effectiveness of monetary policy as an instrument to attain national macroeconomic objectives. Today, of course, it is understood that much depends on whether any trade-off can be assumed to exist between inflation and unemployment over a time horizon relevant to policy-makers—technically, whether there is any slope to the Phillips curve in the short-term. In a strict monetarist model of the sort popular in the 1970s, incorporating the classical neutrality assumption ("purely monetary changes have no real effects"), such a trade-off was excluded by definition. The Phillips curve was said to be vertical at the so-called "natural" (or "non-inflation-accelerating") unemployment rate, determined exclusively by microeconomic phenomena on the supply side of the economy. More recently, however, most theorists have tended to take a more pragmatic approach, allowing that for valid institutional and psychological reasons Phillips-curve trade-offs may well persist for significant periods of time—certainly for periods long enough to make the preservation of monetary independence appear worthwhile to policy-makers. From this perspective, any movement along the continuum in the direction of a common currency will be perceived as a real cost by individual governments.

The key question is how this cost compares with the overall benefit of exchange-rate stabilisation. Here we begin to approach the nub of the issue at hand. My hypothesis is that for each participating country both cost and benefit vary systematically with the degree of policy cooperation, and that it is through the interaction of these costs and benefits that we get the episodic quality of the cooperation process we observe in practice.

Assume absolute monetary independence to start with. Most gains from exchange-rate stabilisation, I would argue, can be expected to accrue "up front" and then decline at the margin for successively higher degrees of policy cooperation. That is because the greatest disadvantage of exchange-rate instability is the damage done to the usefulness of money in its various functions. Any move at all by governments to reduce uncertainty about currency values is bound to have a disproportionate impact on market expectations and, hence, transaction costs in foreign exchange; further steps in the same direction may add to the credibility of the collective commitment but will yield only smaller and smaller savings to participants. Most of the cost of stabilisation, on the other hand, can be expected to be "back-loaded" in the perceptions of the relevant policy-makers. That is because governments have an understandable tendency to discount the disadvantages of foreign agreements until they find themselves really constrained in seeking to attain their domestic objectives—at which point disproportionate importance comes to be attached to the compromises of interests involved. Where initial moves towards coordinated decision-making may be treated as virtually costless, further steps in the same direction tend to be seen as increasingly threatening. Thus, the marginal cost of policy cooperation for each country tends to rise systematically even as the marginal benefit may be assumed to fall. . . .

4. CAN COOPERATION BE "LOCKED IN"?

The dilemma posed by the Unholy Trinity thus helps us to understand why international monetary cooperation is so episodic. The question remains: what, if anything, can be done about it?

One answer can be ruled out from the start: the proposition that the observed inconstancy of policy behaviour could be overcome if only governments could be educated to comprehend their own best interests. If my hypothesis is correct, governments are already acting in their own best interests and behaving in manner consistent with a rational calculus of their own costs and benefits. The issue is not myopia: policy-makers surely are not unaware of the impacts of their behaviour on market expectations . . . and would stick to their commitments if that seemed desirable. Rather, it is a question of how policy incentives change over time as a result of the shifting tide of events. Fundamentally, my reasoning may be understood as a variant of the logic of collective action first elucidated by Mancur Olson more than a quarter of a century ago. A common interest is evident to all, yet individually rational behaviour can, at least part of the time, lead to distinctly sub-optimal outcomes. This is true whether the common interest is understood in terms of policy optimisation or regime preservation.

Moreover, my hypothesis has the advantage of being consistent with a wide range of alternative paradigms that have been employed in the standard international political-economy literature. It is certainly compatible with traditional realist or structuralist approaches in which the sovereign state, for reasons of analytical parsimony, is automatically assumed to behave like a rational unitary actor with its own set of well-defined national interests. It is also consistent with more pluralist models of policy-making, in which conceptions of interest are distilled from the interplay of differing combinations of domestic political and institutional forces; and even with models drawn from public-choice theory, in which policy behaviour is assumed to reflect first and foremost the personal interests of policy-makers (the principal-agent problem). For the purposes of my hypothesis, it really does not matter where the policy preferences of governments come from. It only matters that they act systematically on them.

Assuming education is not the answer, the crux of the issue becomes whether any collective commitment to cooperation once made can be "locked in" in some way. If the problem is that governments find it difficult to sustain their enthusiasm for the process, can a solution be found that will effectively prevent them from retreating?

One obvious possibility is the extreme of a common currency, where individual autonomy is—in principle—permanently surrendered by each participating country. In practice, of course, not even full currency unions have proved indissoluble, as we saw in the case of the East African shilling in the 1970s or as evidently we are about to see in the case of the (former) Soviet Union today. But cases like these usually stem from associations that were something less than voluntary to begin with. When undertaken by consenting sovereign states, full monetary unification generally tends to be irreversible— which is precisely the reason why it is seen so seldomly in the real world. During the *laissez-faire* nineteenth century, when monetary autonomy meant less to governments than it does now, two fairly prominent currency unions were successfully established among formally independent nations—the Latin Monetary Union dating from 1865, and the Scandinavian Monetary Union created in 1873—each built on a single, standardised monetary unit (respectively, the franc and the krone). Both groupings, however, were effectively terminated with the outbreak of World War I. In the twentieth century, the only comparable arrangement has been the Belgium–Luxembourg Economic Union, established in 1921. (Other contemporary currency unions, such as the CFA franc zone and the East Caribbean dollar area, had their origins in colonial relationships.) The recent difficulties experienced by the European Community (EC) in negotiating the details of a formal Economic and Monetary Union (EMU) illustrate just how tough it is to persuade governments even as closely allied as these to make the irrevocable commitment required by a common currency.

Short of the extreme of a common currency, an effective solution would require participating governments to voluntarily pre-commit to some form of external authority over their individual policy behaviour. The authority might be supplied by an international agency armed with collectively agreed decision-making powers—corresponding to what I have elsewhere called the organising principle of supra-nationality. It might also be supplied by one single dominant country with acknowledged leadership responsibilities (the principle of hegemony). Or it might be supplied by a self-disciplining regime of norms and rules accepted as binding on all participants (the principle of automaticity). Unfortunately, neither experience nor the underlying logic of political sovereignty offers a great deal of hope in the practical potential of any of these alternatives. Supra-nationality and automaticity, for example, have always tended to be heavily qualified in international monetary relations. In the G-7 multilateral-surveillance process, the International Monetary Fund (in the person of its managing director) has been given a role, but limited only to the provision of essential data and objective analytical support, and public articulation of any sort of binding rules (regarding, for example, exchange-rate targets) has been strenuously resisted by most governments. Hegemony, in the meantime, may be tolerated where it is unavoidable, as in the sterling area during the 1930s or the Bretton Woods system immediately after World War II. But as both these historical episodes illustrate, dominance also tends to breed considerable resentment and a determined eagerness by most countries to assert individual autonomy as soon as circumstances permit.

The principal exception in recent years has been the joint currency float (the "snake") of the European Community, first implemented in the 1970s by a cluster of smaller countries effectively aligned with West Germany's Deutschemark, and later extended and formalised under the European Monetary System (EMS) starting in 1979. Under the rules of the EC's joint float, national monetary discretion for most members has been distinctly constrained, despite relatively frequent realignments of mutual exchange rates and, until the end of the 1980s, the persistence of significant capital controls in some countries. German policy, on the other hand, has not only remained largely autonomous but has effectively dominated monetary relations within the group. In effect, therefore, the snake has successfully locked in a collective commitment to cooperation through a combination of automaticity and hegemony. Yet not only has the arrangement proved tolerable to its members, over time it has gradually attracted new participants; and now, despite the difficulties of gaining irrevocable commitments to a common currency, may be about to be extended again in the form of EMU.

The reasons for this success quite obviously are unique and have to do most with the distinctive character of the institutional ties that have developed among EC members. Over time, as Robert Keohane and Stanley Hoffmann have recently noted, the EC has gradually built up a highly complex process of policy-making in which formal and informal arrangements are intricately linked across a wide range of issues. Decisions in one sector are closely affected by what is happening elsewhere and often lead to the sort of inter-sectoral "spillover" effects that were first emphasised in early neo-functional theory. (Note that these effects are quite different from those featured in the theoretical case for policy cooperation, which stresses spillovers in a single sector or issue-area.) More generally, member governments have come to fully accept a style of political behaviour in which individual interests are jointly realised through an incremental, albeit fragmented, pooling of national sovereignty—what Keohane and Hoffmann call a "network" form of organisation, "in which individual units are defined not by themselves but in relation to other units." And this, in turn, has been made possible only because of the existence of a real sense of commitment and attachment—of *community*—among all the countries involved. In this sense, the EC truly is the exception that proves the rule. Among states less intimately connected, resistance to any form of external authority over individual policy behaviour is bound to be correspondingly more stubborn and determined.

Does this mean then that nothing can be done about the episodic quality of monetary cooperation? Not at all. In principle, any number of technical innovations can be imagined to moderate underlying tendencies towards recidivism by cooperating governments. As in the G-7 process, for example, meetings could be put on a regular schedule and based on an agreed analytical framework to help ensure greater continuity of policy behaviour. Much the same impact might also be attained by giving more precision as well as greater publicity to policy guidelines and commitments. And there might also be some benefit to be had from establishing a permanent, independent secretariat to provide an institutional memory and ongoing objective analysis of priorities and issues. The issue, however, is not administrative creativity but political acceptability. Each such innovation makes it just that much more difficult for policy-makers to change their minds when circumstances might seem to warrant it. Is the underlying relationship among the states involved sufficiently close to make them willing to take such a risk? This is not a question that can be answered *a priori*; as the exceptional case of the EC demonstrates, it is certainly not a question of monetary relations alone. Ultimately prospects for sustaining any cooperative effort in this crucial area on public policy will depend on how much basic affinity governments feel in other areas as well—in effect, on the extent to which they feel they share a common destiny across the full spectrum of economic and political issues.

16

Globalization and Exchange Rate Policy

JEFFRY A. FRIEDEN

As economic globalization increases, exchange rates become more politicized and more subject to mass and special-interest political pressures. Jeffry A. Frieden argues that this is because currency policies differentially affect the interests of consumers and powerful economic interest groups, and that globalization intensifies these societal conflicts. He then identifies the domestic winners and losers of policies that affect the stability and the level of the exchange rate. Special interests that are heavily involved in foreign commerce and investment are more likely to desire a fixed exchange rate than are domestically oriented interest groups. By the same token, consumers and nontradables producers are more likely to want a strong (relatively appreciated) currency than are tradables producers. Evidence from Latin America supports these predictions. Policy makers also seem to engineer an "exchange rate electoral cycle" in which they boost voters' incomes via currency appreciation in the run-up to an election and impose costs on voters by devaluing only after a new government is in office.

Exchange rates powerfully affect cross-border economic transactions. Trade, investment, finance, tourism, migration, and more are all profoundly influenced by international monetary policies. Many developing-country governments have searched for alternatives to the uncertainty that can prevail on international currency markets. Policy entrepreneurs have rushed to peddle currency nostrums, urging a turn toward dollarization, managed floating, nominal anchors, target bands, or other options.

There are both theoretical and empirical reasons to expect globalization to heighten the importance of the exchange rate. Theoretically, open-economy macroeconomic principles imply that capital mobility profoundly affects exchange rate policy choices. As Robert Mundell showed more than forty years ago, the government of a financially integrated economy faces a choice between monetary policy autonomy and a fixed exchange rate (Mundell 1963). If the government opts for a fixed rate, capital mobility makes impossible a monetary stance different from that of the anchor currency; alternatively, if the government opts to sustain an independent monetary policy, it must allow the currency to move. These constraints mean that the economics and politics of monetary and exchange rate policy are likely to be very different in an economy that is financially open than in an economy that is not. By the same token, inasmuch as international economic integration involves increased exposure to international financial and commercial flows, it heightens the concerns of those involved in or exposed to international trade and finance. In a relatively closed economy, few economic actors care about currency movements. But as economies become "globalized" more firms, investors, and workers find their fortunes linked to the exchange rate, and to its impact on trade and financial flows. This concentrates attention on the exchange rate.

Empirically, the impact of "globalization" on exchange rate politics can be seen both over time and across countries. The exchange rate was an important policy problem in the previous era of high globalization. Between 1870 and 1914, the gold standard was one of the major political controversies of the era. In the economies that first approximated globalized conditions today—the small open economies of Western Europe—the exchange rate was so prominent an issue that monetary unification became the top priority of many Europeans over a twenty-year period. And, in the many economies that have now liberalized commercial and financial relations with the rest of the world, currency policy has similarly become central.

The policy advice that governments receive on exchange rates has typically been presented as technical solutions to technical economic problems. Yet exchange rate policy is highly political. It is chosen by policy-makers often concerned about the impact of currency policy on electoral conditions, and pressures from special interests and mass public opinion can affect its course profoundly. The gap between exchange-rate policy advice and the actual policy environment resembles the gap often found in discussions of policy towards the rule of law, investor protection, and corruption: the recommendations assume away interest groups, mass public opinion, and electoral coalitions—in a word, politics. And this is more than an academic concern. Recommendations that ignore the political economy of policy implementation can have disastrous outcomes. A first-best policy whose implementation is subverted by political realities may well be far worse than a feasible second-best solution.

In this chapter, I set out a rudimentary picture of the political economy of exchange rate policy in developing countries. I start by outlining prevailing approaches to the analysis of currency policy, highlighting the argument that ignoring politics leads to poor policy advice. I then discuss the choices policy-makers face with regard to exchange rate regimes and exchange rate levels, and the tradeoffs among different values that these choices entail. I analyze the political-economy pressures—special-interest, mass political, electoral—faced by policy-makers, with evidence drawn from recent Latin American experiences, before reaching my conclusion.

POLITICS AND THE EXCHANGE RATE

The events of the past twenty years demonstrate the importance of understanding the political economy of currency policy. The European Monetary Union, debates over dollarization in Latin America, currency crises in Mexico, East Asia, Russia, Brazil, Turkey, and Argentina—all are impossible to understand without incorporating the role of pressures from interest groups, from mass publics, and from politicians concerned about their re-election. (The same, of course, is true of the gold standard in the nineteenth and early twentieth centuries.)

Currency policy is made in an intensely political environment. Even apparently apolitical observations often embody political assumptions or assertions. For example, allusions to the unsustainability of a particular exchange rate must be based on some model of political constraints on policy. Technically, no exchange rate is unsustainable; the real economy can be made to fit any nominal exchange rate. Analysts who refer to an unsustainable exchange rate must have in mind that local political conditions will not allow the government to defend the level of the currency. These conditions might include opposition from exporters or import competitors clamoring for a devaluation, or more general concern that a devaluation might reduce local purchasing power in unpopular ways. Whatever the reality, allegations of unsustainability presume something about the political system and the structure of interests within it.

These presumptions are worth making explicit. Yet prevailing analyses of currency policy largely ignore politics, with the result that practical policy discussions tend to abstract from the real and powerful pressures that are brought to bear on exchange rate policy choices.

Two common explanations of exchange rate policy choice focus on optimal currency area criteria and on the currency as an anchor for inflation expectations. The former . . . arguments are well known: currency union between two countries is welfare-improving where factors are mobile between them, or when the countries are subject to correlated exogenous shocks, or when their economic structures are very similar. This reasoning has been extended to explain the choice of a fixed exchange rate, on the principle that currency union is simply an extreme form of fixing.

The second broad category of currency policy explanations emphasizes the use of the exchange rate as a way of overcoming the time-inconsistency of monetary authorities' anti-inflationary commitments. A government attempting to signal its seriousness about non-inflationary policy can peg the exchange rate to a nominal anchor currency. When a government commits to a peg it makes an easily verifiable promise: either it follows macroeconomic policies consistent with the peg, or it does not, in which case the peg collapses. Most contemporary supporters of fixed rates, including dollarization, point to the disciplining characteristics of this policy stance as its main attraction.

There are both theoretical and empirical problems with these two approaches. Theoretically, they presuppose that policy is made on welfare grounds. A welfare-driven policy could be the result of many things, such as that:

- policy-makers do not depend on support from domestic political actors;
- the relevant political pressures are for improvements in aggregate social welfare; or that
- domestic political actors do not have preferences over exchange rate policies other than that they enhance aggregate social welfare.

Needless to say, these theoretical propositions are at odds with decades of theoretical work in political economy.

There is also little or no empirical support for the supposition that policy follows normative welfare principles. For example, there is little evidence that existing currency unions—from Europe's Economic and Monetary Union to dollarized countries—met optimal currency area criteria when they were created. And most empirical work indicates that, except in the extreme case of hyperinflation, it is rare for countries to use nominal anchors for anti-inflationary credibility.

Exchange rate policy motivates the same sorts of special and mass, particularistic and electoral, interests that are to be found in every other realm of economic policy. Recent analyses incorporate the role of interest group and partisan pressures, political institutions, and the electoral incentives of politicians.

CHOICES AND TRADEOFFS

The first analytical task is to understand the tradeoffs faced by politicians and their constituents as they consider national currency policies. Governments making currency policy face decisions on two basic dimensions: on the *regime* by which the currency is managed (fixed or floating, for example), and on the *level* of the currency (strong or weak). In the first instance, policy-makers have to decide whether to float or fix the exchange rate—and if to float, in which of the many possible ways. In the second instance, assuming the currency is not fixed, they need to determine what the preferred level of the exchange rate is. They can, of course, decide to let the currency float completely freely, but in developing countries policy-makers have shown themselves reluctant to do this. Policy-makers often act to avoid a substantial appreciation or depreciation of the currency, which implies that they have preferences over the currency's level.

Regime

FIXED OR FLOATING: STABILITY AND CREDIBILITY OR POLICY FLEXIBILITY? The traditional case for stable exchange rates hinges on the benefits of economic integration. In an open economy, the main advantage of a fixed rate regime is to lower exchange rate risk and transaction costs that can impede international trade and investment. Volatile exchange rates create uncertainty about international transactions, adding a risk premium to the costs of goods and assets traded across borders. By stabilizing the currency, a government can encourage greater trade and investment. More recent analyses emphasize the possibility that an exchange rate peg can enhance monetary-policy credibility, as mentioned above. Both theory and evidence suggest that fixing the exchange rate to the currency of a low-inflation country both promotes international trade and investment and disciplines monetary policy by providing an observable nominal anchor.

But fixing the exchange rate has costs. To gain the benefits of greater economic integration through fixing, governments must sacrifice their capacity to run an independent monetary policy. The "impossible trinity" principle explains that governments must choose two of three goals: capital mobility, exchange rate stability, or monetary independence (Mundell 1963). In a financially integrated economy, domestic interest rates cannot long differ from world interest rates (capital flows induced by arbitrage opportunities quickly eliminate the differential). There is strong evidence that financial integration has progressed so far that capital mobility can be taken more or less as given—which reduces the choice to sacrificing exchange rate stability versus sacrificing monetary independence. Fixed rates require the subordination of domestic monetary policy to currency and balance of payments considerations.

A floating exchange rate, on the other hand, has the great advantage of allowing a government to pursue its own independent monetary policy. This independence is valuable because it provides flexibility to accommodate foreign and domestic shocks, including changes in the terms of trade and world financial conditions. Floating allows the exchange rate to be used as a policy tool: for example, policy-makers can adjust the nominal exchange rate to affect the competitiveness of the tradeable goods sector. In some countries, especially those with a history of high and variable inflation, policy-makers may place an overriding value on monetary stability. But for other countries, achieving monetary stability at the cost of flexibility may involve too great a sacrifice; an autonomous monetary policy might be the best way to cope with the external shocks they face.

In an open economy, then, policy-makers face a tradeoff between two competing sets of values. On the one hand, a fixed rate brings *stability and credibility*; on the other hand, it sacrifices *flexibility*. A fixed rate makes for more currency and monetary stability; a floating rate makes for more policy flexibility. Each set of values is desirable; obtaining each requires forgoing at least some of the other.

Level

HIGH OR LOW: CONSUMERS OR PRODUCERS?   Policy-makers face another set of tradeoffs, and that is on the *level* of the exchange rate. The level of the real exchange rate affects the relative price of traded goods in both local and foreign markets. There is no clear economic-efficiency argument for or against any particular level. A strong (appreciated) currency gives residents greater purchasing power, but the fact that it makes foreign products relatively cheaper also subjects national producers of tradeable products to more foreign competition. When a real appreciation makes domestic goods more expensive relative to foreign, consumers of imports benefit while producers of goods that compete with imports (and exporters) lose. The result is a loss of competitiveness for tradeables producers.

A real depreciation has the opposite effects: it stimulates demand for locally produced tradeable products, which is good for their producers; but it makes consumers worse off by raising the prices they pay for foreign goods and services. In broader macroeconomic terms, a real depreciation can encourage exports, switch expenditures away from imports into domestic goods, invigorate the tradable sectors of the economy, and boost aggregate output. But a real depreciation can also be contractionary, because real money balances shrink as the result of the higher price level. And if a nation relies on imports for many vital items, such as oil, food, or capital goods, depreciation can reduce living standards, retard economic growth, and increase inflation.

Thus, the level of the exchange rate confronts policy-makers with two desirable but mutually exclusive goals—stimulating local tradeables producers, and raising local purchasing power. The benefit of increasing the competitiveness of national producers comes at the cost of reducing the real income of national consumers, and vice versa. To paraphrase Abraham Lincoln, you cannot please all of the people all of the time.

In some instances, especially in developing countries, the tradeoffs discussed above can be collapsed into one dimension. The strongest supporters of exchange rate flexibility and a depreciated currency are typically those producers concerned about their competitiveness in import and export markets. The strongest supporters of a fixed exchange rate are typically those concerned about currency stability and monetary credibility. So in many cases, the principal conflict can be expressed as one between *competitiveness* and *credibility*.

POLITICAL FACTORS IN THE DETERMINATION OF CURRENCY POLICY

Selecting an exchange rate regime is a highly political decision: governments must make tradeoffs among values that are given different importance by different sociopolitical actors. With regard to the regime (fixed or floating), the choice is monetary stability and credibility versus monetary flexibility. With regard to the level (depreciated or appreciated), the choice is between competitiveness and purchasing power. Governments must weigh the relative importance of the stability of nominal macroeconomic variables, the competitiveness of producers of tradable products, and the purchasing power of consumers.

The decisions they make have domestic distributional consequences—a fact that is not lost on interest groups or electorates at large. Governments face pressures:

- for reduced volatility, from those who are internationally exposed, including export producers and those with foreign exchange liabilities, such as firms with dollar debts (suggesting a desire for a fixed exchange rate);
- for favorable relative price effects, especially from tradeables producers (suggesting a desire for a depreciated currency, hence floating);
- for purchasing power, from consumers (suggesting a desire for an appreciated currency).

Below I discuss the pressures exacted by interest groups and by electorates with regard to currency policy, and offer some evidence from Latin America about how governments have responded.

Special Interest Groups

As regards the *exchange rate regime*, we can array groups along a continuum that measures the extent to which they are involved in international or domestic economic activity (Frieden 1991). Groups who are heavily involved in foreign trade and investment—typically including the commercial and financial sectors and foreign currency debtors—should favor exchange rate stability, since currency volatility is an everyday concern that makes their business riskier and more costly. By the same token, these groups care less about a loss of national monetary autonomy, since they typically do business in several countries, and can shift their business or assets abroad if domestic conditions become unfavorable.

By contrast, groups whose economic activity is confined to the domestic economy benefit from a floating regime. The nontradeables sector (for example, services, construction, transport) and import-competing producers of tradeable goods belong in this camp. They are not required to deal in foreign exchange and so are free of the risks and costs of currency volatility. They are highly sensitive to domestic macroeconomic conditions and thus favor the national autonomy made possible by floating.

Tradeables producers are also likely to oppose a fixed rate, for two reasons. First, the adoption of a fixed rate in inflationary conditions—such as have characterized much of Latin America—usually leads to a transitional real appreciation, with detrimental effects on tradeables producers. This has been the experience of most exchange-rate-based stabilization programs. Second, a fixed rate eliminates the possibility of a depreciation to maintain or restore the competitiveness of tradeables producers.

The domestic interest group politics of the *level of the exchange rate* can also be represented simply, separating exporting and import-competing industries that lose, on the one hand, from domestically oriented (nontrade-able) industries that gain from a currency appreciation, on the other. Domestic consumers also gain from an appreciation as the domestic currency prices of imported goods fall, lowering the cost of living. Currency depreciations have the opposite effects, helping exporting and import-competing industries at the expense of domestic consumers and producers of nontraded goods and services.

Among tradeables producers, the degree of concern about currency move-ments depends upon how directly they are affected by changes in the exchange rate. If import-competing firms that face an appreciation of the home cur-rency are able to keep their prices high—as will happen if foreign producers do not pass the expected price decline through to local consumers—they will be less concerned about the appreciation. Generally, tradeables indus-tries with high pass-through are more sensitive to the relative price effects of currency movements than those with low pass-through, since their prices respond more directly to changes in exchange rates. And by extension, the level of the exchange rate is likely to be more politicized in developing than in developed countries, since the former tend to produce standard-ized goods and primary commodities, for which pass-through is high. Cap-turing an industry's sensitivity to exchange rate changes involves measuring the extent to which it sells products to foreign markets, uses foreign-made inputs, and, more directly, competes with foreign manufacturers on the basis of price.

The considerable variation of currency regimes in Latin America provides opportunities for at least a preliminary investigation of interest-group pres-sures. Given the characteristics described above, it seems likely that the manu-facturing sector will prefer more flexible currency regimes in order to maintain the competitiveness of locally produced tradeables. In empirical work reported in Frieden, Ghezzi, and Stein (2001), we found that economies with larger manufacturing sectors were more prone to adopt either floating regimes or backward-looking crawling pegs, both of which tend to deliver more competi-tive exchange rates. . . . This can be seen in Table 1, which shows that countries with larger manufacturing sectors are less likely to have fixed exchange rates (a lower number in the table is associated with a more fixed rate).

Similarly, the larger the manufacturing sector is—indicating greater sensi-tivity to the competitive effects of currency movements—the less likely is a fixed rate. . . . In the closed economies of the import-substitution period, where manufacturers were mostly protected from foreign competition, this rela-tionship was weaker or absent. . . .

It can also be seen that hyperinflationary episodes are associated with the use of a currency peg for credibility-enhancing purposes, whereas episodes of moderate inflation are not. . . . Having inflation greater than 1,000 percent increases the probability of adopting a fixed rate regime by nearly 21 percent-age points.

TABLE 1 Exchange rate regimes are affected by the size of the manufacturing sector, Latin America, 1972–94

Smaller manufacturing sectors			*Larger manufacturing sectors*		
	Man/GDP	Scale of fixed/ floating		Man/GDP	Scale of fixed/ floating
Haiti	8.87	3.19	Dom Republic	17.33	.96
Panama	9.33	0.00	Venezuela	17.42	2.85
Barbados	10.12	0.00	Ecuador	19.37	2.35
Guyana	12.39	5.08	El Salvador	19.48	1.24
Trinidad and Tobago	12.61	2.73	Nicaragua	19.86	1.16
Suriname	13.82	2.08	Colombia	20.31	6.75
Guatemala	15.18	3.58	Chile	21.39	5.79
Honduras	15.24	2.86	Mexico	21.85	6.04
Paraguay	15.71	3.34	Costa Rica	22.83	4.29
Bolivia	16.03	4.80	Peru	23.47	5.79
Belize	16.65	0.00	Uruguay	23.66	6.09
Jamaica	17.22	4.50	Brazil	28.63	7.06
			Argentina	29.35	2.74
Average	13.60	2.68		22.30	4.35

Scale of Fixed/Floating is a 10 point scale with 0 = Fixed for every period, 10 = Floating for every period.

SOURCE: Frieden, Ghezzi, and Stein (2001).

Electoral Considerations

Elections are of recurrent importance in exchange rate policy-making. They may affect exchange rate policy for several reasons. As described in Frieden and Stein (2001), the income effect associated with depreciation reduces the purchasing power of the population; it can make depreciation unpopular and therefore politicians may want to avoid it at election time. Devaluations may also be unpopular because they generate inflation. On the other hand, a real appreciation can deliver an electorally popular reduction in inflation and an increase in purchasing power. In line with this, governments show a strong tendency to allow or engineer a real appreciation in the run-up to elections, which is then reversed after the government changes hands. An exchange rate electoral cycle boosts voters' incomes in the run-up to the election and imposes costs on voters only after the new government is in office. The delay results in a depreciation that is more costly than if it had occurred immediately, but newly elected governments appear to follow the rule of "Devalue immediately and blame it on your predecessors."

FIGURE 1 Exchange Rates in Argentina and Brazil (*pesos* and *reals* per US$)

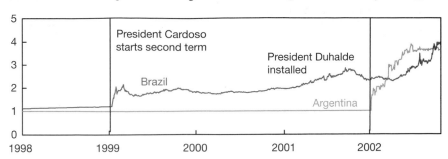

Evidence for Latin America, from individual country studies and a cross-country study, is generally consistent with these arguments (Frieden and Stein 2001). A cross-country study reported in Frieden, Ghezzi, and Stein (2001) examines the behavior of exchange rates before and after elections. Looking at 86 episodes of electoral changes in government, we found that the real exchange rate appreciated nearly 3.5 percent in the months leading to an election and depreciated on average 6 percent during the following four months.

. . . Latin America is a rich repository of experiences in which governments delayed devaluations until after elections: Mexico's ruling PRI party did so with some regularity between 1970 and 1994. More recent Argentine and Brazilian experiences are also expressive. As shown in Figure 1, each government held the exchange rate more or less constant until right after a new president (in the Brazilian case, a re-elected incumbent) took office. In pre-election months, both currencies appreciated substantially in real terms, with a powerful positive impact on the purchasing power of local residents. Immediately after taking office, each government let the currency float—more accurately, sink—to a substantially depreciated level.

The political economy of exchange rate policy is not only important for developing countries. For over thirty years the member states of the European Union have attempted, with varying degrees of success, to stabilize their currencies against one another. The eventual creation of the euro, and the continuing question of whether, when, and how other countries in and around Europe will join the euro zone, certainly respond to powerful domestic and international political pressures (see, for example, Eichengreen and Frieden 2001).

Exchange rates are critical in a wide variety of other settings in the context of an integrated world economy. Commercial and financial relations between the United States and East Asia, for example, have long implicated currency policies, sometimes sparking political conflict. In the early stages of their respective export drives, East Asian nations—first Japan, then South Korea and Taiwan, now China—have typically kept their exchange rates very weak to spur manufactured exports. The results often provoke protests from American manufacturers who press the US government to insist that East Asian governments allow or force their currencies to appreciate.

Conflict over the trade effects of currency values has most recently been played out between the United States and China. The issue has been complicated by the fact that—as was true in the early 1980s when the American target was Japan—the weakness of East Asian currencies is matched by the strength of the US dollar, which itself is in large part due to America's own fiscal policy and the resulting capital inflow. Whatever the ultimate resolution of these "global imbalances"—East Asian trade surpluses and American trade and fiscal deficits—there is little question that highly politicized currency policies played an important role in creating and propagating them. There is also little question that the unwinding of these imbalances will itself provoke political conflict over exchange rates and their effects.

CONCLUSION

Exchange rates are political. They affect the interests of powerful groups and of consumers. They affect elections, and are affected by them. International economic integration only heightens their impact and their political prominence. As the world economy has become more open—and especially as developing countries have become more open—exchange rates have become even more highly politicized, more controversial, and more subject to mass and special-interest political pressures.

Those who ignore the political economy of currency policy will make mistakes in developing feasible exchange rate policies. Both analysts and policymakers would be well advised to pay concentrated attention to political economy factors in exchange rate policy-making.

REFERENCES

Eichengreen, B. and J. Frieden (eds) (2001), *The Political Economy of European Monetary Unification*, 2nd edn. Boulder, CO: Westview Press.

Frieden, J. A. (1991), "Invested Interests: The Politics of National Economic Policy in a World of Global Finance," *International Organization*, 45: 425–451.

Frieden, J. A., P. Ghezzi, and E. Stein (2001), "Politics and Exchange Rates: A Cross-Country Approach to Latin America," in J. A. Frieden and E. Stein (eds), *The Currency Game: Exchange Rate Politics in Latin America*. Baltimore, MD: Johns Hopkins University Press.

Frieden, J. A. and E. Stein (2001), "The Political Economy of Exchange Rate Policy in Latin America: An Analytical Overview," in J. A. Frieden and E. Stein (eds), *The Currency Game: Exchange Rate Politics in Latin America*. Baltimore, MD: Johns Hopkins University Press.

Mundell, Robert A. (1963), "Capital Mobility and Stabilization Policy under Fixed and Flexible Exchange Rates," *Canadian Journal of Economic and Political Science*, 29: 475–485.

17

Divided Opinion, Common Currency: The Political Economy of Public Support for EMU

MATTHEW GABEL

Proposals for common currency arrangements have proliferated in recent years; the most prominent example is Economic and Monetary Union (EMU) in Europe. Matthew Gabel presents research on citizens' attitudes toward European integration suggesting that economic self-interest shapes public support for EMU. He begins by identifying the domestic distributional consequences of EMU and thus which citizens are expected to support or oppose EMU. While Gabel's analytical discussion parallels the domestic societal approach developed by Jeffry Frieden in Reading 16, he evaluates the theory at the individual level of analysis rather than in terms of cross-national variation in policy. In other words, Gabel presents direct evidence that citizens actually adopt the policy attitudes that are predicted by theories that specify individual interests in exchange rate policy. He thus helps bridge the gap between societal interests and the policy choices of governments.

A common approach to the study of international political economy (IPE) and, in particular, the study of monetary unification in the European Union (EU) is to use the distributional consequences of international economic policies to account for the pattern of political conflict over these policies . . . the basic tenet being that individuals favor or oppose particular international economic policies depending on whether the policy increases or decreases their real income. . . . In this chapter, I will address several issues relevant to the application of these models to the politics of economic and monetary union (EMU), and ultimately the politics of managing an EU single currency. In particular, I will examine empirically whether these IPE models accounted for variation in mass support for EMU.

Economic self-interest models have two theoretical components: a theory of the distributional consequences of international economic policies and a political theory of how the distributional consequences relate to policymaking via political agents. In general, IPE scholars identify the distributional consequences through relevant theories of economic welfare for that policy. . . .

On the politics side, there are a variety of different theories of democratic policymaking that identify which political agents' interests are relevant. Of particular interest for this chapter is how these theories treat the mass electorate.

For contrast, we can divide these models into two camps. On one side, scholars assume that voters are generally incapable of holding elected officials accountable for international economic policies and are thus, as an electorate, irrelevant for policymaking. Much evidence from public opinion research supports this assumption, showing that on most international policy issues citizens demonstrate little interest or sophistication. As a result, these scholars assume that organized interest groups are the primary domestic political actors.

On the other side, scholars posit that the threat of electoral penalty endows voters with a strong influence on elected officials and thus policymaking. Although little of this theoretical literature has attended to the issue of voter interest and sophistication, there are both theoretical and empirical reasons to believe that uninformed voters can form meaningful opinions about international economics and pose a credible electoral threat. Several scholars argue that voters do not necessarily need a sophisticated understanding of government policy to identify their economic interests and adopt appropriate political attitudes. Through cues from like-minded elites, citizens may infer sufficient information about the consequences of a policy to adopt political attitudes consistent with their economic interests. And, for elected officials with affected constituents, the economic interests of their voters may influence policy. Consequently, these types of political models assume that the distributional consequences of international economic policies across voters (the mass public) are relevant for policymaking.

There are several reasons to believe that the politics of EMU were consistent with the latter family of political models. First, EMU has been far from an obscure issue to EU citizens. In most EU member states, recent survey evidence shows that the majority of the mass public felt well informed about EMU. In addition, considerable recent media attention and public controversy focused on questions of EMU and membership in a single European currency.

Second, even if interest groups and parties are the primary political agents, one can argue that their political behavior is endogenous to public opinion. Particularly in the EU context, there are good reasons to believe that interest groups and political parties adopted positions toward EMU that reflected their mass constituents' preferences over policy. For one, while organized interests may play a powerful role in policymaking, one source of that influence is their ability to threaten elected officials with electoral penalties for their decisions. For these threats to work, organized interests must be able to deliver the votes of those who share their economic interests. Thus, an interest group's political influence may depend fundamentally on its affiliated voters adopting political attitudes and behavior consistent with their economic interests from international economic policy. Furthermore, there is theoretical and empirical support for the claim that political parties in the EU adopt positions on European integration in response to the economic interests of their electorates. To the extent that parties adopted positions on EMU in a similar manner, we would expect public support to influence policymaking regarding EMU.

Thus, in order to apply the economic self-interest model to the politics of EMU, it seems reasonable to model mass voters as relevant political agents. But for this IPE model to apply to EMU, we must address a second issue: whether the relevant political agents—in this case mass voters—adopted positions on EMU that are consistent with theoretical expectations regarding the distributional consequences of EMU. This chapter focuses on this question. . . .

THEORETICAL EXPECTATIONS

The economic self-interest approach to the politics of EMU assumes that political agents promote or oppose a policy depending on whether the policy increases or decreases their income. As I argued in the introduction, there are several reasons to consider EU citizens as relevant political actors for the politics of EMU. Thus, I am interested in testing the assumption that members of the general public adopted political attitudes (and, presumably, political behavior) consistent with their economic interests related to EMU. To construct an appropriate test, we must first determine theoretical expectations about the distributional consequences of EMU, which will identify which citizens were expected to support or oppose EMU.

There is a vigorous debate about the extent of national and EU-wide economic gains from EMU, as well as about the potential for asymmetric shocks and regional disparities. What I will focus on are theoretical arguments about the distributional implications of EMU at the individual level (as opposed to the national or EU level). At the time of the survey data analyzed here (1993/94), joining EMU represented two different types of policies: a future fixed exchange rate policy with the other EMU member states and a commitment to attain (or maintain) low levels of public debt, public deficits, and inflation. Several scholars offer arguments about the distributional consequences of these policies across EU citizens. Below I briefly describe these theoretical arguments and identify testable hypotheses that connect the purported distributional consequences of EMU with variation in public support for EMU.

Trade-Related Distributional Consequences of Exchange Rate Stability

Several scholars have explored the distributional consequences of exchange rate stability. The basic story is that the value of exchange rate stability differs between producers of tradable goods and producers and consumers of nontradable goods. . . . Thus, those employed in tradable and nontradable sectors will view differently the trade-off between national monetary policy independence and exchange rate stability. Specifically, those citizens' whose welfare depends on trade will support a fixed exchange rate with their trading partners because it eliminates exchange rate volatility. As Frieden (1996, p. 203) argues, "those involved in cross-border investment, traders and exporters of specialized manufactured products all tend to favor exchange rate stability to reduce the risk associated with their business interests in other countries." In contrast, those citizens whose welfare does not depend on trade will prefer national monetary policy independence, since their fortunes depend on domestic business conditions. This latter group includes import-competing traded goods producers and nontradable producers.

In the context of EMU, these distributional effects should have translated into the following patterns of support for EMU. First, those citizens employed in sectors that export to other EU member states should have been more supportive of EMU than those employed in sectors that did not produce tradable goods. And, among those in tradable sectors, support for EMU should have increased with the amount of production for intra-EU export.

Due to data availability, I can only test this claim in an indirect fashion. The Eurobarometer surveys generally did not ask respondents in which sector of the economy they worked. However, in the three surveys I analyze, respondents were classified into four categories: public sector, nationalized industry, private industry, and private services. Applying the theoretical expectations to these groups, I hypothesize that members of the public sector (which is a nontradable sector) were less supportive of EMU than those employed in an industrial sector with at least some intra-EU exports. And, to the extent that services are largely domestically produced and consumed, I expect those respondents employed in services to have been less supportive than those employed in industry.

Although I cannot identify which respondents from the industrial sector worked for firms that were involved in intra-EU exports, I can infer differences in sensitivity to intra-EU trade across industrial sector employees in different member states at the time of the survey. As I describe in the next section, I have constructed an indicator of the percent of total domestic industrial production that was exported to other EU member states. I expect support for EMU to have increased with this indicator because . . . greater production for intra-EU export increases the value to industrial employees of fixed exchange rates between the EU member states. That is, respondents employed in national industrial sectors whose production was largely exported to other EU member states should have been more supportive of EMU than those employed in national industrial sectors whose production was consumed domestically and/or exported outside the EU.

The Politics of Inflation: Class-Based Distributional Consequences of EMU

. . . The distributional consequences of EMU were related to the politics of inflation. The politics of inflation pit the interests of labor and Left political parties against the interests of capital and parties of the Right. The Left supports monetary policy that accommodates wage pressures and tight labor markets. The Right supports slack labor markets and restrictive monetary policy designed to preserve price stability. EMU, by institutionalizing price stability as the goal of monetary policy, settled this political conflict decidedly in the favor of capital and parties of the Right.

This argument has clear implications for connecting the distributive consequences of EMU membership with variation in public support for EMU. First, citizens who are employed as manual workers (labor) should have been less supportive of EMU than citizens employed in management/ownership occupations (executives and professionals). Second, since class conflict has traditionally defined the Left-Right dimension, citizens' placement on this spectrum should have related to their support for EMU. Specifically, citizens' support for EMU should have declined as their placement moved toward the Left end of the spectrum and support should have increased as their ideological placement moved toward the Right pole.

The Distributional Consequences of Cross-Border Shopping and Price Transparency

Those citizens involved in cross-border commerce through cross-border shopping also stand to gain from a fixed exchange rate and a single currency. The elimination of barriers to the movement of goods and people in the EU created cross-border commercial opportunities that are enhanced by a single currency. Consumers residing near intra-EU borders can exploit price differences across nations due to VAT and excise tax rates. Retailers and the border economies in relatively low-tax nations gain from increased demand. EMU was therefore beneficial to these border residents by eliminating commissions on currency exchange and, probably most importantly, facilitating comparative shopping through price transparency.

Thus, I expect residents of border regions to have been more supportive of EMU, on average, than nonborder residents. Also, I expect residents of border regions where price differentials are relatively large to value cross-border commerce (and thereby the single currency) more than border residents where price differences are relatively small. Consequently, among border residents, I expect support for EMU to have increased with the value of cross-border shopping.

The Distributional Consequences of Capital Market Liberalization

EMU also had distributive effects through its liberalization of capital markets. For Scheve (1999, p. 3), the primary economic consequence of EMU for EU citizens was the reduction in transaction costs for cross-border capital investments, thereby completing the capital mobility liberalization of the Single European Act. Scheve developed a formal model of redistributive policymaking that showed how monetary union reduces the amount of national government transfers. . . . The result is a greater return on citizens' occupational skills and financial assets in an integrated capital market and lower spending on government programs.

Consequently, monetary union works to the advantage of those citizens with relatively high occupational skills and asset endowments but to the detriment of likely recipients of redistributive policies (for example, the poor). Applied to EMU, Scheve (1999, p. 8) predicted positive relationships between a citizen's support for EMU and (a) her income relative to the national income distribution, (b) her amount of capital assets, and (c) her occupational skills.

The Distributional Consequences of the Convergence Criteria

The convergence criteria required EMU applicants to attain a low level of inflation, public debt, and public deficit before entry into EMU. In 1993/94, the period I analyze, several member states needed to drastically reduce their national debt and deficits in order to qualify for EMU. While there was no common formula for rectifying the public deficits and debts, clearly there were several groups of citizens more likely to be disadvantaged by any reforms. First, the relatively poor citizens in each nation were more likely to depend on government spending for their income and welfare. The poor therefore stood to lose from their government's attempts to meet the convergence criteria. Consequently, I would expect a citizen's support for EMU to be positively related to her financial position relative to other citizens in her nation. . . .

Second, public employees and those in nationalized industries were likely targets for reductions in government spending through privatizations and restraints on public wages and benefits. This threat to employees of the public sector and nationalized industries increased with the size of their nation's public debt and public deficit. Thus, I expect these economic concerns related to EMU to vary with the size of the national public debt, with support for EMU among respondents in public jobs and nationalized industries inversely related to the size of their public debt.

DATA AND MEASUREMENT

To test these hypotheses, I analyze data from three Eurobarometer surveys merged with several economic indicators. The Eurobarometer survey is conducted in the fall and spring of each year in each member state and consists of roughly 1,000 respondents in each EU member state. I use Eurobarometers 39 to 41, which cover spring 1993 to spring 1994. These were the only surveys with the necessary sectoral occupation question. Also, due to the availability of responses to necessary questions, I will restrict the analysis to citizens from the original twelve member states.

Ideally, I would prefer more recent surveys. It seems likely that the diffusion of information and cues about the costs and benefits of EMU to citizens grew over the 1990s. Thus, examining the hypotheses in the 1993/94 time period may pose a particularly difficult test.

These survey data were pooled into one dataset. The national surveys are analyzed together because I expect the hypotheses to have applied to the EU population and because testing several of the hypotheses requires cross-national variation. The pooling over time is due to the fact that, although the overall sample is large, the number of respondents in key categories (for example, residence in particular border areas) was often very small for any one survey and in any one country.

Dependent Variable

For the dependent variable, I use the following question:

> There should be a European Monetary Union with one single currency replacing by 1999 [National Currency] and all other national currencies of the Member States of the European Community.
>   Response: for; against; don't know

In the analyses reported here, I excluded responses of "don't know," which represented about 6 percent of the sample. However, the results of an analysis that included these respondents as an intermediate response category support very similar statistical inferences to those drawn here. . . .

Explanatory Variables

To distinguish respondents according to their sector of the economy, I created four dummy variables based on the following survey question.

> To those who do or did paid work, are you/were you in . . . ?
> 1. Public Employment
> 2. Nationalized Industry
> 3. Private Industry
> 4. Private Services

To test whether, among respondents in industry, support for EMU increased with the sensitivity of their national industrial sector to intra-EU trade, I created an interaction term. To measure the sensitivity of the national industrial sector to intra-EU trade, I divided the total value of manufacturing exports to the EU in the survey year for each member state by the total value of manufacturing production in the survey year in that member state. This indicator, called *trade sensitivity*, was then interacted with a dummy for industrial employment—called *industry*, which included respondents in both national-ized and private industry. The expectation is that, across those employed in industry, support for EMU increased with *trade sensitivity*.

To test the class-conflict hypothesis, I created three occupational dummy variables: *manual worker, executive*, and *professional*. I expect manual workers to represent unskilled workers, which are a key component of the working class. I expect executives and professionals to represent interests of capital and management. The theoretical expectation is that manual laborers were less supportive of EMU than professionals or executives.

I also created two variables to measure Left–Right ideology, which Oatley identifies as indicative of class conflict. The Eurobarometer survey includes a question asking respondents to place themselves on a ten-point Left–Right scale. . . . The first variable, *left ideology*, is coded zero if a respondent self-identified at five and the variable is coded so that it increases as scores approach one, the left-most position. Similarly, the variable *right ideology* is coded zero for a response of six and is coded so that it increases as the scores approach ten, the right-most position. Thus, both variables range from zero to four, with higher scores representing more extreme ideological positions. The theoretical expectation is that *left ideology* is negatively associated with support for EMU and that *right ideology* is positively related to support for EMU.

To test the hypothesis related to cross-border shopping, I first distinguished respondents by whether or not they resided in a region along an intra-EU land border. I created a dummy variable, *border resident*, coded one for border residents, zero otherwise. The expectation is that border expressed greater support for EMU than nonborder residents.

Second, I created a proxy variable to distinguish among border residents according to the value of cross-border shopping at their border. A 1993 Price Waterhouse study demonstrated that the most important determinant of cross-border shopping was the difference in the price of motor fuel at that border. Specifically, the frequency of cross-border shopping was positively related to the difference in the price of motor fuel at the border. From this finding, I infer that the value to border residents of cross-border shopping increases with the price differential for motor fuel at that border.

I created two variables, based on the absolute value of the difference in the price (in ecu) of 1,000 liters of unleaded motor fuel in the bordering nations in 1993. The first variable, *consumer price difference*, is coded as this price differential only for residents of the relatively high-price side of the border, and zero otherwise. The second variable, *retailer price difference*, is coded as this price difference for residents of the relatively low-price side of the border, and zero otherwise. The reason for creating two variables is to avoid imposing an assumption that the consumer and retailer effects are equal. These variables were then interacted with the variable *border resident*. I expect a positive coefficient for both interaction terms, as I expect support for EMU to have increased with the value to consumers and retailers of cross-border shopping.

To test the hypotheses due to Scheve (1999) about the effects of capital market liberalization on support for EMU, I constructed two variables. First,

Scheve predicted that support for EMU increased with a respondent's income relative to the national distribution of income. Relatively poor respondents in a nation faced fewer fiscal transfers due to EMU and wealthier respondents benefited from higher returns on their assets. To test this hypothesis, I include a variable called *income*, which ranges from zero (lowest quartile) to three (highest quartile) according to where the respondent's income falls in the national income distribution. The expectation is that *income* had a positive relationship with support for EMU. Note that this is also a prediction consistent with the expected distributional consequences of the convergence criteria.

Second, Scheve argued that support for EMU increased with occupational skills. Following Scheve, I use the respondent's level of education as a proxy for occupational skills. I created the variable *education*, which indicates the age at which the respondent finished his formal education. This variable is coded 1 for respondents who finished their education before age fifteen. The variable increases with each year of further education (for example, age 15 is coded as 2). The highest value for this variable is 10, indicating the respondent finished his education after age 22 or is still studying. I expect respondents' support for EMU to have increased with their years of education.

Finally, to capture the distributional effects of the convergence criteria, I created variables to capture the differential effects of the convergence criteria across members of the public sector and nationalized industries. I created two interaction terms. First, I interacted a respondent's national public debt as percent of GDP in the survey year with the dummy variable for public sector employment. Second, I interacted a respondent's national public debt as percent of GDP in the survey year with the dummy variable for nationalized industry employment. The expectation is that, as the size of the public debt increased across members of these economic sectors, support for EMU decreased.

Control Variables

As described in the second section, there are theoretical and empirical reasons for expecting national-level factors to have influenced support for EMU. This is an important issue for this research design because all respondents in Luxembourg and Denmark are coded as border residents. Thus, any results on the *border region* variable or its interaction effects could be confounded by national-level factors. In addition, I want to be sure that the interaction terms measuring cross-national differences within economic sectors are not simply capturing national differences. . . .

I also control for a variety of socioeconomic characteristics (for example, gender, age, and occupation) found in previous studies to relate to support for European integration and that might confound the relationships between the explanatory variables and support for EMU. . . .

STATISTICAL RESULTS

Table 1 reports the results for two heteroskedastic probit models. The first model includes the explanatory and control variables described above. The second model includes controls for nationality. While I have attempted to include theoretically meaningful variables to control for national factors that might influence support for EMU, there is always the chance that some national effects remain. The advantage of this second specification is that it ensures that no unmeasured national effects bias the results. The main disadvantage of this specification is that, the parameter estimates exclusively reflect the impact of the independent variables on intranational variation in support for EMU.

For some hypotheses, this effectively excludes much of the variation in the independent variables from the analysis. For example, some nations (for example, Denmark) have no intranational variation in the price differential for gasoline in a given year, and little difference in the price differential between 1993 and 1994. Thus, the parameter estimates for the independent variables designed to test for the effects of cross-border commerce are based almost exclusively on observations in the nations with border regions that vary in price differentials. And these intranational differences are generally much smaller than the cross-national differences. Similarly, cross-national differences in public deficit and trade sensitivity are also ignored. Since the only intranational variation in these variables is over time and is generally quite small, the bulk of the variation in these variables is omitted from analysis. Consequently, this model specification provides a poor test of the hypotheses related to these variables.

In contrast, the hypotheses for income, education, occupation, and ideology apply to intranational comparisons. The variables designed to test these hypotheses demonstrate considerable intranational variation. Moreover, given the measurement of these variables, the hypotheses call for intranational comparisons. A particular number of years of education may not represent the same level of occupational skills across nations, but within a nation human capital should increase with years of education. Similarly, income is measured in national quartiles, calling for intranational comparison. And the comparison of ideological positions is probably most appropriate in a national political system, which defines that range and content of the Left–Right dimension. Consequently, the model specification provides appropriate tests of these hypotheses.

RESULTS

Across both models, the results are consistent with several hypotheses based on the distributional consequences of capital market liberalization. As expected, respondents from the lowest quartile of their national income

TABLE 1 Heteroskedastic Probit Models of Public Support for EMU

Choice model	Model 1	Model 2
Constant	−0.60*	−3.76*
	(0.057)	(0.62)
Private industry	−0.23*	−0.073*
	(0.035)	(0.022)
Industry* trade sensitivity	0.84*	0.20*
	(0.079)	(0.072)
Public employment	−0.17*	−0.065
	(0.058)	(0.048)
Public employment* public debt	0.0014	0.0004
	(0.0007)	(0.0006)
Nationalized industry	−0.25	0.022
	(0.12)	(0.11)
Nationalized industry* public debt	−0.0005	−0.0016
	(0.002)	(0.0018)
Private services	−0.050	−0.034
	(0.022)	(0.020)
Border resident	−0.88*	−0.042
	(0.052)	(0.047)
Border resident* consumer price difference	0.0085*	0.0007
	(0.0004)	(0.0004)
Border resident* retailer price difference	0.013*	0.0012
	(0.0009)	(0.0008)
Income	0.035*	0.028*
	(0.007)	(0.006)
Education	0.012*	0.013*
	(0.0026)	(0.0028)
Manual laborer	−0.040	−0.021
	(0.040)	(0.035)
Executive	0.056	0.071
	(0.042)	(0.039)
Professional	0.11	0.15*
	(0.053)	(0.051)
Right ideology	0.007	0.012
	(0.009)	(0.0077)
Left ideology	−0.030*	−0.020*
	(0.0077)	(0.0072)
Inflation history	0.0085*	−0.044*
	(0.003)	(0.0092)
Public debt	0.014*	0.0024
	(0.0006)	(0.0034)

(*continued*)

TABLE 1 (*continued*)

Choice model	Model 1	Model 2
Years in ERM	−0.017*	0.25*
	(0.0019)	(0.047)
France	–	0.59*
		(0.054)
Belgium	–	0.67
		(0.31)
Netherlands	–	0.57*
		(0.11)
United Kingdom	–	2.56*
		(0.48)
Italy	–	1.27*
		(0.26)
Denmark	–	0.062
		(0.12)
Ireland	–	1.03*
		(0.17)
Luxembourg	–	0.83*
		(0.17)
Spain	–	3.02*
		(0.45)
Portugal	–	4.10*
		(0.60)
Greece	–	4.41*
		(0.72)
Germany	–	–
Variance model		
France	13.87*	−0.52*
	(0.12)	(0.18)
Denmark	−1.00*	−1.16*
	(0.13)	(0.16)
Education	−0.005	−0.007
	(.006)	(.005)
Heteroskedasticity test		
Likelihood ratio (x^2)	15103.31*	53.72*
Goodness of fit test		
Percent correctly predicted	67%	71%
N	26042	26042

*0.01 significance level

distribution expressed less support for EMU than those from the highest income quartile. For example, in Model 1 the likelihood of supporting EMU increased from 0.64 to 0.68 due to a change from lowest to highest quartile. This is consistent with the expectations of Scheve (1999) and the distributional consequences of the convergence criteria. Also, support for EMU was positively related to level of education, which serves here as a proxy for occupational skills. In Model 1, a respondent who finished her education before age fifteen had, on average, a 0.66 probability of supporting EMU while a respondent who finished education after age 22 had a 0.70 probability of supporting EMU. Thus, public support for EMU varied consistently with the distributional consequences of capital market liberalization identified by Scheve (1999). However, these effects are not substantively large.

The results arc also consistent with the hypotheses based on the distributional consequences of exchange rate stability. The expectation that employees of industry were more supportive of EMU than employees in either the public sector or in private services is difficult to assess because of the interaction of private and nationalized industry with trade sensitivity. The average private industrial employee was employed in an economy where 24 percent of manufacturing production went to intra-EU exports. Thus, for the average private industrial employee, the combined parameter estimate in Model 1 is $(0.24)(0.84) + (-0.23) = -0.028$. The average employee of nationalized industry was employed in an economy where 15 percent of manufacturing production went to intra-EU exports. Thus, for the average employee of nationalized industry, the combined parameter estimate is $(0.15)(0.84) = 0.13$.

Now, we can compare the estimated probability of being in favor of EMU across employees of private and nationalized industry, the public sector, and private services. The probability that a private industrial employee favored EMU is 0.66, that a nationalized industry employee favored EMU is 0.72, that a public sector employee favored EMU is 0.61, and that a private services employee favored EMU is 0.67. Clearly, there is no strong distinction here between the industrial employees and those in the public and services sectors.

However, recall that the hypothesis of sectoral differences in support was predicated on the assumption that industrial sector employees were more sensitive to intra-EU trade than those in the public and services sector. If we compare the industrial sector employees who were the most sensitive to intra-EU trade, the sectoral difference in support for EMU was clearly consistent with expectations. As trade sensitivity increased across industrial sector employees, support for EMU rose. At the upper limit (trade sensitivity = 0.80), a private sector industrial employee had a probability of 0.89 of favoring EMU in Model 1. An employee of a nationalized industry had a 0.87 probability of favoring EMU. Thus, the sectoral differences were apparent when comparing the members of the industrial sector who were the most sensitive to intra-EU trade with those in nontradable sectors. As expected, these sectoral differences were considerably smaller when calculated for Model 2, but the results are consistent with the same conclusions. Thus, variation in public support for EMU—particularly of Model 1—was consistent with the distributional consequences of exchange rate stability. . . .

The results for the class-conflict variables are generally consistent with the hypotheses based on the distributional consequences of EMU related to the inflation. In both models, respondents who identified themselves as ideologically Left were less supportive of EMU than self-identifiers of the Right. In Model 1, the strongest Left respondent had a 0.63 likelihood of supporting EMU while respondents who were in the middle of the ideological dimension or on the Right had a likelihood of 0.67. It is also worth noting that the coefficient for Right ideology is in the expected direction in both models, but is only significant at about the 0.10 level. The results for the occupational dummy variables provide little supporting evidence for the class-based hypothesis. Across both models, professionals were more supportive (at the 0.05 level) of EMU than manual workers. However, there was no difference in the level of support between executives and manual workers.

As for the effects of cross-border commerce, the results provide some evidence consistent with expectations. In Model 1, support for EMU increased with the value of cross-border shopping for residents of both the "consumer" and "retailer" sides of the border. This is consistent with expectations. Note that in Model 1 the coefficient for *border resident* is negative, but the effect of border residence on support for EMU depended on the price differential at the border where the respondent resides. A border resident of a border with the lowest observed price difference (20 ecu/1,000 l.) was, on average, less supportive of EMU than a nonborder resident. This is inconsistent with expectations. However, residents of border regions with the highest price difference (230 ecu/1,000 l.) were much more supportive of EMU than nonborder residents. At this price difference in Model 1, a "consumer" border resident had a 0.94 probability of supporting EMU and a "retailer" border resident had a 0.99 probability of supporting EMU. A nonborder resident had a 0.67 probability of supporting EMU. This finding is consistent with the expectation that support for EMU varies with the benefits of cross-border commerce due to a single currency.

This border effect disappears in Model 2, since the coefficients lose statistical significance. As discussed earlier, this was expected due to the inclusion of national dummy variables, eliminating cross-national variation in border effects from the analysis.

Other results are not consistent with expectations. First, for employees of the public sector and nationalized industries, support for EMU was not related to the size of their public debt as a percentage of GDP, as expected due to the convergence criteria. Second, manual workers did not show a statistically significant difference in support for EMU from executives, although they were on average less supportive of EMU than professionals in Model 2.

The results are partially consistent with the expectations for the national-level control variables. In Model 1, support for EMU increased with the average historical level of inflation and the size of the public debt in the respondent's nation. However, the number of years in the ERM was negatively related to support for EMU. When controls are included for nationality, the results for these variables change dramatically. This is understandable, given that the model effectively includes multiple proxy variables for the same national effects and there are only three time points. . . .

DISCUSSION

A commonly assumed, yet rarely tested, claim in the study of international political economy is that domestic political agents behave so as to further their economic goals related to international economic policy. In particular, some scholars assume that voters connect their economic interests to their political attitudes and behavior regarding international economic policies. Yet there is little evidence to that effect, due largely to the lack of empirical study. This chapter has empirically examined this assumption in the context of public support for economic and monetary union. Based on several theoretical claims about the distributional consequences of EMU, I have examined the relationship between variation in citizens' support for EMU and differences in their expected economic gains/losses from EMU. The analysis reveals that EU citizens did indeed vary in their support for EMU consistent with their economic interests related to the distributional consequences of EMU. These results have important implications for our theoretical conception of the politics of monetary unification in Europe.

Many studies of international economic policy in general and European monetary unification in particular suffer from a level-of-analysis problem. Scholars who employ the economic self-interest model in the study of international economic policy-making often assume that a government's preference in international negotiations reflects its nation's economic interests. However, scholars often leave unopened the black box of how this national preference is formed. Instead, they rely on an assumption that the relevant political actors in the national context pursue their economic interests regarding the international economic policy at issue, thereby endowing the national government with a preference that represents an aggregation of economic interests concerning that policy.

This chapter, by providing a test of this assumption, supports the application of the economic self-interest model to the politics of EMU. The analysis presented here provides evidence at the individual level that citizens adopted political attitudes (and, presumably, behavior) that were consistent with their economic self-interest regarding international economic policy. Moreover, these results obtain in a time period (1993/94) that provides a particularly difficult test of the hypotheses.

In addition, the results contribute to resolving the theoretical debate about which distributional effects of EMU were politically relevant—at least at the mass level. Some scholars contend that the reduced risk in cross-border commerce from a fixed exchange rate accounted for intranational variation in support for EMU. Others argue that EMU was politically divisive because of the consequences of capital market liberalization for redistributive policies and returns on citizens' assets. Still another scholar posits that the politically salient aspect of EMU was that the fixed exchange rate regime imposed restrictive monetary policy on its members, which benefits capital at labor's expense. The empirical analysis provides fairly robust evidence for all three of these claims.

The empirical analysis also indicates that the convergence criteria, particularly the requirement of reduced public debt, had no effect on support for EMU among citizens employed in the public sector. This is a surprising result given that some national governments instituted dramatic reforms of public spending in order to meet the convergence criteria.

It is important to note that the theoretical expectations of the distributional consequences of EMU are also applicable to the politics of the euro. Distributional issues related to a fixed exchange rate, exchange rate stability, inflation, capital market liberalization, and price transparency are all relevant for a European single currency. Thus, to the extent that citizens form attitudes toward the euro in a similar fashion to their attitudes toward EMU, these results have several implications for the politics of the euro. For one, these findings suggest that variation in the distribution of trade by EU member states could upset the balance of domestic political coalitions favoring a single currency. For example, if German industrial exporters were to shift their trade from the EU eastwards (particularly if EU enlargement is postponed), then the analysis indicates that German public support for fixed exchange rates (and thus a single currency) with other EU member states will decline. Specifically, support for the euro among Germans working in the industrial sectors would decline. In contrast, if commercial integration (intra-EU trade as a portion of EU GDP) in the EU continues to increase, then the number of citizens supporting the euro should also increase.

Second, the empirical results indicate that efforts toward tax harmonization may influence the level of public support for the euro. Recent efforts at tax harmonization, particularly harmonization of VAT and excise taxes, may cause a reduction in national price differences for consumer goods. Reduced price differences, in turn, diminish the incentives for cross-border shopping and the value of price transparency provided by a single currency. The results of the analysis suggest that residents of border regions are sensitive to these incentives for cross-border shopping when evaluating a common currency. Specifically, border residents were increasingly supportive of EMU as the price difference at their border increased. Consequently, any reduction in price differences due to tax harmonization is likely to decrease support for the euro among border residents. Since border regions represent significant portions of some nations (for example, Luxembourg is a border region), this may have a significant effect on national public support for the euro in some countries.

BIBLIOGRAPHY

Frieden, Jeffry, 1996, The impact of goods and capital market integration on European monetary politics. *Comparative Political Studies* 29, 193–222.

Scheve, Kenneth, 1999, European economic integration and electoral politics in France and Great Britain. Paper presented at the Annual Meetings of the American Political Science Association, Atlanta, August.

18

Financial Globalization: Gain and Pain for Developing Countries

SERGIO L. SCHMUKLER

In recent decades, advances in information technology and deregulation of domestic financial markets have led countries around the world to become more financially integrated—a process that brings substantial benefits but also carries serious risks. Economist Sergio L. Schmukler presents a balanced view of financial globalization, outlining the benefits and risks that globalization entails for developing countries. On the "benefits" side of the ledger, financial globalization means that more capital is available to lower-income countries, which can foster development, especially of the financial sector. A major downside of financial globalization is that it can lead to financial volatility and crises, due to imperfections in international financial markets that generate bubbles, herding behavior, and speculative currency attacks. Financial globalization is thus a mixed blessing for developing countries. Schmukler considers the net benefits and the policy implications, including his view that more international cooperation is desirable to address the downsides of financial globalization.

The recent wave of globalization has generated an intense debate among economists, attracting both strong supporters and opponents. This paper tries to present a balanced view of financial globalization, outlining the benefits and risks that globalization entails for developing countries. The paper revisits the arguments and evidence that can be used in favor of and against globalization as well as the prospects and policy options.

In this paper, financial globalization is understood as the integration of a country's local financial system with international financial markets and institutions. This integration typically requires that governments liberalize the domestic financial sector and the capital account. Integration takes place when liberalized economies experience an increase in cross-country capital movement, including an active participation of local borrowers and lenders in international markets and a widespread use of international financial intermediaries. Although developed countries are the most active participants in the financial globalization process, developing countries (primarily middle-income countries) have also started to participate. This paper focuses on the integration of developing countries with the international financial system.

From a historical perspective, financial globalization is not a new phenomenon, but the depth and breadth of globalization today are unprecedented. Capital flows have existed for a long time. In fact, according to some measures, the extent of capital mobility and capital flows a hundred years ago is comparable to today's. At that time, however, only a few countries and sectors participated in financial globalization. Capital flows tended to follow migration and were generally directed toward supporting trade flows. For the most part, capital flows took the form of bonds, and the flows were of a long-term nature. International investment was dominated by a small number of free-standing companies, and financial intermediation was concentrated in a few family groups. The international system was dominated by the gold standard, in which gold backed national currencies.

The advent of the First World War represented the first blow to this wave of financial globalization, which was followed by a period of instability and crises ultimately leading to the Great Depression and the Second World War. After these events, governments reversed financial globalization, imposing capital controls to regain monetary policy autonomy. Capital flows reached a historic low during the 1950s and 1960s. The international system was dominated by the Bretton Woods system of fixed but adjustable exchange rates, limited capital mobility, and autonomous monetary policies.

The 1970s witnessed the beginning of a new era in the international financial system. As a result of the oil shock and the breakup of the Bretton Woods system, a new wave of globalization began. The oil shock provided international banks with fresh funds to invest in developing countries. These funds were used mainly to finance public debt in the form of syndicated loans. With the disintegration of the Bretton Woods system of fixed exchange rates, countries were able to open up to greater capital mobility while keeping the autonomy of their monetary policies. The capital inflows of the 1970s and early 1980s to developing countries preceded the debt crisis that started in Mexico in 1982. To solve the debt crisis of the 1980s, Brady bonds were created, which led to the subsequent development of bond markets for emerging economies. Deregulation, privatization, and advances in technology made foreign direct investment (FDI) and equity investments in emerging markets more attractive to firms and households in developed countries. The 1990s witnessed an investment boom in FDI and portfolio flows to emerging markets.

Today, despite the perception of increasing financial globalization, the international financial system is far from being perfectly integrated. There is evidence of persistent capital market segmentation, home country bias, and correlation between domestic savings and investment. The recent deregulation of financial systems, the technological advances in financial services, and the increased diversity in the channels of financial globalization make a return to the past more costly and therefore more difficult. Financial globalization is unlikely to be reversed, particularly for partially integrated economies, although the possibility of a reversal still exists.

The potential benefits of financial globalization will likely lead to a more financially interconnected world and a deeper degree of financial integration of developing countries with international financial markets. Arguably, the main benefit of financial globalization for developing countries is the development of their financial system, which involves more complete, deeper, more stable, and better-regulated financial markets. A better-functioning financial system with more credit is key because it fosters economic growth. There are two main channels through which financial globalization promotes financial development. First, financial globalization implies that a new type of capital and more capital is available to developing countries. Among other things, new and more capital allows countries to better smooth consumption, deepens financial markets, and increases the degree of market discipline. Second, financial globalization leads to a better financial infrastructure, which mitigates information asymmetries and, as a consequence, reduces problems such as adverse selection and moral hazard.

Financial globalization can also carry some risks. These risks are more likely to appear in the short run, when countries open up. One well-known risk is that globalization can be related to financial crises. The crises in Asia and Russia in 1997–98, Brazil in 1999, Ecuador in 2000, Turkey in 2001, Argentina in 2001, and Uruguay in 2002 are some examples that captured worldwide interest. There are various links between globalization and crises. If the right financial infrastructure is not in place or is not put in place during integration, liberalization followed by capital inflows can debilitate the health of the local financial system. If market fundamentals deteriorate, speculative attacks will occur with capital outflows from both domestic and foreign investors. For successful integration, economic fundamentals need to be and remain strong, and local markets need to be properly regulated and supervised. The need for strong fundamentals is key since, other things being equal, financial globalization tends to intensify a country's sensitivities to foreign shocks. Moreover, international market imperfections, such as herding, panics, and boom-bust cycles, and the fluctuating nature of capital flows can lead to crises and contagion, even in countries with good economic fundamentals. Another risk of globalization is the segmentation that it can create between those able to participate in the global financial system and those that need to rely on domestic financial sectors.

The net benefit of financial globalization for developing countries can be large despite the risks. But globalization also poses new challenges for policymakers. One main challenge is to manage financial globalization so that countries can take full advantage of the opportunities it generates while minimizing the risks it implies. This management is important because financial globalization is likely to deepen over time, led by its potential benefits. Another challenge of globalization is that, in a more integrated world, governments are left with fewer policy instruments. Thus, some type of international financial cooperation becomes more important.

This paper discusses the recent developments and main agents of financial globalization and then examines the effects of globalization on the domestic financial sector. The paper also analyzes the potential costs associated with globalization, discusses the net effects, and analyzes the policy options available to deal with financial globalization. The paper concludes with a discussion of the policy implications.

FINANCIAL GLOBALIZATION: LATEST DEVELOPMENTS AND MAIN AGENTS

The last thirty years witnessed many changes in financial globalization. New technological advances and the liberalization of the domestic financial sector and the capital account have led to new developments. The main agents driving financial globalization are governments, private investors and borrowers, and financial institutions.

Important players

Latest Developments in Financial Globalization

The new nature of capital flows and the increasing use of international financial intermediaries constitute two of the most important developments in financial globalization.

NEW NATURE OF CAPITAL FLOWS. Figure 1 shows that net capital flows to emerging economies have increased sharply since the 1970s. Capital flows went from less than U.S.$41 billion in the 1970s to about U.S.$320 billion in 1997 (in real terms), when they peaked. The composition of capital flows to developing countries changed significantly during this period. The importance of official flows more than halved while private capital flows became the major source of capital for a large number of emerging economies. The composition of private capital flows also changed markedly. FDI grew continuously throughout the 1990s. Mergers and acquisitions, especially the ones resulting from the privatization of public companies, were the most important source of this increase. Net portfolio flows grew from U.S.$0.01 billion in 1970 to U.S.$82 billion in 1996 in real terms. New international mutual funds and pension funds helped channel the equity flows to developing countries. The importance of syndicated bank loans and other private flows decreased steadily in relative terms throughout this period, especially after the 1980s debt crises. Figure 1 also shows the abrupt decline in capital flows to emerging markets following the Asian and Russian crises in 1997–98 and the Argentine crisis in 2001.

Even though net private capital flows to developing countries increased in recent years, private capital does not flow to all countries equally. Some countries tend to receive large amounts of inflows while other countries receive little foreign capital. Figure 1 also shows that while flows to developing countries increased in general, the top twelve countries with the highest

FIGURE 1 Net Capital Flows to Developing Countries, 1970–2001

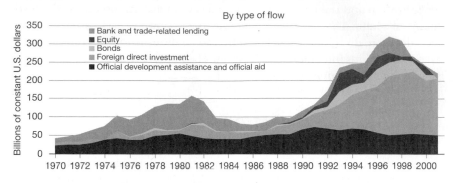

By type of flow

- Bank and trade-related lending
- Equity
- Bonds
- Foreign direct investment
- Official development assistance and official aid

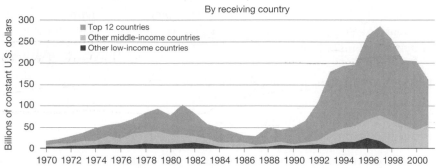

By receiving country

- Top 12 countries
- Other middle-income countries
- Other low-income countries

NOTES: The first panel plots the evolution of private capital flows and official capital flows. Private capital flows are disaggregated into foreign direct investment, portfolio bond flows, portfolio equity flows, and bank and trade-related flows. The second panel depicts the distribution of private capital flows among developing countries. The top twelve receiving developing countries are China, Brazil, Mexico, South Korea, Argentina, Malaysia, Chile, India, Russian Federation, Thailand, Turkey, and South Africa.

flows are receiving the overwhelming majority of the net inflows. Moreover, the top twelve countries are the ones that experienced the most rapid growth in private capital flows during the 1990s. As a consequence, the share of flows dedicated to low- and middle-income countries (outside the top twelve) has decreased over time. This pattern is important because if countries benefit from foreign capital, only a small group of countries are the ones benefiting the most. The unequal distribution of capital flows is consistent with the fact that income among developing countries is diverging although the causality is difficult to determine.

Main Agents

There are four main agents of financial globalization: governments, borrowers, investors, and financial institutions. Each of them is helping countries become more financially integrated.

GOVERNMENTS. Governments allow globalization by liberalizing restrictions on the domestic financial sector and the capital account of the balance of payments. In the past, governments used to regulate the domestic financial sector by restricting the allocation of credit through controls on prices and quantities. Governments also imposed several constraints on cross-country capital movements. The list of instruments used to restrict the capital account is rather extensive, including restrictions on foreign exchange transactions, derivative transactions, lending and borrowing activities by banks and corporations, and the participation of foreign investors in the local financial system.

Even though the domestic financial sector and the capital account were heavily regulated for a long time, the restrictions have been lifted over time. Figure 2 presents the evolution of their index of financial liberalization that takes into account restrictions on the domestic financial system, the stock market, and the capital account. The figure illustrates the gradual lifting of restrictions in developed and emerging countries during the last thirty years. The figure shows that developed countries have tended to use more liberal policies than developing countries have. Although there has been a gradual lifting of restrictions over time, there were periods of reversals in which restrictions were reimposed. The most substantial reversals took place in the aftermath of the 1982 debt crisis, in the mid-1990s, and after the Argentine crisis in Latin America.

FIGURE 2 Financial Liberalization in Developed and Developing Countries (Index)

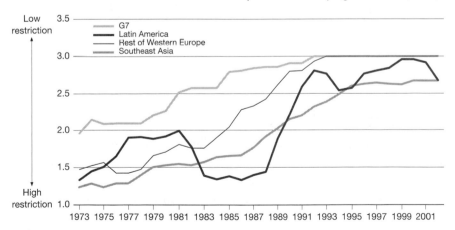

NOTES: The liberalization index is calculated as the simple average of three indexes (liberalization in the capital account, domestic financial system, and stock market) that range between 1 and 3, where 1 means no liberalization and 3 means full liberalization. These data are then aggregated as the simple average between countries of each region.

The literature identifies six main reasons to explain the new wave of liberalization and deregulation by governments of different countries. First, governments found capital controls increasingly costly and difficult to maintain effectively. Second, policymakers have become increasingly aware that government-led financial systems and nonmarket approaches have failed. Third, recent crises have heightened the importance of foreign capital to finance government budgets and smooth public consumption and investment. Also, foreign capital has helped governments capitalize banks with problems, conduct corporate restructuring, and manage crises. Fourth, opening up the privatization of public companies to foreign investors has helped increase their receipts. Fifth, although governments can also tax revenue from foreign capital, they might find this harder to do than with other factors of production because of its footloose nature. Sixth, governments have become increasingly convinced of the benefits of a more efficient and robust domestic financial system for growth and stability of the economy and for the diversification of the public and private sectors' investor base.

BORROWERS AND INVESTORS. Borrowers and investors, including households and firms, have also become main agents of financial globalization. By borrowing abroad, firms and individuals can relax their financial constraints to smooth consumption and investment. Firms can expand their financing alternatives by raising funds directly through bonds and equity issues in international markets and thereby reducing the cost of capital, expanding their investor base, and increasing liquidity. Borrowing countries benefit not only from new capital but also, in the case of FDI, from new technology, know-how, management, and employee training.

More financing alternatives help foreign investors overcome direct and indirect investment barriers. International investors have taken advantage of financial globalization to achieve cross-country risk diversification. If developing countries are to grow faster than developed economies, lenders can expect to obtain higher returns for their investment. As a consequence of the liberalization of financial markets, both institutions and individuals in developed countries can now easily invest in emerging markets through buying shares of international mutual funds (including global, regional, and country funds). Investors can also purchase depositary receipts, cross-listed shares of international companies, and international corporate and sovereign bonds in international capital markets.

FINANCIAL INSTITUTIONS. Financial institutions, through the internationalization of financial services, are also a major driving force of financial globalization. Changes at the global level and changes in both developed and developing countries explain the role of financial institutions as a force of globalization.

At a global level, the gains in information technology have diminished the importance of geography, allowing international corporations to service several markets from one location. The gains in information technology have had three main effects on the financial services industry: (1) They promoted a more intensive use of international financial institutions, (2) they led to a major consolidation and restructuring of the world financial services industry, and (3) they gave rise to global banks and international conglomerates that provide a mix of financial products and services in a broad range of markets and countries, blurring the distinctions between financial institutions and the activities and markets in which they engage. Demographic changes and the increased sophistication of small investors around the world have intensified competition for savings among banks, mutual funds, insurance companies, and pension funds. Households have bypassed bank deposits and securities firms to hold their funds with institutions better able to diversify risks, reduce tax burdens, and take advantage of economies of scale.

In developed countries, increased competition has led banks and nonbank financial firms to look for expanding their market shares into new businesses and markets, attracting customers from other countries, which allows them to diversify risk. Decreasing costs due to deregulation and technical improvements were accompanied by more competition. Deregulation has meant that banks can enter business that had been off limits (such as securities, insurance, and asset management). Nonbank financial institutions have been slowly competing with traditional banks, offering financial services traditionally provided exclusively by banks, adopting new financial risk calculation methods, and penetrating traditional banking activities in credit markets, such as syndication of loans and bridge loans via new structured financial instruments.

In developing countries, the liberalization of the regulatory systems has opened the door for international firms to participate in local markets. The privatization of public financial institutions has provided foreign banks an opportunity to enter local financial markets. Macroeconomic stabilization, a better business environment, and stronger fundamentals in emerging markets have ensured a more attractive climate for foreign investment.

FINANCIAL GLOBALIZATION AND FINANCIAL SECTOR DEVELOPMENT

Financial globalization can lead to the development of the financial system. A well-functioning financial sector provides funds to borrowers (households, firms, and governments) that have productive investment opportunities. Financial systems do not usually operate as desired because lenders confront problems of asymmetric information; lenders know less about the particular project than the borrower. Asymmetric information can lead to adverse selection and moral hazard. Adverse selection means that low-quality borrowers are the ones more likely to seek out funds in the market. Low-quality borrowers are the ones less concerned about paying back a loan. Adverse selection might lead to credit rationing, in the sense that lenders are not willing to lend even at high interest rates; lenders realize that low-quality borrowers are the ones most attracted to high rates. Moral hazard means that, after obtaining the funds, borrowers have incentives to take risky positions or to use the funds in certain ways that are not beneficial to lenders. Thus, borrowers can obtain large gains if their bets pay off and can default otherwise.

One of the primary potential benefits of financial globalization is the development of the financial sector, enhancing the provision of funds for productive investment opportunities. Financial globalization helps improve the functioning of the financial system through two main channels: by increasing the availability of funds and by improving the financial infrastructure, which can reduce the problem of asymmetric information. As a consequence, financial globalization decreases adverse selection and moral hazard, thus enhancing the availability of credit.

New and More Capital Is Available

As described above, both borrowers and investors have incentives to move funds across countries. In a financially integrated world, funds can flow freely from countries with excess funds to countries where the marginal product of capital is high. In this context, both foreign institutions and individuals might provide capital to developing countries if they expect these countries to grow faster than developed economies. As a consequence, countries can smooth consumption and make investments financed by foreign capital. This flow of capital from developed to developing countries is reflected in the large current account deficits typically observed in many developing nations.

The effects of capital flows on financial development take place because new sources of funds and more capital become available. New sources of funds mean that borrowers not only depend on domestic funds but they can also borrow from foreign countries willing to invest in domestic assets. The capital available from new sources means that market discipline is now stronger both at the macroeconomic level and at the financial sector level, as now local and foreign investors enforce market discipline on private and public borrowers. Foreign capital is particularly effective in imposing this kind of discipline given its footloose nature; foreign capital can more easily shift investment across countries. Domestic capital tends to have more restrictions against investing internationally.

More capital leads to a deepening and increased sophistication of financial markets, including an increase in the sources and uses of financing, and expands the scope of products, instruments, and services available to nationals. As a consequence, borrowers and lenders have more financial opportunities; more assets and liabilities of domestic borrowers and investors become available and transacted. More instruments and investors allow better risk diversification within and across countries. By issuing to global investors, borrowers can lower their cost of capital, in part because international investors are more diversified and, therefore, ready to pay higher prices for domestic equity and bonds. Also, the shift to a foreign jurisdiction can allow borrowers to lengthen their debt duration because this shift would reduce the overall risk for the investor (for instance, by improving contract enforcement, transparency, and market infrastructures). For a given level of risk appetite, reducing the risk would make room for the investor to increase duration risk. Finally, foreign direct investment brings not only capital but also new technology, know-how, and management and employee training, all of which contribute to increase productivity and foster economic growth.

Thanks in part to the availability of more capital, developing economies have developed their stock and bond markets as well as some of their local financial services industry. Capital markets have developed in the sense that more domestic equity and bonds are issued and traded, but this development does not imply that all domestic financial institutions have become more important. As discussed above, borrowers and investors can just use international financial intermediaries, like stock exchanges and banks, to conduct their financial transactions. In fact, domestic financial institutions can actually shrink as a result of competition with international financial institutions. . . .

Improvement in the Financial Infrastructure

Financial globalization tends to improve the financial infrastructure. An improved financial sector infrastructure means that borrowers and lenders operate in a more transparent, competitive, and efficient financial system. In this environment, problems of asymmetric information are minimized and credit is maximized.

In theory, there are different channels through which financial globalization can lead to improvements in the financial sector infrastructure. First, financial globalization can lead to greater competition in the provision of funds, which can generate efficiency gains. Second, the adoption of international accounting standards can increase transparency. Third, the introduction of international financial intermediaries would push the financial sector toward the international frontier. Fourth, financial globalization improves corporate governance; new shareholders and potential bidders can lead to a closer monitoring of management. Fifth, the increase in the technical capabilities for engaging in precision financing results in a growing completeness of local and global markets. Sixth, the stringent market discipline imposed by financial globalization has consequences not only on the macroeconomy but also on the business environment and other institutional factors.

Foreign bank entry is another way through which financial globalization improves the financial infrastructure of developing countries. Foreign banks enhance financial development for at least three main reasons. First, foreign banks have more diversified portfolios as they have access to sources of funds from all over the world, which means that they are exposed to less risk and are less affected by negative shocks to the home country economy. Second, foreign entry can lead to the adoption of best practices in the banking industry, particularly in risk management but also in management techniques, which leads to a more efficient banking sector. Third, if foreign banks dominate the banking sector, governments are less likely to bail out banks when they have solvency problems. A lower likelihood of bailouts encourages more prudent behavior by banking institutions, an increased discipline, and a reduction in moral hazard. . . .

RISKS AND NET EFFECTS OF GLOBALIZATION

Although financial globalization has several potential benefits, it can also carry some risks. The recent stream of financial crises and contagion after countries liberalized their financial systems and became integrated with world financial markets might lead some to suggest that globalization generates financial volatility and crises.

Even though domestic factors tend to be key determinants of crises, there are different channels through which financial globalization can be related to crises. First, when a country liberalizes its financial system, it becomes subject to market discipline exercised by both foreign and domestic investors. When an economy is closed, only domestic investors monitor the economy and react to unsound fundamentals. In open economies, the joint force of domestic and foreign investors might prompt countries to try to achieve sound fundamentals although this process might take a long time.

Second, globalization can also lead to crises if there are imperfections in international financial markets, which can generate bubbles, irrational behavior, herding behavior, speculative attacks, and crashes, among other things. Imperfections in international capital markets can lead to crises even in countries with sound fundamentals. For example, if investors believe that the exchange rate is unsustainable they might speculate against the currency, which can lead to a self-fulfilling balance-of-payments crisis regardless of market fundamentals. . . . Imperfections can also deteriorate fundamentals. For example, moral hazard can lead to overborrowing syndromes when economies are liberalized and implicit government guarantees exist, increasing the likelihood of crises.

Third, globalization can lead to crises as a result of the importance of external factors, even in countries with sound fundamentals and even in the absence of imperfections in international capital markets. If a country becomes dependent on foreign capital, sudden shifts in foreign capital flows can create financing difficulties and economic downturns. These shifts do not necessarily depend on country fundamentals. External factors are important determinants of capital flows to developing countries. In particular, . . . world interest rates were a significant determinant of capital inflows into Asia and Latin

America during the 1990s. Economic cyclical movements in developed countries, a global drive towards diversification of investments in major financial centers, and regional effects tend to be other important global factors. . . .

Fourth, financial globalization can also lead to financial crises through *transmission* contagion, namely by shocks that are transmitted across countries. Three broad channels of contagion have been identified in the literature: real links, financial links, and herding behavior, or "unexplained high correlations." Real links have usually been associated with trade links. When two countries trade among themselves or if they compete in the same external markets, a devaluation of the exchange rate in one country deteriorates the other country's competitive advantage. As a consequence, both countries will likely end up devaluing their currencies to rebalance their external sectors. Financial links exist when two economies are connected through the international financial system. One example of financial links is leveraged institutions facing margin calls. When the value of their collateral falls as a result of a negative shock in one country, leveraged companies need to increase their reserves. Therefore, they sell part of their valuable holdings in the countries that are still unaffected by the initial shock. This mechanism propagates the shock to other economies. Finally, financial markets might transmit shocks across countries as a result of herding behavior or panics. At the root of this herding behavior is asymmetric information. Information is costly, so investors remain uninformed. Therefore, investors try to infer future price changes on the basis of how other markets are reacting. In this context, a change in Thailand's asset prices might be useful information about future changes in Indonesia or Brazil's asset prices. Additionally, in the context of asymmetric information, what the other market participants are doing might convey information that each uninformed investor does not have. This type of reaction leads to herding behavior, panics, and "irrational exuberance."

Net Effects

The previous sections argued that globalization can bring benefits by developing the domestic financial system. But globalization can also be associated with crises and contagion. This link is inescapable in a world of asymmetric information and imperfect contract enforcement. Though many crises are triggered by domestic factors and countries have had crises for a long time (even in periods of low financial integration), globalization can increase the vulnerability of countries to crises. In open economies, countries are subject to the reaction of both domestic and international markets, which can trigger fundamental-based or self-fulfilling crises. Moreover, the cross-country transmission of crises is characteristic of open economies. Completely closed economies should be isolated from foreign shocks. But when a country integrates with the global economy, it becomes exposed to contagion effects of different types and, more generally, to foreign shocks.

Is the link between globalization, crises, and contagion important enough to outweigh the benefits of globalization? The evidence is still very scarce, but it is far from clear that open countries are more volatile and suffer more from crises. The evidence suggests that, in the long run, volatility tends to decrease following liberalization and integration with world markets, probably thanks to the development of the financial sector. The evidence holds even when including crisis episodes, which might be considered particular events.

Any potential increase in volatility tends to occur in the short run, right after liberalization. When countries first liberalize their financial sector, volatility and crises might arise, particularly in countries with vulnerable fundamentals. If the domestic financial sector is not prepared to cope with foreign

FIGURE 3 Average Boom-Bust Cycles and Financial Liberalization

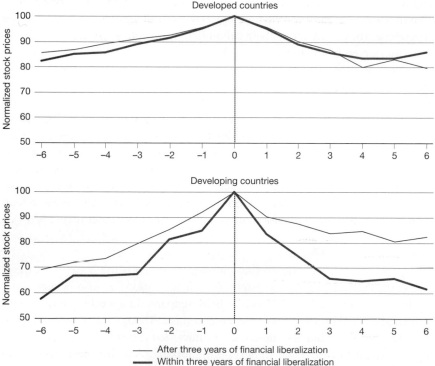

NOTES: The figures show the average boom-bust cycle in financial markets for selected countries. Date 0 is the date of the peak in stock market prices. All stock market indices are normalized to 100 at the peak. Developed countries are Canada, France, Germany, Italy, Japan, the United Kingdom, the United States, Denmark, Finland, Ireland, Norway, Portugal, Spain, and Sweden. Developing countries are Argentina, Brazil, Chile, Colombia, Mexico, Peru, Venezuela, Hong Kong, Indonesia, Korea, Malaysia, the Philippines, Taiwan, and Thailand. Financial liberalization occurs when countries substantially lift the restrictions on cross-country capital movements.

flows and is not properly regulated and supervised, financial liberalization can lead to domestic crises. This result is shown in Figure 3, which displays the typical boom-bust episode in stock markets. Three years after liberalization the cycles in the stock market become less pronounced while they become more pronounced in the aftermath of liberalization.

There is also some evidence of the positive impact of financial liberalization on output growth. . . . Financial liberalization leads to higher average long-run growth even though it also leads to occasional crises. This gain in growth is over and above the gain derived from trade liberalization. The growth-enhancing financial deepening that follows liberalization is not a smooth process but takes place through boom-bust cycles. In the presence of severe contract enforceability problems, occasional crises are the price that has to be paid to attain higher growth. The first best alternative would be to improve domestic credit markets by implementing judicial reform. In the absence of such reform, liberalization allows financially constrained firms to attain greater leverage and invest more at the cost of undertaking credit risk. Credit risk creates an environment with high growth and financial fragility.

POLICY OPTIONS

There are different views on how governments can maximize the benefits of globalization and minimize its risks. As discussed above, one of the most important benefits of financial globalization is the development of the financial sector. This development tends to lead to deeper and less volatile financial markets. But, on the other hand, globalization can also be associated with some costs. The most important one involves a higher sensitivity to crises and contagion. The gains are likely to materialize in the long run, while the costs will tend to be more prevalent in the short run. In all the aspects of globalization, the action or inaction of governments can be important.

Three Views on the Role of Government

In the past, the mood might have favored unfettered capitalism, but the fact that globalization has been associated with crises and contagion has led many economists to believe that some degree of government intervention can be beneficial. Most economists would now agree that financial integration with the rest of the world is beneficial, and only a few would suggest policies that isolate countries. However, the recent experience with crises and contagion has generated large disagreements on how to integrate and on the policy recommendations. There are different views on what governments should do regarding financial integration.

A first view argues that government intervention is at the root of recent crises. This view believes that international capital markets are efficient and developed (or at least international financial markets are more efficient than financial markets in developing countries). Therefore, countries with underdeveloped financial markets would benefit from full financial liberalization, with minimal government intervention. Certain types of government intervention create distortions that can lead to moral hazard and crises. Government guarantees can induce firms to go broke at society's expense (looting). Once looting becomes established in one sector, it can distort production in other sectors.

A second view claims that cross-country capital flows should be restricted. According to this view, inefficient international financial markets debilitate the argument for unregulated financial integration. Anomalies such as asymmetric information, moral hazard, asset bubbles, speculative attacks, herding behavior, and contagion are present in international financial markets. So economies open to capital flows suffer the consequences of these imperfections. The recent crises showed that international financial markets punished similarly countries with different fundamentals and policies. Given this evidence, government intervention to restrict cross-country capital movements can be socially beneficial. . . . Governments can mitigate the cost of volatile capital flows, reducing excessive risk taking and making markets less vulnerable to external shocks, and still pursue integration with international financial markets.

A third view concentrates on risk management. This view focuses on strengthening the domestic financial sector and sequencing financial liberalization and argues that opening a weak domestic financial sector to large capital movements is potentially risky. If the domestic financial sector does not manage risk properly, does not have sufficient reserves and capital, or does not have the right incentives, large capital inflows and outflows can create severe problems in the domestic financial sector. Foreign competition can also debilitate local financial intermediaries. Since financial crises can be very costly, this view proposes an adequate regulation and supervision of the domestic financial system without distinguishing between foreign capital and domestic capital. Additional proposals include the use of countercyclical fiscal policy, the stability of prices, the active management of reserve requirements, and the implementation of contingent liquidity arrangements. Also, improved prudential regulation and increased market discipline, through more transparency and information, have been recommended as a way to avoid excessive risk taking.

Fewer Policy Instruments

One of the main consequences of globalization for policymaking is that the number of instruments at the country level diminishes when the economy is integrated. When the domestic financial system integrates with the rest of the world, it is more difficult for countries to monitor and regulate the transactions outside its borders. For example, local authorities are able to regulate the activities of the local subsidiary of an international bank, but it is more difficult to regulate the parent company and subsidiaries in other countries, which can be linked to the local bank. Also, the ability of capital to move freely in and out of the country makes government intervention less effective.

The initial conditions matter. There are more policy options at the domestic level when countries have a low level of financial integration. As countries become more integrated, the need for some kind of international financial cooperation grows.

The rest of the section illustrates, with three examples, how financial globalization influences the policies available to policymakers. These policies have received significant attention in the discussions surrounding crises and financial globalization. The policies discussed below are the ones related to capital controls, risk management, and the choice of monetary and exchange rate regimes.

CAPITAL CONTROLS.   The proposals on capital controls are designed to reduce the probability or mitigate the effects of sudden shifts in foreign capital. These proposals suggest that international capital flows should be restricted in very particular and judicious ways. The main proposals can be divided into four different categories: (1) controls on outflows, which restrict investors to move capital outside the country; (2) controls on aggregate inflows, which are intended to keep capital from flowing into the country rather than restricting the exit of capital once it is in the country; (3) controls on short-term inflows, à la Chile, to avoid the build up of short-term debt; and (4) controls on foreign exchange transactions, or a "Tobin tax," aimed at imposing a small uniform tax on all foreign exchange transactions, regardless of their nature.

There is a very large literature on the effects of capital controls. On the whole the literature is inconclusive about the effects of capital controls. The literature consists primarily of interesting case studies, with little systematic cross-country evidence. Some papers suggest that controls work as expected while others find no controls or negative effects of controls. The evidence suggests that when controls work, they do so on a temporary basis. As time passes, controls become ineffective; market participants find ways to circumvent the controls. A brief review of part of the empirical evidence follows.

The country that has received most of the attention is probably Chile, given the attractiveness of its scheme, which imposed capital controls on short-term inflows through unremunerated reserve requirements. Chile was also widely studied because it systematically put limits to capital flows in both episodes of international capital inflows to emerging markets (1978–81 and 1990–96). The evidence from several studies suggests that controls on inflows introduced a wedge between domestic and foreign returns and allowed Chile's central bank to undertake a more independent monetary policy. This finding holds only when external shocks were small. Controls were not effective in preventing spillovers from very large shocks, such as the ones observed in the midst of the Asian crisis in 1997. Even though controls in Chile appear to have shifted the composition or at least the denomination of capital flows to long-term flows, the effects were confined only to the short run. The effectiveness of the controls was reduced over time as investors found ways to circumvent them. . . .

RISK MANAGEMENT.   As an alternative to capital controls, some economists have proposed focusing on managing risk by regulating and supervising the financial system, without distinguishing between domestic and foreign capital. When economies are partially integrated with the rest of the world, distinguishing between domestic and foreign capital becomes more difficult, which is why capital controls tend to be ineffective. In this case, governments can benefit by focusing on the stability of the overall financial sector to avoid financial crises or to make crises less costly. If there are imperfections in capital markets, it becomes even more important to avoid excessive risk taking. So the discussion shifts toward risk management.

Governments might want to regulate and supervise financial systems to ensure that the financial sector is managing risk well. Governments might want to avoid large asset-liability mismatches, like unhedged foreign exchange borrowings invested in nontradable sectors and short-term assets for long-term investments, which can leave banks vulnerable to exchange rate depreciations and to interest rate surges. Also, the regulation and supervision should ensure that banks are sufficiently capitalized with appropriate loan classification and adequate loan loss provisions. Transparency for investors and depositors through mandatory public disclosure of audited financial statements will help enforce market discipline. The removal of explicit or implicit government guarantees and sharing risk with investors will decrease the potential for moral hazard. . . .

The policies toward the financial sector should also be accompanied by the right incentives for sound corporate finance. Clear rules and adequate financial disclosure help regulators and market participants monitor corporations, pushing corporations to achieve good practices. Clear governance rules help prevent insider and group lending not subject to loan evaluation and creditworthiness standards. Developed corporate bond and equity markets help companies obtain external financing, become more transparent, and be subject to market discipline. . . .

Proper risk management helps avoid and manage crises. First, as a preventive measure, countries with solid financial sectors will probably suffer fewer crises and less pronounced recessions. Second, countries with sound financial sectors will have more flexibility to cope with external shocks and to take corrective measures during a crisis. Countries with a solvent banking sector and low corporate leverage ratios will be able to some extent to raise interest rates to contain speculative attacks on the exchange rate. Countries with large foreign exchange reserves and access to contingent liquidity facilities will be able to inject liquidity into the system, avoiding credit squeezes and bank runs.

The recent experiences with crises and contagion stress the importance of adequate risk management. One of the most important lessons of the East Asian crisis is that highly leveraged and vulnerable corporate sectors were a key determinant of the depth of the crisis. Currency devaluations suddenly inflated the size of external debt (measured in terms of the domestic currency) and debt service obligations, thereby driving the domestic corporations into financial distress. High interest rates also sharply increased domestic debt service obligations of the corporations. These vulnerabilities affected the banks with exposures to the corporations. . . . Currency crises lead to an increase in foreign denominated debt, which, combined with declining sales and higher interest rates, weakens the corporate sector and in turn the financial system. . . .

Can financial liberalization occur without the appropriate risk management in place? This question leads to the issue of sequencing of liberalization. Having a robust financial sector is key for a successful globalization. A standard recommendation on sequencing is to first clean up domestic financial institutions and change government institutions and then deregulate the industry and open up the capital account. But this discussion may be irrelevant if the timing is such that reforms never predate liberalization, with institutional changes happening mostly as a result of financial deregulation. . . . The evidence for emerging and mature markets suggests that reforms to institutions occur mostly after liberalization is implemented. These results cast doubts on the notion that governments tend to implement institutional reforms before they start deregulating the financial sector. On the contrary, the evidence suggests that partial liberalization fuels institutional reforms.

There are several reasons that can explain why financial liberalization might prompt institutional reforms. First, well-established firms may oppose reforms that promote financial development because it breeds competition. These firms can even be hurt by financial development because it implies better disclosure rules and enforcement (reducing the importance of these firms' collateral and reputation) and permits newcomers to enter and compete away profits. Also, incumbents may oppose the removal of capital controls as capital can flow away to more attractive destinations, limiting their sources of funds. However, opposition may be weaker in the presence of worldwide abundance of trade and cross-border flows. In these times, free access to international capital markets will allow the largest and best-known domestic firms to tap foreign markets for funds, with the support for financial liberalization becoming stronger. But financial liberalization sows the seeds of destruction of the old protected and inefficient financial sector because foreign and domestic investors (now with access to international capital markets) require better enforcement rules.

Second, as mentioned before, the liberalization and the gradual integration of emerging markets with international financial markets by itself may help to fortify the domestic financial sector. Foreign investors have overall better skills and information and can thus monitor management in ways local investors cannot. Liberalization, moreover, allows firms to access mature capital markets. Firms listing on foreign stock markets are also in the jurisdiction of a superior legal system and have higher disclosure standards. Third, the integration with world markets and institutions tends to speed up the reform process to achieve a resilient financial system. Capital markets can help supervise domestic financial institutions, imposing stricter market discipline, increasing transparency and the diffusion of information, and even pushing governments into guaranteeing that their financial systems are well supervised and regulated.

MONETARY AND EXCHANGE RATE POLICY. The choice of exchange rate regime (floating, fixed, or somewhere in between) has been a recurrent question in international monetary economics. Different historical phases of financial globalization can be understood in terms of the impossible trinity. According to this proposition, a country can consistently pursue only two out of the three policy objectives: free capital mobility, a fixed (or highly stable) nominal exchange rate, and an autonomous monetary policy. International capital mobility has thus prevailed in periods of political support either for subordinating monetary policy to exchange rate stability (as in the gold standard, 1880–1914) or for giving up exchange rate stability so as to enable monetary policy to pursue domestic objectives (as in the post–Bretton Woods era, 1971–2003). In contrast, when countries attempted simultaneously to target their exchange rates and use monetary policy in pursuit of domestic objectives (for example, to combat the slowdown of economic activity in the interwar period), they had to impose controls to curtail capital movements, as in the interwar (1914–45), and Bretton Woods (1945–71) periods. After the crises of the 1990s economists have become in favor of corner exchange rate regimes; according to which countries will either firmly fix their exchange rate or follow a flexible regime without precommitments, allowing for free capital movements.

By fixing the exchange rate, countries tend to reduce transaction costs and exchange rate risk that can discourage trade and investment. At the same time, a fixed exchange rate has been used as a credible nominal anchor for monetary policy. On the other hand, a flexible exchange rate allows a country to pursue independent monetary policy. A flexible exchange rate allows countries to respond to shocks through changes in the exchange rate and interest rate to avoid going into recession. Under the combination of fixed exchange rates and complete integration of financial markets, monetary policy becomes completely powerless. Any fluctuations in the currency or currencies to which the country fixes its exchange rate will affect the domestic currency. Under a fixed exchange rate regime, other variables need to do the adjusting.

Even though countries can choose a flexible exchange rate regime, some papers have argued that countries are not allowing their exchange rates to move in part because of the high degree of financial globalization. "Fear of floating" prevents countries with de jure flexible regimes from allowing their exchange rates to move freely. According to this view, factors like lack of credibility, exchange rate pass-through, and foreign-currency liabilities prevent countries from pursuing an independent monetary policy, regardless of their announced regime. Therefore, many countries, even if formally floating, are de facto "importing" the monetary policy of major-currency countries, much as those with pegs.

The empirical evidence seems to suggest that countries are not able or do not choose to pursue a completely independent monetary policy. The evidence from recent papers shows that local interest rates exhibit high sensitivity to international rates, regardless of the exchange rate regime. . . .

Even though countries with flexible exchange rate regimes cannot benefit from fully independent monetary policy in integrated countries, they should not be forced to adopt a fixed regime. There are credible ways to adopt a flexible regime if the right monetary institutions are in place and if countries can commit to an inflation targeting policy. In this way, countries may benefit at least partially from conducting their own monetary policy without giving up credibility.

. . . The choice of exchange rate regime is likely to be of second order importance to the development of good fiscal, financial, and monetary institutions in producing macroeconomic success in emerging market countries. A focus on institutional reforms rather than on the exchange rate regime may encourage emerging market countries to be healthier and less prone to crises.

CONCLUSIONS

In the last decades, countries around the world have become more financially integrated, driven by the potential benefits of financial globalization. One of the main benefits of financial globalization is the development of the financial sector. Financial markets become deeper and more sophisticated when they integrate with world markets, increasing the financial alternatives for borrowers and investors. Financial markets operating in a global environment enable international risk diversification and facilitate consumption smoothing. Although financial globalization has several potential benefits, it also poses new challenges. The crises of the 1990s, after many countries liberalized their financial system, have questioned in part the gains of globalization. Countries become exposed to external shocks and crises not only generated in their own country but also from contagion effects. In the initial stages of liberalization, if the right infrastructure is not in place or put in place, financial liberalization can lead to increased risks. Moreover, in a financially integrated economy, policymakers have fewer policy instruments to conduct economic policy.

The recent experiences with financial globalization yield some useful lessons for policymaking.

Countries Can Benefit from Globalization

Countries can benefit from financial globalization and should take advantage of it. Financial liberalization tends to develop the financial system, enhancing the financing opportunities, reducing the cost of capital, and increasing investment and liquidity. At the same time, the evidence does not suggest that financial volatility increases after financial liberalization. It is true that crises have had a very large impact on growth in some countries like Indonesia. But in other cases the recovery has been rapid, as in South Korea and Mexico. Also, it would be hard to argue that economies would have grown as fast as they did if they had remained closed.

Though the potential benefits can be large, we are far from full financial globalization. Even in open countries there is still an important home bias. Given the potential benefits of globalization, there is scope for a much deeper financial globalization and for much larger gains. Many countries are already partially open, and the prospect is for an increased globalization of financial markets. Paradoxically, the increased globalization can reduce the scope for risk diversification because integrated financial markets tend to be more correlated.

Importance of Sound Fundamentals and Strong Institutions

Sound macroeconomic and financial fundamentals are key in lowering the probability of crises and contagion and in enabling more effective management of crises. Preventing currency and banking crises should be one of the primary objectives of any policymaker because of the high cost of crises. This objective is more important in a world of free capital mobility because both foreign and domestic investors exercise market discipline and because foreign crises might have contagion effects at home. Attacks on currencies can occur whenever confidence is lost even if a country has sound fundamentals. A crisis in a foreign country can rapidly trigger a crisis at home. Weak fundamentals tend to scare investors more easily and make crisis management more difficult. Countries with bad fundamentals—for example, with large fiscal deficits and public debt—have fewer instruments to use in the midst of a crisis. Therefore, countries should focus on key policies that help them prevent and manage crises. These policies include avoiding large current account deficits financed through short-term private capital inflows and large asset-liability currency mismatches.

Improving the contractual and regulatory environment is also important. Better institutions make an emerging country more fit to join in the financial globalization process. In particular, they increase the capacity of the domestic financial system to intermediate prudently large international capital flows. Also, improvements in the contractual and regulatory framework can enhance the access of resident corporations (at least in the case of larger countries and for the larger corporations) to financial services supplied abroad.

Initial Conditions Matter

Measures to isolate countries (like capital controls) are unlikely to work in the long run. When there were attempts to isolate partially open economies, investors have tended to find ways to avoid the restrictions over time.

The initial conditions matter; the effectiveness of policies relies on the degree of integration with world markets. Countries with a very low degree of integration with world capital markets and with underdeveloped financial markets are more able to delay or reverse the process of financial globalization than countries already partially integrated. A country with a low level of integration should ensure that its financial sector is prepared to cope with open capital markets. If the domestic financial sector does not manage risk properly, does not have sufficient reserves and capital, or does not have the right incentives, large capital inflows and outflows can create severe problems in the domestic financial sector. However, it is not the case that all the conditions need to be met before governments liberalize the financial sector. As the discussion on sequencing shows, the process of integration itself can in some ways help improve the conditions of the domestic financial sector.

When countries develop, more comprehensive policies for risk management will be needed. These measures should try to avoid imperfections in capital markets and the buildup of vulnerabilities. In more open economies, the distinction between foreign and domestic capital becomes increasingly difficult. As the economy becomes integrated with the rest of the world, restraints to capital movements are more difficult to make effective since they can be circumvented easily. Therefore, a more comprehensive approach will be needed to build solid financial economies. This approach involves proper regulation and supervision of the financial system.

Need for International Financial Cooperation

As economies become more integrated, governments have fewer policy instruments and have to rely more on international financial policies. For example, governments tend to have fewer options about their monetary policy and exchange rate policy. In open economies there is a higher transmission of international interest rates and prices to the domestic economy. Moreover, bank regulation and supervision by one government is more difficult when liabilities and prices are denominated in foreign currency and when the banking sector is part of an international banking system. Also, in the midst of contagious crises, governments tend to lack sufficient resources to stop a currency attack, and individual governments can do little to stop crises being originated in foreign countries. In these cases, international financial coordination can help individual governments achieve their goals.

There are different policies in which there is scope for cooperation. One policy is the timely mobilization of external liquidity of sufficient magnitude to reverse market expectations in a context of sound policies. That liquidity usually comes from the international financial institutions. Given the magnitude of capital flows and the clustering of crises, isolated actions of individual governments or institutions are not sufficient to gain the required confidence. A coordinated action among governments and the international financial institutions is necessary to overcome crises and contagion at both regional and global levels. To minimize potential moral hazard, it would be necessary to involve the private sector so that private international investors share in the costs as a penalty for excessive risk taking.

V

TRADE

The international trade regime constructed under American leadership after World War II and now embodied in the World Trade Organization (WTO) has facilitated the emergence of the most open international economy in modern history. After World War II, political leaders in the United States and many other advanced industrialized countries believed, on the basis of their experience during the Great Depression of the 1930s, that protectionism contributes to depressions, depressions magnify political instability, and protectionism therefore leads to war. Drawing on these beliefs, the United States led the postwar fight for a new trade regime to be based on the economic principle of comparative advantage. Tariffs were to be lowered, and each country would specialize in those goods that it produced best and trade for the products of other countries, as appropriate. To the extent this goal was achieved, American decision makers and others believed that all countries would be better off and prosperity would be reinforced.

The American vision for the postwar trade regime was originally outlined in a plan for an International Trade Organization (ITO), which was intended to complement the International Monetary Fund. As presented in 1945, the American plan offered rules for all aspects of international trade relations. The Havana Charter, which created the ITO, was finally completed in 1947. A product of many international compromises, the Havana Charter was the subject of considerable opposition within the United States. Republican protectionists opposed the treaty because they felt it went too far in the direction of free trade, while free-trade groups failed to support it because it did not go far enough. President Harry Truman, knowing that the treaty faced almost certain defeat, never submitted the Havana Charter to Congress for ratification. In the absence of American support, the nascent ITO died a quick and quiet death. The General Agreement on Tariffs and Trade (GATT) was drawn up in 1947 to provide a basis for the trade negotiations then under way in Geneva. Intended merely as a temporary agreement to last only until the Havana Charter was fully implemented, the GATT became, by default, the principal basis for the international trade regime. The GATT was finally replaced by the WTO in 1995.[1]

Despite its supposedly temporary origins, the GATT was, for decades, the most important international institution in the trade area. Trade negotiations within the GATT—and now, the WTO—proceed in "rounds," typically initiated by new grants of negotiating authority delegated from the United States Congress to the president. Since 1947, there have been eight rounds of negotiations, each resulting in a new treaty, which was subsequently ratified by member states under their individual constitutional provisions.

The WTO is based on three primary norms. First, all members agree to extend unconditional most-favored-nation (MFN) status to one another. Under this agreement, no country receives any preferential treatment not accorded to all other MFN countries. Additionally, any benefits acquired by one country are automatically extended to all MFN partners. The only exceptions to this rule are customs unions, such as the European Union.

Second, the WTO is based on the norm of reciprocity—the concept that any country that benefits from another's tariff reduction should reciprocate to an equivalent extent. This norm ensures fair and equitable tariff reductions by all countries. In conjunction with the MFN (or nondiscrimination) norm, it also serves to reinforce the downward spiral of tariffs initiated by the actions of any one country.

Third, "safeguards," or loopholes and exceptions to other norms, are recognized as acceptable if they are temporary and imposed for short-term balance-of-payments reasons. Exceptions are also allowed for countries experiencing severe market disruptions from increased imports.

The GATT and WTO have been extremely successful in obtaining the declared goal of freer trade and lower tariffs. By the end of the Kennedy Round of the GATT in 1967 (initiated by President John F. Kennedy in 1962), tariffs on dutiable nonagricultural items had declined to approximately 10 percent in the advanced industrialized countries. In the Tokyo Round, concluded in 1979, tariffs in these same countries were reduced to approximately 5 percent, and member countries pledged to reduce their remaining tariffs by a further 40 percent in the Uruguay Round, concluded in late 1993. These significant reductions initiated an era of unprecedented growth in international trade, which continues today. The two most rapidly increasing areas are the overlapping realms of trade between advanced industrialized countries and intrafirm trade (the exchange of goods within, rather than between, corporations).

The GATT and WTO continued to be an active force for liberalization in the late 1980s and early 1990s, as the Uruguay Round produced new agreements on the thorny issues of services and agricultural trade—two areas that had been excluded from earlier negotiations. Governments have long regulated many of their domestic service industries, such as insurance, banking, and financial services. Often differing dramatically from country to country, these regulations operate like politically contentious barriers to trade. Like-wise, governments in most developed countries subsidize their agricultural sectors, leading to reduced imports and increasing surpluses that can only be managed through substantial sales abroad. Nearly all analysts agree that national and global welfare could be enhanced by reducing agricultural sub-sidies and returning to trade based on the principle of comparative advan-tage; yet as the prolonged negotiations of the Uruguay Round demonstrated, politicians found it difficult to resist demands from farmers for continued government intervention. Here, as in other areas, the tension between national wealth and the self-seeking demands of domestic interest groups has created a difficult diplomatic issue—but one that, after years of comparative neglect, finally made it onto the trade liberalization agenda. The Uruguay Round did make substantial progress on many fronts, including services and agricul-tural trade; the primary exception, from the American point of view, was entertainment products such as films, which were excluded from the final agreement at the insistence of the European Union.

In the aftermath of the Uruguay Round, farm subsidies are once again a major sticking point in progress toward further trade liberalization. Bargain-ing in the current "Doha Round" of WTO trade negotiations, which began at a WTO ministerial meeting in 2001 in Doha, Qatar, has stalled repeatedly over agricultural policies. The most significant differences are between developed nations with extensive agro-subsidy programs (e.g., the European Union, the United States, and Japan) and developing countries that want greater access to rich-country agricultural and industrial markets (e.g., Brazil, India, China, and South Africa). As the most heavily protected sector in world trade, agri-cultural reform stands to deliver the greatest economic benefits. Ironically, agriculture appears to be the sector most resistant to change.

Outside of agriculture, tariffs have been declining and trade increasing, but new threats have emerged to the free-trade regime. With the success of trade liberalization, more and more industries have been exposed to increased international competition. Industry demands for some form of protection have multiplied in nearly all countries, and increasingly, governments have sought to satisfy these demands for protection through nontariff barriers to trade (NTBs). The most important of these NTBs are voluntary export restraints, in which exporters agree to restrain or limit their sales in the importer's market. Estimates suggest that almost 20 percent of all goods imported into the Euro-pean Union, for instance, enter under some type of NTB.[2] Although the Uru-guay Round agreement has helped to bring their growth under control and even produced reductions in some areas, NTBs remain an important threat to free trade and a source of concern to observers of the international economy.

The readings in this section address the causes and implications of trade policy. Cletus C. Coughlin (Reading 19) reviews the classic economic argument for free trade and surveys explanations for protection. The remaining articles use economic insights to address the politics of international trade. Ronald

Rogowski (Reading 20) examines how changing exposure to international trade influences political cleavages within states. In this international economic perspective, political coalitions are a product of a country's position within the international division of labor and of exogenous changes in the costs of trade. Building on the insights offered by Rogowski and then extending their analysis to other models of trade policy, James E. Alt and Michael Gilligan (Reading 21) synthesize domestic societal and domestic institutional theories into a broad explanation of trade policy. Richard B. Freeman (Reading 22) then examines what is sometimes referred to as the "trade and wages" debate. In theory, less-skilled labor in the United States and Europe should have been harmed by increasing international trade, and real wages have fallen for such workers. Nonetheless, identifying the independent effects of international trade remains quite difficult, and as Freeman concludes, trade probably accounts for only a fraction of the decline. Alan V. Deardorff and Robert M. Stern (Reading 23) consider the case for free trade and examine the controversy surrounding the WTO—the international institution charged with promoting trade liberalization. While domestic distributional politics motivate much of the controversy, the authors also note that the WTO's international power has made it a target for social activists, who seek to leverage the WTO's influence to promote environmental and other social agendas.

Our final article in this section illustrates the importance of domestic institutional factors in the process of trade liberalization. Michael Bailey, Judith Goldstein, and Barry R. Weingast (Reading 24) argue that trade policy outcomes in the United States are strongly influenced by the rules and procedures of making trade policy.

NOTES

1. The GATT continues to exist as a legal entity related to the WTO. Nonetheless, the GATT secretariat and director general were transferred to the WTO, and the latter organization is expected to subsume, and fully replace, its predecessor over time. Except where specifically referring to the GATT, we refer to the international trade regime as the WTO.

2. Based on import coverage ratio from Organization for Economic Co-operation and Development (OECD), *Indicators of Tariff and Non-Tariff Trade Barriers*. (Paris: OECD, 1997), p. 53.

19

The Controversy over Free Trade: The Gap between Economists and the General Public

CLETUS C. COUGHLIN

Nearly all economists think that free trade is the best policy, but free trade is highly controversial among the general public. In this selection, economist Cletus C. Coughlin explores the reasons why the general public is reluctant to support the free trade policies espoused by most economists. Beginning with an exposition of the principle of comparative advantage, the author reviews the arguments in favor of free trade in light of new theories and evidence. He concludes that free trade remains the optimal policy for all countries. To explain why many people nonetheless oppose free trade, the author emphasizes societal theories focusing on the distributional effects of trade policy, as well as public concerns about labor rights and the environment.

In contrast to their divergent opinions on many public-policy issues, most economists strongly support free trade policies. Nonetheless, there is substantial public opposition for such policies—from the right as well as the left ends of the political spectrum. Because public opinion affects policy decisions, understanding why this gap exists is a first step in devising strategies to increase public support for free trade. In light of arguments and evidence indicating that free trade yields substantial benefits, attempts to influence public opinion seem warranted.

In the next section I report survey information highlighting the gap between the views of economists and the general public on free trade policies. The primary focus of this paper is on the "whys" of this gap in the United States. After examining why most economists support free trade policies. I explore why free trade is controversial. To ensure that this discussion about controversial issues is of a reasonable length, I focus on trade arguments involving either labor or environmental issues. Next, I examine suggestions for increasing the support for free trade. A summary of key points completes the paper.

DIFFERING VIEWS ON FREE TRADE POLICIES

Surveys have consistently shown strong support among economists for free trade policies. In a 1990 survey of economists employed in the United States, more than 90 percent agreed generally with the proposition that tariffs and import quotas usually reduce general economic welfare. This consensus mirrored the results of a similar survey in 1976. . . .

On the other hand, the general public is not as strongly in favor of reducing trade barriers as economists. Based on answers to a question in a survey by the Chicago Council on Foreign Relations, it is clear that the general public in the United States has major reservations about free trade. In response to a question in 1998 pointing out that the elimination of tariffs and other import restrictions would lead to lower prices but that certain jobs in import-competitive industries would likely be eliminated, only 32 percent of the general public were in favor of eliminating tariffs in this case. Meanwhile, 49 percent were more sympathetic to the argument that tariffs are necessary to protect jobs.

Survey results suggest that Americans recognize both the benefits and costs of international trade. Large majorities of Americans think that freer trade generates benefits in terms of lower prices, increased product variety, and more innovation. On the other hand, a majority of Americans think that trade results in fewer jobs and lower wages for some segments of the labor force. Relative to economists, however, survey respondents tend to emphasize the costs rather than the benefits. For example, the 1999 Program on International Policy Attitudes survey asked whether free trade was a good idea because it could lead to lower prices and faster growth or a bad idea because it could lead to lower wages and lost jobs. Survey respondents were nearly evenly divided, with 51 percent saying free trade was a good idea and 44 percent saying it was a bad idea. Five percent did not know or refused to answer.

WHY ECONOMISTS SUPPORT FREE TRADE POLICIES

Underlying the consensus among economists on the desirability of free trade is the judgment that nations are better off with free trade than with policies restricting trade. Trade can affect a nation's income and its economic well-being through numerous channels. For example, the reduction of trade barriers allows for gains stemming from (i) specialization and exchange according to comparative advantage, (ii) increasing returns to scale from larger markets, (iii) the exchange of ideas through communication and travel, and (iv) the spread of technology by means of investment and exposure to new goods. Numerous models have been developed that show how a nation benefits from free trade. Rather than discuss numerous models, I examine the key ideas that economists stress when discussing the gains from trade. I complete this section by discussing some studies that measure the gains/losses that are likely to accompany specific trade policies.

The Gains from Trade: A Historical View

The most famous demonstration of the gains from trade appeared in 1817 in David Ricardo's *Principles of Political Economy and Taxation*. In his example,

England and Portugal produce the same two goods, wine and cloth, and the only production costs are labor costs. The amount of labor (e.g., worker-days) required in each country to produce one bottle of wine or one bolt of cloth is listed below.

	Wine	*Cloth*
England	3	7
Portugal	1	5

Because both goods are more costly to produce in England than in Portugal, England is absolutely less productive in producing both goods than its prospective trading partner. Portugal has an absolute advantage in both wine and cloth. Intuitively, one might be inclined to conclude that absolute advantage eliminates the possibility of mutual gains from trade. Thus, a high productivity (i.e., high income) country could not engage in mutually beneficial trade with a low productivity (i.e., low income) country. Productivity is crucial in determining wages. In view of absolute advantage, workers in the country with higher productivity will receive higher wages. However, absolute advantage is irrelevant in whether trade can benefit both countries.

What is crucial is that the ratio of the production costs for the two goods is different in the two countries. In England, a bottle of wine will exchange for 3/7 of a bolt of cloth because the labor content of the wine is 3/7 of that of cloth. In Portugal, a bottle of wine will exchange for 1/5 of a bolt of cloth. Thus, wine is relatively cheaper in Portugal than in England and, conversely, cloth is relatively cheaper in England than in Portugal. Economists say that Portugal has a comparative advantage in wine production and England has a comparative advantage in cloth production.

The different relative prices provide the basis for both countries to gain from international trade. The gains arise from both *exchange* and *specialization*.

The gains from *exchange* can be shown in the following manner. If a Portuguese wine producer sells five bottles of wine at home, he receives one bolt of cloth. If he trades in England, he receives more than two bolts of cloth for five bottles of wine. Hence, he can gain by exporting his wine to England. English cloth producers are willing to trade in Portugal; for every 3/7 of a bolt of cloth they sell there, they receive just over two bottles of wine, which is better than the one bottle of wine they would receive in England. Overall, the English gain from exporting cloth to (and importing wine from) Portugal, and the Portuguese gain from exporting wine to (and importing cloth from) England. Each country gains by exporting the good in which it has a comparative advantage and by importing the good in which it has a comparative disadvantage.

Gains can also arise from *specialization*. Assume initially that each country is producing some of both goods. Suppose that, as a result of trade, 21 units of labor are shifted from wine to cloth production in England and that 10 units

of labor are shifted from cloth to wine production in Portugal. This reallocation of labor does not change the total amount of labor used in the two countries; however, it causes the production changes listed [below]:

	Bottles of Wine	Bolts of Cloth
England	–7	+3
Portugal	+10	–2
Net	+3	+1

The shift of English labor causes cloth production to increase by three
bolts and wine production to decline by seven bottles. Meanwhile, the shift of
Portuguese labor causes cloth production to decrease by two bolts and wine
production to increase by ten bottles. Overall, the production of both goods
increases. This increased output of three bottles of wine and one bolt of cloth
allows both countries to increase their consumption of both goods. Thus,
specialization due to trade based on comparative advantage provides mutual
benefits.

The Gains from Trade: Selected Developments since Ricardo

Not surprisingly, trade theory has progressed since Ricardo. Some of the developments provide alternative explanations of comparative advantage, while others use different explanations of trade flows.

The most well-known alternative explanation of comparative advantage is
the Heckscher-Ohlin model of international trade. This model is based on (i)
the fact that countries differ from each other in terms of their productive
resources (e.g., labor, capital, natural resources) and (ii) the fact that goods
are produced using different proportions of those resources.

To illustrate the theory, assume two countries, China and Japan; two productive resources, labor and capital; and two goods, automobiles and clothing.
Assume further that China's endowment of labor relative to capital exceeds
that of Japan. In this case China is relatively well endowed with labor. Conversely, Japan is relatively well endowed with capital. Thus, one should expect
that the price of labor relative to capital would be lower in China than in
Japan.

Next, assume that in the production of clothing the use of labor relative to
capital is greater than in the production of automobiles. In this case, clothing
is produced by relatively labor-intensive methods and, conversely, automobiles are produced by relatively capital-intensive methods.

The Heckscher-Ohlin theory states the following: A country will be able to
produce a good at a relatively lower cost if its production requires a relatively
larger proportion of a relatively abundant resource in that country. (That is, a
relatively abundant resource would be a relatively less expensive factor of

production.) In the present example, this implies that China should have a comparative advantage in clothing and Japan should have a comparative advantage in automobiles. As in the Ricardian case, the different relative prices provide the basis for both countries to gain from international trade by means of exchange (i.e., Japan will export automobiles and import clothing and China will export clothing and import automobiles) and specialization (i.e., Japan will increase its production of automobiles and China will increase its production of clothing).

An appealing feature of the Heckscher-Ohlin model is that it can generate insights into the political economy of trade policy. The preceding discussion suggests that allowing for free trade sets in motion a number of price changes. Specifically, the relative prices of goods in the two countries should tend to equalize, as well as the prices of the productive resources. In the two-country, two-good, two-resource world discussed above, the payments to one factor in a specific country will rise and the payments to the other factor will fall.

The Stolper-Samuelson theorem states that free international trade benefits a country's abundant resource and harms that country's scarce resource. In the preceding example, this means that capital will benefit and labor will be harmed in Japan. Meanwhile, labor will benefit and capital will be harmed in China. As a result, it is easy to see why labor in Japan would be opposed to the reduction of trade barriers with China and that capital would support such a change. Later in the paper I use the Stolper-Samuelson theorem in the context of U.S. trade policy.

The Heckscher-Ohlin model focuses on inter-industry trade. This trade exists when a country exports goods produced by one industry in exchange for goods produced by another industry in a second country. For example, the United States exports machinery to China in exchange for clothing. A common feature of the trade between industrialized countries is that they export and import similar types of products, which is known as intra-industry trade. For example, industrialized countries export and import different models of automobiles. Such trade likely requires explanations other than those based on comparative advantage. One explanation revolves around increasing returns to scale, which are said to exist when an identical percentage increase in the use of each productive input causes an even larger percentage increase in output. For example, if the use of each input were increased by 10 percent, output would increase by more than 10 percent. If increasing returns exist, then the cost per unit for the firm (industry) declines as its output increases.

In a world with increasing returns to scale, benefits from free trade arise because removing trade barriers allows a country to specialize in industries where average costs decline as output expands. Another view of this phenomenon is that productivity in the industry increases as more resources are utilized. These productivity increases are an important source of the gains from trade.

The existence of increasing returns to scale complicates the analysis of international trade by forcing the consideration of market structures other than perfect competition and raises the possibility that both countries do not gain from trade. Overall, however, recent theoretical developments have likely strengthened the case for an open trading system by highlighting three sources of gains from trade. First, as highlighted in the preceding paragraph, as the market potentially served by firms expands, there are gains associated with declining per-unit production costs. A second source of gains results from the reduction in the monopoly power of domestic firms, who face increased pressures from foreign competitors to produce output demanded by consumers at the lowest possible cost. The third gain is that consumers enjoy increased product variety and lower prices.

The Gains from Trade: A Graphical View

Many of the key ideas discussed previously can be illustrated graphically. For space reasons I limit my focus to the static gains from trade by using a partial equilibrium approach. Static gains refer to one-time benefits of reducing trade barriers that arise as national (domestic) prices move closer to global (world) prices. The price changes stemming from the liberalization of trade cause productive resources to be reallocated and consumption patterns to change, which result in the gains from specialization and exchange identified by Ricardo.

The illustration of the static gains from free trade using partial equilibrium analysis assuming perfectly competitive markets is straightforward. As discussed previously, different relative prices for the same good in two countries provide a fundamental reason for international trade. If the price in the United States is higher than the price abroad when no trade is allowed, then the good will be imported into the United States when free trade is allowed. On the other hand, if the price in the United States is lower than the price abroad when no trade is allowed, then the good will be exported from the United States when free trade is allowed. Consequently, two cases—one in which the good is imported into the United States and the other in which the good is exported from the United States—are examined.

In the first case, the price of a hypothetical good abroad is assumed to be lower than that in the United States. In Figure 1 the lines S_{US} and D_{US} are the U.S. supply and demand curves for the hypothetical good. Their intersection at B results in the equilibrium values for price, P_{US}, and quantity, Q_{US}, of the good. Meanwhile, S_W is the supply curve abroad. This curve, represented by a horizontal line, is based on an assumption that U.S. purchases will not affect the price abroad, which in this case is P_W. If one allows for free trade, this lower price abroad has two effects in the United States. First, U.S. consumers will increase their purchases of this good from Q_{US} to the free trade level of QD_{FT}. Second, U.S. producers will decrease their production of this good

FIGURE 1   The Gains from Trade: The United States as an Importer

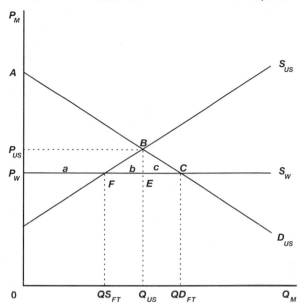

from Q_{US} to the free-trade level of QS_{FT}. U.S. purchases in excess of U.S. production (i.e., QD_{FT} less QS_{FT}) reflect the quantity of imports.

The lower price simultaneously benefits the U.S. consumers of this product
and harms the U.S. producers of this product, a fact that can be used to explain
why a free-trade policy is controversial. The magnitude of these gains and
losses can be seen in Figure 1 using the concepts of consumer and producer
surplus.

First, we look at consumers, who gain in two ways. Prior to free trade, consumers purchased Q_{US} at a price per unit of P_{US}. With free trade, they pay the
lower price per unit of P_W for Q_{US}. This gain in consumer surplus is represented by the rectangle $P_{US}BEP_W$. In addition, consumers gain because the
lower price induces consumers to increase their purchases from Q_{US} to QD_{FT}.
This additional increase in consumer surplus is represented by the triangle
BCE. Thus, the total gain for consumers is the area $P_{US}BCP_W$ or, using lower
case letters to represent specific areas, $a+b+c$.

Analogously, producers lose because of the lower price per unit they receive
for their output, QS_{FT}, and the contraction of production from Q_{US} to QS_{FT}.
Thus, the total loss incurred by producers is the area $P_{US}BFP_W$ or a. Overall,
the United States gains because the consumer gains exceed the producer
losses by $b+c$.

The preceding analysis can also be used for the case when the good is
exported from the United States under free trade. The key modification of

Figure 1 to create Figure 2 is that the price of the good prior to free trade is higher abroad than in the United States. The horizontal supply curve abroad, S_W, is based on the assumption that U.S. production will not affect the world price. Consequently, if one allows for free trade, the higher price abroad has two effects in the United States. First, U.S. consumers will decrease their purchases of this good from Q_{US} to the free-trade level of QD_{FT}. Second, U.S. producers will increase their production of this good from Q_{US} to the free-trade level of QS_{FT}. U.S. production in excess of U.S. purchases (i.e., QS_{FT} less QD_{FT}) reflects the quantity of exports.

The higher price simultaneously harms the U.S. consumers of this product and benefits the U.S. producers of this product. U.S. consumers lose because with free trade they are paying a higher price per unit. P_W versus P_{US}, for a smaller quantity of the export good, QD_{FT} versus Q_{US}. The reduction in consumer surplus is represented by the area $P_{US}BHP_W$ or $e+f$. Meanwhile, U.S. producers benefit from the higher price they receive for their prior output. In addition, they receive increased producer surplus as they expand production from Q_{US} to QS_{FT}. The total gain for producers is the area $P_{US}BGP_W$ or $e+f+g$. Overall, the U.S. benefits because the producer gains exceed the consumer losses by g.

The preceding partial equilibrium analysis is suggestive of the gains that the United States would generate as it moved from self-sufficiency to free trade. . . .

FIGURE 2 The Gains from Trade: The United States as an Exporter

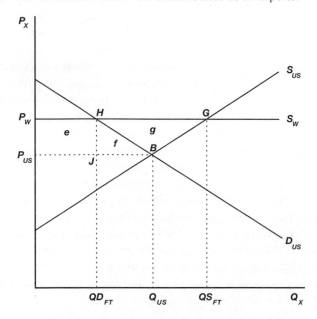

The Dynamic Gains from Free Trade

Free trade can also contribute to economic growth, which is another source of gains. Such dynamic gains are potentially more important than the static gains. Most economic models suggest that trade liberalization will have a positive effect on economic growth. An economy grows over time as a result of increases in its productive resources or technological innovation; both developments increase the capacity of an economy to produce goods and services. In addition, reducing trade barriers might increase competitive pressures that would force the efficient use of a nation's resources. Economic theory suggests a number of routes by which freer trade can stimulate growth.

One route is through increased savings that ultimately fund investment spending. Such spending increases the amount of capital. As argued previously, trade raises the level of real income, some of which can be saved. This higher level of savings translates into a greater availability of funds for investment spending. Free trade also allows the possibility for a country to borrow the savings of other countries. When a country imports more than it exports, a country is effectively borrowing funds from the rest of the world. If these funds are being used to finance the imports of capital goods, then a country's capital is increased.

A country, however, need not run trade deficits to import capital goods. When a country imports capital goods in exchange for consumer goods, then its productive capacity increases. This productive capacity allows for subsequent increases in output.

A related idea is that free trade increases the possibility that a firm importing a capital good will be able to locate a supplier who will provide a good that more nearly meets its specifications. The better the match, the larger is the resulting increase in productivity, which ultimately translates into higher incomes.

International trade may also spur the diffusion of technology by increasing the commercial contacts between employees in firms from different countries. Such interactions serve to transfer information about new products and production processes. Of course, formal transactions may also facilitate the transfer of technology. Licensing is a common practice that allows the international transfer of technology. In addition, technology is embodied in new capital equipment. Thus, freer international trade facilitates the transfer of technology internationally and spurs economic growth.

Another potential route for economic growth results from the competitive pressures associated with international trade. Opening a country's markets to foreign firms tends to reduce the market power of domestic firms. For example, domestic monopolists are subjected to competitive pressures. As a result, the domestic firms are forced to become more efficient or else they perish. Either way, a nation's productive resources will be used more efficiently in producing the goods that consumers desire.

A final route is related to the prior discussion suggesting that, as international trade expands the size of a market that firms face, firms might be able to exploit economies of scale. Recall that increased output at lower per unit cost is a clear-cut gain. Moreover, the larger market size might also spur research and development spending because the spending can be spread over larger levels of output. If successful, the spending would increase the productive capacity of the country.

Empirical Studies of the Gains from Trade and the Losses from Protectionist Policies

The preceding discussion of international trade theory provides many reasons why economists support free trade policies. Empirical studies provide additional reasons. As discussed previously, a fundamental proposition is that international trade allows a country to achieve a higher real income than would otherwise be attained. Empirical evidence tends to confirm this proposition. . . . [P]olicies restricting international trade can result in substantial costs in terms of actual per capita income falling short of potential per capita income.

Additional empirical evidence focused directly on the issue of free trade has also been generated. Numerous estimates of the static and dynamic costs/benefits using partial as well as general equilibrium approaches have been produced assessing the consequences of trade policy changes. Using a partial equilibrium approach, it is easy to illustrate the effects of a trade policy change via supply and demand curves. Figure 3 shows the supply and demand curves for a hypothetical good imported into the United States that is subject to a tariff. Identical to Figure 1 the free trade results reveal, given the free trade price of P_W, U.S. consumption of QD_{FT}, production of QS_{FT}, and imports equal to the difference between QD_{FT} and QS_{FT}. Assume a tariff is imposed, causing the price in the United States to increase to P_T. The price in the United States now exceeds the price in the world by the amount of the tariff, $P_W P_T$.

The higher U.S. price causes consumer purchases to decrease from QD_{FT} to QD_T, production to increase from QS_{FT} to QS_T, and imports to decrease from $QS_{FT}QD_{FT}$ to QS_TQD_T. The imposition of the tariff causes consumers to lose $d + e + f + g$, while producers gain d. Thus, domestic producers are protected from foreign competition at the expense of domestic consumers. One complication is that the government collects tariff revenue. This revenue, which can be viewed as a gain for the government, equals the tariff, $P_W P_T$, times the quantity of imports, QS_TQD_T. This revenue is represented by area f.

Overall, the United States loses because the losses of consumers, $d + e + f + g$, exceed the gains of producers, d, and of government, f. The net national loss is $e + g$. Area e is called a "deadweight production loss" and reflects the loss from inefficient (excessive) production, while area g is called a "deadweight consumption loss" and reflects the loss from inefficient (too little) consumption.

FIGURE 3 The Effects of a U.S. Tariff

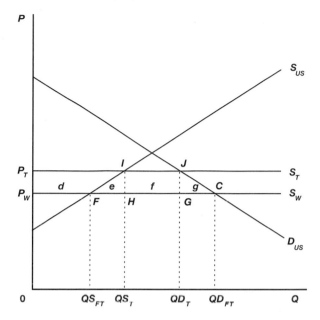

Hufbauer and Elliott (1994) have generated estimates of the potential net national gains by industry, as well as the consumer gains and producer losses, if the United States were to liberalize trade in 21 industries. Table 1 reveals that the gains for consumers in the apparel industry would exceed $21 billion if protection were removed. Not surprisingly, a substantial portion of this gain would come at the expense of producers whose losses would by nearly $10 billion. The net national gain from liberalizing trade in the apparel industry would be $7.7 billion.

Additional perspective is provided by expressing the consumer and national gains relative to the job losses in the apparel industry resulting from the liberalization. The consumer gain per job lost is $139,000, and the net national gain per job lost is $51,000. What this means is that consumers were effectively paying an average of $139,000 for each job protected in 1990 in the apparel industry, an industry in which the average pay of a production worker was less than $15,000.

Clearly, the net national gains from liberalizing trade in the apparel industry exceed by a large amount the potential gains from liberalizing other industries. However, there are large gains that could be realized by liberalizing trade in a number of other industries. Net national gains exceed $500 million dollars in the textiles, sugar, and maritime transport industries. Moreover, the consumer gain per job lost in the sugar industry is $600,000 and the net national gain per job lost is $257,000. It is also noteworthy how much consumers can

TABLE 1 Welfare Effects of Liberalizing Trade in Certain U.S. Industries, 1990 (millions of dollars)

Industry	Tariff or equivalent	Consumer gain	Producer loss	Net national gain	Consumer gain per job lost (dollars)	Net national gain per job lost (dollars)
Ball bearings	11.0%	64	13	1	438,356	6,849
Benzenoid chemicals	9.0	309	127	10	>1,000,000	46,296
Canned tuna	12.5	73	31	10	187,179	25,641
Ceramic articles	11.0	102	18	2	244,019	4,785
Ceramic tiles	19.0	139	45	2	400,576	5,764
Costume jewelry	9.0	103	46	5	96,532	4,686
Frozen orange juice concentrate	30.0	281	101	35	461,412	57,471
Glassware	11.0	266	162	9	180,095	6,093
Luggage	16.5	211	16	26	933,628	115,044
Polyethylene resins	12.0	176	95	20	590,604	67,114
Rubber footwear	20.0	208	55	12	122,281	7,055

Softwood lumber	6.5	459	264	12	758,678	19,835
Women's footwear, except athletic	10.0	376	70	11	101,567	2,971
Women's handbags	13.5	148	16	13	191,462	16,818
Dairy products	50.0	1,184	835	104	497,897	43,734
Peanuts	50.0	54	32	22	136,020	55,416
Sugar	66.0	1,357	776	581	600,177	256,966
Maritime transport	85.0	1,832	1,275	556	415,325	126,049
Apparel	48.0	21,158	9,901	7,712	138,666	50,543
Textiles	23.4	3,274	1,749	894	202,061	55,175
Machine tools	46.6	542	157	385	348,329	247,429

NOTE: Tariffs are the primary protective device for the first 14 industries in the Table. Import quotas are used for dairy products, peanuts, sugar, and maritime transport. Voluntary export restraints are used for apparel, textiles, and machine tools.

SOURCE: Derived from Tables 1.2 and 1.3 in Hufbauer and Elliott (1994).

gain per job lost in other industries. In the benzenoid chemicals industry the consumer gain per job lost exceeds $1 million; in the luggage industry the consumer gain per job lost exceeds $900,000. In the latter case, the net national gain per job lost is $115,000.

A recent study by the U.S. International Trade Commission (1999) uses a general equilibrium approach to explore the consequences of liberalizing trade in industries subject to significant trade restrictions. Based on 1996 data, the simultaneous liberalization of all significant restraints causes a net national gain of $12.4 billion, as shown in Table 2. Given the results in Hufbauer and Elliott (1994), it is not surprising that the elimination of trade barriers in the textiles and apparel sector yields the majority of the gains. Nor is it surprising that the maritime transport, sugar, footwear, and dairy industries are the sources for the majority of the rest of the gains.

The preceding examples reveal the possibility of substantial gains by liberalizing trade in selected industries. Overall, however, U.S. trade policy can be characterized as "open" relative to the policies of other countries. Consequently, estimates of the gains from trade do not reflect a change from the prohibition of trade to free trade, but rather a change from some level of trade restriction to free trade. From this perspective it should not be surprising that, relative

TABLE 2 Welfare Estimates of Liberalizing Trade in Highly Protected Sectors, 1996 (millions of dollars)

Sector	Welfare increase
Simultaneous sector liberalization of all significant restraints	12,402
Individual liberalization:	
Textiles and apparel	10,376
Maritime transport (Jones Act)	1,324
Sugar	986
Footwear	501
Dairy	152
Ball and roller bearings, and parts	49
Frozen fruit, fruit juices, and vegetables	28
Costume jewelry and costume novelties	19
Leather gloves and mittens	16
Personal leather goods	14
China tableware	12
Ceramic tile	9
Cutlery	4

SOURCE: U.S. International Trade Commission (1999, Table ES-1).

to total U.S. economic activity, the static gains from eliminating trade barriers (or the costs stemming from the existing trade barriers) are relatively small. Of course, one might argue that gains exceeding $12 billion are still substantial. . . .

In contrast to the findings concerning the static gains, one finds that the empirical literature assessing the relationship between trade policy and economic growth is far from definitive. Numerous problems with this empirical analysis preclude an unqualified conclusion. Many studies, using different data sets, countries, and methodologies, have found that countries with more-open trade policies (i.e., those closer to free trade) tend to grow faster than countries with less-open trade policies. . . .

In summary, the empirical literature clearly indicates that liberalizing trade in highly protected industries is likely to yield gains. Whether those gains are large is in the eye of the beholder. The evidence concerning the dynamic gains from trade reveals that economies that are more open are likely to grow faster. If the faster growth is long-lived, substantial increases in well-being can be generated.

WHY FREE TRADE IS CONTROVERSIAL

What Does Research Based on Self-Interested Behavior Reveal?

To understand the opposition to free trade, one must understand the preferences of individuals as they relate to the policy choices available to policymakers. Unfortunately, most economic research does not provide direct evidence on the preferences of individuals. Generally speaking, empirical research on the political economy of trade policy focuses on trade policy outcomes. Because representatives do respond to the economic interests of their constituents, these outcomes certainly depend on the preferences of individuals. However, there are a number of other factors that come into play, such as the influence of interest groups, the preferences of policymakers, and the institutional structure of government. These other factors preclude the researcher from making definitive statements about individual preferences.

Nonetheless, the voluminous literature on the determinants of protection does provide some results suggestive of individual preferences. For example, protection received by an industry is higher when it is a labor-intensive, low-skill, low-wage industry. This suggests that individuals are willing to support trade restrictions to improve the job and income prospects of low-income workers.

A recent study by Scheve and Slaughter (2001b) focuses specifically on individual preferences. They find that the lower the skill level of a worker, measured by education or average occupational earnings, the stronger is the worker's support for new trade barriers. This result is consistent with a Heckscher-Ohlin trade model in which the United States is well endowed with skilled labor.

Recalling the prior discussion of the Stolper-Samuelson theorem, the movement to free trade would tend to increase the incomes of skilled labor. Meanwhile, the incomes of unskilled labor would fall further behind. Because less-skilled workers have experienced sharp declines in their wages relative to more-skilled workers, Scheve and Slaughter (2001a) argue that the differences in their attitudes toward free trade may reflect the different wage-growth experiences of these groups since the early 1970s. Arguably, the poor labor-market results of low-skilled workers, both absolutely and relative to high-skilled workers, could be due to other factors such as technological changes favoring high-skilled workers. Scheve and Slaughter argue that, regardless of the reasons for their poor labor-market experience, those with relatively less education and skill expect the labor-market results stemming from additional international trade flows to be harmful.

More generally, the public fails to see any broad-based gains from trade. . . . The difficulty of envisioning broad-based gains might simply reflect the difficulty of envisioning any gains. As discussed previously, the static gains for an average individual of implementing free trade for the United States are small. Moreover, it is likely difficult for non-economists to envision how free trade will spur economic growth that will improve their economic well-being. Thus, because they do not see personal benefits, it is easy to see why individuals lack enthusiasm about trade negotiations.

Other Perspectives: The Social Dimensions of Trade

A foundation of economic analysis is self-interested behavior. In the present context, this implies that individuals evaluate trade policy based on how their current well-being is affected without regard for national well-being. However, people act for various reasons, some of which are materialistic and some of which are humanitarian. The allowance for self-interested behavior beyond those satisfying material demands complicates economic analysis. Nonetheless, such motives might well be important in understanding the opposition to free trade policies.

EMPLOYMENT/INCOME CONCERNS. The survey information cited previously indicates one of the reasons that the general public remains reluctant to support the free trade policies espoused by most economists: concern about jobs, but not necessarily their own. One might view this reason as reflecting humanitarian motives. . . .

Note how such preferences conflict with the analysis underlying Figure 1. In Figure 1 a given value of losses suffered by producers were netted, dollar for dollar, against the larger value of gains received by consumers. However, it is possible that it is not that simple. For example, assume a change in trade policy that would cause a $105 gain for a high-income individual but a $100 loss for a low-income individual. Despite a net national gain of $5, it is possible that a third party might oppose such a change because the adverse effect for the low-income individual might be viewed as outweighing the beneficial effect for the high-income individual.

In addition, there are short-run adjustment costs stemming from changes in trade policy that might generate opposition. Because some industries will reduce production, some workers will lose their jobs. Being unemployed, regardless of its length, is a noteworthy cost that generates opposition to proposed trade-policy changes from both those likely to be adversely affected and those who sympathize with them.

. . . Evidence suggests that U.S. consumers care about the conditions of the workers in developing countries. Elliott and Freeman (2001) concluded that the vast majority of people are willing to pay higher prices for items produced under better working conditions in developing countries. In addition, most Americans favor linking labor standards to trade. The 1999 Program on International Policy Attitudes survey found that 93 percent of respondents felt that as part of international trade agreements countries should be required to maintain minimum standards for working conditions (University of Maryland, 2000). In this same survey, three-quarters of the respondents felt morally obligated to help workers faced with poor working conditions. Moreover, roughly the same percentage reported a willingness to pay $5 more for a $20 garment if they knew it was not made in a sweatshop. Overall, most respondents found the arguments for minimum standards (that harsh conditions are immoral and that standards eliminate cost advantages due to exploitation) to be more convincing than the arguments against standards (that the standards might hinder exports and reduce jobs in developing countries, as well as impinge on national sovereignty).

Note, however, that self-interest might provide a reason for some to argue for the linking of labor standards with international trade. Even when differing labor standards are appropriate given the specific situations of individual countries (i.e., the benefits exceed the costs at the national level), differing labor standards do provide cost advantages to firms in countries with relatively low standards. These advantages cause competitive problems for firms in countries, such as the United States, with relatively high standards. Such competitive problems are especially pronounced for those firms and workers in labor-intensive industries. Thus, higher standards would serve the interests of those being harmed by the imports from low-cost competitors. Not surprisingly, countries with low standards view the proposals to link labor standards with trade measures as protectionist because such proposals would tend to eliminate some of the cost advantages possessed by the firms in these countries.

ENVIRONMENTAL CONCERNS. Similar to linking labor standards to trade, sentiment exists for linking environmental issues to trade. A fundamental concern is that free trade will stimulate economic growth and that this growth will harm the environment. This argument illustrates a basic source for conflict between free traders and environmentalists. Proponents of free trade want to remove governmentally imposed trade barriers so that markets can generate efficient results, while environmentalists see free trade as generating consequences that require additional governmental regulations.

The 1999 Program on International Policy Attitudes survey revealed that 77 percent of respondents felt there should be more international agreements on environmental standards. Underlying this result is a belief by many that environmental problems, such as acid rain and greenhouse gases, are global in nature. Clearly, acid rain and greenhouse gases are international issues that require a solution among governments; however, many economists would argue that many environmental problems are domestic issues that require a national solution. Views of what constitutes a strictly domestic environmental problem and what constitutes an international one can differ.

Some of the concern about the environment, however, can be linked to U.S. jobs. For example, 67 percent of respondents felt that the absence of international environmental standards would threaten U.S. jobs, as well as the environment, because lower environmental standards abroad would make the United States a less competitive location and would induce U.S. companies to relocate. This view that diversity in environmental standards would affect the desirability of maintaining/locating production in the United States tends to make allies of U.S. companies, labor unions, and environmentalists. In terms of trade negotiations, this view requires that environmental regulations must be harmonized with, at least, existing U.S. standards prior to allowing for free trade. Many economists, however, would argue that domestic environmental problems should be handled nationally and that international differences in environmental standards are natural.

Generally speaking, the survey respondents did not support views on environmental issues based on either national sovereignty or fairness. Only 33 percent supported the view that each country should decide how to deal with environmental issues. Only 37 percent supported the view that, because the costs of complying with international environmental standards would vary across countries, such standards would be unfair for countries with relatively high compliance costs. The prevailing views in this survey likely conflict with views that most economists hold. For example, most economists would argue that a national problem requires a national solution and that the costs as well as the benefits of any proposed solution be considered.

Clearly, the protection of U.S. jobs underlies the environmental position of many. Nonetheless, there is evidence that, when faced with a trade-off between protecting the environment and increasing jobs and economic growth, a majority of Americans, 52 percent, chose protecting the environment. Of the remainder, 37 percent chose jobs and 10 percent viewed the environment and jobs as equally important.

BRIDGING THE GAP

Three approaches have been suggested to move public opinion toward supporting free trade. The first approach is to increase economic education on free trade. The second approach reduces the costs borne by those who are harmed by the implementation of free trade policies. In other words, those incurring job losses and wage reductions might be compensated to ameliorate these costs. As a result, those facing job and wage uncertainty related to proposed trade agreements, as well as those concerned about these individuals, might be more inclined to support trade liberalization. The third approach attempts to increase support for free trade by expanding the agenda encompassed by trade negotiations. By addressing additional issues, such as those of concern to labor and environmental interests, support for trade liberalization efforts may be increased.

Education

Because economists find the arguments for free trade to be convincing, they are inclined to think that increased economic knowledge would increase public support for free trade. . . .

In terms of influencing public opinion, an important issue is how to communicate with those not likely to take an international economics course. . . . As discussed previously, economists focus on consumption; however, public discussions tend to focus on production. The economist stresses that free trade allows for increases in well-being because consumers can buy more and varied goods at lower prices. Meanwhile, public discussions frequently argue that exports are good, but imports are bad; exports support jobs, frequently well paying ones, but imports destroy domestic job opportunities.

Thus, the economist's view of imports as good rather than evil is ignored by many. Imports provide consumers with increased choices of items that might be of higher quality, lower price, or more suited to one's tastes than would otherwise be available. Exports help us buy imports, but our enjoyment comes from consuming goods rather than from producing goods. To point out the folly of viewing exports as good and imports as bad, nineteenth-century economist Frédéric Bastiat satirically wondered whether the best outcome would be for ships transporting goods between countries to sink. As a result, countries could have exports without imports.

As noted here previously, the nature of the popular discussion tends to strengthen the arguments against free trade in relation to the arguments for free trade. . . . The opposition to free trade is strengthened by its visual appeal. For example, when international trade is identified as the reason for a plant closure or a layoff, a picture of a closed plant can be provided or the consequences for a specific family can be told. Meanwhile, the case for free trade is more difficult to present in concrete terms.

A closely related asymmetry is that the intensity of the argument likely favors the opponents of free trade. The opposition to free trade comes from workers who may lose their jobs. It is easy to see why such a group would be passionately opposed to international trade. Conversely, the beneficiaries of free trade are likely to be more diffuse. Their individual benefits are more likely to be small and frequently hard to identify precisely. Thus, passionate support is unlikely on this side of the argument.

Finally, the arguments against free trade are more readily appreciated than those for free trade. For example, it is relatively easy to understand that competition as a result of imports makes it more difficult for a domestic company to generate profits. Moreover, the competition puts downward pressure on wages and causes layoffs. Arguments in favor of free trade that rely on comparative advantage and the gains from specialization and exchange are not likely to be very convincing, especially in light of the limited knowledge many citizens possess about how markets function.

Given the preceding obstacles of influencing the general public, economists must use approaches and arguments that overcome these obstacles. . . .

Frequently, proponents of free trade suggest that exports create jobs. On the other hand, opponents of free trade stress that imports destroy jobs. It is possible that the focus on jobs distorts one's view of free trade. Recall that the previously discussed survey asked the general public their views about eliminating tariffs by stating that prices would decline, but that certain jobs would likely be eliminated. No mention was made of the fact that jobs would also be created so that the net job effect would likely be negligible. The bottom line is that trade policy does affect the distribution of jobs, but is unlikely to affect substantially the net number of jobs.

. . . Despite the argument that the removal of a tariff generates benefits to consumers that exceed the losses of producers, the producers as well as the workers who are adversely affected are not always compensated for their losses. Rather than duck this issue, it should be acknowledged. In addition, policies to assist those incurring losses, which are discussed later, could be stressed.

. . . Students in economics classes might be convinced of the wisdom of free trade policies using the economic theory and tools that economists find convincing, but the general public would probably ignore such a discussion. A compelling case likely requires an illustration of the gains from trade in the form of specific examples or reasonable hypothetical examples. As discussed previously, many individuals do not see how they gain from free trade or how they are harmed by trade restrictions. Expressing the gains of reducing trade barriers in terms of consumer gains (or national gains) per job lost is one way to argue convincingly. Another specific example is to show how per capita income in the United States would increase over a ten-year period if free trade led to an increased U.S. growth rate of 1 percent per year. In this case

U.S. per capita gross domestic product in 2000 would have been more than $3,500 higher than its level of $35,400. Most individuals can appreciate the effect of a roughly 10 percent pay increase. Moreover, stressing the beneficial growth effects of free trade moves the focus from a winners-versus-losers focus to the possibility of everyone sharing in the benefits of increased growth.

However, the benefits of economic growth are unlikely to convince some individuals and groups to support free trade. As international trade has become more important, its potential economic and social effects have increased. One consequence is increased demands that trade discussions encompass a broader range of economic and social issues. Moreover, Americans do not see the growth of trade as a key priority. They see international trade as a goal that should be balanced with other goals, such as protecting workers, the environment, and human rights.

Not surprisingly, expanding the range of issues complicates trade negotiations. Resolving social issues is especially difficult because of the trade-offs that are required to satisfy competing objectives—trade-offs, in fact, for which policymakers lack precise information. . . . For example, although child labor may be deplorable, it is possible that the earnings may be necessary to keep the children alive. A cleaner environment is desirable, but maybe not if the cost pushes the poorest countries further into poverty. Human rights are valuable, but so is national sovereignty. Obviously, disagreements on the "right" balance are inevitable. . . .

Reducing the Cost for Those Harmed

As highlighted previously, changes in trade policy cause gains for some individuals and losses for others. Generally speaking, high-skilled workers in the United States tend to benefit relative to low-skilled workers when trade barriers are reduced. Those suffering job losses as a result can incur income losses, reductions in health and pension benefits, costs associated with relocating, and the psychological costs of losing a job. The trade adjustment assistance program, which is administered by the U.S. Department of Labor, allows workers who lose their jobs because of increased imports to receive unemployment compensation for an additional period beyond that received by other displaced workers. In addition, trade adjustment assistance recipients can also participate in retraining programs plus receive out-of-area job search allowances and moving expenses.

Among the arguments to justify the trade adjustment assistance program is that the program reduces workers' lobbying efforts against trade liberalization. Even if voters are motivated by their perceptions of collective well-being and not simply their own individual well-being, trade adjustment assistance might increase support for free trade by both those who gain and those who lose. . . .

. . . A more effective trade adjustment program is likely to generate an increased willingness to support trade liberalization.

Another proposal to ameliorate the problems faced by displaced workers and reduce the opposition to trade liberalization is to provide wage insurance. As noted by the U.S. Trade Deficit Review Commission, many displaced workers, especially those with much tenure, suffer not only during the period between jobs but also after they become reemployed. For example, the weekly earnings of all reemployed workers fell 5.7 percent on average during 1995–97. Those displaced from high-tenure jobs experienced a wage decline of over 20 percent. Wage insurance would provide earnings supplements for a set period to workers who become reemployed at a lower wage.

Proponents of wage insurance . . . argue that it provides an incentive for workers to find a new job quickly as contrasted with unemployment insurance, which provides an incentive to delay looking for work. For younger workers, the quicker reemployment might make it easier for them to acquire training and new skills that will make them more employable and productive over their working lives. For older workers, the wage insurance might allow them to reach retirement without lowering their standard of living or altering their retirement plans. . . .

Expanding the Trade Agenda

During recent years many have argued that policymakers should expand the agenda for trade negotiations occurring under the World Trade Organization (WTO) and other bodies. Prior negotiations have produced substantial reductions in tariff barriers. One result is that the remaining trade barriers are in the most sensitive industries and involve the most complex issues. As discussed previously, sentiment is strong for linking labor and environmental issues with trade negotiations. What is unclear is whether such changes would ultimately increase the prospects for liberalizing trade. Expanding the agenda might provide negotiators with more opportunities for compromise; however, expanding the agenda might also bog down negotiations by introducing issues upon which compromise is very difficult. In fact, many have come to the conclusion that expanding the trade agenda would be detrimental to liberalizing trade in the United States and throughout the world.

. . . The priorities of member countries are unlikely to coincide with each other or with the WTO. For example, the United States argues for rigorously enforcing high labor standards. On the other hand, developing countries desire minimal standards and enforcement because they fear the standards will provide a cover for protectionism. Meanwhile, the WTO may resist enforcing labor standards because they are not related to their original mission of fostering free trade. The bottom line is that such a linkage is not a promising approach for generating gains from trade. . . .

CONCLUSION

The economic case for free trade is compelling for nearly all economists. Free trade policies enable free market forces to allocate resources to their most productive activities. This allows a nation to maximize the value of the goods and services produced within its borders. Free trade also allows consumers to allocate their incomes to maximize the value of the goods and services that they purchase and consume. Numerous models also suggest that the growth prospects of a nation are improved by using free trade policies. Moreover, the findings of empirical studies reinforce economic theory.

Despite these economic benefits, free trade policies are opposed by a large percentage of the U.S. public. The opposition consists of various groups, such as protectionists, labor unions, environmentalists, human rights activists, and economic nationalists. Clearly, the implementation of trade policies creates winners and losers. Not surprisingly, potential losers oppose free trade policies. Moreover, some oppose free trade because of their recognition that others will lose. This clash suggests that many in the general public differ from economists in how they weigh the costs and benefits of free trade policies. Others oppose free trade because of concerns that free trade contributes to the abuse of workers throughout the world, as well as to environmental degradation. Thus, these individuals will oppose reductions in trade barriers until these issues are addressed.

In view of the potential gains of free trade, an important question is how to reduce the opposition to free trade. A first step would be increased education concerning the benefits of free trade. Such a step is not controversial; however, to date, economists have been only moderately successful in spreading this good news to a large audience. Illustrating the gains from free trade using concrete and personal examples, as opposed to theoretical arguments, is one suggestion for convincing a larger audience.

A second step involves reducing the cost to the losers from free trade. A standard view is that the costs of liberalizing trade fall disproportionately upon less-skilled workers. Trade adjustment assistance is one policy option that has generated much political support. A more controversial policy is wage insurance. Questions about the cost-effectiveness of both policies, especially the latter, have been raised.

The most controversial step is to attempt to increase political support for free trade by expanding the issues covered in trade negotiations. Many Americans have real demands that the well-being of workers be safeguarded in developing countries and that the environment be protected. Whether these demands can be best served by linking them to trade agreements is controversial. Arguably, there are better ways to resolve many of these issues. The inclusion of labor and environmental issues in trade negotiations, as well as other issues, may or may not increase domestic political support. However, even if the inclusion of these other issues generated additional domestic support for free trade, it would not necessarily ensure success in negotiations to reduce trade barriers: foreign opposition to the inclusion of these issues, especially in developing countries, might negate any newly gained domestic support.

The fact that highly controversial steps are being suggested as necessary to propel trade negotiations points to one clear fact. Just as there are no quick fixes for the social issues that are increasingly linked to trade issues, there is no quick fix for generating political support for one of the few things that most economists agree upon—a nation's economic well-being is best served by free trade.

REFERENCES

Elliott, Kimberly Ann, and Freeman, Richard B. "White Hats or Don Quixotes? Human Rights Vigilantes in the Global Economy." Working Paper 8102, National Bureau of Economic Research, January 2001.

Hufbauer, Gary Clyde, and Elliott, Kimberly Ann. *Measuring the Costs of Protection in the United States*. Washington, DC: Institute for International Economics, 1994.

Ricardo, David. *On The Principles of Political Economy and Taxation*. New York: Penguin, 1971.

Scheve, Kenneth F., and Slaughter, Matthew J. *Globalization and the Perceptions of American Workers*. Washington, DC: Institute for International Economics, 2001a.

———. "What Determines Individual Trade-Policy Preferences?" *Journal of International Economics*, August 2001b, *54*(2), pp. 267–92.

University of Maryland, Program on International Policy Attitudes. *Americans on Globalization: A Study of Public Attitudes*. College Park, MD, March 2000. <http://www.pipa.org/OnlineReports/Globalization/contents.html>.

U.S. International Trade Commission. *The Economic Effects of Significant U.S. Import Restraints*. Washington, DC: U.S. Government Printing Office, May 1999.

20

Commerce and Coalitions: How Trade Affects Domestic Political Alignments

RONALD ROGOWSKI

According to the Stolper-Samuelson theorem, free trade benefits locally abundant factors of production—such as land, labor, or capital—and harms locally scarce factors of production. Building on this insight, Ronald Rogowski offers a compelling theoretical and empirical account of political cleavages within countries. He extends the Stolper-Samuelson theorem to reason that increasing exposure to trade—say, because of falling transportation costs—will increase the political power of locally abundant factors, whereas decreasing exposure to trade will hurt these factors. Although not seeking to explain trade policy outcomes (such as the level of protection within a country), Rogowski provides a powerful explanation of the political coalitions and the politics surrounding trade policy. This essay shows how international economic forces can exert a profound effect on domestic politics.

THE STOLPER-SAMUELSON THEOREM

In 1941, Wolfgang Stolper and Paul Samuelson solved conclusively the old riddle of gains and losses from protection (or, for that matter, from free trade). In almost any society, they showed, protection benefits (and liberalization of trade harms) owners of factors in which, relative to the rest of the world, that society is *poorly* endowed, as well as producers who use that scarce factor intensively. Conversely, protection harms (and liberalization benefits) those factors that—again, relative to the rest of the world—the given society holds *abundantly*, and the producers who use those locally abundant factors intensively. Thus, in a society rich in labor but poor in capital, protection benefits capital and harms labor; and liberalization of trade benefits labor and harms capital.

So far, the theorem is what it is usually perceived to be, merely a statement, albeit an important and sweeping one, about the effects of tariff policy. The picture is altered, however, when one realizes that *exogenous* changes can have exactly the same effects as increases or decreases in protection. A cheapening of transport costs, for example, is indistinguishable in its impact from an across-the-board decrease in every affected state's tariffs; so is any change in the international regime that decreases the risks or the transaction costs of

365

trade. The converse is of course equally true: when a nation's external transport becomes dearer or its trade less secure, it is affected exactly as if it had imposed a higher tariff.

The point is of more than academic interest because we know, historically, that major changes in the risks and costs of international trade have occurred: notoriously, the railroads and steamships of the nineteenth century brought drastically cheaper transportation; so, in their day, did the improvements in shipbuilding and navigation of the fifteenth and sixteenth centuries; and so, in our own generation, have supertankers, cheap oil, and containerization. According to the familiar argument, . . . international hegemony decreases both the risks and the transaction costs of international trade; and the decline of hegemonic power makes trade more expensive, perhaps—as, some have argued, in the 1930s—prohibitively so. . . .

Global changes of these kinds, it follows, should have had global consequences. The "transportation revolutions" of the sixteenth, the nineteenth, and scarcely less of the mid-twentieth century must have benefited in each affected country owners and intensive employers of locally abundant factors and must have harmed owners and intensive employers of locally scarce factors. The events of the 1930s should have had exactly the opposite effect. What, however, will have been the *political* consequences of those shifts of wealth and income? To answer that question, we require a rudimentary model of the political process and a somewhat more definite one of the economy.

SIMPLE MODELS OF THE POLITY AND THE ECONOMY

Concerning domestic political processes, I shall make only three assumptions: that the beneficiaries of a change will try to continue and accelerate it, while the victims of the same change will endeavor to retard or halt it; that those who enjoy a sudden increase in wealth and income will thereby be enabled to expand their political influence as well; and that, as the desire and the means for a particular political preference increase, the likelihood grows that political entrepreneurs will devise mechanisms that can surmount the obstacles to collective action.

For our present concerns, the first assumption implies that the beneficiaries of safer or cheaper trade will support yet greater openness, while gainers from dearer or riskier trade will pursue even greater self-sufficiency. Conversely, those who are harmed by easier trade will demand protection or imperialism; and the victims of exogenously induced constrictions of trade will seek offsetting reductions in barriers. More important, the second assumption implies that the beneficiaries, potential or actual, of any such exogenous change will be strengthened politically (although they may still lose); the economic losers will be weakened politically as well. The third assumption gives us reason to think that the resultant pressures will not remain invisible but will actually be brought to bear in the political arena.

The issue of potential benefits is an important one, and a familiar example may help to illuminate it. In both great wars of this century, belligerent governments have faced an intensified demand for industrial labor and, because of the military's need for manpower, a reduced supply. That situation has positioned workers—and, in the U.S. case, such traditionally disadvantaged workers as blacks and women—to demand greatly increased compensation: these groups, in short, have had large *potential* gains. Naturally, governments and employers have endeavored to deny them those gains; but in many cases—Germany in World War I, the United States in World War II, Britain in both world wars—the lure of sharing in the potential gains has induced trade union leaders, and workers themselves, to organize and demand more. Similarly, when transportation costs fall, governments may at first partially offset the effect by imposing protection. Owners of abundant factors nonetheless still have substantial *potential* gains from trade, which they may mortgage, or on which others may speculate, to pressure policy toward lower levels of protection.

So much for politics. As regards the economic aspect, I propose to adopt with minor refinements the traditional three-factor model—land, labor, and capital—and to assume . . . that the land-labor ratio informs us fully about any country's endowment of those two factors. . . . No country, in other words, can be rich in both land and labor: a high land-labor ratio implies abundance of land and scarcity of labor; a low ratio signifies the opposite. Finally, I shall simply define an *advanced* economy as one in which capital is abundant.

This model of factor endowments . . . permits us in theory to place any country's economy into one of four cells (see Figure 1), according to whether it is advanced or backward and whether its land-labor ratio is high or low. We recognize, in other words, only economies that are: (1) capital rich, land rich, and labor poor; (2) capital rich, land poor, and labor rich; (3) capital poor, land rich, and labor poor; or (4) capital poor, land poor, and labor rich.

POLITICAL EFFECTS OF EXPANDING TRADE

The Stolper-Samuelson theorem, applied to our simple model, implies that increasing exposure to trade must result in *urban-rural conflict* in two kinds of economies, and in *class conflict* in the two others. Consider first the upper right-hand cell of Figure 1: the advanced (therefore capital-rich) economy endowed abundantly in labor but poorly in land. Expanding trade must benefit both capitalists and workers; it harms only landowners and the pastoral and agricultural enterprises that use land intensively. Both capitalists and workers—which is to say, almost the entire urban sector—should favor free trade; agriculture should on the whole be protectionist. Moreover, we expect

FIGURE 1 Four Main Types of Factor Endowments

Land-Labor Ratio

	High	Low
Economy Advanced	ABUNDANT: Capital Land SCARCE: Labor	ABUNDANT: Capital Labor SCARCE: Land
Economy Backward	ABUNDANT: Land SCARCE: Capital Labor	ABUNDANT: Labor SCARCE: Capital Land

the capitalists and the workers to try, very likely in concert, to expand their political influence. Depending on preexisting circumstances, they may seek concretely an extension of the franchise, a reapportionment of seats, a diminution in the powers of an upper house or of a gentry-based political elite, or a violent "bourgeois" revolution.

Urban-rural conflict should also arise in backward, land-rich economies (the lower left-hand cell of Figure 1) when trade expands, albeit with a complete reversal of fronts. In such "frontier" societies, both capital and labor are scarce; hence both are harmed by expanding trade and, normally, will seek protection. Only land is abundant, and therefore only agriculture will gain from free trade. Farmers and pastoralists will try to expand their influence in some movement of a "populist" and antiurban stripe.

Conversely, in backward economies with low land-labor ratios (the lower right-hand cell of Figure 1), land and capital are scarce and labor is abundant. The model therefore predicts *class conflict*: labor will pursue free trade and expanded political power (including, in some circumstances, a workers' revolution); landowners, capitalists, and capital-intensive industrialists will unite to support protection, imperialism, and a politics of continued exclusion.

The reverse form of class conflict is expected to arise in the final case, that of the advanced but land-rich economy (the upper left-hand cell of Figure 1) under increasing exposure to trade. Because both capital and land are abundant, capitalists, capital-intensive industries, and agriculture will all benefit from, and will endorse, free trade; labor being scarce, workers and labor-intensive industries will resist, normally embracing protection and (if need be) imperialism. The benefited sectors will seek to expand their political power, if not by disfranchisement then by curtailment of workers' economic preroga-tives and suppression of their organizations.

These implications of the theory of international trade (summarized in Figure 2) seem clear, but do they in any way describe reality? . . . [I]t is worth observing how closely the experience of three major countries—Germany, Britain, and the United States—conforms to this analysis in the period of rapidly expanding trade in the last third of the nineteenth century; and how far it can go to explain otherwise puzzling disparities in those states' patterns of political evolution.

Germany and the United States were both relatively backward (i.e., capital-poor) societies: both imported considerable amounts of capital in this period, and neither had until late in the century anything like the per capita industrial capacity of the United Kingdom or Belgium. Germany, however, was rich in labor and poor in land; the United States, of course, was in exactly the opposite position. (Again, we observe that the United States imported, and Germany

FIGURE 2   Predicted Effects of Expanding Exposure to Trade

Land-Labor Ratio

	High	**Low**
Economy Advanced	CLASS CLEAVAGE: Land and Capital free-trading, assertive; Labor defensive, protectionist	URBAN-RURAL CLEAVAGE: Capital and Labor free-trading, assertive; Land defensive, protectionist **Radicalism**
Economy Backward	URBAN-RURAL CLEAVAGE: Land free-trading, assertive; Labor and Capital defensive, protectionist **U.S. Populism**	CLASS CLEAVAGE: Labor free-trading, assertive; Land, Labor and Capital defensive, protectionist **Socialism**

exported—not least to the United States—workers, which is not surprising since, at midcentury, Prussia's labor-land ratio was fifteen times that of the United States.)

The theory predicts class conflict in Germany, with labor the "revolvtion-ary" and free-trading element, and with land and capital united in support of protection and imperialism. Surely this description will not ring false to any student of German socialism or of Germany's infamous "marriage of iron and rye." For the United States, conversely, the theory predicts—quite accu-rately, I submit—urban-rural conflict, with the agrarians now assuming the "revolutionary" and free-trading role; capital and labor unite in a protection-ist and imperialist coalition. . . .

Britain, on the other hand, was already an advanced economy in the nine-teenth century. Its per capita industrial output far exceeded that of any other nation, and it exported capital in vast quantities. That it was also rich in labor is suggested by its extensive exports of that factor to the United States, Can-ada, Australia, New Zealand, and Africa; in fact, Britain's labor-land ratio then exceeded Japan's by 50 percent and was over thirty times that of the United States. Britain therefore falls into the upper right-hand quadrant of Figure 1 and is predicted to exhibit a rural-urban cleavage whose fronts are opposite those found in the United States: capitalists and labor unite in sup-port of free trade and in demands for expanded political power, while land-owners and agriculture support protection and imperialism.

Although this picture surely obscures important nuances, it illuminates cru-cial differences—between, for example, British and German political develop-ment in this period. In Britain, capitalists and labor united in the Liberal party and forced an expanded suffrage and curtailment of (still principally land-owning) aristocratic power. In Germany, liberalism shattered, the suffrage at the crucial level of the individual states was actually contracted, and—far from eroding aristocratic power—the bourgeoisie grew more and more *ver-junkert* in style and aspirations.

POLITICAL EFFECTS OF DECLINING TRADE

When rising costs or declining security substantially increases the risks or costs of external trade, the gainers and losers in each situation are simply the reverse of those under increasing exposure to trade. Let us first consider the situation of the highly developed (and therefore by definition capital-rich) economies.

In an advanced economy with a high land-labor ratio (the upper left-hand cell of Figure 1), we should expect intense *class conflict* precipitated by a newly aggressive working class. Land and capital are both abundant in such an economy; hence, under declining trade owners of both factors (and pro-ducers who use either factor intensively) lose. Moreover, they can resort to no such simple remedy as protection or imperialism. Labor being the only scarce resource, workers and labor-intensive industries are well positioned to reap a significant windfall from the "protection" that dearer or riskier trade affords; and, according to our earlier assumption, like any other benefited class they will soon endeavor to parlay their greater economic power into greater political power. Capitalists and landowners, even if they were previously at odds, will unite to oppose labor's demands.

Quite to the contrary, declining trade in an advanced economy that is labor rich and land poor (the upper right-hand cell of Figure 1) will entail renewed *urban-rural* conflict. Capital and labor are both abundant, and both are harmed by the contraction of external trade. Agriculture, as the intense exploiter of the only scarce factor, gains significantly and quickly tries to translate its gain into greater political control.

Urban-rural conflict is also predicted for backward, land-rich countries under declining trade; but here agriculture is on the defensive. Labor and capital being both scarce, both benefit from the contraction of trade; land, as the only locally abundant factor, is threatened. The urban sectors unite, in a parallel to the "radical" coalition of labor-rich developed countries under expanding trade discussed previously, to demand an increased voice in the state.

Finally, in backward economies rich in labor rather than land, class conflict resumes, with labor this time on the defensive. Capital and land, as the locally scarce factors, gain from declining trade; labor, locally abundant, suffers economic reverses and is soon threatened politically.

Observe again, as a first test of the plausibility of these results—summarized in Figure 3—how they appear to account for some prominent disparities of political response to the last precipitous decline of international trade, the depression of the 1930s. The U.S. New Deal represented a sharp turn to the left and occasioned a significant increase in organized labor's political power. In Germany, a depression of similar depth (gauged by unemployment rates and declines in industrial production) brought to power first Hindenburg's and then Hitler's dictatorship. Landowners exercised markedly greater influence than they had under Weimar; and indeed a credible case can be made that the rural sector was the principal early beneficiary of the early Nazi regime. Yet this is exactly the broad difference that the model would lead us to anticipate, if we accept that by 1930 both countries were economically advanced—although Germany, after physical reparations and cessions of industrial regions, was surely less rich in capital than the United States—but the United States held land abundantly, which in Germany was scarce (respectively, the left- and right-hand cells of the upper half of Figure 3). Only an obtuse observer would claim that such factors as cultural inheritance and recent defeat in war played no role; but surely it is also important to recognize the sectoral impact of declining trade in the two societies.

As regards the less developed economies of the time, it may be profitable to contrast the depression's impact on such South American cases as Argentina

FIGURE 3 Predicted Effects of Declining Exposure to Trade

Land-Labor Ratio

	High	Low
Economy Advanced	CLASS CLEAVAGE: Labor assertive, Land and Capital defensive **U.S. New Deal**	URBAN-RURAL CLEAVAGE: Land assertive, Labor and Capital defensive **W. European Fascism**
Economy Backward	URBAN-RURAL CLEAVAGE: Labor and Capital assertive, Land defensive **South American Populism**	CLASS CLEAVAGE: Land and Capital assertive, Labor defensive **Asian & East European Fascism**

and Brazil with its effects in the leading Asian country, Japan. In Argentina and Brazil, it is usually asserted, the depression gave rise to, or at the least strengthened, "populist" coalitions that united labor and the urban middle classes in opposition to traditional, landowning elites. In Japan, growing military influence suppressed representative institutions and nascent workers' organizations, ruling in the immediate interest—if hardly under the domination—of landowners and capitalists. (Similar suppressions of labor occurred in China and Vietnam.) In considering these contrasting responses, should we not take into account that Argentina and Brazil were rich in land and poor in labor, while in Japan (and, with local exceptions, in Asia generally) labor was abundant and land was scarce? . . .

POSSIBLE OBJECTIONS

Several objections can plausibly be raised to the whole line of analysis that I have advanced here. . . .

1. It may be argued that the effects sketched out here will not obtain in countries that depend only slightly on trade. Belgium, where external trade (taken as the sum of exports and imports) roughly equals gross domestic product (GDP), can indeed be affected profoundly by changes

in the risks or costs of international commerce; but a state like the United States in the 1960s, where trade amounted to scarcely a tenth of GDP, will have remained largely immune.

This view, while superficially plausible, is incorrect. The Stolper-Samuelson result obtains at any margin; and in fact holders of scarce factors have been quite as devastated by expanding trade in almost autarkic economies—one need think only of the weavers of India or of Silesia, exposed in the nineteenth century to the competition of Lancashire mills—as in ones previously more dependent on trade.

2. Given that comparative advantage always assures gains from trade, it may be objected that the cleavages described here need not arise at all: the gainers from trade can always compensate the losers and have something left over; trade remains the Pareto-superior outcome. As Stolper and Samuelson readily conceded in their original essay, this is perfectly true. To the student of politics, however, and with even greater urgency to those who are losing from trade in concrete historical situations, it remains unobvious that such compensation will in fact occur. Rather, the natural tendency is for gainers to husband their winnings and to stop their ears to the cries of the afflicted. Perhaps only unusually strong and trustworthy states, or political cultures that especially value compassion and honesty, can credibly assure the requisite compensation . . . and even in those cases, substantial conflict over the nature and level of compensation will usually precede the ultimate agreement.

3. Equally, one can ask why the cleavages indicated here should persist. In a world of perfectly mobile factors and rational behavior, people would quickly disinvest from losing factors and enterprises (e.g., farming in Britain after 1880) and move to sectors whose auspices were more favorable. Markets should swiftly clear; and a new, if different, political equilibrium should be achieved.

To this two answers may be given. First, in some cases trade expands or contracts so rapidly and surprisingly as to frustrate rational expectations. Especially in countries that experience a steady series of such exogenous shocks—the case in Europe, I would contend, from 1840 to the present day—divisions based on factor endowments (which ordinarily change only gradually) will be repeatedly revived. Second, not infrequently some factors' privileged access to political influence makes the extraction of rents and subsidies seem cheaper than adaptation: Prussian *Junkers* familiarly, sought (and easily won) protection rather than adjustment. In such circumstances, adaptation may be long delayed, sometimes with ultimately disastrous consequences.

At the same time, it should be conceded that, as improved technology makes factors more mobile . . . and anticipation easier, the theory advanced here will likely apply less well. Indeed, this entire analysis may be a historically conditioned one, whose usefulness will be found to have entered a rapid decline sometime after 1960. . . .

4. This analysis, some may contend, reifies such categories as "capital," "labor," and "land," assuming a unanimity of preference that most countries' evidence belies. In fact, a kind of shorthand and a testable hypothesis are involved: a term like "capital" is the convenient abbreviation of "those who draw their income principally from investments, plus the most capital-intensive producers"; and I indeed hypothesize that individuals' political positions will vary with their derivation of income—or, more precisely, of present value of all anticipated future income—from particular factors.

   A worker, for example, who derives 90 percent of her income from wages and 10 percent from investments will conform more to the theory's expectation of "labor"'s political behavior than one who depends half on investments and half on wages. An extremely labor-intensive manufacturer will behave less like a "capitalist" than a more capital-intensive one. And a peasant (as noted previously) who depends chiefly on inputs of his own labor will resemble a "worker," whereas a more land-intensive neighbor will behave as a "landowner."

5. Finally, it may be objected that I have said nothing about the outcome of these conflicts. I have not done so for the simple reason that I cannot: history makes it all too plain, as in the cases of nineteenth-century Germany and America, that the economic losers from trade may win politically over more than the short run. What I have advanced here is a speculation about *cleavages*, not about outcomes. I have asserted only that those who gain from fluctuations in trade will be strengthened and emboldened politically; nothing guarantees that they will win. Victory or defeat depends, so far as I can see, both on the relative size of the various groups and on those institutional and cultural factors that this perspective so resolutely ignores.

CONCLUSION

It is essential to recall what I am *not* claiming to do. . . . I do not contend that changes in countries' exposure to trade explain all, or even most, of their varying patterns of political cleavage. It would be foolish to ignore the importance of ancient cultural and religious loyalties, of wars and migrations, or of such historical memories as the French Revolution and the *Kulturkampf*. Other cleavages antedate, and persist through, the ones I discuss here, shaping, crosscutting, complicating, and indeed sometimes dominating their political resolution. . . .

In the main, I am presenting here a theoretical puzzle, a kind of social-scientific "thought experiment" in Hempel's original sense: a teasing out of unexpected, and sometimes counterintuitive, implications of theories already widely accepted. For the Stolper-Samuelson theorem *is* generally, indeed almost universally, embraced; yet, coupled with a stark and unexceptionable model of the political realm, it plainly implies that changes in exposure to trade must profoundly affect nations' internal political cleavages. Do they do so? If they do not, what conclusions shall we draw, either about our theories of international trade, or about our understanding of politics?

21

The Political Economy of Trading States: Factor Specificity, Collective Action Problems, and Domestic Political Institutions

JAMES E. ALT AND MICHAEL GILLIGAN

In this essay, James Alt and Michael Gilligan contrast Rogowski's factor-based approach to political coalitions (see Reading 20) with a sectoral approach drawn from the Ricardo-Viner, or "specific factors," model of international trade. They explain under what circumstances political coalitions will take the form of broad classes, as predicted by Rogowski, and under what circumstances they will organize along the lines of specific industries. The authors then examine how collective action costs (the costs incurred by groups in organizing for political action) and domestic political institutions influence the formation of political coalitions, and they conclude that these constraints may exert a more important effect than strictly economic considerations. Alt and Gilligan provide a broad survey of the most important theoretical concepts used by contemporary analysts and develop a synthetic approach to the domestic politics of international trade.

I. INTRODUCTION

The fundamental problem that international trade poses for states is this. Trade typically offers cheaper goods, with more choice for consumers and the greatest economic output for society as a whole. But at the same time, it is also very disruptive to individuals' lives, tying their incomes to the vagaries of international markets. In so doing, trade affects the distribution of wealth *within* the domestic economy, raising questions of who gets relatively more or less, and what they can do about it politically. Trade also has important effects, naturally, on aggregate domestic economic welfare and on the distributions of wealth and power among national societies. Anyone theorizing about "trading states" (states of trading societies) should consider the state's problem of how to weigh the aggregate, external effects against the internal, distributional effects—and indeed against the costs or disturbances that those internal redistributions may bring.

All too often, however, theories of states and trade neglect the domestic political dimension. The purpose of this article is to present a manual (or perhaps a map) explicating what is required to understand the domestic consequences of a society's "choosing to trade." It discusses considerations fundamental to answering a range of questions, from "Can a state enhance aggregate welfare by intervening in a trading economy?" to "What consequences would/should an increase in trade have for the design of state institutions?"

In domestic politics the conflict over these distributional consequences will reflect the trade policy coalitions that form around shared interests in liberalization as opposed to protection. Whether trade policies are taken to be chosen democratically or imposed from above, whether those coalitions are engaged in vote mobilization or protest, the balance between the opposed coalitions favoring freer trade and those favoring protection creates the "demand" by society for liberalization or protection. At one level, our central concern is with explaining how and why these coalitions take the form they do. In these terms, the essential problem for the state of a trading economy (or indeed for any government which seeks to stay in office) may become weighing the good of the many, which is often served by relatively free trade, against the good of the powerful few which may be served by restricting trade. At other times and places, however, the battle may be between two groups of the few or between two groups of the many. . . .

II. COLLECTIVE ACTION FROM PARETO TO THE PRESENT

Let us first consider the problem as one purely of collective action. Seventy years ago the Italian economist Vilfredo Pareto argued:

> In order to understand how those who champion protection make themselves heard so easily it is necessary to add the consideration which applies to social movements generally . . . If a certain measure A is the cause of a loss of one franc to each of a thousand persons, and of a one thousand franc gain to one individual, the latter will expend a great deal of energy, whereas the former will resist weakly; and it is likely that, in the end, the person who is attempting to secure the thousand francs via A will be successful.
>
> A protectionist measure provides large benefits to a small number of people, and causes a very great number of consumers a slight loss. This circumstance makes it easier to put a protection measure in practice.[1]

Similarly, in his classic study of the Smoot-Hawley Act of 1930 Schattschneider explained the costly increase in protection by arguing, "Benefits are concentrated while costs are distributed."[2] It is vital to note that Pareto's and Schattschneider's statements are empirical observations, not general theoretical

1. Pareto 1927, p. 379.
2. Schattschneider 1935, pp. 127–8.

points. In what follows we will discuss the conditions under which we would expect to observe what they describe. . . . Collective action problems continue to be a major component of explanations in trade policy today, particularly in the endogenous tariff literature in economics.

There are really two interactive problems of organizing or taking collective political action: one is "excludability" and the other is the cost of organizing a group. The problem of excludability stems from the fact that collective political action is a public good: all members of a group benefit from acting in favor of their preferred trade policy whether they contribute to that effort or not, so each has an incentive to free ride. . . .

. . . Since each member can consume the lobbying supplied by all the other members of the group, they receive less benefit from the lobbying that they actually pay for and consequently buy less than they would if they could not consume the lobbying of others. This is essentially where the free rider problem comes from. . . .

Even though the problem of free-riding is less in smaller groups, . . . they should not always be expected to win. We are still left with Pareto and Schatt-schneider's empirical puzzle: how policies which benefit a small minority of the population are enacted. Two answers to the puzzle are possible. First, there may be *per person* transaction costs in organizing groups. Second, if policy outcomes are probabilistic, members of large groups with small per person stakes and contributions may suppose that their own contributions will be insignificant to the political outcome and therefore not make them. On the other hand, members of smaller groups, with their larger stakes and contributions per person, may see that their contribution has a non-negligible impact on the likelihood that a policy will be enacted, and therefore they will make their contributions. . . .

First, if transaction costs are fixed per person, larger groups will find it costlier to organize than smaller groups. These per person transaction costs may be paid by the organization (for instance the costs of soliciting contributions door to door or through the mail) or they may be borne by the members of the group (through the costs of learning which groups are active on an issue and how a new member can help). . . .

A second reason why smaller groups may have an advantage over larger groups is that outcomes of political action are uncertain. Members of each group will only be concerned with the probability that their contribution will decide the political outcome. . . . [I]n smaller groups individuals' contributions will be larger, and as a result their probabilities of deciding the outcome will be larger. In very large groups like consumer groups, on the other hand, individual contributions will be quite small, and as a result individual probabilities of deciding outcomes will be small as well—so small, perhaps, as to make the expected benefits of a contribution negligible.

In other words, expected benefits will outweigh expected costs only at fairly high contributions, because only high contributions have a non-negligible chance of deciding the outcome. Furthermore, these contributions will only be made by individuals with fairly high individual stakes, which is to say, people in the smaller group. So because the members of the smaller group make larger contributions per person, they also have a larger effect on the probability of changing the outcome and therefore benefits can outweigh costs. On the other hand members of large groups have very small stakes per person in the issue: their contributions are small, and therefore so too are their chances of changing the outcome also small. Consequently the expected benefits are too small to outweigh even the small cost of a contribution. To bring it down to earth, a one million dollar lobbying contribution from GM will likely have a large effect on trade policy. A ten dollar contribution from an individual auto consumer will have virtually no effect. Thus even though the cost of the auto consumer's contribution is negligible, the expected benefits are even more negligible.

III. A BRIEF PRIMER OF THE STOLPER-SAMUELSON AND RICARDO-VINER MODELS

The expected costs facing organizers of potential collective political actions are a feature of the domestic political and economic environment, affected by but also largely independent of the variables we discuss (namely, political institutions, and factor abundance and mobility). But these economic variables cannot be ignored if one is to understand the demand for political outcomes, independently of the costs of collective action. These variables, in short, determine the "stakes," which we held constant in the last section. We need to understand their role in determining individual-level preferences, reflected in the incentives to form coalitions and demand political redress, in who goes with whom and at what cost. To illustrate this for the case of international trade, we organize our discussion around two models, the Stolper-Samuelson or "mobile factors" approach (central in Rogowski's work; see Reading 20) and the Ricardo-Viner or "specific factors" model. . . .

A. The Stolper-Samuelson Model

In 1944 Wolfgang Stolper and Paul Samuelson seemingly settled a long debate within economics about the effects of a change in the price of a product on the real incomes of the owners of factors (such as labor and capital) that produce that product and other products in the economy. The Stolper-Samuelson theorem, as it was later called, argued that a change in the price of a product—for the sake of argument, let us say an increase—would *more than proportionally* increase the return to the factor that is used intensively in the production of that good. Therefore the real incomes of owners of that intensively-used factor will unambiguously rise, giving them, in our terms, a stake in bringing about that change in prices. So, for example, an increase in the price of the labor-intensive good leads to an increase in the real wage rate of labor throughout the economy and an increase in the real incomes of laborers. Furthermore, if there are only two factors of production, the theorem shows that the real incomes of the owners of the factor that is used less intensively will fall.

It takes a few steps to establish this overall result. First, protection of an industry will raise the price of the good produced by that industry. That is where the change in relative prices comes from. Protection increases the returns to the owners of the factors that are used most intensively in the protected (import-competing) industry and less intensively in the unprotected (export) industry; and it reduces the returns to those factors that are used less intensively in the protected industry and more intensively in the unprotected industry. The big consequence from our point of view is that, because factors are assumed to be mobile between sectors, owners of the same factor have the same change to its returns, *regardless of whether it is actually employed in the protected industry* or in the unprotected industry. Therefore the conflict is between the factors of production, regardless of the industry in which they work.

Second, let us reground the prediction of which groups within a country will be relatively more disposed to favor protection or free trade. Instead of basing that prediction, as before, on intensity of use let us instead base it a point prior to that: the country's actual endowments. To do this, combine the Stolper-Samuelson theorem's predictions about factor price changes and income changes with the Hecksher-Ohlin theorem. This theorem states that a country will export the good which intensively uses whichever factor of production is relatively abundant in that country. Therefore, according to the Hecksher-Ohlin theorem, if there are two factors of production (say, capital and labor) a country which is relatively abundant in capital will export capital-intensive products and import labor-intensive products, while a country that is relatively abundant in labor will export labor-intensive products and import capital-intensive products. Combining this prediction with the Stolper-Samuelson theorem yields the usual conclusion that, other things being equal, in a relatively capital-abundant country labor will favor protection because it cannot be intensively used in exports, while capital will favor relatively free trade. Conversely, in a relatively labor-abundant country capital will favor protection and labor will favor relatively free trade. These were Rogowski's main arguments.

Finally, to predict individual preferences over policy outcomes we need to add one further consideration. The "magnification effect" allows us to translate "returns to factors" into real incomes and thus establish the Stolper-Samuelson theorem's central point, which is that trade policy can more than proportionally increase the real incomes of owners of the factor that is used intensively in making that product. The mechanism through which the Stolper-Samuelson theorem works is known as the "Rybczynski theorem." Suppose that in a capital-rich country (which imports labor-intensive products) some shock increases imports, thus producing lower relative prices for the imported (that is to say, labor-intensive) good and higher relative prices for the exported (that is to say, capital-intensive) good. This reduction in the relative price of the imported good leads to reduced production in the labor-intensive industry, while the increase in the relative price of the exported good leads to an increase in production in the export industry. To accommodate these changes in production in each of the two industries, labor and capital are freed up in the labor-intensive industry, and the need for labor and capital is increased in the capital-intensive industry. Since it is after all a capital-intensive industry, in order to increase production that industry needs relatively *less* labor and relatively *more* capital than would a labor-intensive industry. Meanwhile, as it reduces production the labor-intensive industry sheds relatively *more* labor and relatively *less* capital (it is after all a labor-intensive industry). Therefore, there is excess labor on the market, and the relative price of labor falls to bring the market back into equilibrium. Meanwhile, there is excess demand for capital, so the price for capital is bid up to bring the market back into equilibrium.

Precisely because relatively more labor is freed up from the labor-intensive industry and it is needed less by the capital-intensive industry, the wage falls proportionally more than the relative price of the import-competing good. Similarly, precisely because relatively less capital is freed up from the labor-intensive industry while it is needed more by the capital-intensive industry, the price of capital increases by relatively more than the increase in relative price for the capital-intensive good. This magnification effect of changes in relative prices of goods on the rewards to the factors that produce them is the heart of the Stolper-Samuelson theorem. The logic may be somewhat involved, but the bottom line is not: in this example of a capital-abundant country, labor loses and capital wins from freer trade.

B. The Ricardo-Viner (Specific Factors) Model

The assumption that factors are mobile between sectors of the economy is crucial to the derivation of the Stolper-Samuelson theorem. It is only because capital can flow from the import-competing (labor-intensive industry) to the capital-intensive industry that it is able to enjoy the effect of the increased production of the capital-intensive good. But what if the capital used in the labor-intensive industry is different from the capital used in the capital-intensive industry? To bring the example back down to earth, what if knitting machines cannot be used to make microchips? Indeed, in many real world situations it seems intuitively likely that this will be the case: capital (or certain kinds of labor, for that matter) will not be able to flow easily from a declining sector to a rising sector. A different set of assumptions is needed for this contingency. According to the assumptions of the Ricardo-Viner model (or "specific factors" model as it is often called), factors of production are "specific" to a particular industry, and when that industry declines they cannot move to the rising industry.

"Cannot move" is a matter of degree. Specificity corresponds to the loss of value in moving an asset from its current to its next-best use. Specificity relates to ways in which investments are tied to particular production relationships: it can involve location, human capital (expertise) and many other forms in which assets may be dedicated to a particular use. What specific assets have in common is that, apart from their present use, they just do not have any very good alternate uses. Various social characteristics can increase the general level of specific assets in an economy. *Economic development*, to the extent that it involves increasingly taking advantage of differentiation and specialization, probably increases the frequency of specific factors. Any general increase in *transaction costs*, even if narrowly construed to involve only monitoring and policing, probably increases specificity throughout an economy. Such disparate factors as *geographical separation* and *ethnic rivalries* can reduce the ability of labor to move freely. In fact, all sorts of *entry barriers* increase specificity: insofar as entry to one sector involves exit from another, specificity just reflects costs of exit. In this sense, specificity is probably very high in *centrally planned* economies, where factor owners would not think of moving without asking the permission of bureaucrats.

In this situation, what are the effects of the relative price changes following an increase in imports? Let us assume for exposition that there are two industries, the export industry and the import industry, and that each industry has a factor that is specific to it. Let us further assume that there is also a mobile factor, which we will call labor, that is needed by both industries and that can move easily between them. To continue now with the example from the previous section, as the price of the import-competing good decreases as a result of the increased competition from imports, production will also decrease in that industry; and the mobile factor, labor, will flow out of that sector, just as before. However, the factor that is specific to that industry must obviously remain in that industry. The specific factors remaining in that industry still need labor to produce their product. But as labor flows out of the import-competing industry, they find it increasingly hard to get it and become less productive in consequence. Because of this productivity decline, the income of the specific factor in the import-competing industry will fall with respect to the price of both the export good and the imported good. Meanwhile, labor will flow into the export industry, since the relative price of the export good will increase as a result of the falling price of the import-competing good. Factors of production that are specific to the export industry will become more productive (because of the extra labor that they can now use) and as a result the return to that factor will increase relative to the price of both the export good and the imported good.

In the Ricardo-Viner model, the effect on the real income of the mobile factor is ambiguous. It depends not only on intensities of use (which work much as described in the previous part) but also on consumption patterns. Since the labor-intensive industry is in our running example the one in decline, wages have to fall. . . . The second part of the effect, the consumption effect, is however more complicated. First, the nominal wage paid to the mobile factor will fall, but by less than the reduction in the price of the imported good: thus owners of the mobile factor enjoy an increase in their wage, relative to the price of the imported good. Second, however, the price of the exported good remains the same, so the wage rate falls relative to it. The net effect on each owner of the mobile factor of the price changes and the change in the return to the mobile factor therefore depends on (a) the size of the nominal reduction in the wage rate and (b) the share of each of the two products in each person's budget. If workers consume a great deal of the import good, their real incomes are more likely to rise because their wages have risen relative to the price of the import good. If they consume a great deal of the export good, their incomes are likely to fall because their real incomes have fallen relative to the export good. . . .

What changes in moving from the Stolper-Samuelson to the Ricardo-Viner model? First, we lose the simple derivation, working through relative intensity of use, of economic interest from factor abundance. In the specific factors model, there is a zero-sum conflict of interest between exporting and import-competing sectors: their interests are diametrically opposed; whatever one side gains the other loses, rather than gains and losses being distributed according to factor ownership within both sectors. However, the interests of one of these groups of factor owners will in general be aligned with the interests of the owners of the mobile factor(s). It seems probable that the stakes of the mobile factor owners will be smaller than those of the the specific factor owners. Supposing however that the mobile factor could be more or less scarce and supposing that scarcer factors mean fewer owners of that factor, the per capita stakes will be the larger. This opens up intriguing possibilities for coalition formation even in a specific factors model.

IV. TRADE POLICY COALITIONS: FACTOR SPECIFICITY, COLLECTIVE ACTION AND DOMESTIC INSTITUTIONS

From these economic models, we can thus infer individuals' preferences from the stakes facing them in potential situations of collective action. Let us now, reflecting on the collective action literature, consider how people might respond. In so doing we shall initially set aside, and then reintroduce, the effects of institutional context.

A. From Preferences to Trade Policy Coalitions

The implication for politics of the "mobile factors" approach is just this: the scarce factor (labor, in the above example) will favor restricting trade, and the abundant factor (capital, in the above example) will have incentives to favor liberalizing trade, no matter where in the economy those factors are employed. Let us further assume, for the moment, that there are no barriers to collective action (or that any that exist are easily surmounted) and that one or another coalition can actually get what it wants. (These are not always good assumptions about politics, as we will argue below, but for now let us make them in order to highlight the effects of economic variables on trade policy coalitions.) It then follows from the "mobile factors" model that owners of the abundant factor will favor liberalization while the scarce factor will favor protection. . . .

The predictions about trade policy coalitions flowing from the Ricardo-Viner model are somewhat more complicated. We proceed in two steps, continuing throughout to focus on the case where labor is the mobile factor. First, were we to assume away the interests of the mobile factor, . . . the coalitions predicted by the Ricardo-Viner model would be simply the specific factors used in the export industry versus the specific factors used in the import industry. As argued above, the former unambiguously gains from the relative price reduction of the imported good, while the latter unambiguously loses. As the mobile factor flows out of the import-competing industry and into the export industry, the specific factor in the import-competing industry becomes less productive and its real return falls. Meanwhile, the real return to the specific factor in the export industry rises, as that factor becomes more productive due to the larger pool of the mobile factor available to it. As Figure 1 shows, pro-liberalization (protectionist) groups will always include the specific factor in the export (import-competing) industry. But where will the mobile factor, labor, be allied?

. . . [W]here the export industry is labor-intensive and labor consumes relatively much of (spends a disproportionate share of its consumption budget on) the imported good, labor has an interest in liberalization; so too, naturally, does the owner of the specific factor in the export industry. Set against this pro-liberalization coalition is the specific factor in the import-competing industry alone. Change the relative labor intensities of the two industries, and switch labor's consumption of imports to "relatively low," and we move to . . . [a situation where] the owners of the export industry's specific factor stand alone in wanting liberalization, other things equal. . . . The underlying logic is simply this: the factor that is politically *advantaged* is that which is specific to the good which *uses labor intensely*, if labor does not disproportionately consume that as well.

But what if the direct effect of relative price changes on the mobile factor is ambiguous? Even then, each of the two specific factors may want to pull the mobile factor into its coalition. To do so, they may be willing to offer side-payments to labor to bring it into their coalition. . . . In these cases, which coalition labor allies with (or at least is bought by more cheaply) will depend on whether the effects of the consumption bundle or of factor intensity are stronger.

FIGURE 1 Trade Policy Coalitions under the Stolper-Samuelson and Ricardo-Viner Assumptions

Stolper-Samuelson		Ricardo-Viner	
		Export Industry Relatively Labor-Intensive	**Import Industry Relatively Labor-Intensive**
Pro-trade	**Abundant Factor**	*High* Consumption of Imported Good — Export Industry Specific Factor and Labor	Export Industry Specific Factor Labor "Biddable"
		Low — Export Industry Specific Factor Labor "Biddable"	Export Industry Specific Factor
		Export Industry Relatively Labor-Intensive	**Import Industry Relatively Labor-Intensive**
Protectionist	**Scarce Factor**	*High* Consumption of Imported Good — Import-Competing Specific Factor	Import-Competing Specific Factor Labor "Biddable"
		Low — Import-Competing Specific Factor Labor "Biddable"	Import-Competing Specific Factor and Labor

In any case, it would be wrong to assume that, in the Ricardo-Viner model, the mobile factor will not take sides in the trade policy coalitions. This is particularly true in political systems where "numbers matter"—that is, where a majority or at least fairly large numbers must be behind a particular policy for it to be enacted. In such political systems the mobile factor holds a very powerful political position. If the changes in its income resulting from a change in relative prices are smaller than the changes in the income of the specific factors involved, the mobile factor is in a sense the median group between the two specific factors. If so, it commands what is sometimes important political turf, and it might therefore be courted by the two specific factors. This consideration is our link to the role of institutions.

B. The Relationship between Factor Mobility, Institutions, and Collective Action Costs

What, then, determines the policy outcomes? Partly the distribution of benefits, as described before: that is the demand side. But neither the Stolper-Samuelson nor the Ricardo-Viner models are by themselves sufficient to understand coalition formation on trade policy issues. The severity of collective action problems—the difficulty of mobilizing or organizing resources in order to secure a favorable political decision—also has a role in the maintenance and extension of protection. Let us, purely for the sake of analytic convenience, disaggregate "collective action problems" into three parts: (1) those which relate systematically to factor mobility or specificity, (2) those which relate directly to the nature of domestic political institutions and (3) all the rest. Much more might be said about this last category, but for our purposes it will serve merely as a residual category reflecting the effects of ease of communication, geographical concentration and pre-existing collective organizations, all of which reduce the cost of collective action in any particular case.

Factor mobility has obvious effects on possibilities for collective action. Mobility automatically disperses the benefits of any trade policy across all the owners of a particular factor, regardless of which industry employs them. This produces non-excludability, which in turn opens up the possibility of free-riding. Collective action is easier the more any non-participant can be excluded from the benefits: factor mobility, conversely, makes collective action harder. With perfect factor mobility, the scarce factor in the economy will benefit from protection (and from the lobbying that secures it) wherever it is employed. Contrast that with the case in which, when protection is granted to one industry, the benefits of that protection flow only to the specific factors employed in that industry (and possibly the mobile factor): there, the benefits of protection would be more excludable, mitigating the free-rider problem. With mobile factors, however, the benefits are more broadly dispersed, and thus the result should be that they are less excludable.

Ignore now, for a moment, factor mobility. Focus instead on political institutions, and where the jurisdiction for taking decisive actions on trade policy lies. Many possibilities exist. One is that action is taken directly by majoritarian voting, as in a referendum. Here, to obtain a favorable outcome one needs (relatively) large numbers of supporters. The Stolper-Samuelson model, in which one's "interest" depends on how large a share of one's income is derived from each of the factors of production, interacts with such majoritarian politics in a straightforward way: if, for example, the great mass of the population derives most of its income from labor then there will be a standing majority ready to vote the interest of labor. Another possibility, not quite so extreme, is that policy is made in a legislature by party bloc voting. Large numbers of supporters are once again involved, although the possibilities for using organizational channels facilitate some collective action that might be too costly if everyone affected had to be mobilized individually.

Where numbers count most, outcomes depend on the distribution of income, which can be used as shorthand for distribution of factor ownership. This, combined with the level of development of an economy (which is to say, whether capital is scarce or abundant), determines trade policy outcomes. A capital-rich country in which capital is highly concentrated in a few hands (strictly speaking, a country in which a large majority have little capital or derive little of their income from capital) should adopt trade restrictions, because the majority of the population would benefit from them. The more equitable the distribution of income (again, technically, the greater the extent to which a majority of the population derive most of their income from capital) the lower trade barriers should be, since a larger share of the population would own capital and would be hurt by trade barriers.

At the other end of the scale, imagine decision-making institutions completely insulated from majoritarian pressures. All one has to do to get protection, say, is to convince a bureaucrat (perhaps just a regional administrator) in a centrally planned economy. Or maybe it is one or a small group of legislators, whose interest in maintaining office requires pleasing only a relatively small, sector-specific, geographically differentiated constituency. Or maybe the outcome can be achieved by bargaining between ministers or even within ministries. In cases such as these, support from large segments of the population is not necessary for a policy to be enacted. Much more important for a group's success is its ability to access and to influence the decision-making system. There is then no need for an interest group to make sure that its preferred policy benefits a large share of the population—to do so would only lower the per-person benefits within the group and increase the organizational costs of political action. The point is that majoritarian institutions force groups to disperse benefits more broadly than do non-majoritarian systems. For any aggregate amount of benefit that would flow from some trade policy change, the less majoritarian the institution the fewer who will share in the benefit, either directly or indirectly (through compensatory payments).

This effect of political institutions is not the same as the effect of factor mobility, however. Benefits can in principle be as excludable as you like in a majoritarian politics model. Majoritarianism affects the number of supporters that must be brought within a winning coalition, and thus the dispersion of benefits across members of that coalition. In majoritarian political systems the benefits must be spread across a large number of individuals to make the policy politically viable. Non-excludability, on the other hand, means that the benefits of a trade policy will flow to many regardless of whether or not they participate in the winning coalition, which will be more of a problem in a Stolper-Samuelson world because the benefits of a particular trade policy accrue to a particular factor regardless of where in the economy it is employed. The effect of these two variables—factor mobility and political institutions—is in another sense the same, however. Other things being equal, majoritarian political systems and factor mobility will both mean that benefits will be more dispersed and, therefore, that it will be harder to organize a successful interest group.

It is not only the case that factor mobility and majoritarian institutions produce their effects in different ways. They also vary independently of each other to some extent. That is not to say that the two do not affect each other.

The existence of non-majoritarian institutions probably does make it easier for the owners of specific factors to invest in securing policies which in fact make factors more specific, and even to seek institutional changes which make it easier to achieve such policies. But deciding to make trade policy by referendum would not by itself make all factors of production mobile, nor would inventing legislative subcommittees necessarily make factors sticky. Neither does the mobility of factors by itself generate complementary political institutions. There may be some effects in each direction. But when considering costs of collective action facing a possible interest group in securing trade policy outcomes, factor mobility and political institutions are independent variables.

C. Collective Action Costs and Trade Policy Coalitions

What coalitions, then, are we actually likely to observe? To see how the effects of the costs of collective action work, let us first hold the institutional variable constant. Then the implications of collective action costs and factor mobility for trade policy coalitions are as summarized in Figure 2. The horizontal axis specifies the severity of collective action costs, net of institutions and factor mobility—that is, how costly it is to organize an interest group, holding constant the problems of non-excludabilty and dispersion of benefits that may arise due to factor mobility or political institutions. The vertical axis specifies whether the Stolper-Samuelson or the Ricardo-Viner model is appropriate for the degree of factor mobility between industrial sectors.

The northeast quadrant contains the assumptions underlying Rogowski's book (excerpted in Reading 20). The absence of collective action problems and the complete mobility of labor and capital (and perhaps land) between sectors of the economy imply a cleavage between scarce and abundant factors,

FIGURE 2 Coalition Possibilities: The Effects of Factor Mobility and Collective Action Costs

Collective Action Costs

	High	Low
Factors Mobile	Rampant free riding No trade policy coalitions	Rogowski
Factors Specific	Standard trade policy models (Pareto, Olson, etc.)	Many interest groups Consumers active Coalitions between the specific and mobile factors

which Rogowski interpreted (depending on which was the scarce factor) as class and urban-rural conflict. Notice that the assumptions of both perfect mobility and small collective action costs are necessary for his argument. With less than perfect factor mobility, the costs of increased international trade would be concentrated primarily on the factor specific to production of the particular traded good in question (and perhaps the perfectly mobile factor). Therefore, other factors in the economy would have no reason to oppose freer trade of that good; indeed, they should support it, and the broad coalitions Rogowski speaks of would not form.

Furthermore, even if factors were perfectly mobile, high costs of collective action might mean that many of the factor owners would have little incentive to take costly political action to affect trade policy, free-riding instead on the political action of others. Then, as in the northwest quadrant of the Figure 2, it is likely that there would be no coalitions over trade issues (except perhaps in some cases where capital is the scarce factor). In a capital-rich country, for instance, labor in one industry would let labor in other industries lobby for protection, and as a result very little lobbying would be done. Depending on how far you push the assumption of mobility, it could even be that exit—in the form of moving to another employment, emigration or capital flight—would be a far more common response than lobbying.

Let us now revert to the assumption of easy collective action, but assume factors are specific. The southeast corner describes just such a political economy, where individual industries seeking protection for their products are opposed by the consumers of those products. Assuming no collective action problems in this domestic political economy, however, *any* consumers might participate in trade politics, however small their stake in the issue; they would not free ride, relying on their fellow consumers to do the lobbying for them. An industry interested in protection could only really win, then, if it banded together with other industries interested in protection and lobbied for protection for all of them. The coalition that would emerge in such a situation would pit import competers against non-tradeable producers and exporters. The problem with this coalition is that all the protected industries might be worse off from this "universalistic logroll" than if they simply accepted free trade, since the costs to them of the protection to all the other industries might very well be higher than their gains from protection of their own industry. Therefore, such a coalition is inherently unstable. The existence of collective action problems is, thus, essential to the Ricardo-Viner explanation of trade policy coalitions generating protection for individual industries, as this quadrant serves to show.

The southwest quadrant contains the ideal type of trade policy "coalition" described by Pareto, Schattschneider, Olson and the endogenous tariff literature. In that ideal type, collective action problems exclude most of the public from participating in trade politics. In fact, there really are no coalitions at all: there are simply individual industries requesting, and often receiving, protection for their particular products. They may be opposed, in that request, by the consumers of that product if those consumers are sufficiently concentrated (if, for example, they are industrial consumers who need the product for their production); but otherwise trade policy will be dominated by special interests seeking protection.

D. The Effect of Institutions

Of course, domestic political institutions also affect the severity of collective action problems and, through them, trade policy coalitions as well. To illustrate this, we transform Figure 2 into Figure 3 by adding a further distinction between majoritarian and non-majoritarian institutions. Collective action costs still vary across the horizontal axis. The vertical axis reflects the individual's share of a given aggregate gain, allowing for the effects of both dispersion and nonexcludability, with per capita benefits being lowest at the top and highest at the bottom (although the two middle rows on the vertical axis could actually be in either order).

The two polar "ideal types" are still present, in opposite corners. The Rogowski model is in the upper right: factor mobility means that benefits are relatively nonexcludable, and thus the numbers (and hence coalitions) of those affected will be larger; majoritarian institutions mean that large numbers

FIGURE 3 Coalition Possibilities: The Effects of Factor Mobility, Collective Action Costs, and Domestic Political Institutions

Collective Action Costs

	High	**Low**
Factors Mobile Majoritarian Institutions	Rampant free riding No trade policy coalitions Exit (?)	Rogowski
Factors Mobile Non-majoritarian Institutions	Rampant free-riding Trade Policy coalitions Exit (?)	Class based coalitions possible, but not necessary for victory
Factors Specific Majoritarian Institutions	Individual interest groups unable to affect trade policy Consumer groups inactive Universalistic logroll (?)	Cross sector coalitions (logrolling) or coalitions with labor Consumer groups active
Factors Specific Non-majoritarian Institutions	Standard trade policy Model (Pareto, Olson, etc.) Lobbying for protection Consumer groups inactive	Cross sector coalitions (logrolling) or coalitions with labor possible, but not necessary for victory Consumer groups active

are needed to win, and costs of collective action must (other things being equal) be small enough to allow such large organizations to develop. Clearly, as you increase costs of collective action (moving leftward in the first row of Figure 3) exit once again becomes more appealing: thus, there really seems to be a natural affinity between the Stolper-Samuelson model and majoritarian politics.

In the second row, given any significant costs of collective action, factor mobility would mean that free-riding should be rampant, inhibiting collective action. If conversely the cost of collective action goes to zero, any coalition should form. These should be large because the costs of collective action are low and benefits are non-excludable. There would be little incentive to build large coalitions, however, because size would not guarantee victory in this case: the political institutions are non-majoritarian. This cell seems to yield few interesting predictions.

Where factors are specific a number of different cases arise, surrounding the "classic" case of interest-group lobbying in the lower left corner. Protectionism is the likely outcome in this cell. There, costs of collective action are high, thus excluding consumers (who are, after all, a very large group with non-excludable benefits) from trade politics. The benefits of trade policy are concentrated on particular industries, due to factor specificity. Thus, these industries have an incentive to pay the collective action costs, even though they are high, in order to gain their favored trade policy.

In the penultimate row, where factors are specific but majorities are needed to win, exit is costly (because factors are specific) but high costs of collective action mean that groups must be small or benefits concentrated to form. In such situations, the universal logroll mentioned above would be a possibility. In this case, as costs of collective action decrease and large groups are needed to gain victory, alliances between a specific factor and the mobile factor become more likely, as do alliances between various specific factors. The numbers of the mobile factor group are large enough to make it worthwhile for specific factor groups to try to bring them into a coalition, provided the stake can be made large enough to motivate their participation.

Finally, in the lower-right corner (where factors are specific and institutions non-majoritarian, but costs of collective action are low) even dispersed losers can organize because costs are low. Any group could win, however, because the size of a group is not important to political victory. This cell, too, appears to yield few interesting predictions.

As should be clear from Figure 3, the two major models of international trade policy coalitions carry with them hidden assumptions—one about the severity of costs of collective action, the other about the domestic political institutions which make trade policy. In any case the models presume ideal types of political organization which may not exist. Without considering political variables, economic explanations are biased, and vice versa.

V. CONCLUSIONS

The narrowest purpose of this paper has been to review the determinants of trade policy coalitions. Although recent studies have stressed economic factors such as abundance and mobility of factors of production, we have argued that other more political factors (collective action costs, political institutions) are likely to be just as important. Furthermore, we have argued that these effects are interactive, the effects of some of these variables depending on the levels of others. The Stolper-Samuelson model really requires that collective action costs be low for Rogowski's broad trade policy coalitions to emerge: if there are collective action problems and factors are perfectly mobile, trade policy coalitions will not necessarily form along class lines and in fact may not form at all, due to familiar collective action problems. The Ricardo-Viner model, in contrast, is much more amenable to the incorporation of varying degrees of collective action costs. We made a related argument regarding domestic political institutions, suggesting that the Stolper-Samuelson theorem is more consistent with a majoritarian mode of policy making, while the Ricardo-Viner model is more consistent with a non-majoritarian or interest group politics model. In all these ways the paper raises broader issues about the interplay of politics and economics, while laying out a calculus of preferences, effects and likely actions and outcomes which anyone contemplating the domestic effects of trade needs to consider. . . .

REFERENCES

Olson, Mancur, Jr. 1965. *The Logic of Collective Action.* Cambridge, Mass.: Harvard University Press.

Pareto, Vilfredo. 1927. *Manual of Political Economy.* New York: A. M. Kelley.

Schattschneider, E. E. 1935. *Politics, Pressures and the Tariff.* New York: Prentice Hall.

22

Are Your Wages Set in Beijing?

RICHARD B. FREEMAN

During the 1990s, the wages of unskilled workers in the United States fell in real (inflation-adjusted) terms. In Europe, in an analogous trend, real wages have remained stable, but unemployment levels for unskilled workers have dramatically increased. Economist Richard B. Freeman surveys the growing literature on the effect of trade on wages and employment. Drawing on the theories used to understand the political economy of trade in earlier readings (Rogowski, Reading 20; Alt and Gilligan, Reading 21), Freeman argues that there are good economic reasons for expecting trade to lead to the "immiseration" of low-skilled workers in developed or capital-abundant states. Factor prices, including wages, in different national markets that are open to trade should tend to converge.

Freeman then examines the empirical evidence and finds the picture more mixed. The consensus opinion is that trade may have contributed to a fall in real wages for low-skilled workers, but it cannot itself account for the scope of the existing problem. Estimates of the future effects of trade are even more uncertain. Freeman has analyzed an important trend within the international economy. Whether the effects of trade are real or partly exaggerated, his analysis helps explain why in many developed countries labor is moving into the protectionist camp.

In the 1980s and 1990s, the demand for less-skilled workers fell in advanced countries. In the United States, this showed up primarily in falling real wages for less-educated men, although hours worked by these men also declined. In OECD-Europe, it took the form of increased unemployment for the less skilled. Over the same period, manufacturing imports from third world countries to the United States and OECD-Europe increased greatly. In 1991, the bilateral U.S. merchandise trade deficit with China was second only to its deficit with Japan.

The rough concordance of falling demand for less-skilled workers with increased imports of manufacturing goods from third world countries has created a lively debate about the economic consequences of trade between advanced and developing countries. This debate differs strikingly from the debate over the benefits and costs of trade in the last few decades. In the 1960s and 1970s, many in the third world feared that trade would impoverish them, or push them to the periphery of the world economy; virtually no one in advanced countries was concerned about competition from less-developed countries. In the 1980s and 1990s, by contrast, most of the third world has embraced the global economy; whereas many in the advanced world worry over the possible adverse economic effects of trade. The new debate focuses on one issue: whether in a global economy the wages or employment of low-skill workers in advanced countries have been (or will be) determined by the global supply of less-skilled labor, rather than by domestic labor market conditions. Put crudely, to what extent has, or will, the pay of low-skilled Americans or French or Germans be set in Beijing, Delhi and Djakkarta rather than in New York, Paris or Frankfurt?

On one side of the new debate are those who believe in factor price equalization—that in a global economy the wages of workers in advanced countries cannot remain above those of comparable workers in less-developed countries. They fear that the wages or employment of the less skilled in advanced countries will be driven down due to competition from low-wage workers overseas. On the other side of the debate are those who reject the notion that the traded goods sector can determine labor outcomes in an entire economy or who stress that the deleterious effects of trade on demand for the less skilled are sufficiently modest to be offset readily through redistributive social policies funded by the gains from trade. They fear that neo-protectionists will use arguments about the effect of trade on labor demand to raise trade barriers and reduce global productivity. . . .

This paper provides a viewer's guide to the debate. I review the two facts that motivate the debate: the immiseration of less-skilled workers in advanced countries and the increase in manufacturing imports from less-developed countries. Then I summarize the arguments and evidence brought to bear on them and give my scorecard on the debate. I conclude by examining the fear that, whatever trade with less-developed countries did in the past, it will impoverish less-skilled Americans and western Europeans in the future, as China, India, Indonesia and others make greater waves in the world economy.

THE IMMISERATION OF LOW-SKILL WORKERS IN THE UNITED STATES AND EUROPE

An economic disaster has befallen low-skilled Americans, especially young men. Researchers using several data sources—including household survey data from the Current Population Survey, other household surveys, and establishment surveys—have documented that wage inequality and skill differentials in earnings and employment increased sharply in the United States from the mid-1970s through the 1980s and into the 1990s. The drop in the relative position of the less skilled shows up in a number of ways: greater earnings differentials between those with more and less education; greater earnings differentials between older and younger workers; greater differentials between high-skilled and low-skilled occupations; in a wider earnings distribution overall and within demographic and skill groups, and in less time worked by low-skill and low-paid workers.

If the increase in earnings inequality had coincided with rapidly growing real earnings, so that the living standards of low-skill workers increased or fell a trifle, no one would ring alarm bells. But in the past decade or two, real earnings have grown sluggishly at best, and fallen for men on average. The economic position of low-skill men has fallen by staggering amounts. For instance, the real hourly wages of males with 12 years of schooling dropped by some 20 percent from 1979 to 1993; for entry-level men with 12 years, the drop has been 30 percent! The real hourly earnings of all men in the bottom decile of the earnings distribution fell similarly since the early or mid-1970s, while that of men in the upper decile has risen modestly—producing a huge increase in inequality.

Similar economic forces have led to somewhat different problems in Europe. For most of the period since World War II, OECD-Europe had lower unemployment rates than the United States. For example, in 1973, the rate of unemployment was 2.9 percent for OECD-Europe compared to 4.8 percent for the United States, and the ratio of employment to population was as high in Europe as in the United States. This changed in the 1980s. From 1983 to 1991 unemployment averaged 9.3 percent in OECD-Europe compared to 6.7 percent in the United States. Unemployment in OECD-Europe seems destined to remain above American levels throughout the '90s decade. The ratio of employment to the population of working age and the hours worked per employee has also fallen in Europe relative to the United States, adding to the U.S.-Europe gap in the utilization of labor. In addition, unemployment has been highly concentrated in Europe: in OECD-Europe, nearly half of unemployed workers are without jobs for over a year, compared to less than 10 percent of unemployed workers in the United States. . . .

If wage inequality had risen in Europe as much as in the United States, or was near U.S. levels, or if the real wages of low-skill Europeans had fallen, high joblessness would be a devastating indictment of European reliance on institutional forces to determine labor market outcomes. In effect, Europe would be suffering unemployment with no gain in equality. But in general, Europe has avoided an American level of inequality or changes in inequality, and wages at the bottom of the distribution rose rather than fell. By the early 1990s, workers in the bottom tiers of the wage distribution in Europe had higher compensation than did workers in the bottom tiers in the United States. Western Europe's problem was one of jobs, not of wages: the workers whose wages have fallen through the floor in the United States—the less skilled and (except in Germany) the young—were especially likely to be jobless in Europe.

The rise in joblessness in Europe is thus the flip side of the rise in earnings inequality in the U.S. The two outcomes reflect the same phenomenon—a relative decline in the demand against the less skilled that has overwhelmed the long-term trend decline in the relative supply of less-skilled workers. In the United States, where wages are highly flexible, the change in the supply-demand balance lowered the wages of the less skilled. In Europe, where institutions buttress the bottom parts of the wage distribution, the change produced unemployment. The question then is not simply why the United States and Europe experienced different labor market problems in the 1980s and 1990s, but what factors depressed the relative demand for low-skill labor in both economies?

TRADE BETWEEN THE UNITED STATES AND EUROPE WITH THE THIRD WORLD

One thing that distinguishes the 1980s and 1990s from earlier decades following World War II is the growth of the global economy, which in practical terms can be seen in reduced trade barriers, increased trade, highly mobile capital, and rapid transmission of technology across national lines. Multinationals, who locate plants and hire workers almost anywhere in the world, have replaced national companies as the cutting edge capitalist organization. The most commonly used indicator of globalization is the ratio of exports plus imports to gross domestic product. In the United States, this ratio rose from 0.12 in 1970 to 0.22 in 1990. Trade ratios rose substantially throughout the OECD. Although most trade is among advanced countries, trade with less-developed countries increased greatly. By 1990, 35 percent of U.S. imports were from less-developed countries, compared with 14 percent in 1970. In the European Community, 12 percent of imports were from less-developed countries, compared with 5 percent in 1970. (The less-developed country portion of European trade is lower largely because trade among U.S. states doesn't count as imports and exports, while trade among European countries does, thus inflating the overall total of intra-Europe trade.) In 1992, 58 percent of less-developed country exports to the western industrialized nations consisted of (light) manufacturing goods, compared with 5 percent in 1955.

The increase in manufacturing imports from less-developed countries presumably reflects the conjoint working of several forces. Reductions in trade barriers must have contributed: why else the huge international effort to cut tariff and nontariff barriers embodied in GATT, NAFTA, WTO and other agreements? The shift in development strategies of less-developed countries, from import substitution to export promotion, must also have played a part. Perhaps World Bank and IMF pressures on less-developed countries to export as a way of paying off their debts contributed as well. Advanced country investments in manufacturing in less-developed countries also presumably increased their ability to compete in the world market.

Changes in the labor markets of less-developed countries have also contributed to the increased role of those countries in world markets. The less-developed country share of the world workforce increased from 69 percent in 1965 to 75 percent in 1990; and the mean years of schooling in the less-developed country world rose from 2.4 years in 1960 to 5.3 years in 1986. The less-developed country share of world manufacturing employment grew from 40 percent in 1960 to 53 percent in 1986. Finally, diffusion of technology through multinational firms has arguably put less-developed countries and advanced countries on roughly similar production frontiers. Skills, capital infrastructure, and political stability—rather than pure technology—have become the comparative advantage of advanced countries.

Given these two facts, it is natural to pose the question: to what extent might trade with less-developed countries be reducing demand for less-skilled labor in the advanced countries?

ECONOMIC THEORY: FACTOR PRICE EQUALIZATION

At the conceptual heart of the debate over the effects of trade on the labor market is the strength of forces for factor price equalization. Consider a world where producers have the same technology; where trade flows are determined by factor endowments, so that advanced countries with many skilled workers compared to unskilled workers import commodities made by less-skilled workers in developing countries, while developing countries with more unskilled labor import commodities made by skilled labor in advanced countries; and where trade establishes a single world price for a good. Trade makes less-skilled labor in advanced countries and skilled labor in developing countries less scarce and can thus be expected to reduce their wages. By contrast, trade will increase the production of goods made by skilled labor in advanced countries and by less-skilled labor in developing countries and can thus be expected to raise their wages. In equilibrium, under specified conditions, the long-term outcome is that factor prices are equalized throughout the world: the less-skilled worker in the advanced country is paid the same as his or her competitor in a developing country; and similarly for the more-skilled workers.

But does factor price equalization . . . capture economic reality? For years, many trade economists rejected factor price equalization as a description of the world. The wide, and in some cases increasing, variation in pay levels among countries seemed to make it a textbook proposition of little relevance. . . .

To labor economists, the observation that trade with less-developed countries places some economic pressures on low-skill westerners is a valuable reminder that one cannot treat national labor markets in isolation. If the West can import children's toys produced by low-paid Chinese workers at bargain basement prices, surely low-skilled westerners, who produce those toys at wages 10 times those of the Chinese, will face a difficult time in the job market. It isn't even necessary that the West import the toys. The threat to import them or to move plants to less-developed countries to produce the toys may suffice to force low-skilled westerners to take a cut in pay to maintain employment. In this situation, the open economy can cause lower pay for low-skilled westerners even without trade; to save my job, I accept Chinese-level pay, and that prevents imports. The invisible hand would have done its job, with proper invisibility.

For the factor price equalization argument to carry weight, advanced countries should export commodities to less-developed countries made with relatively skilled labor and import commodities from less-developed countries produced by unskilled labor. U.S. trade operates in just this way. American exports are skill intensive: our net exports are positive for such goods as scientific instruments, airplanes, and in intellectual property, including software. Imports make less intensive use of skilled labor: our net imports are positive for toys, footwear and clothing. Europe also imports low skill intensive goods from less-developed countries and exports high skill intensive goods. While factors other than labor skills affect trade—natural resource endowments, infrastructure capital, perhaps capital overall, technological changes that diffuse slowly—the flows of goods between advanced countries and less-developed countries seems to fit the Hecksher-Ohlin model well enough to raise the specter of factor price equalization for low-skilled westerners.

The argument for complete factor price equalization is, to be sure, an extreme one. It implies that in an economy fully integrated in the world trading system, domestic market developments have *no* effect on wages. Instead, there is a single global labor market that sets the factor prices for inputs, even if trade is only a small part of the economy. Whether 5 percent or 95 percent of less-skilled workers are employed in import-competing activities, their pay is determined in Beijing. Transportation costs, immediacy of delivery, and such factors are assumed to be irrelevant in differentiating the location of production. If unskilled labor can readily switch from traded goods to nontraded goods, it would be a single factor, so that the pay of even those working in nontraded goods or services would be set in the global market. Only when *all* less-skilled workers are employed in nontraded activities or if those in nontraded activities have sector-specific skills that make them "different" from workers in traded activities (for some period) will their pay depend on domestic market considerations.

These predictions run counter to a wide body of evidence that domestic developments do affect wages: for instance, that the baby boom affected the pay of young workers; that the relative number of college graduates altered the premium paid for education; that sectoral developments affect pay in certain industries; that your wages are likely to be higher if your firm does well than if it is doing poorly. In the United States, wage differences among states and localities have persisted for decades despite free trade, migration, and capital flows. Among countries, wage differences between workers with seemingly similar skills have also persisted for decades, albeit exaggerated by the divergence between purchasing power parities and exchange rates, and by differences in skills that are hard to measure.

Given these considerations, factor price equalization should not be viewed as the Holy Grail giving the answer of economic science as to why demand fell for low-skill western workers in the 1980s and 1990s. Instead, the theory is a flag alerting us to the possibility that increased linkages with less-developed countries *may have* contributed to the immiseration of the less skilled, and pointing to some routes through which such linkages *may have* worked. The gap between "may have" contributed and "has" contributed is large—bridgeable only by empirical analysis, with all of its compromises and difficulties.

EMPIRICAL WORK

The effort to see whether or not trade has contributed to the growing immis-eration of low-skill workers in developed economies has taken two forms. One set of studies exploits data on the "factor content" of import and export industries to estimate the implicit change in factor endowments in advanced countries due to trade. A second set of studies exploits price data to see if increased imports from less-developed countries have induced sizable drops in the prices of goods produced by low-skilled westerners, which would reduce demand for their labor and lower their pay or disemploy them. The debate has drawn attention to problems with both sets of calculations.

Factor Content Analysis: Can the Tail Wag the Dog?

In factor content studies, analysts estimate the impact of trade on the demand for labor at given wages or, alternatively, on the nation's "effective" factor endowments, that is, the domestic *and* foreign labor inputs used to produce society's consumption bundle. Since the U.S. imports goods that make heavy use of low-skilled labor, and exports goods that make heavy use of high-skilled labor, trade with developing countries reduces the relative demand for less-skilled labor in the United States, or, if you prefer, increases the relative supply of less-skilled labor. Given estimates of the labor skills used in various sectors, one can estimate how changes in imports and exports altered the demand-supply balance for high- and low-skilled labor at given relative wages and prices. To see how the changed supply-demand balance for labor skills affected relative wages (the variable of interest in the United States), analysts transform the calculated shifts in quantities into changes in wages using esti-mates of the effect of changes in supply and demand on relative pay from other studies (for instance, studies of how the increase in the relative supply of college graduates on the domestic labor market affects their relative pay).

For example, if the United States imported 10 additional children's toys, which could be produced by five American workers, the effective supply of unskilled workers would increase by five (or alternatively, domestic demand for such workers would fall by five), compared with the alternative in which those 10 toys were produced domestically. This five-worker shift in the supply-demand balance would put pressure on unskilled wages to fall, causing those wages to fall in accord with the relevant elasticity. Any trade-balancing flow of exports would, contrarily, reduce the effective endowment of skilled workers (raise their demand) and thus increase their pay. . . .

Several recent studies . . . find that changes in actual trade flows have not displaced all that many low-skill workers from manufacturing (taken as the major traded goods sector) for one basic reason: that only a moderate proportion of workers now work in manufacturing. In 1993, roughly 15 percent of American workers were employed in manufacturing. The vast majority of unskilled workers were in nontraded goods, such as retail trade and various services. In such a world it is hard to see how pressures on wages emanating from traded goods can determine wages economy-wide. To be sure, the strong version of factor price equalization argues that the wage of low-skilled labor is set in a global market, affecting workers in both traded goods and untraded services. But this seems implausible. Compare two situations: in the first, 50 percent of the nation's unskilled workers are in import-competing industries, and increased trade with less-developed countries displaces one in 10 of them; in the second, only 1 percent of unskilled workers are in import-competing industries, and trade displaces one in 10 of them. To argue that trade would have the same effect in both cases seems far-fetched, dependent on the simplifying assumptions of the trade model (notably that elasticities of supply are infinite, with no variation in products produced in developed and less-developed countries).

However, Adrian Wood's (1994) factor content study . . . reaches a different conclusion. Wood argues that standard factor content analyses understate the effect of trade on employment. Once the proper corrections are made, he argues, trade becomes the root cause of the fall in demand for less-skilled workers in advanced countries.

Wood begins by arguing that estimated changes in effective labor endowments, based on existing labor input coefficients in advanced countries, are biased against finding a big disemployment effect. The reason is that less-developed countries export different and noncompeting goods within sectors than the goods produced by advanced countries; for example, the United States might make high-tech toys, while the Chinese make low-tech toys. The typical factor content analysis would observe the import of low-tech Chinese toys and then multiply that by the quantity of labor, of various skills, used in the U.S. manufacture of high-tech toys. But if the low-tech toys were made in the United States, manufacturers would in fact use more less-skilled labor than in producing high-tech toys. To correct for this possible bias, Wood uses the labor input coefficients for developing countries, adjusted for labor demand responses to higher western wages, rather than those for the advanced countries. With this procedure, he estimates that labor demand due to imports of manufactures fell by "ten times the conventional ones" (Wood, 1994, p. 10).

The problem of differing mixes of products within industries is real. Ideally, one would like the change in labor input coefficients associated with the actual change in goods produced domestically as a result of imports. My guess is that the conventional factor content approach does underestimate the effect of trade on demand for low-skilled labor, but I also suspect that Wood's upward adjustment is probably excessive.

Wood (1994) also asserts that trade with less-developed countries induced substantial labor-saving innovation in the traded goods sector. This further reduces demand for unskilled labor. Although there is no reason to expect innovation to respond to import competition any more or less than to any other form of competition, the problem of induced technical change is a real one, and Wood's adjustment is potentially in the right direction. But he may be claiming too much for this factor. . . . As the evidence stands, the claim that trade induces large labor-saving technological change in low-skill industries is not especially strong.

Standard factor content analysis studies indicate that trade can account for 10–20 percent of the overall fall in demand for unskilled labor needed to explain rising wage differentials in the United States or rising joblessness in Europe. If one accepts Wood's (1994) adjusted factor content analysis for traded goods and his estimate of induced technological change, then trade accounts for about half of the requisite fall in demand for labor. Where can we find the other half?

As a final step, Wood assumes that trade-induced labor-saving technological changes spill over to nontraded sectors, where most nonskilled workers are employed. This final assumption leads him to conclude that increased trade with less-developed countries accounts for all of the rise of inequality in the United States and all of the increase in unskilled unemployment in Europe.

If one is going to use a factor content approach to attribute immiseration of the less skilled in the West to globalization, Wood's clear and careful approach shows the way. But as he is fully aware, some of the steps along the way are arguable or problematic. . . .

Price Effects Studies and Other Evidence

Two additional bodies of evidence have been brought to bear on this debate: price data on the goods produced by low-skill labor; and data on changes in the employment of skilled and less-skilled workers in industries that produce traded and nontraded goods. In the trade model, price declines in import-competing sectors should lower the relative wages of unskilled labor, which those sectors use intensely, and ultimately the prices of all goods and services produced by those workers. The lower relative pay of the less skilled ought further to lead firms to substitute them for more expensive skilled labor throughout the economy.

Two studies have looked for evidence that the prices of sectors that extensively use unskilled labor have fallen greatly. Lawrence and Slaughter (1993) correlate changes in import prices with the share of production workers across industries and find that when prices are adjusted for changes in total factor productivity, the prices of less skill intensive goods fell only slightly. Sachs and Shatz (1994) examine output prices for all of manufacturing, not just imports, which provides a larger sample of industries. After adjusting for productivity changes that should independently affect prices, they find a modest negative relation between the production worker share of employment and changes in industry prices. They also find that prices fell faster in sectors that make more intensive use of low-skilled workers in the 1980s than in previous decades compared with sectors that use fewer low-skilled workers. They conclude that relative prices exerted some pressure on the pay of the less skilled, but not by enough to account for a significant widening of wage inequality. . . .

Like the factor content studies, price studies provide a clue to how trade could affect relative wages—the greater the estimated import-induced reduction in the prices of goods produced by low-skill labor, the greater the likely trade effect on wages and employment—but they also are far from the final word. . . .

CONCLUSION

The debate over whether increased trade with less-developed countries is the main cause of the immiseration of the less-skilled has raised numerous conceptual and empirical issues, as well as some hackles. Adherents of one side in the debate, or of one approach to the problem, have found it easy to criticize the other. Most criticisms have at least an element of truth, making scoring the debate a bit of a judgment call. Largely because neither the factor content nor the price analysis comes up with a smoking gun, and because demand for the less skilled has fallen even in nontraded goods sectors, my scorecard reads: trade matters, but it is neither all that matters nor the primary cause of observed changes.

That we lack compelling evidence that trade underlies the problems of the less skilled in the past does not, of course, rule out the possibility that trade will dominate labor market outcomes in the future. Indeed, it is commonplace in the trade-immiseration debate for those who reject trade as *the* explanation of the past decline in the demand for the less skilled to hedge their conclusion by noting that there is a good chance that in the future, pressures for factor price equalization will grow. Maybe your wages were not set in Beijing yesterday or today, but tomorrow they will be.

I have problems with this prognostication. Economists do not have a good record as soothsayers, and neither trade nor labor economists are exceptions.

Trade economists once worried about the perpetual dollar shortage; believed that flexible exchange rates would be more stable than fixed exchange rates; and saw the Common Market as the cure-all to European problems. Labor economists declared unions were dead just before the formation of the CIO; worried about the falling return to skills and were as shocked as anyone else by the increased inequality of the 1980s; did not expect the Civil Rights Act to raise the demand for black workers; and so on. For what it is worth, I am not convinced that continued expansion of trade with less-developed countries spells doom for low-skill westerners. As more and more low-skilled western workers find employment in the nontraded goods service sector, the potential for imports from less-developed countries to reduce their employment or wages should lessen. In the standard trade model, a factor used exclusively in nontraded goods has its pay determined by the domestic economy. The closer western economies get to this situation, the smaller should be the trade-induced pressures on low-skilled workers. Wildly heralded trade agreements such as the U.S.-Canadian agreement, the Common Market, and NAFTA have not dominated our wages and employment in the ways their advocates or opponents forecast.

In the past, other factors have been more important than trade in the well-being of the less skilled: technological changes that occur independent of trade; unexpected political developments, such as German reunification and instability in various regions of the world; policies to educate and train work-ers; union activities; the compensation policies of firms; and welfare state and related social policies. In the future, I expect that these factors will continue to be more important. I could, of course, be utterly wrong. The best we can do is probe and poke at the evidence and arguments, and present our analyses and prognostications with appropriate humility.

REFERENCES

Lawrence, Robert, and Matthew Slaughter, "Trade and U.S. Wages: Great Sucking Sound or Small Hiccup?" In *Brookings Papers on Economic Activity, Microeconomics.* Vol. 2. Washington, D.C.: Brookings Institution, 1993.

Sachs, Jeff, and Howard Shatz, "Trade and Jobs in U.S. Manufacturing," *Brookings Papers on Economic Activity.* Vol. 1. Washington, D.C.: Brookings Institution, 1994, pp. 1–84.

Wood, Adrian, *North-South Trade, Employment and Inequality.* Oxford: Clarendon Press, 1994.

23

What You Should Know about
Globalization and the World Trade Organization

ALAN V. DEARDORFF AND ROBERT M. STERN

Economists have long recognized the gains from international trade; in fact, the study of these gains is where modern economics began. Why, then, has the World Trade Organization (WTO)—the institution at the center of the world trading system—provoked so much opposition? In this article, Alan V. Deardorff and Robert M. Stern review the case for freer trade and examine the role of the WTO in promoting trade liberalization. They note that domestic distributive concerns underlie much of the controversy: opponents are spurred by fears that the WTO accelerates the opening of global markets to the detriment of scarce factors, industry-specific factors, and factors that are unable to move or retrain. The authors also note that the WTO constrains the policies of powerful nations and thereby helps to defend smaller, weaker nations from the nationalistic actions of great powers. Recognition of the WTO's international power has motivated social activists to try and leverage that influence to promote other agendas, such as improving the environment and protecting human rights.

1. INTRODUCTION

The term "globalization" has only recently become commonplace, yet trade economists like us have been studying it and teaching about it for decades, even centuries. The institution of the World Trade Organization (WTO) has only recently come to exist, yet legal experts on international trade have been studying and teaching for almost half a century about its predecessor, the GATT, as well. In both cases, specialists in international trade have argued the benefits, but also acknowledged the costs, of international economic integration and the institutions that facilitate it. Yet until recently ours was a specialty that only a few paid attention to, especially in the United States where the size of domestic markets seemed to render the rest of the world of only secondary importance. Only in the 1990s did America begin to wake up to the significance of world markets and institutions. By the end of the decade, at the Seattle ministerial meeting of the WTO in December 1999, a host of voices were raised against both. This has turned our academic specialty from obscure to reviled in barely a moment. In this paper we try to set the record straight.

Our purpose is to clarify, for both globalization and the WTO, what they are and what they mean to the world. We do not primarily intend to be advocates of either, and we will acknowledge and explain both the costs and benefits of both. But inevitably, having spent our careers consistently finding the benefits to outweigh the costs, we will conclude that here. Yes, there are those who lose from world markets and institutions, and some of them are understandably opposed when these intrude into their lives. But overall, we agree with almost all others who have looked at these issues carefully and objectively (and many, admittedly, who have not), that the vast majority of people in the world are ultimately made better off by the spread of global markets and the efforts of the WTO to keep those markets reasonably free. To be sure, there are problems that need to be addressed, and we will mention them too and possible solutions for them. But even in their current imperfect form, the WTO and the open international markets that it has fostered are far better for the world economy than the alternatives that would likely arise if they were disbanded and reversed.

Our paper will be in two parts, the first on globalization and the second on the WTO. In both, we will first define and document the phenomena at issue, then identify the major groups who benefit and lose from their effects. Much of this discussion, especially for globalization, will inevitably repeat what trade economists have been saying about trade for two centuries, for the issues are not new. However, they have taken new forms in recent years, and the WTO has likewise expanded the institutional scope of its predecessor, the GATT, in ways that also need to be addressed. In particular, events in Seattle raised many issues that had only recently been seen in discussions of international trade, and we will do our best to describe what these were and what actually happened in Seattle. In both parts of the paper, we will conclude with some discussion of what the options are for action, if any, and what we believe should be done. The paper concludes with a final section that tries in much briefer form to answer the question of our title, listing what we believe to be the most important things that the public should know about globalization and the WTO.

2. GLOBALIZATION

What Is It?

Everybody is writing about globalization these days, and the word means different things to different people. We take it to mean the increase in international transactions in markets for goods, services, and some factors of production, plus the growth and expanded scope of institutions that straddle national borders—including firms, governments, international institutions, and nongovernmental organizations (NGOs). At the most basic level, globalization is growth of international trade. But it is also the expansion of much else, including foreign direct investment (FDI), multinational corporations (MNCs), integration of world capital markets and resulting financial capital flows, extraterritorial reach of government policies, attention by NGOs to issues that span the globe, and the constraints on government policies imposed by international institutions. All of this has fostered an increasing sense of helplessness among many who feel that their lives and their economic options are being determined not by themselves, or even by their countrymen and their own governments, but by external forces over which they have no control. Residents of small countries may have experienced this long ago, but in the United States and other large countries, this is a new experience, and for many it is disagreeable.

Evidence of globalization is not hard to find, although the surprise may be that the current wave of globalization is not the first. In many ways, the world economy reached a peak of globalization just before World War I, when trade and FDI attained what were then unprecedented levels that are still quite remarkable given the technologies that were available for transportation and communication. But the current wave of globalization has far surpassed that of a century ago.

Figure 1 shows one indicator of the growth of trade over the last half century. Measured as an index of the ratio of world exports to world GDP (1990=100), the graph shows that this ratio increased fairly steadily through the early 1970s. It then stalled until the mid-1980s, when its growth resumed, and it grew especially fast in the mid-1990s. By 1998 it was more than three times what it was in 1950. . . .

FIGURE 1   Index (1990 = 100) of Ratio of World Merchandise Exports to World GDP (Adapted from WTO, International Trade Statistics, 1999)

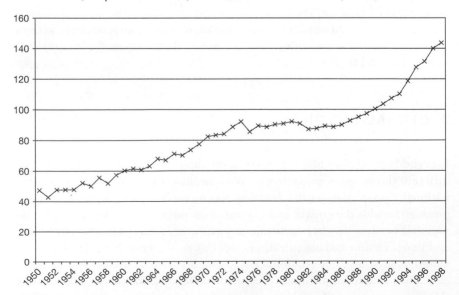

FIGURE 2 Foreign Assets as a Percentage of World GDP (Adapted from Crafts, 2000)

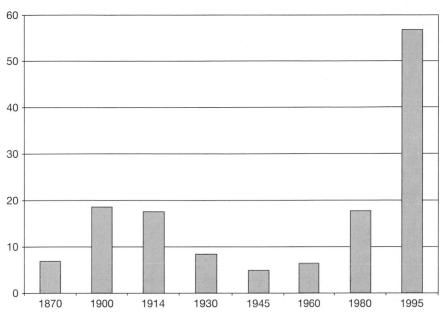

Increased international capital flows have been most pronounced in portfolio investment, which, like trade, displayed an earlier peak prior to World War I. Figure 2 shows foreign assets as a percentage of world GDP for selected years. The pre-WWI levels were not reached again until around 1980, after which they grew threefold by 1995. We do not have exactly comparable information on FDI or the presence of MNCs in the world economy, although information reported by Crafts (2000) shows that both were also important in 1914. The real stock of FDI relative to world GDP rose by 59% from 1960 to 1995. Thus, at least in the second half of the twentieth century, both international trade and international capital flows of various kinds were increasing steadily, and this is much of what has come to be called globalization.

What has caused these changes? Two obvious reasons are technology and policy. Improvements in both transportation and communication have increased globalization in all markets, trends that may be accelerating today with the Internet. Policies, in contrast, have alternated direction over the years, restricting international transactions and mobility after World War I, then opening up after World War II. . . .

Is this, then, all there is to globalization—increased trade and capital flows caused by improved technology and reduced policy barriers? Not really.

Other aspects of economic life have also become globalized. Governments are increasingly sensitive to policies used by other countries. NGOs look increasingly beyond borders, either because their issues are intrinsically global (the hole in the ozone layer), or because they view their causes to be of worldwide importance (human rights). Corporations increasingly operate across national borders, and have grown to sizes that dwarf some countries, achieving leverage over national governments that may free the companies from control. Again, all of these changes had counterparts in the nineteenth century, but that does not make their importance today any less.

Finally, the designers of the postwar institutions explicitly envisioned the need for countries to cooperate, and sometimes to sacrifice narrow national interests for the greater good. These institutions have been very successful, at least in expanding their own power and importance. The World Bank, the IMF, and now perhaps the WTO have reached the size that they can now grow on their own momentum. Some find these changes gratifying; others find them threatening. And all are part of globalization.

Whom Does It Help and Whom Does It Hurt?

At its core, globalization means that international markets are becoming more integrated. Such integration has been the subject of international trade theory for two centuries, and economists have a good understanding of its effects. In this section, we review these insights from trade theory.

STATIC EFFECTS OF TRADE. Who gains from trade? The first answer is consumers. That is, everybody in a country stands to gain from trade in their role as consumers of goods and services. For many reasons—including comparative advantage, economies of scale, increased competition, and access to a greater variety of products—a country's average consumer, with an average income, is better off with trade than without. That is, the average person's income will buy a larger, more desirable bundle of goods and services with trade than without, increasing their material standard of living. This proposition, called the "gains from trade," has been shown theoretically in all sorts of economic models. With only a few exceptions—which economists generally view as unlikely to reverse the broad conclusion in practice—it applies to all countries comparing trade to not trading at all. The argument extends to further degrees of openness, as well as to other kinds of openness such as international movement of capital. Thus, the fundamental case for trade and globalization is that it raises the average person's standard of living.

However, this benefit applies to the average person, with average income. Income is not equally distributed, and trade may not benefit everybody. A fundamental result of trade theory, the Stolper–Samuelson (SS) theorem, identifies winners and losers from trade in terms of the national abundance and scarcity of factors of production, such as labor and capital, from which they derive their incomes. Owners of abundant factors tend to gain more than average from trade, while owners of scarce factors are made unambiguously worse off. More general models allow for additional sources of gain from trade and suggest that even owners of scarce factors may gain, in which case SS says only that they gain less than average. But the possibility remains that they actually lose.

So trade theory tells us that, indeed, there may be losers as well as gainers from trade and globalization. Who are the losers? In the United States, with its abundance of capital, education, and land, the scarce factor is clearly labor. Not that we have a small labor force—we do not. But we have even more of everything else. In this relative sense, we are especially scarce in those workers without a great deal of education, what we will simply call labor. Therefore, trade theory tells us that the group in the United States most likely to lose from globalization, or at best to gain less than everyone else, is labor. This is hardly a surprise. Growing opposition to globalization by organized labor shows that they are well aware of this. The surprise may be that economists, who tend to favor trade, would agree. But we do.

It follows from this, too, that trade is likely to increase income inequality in advanced countries. Because labor has lower income than those with income from other sources, and because trade lowers the relative wage, it tends to make the poor relatively poorer. Leaving aside the legitimate question of whether an increased return to some other factors, such as the return to education, may actually increase the opportunity to escape poverty by becoming skilled, we therefore expect in the short run at least that globalization will increase inequality in rich countries like the United States. Empirical studies . . . confirm that increased trade accounts for a portion (although much less than half) of the increased inequality observed in the United States since 1980.

Why, then, do we claim that there are gains from trade? Because we are confident from both theory and experience that the winners gain more than the losers lose, enough so that policy could potentially compensate them, leaving everyone better off. In the long run, with some mobility across population groups and with programs to permit the whole population to share in the country's income, most people can expect to be better off with trade than without.

The Stolper—Samuelson theorem applies also to LDCs, but there the scarce factor is different. Being poor, LDCs are the mirror image of the United States, with labor abundant and most other factors scarce, especially capital and education. These belong to the elite, who therefore lose from trade, according to SS. Labor in LDCs will gain. Since labor in LDCs is far poorer than labor in developed countries, globalization can be expected to reduce income inequality worldwide, even while it may increase inequality within rich countries.

Are there other gainers and losers from trade, besides the owners of abundant and scarce factors? Yes, and many of them are obvious. Through trade, some industries expand and others contract. Many people are invested in "industry specific" capital, human and/or physical, in particular industries— skills and equipment that are useful only within an industry. These people gain or lose along with their industries, and some can find the basis for their livelihoods destroyed, a serious cost that public policy can usually only partially acknowledge. For some, these costs continue for months or even years, as they relocate, retrain, reinvest, and otherwise readjust. Others, especially those later in life, may never recover. Trade theory does not in any way dismiss these costs as unimportant or even as smaller than other gains. Economists therefore usually favor only gradual movement toward freer trade, so that these adjustment costs can be accommodated within the routine ups and downs of markets.

Nonetheless owners of contracting-industry specific factors are a major source of concern in response to globalization. These include, for example, American owners and workers in textile and apparel firms, India's skilled workers in steel mills that were built as it attempted self-sufficient industrialization, and Mexico's small farmers of corn (maize) who now compete with more productive farms in the Midwest United States. These are only a few of the many groups throughout the world who have reason to be leery of globalization because of their dependence on industry-specific factors.

It is not only whole industries that expand and contract owing to trade. Within an industry, particular firms also win and lose, and firms that have prospered in a protected domestic market may not be the same ones that do well in a globalized economy. Anticipating in advance the identities of winners and losers may be impossible; but once the process is under way, particular firms will try to speed it up or slow it down, depending on how well they deal with its competitive pressures.

DYNAMIC EFFECTS OF TRADE. This discussion of gains and losses by particular firms and by specific factors is appropriate primarily to the short run, because in the longer run, people relocate, retrain, and otherwise readjust to changing circumstances. Gains and losses to abundant and scarce factors, in contrast, last longer, continuing even after factors have moved from failing firms and contracting industries into new and expanding ones. However, this is not the end of the story. Over even longer time horizons, the total of a country's factors changes with economic growth. It is reasonable to ask, then, who gains and loses from trade in the *very* long run, as sizes of countries and their rates of economic growth may change.

An easy answer to who gains and loses from trade in the very long run is: "Not us." Keynes said that in the long run we are all dead, and he was probably right. Thus whoever may be the long-run gainers and losers from globalization, they will be subsequent generations, not ourselves. That makes it harder to predict how they will fare, since we know less about them than we do about ourselves. In a dynamic economy like the United States, the owners of tomorrow's capital, land, and human capital may not be the descendants of those who own these factors today. Therefore, even without economic growth, our best bet for helping future generations is to maximize total income. Globalization does exactly that. Therefore we have some confidence that "everyone" in future generations will benefit from it.

Allowing for economic growth, this conclusion becomes still more likely, although the theoretical basis for it is less certain than the aggregate gains from trade in the shorter run. Economists do not in fact have a solid theoretical grasp of how trade affects economic growth, perhaps because growth itself is less well understood than the economics of static markets. Instead, there exist a variety of models of growth, and even more ideas of how trade may interact with growth. Some predict only that trade permits a country to grow larger than it otherwise would; others suggest that trade lets countries grow faster indefinitely. And there are also models where trade may be bad for growth.

But empirical evidence is much clearer that trade and globalization are good for growth. For half a century, most countries that have minimized trade have failed to grow, while those that have stressed exports have done much better. After a few successful countries demonstrated the benefits of trade for growth—especially the "four tigers" of Hong Kong, Singapore, South Korea, and Taiwan—other countries opened their markets and grew faster as well. This process has had setbacks, but few economists today doubt that open markets are beneficial for growth, even if we do not entirely know why.

If so, the case is even stronger that, in the very long run, entire populations gain from globalization. Those who are hurt by trade in the short run may lose relative to others. But because they will have a smaller slice of a larger pie, they may well be better off absolutely. That will surely be true if trade permits countries not just to grow to larger size, but to continue growing at faster rates indefinitely. In that case, globalization and trade are beneficial for everyone who will ultimately be alive.

EFFECTS OF INTERNATIONAL CAPITAL FLOWS. All of our discussion so far refers to the gainers and losers from trade. To a great extent, the gainers and losers from international capital flows are the same, since capital tends to flow in response to the same market forces as trade. There is, however, the added proviso that those who are internationally mobile tend to do better than those who are not. In a globalized economy where some groups are mobile and others are not, those who can move tend to benefit at the expense of others. In the last half century, capital has become increasingly mobile, while labor has not. We therefore expect some additional tendency for labor to lose, and capital to gain, from globalization.

This may account in part for a widely held perception that globalization is mostly for the benefit of large corporations. . . . It is certainly true that large corporations often (but not always) prosper in the international environment, and those small corporations who also prosper become large as a result. This is partly due to their ability to shift operations around the world to wherever makes the most economic sense. If they do this well, their stockholders gain. Of course, the larger the corporation the more likely is its stock to be widely held, including in the retirement funds of workers. Therefore the gains that accrue to capital accrue in part to those workers who manage to save during their working years.

Capital mobility has another quite different implication, however, that has little to do with returns to factors of production. Financial capital often takes very short-term forms, and it is highly liquid—able to move quickly into and out of a country or a currency in response to speculative expectations. Such movements generate another class of winners and losers: those who bet correctly and incorrectly on changes in financial markets. More important, however, are other victims of short-term capital flight. When expectations turn against a country or its currency, the resulting capital outflow batters many of those within the country. Borrowers default, banks become insolvent, credit to finance exports dries up, and the damage spreads through domestic markets causing recession that hurts much of the population regardless of their apparent exposure to foreign markets. This is the story of the Asian crisis of 1997, but it had happened before, and will probably happen again. The harm here is a byproduct of globalization, but also of the prosperity that globalization has previously contributed to via capital inflows.

OTHER EFFECTS OF GLOBALIZATION.   This completes our list of gainers and losers from globalization. But the discussion would be incomplete without mentioning several additional benefits and costs.

On the side of benefits, many say that globalization has reduced inflation. Inflation rates in many countries are low, and inflationary pressures have so far been restrained even where unemployment rates are also low. Some attribute this to a "new economy," in which technology and global markets together restrain firms from raising prices. If this continues and if it truly is a byproduct of globalization, then the lower inflation rate and the associated lower sustainable rate of unemployment benefit almost everyone.

Another possible benefit of globalization is an increased rate of technological progress and productivity growth. The slowdown in productivity growth that began in the mid-1970s appears to have reversed in the late 1990s, although it is too soon to know whether this will last. Here too, some argue that increased international competition has forced firms to innovate and to economize on labor, increasing productivity, and that this may be a lasting benefit of globalization. We see even less evidence to support this conclusion than the previous one, but it deserves mention.

Finally, globalization affects local cultures, causing changes that are sometimes admired, sometimes deplored. International trade, travel, and capital flows have exposed people everywhere to the products and sometimes the customs of other countries. This is evident in the United States, for example, with the variety of national cuisines now available in restaurants and super-markets. The same is happening even more in reverse, although many are unhappy to see it. US culture is spreading throughout the globe through trade, especially US exports of movies, music, and television programs. Young people around the world are adopting American styles of dress, music, and behavior, to the dismay of some of their elders and of those who fear the loss of their own cultural traditions. As economists, we are reluctant to dis-count the choices made freely by consumers anywhere. But cultures are public goods, and fragile ones at that. Globalization may bring cultures into conflict, and new policies for protecting them may be needed.

What Should Be Done about Globalization?

We have heard it said that globalization has so much momentum that it can-not be stopped. We disagree. Unforeseen events, and even deliberate policies with unforeseen consequences, could conceivably reverse the process of glo-balization, just as World War I and the Great Depression did once before. There is little reason to believe that the world is now immune from the sorts of worldwide disruptive events that have wracked it twice before within the last century. If such occur, much will depend on the wisdom and expertise of the world's leaders and their efforts to repair and restore the institutions of the world economy afterwards.

It is also conceivable that public policy could change direction and reverse globalization more deliberately. The institutions of the global economy—the World Bank, IMF, and WTO—would be incapacitated if the United States or Europe withdrew support, and considering recent controversies, this could happen. Without them, especially the WTO, the world could descend into a trade war or a series of competitive devaluations and tariff increases, just as in the 1930s. These were *not* irrational acts by uninformed policy-makers, mistakes that we would not repeat today. Instead, like the uncooperative strat-egies in the "prisoners' dilemma" of game theory, they were rational individ-ual responses to situations. Without some mechanism for international cooperation, the same could easily happen again.

While we believe that the benefits outweigh the costs for both trade and FDI, we are less sure of the free movement of financial capital. The disrup-tion and hardship caused by recent financial crises could perhaps have been avoided through better policies and decisions on the part of governments and international organizations, but a case can also be made for limited restric-tion on international movement of short-term capital. This is not our area of expertise, and we are reluctant to take a position on it. We merely note that smart people disagree on this issue, and leave it at that.

Aside from financial capital markets, then, what policies should be pursued with regard to globalization? As we have said, we believe that globalization has been largely a good thing, with the benefits exceeding the costs. Therefore we certainly do not want to see any reversal of direction, or a return to protection. Since most of the costs of globalization are costs of adjustment, analogous costs would arise again if we moved back in the other direction. Indeed, given the progress toward global and efficient markets, continued liberalization may be less painful than what has come before. In any case, we favor continuing liberalization of both trade and direct investment.

Many of the concerns of those who oppose globalization are legitimate, however, and should not be ignored. National governments and international institutions must address their concerns, assisting those who lose most from globalization wherever they can without undermining the process. How this can best be done deserves greater study and perhaps experimentation, but programs of adjustment assistance, wage insurance, and retraining should be considered.

3. THE WORLD TRADE ORGANIZATION

What Is It?

The World Trade Organization, created in 1995, is the successor to, and incorporates within it, the GATT—the General Agreement on Tariffs and Trade—which was a treaty among Western market economies at the end of World War II. Member countries agree to rules about when they may increase trade barriers, especially tariffs, in order to prevent them using trade policies that harm other countries. The GATT was also a forum for negotiation to reduce trade barriers. Presumably the WTO will do this as well, although it has not yet. The GATT oversaw eight rounds of multilateral trade negotiations, culminating in the Uruguay Round that created the WTO. The WTO also took on issues that GATT had not covered, including trade in services, tariffication in agriculture, and intellectual property protection.

The most important change in the WTO, compared to the GATT, may be its dispute settlement mechanism (DSM). The GATT permitted countries to complain against other countries for violating its rules. Each complaint was handled by a "panel" of experts who issued a report that, if adopted unanimously by GATT members, would require the offending party to either change its behavior or be subject to sanctions. However, unanimity meant that the offending party could block a report, in effect giving every country veto power over findings against itself. The surprise was that this ever worked at all, which it did.

The WTO reversed this bias, requiring instead a unanimous decision to block a report, and it therefore made the DSM much more effective. It also made other improvements, including the right to appeal. The intent was to provide viable enforcement for WTO rules, and it appears to have worked. The DSM has been used much more often than under the GATT, both by and against a wide range of countries. . . . Just as important, large countries (the US) have stopped going outside the GATT with their most important complaints.

Inevitably, however, the DSM has not worked to everyone's satisfaction. The WTO restricts policies that harm other countries, not only deliberately, but also inadvertently, as when policy restricts the options of another country's citizens. A contentious example was the "shrimp–turtle" case. A US law protected sea turtles from death in the nets of shrimp fishermen by prohibiting imports of shrimp caught without "turtle exclusion devices" (TEDs). Since it is impossible to tell from looking at a shrimp how it was caught, the law restricted imports from certain countries. These took the case to the WTO, which decided against the United States. In effect, this decision struck down US law, an intrusion into sovereignty that offended environmentalists and others. There have been other, similar examples.

The potential of the WTO to intrude in national affairs was also increased by its expanded coverage. The GATT was limited to trade in goods, even excluding certain sectors such as agriculture and textiles/apparel. The latter was covered instead by the GATT-sanctioned Multi-Fibre Arrangement (MFA), restricting developing-country exports to developed countries. The WTO changed all that, or at least it promises to. The Uruguay Round scheduled the elimination of the MFA, though the most difficult liberalization is postponed ("backloaded") for ten years. First steps were also taken in agriculture, converting existing NTBs to tariffs (tariffication) so as later to negotiate them downward. And trade in services was covered in a parallel agreement to the GATT, the General Agreement on Trade in Services (GATS).

The WTO also expanded to new areas. Most prominent and effective is its TRIPS (Trade Related Intellectual Property) Agreement covering intellectual property—primarily patents, copyrights, and trademarks. In addition, the WTO includes (as the GATT had before, actually) some small ways that countries may use trade policies for environmental purposes. However, the one area—much discussed—where the WTO has *not* been extended is labor standards and rights. Despite many in developed countries who favor using trade policies for this purpose, resistance from the developing world, as well as from corporations who employ labor there, has prevented it from even being discussed.

Whom Does It Help and Whom Does It Hurt?

With its expanded role, the WTO will affect many groups. But fundamentally it is still, like the GATT, a force for increased trade, and thus for much of globalization. The WTO has not, yet, done much on international capital movements, although its agreement on financial services will lower transactions costs for movements of financial capital. But it has done much to facilitate international trade. Those who gain and lose from the WTO, then, are also those who gain and lose from globalization.

Therefore, all that we said above applies here as well, about gains and losses to abundant and scarce factors, to industry-specific factors, and to factors unable to move or retrain. Because the WTO extends to previously excluded sectors—textiles, apparel, agriculture, and services—those principles will apply especially strongly to them. For example, developed-country textile workers, who have been protected for decades, have particular reason now to be concerned, if indeed the MFA will disappear. Developing-country textile workers have corresponding reason to be hopeful.

More generally, however, the WTO has an important institutional role beyond just fostering trade: to constrain countries from using trade policies that will hurt each other and themselves. Without such constraints, two things would guide countries' uses of trade policies. First, large countries would be able to use policies to gain at small countries' expense. Second, weak and misguided governments would be able to use policies to benefit themselves and their "cronies." The WTO, with its rules and its DSM for enforcement, deters both. It protects weak countries from strong countries, and also weak countries from themselves. This is true especially for poor countries. Thus, even though the WTO was mostly designed by rich countries and even corporations, its greatest beneficiaries may well be in the developing world.

Who loses from the WTO? Again, some of the losers are simply those who lose most from trade, and here we must point again to relatively unskilled labor in developed countries. It makes perfect sense that organized labor in developed countries should be skeptical of the benefits from the WTO, for theory predicts that greater trade will indeed hurt their members, at least relatively.

Aside from these effects of globalization itself, the rules of the WTO will also hurt those who would wish to break them. If there are large countries that seek to use their economic size at other countries' expense, then they will be frustrated by the WTO. Fortunately, we see little evidence in recent decades that the most powerful countries have sought to do this.

More likely losers, therefore, are those who seek to use trade policy for other legitimate purposes but run afoul of the WTO, as in the shrimp/turtle case. Those who seek to halt environmental degradation naturally wish to use trade policies to pursue their aims, since few other policies work across borders. Yet to do so risks violating the strictures of the WTO. Environmentalists have therefore sometimes been hamstrung by WTO rules, and they believe that they—or the environment—are hurt by the WTO.

It is true that the WTO makes the objectives of environmentalists harder to attain. Policies impose costs, and some are borne by other countries when one country unilaterally uses trade policies for environmental purposes. The WTO gives those costs more weight than if countries could act alone. This means that a lower level of environmental protection will result when these costs are factored in. This is as it should be, however, since global policy decisions should be based on global costs and benefits, including all aspects of all people's lives, not just the environment or one country. Environmentalists, whose role is narrower, will indeed make less progress when their interests are balanced against those of others.

Environmentalists might say, "Fine, but the WTO does not just balance other interests against the environment: it rules the environment out of court. All we want is for environmental concerns to be heard in the WTO." In fact, the WTO does include several environmental clauses, so even here the question is one of balance. How much role should environmental concerns play in justifying trade policies? Arguably, the current system has not done badly. The problem with using trade policies for environmental and other purposes is that they too easily push the cost onto others. The WTO has forced their advocates to find fairer ways to achieve those purposes. For example, the shrimp–turtle brouhaha led, more quietly, to shrimp fishermen being equipped with TEDs at developed country expense. We would say that this was the right solution all along.

There are other issues, besides the environment, whose advocates wish to use trade policies, including human rights and labor standards. For both, the United States especially has used trade policies in the past, against non-WTO members like China, and in our implementation of preferential trading arrangements. Some see the WTO as an enemy of human rights and labor standards. That conclusion is way too strong; but as with the environment, as the WTO interferes with policies that would otherwise be available to pursue these ends, the ends themselves will not be attained as fully.

In the case of human rights, the WTO does permit some use of trade policies, such as the economic sanctions that were used against Rhodesia in 1965 and against South Africa in 1985. Formally, these were permitted under GATT Article XXI, based on actions under the United Nations Charter for purposes of peace and security. The WTO does not permit unilateral sanctions for human rights, however.

In the case of labor standards and labor rights, the issue is more complex, partly because it is so difficult to separate the moral from the economic, and partly because of different views of what labor standards mean economically. Some labor standards, such as the prohibition of slave labor and exploitative child labor, are clearly moral issues. Others, such as a minimum wage, are economic. And still others, such as working conditions and child labor with the approval of caring parents, are somewhere in between. Where to draw the line, and who should draw it, are hard to say.

Economically, most labor standards affect the cost of labor, even when not explicitly about wages. But their effects depend on how one believes that wages are determined. From the perspective of competitive markets, which guides most economists on this issue, labor standards are mostly about the remuneration of labor in poor versus rich countries, and higher labor standards in the former primarily benefit the latter, putting developing country workers out of work. Another view, however, is that all labor remuneration is at the expense of capital, so that higher labor standards merely reduce profits. In economics, this second view makes most sense if employers have market power, something that globalization is in fact likely to undermine. But not everyone believes market economics, especially noneconomists, and there are plenty of subscribers to this second view among opponents of the WTO. In their view, by excluding labor standards as a basis for trade policy, the WTO helps capitalists and hurts workers, everywhere. But modern economics suggests that only developed-country workers may be hurt, while the true beneficiaries of the WTO are the developing-country workers whom labor standards are ostensibly meant to help.

The latter view, which we share, is voiced prominently by economists and by most leaders of developing countries. They perceive labor standards, when enforced by trade sanctions, as thinly disguised protection for developed-country labor. The WTO excludes labor standards as part of its broader role of protecting the weak from the strong. We agree with the position taken at the 1996 GATT Ministerial Meeting in Singapore that issues of labor standards should be handled in the International Labor Organization, although we also favor some increase in that organization's resources and effectiveness.

Other Objections to the WTO

Even among those who think the WTO has it right on environment and labor standards, the WTO does nonetheless have flaws. One is its lack of transparency. The proceedings of the DSM panels are secret, and the panelists get information only from governments. Some regard this mechanism as undemocratic, and they fear its capture by corporations with financial stake in the outcome. They would like interested NGOs to be able to provide input to the process, and perhaps to have the panelists themselves selected by a process that NGOs could influence.

The complaint about undemocratic procedures is ironic, since the WTO works by consensus among mostly democratic governments, whereas NGOs are by definition self-appointed special interests. More important, however, is a concern from developing countries, that opening the DSM to public scrutiny and influence would cause its capture by precisely these special interests, at developing-country expense.

Nonetheless, even defenders of the WTO are coming to see the DSM's secrecy as counterproductive. It is also inconsistent with other WTO procedures, which have always been open if anyone cared to look at them. Therefore many say the DSM should permit NGOs and others to file "friend of the court briefs." Some also argue that a more permanent body should replace the panels themselves, instead of being assembled case-by-case. If so, then greater public input to selection of that body might be natural.

Another concern has long been that a few rich countries dominate the WTO, developing countries having little role. This is true in spite of—or even because of—its formal reliance on consensus. With 140 member countries, consensus is not practical, and therefore a smaller group has typically sought agreement among themselves, then come to the larger group for approval. This smaller group, named the "green room group" after the room in which they have sometimes met at WTO headquarters in Geneva, has been assembled on an ad hoc basis by the Director General and has included both developed and developing countries based on their interest in the issues being addressed. However, many developing countries—especially smaller ones—have been excluded and were not formally represented, not by design because there was no design, but by default. Exactly how to change this is not clear, but it must be changed.

As already noted, a common objection to the WTO is that it overrules domestic laws. This is true, for that is its purpose. The GATT was a treaty among countries to prevent them from using certain laws and policies that would adversely affect each other. The WTO continues that purpose. However, while the original GATT dealt only with tariffs, over time the GATT/WTO has expanded to many other policies, such as environmental laws, whose main purposes are not international. Critics object that the WTO undermines domestic policies, not just tariffs. Countries might well want to reconsider membership if these new restrictions are too onerous. Had the WTO existed for 50 years without the opportunity to withdraw, this might be a big concern. However, since all members joined only six years ago, it would be surprising if many were now to pull out.

A troubling feature of the WTO for many is that countries may not restrict imports based upon the process by which they were produced. The WTO permits countries to exclude goods deemed harmful to health or the environment, for example, but only based on observable characteristics of the products themselves. In practice countries often want to exclude imports that were produced by a process that has harmed the environment, has violated labor standards or human rights, has adverse health consequences for consumers, or may be otherwise undesirable. These are often legitimate concerns, and if the process could be inferred from a product characteristic at the border, the WTO might permit their exclusion. But without that, exclusion must be based on the country where they were produced and some judgment about practices there. This runs the risk of excluding products that did not use the offending process, and also of undermining a producing country's legitimate comparative advantage.

A final concern of many WTO critics is that it is dominated by large corporations. This is true and probably inevitable, since it is large corporations that do most trade. Corporations have both the incentive and the resources to influence policies, and they do, both within countries and internationally. This means that the WTO has elements that would not be there without corporate lobbying, and some of these elements are undesirable. For example, antidumping statutes are economically nonsensical and pernicious, and yet the GATT has always permitted them, for the obvious reason that many corporations want them. More recently, in response to corporate lobbying the Uruguay Round added intellectual property rights to the WTO, in spite of strong resistance from developing countries that ultimately was overcome by the promise of market opening in textiles and apparel.

The WTO, then, is not a perfect organization. It could be improved, but many of its flaws will inevitably remain, because they are there in response to political realities. Overall, it seems clear to us that the WTO serves an extremely useful purpose and that it serves it surprisingly well.

One indication that the WTO is not too far off the mark comes from its opponents. Although they share unhappiness with the WTO, some say that it does too much, others that it does too little. Environmentalists usually complain that it does too much, ruling against national efforts to improve the environment, and they want it weakened or destroyed so that national policies can proceed unhindered. Labor activists, on the other hand, complain that it does too little, not enforcing labor standards around the world. They want the WTO to take on more issues, and interfere more with national policies. . . .

4. CONCLUSIONS

In this conclusion, we try to distill what we have said into a list of the essentials.

On Globalization

- Globalization refers to the most recent expansion of global trade, together with expanding flows of real and financial capital across national borders.
- Globalization increases average real incomes in all countries, but within countries the gains are shared unequally and some may lose.
- Losers from globalization include owners of scarce factors, as well as those in contracting industries, if they cannot easily change their location, skills, or industry of employment.

On the WTO

- The WTO was formed by governments for the purpose of promoting globalization and preventing countries from doing harm with their trade policies.
- Those who gain most from the WTO are those who gain from globalization, especially small, poor countries who would be most hurt by nationalistic trade policies.
- The WTO limits those who would use trade policies for other goals, including environment, labor standards, and human rights, forcing them to pursue their objectives at less cost to other countries.

- The WTO provides a dispute settlement mechanism that has been quite effective, but its operation has been less transparent than it could be.
- The WTO operates by consensus, but its large membership makes that process unwieldy and exclusionary in practice, leaving many developing countries especially without a voice. . . .

24

The Institutional Roots of American Trade Policy: Politics, Coalitions, and International Trade

MICHAEL BAILEY, JUDITH GOLDSTEIN, AND BARRY R. WEINGAST

Before 1934, U.S. trade policy was protectionist and partisan. When Republicans were in control of Congress and the presidency, they raised tariffs, culminating in the infamous Smoot-Hawley Tariff of 1930 (see Reading 2). Shortly thereafter, free-trading Democrats took control of government and passed the Reciprocal Trade Agreements Act (RTAA) of 1934. According to Michael Bailey, Judith Goldstein, and Barry R. Weingast, the RTAA fundamentally changed not only the process but also the course of U.S. trade policy. In passing the RTAA, Congress delegated to the executive branch the authority to reduce tariffs through reciprocal trade agreements with other countries. These institutional changes generated broader bipartisan support for freer trade, and the RTAA went on to serve as the basis for more than half a century of U.S. trade liberalization.

While economists are unanimous in their agreement that free trade yields significant welfare gains, no consensus exists on the political conditions that will support such a policy. According to conventional views, even if politicians recognize that society gains from trade, they are constrained because of an organizational bias in society: those who lose from increased trade have a greater incentive to organize than those who benefit from the policy. The outcome is an overrepresentation of protectionist interests and constant pressure on governments to close markets. Although logically consistent, the conventional view suffers from the empirical problem that democracies have and continue to support free-trade policies. We argue that political institutions, by structuring conflict over trade policy, provide an explanation for the divergence between analyses that predict economic closure and the empirical reality of relatively free trade.

The importance of institutional rules is no more apparent than in the case of the creation and sustenance of a liberal trade policy in the United States. For most of the nineteenth century, protectionist interests successfully pressured Congress to maintain high barriers to trade. Although the interest of manufacturers in cheap raw materials periodically led Congress to enact a "free list" for such products, the interests of consumers and exporters were largely ignored. This situation changed dramatically with the passage of the Reciprocal Trade Agreements Act (RTAA) in 1934, which changed the way trade policy was determined and set the stage for American leadership in efforts to expand international trade.

Trade liberalization in the United States was neither inevitable nor irrevocable; the structure of American politics in the middle of the twentieth century made trade policy still vulnerable to protectionist impulses that were difficult to contain. Hence, any explanation of American trade policy must account not only for the passage of the RTAA but also for how and why Congress sustained the trade liberalization program in the ensuing decades.

This essay offers an explanation for the timing, form, and efficacy of this institutional innovation. The argument has two parts. First, we ask what explains the choice of the rules and procedures that characterized the 1934 foundational legislation. Two rule changes distinguished the Reciprocal Trade Agreements Act from its predecessors: (1) it mandated reciprocal, not unilateral, tariff reductions, and (2) it authorized trade agreements on the basis of a simple majority vote instead of the supermajority mandated in the Constitution. We argue that these changes in trade rules reflected efforts by the Democratic Party to build support for free trade within the party and to insulate trade policy from a future Republican Congress.

Second, the essay demonstrates how these two institutional changes shifted American policy to a more liberal equilibrium. The real significance of the RTAA was not just that it was passed; had it been overturned a few years later, after all, it would be nothing but a footnote to American trade history. Rather, the RTAA had an impact because it created a dynamic of political support for free trade. In contrast to perspectives in which Congress is seen to have abdicated control of trade policy, we focus on how presidential agreements affected congressional preferences. The president's "bundling" of international and domestic tariffs made low tariffs politically durable. The ensuing increases in world trade made members of Congress more willing to trade off the political risk of reducing U.S. tariffs for the political benefits of gaining access to foreign markets. This change in preference enabled presidents to ask for and receive ever broader authority to negotiate tariff reductions.

We divide this essay into three sections. Section I begins with the empirical observation of the breakdown of partisan divisions on trade and the emergence of a free-trade coalition, a puzzling occurrence given the previous decades of trade closure and continued congressional involvement in trade policy. Section II explains the origins of the RTAA and shows how political factors changed the institutional environment of trade policy. We offer a model in which members of Congress, the president, and a generic foreign government interact on trade policy. Section III examines the dynamic effects of the RTAA and shows how its institutional structure changed the political environment of trade policy. Not only did the RTAA dramatically increase the political durability of low tariffs, but, as we show through an empirical examination of congressional voting in 1953 and 1962, the rise in exports that it brought about also led to changes in congressional preferences on trade.

I. BIPARTISAN SUPPORT FOR TRADE POLICY

One of the anomalies in the history of U.S. politics involves the relatively rapid change in the political salience of trade policy. Where trade policy was a defining issue of partisan politics in the late nineteenth and early twentieth centuries, it all but disappeared from the political arena by the 1950s. Indicative of the charged political climate of early tariff policy-making were policy shifts that followed changes in control of government. . . . Trade policy through 1934 shows tremendous predictability. In general, when Democrats took office, they lowered tariffs; when Republicans held office, they did the opposite. This ability to predict policy based on party control disappears in midcentury. After World War II the parties look increasingly similar in their voting behavior. (See Figures 1 and 2.) What explains this change in congressional preferences?

There is an impressive body of literature suggesting that change occurred because Congress abdicated its control over trade policy when the RTAA transferred authority for setting tariffs to the president. By one account, the work associated with tariff legislation had become so onerous that members of Congress chose to remove themselves from the process. While revision of tariff schedules had never been a simple matter, the process had degenerated into a frenzy of special-interest lobbying and deal making with the Smoot-Hawley Tariff Bill of 1930. Schattschneider wrote of the "truly Sisyphean labor" to which the legislation condemned Congress—eleven

FIGURE 1 Voting in Senate on Passage of Major Trade Legislation by Party 1913–1962

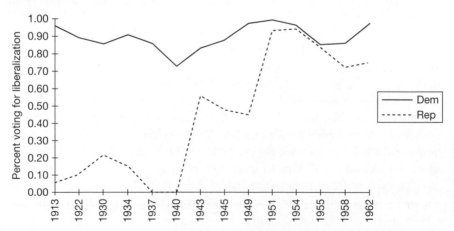

FIGURE 2 Voting in House on Passage of Major Trade Legislation by Party 1913–1962

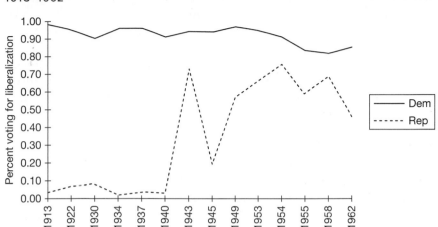

thousand pages of testimony and briefs collected over forty-three days and five nights of hearings.[1] Many therefore viewed the congressional move to delegate authority to change tariffs as a means of avoiding months of tedious hearings and negotiations.

Several factors make it difficult to accept that the fundamental motivation for the RTAA was a desire to reduce workload. First, the easiest way to reduce workload is to do nothing. Clearly this was not the choice of Congress. Second, there were many other ways to streamline the process than by delegating to the president: existing organizations could have been used differently, new committees and commissions could have been created, and rules and formulas could have been established. There is no specific reason to choose delegation to the president over these other possibilities.

An alternative explanation, the "lesson thesis," suggests that the disastrous results of the Smoot-Hawley Tariff led members of Congress to the realization that they were politically incapable of passing a rational tariff policy. Destler, for example, states that members of Congress chose to delegate in order to "protect themselves from the direct one-sided pressure from producer interests that had led them to make bad law."

This perspective, too, is problematic. First, one should be wary of models of congressional behavior in which members of Congress act against one-sided political pressure in the interest of good public policy for no political reason. If such behavior were the norm, one would expect Congress to "protect" itself

1. E. E Schattschneider, *Politics, Pressure and the Tariff: A Study of Free Private Enterprise in Pressure Politics as Shown in the 1929–1930 Revision of the Tariff* (Hamden, Conn.: Archon Books, 1935), 29, 36.

from the American Association of Retired People, the National Rifle Association, farmers, oil producers, and almost all other interests as well. Needless to say, this is not generally the case; even on trade, Congress has continued to represent producer interests on more than a few occasions.

Second, problems with the process in 1930 do not prove that Congress was incapable of getting the process back under control. A new set of congressional leaders with different priorities could have organized procedures differently so as to achieve a better outcome than that of 1930. Congress had gone through such reorganizations in 1894, 1909, and 1913; and it did it again in 1934, when the Senate defeated many amendments seeking exemptions for particular industries, precisely the type of amendments that had spun the process out of control in 1930.[2]

Third, . . . if congressional learning did in fact occur between 1930 and 1934, one would expect to see a substantial number of members who voted for the Smoot-Hawley Tariff coming around to support the RTAA. To the contrary, however, voting on *both* the Smoot-Hawley Tariff and the RTAA was almost wholly partisan: Republicans favored the former and opposed the latter, whereas Democrats opposed the former and favored the latter. Of 225 representatives and senators who voted on both bills, only nine voted in a manner consistent with the lesson thesis. The remaining 96 percent voted either along party lines or in a manner inconsistent with the lesson thesis. The difference between 1930 and 1934 is therefore not that protariff members of Congress learned from their mistake, but rather that there were too few Republicans in 1934 to oppose the Democrats' initiative.

As well as disagreeing on why Congress would grant new tariff-setting powers to the president, analyses differ over the actual effect of the RTAA on American policy. One view, consistent with the deflection and lesson theses, holds that the RTAA allowed Congress to wash its hands of tariffs, leaving the president free to pursue rational liberalization of U.S. trade policy unburdened by members of Congress or the special interests they represented.

This view is overstated. While congressional activity on tariffs declined dramatically after the RTAA, it still remained substantial; Congress continued to play a central role at every step along the path to trade liberalization. Congress extended the RTAA ten times between 1934 and 1962, debating and often modifying the legislation. In 1937, for example, an amendment to limit reductions on agricultural duties to whatever level would be necessary to equalize production costs initially passed the Senate and was only defeated on a revote. In 1948, 1951, and 1955, Congress added peril-point provisions that tied duties to the minimum rates necessary to protect domestic producers

2. Stephan Haggard, "The Institutional Foundations of Hegemony: Explaining the Reciprocal Trade Agreements Act of 1934," in G. John Ikenberry, David Lake, and Michael Mastanduno, eds., *The State and American Foreign Economic Policy* (Ithaca, N.Y.: Cornell University Press, 1988), 113.

against imports. In 1953 Republicans in Congress agreed to a one-year renewal only when the president promised not to enter into any new trade negotiations. While Congress never overturned the RTAA, members were clearly always ready to make significant changes if they thought them necessary. . . .

What does explain the passage of the RTAA in 1934 if not that Congress abdicated control or sought to deflect political pressure? Our answer is simple: the Democratic leadership wanted lower tariffs that would pass an increasingly skeptical Congress and would be able to outlive Democratic control of Congress. The institutions they designed met this goal. In that the Democrats chose to lower tariffs through reciprocal "bundled" agreements with other nations, some delegation to the president to negotiate these agreements was necessary. The significant change, however, was not delegation to the president per se. Rather, the RTAA marks a turning point in American trade history because first, it moved Congress away from legislating unilateral tariffs, and second, it granted these bilateral agreements the status of treaties without a two-thirds supermajority.

II. THE POLITICAL ORIGINS OF THE RTAA

With its passage of the RTAA in 1934, Congress ushered in a new era of trade policy. The legislation amended the 1930 Smoot-Hawley Tariff Act to allow the president to negotiate reciprocal trade agreements with foreign governments. In exchange for increased access to foreign markets, the president was authorized to reduce U.S. duties by up to 50 percent. No specific duties were established or changed by the act and no congressional approval of agreements was required.

That such legislation was passed in 1934 is somewhat surprising in light of the fact that there was no groundswell of support for tariff reductions. Although highly critical of Hoover's tariff policy during the 1932 campaign, Roosevelt was no staunch free trader. While he associated himself with the Wilsonian international wing of the Democratic Party, at times he sounded very much like a protectionist. In the 1932 presidential campaign he announced that his trade doctrine was "not widely different from that preached by Republican statesmen and politicians" and that he favored "continuous protection for American agriculture as well as American industry."[3]

In addition, many in the Roosevelt administration, including leading members of Roosevelt's brain trust, such as Rexford Tugwell, Raymond Moley, and Adolf Berle, placed a low priority on trade liberalization. They considered America's problems to be domestic in nature, requiring domestic solutions. Many members of the administration were thus willing to impose higher

3. Haggard (fn. 2), 106–7.

duties in the interests of insulating the domestic economy from the world economy. Such sentiment manifested itself in provisions of the National Industrial Recovery Act (NIRA) and the Agriculture Assistance Act (AAA), which allowed the government to limit imports if they were deemed to be interfering with the operation of the programs.

Rank-and-file Democrats also were not united in favor of lower tariffs. The increase in blue-collar and immigrant labor in the party proved a counterweight to southern preferences for lower tariffs. Led by Al Smith, 1928 presidential nominee and 1932 contender for the nomination, a major wing of the party supported high tariffs. Indicatively, during the debate on the Smoot-Hawley Tariff of 1930, most Democrats tempered their opposition to high tariffs.

The Great Depression did little to enhance the appeal of lower tariffs for these Democrats. During this period, efforts to cut tariffs unilaterally were dismissed as politically foolhardy. In 1931 Democratic representative and future speaker Henry Rainey of Illinois argued that such a unilateral reduction of tariffs would trigger a flood of imports. During the 1932 presidential campaign, Roosevelt's advisers roundly criticized Hull's proposal of unilateral reductions, and when Roosevelt was given a draft of a speech calling for a flat 10 percent reduction in tariffs, Democratic senators Pittman (Nevada) and Walsh (Montana) warned him that support for such a measure would be politically dangerous. Even after the election, reciprocal cuts were so politically risky that Roosevelt delayed introducing the RTAA to Congress for a year, out of fear that controversy over trade would derail high-priority items like NIRA.

Thus, the Democratic Party faced two constraints in fashioning a trade policy. First, its old platform of unilateral tariff reductions had questionable support, both within and outside the party. Roosevelt's promise of tariff reform would need to be fulfilled some other way. Second, Democrats wanted to provide some durability for their preferred policies. . . . Democratic tariffs had lasted only as long as the Democrats' tenure in power. Although we now consider 1932 as a watershed election in American history, it was not perceived as such at the time. In 1934 the electoral future looked highly uncertain to Democrats. The Republicans after all had dominated national elections for the previous seventy years, and were it not for the depression, they would probably still have been in office. Given this uncertainty, Democrats were looking for a way to make their tariff policy last beyond their tenure. House members were facing midterm elections in November and the president was in the second year of what could be a single four-year term. Party members had not forgotten their last effort at tariff reform, in 1913, when Woodrow Wilson fought long and hard for the Tariff Act, only to see it scuttled when the Republicans regained office.

The institutional form of the legislation introduced in 1934 should be understood as serving dual purposes. The key innovation—coupling liberalization of U.S. tariffs with reductions in foreign tariffs—accomplished two tasks. First, the form of tariff reduction served to broaden the range of tariff cuts acceptable to a majority in Congress. As shown below, it is easier to build majority support for reductions (and harder to form a coalition to negate an agreement) when tariffs are coupled with changes in access to foreign markets. Second, it provided durability for the reform efforts. Granting the president the right to negotiate "bundled" tariff treaties increased the costs to Republicans of increasing tariffs. Under the RTAA, even small adjustments could unravel many agreements and harm U.S. export interests. We take up each of these points in turn.

Building a Coalition in Favor of Free Trade

We begin with a spatial model to show how the RTAA enabled the Democrats to ensure domestic political support for lower tariffs. The preferences of political actors in a two-dimensional policy space are shown in Figure 3. The horizontal axis represents the level of domestic tariffs, ranging from low to high. The vertical axis represents the level of foreign tariffs. Political actors have ideal policies, that is, tariff rates they prefer over all others. They prefer policies closer to their ideal policy to those farther away. To simplify matters, we consider the rest of the world to be one nation that sets the foreign tariff levels. For simplicity, we also assume Congress is unicameral.

The historical record is clear about the location of actors in this space. First, all American political actors prefer foreign tariffs to be as low as possible. Therefore their ideal points line the horizontal axis in Figure 3. Second, in the late nineteenth and early twentieth centuries the parties had distinct preferences, with Republicans the party of high tariffs and Democrats the

FIGURE 3 Actor Preferences and Predicted Tariff under Pre-RTAA System

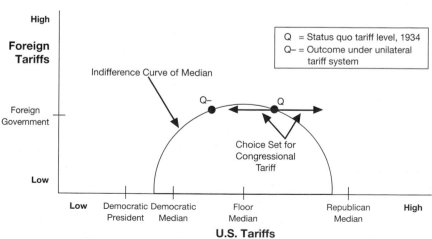

party of low tariffs. The median in Congress (the "floor median") is located between the Democratic median and the Republican median. During periods of Republican majority, the median was among the Republicans with the lowest ideal rates; during Democratic majorities, it was among the Democrats with the highest ideal rates.

While presidents shared the partisan inclinations on trade, their national constituencies and their more direct concern with international diplomacy made them less protectionist than the median member of their parties. The foreign government is assumed to be a unitary actor with an ideal point along the vertical axis, preferring U.S. tariffs to be as low as possible.

We also need an assumption about who controls the agenda in Congress. The literature on Congress propounds various views on the question—that committee, party, or the median controls the agenda. Because committee and party leaders took a leading role in the passage of the RTAA, we assume here that the agenda setter is some party leader who is distinct from the floor median. For convenience, we refer to this actor as the Democratic or Republican median.

To analyze congressional choice on the RTAA, we compare outcomes with and without the RTAA. We assume that the Democrats control the presidency and Congress, as they did in 1934. First, consider the situation without the RTAA. Under the existing tariff system, the Democratic median proposes unilateral changes in U.S. tariffs that are passed or rejected by the floor median. Because the tariff changes are unilateral, the Democratic median is constrained to making proposals along a horizontal line extending in both directions from the status quo Q. In other words, the Democratic median treats the foreign tariff level as fixed and makes a proposal affecting only U.S. tariff levels.

The Democratic median will propose a policy that makes it better off than the current status quo and is preferred by the median to the current status quo. In this situation, the status quo is the protectionist level of the Smoot-Hawley tariff. The Democratic median would maximize its utility by proposing Q−, the policy closest to the Democratic median among those preferred by the floor median to the status quo. Figure 3 illustrates the Democratic median's choice.

Such an outcome is suboptimal for many actors. There is a range of policies that would make the Democratic median, the floor median, and the foreign government better off than Q−. In Figure 4 we have drawn the preferred sets of the floor median and the foreign government to Q−; all points in the interior of the indifference curves are preferred to Q−. The shaded region at the intersection of the two preferred sets is an area of potential mutual gain; both of those actors and the Democratic median would be better off at any other outcome in the region than at Q−. When decision making is unilateral, however, Congress cannot move outcomes into this region.

FIGURE 4   Gains from Reciprocity

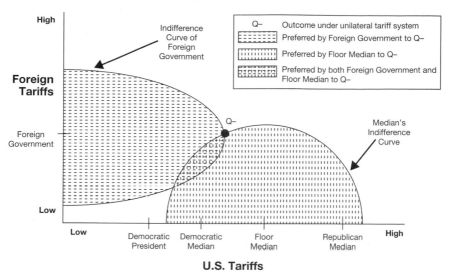

Next consider outcomes under the RTAA. First, the president proposes an agreement to the foreign government subject to the minimum tariff provisions enacted by Congress. The foreign government then accepts or rejects the proposal. Even if there is no agreement, Congress still has the option of passing tariff legislation. The criterion for the foreign government is whether the proposal would leave it better off than if there were no proposal. From above we know that if there is no agreement, Congress will pass a unilateral tariff bill and the outcome will be Q–. The foreign government will therefore accept the proposal if the proposal makes it better off than Q–.

In making the proposal, the president seeks to bring the policy as close as possible to his ideal point. If the president proposes an agreement that is rejected by the foreign government, Congress would then set tariffs as if there were no agreement and choose Q–. Since the president is to the left of the Democratic median and the median, he would seek larger reductions, if possible. In particular, he would choose the point closest to his ideal point among policies above the congressional minimum tariff level and preferred to Q– by the foreign government. Agreement A* in Figure 5 is such a point: of the points above the minimum tariff level and preferred by the foreign government to Q–, it is the point closest to the president's ideal policy.

It is essential, then, that the Democratic median choose an appropriate minimum tariff level. If the minimum tariff level is too low—that is, if the president is able to choose a policy that makes the median worse off than the status quo—the floor median will not support the RTAA. Therefore, the Democratic median will set the minimum tariff level such that policy chosen

FIGURE 5   Predicted Tariff under the RTAA

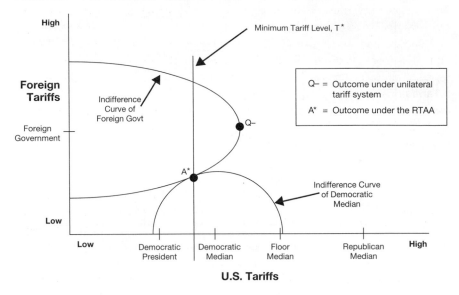

by the president is as close as possible to its ideal point given that the policy is still preferred by the floor median to the status quo. As in Figure 5, such a minimum tariff level will go through the point of tangency between an indifference curve of the Democratic median and the indifference curve of the foreign government through Q–. The floor median will prefer the outcome chosen by the president, A*, to Q–.

The result is that under the RTAA, the Democratic median maintains a minimum tariff level of T*, the floor median supports the RTAA, and the president proposes an agreement at A* that is accepted by the foreign government. The implication is that the RTAA makes perfect sense given the preferences of American political actors and an assumption of strategic behavior. No extra assumptions about congressional laziness or congressional antipathy toward special interests are necessary. Moreover, it is not a story of congressional abdication.

This framework can also be used to explain why other means of trade liberalization were not chosen. First, we can see why congressional Democrats were not satisfied with letting the president use existing treaty-making powers. The Constitution requires that a treaty must be approved by a two-thirds vote in the Senate. Hence, the president would be constrained to please the member at the sixty-seventh percentile of protectionists in order to achieve mutual reduction in tariffs. In fact, the inability to garner a two-thirds majority in the Senate had repeatedly nullified trade treaties negotiated in the nineteenth century. Under the RTAA, by contrast, the process was structured to require only a simple majority to pass tariff reductions—a clever institutional innovation that allowed the Democrats to sidestep the constraints of the existing institutional structure.

A second possible alternative to the RTAA was that Congress could have tried to devise a strategy to induce foreign reductions in tariffs. However, the sequential nature of tariff making could undermine such efforts. Consider first the commitment problems in trying to effect mutual lowering of tariffs. Suppose the status quo is Q and Democrats take over Congress and are considering tariff reductions. We know Congress can pass Q–. Suppose, however, that the Democrats propose some reduction beyond Q– and argue that this large cut in U.S. tariffs will be accompanied by a cut in foreign tariffs. It would be difficult for such a strategy to work. First, the foreign country will be sorely tempted not to lower tariffs, because it favors low U.S. tariffs and high foreign tariffs over low U.S. tariffs and low foreign tariffs. To avoid this outcome, the Democrats would have to commit to raising tariffs if foreign tariffs were not lowered. But here, the temptation would be on the Democrats. Would they be willing to raise tariffs even though they prefer low tariffs? How credible would their threat be? Both the foreign country and the median in Congress would have good reason to doubt that the Democrats would carry out their threat.

These commitment problems would be exacerbated by problems associated with political uncertainty. Even if the Democrats were to lower tariffs beyond Q– and the foreign country responded in kind, the Democrats could lose an election and the incoming Republicans could raise tariffs back to Q. The foreign country would be forced to retreat from its reduction of tariffs. This possibility could make the foreign government reluctant to lower tariffs in the first place.

The RTAA and Political Durability

The second need for congressional Democrats was to provide some political durability for the tariff cuts. To demonstrate the increase in durability of trade liberalization under the RTAA, we first model the extreme volatility of trade policy under the pre-RTAA institutional structure. Under that regime, changes in trade policy followed the classic American legislative process. Parties originated legislation in Congress. If Congress passed a tariff bill, it went to the president. If the president signed the legislation, it became law; if he vetoed it, it went back to Congress where a two-thirds majority was required to override the veto.

Given this framework, we can determine equilibrium outcomes for different states of the world. Because tariffs were set unilaterally by each country, choices can be represented in one dimension. Consider a period in which there is a Republican majority in Congress, a Republican president, and a status quo tariff rate of Q, as in Figure 3. As long as the Republicans maintain their majority, Q is stable. While the median prefers all points between Q and Q–, defined to be a point equidistant from the median as Q but on the left side of the median, the congressional Republicans prefer none of these points.

Now suppose that after an election, the Democrats become the majority party. The status quo, Q, is no longer an equilibrium, as there are points that both the Democratic agenda setters and the median prefer to such a policy. In order for the Democrats to get as close to the Democratic median as possible, given that the bill must be approved by the median, they will introduce and pass the policy Q–. The Democratic president will prefer Q– to Q and will not veto the legislation. Once at this point, policy remains stable as long as the Democrats remain in power. As soon as the Republicans recapture Congress and the presidency, however, the status quo inherited from the Democrats is no longer an equilibrium. By similar reasoning as above, the Republicans would pass Q.

According to this logic, tariff shifts should occur when a new party obtains control of government. In fact, this is what occurred. In 1860, 1897, and 1920 the Republicans gained unified control of government after periods of unified Democratic control. Every time, they raised tariffs. In 1845, 1892, 1912, and 1930 the Democrats gained unified control of government after periods of unified Republican control. Every time, they lowered tariffs.

The dynamics of trade policy under the RTAA provide a stark contrast. To demonstrate the implications of the RTAA for the durability of low tariffs, we analyze two situations, one in which preferences are constant and one in which preferences change. First, we assume that the ideal point of the floor median remains constant, even as parties change. This is plausible if, say, moderate Democrats are replaced by moderate Republicans. We have already seen that the status quo after the passage of the RTAA is A*.

What happens after an election? If Democrats retain the presidency and Congress, there is no change: the minimum tariff level prevents the president from negotiating further tariff reductions, and congressional agenda setters desire no change. If the Republicans win control of both the presidency and Congress, change will be possible only if the median prefers the unilateral tariff of the foreign country to A*. However, since the RTAA moved the median to an outcome preferred over Q (and Q–), this will not be the case and no change will be possible.

Of course, members of Congress are likely to change their preferences after an election. We therefore consider the kind of changes in preferences that would be necessary to allow Congress to overturn the RTAA and resume unilateral tariff making. The president's preferences play a key role. If a protectionist president were elected, the floor median would have to shift to the right to the extent that he or she prefers some point along the foreign unilateral tariff line to the RTAA outcome, A*. In Figure 6 the floor median would have to shift

FIGURE 6 Stability of Tariffs under the RTAA

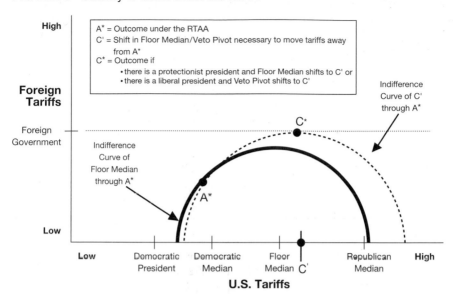

to a point equidistant from A* and the foreign unilateral tariff line. To determine this point, we find an ideal point, C', at which the indifference curve through A* touches the foreign unilateral tariff line. If the change were any smaller, no protectionist legislation would be possible, as the floor median would not be satisfied with any possible unilateral tariff legislation.

On the other hand, if a Democratic or internationalist Republican president were elected, protectionist legislation would have to overcome a presidential veto. Hence legislative success would depend, not on the floor median, but on the veto pivot. The veto pivot in this case is the member at the sixty-sixth percentile (ranked from least to most liberal); if this member and all more protectionist members prefer a bill to the status quo, then Congress can pass the legislation over the veto of the president. In this case, then, preferences in Congress would have to change such that the veto pivot—one of the more liberal members of Congress—would shift to C' on the right of the current median (as in Figure 6). In other words, if the president is a free trader, Congress would almost certainly not be able to raise tariffs, even if the Republicans were to take power.

Could we expect the president to be liberal on trade? Two factors indicate yes. First, being elected from a national constituency makes a president less susceptible to narrow demands for protection and more interested in policies that benefit the whole country. Second, the president's international role often inclines him to use trade liberalization as a tool in achieving geopolitical goals.

III. LONG-TERM EFFECTS OF THE RTAA

The importance of the RTAA was more than simply creating the mechanism for short-term tariff reform. More important, it set up a self-reinforcing dynamic that led to increasingly lower tariffs. In this section, we discuss the effects of RTAA-induced increases in trade on congressional and foreign preferences. We argue that congressional support for the expansion of presidential authority to negotiate cuts in American and foreign tariffs was forthcoming because the RTAA increased the importance of exports to constituents in congressional districts, which, in turn, changed the trade policy preferences of key congressional representatives. This section illustrates how RTAA structures influenced support for free trade. First, we show that trade did expand under the RTAA. Second, we model how expanding trade affects political preferences. Third, we present empirical evidence that increasing exports were a significant factor in transforming trade from a partisan to a bipartisan issue.

Tariffs declined precipitously and trade expanded dramatically during the tenure of the RTAA. In 1934 American duties averaged over 46 percent; by 1962 they had fallen to 12 percent. World trade increased from 97 trillion dollars at the war's end to 270 trillion at the time of the 1962 Trade Act. U.S. exports grew from $2.1 billion in 1934 to $3.3 billion in 1937 and from $9.8 billion in 1945 to over $20 billion in 1962.

While much of this increase in world trade can be attributed to the emergence of the world economy out of depression and war, two factors point to the substantial role of the RTAA. First, the RTAA allowed the president to take the lead in fighting for increased international openness. After the Smoot-Hawley Tariff Act of 1930, a retaliatory spiral of beggar-thy-neighbor policies had left the world with monumentally high tariffs. Given protectionist pressures inherent in democracies, we have good reason to believe that without the RTAA, tariffs would have moved downward at a far slower pace. Second, there is evidence that U.S. trade with treaty nations increased more rapidly than with nontreaty nations. For example, in the first three years of the program, exports to twenty-two nations with which agreements existed increased by 61 percent as compared with a 38 percent increase to other nations.

There are two ways such changes in trade flows could change political preferences. First, the ideal points could shift. Since we assume that all members of Congress prefer zero foreign tariffs, the only room for movement would be along the horizontal axis. For any given level of foreign tariffs, that is, a member's ideal level of U.S. tariffs could shift. Such a shift could mean members of Congress would prefer unilateral reductions in U.S. tariffs.

A second possible change is that the relative weight members put on the two dimensions may change. Consider a generic situation in which a political actor has preferences over a two-dimensional policy space, with a level of X on the horizontal axis and a level of Y on the vertical axis. If the actor places equal weight on each dimension, the actor's indifference curves will be circular; the actor is willing to trade off loss of units of X in equal proportion to gain in units of Y. Suppose the actor comes to place greater weight on the X dimension such that she is willing to exchange a small gain in X for a larger loss in Y. The indifference curves would then become vertical ellipses; small changes in X would require large changes in Y in order to make her indifferent. By contrast, if the actor comes to place a greater weight on dimension Y, her indifference curves will be horizontal ellipses; small changes in Y would require large changes in X to make the actor indifferent.

We emphasize this latter process; that is, changing weights on issue dimensions allowed the president to expand the coalition in favor of free trade. Increasing trade flows increased the size and profits of export interests but had a lesser effect on import-competing interest (as some industries facing import competition disappeared). A similar effect occurred abroad, as exports to the U.S. activated foreign export interests. The net effect was that the importance placed on foreign access increased relative to the importance of protecting domestic industry. Indifference curves of actors in each nation changed, with American curves being transformed from circles to flat horizontal ellipses and foreign indifference curves becoming vertical ellipses.

Consider Figure 7 in which A* (from Figure 5) is the status quo. The only way that Congress will lower the minimum tariff level is if doing so makes congressional agenda setters (the Democratic median) better off. If the

FIGURE 7 How Tariffs Shift in Response to Changes in Preferences

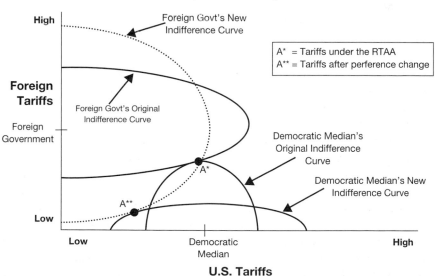

preferences of the Democratic leaders—both in terms of the location and relative weights—remain the same, no such policy will exist. If, however, increasing trade has led the foreign government and members of Congress to place relatively more weight on export interests, the indifference curves will shift. The indifference curves of U.S. actors will flatten and those of the foreign government will broaden, as indicated by the dotted lines in Figure 7. This means that the set of policies preferred over the status quo by the agenda setters will no longer be empty and a new equilibrium at a point such as A** will be possible.

The implication for the dynamics of trade liberalization is now apparent: increasing trade leads members of Congress and foreign actors to place more weight on access to foreign markets, indifference curves then shift, and greater liberalization is possible.

Changing Congressional Preferences

We can now return to our original query: what explains the depoliticization of American trade policy after World War II? We noted that trade was a highly partisan issue in the pre-RTAA period. Historically, Democrats voted for tariff reductions; Republicans voted for tariff increases. Figures 1 and 2 indicate that voting in Congress on trade measures before the RTAA generally followed party lines.

As the RTAA program progressed, the partisan composition of trade voting began to change in important ways. In 1943 some Republicans voted for the program for the first time, and by the mid-1950s many Republicans supported the program. Of course, Republicans were still more protectionist than Democrats and many voted for protectionist amendments to the RTAA renewal legislation. Nevertheless, their support for the general principles of the RTAA was no longer in doubt. In our empirical analysis, we concentrate on the period from 1953 to 1962, a time that saw the beginnings of substantial changes in partisan voting patterns on trade.

The logic we offer above suggested that changes in votes will be a function of export interests in congressional districts. With passage of increasing numbers of trade agreements, highly competitive American products were pouring into foreign markets. This increased flow of trade led to growth in the size, number, and profitability of export industries. Import competition was more than offset by increased opportunities in the export sector, so at least until the mid-1960s the overall effect was that producers and their representatives placed increased importance on foreign access relative to the importance of protecting domestic industry.

To explore the relationship between exports and congressional preferences, we estimated probit models on congressional voting on major trade bills in 1953 and 1962. . . .

In the estimations, we controlled for party and ideology, recognizing that these factors have traditionally been important determinants of a representative's trade preferences. . . .

We analyzed votes that occurred in 1953 and 1962, years that spanned the important development of bipartisan support for free trade. For 1953 we considered three votes: the Curtis Motion to recommit an RTAA alternative trade bill; the Smith Motion to recommit the RTAA; and the renewal of the RTAA. Of the three, the most controversial, and thus the most divisive, was the Curtis Motion. The motion recommitted a protectionist trade bill that had been introduced as a substitute for the renewal of the trade agreements program. (The vote on final passage of the renewal was very lopsided [363–34] and is therefore not amenable to probit analysis. To compensate for the skewed vote, we used ordered probit analysis, combining the vote on passage and the Smith Motion.) For 1962 we analyzed the Mason Motion, a protectionist effort to substitute a one-year extension of the RTAA for the Trade Expansion Act and the vote on the final passage of the bill. . . .

Because the estimated coefficients from probit analysis are not directly interpretable, we provide estimates of the effect of change in exports on the probability of liberal trade voting for different groups within Congress. Table 1 does this for the 1953 vote on the Curtis Motion and Table 2 does this for the 1962 vote on final passage. The first column is the predicted probability of voting for trade liberalization by an "average" representative, computed as someone with average levels of all independent variables for the whole subgroup. The second column is the predicted probability of voting for trade

TABLE 1 Estimated Probabilities of Liberal Trade Voting in 1953 by Group and Change in Exports

	Probability of voting for trade liberalization		
	Exports	*Average exports plus 1 standard deviations*	*Average exports plus 2 standard deviations*
All	0.65	0.75	0.84
Republicans	0.49	0.63	0.75
Democrats	0.78	0.85	0.90

TABLE 2 Estimated Probabilities of Liberal Trade Voting in 1962 by Group and Change in Exports

	Probability of voting for trade liberalization		
	Average exports	*Average exports plus 1 standard deviations*	*Average exports plus 2 standard deviations*
All	0.78	0.85	0.90
Republicans	0.47	0.58	0.68
Democrats	0.90	0.94	0.96

liberalization when exports are increased by one standard deviation and all other variables are held constant at their average levels. The third column repeats the exercise for an increase of two standard deviations in exports.

From Tables 1 and 2 we see that exports explain why—for the first time in a century—members of the Republican Party abandoned their party's traditional stance on trade. Table 1 shows for 1953 that a two standard deviation increase in export share of production increased the probability of a free trade vote from 65 percent to 84 percent for an "average" representative. The effect is stronger for Republicans, moving them from a 49 percent probability of voting for free trade at average levels of exports to a 75 percent probability of a free-trade vote when export shares increased by two standard deviations. The effect of exports was less important for Democrats, but most Democrats were already committed to free trade.

Table 2 reveals a similar story for the 1962 vote. An increase in two standard deviations of export shares of production raised the probability of a free-trade vote by 12 percent for all members. For Republicans, those least likely to vote for free trade in 1962, the effect was an increase of 21 points. Democrats in 1962 were still highly likely to vote for free trade, but an increase of two standard deviations in export share of production increased their likelihood to vote for free trade by 6 percent.

The general conclusion that emerges from this analysis is that exports affect congressional voting on trade. Higher levels of exports led to increased support for free trade. Although analysts have often suggested that exports should play such a role, the effect has been difficult to demonstrate. It is hard to get export data on the district level, and often the effects are overwhelmed by the more traditional variables of party, region, and ideology. By extrapolating export shares of production from district-level industrial data and using probit simulations, we have shown that an export effect was felt by congressional representatives. Members of Congress do vote based on constituent interests, and their views on American trade policy shifted as exports grew.

CONCLUSION

Through detailed analysis of both the logic and empirical effects of liberalization, this paper provides a new interpretation of the transformation of U.S. trade policy in the middle of the century. By examining both the causes and economic ramifications of the RTAA, we are able to explain how political factors shaped the institutional environment and, in turn, how the institutional factors shaped the political environment.

Two sets of puzzles have driven the analysis. The first set revolves around the initial legislation. Why would Congress ever agree to forfeit so much power to the president? And, more curiously, why would Congress choose to do so at a time when the commitment to free trade was not particularly strong? The second puzzle revolves around the expansion of the RTAA, especially after the Second World War. What was the mechanism that allowed trade liberalization to move continuously forward throughout the twenty-eight-year life span of the RTAA? Liberalization goes counter to a conventional logic that assumes that pro-protection interests should have been overrepresented in the policy process because of the distributional inequalities that obtained from a liberal trade policy.

The existing literature provides incomplete answers to both puzzles. Many analyses of the original delegation emphasize congressional efforts to reduce its workload or to avoid serving special interests. In contrast, we argue that a model positing only policy-oriented, strategic political actors can explain the initial delegation. The RTAA allowed congressional Democrats to satisfy reluctant free traders and to durably reduce tariffs by coupling U.S. tariff cuts with foreign cuts. Further, it created a mechanism for lowering tariffs without having to meet the demanding constitutional requirement for two-thirds support that had undermined previous treaty efforts.

Many analyses of the effects of the RTAA are also suspect. Some claim that the RTAA removed trade policy from the constraints of a protectionist Congress; others argue that delegating authority and its accompanying agenda-setting power to the president was the key to trade liberalization in the period. But neither of these views can explain the clear and continued congressional involvement in tariff policy, even under the RTAA.

We agree with the consensus that congressional delegation to the president was an important element of the trade liberalization program. Nevertheless, the president's involvement in lowering trade barriers should not be exaggerated. Once Congress eschewed unilateral tariff reductions, presidential involvement was inevitable—it is the president's constitutional prerogative to negotiate treaties with foreign nations. But presidents had negotiated trade treaties throughout American history. Few, however, made it past a congressional veto. The RTAA should be remembered not because it delegated power to the president but because it mandated reciprocal tariff cuts under an innovative voting rule that bypassed the need for ex post approval by a supermajority in Congress.

The radical change in underlying preferences that allowed the liberalization of American trade policy cannot be explained either by the insulation of trade policy making or by presidential agenda control. Rather, trade liberalization endured because the RTAA changed the strategic environment of policy setting and later, the optimal policy choices of elected officials. First, the RTAA increased support for trade liberalization by "bundling" domestic and foreign reductions into one package. This not only garnered a larger base of support than did unilateral tariff reductions, but it also made it more difficult to change policy, even with an alteration in political control of government. By tying domestic reductions to foreign reductions, a greater pool of representatives found themselves in the proliberalization coalition. The existence of treaty obligations and the direct loss of foreign markets in response to a tariff hike made tariff reform far more durable than in any previous period of U.S. history. The RTAA was not simply a bill to lower tariffs; it was as well, an attempt to institutionalize a low tariff policy.

Second, and as important, tariff reform under the RTAA began an endogenous process of tariff reduction. Tariff reductions were matched with export growth. Increased export dependence in districts led to a more fundamental and enduring change in the political preferences of key actors in Congress. Although not the only factor, the RTAA was instrumental in increasing world trade, which spurred political interest in increasing access to foreign markets. This made increasing numbers of politicians willing to trade off support from import-competing interests that stood in the way of trade liberalization in exchange for support from export groups.

Empirical analysis of voting on trade bills supports our argument. Before the RTAA, voting on trade was almost wholly partisan, with Democrats in favor of and Republicans opposed to reductions in U.S. tariffs. After World War II partisan voting broke down, as more Democrats voted for protection and many more Republicans voted for trade liberalization.

Overall, the shift in American policy exceeded everyone's expectations. Trade increased dramatically, and the U.S. sustained a policy of relatively open borders. Our analysis strongly suggests that part of this shift should be attributed to an increase in the importance of exports at the district level.

In summary, the early history of liberalization in the U.S. provides a picture of how domestic politics, institutional choice, and the international economy are interlinked. Domestic politics led to an institutional innovation, the RTAA. The institutional innovation led both directly and indirectly to increased world trade. And, in turn, increased world trade led members of Congress and foreign actors to put more weight on increasing access to international markets. These preference changes expanded the coalition supporting free trade and allowed trade liberalization to continue to move forward.

VI

ECONOMIES IN DEVELOPMENT

The liberal international economy created after 1945 and the increase in international finance and trade (discussed in previous sections) have helped produce unprecedented levels of national and global growth. Within this broad pattern of economic success, however, there are important variations. While some countries and people enjoy the highest standards of living in human history, many more remain mired in poverty.

Indeed, the gap between the richest and the poorest people on earth not only is large but also is growing wider every year. As of 2007, the richest one-fifth of the world's population accounted for 76.6 percent of the world's private consumption, while the world's poorest one-fifth accounted for only 1.5 percent. And while the ratio between the income of the richest 20 percent and the poorest 20 percent of the world's population was 30:1 in 1960, it grew to 45:1 in 1980 and then to 82:1 in 1995.

This pattern is replicated at the level of individual countries as well. Where all developing countries have seen their gross national product (GNP) per capita rise from 5.0 percent of the industrialized countries in 1960 to 7.0 percent in 1995, the "least" developed countries (those with a GNP per capita of $300 or less) fell from 3.5 percent to 1.8 percent. These income trends are repeated in the areas of trade, savings, and investment.[1] While economic growth has increased over the post-1945 period, raising the average standard of living around the globe, the gaps between the world's wealthiest and poorest societies have increased even faster. As Jeffrey G. Williamson points out in Reading 27, the comparisons between current trends—in income differentials both among countries and within them—and those of the nineteenth and early twentieth centuries is illuminating and potentially worrisome.

For decades, scholars and practitioners have debated the sources of economic growth and the best strategies for producing rapid increases in standards of living. Many analysts argue that development, at least in its initial

443

stages, requires that the country insulate itself from more established economic powers and stimulate key industries at home through trade protection and government subsidies. Indeed, Alexander Hamilton, the first secretary of the treasury of the United States, argued for just such a policy in his famous *Report on Manufactures,* which he presented to the House of Representatives in 1791.

Starting in the 1930s with the collapse of the international economy in the Great Depression, many so-called developing countries began de facto strategies of import-substituting industrialization (ISI) in order to increase domestic production to fill the gap created by the decrease in foreign trade. After World War II, especially in Latin America but elsewhere as well, this de facto strategy was institutionalized de jure in high tariffs and explicit governmental policies of industrial promotion. Behind protective walls, countries sought to substitute domestic manufactures for foreign imports, first in light manufactures, such as textiles, apparel, and food processing, and later in intermediate and capital goods production.

Beginning in the 1960s, however, ISI started to come under increasing criticism. Government incentives for manufacturing benefited industry at the expense of agriculture—increasing rural-to-urban migration and often worsening income distribution—and produced many distortions and inefficiencies in the economy. The later stages of ISI, which focused on intermediate and capital goods production and were often more dependent on technology and economies of scale in production, also had the paradoxical effect of increasing national dependence on foreign firms and capital. Yet despite these criticisms, virtually all countries that have industrialized successfully have also adopted ISI for at least a brief period. While many economists argue that success occurs in spite of trade protection and government policies of industrial promotion, historical experience suggests that some degree of import substitution may be a necessary prerequisite for economic development.

In the 1980s, ISI generally gave way to policies of export-led growth. Many developing countries came to recognize the economic inefficiencies introduced by protectionist policies. The debt crisis of the early 1980s and the subsequent decline in new foreign lending increased the importance of exports as a means of earning foreign exchange. Rapid technological changes made "self-reliance" less attractive. There were also important political pressures to abandon ISI. The World Bank and International Monetary Fund (IMF), important sources of capital for developing countries, pressed vigorously for more liberal international economic policies. Proclaiming the "magic of the marketplace," the United States also pushed for more liberal economic policies in the developing world.

Particularly important in reorienting development policy was the success of the newly industrializing countries (NICs) of East Asia: South Korea,

Taiwan, Hong Kong, and Singapore. All these states achieved impressive rates of economic growth and industrialization through strategies of aggressive export promotion. While they all adopted ISI during their initial stages of development, the NICs generally sought to work with, rather than against, international market forces. With well-educated labor forces but limited raw materials, the NICs exploited their comparative advantage in light manufactures and, over time, diversified into more capital-intensive production. Today, the NICs are among the most rapidly growing countries in the world, and they have achieved this result with relatively egalitarian income distributions.

The opening to the world economy of large developing countries, such as China and India, is further evidence that strategies of development now hinge on globalization. Prior to the 1980s, China and India had almost totally closed economies. Since then, they—and many other developing countries—have experienced high rates of growth while pursuing outward-oriented policies.

The sources of development are controversial, however. Some analysts give primacy to the outward-oriented strategies adopted by China, India, and other recent globalizers. This view is represented in the article by David Dollar (Reading 25). Others argue that domestic institutions are the fundamental sources of development. For example, Daron Acemoglu (Reading 26) maintains that the prerequisites for development are domestic institutions that protect property rights, promote investment, and constrain the ability of politicians and powerful interest groups to expropriate the wealth of others.

For many developing countries, the road to economic and political reform has been long and arduous. According to Razeen Sally (Reading 28), the process of moving from ISI and central planning to open markets and limited governments has been so difficult and protracted that it has engendered widespread opposition to further reform. This problem, and the problem of development more generally, raises questions central to the study of international political economy. How, and under what circumstances, should countries seek to integrate themselves into the international market? How can the international economy be structured so as to fulfill the needs of separate nation-states? How does the international economy affect politics within states?

An examination of the historical and contemporary international political economy can shed important light on these questions and produce essential insights into the future of the economies in development. Nonetheless, the final outcome of this process will not be known for many years and depends fundamentally on the weight of decades of past developments. As Karl Marx wrote in 1852: "Men make their own history, but they do not make it just as they please; they do not make it under circumstances chosen by themselves, but under circumstances directly encountered, given and transmitted from the past."[2]

NOTES

1. These figures are from United Nations Development Programme (UNDP), *Human Development Report 1992* (New York: Oxford University Press, 1992), pp. 35, 141; and UNDP, *Human Development Report 1998* (New York: Oxford University Press, 1998), pp. 2, 29–30, 206; UNDP, *Human Development Report 2003* (New York: Oxford University Press, 2003), p. 39; and World Bank, *World Development Indicators 2008* (New York: World Bank Publications), p. 4.

2. Karl Marx, *The Eighteenth Brumaire of Louis Napoleon*, 1852.

25

Globalization, Poverty, and Inequality since 1980

DAVID DOLLAR

One of the most contentious contemporary issues is the effect of global economic integration on inequality and poverty. David Dollar, at the time a research economist with the World Bank, documents a number of trends in inequality and poverty during the modern era of globalization. He shows that poor countries are growing at a faster rate than rich countries for the first time in modern history. He also finds that the number of people in the world living in extreme poverty has declined significantly since 1980—another first in modern history—and that there is no general trend toward higher inequality within countries. While not all his news is good, most of it suggests that the developing countries are, in fact, on the path to development and that poverty is in decline. Furthermore, the trends toward faster growth and poverty reduction are strongest in the developing countries in which there has been the most rapid integration with the global economy, supporting the view that globalization has been a positive force for improving people's lives in the developing world.

There is an odd disconnect between debates about globalization in developed economies and developing economies. Among intellectuals in developed areas one often hears the claim that global economic integration is leading to rising global inequality—that is, that integration benefits rich people proportionally more than poor people. In the extreme claims poor people are actually made out to be worse off absolutely. In developing economies, though, intellectuals and policymakers often view globalization as providing good opportunities for their countries and people. To be sure, they are not happy with . . . rich countries for their protectionism against poor countries. . . . But the point of these critiques is that integration—through foreign trade, foreign investment, and immigration—is basically a good thing for poor countries and that rich countries could do a lot more to facilitate integration—that is, make it freer. The claims from antiglobalization intellectuals in rich countries, however, lead inescapably to the conclusion that integration is bad for poor countries and that therefore trade and other flows should be more restricted.

The first goal of this article is to document what is known about trends in global inequality and poverty over the long term and during the recent wave of globalization that began around 1980. Global inequality is used to mean different things in different discussions—distribution among all the citizens of the world, distribution within countries, distribution among countries, distribution among wage earners—all of which are used in this article. A second goal of the article is to relate these trends to globalization.

The first section briefly discusses the growing integration of developing economies with industrialized countries and with each other, starting around 1980. The opening of large developing countries, such as China and India, is arguably the most distinctive feature of this wave of globalization. The second section, the heart of the article, presents evidence in support of five trends in inequality and poverty since 1980:

- Growth rates in poor countries have accelerated and are higher than growth rates in rich countries for the first time in modern history.
- The number of extremely poor people (those living on less than $1 a day) in the world has declined significantly—by 375 million people—for the first time in history, though the number living on less than $2 a day has increased.
- Global inequality has declined modestly, reversing a 200-year trend toward higher inequality.
- Within-country inequality is generally not growing.
- Wage inequality is rising worldwide. This may seem to contradict the fourth trend, but it does not because there is no simple link between wage inequality and household income inequality.

The third section then tries to draw a link between the increased integration and accelerated growth and poverty reduction. Individual cases, cross-country statistical analysis, and micro-evidence from firms all suggest that opening to trade and direct investment has been a good strategy for such countries as China, India, Mexico, Uganda, and Vietnam. The conclusions for policy in the fourth section are . . . Developing economies have a lot to do to develop in general and to make effective use of integration as part of their development strategy. Rich countries could do a lot more with foreign aid to help with that work. Access to markets in rich countries is important. A lot of protections remain in Organisation for Economic Co-operation and Development (OECD) markets from the goods and people of developing economies, and globalization would work much better for poor people if developing areas had more access to those markets.

GROWING INTEGRATION BETWEEN DEVELOPED AND DEVELOPING ECONOMIES

Global economic integration has been going on for a long time. In that sense, globalization is nothing new. What is new in this most recent wave of globalization is the way developing countries are integrating with rich countries. As in previous waves of integration, this change is driven partly by technological advances in transport and communications and partly by deliberate policy choices. . . .

Recent Wave of Globalization

The most recent wave of globalization started in 1978 with the initiation of China's economic reform and opening to the outside world, which roughly coincides with the second oil shock, which contributed to external debt crises throughout Latin America and in other developing economies. In a growing number of countries in Latin America, South Asia, and Sub-Saharan Africa political and intellectual leaders began to fundamentally rethink development strategies. The distinctive part of this latest wave of globalization is that the majority of developing economies (in terms of population) shifted from an inward-focused strategy to a more outward-oriented one.

This altered strategy can be seen in the huge increases in trade integration of developing areas over the past two decades. China's ratio of trade to national income has more than doubled, and countries such as Mexico, Bangladesh, Thailand, and India have seen large increases as well (figure 1). But several developing economies trade less of their income than two decades ago, a fact that will be discussed later. The change has not been only in the

FIGURE 1 Change in Trade as a Share of GDP, Selected Countries, 1977–1997 (%)

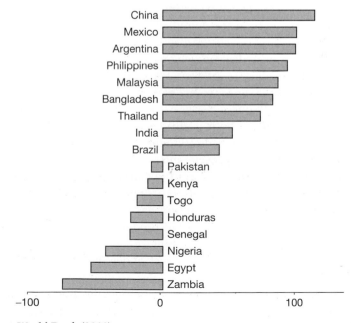

SOURCE: World Bank (2002).

FIGURE 2   Developing Country Exports by Sector, 1965–1999 (% of total)

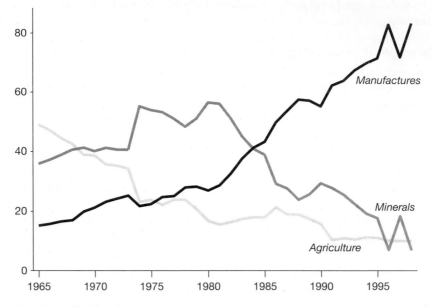

SOURCE: World Bank (2002).

amount, but also in the nature of what is traded. Twenty years ago, nearly 80 percent of developing country merchandise exports were primary products: the stereotype of poor countries exporting tin or bananas had a large element of truth. The big increase in merchandise exports in the past two decades, however, has been of manufactured products, so that 80 percent of today's merchandise exports from developing countries are manufactures (figure 2). Garments from Bangladesh, CD players from China, refrigerators from Mexico, and computer peripherals from Thailand—these are the modern face of developing economy exports. Service exports from developing areas have also increased enormously—both traditional services, such as tourism, and modern ones, such as software from Bangalore, India.

Manufactured exports from developing economies are often part of multinational production networks. Nike contracts with firms in Vietnam to make shoes; the "world car" is a reality, with parts produced in different locations. So part of the answer to why integration has taken off must lie with technological advances that make integrated production feasible (. . . dramatic declines in the cost of air transport and international communications). But part of the answer also lies in policy choices of developing economies. China and India had almost totally closed economies, so their increased integration would not have been possible without steps to gradually liberalize trade and direct foreign investment.

Some measure of this policy trend can be seen in average import tariff rates for developing economies. Since 1980 average tariffs have declined sharply in South Asia, Latin America and the Caribbean, and East Asia and Pacific, whereas in Africa and the Middle East there has been much less tariff-cutting. These reported average tariffs, however, capture only a small amount of what is happening with trade policy. Often the most pernicious impediments are nontariff barriers: quotas, licensing schemes, restrictions on purchasing foreign exchange for imports, and the like. China started to reduce these nontariff impediments in 1979, which led to a dramatic surge in trade. . . .

Another major impediment to trade in many developing areas is inefficient ports and customs administration. For example, it is much more expensive to ship a container of textiles from a Mombasa, Kenya, port to the East Coast of the United States than from Asian ports such as Mumbai, Shanghai, Bangkok, or Kaohsiung, Taiwan (China), even though Mombasa is closer. The extra cost, equivalent to an 8 percent export tax, is due to inefficiencies and corruption in the port. Long customs delays often act as import and export taxes. Developing economies that have become more integrated with the world economy have reasonably well-functioning ports and customs, and their improvement has often been a deliberate policy target. Several countries, including Kenya, trade less of their income today than 20 years ago; surely this is partly the result of restrictive trade policies, defined broadly to include inefficient ports and customs.

Thus, one key development in this current wave of globalization is a dramatic change in the way many developing countries relate to the global economy. Developing economies as a whole are a major exporter of manufactures and services—many of which compete directly with products made in industrialized countries. The nature of trade and competition between rich and poor countries has fundamentally changed.

ACCELERATED GROWTH AND POVERTY REDUCTION IN DEVELOPING ECONOMIES

Some of the debate about globalization concerns its effects on poor countries and poor people. . . . Thus, this section focuses on the trends in global poverty and inequality, and the following section links them to global integration. The trends of the last 20 years highlighted here are:

- Growth rates of developing economies have accelerated and are higher than those of industrialized countries.
- The number of extremely poor people (those living on less than $1 a day) has declined for the first time in history, though the number of people living on less than $2 a day has increased.

- Measures of global inequality (such as the global Gini coefficient) have declined modestly, reversing a long historical trend toward greater inequality.
- Within-country inequality in general is not growing, though it has risen in several populous countries (China, India, the United States).
- Wage inequality in general has been rising (meaning larger wage increases for skilled workers than for unskilled workers).

The fifth trend may seem to run counter to the fourth trend; why it does not will be explained here. The fifth trend is important for explaining some of the anxiety about globalization in industrialized countries.

Growth Rates in Developing Economies Have Accelerated

Reasonably good data on economic growth since 1960 for about 100 countries that account for the vast majority of world population are summarized in the Penn World Tables (Center for International Comparisons 2004). Aggregating data on growth rates for industrialized countries and developing economies for which there are data since 1960 shows that in general growth rates have declined in rich countries while accelerating in developing countries (figure 3). In particular, in the 1960s growth of OECD countries was about twice as fast as that of developing areas. Per capita growth rates in rich

FIGURE 3 GDP per Capita Growth Rate, by Country Type, 1960s–1990s (%)

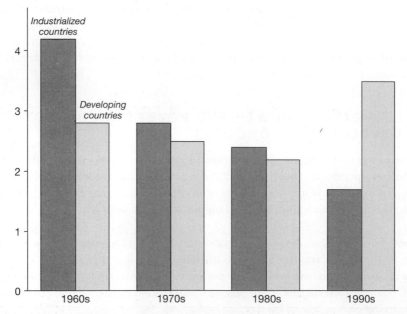

SOURCE: Center for International Comparisons (2004).

countries have gradually declined from about 4 percent in the 1960s to 1.7 percent in the 1990s—close to the long-term historical trend rate of the OECD countries. The rapid growth in the 1960s was still to some extent a rebound from the destruction of World War II as well as a payoff to economic integration among rich countries.

In the 1960s and early 1970s, the growth rate of developing economies was well below that of rich countries, a paradox whose origin has been long debated. The slower growth of less developed economies was a paradox because neoclassical growth theory suggested that other things being equal poor countries should grow faster. This pattern finally emerged in the 1990s, with per capita growth in developing countries of about 3.5 percent—more than twice the rate of rich countries.

This high aggregate growth depends heavily on several large countries that were among the poorest in the world in 1980 but that have grown well since then. Ignoring differences in population and averaging growth rates in poor countries over 1980–2000 result in an average growth of about zero for poor countries. China, India, and several small countries, particularly in Africa, are among the poorest quintile of countries in 1980. Ignoring population, the average growth of Chad and China is about zero, and the average growth of India and Togo is about zero. Accounting for differences in population, though, the average growth of poor countries has been very good in the past 20 years. China obviously carries a large weight in any calculation of the growth of poor countries in 1980, but it is not the only poor country that did well: Bangladesh, India, and Vietnam also grew faster than rich countries in the same period. Several African economies, notably Uganda, also had accelerated growth.

The Number of Extremely Poor People Has Declined by 375 Million Globally

The most important point in this section is that poverty reduction in low-income countries is very closely related to the GDP growth rate. The accelerated growth of low-income countries has led to unprecedented poverty reduction. By poverty I mean subsisting below some absolute threshold. Most poverty analyses are carried out with countries' own poverty lines, which are set in country context and naturally differ.

China, for example, uses a poverty line defined in constant Chinese yuan. The poverty line is deemed the minimum amount necessary to subsist. In practice, estimates of the number of poor in a country such as China come from household surveys carried out by a statistical bureau. These surveys aim to measure what households actually consume. Most extremely poor people in the world are peasants, and they subsist to a large extent on their own agricultural output. To look only at their money income would not be very relevant, because the extremely poor have only limited involvement in the money economy. Thus measures ask households what they actually consume and attach a value to their consumption based on the prices of different commodities. So a poverty line is meant to capture a certain real level of consumption. Estimating the extent of poverty is obviously subject to error, but in many countries the measures are good enough to pick up large trends. In discussing poverty it is important to be clear on the poverty line being used. In global discussions international poverty lines of either $1 a day or $2 a day, calculated at purchasing power parity, are used. For discussions of global poverty a common line should be applied to all countries.

Chen and Ravallion (2004) used household survey data to estimate the number of poor people worldwide based on the $1 a day and $2 a day poverty lines back to 1981. They found that the incidence of extreme poverty (consuming less than $1 a day) was basically cut in half in 20 years, from 40.4 percent of the population in developing economies in 1981 to 21.1 percent in 2001. It is interesting that the decline in $2 a day poverty incidence was not as great, from 66.7 percent to 52.9 percent, over the same period.

Poverty incidence has been gradually declining throughout modern history, but in general population growth has outstripped the decline in incidence so that the total number of poor people has actually risen. Even in 1960–80, a reasonably prosperous period for developing economies, the number of extremely poor people continued to rise. Most striking in the past 20 years is that the number of extremely poor people declined by 375 million, while at the same time world population rose by 1.6 billion. But the decline was not steady: in 1987–93 the number of extremely poor people rose, as growth slowed in China and India underwent an economic crisis. After 1993 growth and poverty reduction accelerated in both countries.

The 1981–2001 decline in the number of extremely poor people is unprecedented in human history. At the same time many of those who rose above the very low $1 a day threshold are still living on less than $2 a day. The number of people living on less than $2 a day increased between 1981 and 2001 by nearly 300 million. About half the world's population still lives on less than $2 a day, and it will take several more decades of sustained growth to bring this figure down significantly.

Although the overall decline in extreme poverty is positive news, performance has varied by region. South Asia and East Asia and Pacific grew well and reduced poverty, but Sub-Saharan Africa had negative growth between 1981 and 2001 and a rise in poverty: the number of extremely poor people there increased from 164 million (41.6 percent of the population) to 316 million (46.9 percent of the population). Two-thirds of extremely poor people still live in Asia, but if strong growth there continues, global poverty will be increasingly concentrated in Africa.

Global Inequality Has Declined Modestly

Global inequality is casually used to mean several things, but the most sensible definition is the same as for a country: line up all the people in the world from the poorest to the richest and calculate a measure of inequality among their incomes. There are several measures, of which the Gini coefficient is the best known. Bhalla (2002) estimates that the global Gini coefficient declined from 0.67 in 1980 to 0.64 in 2000 after rising from 0.64 in 1960. Sala-i-Martin (2002) likewise finds that all the standard measures of inequality show a decline in global inequality since 1980. . . .

For historical perspective, Bourguignon and Morrisson (2002) calculate the global Gini coefficient back to 1820. Although confidence in these early estimates is not high, they illustrate an important point: global inequality has been on the rise throughout modern economic history. Bourguignon and Morrisson estimate that the global Gini coefficient rose from 0.50 in 1820 to about 0.65 around 1980. Sala-i-Martin (2002) estimates that it has since declined to 0.61.

Other measures of inequality such as mean log deviation show a similar trend, rising until about 1980 and then declining modestly after. Roughly speaking, the mean log deviation is the percent difference between average income in the world and the income of a randomly chosen individual who represents a typical person. Average per capita income in the world today is around $5,000, but the typical person lives on 20 percent of that, or $1,000. The advantage of the mean log deviation is that it can be decomposed into inequality between countries (differences in per capita income across countries) and inequality within countries. This decomposition shows that most inequality in the world can be attributed to inequality among countries. Global inequality rose from 1820 to 1980, primarily because already relatively rich countries (those in Europe and North America) grew faster than poor ones. As noted in the discussion of the first trend, that pattern of growth was reversed starting around 1980, and the faster growth in such poor countries as Bangladesh, China, India, and Vietnam accounts for the modest decline in global inequality since then. (Slow growth in Africa tended to increase inequality, faster growth in low-income Asia tended to reduce it, and Asia's growth modestly outweighed Africa's.)

Thinking about the different experiences of Africa and Asia, as in the last section, helps give a clearer picture of what is likely to happen in the future. Rapid growth in Asia has been a force for greater global equality because that is where the majority of the world's extremely poor people lived in 1980—and they benefited from growth. But if the same growth trends persist, they will not continue to be a force for equality. Sala-i-Martin (2002) projects future global inequality if the growth rates of 1980–98 persist: global inequality will continue to decline until about 2015, after which global inequality will rise sharply. A large share of the world's poor people still lives in India and other Asian countries, so that continued rapid growth there will be equalizing for another decade or so. But increasingly poverty will be concentrated in Africa, so that if slow growth persists there, global inequality will eventually rise again.

Within-Country Inequality Is in General Not Growing

The previous analysis shows that inequality within countries has a relatively small role in measures of global income inequality. But people care about trends in inequality in their own societies (arguably more than they care about global inequality and poverty). So a different question is what is happening to income inequality within countries. One common claim about globalization is that it leads to greater inequality within countries and thus fosters social and political polarization.

To assess this claim Dollar and Kraay (2002) collected income distribution data from more than 100 countries, in some cases going back decades. They found no general trend toward higher or lower inequality within countries. Focusing on the share of income going to the bottom quintile, another common measure of inequality, they found increases in inequality for some countries (for example, China and the United States) in the 1980s and 1990s and decreases for others. They also tried to use measures of integration to explain the changes in inequality that have occurred, but none of the changes were related to any of the measures. For example, countries in which trade integration increased showed rises in inequality in some cases and declines in others. They found the same results for other measures, such as tariff rates and capital controls. Particularly in low-income countries, much of the import protection benefited relatively rich and powerful groups, so that integration with the global market went hand in hand with declines in income inequality. It is widely recognized that income distribution data have a lot of measurement error, which makes it difficult to identify systematic relationships, but given the available data, there is no robust evidence that integration is systematically related to higher inequality within countries.

There are two important caveats to this conclusion. First, inequality has risen in several very populous countries, notably China, India, and the United States. This means that a majority of citizens of the world live in countries in which inequality is rising. Second, the picture of inequality is not so favorable for rich countries in the past decade. The Luxembourg Income Study, using comparable, high-quality income distribution data for most rich countries, finds no obvious trends in inequality through the mid- to late 1980s. Over the past decade, though, inequality has increased in most rich countries. Because low-skilled workers in these countries now compete more with workers in developing economies, global economic integration can create pressure for higher inequality in rich countries while having effects in poor countries that often go the other way. The good news from the Luxembourg Income Study is that "domestic policies and institutions still have large effects on the level and trend of inequality within rich and middle-income nations, even in a globalizing world. . . . Globalization does not force any single outcome on any country" (Smeeding 2002, p. 179). In other words, some rich countries have maintained stable income distributions in this era of globalization through their social and economic policies (on taxes, education, welfare, and the like).

Wage Inequality Is Rising Worldwide

Much of the concern about globalization in rich countries relates to workers, wages, and other labor issues. The most comprehensive examination of globalization and wages used International Labour Organization data from the past two decades (Freeman and others 2001). These data look across countries at what is happening to wages for very specific occupations (for example, bricklayer, primary schoolteacher, nurse, autoworker). The study found that wages have generally been rising fastest in more globalized developing economies, followed by rich countries, and then less globalized developing economies. . . . The fastest wage growth is occurring in developing economies that are actively increasing their integration with the global economy.

Although the general rise in wages is good news, the detailed findings from Freeman and others (2001) are more complex and indicate that certain types of workers benefit more than others. First, increased trade is related to a decline in the gender wage gap. More trade appears to lead to a more competitive labor market in which groups that have been traditionally discriminated against—women, for example—fare especially well. Second, the gains from increased trade appear to be larger for skilled workers. This finding is consistent with other work showing a worldwide trend toward greater wage inequality—that is, a larger gap between pay for educated workers and pay for less educated and unskilled workers. . . . Wages in skill-intensive industries, such as aircraft production, have been going up faster than wages in low-skill industries, such as garments.

If wage inequality is going up worldwide, how can income inequality not be rising in most countries? There are several reasons. First, in the typical developing economy wage earners make up a small share of the population. Even unskilled wage workers are a relatively elite group. Take Vietnam, for example, a low-income country with a survey of the same representative sample of households early in liberalization (1993) and five years later. The majority of households in the country (and thus in the sample) are peasants. The household data show that the price of the main agricultural output (rice) went up dramatically while the price of the main purchased input (fertilizer) actually went down. Both movements are related directly to globalization because over the survey period Vietnam became a major exporter of rice (raising its price) and a major importer of fertilizer from cheaper producers (lowering its price). Poor families faced a much bigger wedge between rice's input price and output price, and their real income went up dramatically. So, one of the most important forces acting on income distribution in this low-income country had nothing to do with wages.

Several rural households also sent a family member to a nearby city to work in a factory for the first time. In 1989 the typical wage in Vietnamese currency was the equivalent of $9 a month. Today, factory workers making contract shoes for U.S. brands often make $50 a month or more. So the wage for a relatively unskilled worker has gone up nearly fivefold. But wages for some skilled occupations, for example, computer programmers and English interpreters, may have gone up 10 times or more. Thus, a careful study of wage inequality is likely to show rising inequality. But how wage inequality translates into household inequality is very complex. For a surplus worker from a large rural household who obtains a newly created job in a shoe factory, earnings increase from $0 to $50 a month. If many new wage jobs are created, and if they typically pay much more than people earn in the rural or informal sectors, a country can have rising wage inequality but stable or even declining income inequality. . . .

In rich countries most household income comes from wages, but household income inequality and wage inequality do not have to move in the same direction. If there are changes in the way that people partner and combine into households, household inequality can rise even if wage inequality stays the same. Another point about wage inequality and household income inequality relevant to rich countries is that measures of wage inequality are often made before taxes are taken out of earnings. If the country has a strongly progressive income tax, inequality measures from household data (which are often made after taxes are taken out of earnings) do not have to follow pretax wage inequality. Tax policy can offset some of the trends in the labor market.

Finally, households can respond to increased wage inequality by investing more in their children's education. A higher economic return to education is not a bad thing, as long as there is equal access to education for all. Vietnam saw a tremendous increase in the secondary school enrollment rate in the 1990s—from 32 percent in 1990–91 to 56 percent in 1997–98. This increase partly reflects society's and the government's investment in schools (supported by aid donors) and partly reflects households' decisions. If little or no return to education is perceived (that is, no jobs at the end of the road), it is much harder to convince families in poor countries to send their children to school. Where children have decent access to education, a higher skill premium stimulates a shift of the labor force from low-skill to higher-skill occupations.

It should also be noted that there has been a large decline in child labor in Vietnam since the country started integrating with the global market. There is ample evidence that child labor is driven primarily by poverty and educational opportunities. Child labor is more prevalent in poor households, but between 1993 and 1998 it declined for all income groups. The change resulted from the fact that everyone was richer than they were five years earlier and from the expansion of schooling opportunities.

From this discussion of wage trends, it is easy to see why some labor unions in rich countries are concerned about integration with developing economies. It is difficult to prove that integration is increasing wage inequality, but it seems likely that integration is one factor. Concerning the immigration side of integration, Borjas and others (1997) estimate that flows of unskilled labor into the United States have reduced wages for unskilled labor by 5 percent from where they otherwise would be. Immigrants who find new jobs earn much more than they did before (10 times as much, according to World Bank 2002), but their competition reduces the wages of U.S. workers already doing such jobs. Similarly, imports of garments and footwear from countries such as Bangladesh and Vietnam create jobs for workers that pay far more than other opportunities in those countries but put pressure on unskilled wages in rich countries.

Thus overall the era of globalization has seen unprecedented reduction of extreme poverty and a modest decline in global inequality. But it has put real pressure on less skilled workers in rich countries—a key reason why the growing integration is controversial in industrialized countries.

IS THERE A LINK BETWEEN INTEGRATION AND POVERTY REDUCTION?

Developing economies have become more integrated with the global economy in the past two decades, and growth and poverty reduction have accelerated. A natural question is whether there is a link between the two. In other words, could countries such as Bangladesh, China, India, and Vietnam have grown as rapidly if they had remained as closed to foreign trade and investment as they were in 1980? This cannot be answered with scientific certainty, but several different types of evidence can be brought to bear on it.

It is useful to begin with what to expect from economic theory. . . . Traditional growth theory focuses on accumulation and the "object gap" between poor countries and rich ones. If increasing the number of factories and workplaces is the only important action, it does not matter whether the environment is closed or dominated by the state. This model was followed in the extreme by China and the Soviet Union, and to a lesser extent by most developing economies, which followed import-substituting industrialization strategies throughout the 1960s and 1970s. The disappointing results from this approach led to new thinking by policymakers in developing areas and economists studying growth. . . . The new growth theory . . . emphasized how innovation occurs and is spread and the role of technological advance in improving the standard of living. Different aspects of integration—sending students abroad to study, connecting to the Internet, allowing foreign firms to open plants, purchasing the latest equipment and components—can help overcome the "idea gap" that separates poor countries from rich countries.

What is the evidence on integration spurring growth? Some of the most compelling evidence comes from case studies that show how this process can work in particular countries. Among the countries that were very poor in 1980, China, India, Uganda, and Vietnam provide an interesting range of examples:

China

China's initial reforms in the late 1970s focused on the agricultural sector and emphasized strengthening property rights, liberalizing prices, and creating internal markets. Liberalizing foreign trade and investment were also part of the initial reform program and played an increasingly important role in growth as the 1980s proceeded. The role of international links is described in a case study by Eckaus (1997, pp. 415–37):

> China's foreign trade began to expand rapidly as the turmoil created by the Cultural Revolution dissipated and new leaders came to power. Though it was not done without controversy, the argument that opening of the economy to foreign trade was necessary to obtain new capital equipment and new technology was made official policy. . . . Most obviously, enterprises created by foreign investors have been exempt from the foreign trade planning and control mechanisms. In addition, substantial amounts of other types of trade, particularly the trade of the township and village enterprises and private firms, have been relatively free. The expansion of China's participation in international trade since the beginning of the reform movement in 1978, has been one of the most remarkable features of its remarkable transformation.

India

It is well known that India pursued an inward-oriented strategy into the 1980s with disappointing results in growth and poverty reduction. . . .

Under this policy regime India's growth in the 1960s (1.4 percent a year) and 1970s (–0.3 percent) was disappointing. During the 1980s India's economic performance improved, but this surge was fueled by deficit spending and borrowing from abroad that was unsustainable. In fact, the spending spree led to a fiscal and balance of payments crisis that brought a new, reform government to power in 1991. Srinivasan (1996, p. 245) describes the key reform measures and their results:

> In July 1991, the government announced a series of far reaching reforms. These included an initial devaluation of the rupee and subsequent market determination of its exchange rate, abolition of import licensing with the important exceptions that the restrictions on imports of manufactured consumer goods and on foreign trade in agriculture remained in place, convertibility (with some notable exceptions) of the rupee on

the current account; reduction in the number of tariff lines as well as tariff rates; reduction in excise duties on a number of commodities; some limited reforms of direct taxes; abolition of industrial licensing except for investment in a few industries for locational reasons or for environmental considerations, relaxation of restrictions on large industrial houses under the Monopolies and Restrictive Trade Practices (MRTP) Act; easing of entry requirements (including equity participation) for direct foreign investment; and allowing private investment in some industries hitherto reserved for public sector investment.

In general, India has seen good results from its reform program, with per capita income growth above 4 percent a year in the 1990s. Growth and poverty reduction have been particularly strong in states that have made the most progress liberalizing the regulatory framework and providing a good environment for delivery of infrastructure services.

Uganda

Uganda has been one of the most successful reformers in Africa during this recent wave of globalization, and its experience has interesting parallels with Vietnam's. It, too, was a country that was quite isolated economically and politically in the early 1980s. The role of trade reform in its larger reform context is described in Collier and Reinikka (2001, pp. 30–39):

> Trade liberalization has been central to Uganda's structural reform program. . . . In 1986 the NRM government inherited a trade regime that included extensive nontariff barriers, biased government purchasing, and high export taxes, coupled with considerable smuggling. The nontariff barriers have gradually been removed since the introduction in 1991 of automatic licensing under an import certification scheme. Similarly, central government purchasing was reformed and is now subject to open tendering without a preference for domestic firms over imports. . . . The average real GDP growth rate was 6.3 percent per year during the entire recovery period (1986–99) and 6.9 percent in the 1990s. The liberalization of trade has had a marked effect on export performance. In the 1990s export volumes grew (at constant prices) at an annualized rate of 15 percent, and import volumes grew at 13 percent. The value of noncoffee exports increased fivefold between 1992 and 1999.

Vietnam

The same collection that contains Eckaus's (1997) study of China also has a case study of Vietnam, analyzing how the country went from being one of the poorest countries in the 1980s to being one of the fastest growing economies in the 1990s (Dollar and Ljunggren 1997, pp. 452–55):

That Vietnam was able to grow throughout its adjustment period can be attributed to the fact that the economy was being increasingly opened to the international market. As part of its overall effort to stabilize the economy, the government unified its various controlled exchange rates in 1989 and devalued the unified rate to the level prevailing in the parallel market. This was tantamount to a 73 percent *real* devaluation; combined with relaxed administrative procedures for imports and exports, this sharply increased the profitability of exporting.

This . . . policy produced strong incentives for export throughout most of the 1989–94 period. During these years real export growth averaged more than 25 percent per annum, and exports were a leading sector spurring the expansion of the economy. Rice exports were a major part of this success in 1989; and in 1993–94 there was a wide range of exports on the rise, including processed primary products (e.g., rubber, cashews, and coffee), labor-intensive manufactures, and tourist services. . . . In response to stabilization, strengthened property rights, and greater openness to foreign trade, domestic savings increased by twenty percentage points of GDP, from negative levels in the mid-1980s to 16 percent of GDP in 1992.

Are These Individual Country Findings Generalizable?

These cases provide persuasive evidence that openness to foreign trade and investment—coupled with complementary reforms—can lead to faster growth in developing economies. But individual cases always beg the question, how general are these results? Does the typical developing economy that liberalizes foreign trade and investment get good results? Cross-country statistical analysis is useful for looking at the general patterns in the data. Cross-country studies generally find a correlation between trade and growth. To relate this to the discussion in the first section, some developing economies have had large increases in trade integration (measured as the ratio of trade to national income), and others have had small increases or even declines. In general, the countries that had large increases also had accelerations in growth. The group of developing economy globalizers identified by Dollar and Kraay (2004) had population-weighted per capita growth of 5 percent in the 1990s, compared with 2 percent in rich countries and –1 percent for other developing countries (figure 4). This relationship between trade and growth persists after controlling for reverse causality from growth to trade and for changes in other institutions and policies.

A third type of evidence about integration and growth comes from firm-level studies. . . . Developing economies often have large productivity dispersion across firms making similar things: high-productivity and low-productivity firms coexist, and in small markets there is often insufficient competition to spur innovation. A consistent finding of firm-level studies is that openness leads to lower productivity dispersion. High-cost producers exit the market

FIGURE 4 Per Capita GDP Growth Rates, by Country Type, 1990s (%, based on GDP in purchasing power parity terms)

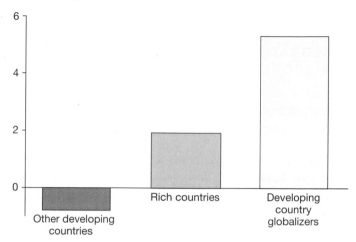

SOURCE: Dollar and Kraay (2004).

as prices fall; if these firms were less productive or were experiencing falling productivity, their exits represent productivity improvements for the industry. Although the destruction and creation of new firms is a normal part of a well-functioning economy, attention is simply too often paid to the destruction of firms—which misses half the picture. The increase in exits is only part of the adjustment—granted, it is the first and most painful part—but if there are no significant barriers to entry, there are also new entrants. The exits are often front loaded, but the net gains over time can be substantial.

Wacziarg (1998) uses 11 episodes of trade liberalization in the 1980s to examine competition and entry. Using data on the number of establishments in each sector, he calculates that entry rates were 20 percent higher in countries that liberalized than in countries that did not. This estimate may reflect other policies that accompanied trade liberalization, such as privatization and deregulation, so this is likely to be an upper bound of the impact of trade liberalization. However, it is a sizable effect and indicates that there is plenty of potential for new firms to respond to the new incentives. . . .

The higher turnover of firms is an important source of the dynamic benefit of openness. In general, dying firms have falling productivity and new firms tend to increase their productivity over time. Aw and others (2000) find that in Taiwan (China) within a five-year period the replacement of low-productivity firms with new, higher-productivity entrants accounted for half or more of the technological advance in many Taiwanese industries.

Although these studies shed some light on why open economies are more innovative and dynamic, they also show why integration is controversial. There will be more dislocation in an open, dynamic economy—with some firms closing and others starting up. If workers have good social protection and opportunities to develop new skills, everyone can benefit. But without these policies there can be some big losers. . . .

MAKING GLOBALIZATION WORK BETTER FOR POOR PEOPLE

So far, the most recent wave of globalization starting around 1980 has been associated with more rapid growth and poverty reduction in developing economies and with a modest decline in global inequality. These empirical findings from a wide range of studies help explain what otherwise might appear paradoxical: opinion surveys reveal that globalization is more popular in poor countries than in rich ones. In particular, the Pew Research Center for the People and the Press (2003) surveyed 38,000 people in 44 countries in all developing regions. In general, there was a positive view of growing economic integration worldwide. But what was striking in the survey was that views of globalization were distinctly more positive in low-income countries than in rich ones.

Although most people expressed the view that growing global trade and business ties are good for their country, only 28 percent of people in the United States and Western Europe thought that such integration was "very good." By contrast, the share who thought integration was very good was 64 percent in Uganda and 56 percent in Vietnam. These countries stood out as particularly proglobalization, but respondents from developing economies in Asia (37 percent) and Sub-Saharan Africa (56 percent) were also far more likely to find integration "very good" than respondents from rich countries. Conversely, a significant minority (27 percent) in rich countries thought that "globalization has a bad effect" on their country, compared with a negligible number of households in developing economies in Asia (9 percent) or Sub-Saharan Africa (10 percent).

Developing economies also had a more positive view of the institutions of globalization. Some 75 percent of households in Sub-Saharan Africa thought that multinational corporations had a positive influence on their country, compared with only 54 percent in rich countries. Views of the effect of the International Monetary Fund, the World Bank, and the World Trade Organization (WTO) were nearly as positive in Africa (72 percent of households said they had a positive effect on their country). By contrast, only 28 percent of households in Africa thought that antiglobalization protestors had a positive effect on their country. Views of the protestors were more positive in the United States and Western Europe (35 percent said the protestors had a positive effect on their country).

Although global economic integration has the potential to spur further growth and poverty reduction, whether this potential is realized depends on the policies of developing economies and the policies of industrialized countries. True integration requires not just trade liberalization but also wide-ranging reforms of institutions and policies, as the cases of China and India illustrate so clearly. Many of the countries that are not participating very much in globalization have serious problems with the overall investment climate, for example, Kenya, Myanmar, Nigeria, and Pakistan. Some of these countries also have restrictive policies toward trade. But even if they liberalize trade, not much is likely to happen without other measures. It is not easy to predict the reform paths of these countries. (Consider the relative successes cited here: China, India, Uganda, Vietnam. In each case their reform was a startling surprise.) As long as there are locations with weak institutions and policies, people living there are going to fall further behind the rest of the world in terms of living standards.

Building a coalition for reform in these locations is not easy, and what outsiders can do to help is limited. But one thing that industrialized countries can do is make it easy for developing areas that do choose to open up to join the club of trading nations. Unfortunately, in recent years rich countries have made it harder for poor countries to do so. The General Agreement on Tariffs and Trade was originally built around agreements concerning trade practices. Now, however, a certain degree of institutional harmonization is required to join the WTO, for example, on policies toward intellectual property rights. The proposal to regulate labor standards and environmental standards through WTO sanctions would take this requirement for institutional harmonization much farther. Developing economies see the proposal to regulate their labor and environmental standards through WTO sanctions as a new protectionist tool that rich countries can wield against them.

Globalization will proceed more smoothly if industrialized countries make it easy for developing economies to have access to their markets. Reciprocal trade liberalizations have worked well throughout the postwar period. There still are significant protections in OECD countries against agricultural and labor-intensive products that are important to developing economies. It would help substantially to reduce these protections. At the same time, developing economies would benefit from opening their own markets further. They have a lot to gain from more trade in services. Also, 70 percent of the tariff barriers that developing areas face are from other developing economies. So there is much potential to expand trade among developing areas, if trade restrictions are further eased. But the trend to use trade agreements to impose an institutional model from OECD countries on developing economies makes it more difficult to reach trade agreements that benefit poor countries. . . .

Another reason to be pessimistic about further integration of poor economies and rich ones is geography. There is no inherent reason why coastal China should be poor—or southern India, or Vietnam, or northern Mexico. These locations were historically held back by misguided policies, and with policy reform they can grow very rapidly and take their natural place in the world income distribution. However, the same reforms are not going to have the same effect in Chad and Mali. Some countries have poor geography in the sense that they are far from markets and have inherently high transport costs. Other locations face challenging health and agricultural problems. So, it would be naive to think that trade and investment can alleviate poverty in all locations. Much more could be done with foreign aid targeted to developing medicines for malaria, HIV/AIDS, and other health problems in poor areas and to building infrastructure and institutions in these locations. The promises of greater aid from Europe and the United States at the Monterrey Conference were encouraging, but it remains to be seen if these promises will be fulfilled.

So integration of poor economies with rich ones has provided many opportunities for poor people to improve their lives. Examples of the beneficiaries of globalization can be found among Chinese factory workers, Mexican migrants, Ugandan farmers, and Vietnamese peasants. Lots of nonpoor people in developing and industrialized economies alike also benefit, of course. But much of the current debate about globalization seems to ignore the fact that it has provided many poor people in developing economies unprecedented opportunities. After all the rhetoric about globalization is stripped away, many of the practical policy questions come down to whether rich countries are going to make it easy or difficult for poor communities that want to integrate with the world economy to do so. The world's poor people have a large stake in how rich countries answer these questions.

REFERENCES

Aw, B. Y., S. Chung, and M. J. Roberts. 2000. "Productivity and the Decision to Export: Micro Evidence from Taiwan and South Korea." *World Bank Economic Review* 14(1):65–90.

Bhalla, Surjit. 2002. *Imagine There Is No Country: Poverty, Inequality, and Growth in the Era of Globalization.* Washington, D.C.: Institute of International Economics.

Borjas, G. J., R. B. Freeman, and L. F. Katz. 1997. "How Much Do Immigration and Trade Affect Labor Market Outcomes?" *Brookings Papers on Economic Activity* 1:1–90.

Bourguignon, F., and C. Morrisson. 2002. "Inequality among World Citizens: 1820–1992." *American Economic Review* 92(4):727–44.

Center for International Comparisons. 2004. *Penn World Tables.* Philadelphia: University of Pennsylvania.

Chen, S., and M. Ravallion. 2004. "How Have the World's Poorest Fared since the Early 1980s?" Policy Research Working Paper 3341. World Bank, Washington, D.C.

Collier, P., and R. Reinikka. 2001. "Reconstruction and Liberalization: An Overview." In *Uganda's Recovery: The Role of Farms Firms, and Government.* Regional and Sectoral Studies. Washington, D.C.: World Bank.

Dollar, David, and Aart Kraay. 2002. "Growth Is Good for the Poor." *Journal of Economic Growth* 7(3):195–225.

———. 2004. "Trade, Growth, and Poverty." *Economic Journal* 114(493):F22–F49.

Dollar, David, and Borje Ljunggren. 1997. "Going Global, Vietnam." In Padma Desai, ed., *Going Global: Transition from Plan to Market in the World Economy.* Cambridge, Mass.: MIT Press.

Eckaus, R. 1997. "Going Global: China." In Padma Desai, ed., *Going Global: Transition from Plan to Market in the World Economy.* Cambridge, Mass.: MIT Press.

Freeman, R., R. Oostendorp, and M. Rama. 2001. "Globalization and Wages." World Bank, Washington, D.C.

Pew Research Center for the People and the Press. 2003. *Views of a Changing World: June 2003.* Second Major Report of the Pew Global Attitudes Project. Washington, D.C.

Sala-i-Martin, X. 2002. "The Disturbing 'Rise' of Global Income Inequality." Columbia University, New York.

Smeeding, T. M. 2002. "Globalization, Inequality and the Rich Countries of the G-20: Updated Results from the Luxembourg Income Study (LIS) and Other Places." Prepared for the G-20 Meeting, Globalization, Living Standards and Inequality: Recent Progress and Continuing Challenges, May 26–28, Sydney, Australia.

Srinivasan, T. N. 1996. "Indian Economic Reforms: Background, Rationale, Achievements, and Future Prospects." Yale University, Department of Economics, New Haven, Conn.

Wacziarg, R. 1998. "Measuring Dynamic Gains from Trade." Policy Research Working Paper 2001. World Bank, Washington, D.C.

World Bank. 2002. *Globalization, Growth, and Poverty: Building an Inclusive World Economy.* Oxford, U.K.: Oxford University Press.

26

Root Causes: A Historical Approach to Assessing the Role of Institutions in Economic Development

DARON ACEMOGLU

There are enormous differences in the wealth of nations and living standards across the globe, and the causes of these differences are hotly debated. In this selection, economist Daron Acemoglu develops the empirical and theoretical case that differences in domestic political institutions are the fundamental cause of differences in economic development. The author builds his case by conducting a "natural experiment" from history in which variation in the early colonization experiences of developing countries is considered the "treatment." In colonies where European settlers established political institutions that constrained the political power of elites, protected property rights for investors, and provided incentives to develop new technologies, growth rates were high regardless of initial geographic conditions. By contrast, today's development failures are often former colonies that were rich in the fifteenth and sixteenth centuries. But because Europeans installed extractive institutions to plunder resources or exploit the indigenous population, these countries have underperformed their potential. In short, the author claims that political institutions are most important for understanding the wealth of nations.

Tremendous differences in incomes and standards of living exist today between the rich and the poor countries of the world. Average per capita income in sub-Saharan Africa, for example, is less than one-twentieth that in the United States. Explanations for why the economic fortunes of countries have diverged so much abound. Poor countries, such as those in sub-Saharan Africa, Central America, or South Asia, often lack functioning markets, their populations are poorly educated, and their machinery and technology are outdated or nonexistent. But these are only *proximate* causes of poverty, begging the question of why these places don't have better markets, better human capital, more investments, and better machinery and technology. There must be some *fundamental* causes leading to these outcomes, and via these channels, to dire poverty.

The two main candidates to explain the fundamental causes of differences in prosperity between countries are geography and institutions. The *geography hypothesis*, which has a large following both in the popular imagination and in academia, maintains that the geography, climate, and ecology of a society shape both its technology and the incentives of its inhabitants. It emphasizes forces of nature as a primary factor in the poverty of nations. The alternative, the *institutions hypothesis*, is about human influences. According to this view, some societies have good institutions that encourage investment in machinery, human capital, and better technologies, and, consequently, these countries achieve economic prosperity.

Good institutions have three key characteristics: enforcement of property rights for a broad cross section of society, so that a variety of individuals have incentives to invest and take part in economic life; constraints on the actions of elites, politicians, and other powerful groups, so that these people cannot expropriate the incomes and investments of others or create a highly uneven playing field; and some degree of equal opportunity for broad segments of society, so that individuals can make investments, especially in human capital, and participate in productive economic activities. These good institutions contrast with conditions in many societies of the world, throughout history and today, where the rule of law is applied selectively: property rights are nonexistent for the vast majority of the population; the elites have unlimited political and economic power; and only a small fraction of citizens have access to education, credit, and production opportunities.

GEOGRAPHY'S INFLUENCE

If you want to believe that geography is the key, look at a world map. Locate the poorest places in the world where per capita incomes are less than one-twentieth those in the United States. You will find almost all of them close to the equator, in very hot regions that experience periodic torrential rains and where, by definition, tropical diseases are widespread.

However, this evidence does not establish that geography is a primary influence on prosperity. It is true there is a *correlation* between geography and prosperity. But correlation does not prove causation. Most important, there are often omitted factors driving the associations we observe in the data.

Similarly, if you look around the world, you'll see that almost no wealthy country achieves this position without institutions protecting the property rights of investors and imposing some control over the government and elites. Once again, however, this correlation between institutions and economic development could reflect omitted factors or reverse causality.

To make progress in understanding the relative roles of geographic and institutional factors, we need to find a source of exogenous variation in institutions—in other words, a natural experiment where institutions change for reasons unrelated to potential omitted factors (and geographic factors remain constant, as they almost always do).

The colonization of much of the globe by Europeans starting in the fifteenth century provides such a natural experiment. The colonization experience transformed the institutions in many lands conquered or controlled by Europeans but, by and large, had no effect on their geographies. Therefore, if geography is the key factor determining the economic potential of an area or a country, the places that were rich before the arrival of the Europeans should have remained rich after the colonization experience and, in fact, should still be rich today. In other words, since the key determinant of prosperity remains the same, we should see a high degree of persistence in economic outcomes. If, on the other hand, it is institutions that are central, then those places where good institutions were introduced or developed should be richer than those in which Europeans introduced or maintained extractive institutions to plunder resources or exploit the non-European population.

Historical evidence suggests that Europeans indeed pursued very different colonization strategies, with very different associated institutions, in various colonies. At one extreme, Europeans set up exclusively extractive institutions, exemplified by the Belgian colonization of the Congo slave plantations in the Caribbean, and forced labor systems in the mines of Central America. These institutions neither protected the property rights of regular citizens nor constrained the power of elites. At the other extreme, Europeans founded a number of colonies where they created settler societies, replicating—and often improving—the European form of institutions protecting private property. Primary examples of this mode of colonization include Australia, Canada, New Zealand, and the United States. The settlers in these societies also managed to place significant constraints on elites and politicians, even if they had to fight to achieve this objective.

REVERSAL OF FORTUNE

So what happened to economic development after colonization? Did places that were rich before colonization remain rich, as suggested by the geography hypothesis? Or did economic fortunes change systematically as a result of the changes in institutions?

The historical evidence shows no evidence of the persistence suggested by the geography hypothesis. On the contrary, there is a remarkable *reversal of fortune* in economic prosperity. Societies like the Mughals in India and the Aztecs and the Incas in America that were among the richest civilizations in 1500 are among the poorer societies of today. In contrast, countries occupying the territories of the less developed civilizations in North America, New Zealand, and Australia are now much *richer* than those in the lands of the Mughals, the Aztecs, and the Incas. Moreover, the reversal of fortune is not confined to this comparison. Using various proxies for prosperity before modern times, we can show that the reversal is a much more widespread phenomenon. For example, before industrialization, only relatively developed societies could sustain significant urbanization, so urbanization rates are a relatively good proxy for prosperity before European colonization. The chart here shows a strong negative relationship between urbanization rates in 1500 and income per capita today. [See Figure 1.] That is, the former Euro-

FIGURE 1 Shifting Prosperity: Countries That Were Rich in 1500 Are Among the Less Well Off Societies Today

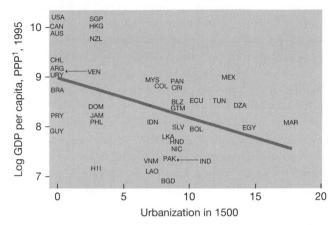

NOTE: ARG = Argentina, AUS = Australia, BGD = Bangladesh, BLZ = Belize, BOL = Bolivia, BRA = Brazil, CAN = Canada, CHL = Chile, COL = Colombia, CRI = Costa Rica, DOM = Dominican Republic, DZA = Albania, ECU = Ecuador, EGY = Egypt, GTM = Guatemala, GUY = Guyana, JAM = Jamaica, HKG = Hong Kong SAR, HND = Honduras, HTI = Haiti, IDN = Indonesia, IND = India, LAO = Lao People's Democratic Republic, LKA = Sri Lanka, MAR = Morocco, MEX = Mexico, MYS = Malaysia, NIC = Nicaragua, NZL = New Zealand, PAK = Pakistan, PAN = Panama, PER = Peru, PHL = Philippines, PRY = Paraguay, SGP = Singapore, SLV = El Salvador, TUN = Tunisia, URY = Uruguay, USA = United States, VEN = Venezuela, VNM = Vietnam.

[1]Purchasing power parity.

SOURCE: Author.

pean colonies that are relatively rich today are those that were poor before the Europeans arrived.

This reversal is prima facie evidence against the most standard versions of the geography hypothesis discussed above: it cannot be that the climate, ecology, or disease environments of the tropical areas have condemned these countries to poverty today, because these same areas with the same climate, ecology, and disease environment were richer than the temperate areas 500 years ago. Although it is possible that the reversal may be related to geographic factors whose effects on economic prosperity vary over time—for example, certain characteristics that first cause prosperity then condemn nations to poverty—there is no evidence of any such factor or any support for sophisticated geography hypotheses of this sort.

Is the reversal of fortune consistent with the institutions hypothesis? The answer is yes. In fact, once we look at the variation in colonization strategies, we see that the reversal of fortune is exactly what the institutions hypothesis predicts. European colonialism made Europeans the most politically powerful group, with the capability to influence institutions more than any indigenous group was able to at the time. In places where Europeans did not settle and cared little about aggregate output and the welfare of the population, in places where there was a large population that could be coerced and employed cheaply in mines or in agriculture or simply taxed, in places where there were resources to be extracted, Europeans pursued the strategy of setting up extractive institutions or taking over existing extractive institutions and hierarchical structures. In those colonies, there were no constraints on the power of the elites (which were typically the Europeans themselves and their allies) and no civil or property rights for the majority of the population; in fact, many of them were forced into labor or enslaved. Contrasting with this pattern, in colonies where there was little to be extracted, where most of the land was empty, where the disease environment was favorable, Europeans settled in large numbers and developed laws and institutions to ensure that they themselves were protected, in both their political and their economic lives. In these colonies, the institutions were therefore much more conducive to investment and economic growth.

This evidence does not mean that geography does not matter at all, however. Which places were rich and which were poor before Europeans arrived might have been determined by geographic factors. These geographic factors also likely influenced the institutions that Europeans introduced. For example, the climate and soil quality in the Caribbean made it productive to grow sugar there, encouraging the development of a plantation system based on slavery. What the evidence shows instead is that geography neither condemns a nation to poverty nor guarantees its economic success. If you want to understand why a country is poor today, you have to look at its institutions rather than its geography.

NO NATURAL GRAVITATION

If institutions are so important for economic prosperity, why do some societies choose or end up with bad institutions? Moreover, why do these bad institutions persist long after their disastrous consequences are apparent? Is it an accident of history or the result of misconceptions or mistakes by societies or their policymakers? Recent empirical and theoretical research suggests that the answer is no: there are no compelling reasons to think that societies will naturally gravitate toward good institutions. Institutions not only affect the economic prospects of nations but are also central to the distribution of income among individuals and groups in society—in other words, institutions not only affect the size of the social pie, but also how it is distributed.

This perspective implies that a potential change from dysfunctional and bad institutions toward better ones that will increase the size of the social pie may nonetheless be blocked when such a change significantly reduces the slice that powerful groups receive from the pie and when they cannot be credibly compensated for this loss. That there is no natural gravitation toward good institutions is illustrated by the attitudes of the landed elites and the emperors in Austria-Hungary and in Russia during the nineteenth century. These elite groups blocked industrialization and even the introduction of railways and protected the old regime because they realized capitalist growth and industrialization would reduce their power and their privileges.

Similarly, European colonists did not set up institutions to benefit society as a whole. They chose good institutions when it was in their interests to do so, when they would be the ones living under the umbrella of these institutions, as in much of the New World. In contrast, they introduced or maintained existing extractive institutions when it was in their interest to extract resources from the non-European populations of the colonies, as in much of Africa, Central America, the Caribbean, and South Asia. Furthermore, these extractive institutions showed no sign of evolving into better institutions, either under European control or once these colonies gained independence. In almost all cases, we can link the persistence of extractive institutions to the fact that, even after independence, the elites in these societies had a lot to lose from institutional reform. Their political power and claim to economic rents rested on the existing extractive institutions, as best illustrated by the Caribbean plantation owners whose wealth directly depended on slavery and extractive institutions. Any reform of the system, however beneficial for the country as a whole, would be a direct threat to the owners.

European colonialism is only one part of the story of the institutions of the former colonies, and many countries that never experienced European colonialism nonetheless suffer from institutional problems (while certain other former European colonies have arguably some of the best institutions in the world today). Nevertheless, the perspective developed in this article applies to these cases as well: institutional problems are important in a variety of instances, and, in most of these, the source of institutional problems and the difficulty of institutional reform lie in the fact that any major change creates winners and losers, and the potential losers are often powerful enough to resist change.

The persistence of institutions and potential resistance to reform do not mean that institutions are unchanging. There is often significant institutional evolution, and even highly dysfunctional institutions can be successfully transformed. For example, Botswana managed to build a functioning democracy after its independence from Britain and become the fastest-growing country in the world. Institutional change will happen either when groups that favor change become powerful enough to impose it on the potential losers, or when societies can strike a bargain with potential losers so as to credibly compensate them after the change takes place or, perhaps, shield them from the most adverse consequences of these changes. Recognizing the importance of institutions in economic development and the often formidable barriers to beneficial institutional reform is the first step toward significant progress in jump-starting rapid growth in many areas of the world today.

27

Globalization and Inequality, Past and Present

JEFFREY G. WILLIAMSON

The gap between the rich and the poor is a source of much political strife, both within countries and among them. Economic historian Jeffrey Williamson analyzes the experience of the past 150 years with an eye to the impact of globalization on inequality and finds that international economic integration before World War I exacerbated inequality in many developing countries, especially those with relatively abundant natural resources. This increased inequality may have contributed to a backlash against the international economy in the interwar period. Inasmuch as there is evidence of similar trends in income inequality in the past thirty years, Williamson's historical analysis suggests that we may see similar political conflict over the global economy in the future.

Economic growth after 1850 in the countries that now belong to the Organization for Economic Cooperation and Development (OECD) can be divided into three periods: the late nineteenth century belle epoque, the dark middle years between 1914 and 1950, and the late twentieth century renaissance. The first and last epochs were characterized by rapid growth; economic convergence as poor countries caught up with rich ones; and globalization, marked by trade booms, mass migrations, and huge capital flows. The years from 1914 to 1950 are associated with slow growth, a retreat from globalization, and economic divergence. Thus history offers an unambiguous positive correlation between globalization and convergence. When the pre–World War I years are examined in detail, the correlation turns out to be causal: globalization was *the* critical factor promoting economic convergence.

Because contemporary economists are now debating the impact of the forces of globalization on wage inequality in the OECD countries, the newly liberalized Latin American regimes, and the East Asian "tigers," it is time to ask whether the same distributional forces were at work during the late nineteenth century. A body of literature almost a century old argues that immigration hurt American labor and accounted for much of the rise in income inequality from the 1890s to World War I. The decision by a labor-sympathetic Congress to enact immigration quotas shows how important the issue was to the electorate. An even older literature argues that cheap grain exported from the New World eroded land rents in Europe so sharply that landowner-dominated continental parliaments raised tariffs to protect domestic growers from the impact of globalization. But nowhere in this historical literature had anyone constructed data to test three contentious hypotheses with important policy implications:

> *Hypothesis 1:* Inequality rose in resource-rich, labor-scarce countries such as Argentina, Australia, Canada, and the United States. Inequality fell in resource-poor, labor-abundant agrarian economies such as Ireland, Italy, Portugal, Scandinavia, and Spain. Inequality was more stable among the European industrial leaders, including Britain, France, Germany, and the Lowland countries, all of whom fell in between the rich New World and poor Old World.
>
> *Hypothesis 2:* If the first hypothesis is true, a second follows: these inequality patterns can be explained largely by globalization.
>
> *Hypothesis 3:* If this second hypothesis holds, then these globalization-induced inequality trends help explain the retreat from globalization between 1913 and 1950.

This article reviews the historical debate about the first globalization boom in the late nineteenth century and attempts to tie it to the current debate about the globalization boom in the late twentieth century. The two debates are strikingly similar. They also share a shortcoming in the empirical analysis: nobody has yet explored this issue with late nineteenth century panel data across poor and rich countries, and, with the important exception of Wood (1994), few have done so for the late twentieth century debate either. Indeed, until very recently, most economists had focused solely on the American experience. The central contribution of this paper is to explore a database for the late nineteenth century that includes both rich and poor countries or, in the modern vernacular, North and South.

It appears that globalization did contribute to the implosion, deglobalization, and autarkic policies that dominated between 1913 and 1950. Indeed, during these years of trade suppression and binding migration quotas, the connection between globalization and inequality completely disappeared. It took the globalization renaissance of the early 1970s to renew this old debate.

GLOBALIZATION AND INEQUALITY IN THE LATE TWENTIETH CENTURY

From 1973 through the 1980s, real wages of unskilled workers in the United States fell as a result of declining productivity growth and an increasing disparity in wages paid to workers with different skills. This difference was manifested primarily by higher wages for workers with advanced schooling and age-related skills. The same trends were apparent elsewhere in the OECD in the 1980s, but the increase in wage gaps was typically far smaller. The widening of wage inequalities coincided with the forces of globalization, both in the form of rising trade and increased immigration, the latter characterized by a decline in the skill levels of migrants. Trade as a share of gross national product in the United States increased from 12 percent in 1970 to 25 percent in 1990 (Lawrence and Slaughter 1993), while exports from low-income countries rose from 8 percent of total output in 1965 to 18 percent in 1990. These developments coincided with a shift in spending patterns that resulted in large trade deficits in the United States.

The standard Heckscher-Ohlin trade model makes unambiguous predictions: every country exports those products that use abundant and cheap factors of production. Thus a trade boom induced by a drop in tariffs or in transport costs will cause exports and the demand for the cheap factor to boom as well. Globalization in poor countries should favor unskilled labor; globalization in rich countries should favor skilled labor. . . .

Thus far the discussion has focused mainly on the United States, perhaps because rising inequality and immigration have been greatest there. But the question is not simply why the demand for unskilled labor in the United States and even Europe was depressed in the 1980s and 1990s but whether the same factors were *stimulating* the relative demand for low-skill labor in developing countries. This is where Adrian Wood (1994, ch. 6) enters the debate. Wood was one of the first economists to systematically examine inequality trends across industrial and developing countries.

Wood distinguishes three skill types: uneducated workers, those with a basic education, and the highly educated. The poor South has an abundance of uneducated labor, but the supply of workers with basic skills is growing rapidly. The rich North, of course, is well endowed with highly educated workers; its supply of labor with basic skills is growing slowly. Wood assumes that capital is fairly mobile and that technology is freely available. As trade barriers fall and the South improves its skills through the expansion of basic education, it produces more goods that require only basic skills, while the North produces more high-skill goods. It follows that the ratio of the unskilled to the skilled wage should rise in the South and fall in the North. The tendency toward the relative convergence of factor prices raises the relative wage of workers with a basic education in the South and lowers it in the North, producing rising inequality in the North and falling inequality in the South.

Wood concludes that the decline in the relative wages of less-skilled northern workers is caused by the elimination of trade barriers and the increasing abundance of southern workers with a basic education. . . .

Wood's research has met with stiff critical resistance. Since his book appeared in 1994, more has been learned about the link between inequality and globalization in developing countries. . . . [A] study of seven countries in Latin America and East Asia shows that wage inequality typically did not fall after trade liberalization but rather *rose*. This apparent anomaly has been strengthened by other studies, some of which have been rediscovered since

Wood's book appeared. . . . None of these studies is very attentive to the simultaneous role of emigration from these countries, however, leaving the debate far from resolved.

GLOBALIZATION AND INEQUALITY IN THE LATE NINETEENTH CENTURY

The spread between real wages from 1854 to 1913 in fifteen countries is shown in figure 1. The downward trend confirms what new-growth theorists call convergence, that is, a narrowing in the economic distance between rich and poor countries. The convergence is more dramatic when America and Canada—which were richer—or when Portugal and Spain—who failed to play the globalization game—are excluded. . . . Most of this convergence was the combined result of the trade boom and the prequota mass migrations.

Trade Issues

The late nineteenth century was a period of dramatic integration of commodity markets: railways and steamships lowered transport costs, and Europe moved toward free trade in the wake of the 1860 Cobden-Chevalier treaty. These developments implied large trade-induced price shocks that affected every European participant. The drop in grain prices was the canonical case: wheat prices in Liverpool were 60 percent higher than those in Chicago in 1870, for example, but they were less than 15 percent higher in 1912, a decline of forty-five percentage points. The commodity price differential declined by even more when the spread is measured from wheat-growing regions outside of Chicago. Furthermore, prices of all tradables, not just grain, were affected. . . .

The standard trade model argues that, as countries everywhere expand the production and export of goods that use their abundant (and cheap) factors relatively intensively, the resultant market integration would lead to an international convergence of factor prices. Under this theory, then, the late nineteenth century trade boom accounted for 10 to 20 percent of the convergence in GDP per worker hour and in the real wage. It also had distributional implications for poor countries: it meant rising wages for unskilled workers relative to land rents and skilled wages. For rich countries, it meant that unskilled wages fell relative to land rents and skilled wages.

Migration Issues

The correlation between real wages or GDP per worker hour and migration rates is positive and highly significant. The poorest Old World countries tended to have the highest emigration rates, while the richest New World countries tended to have the highest immigration rates. The correlation is not perfect since potential emigrants from poor countries often found the cost of the move too high, and some New World countries restricted inflows of such

FIGURE 1 Real Wage Dispersion, 1854–1913

Coefficient of Variation

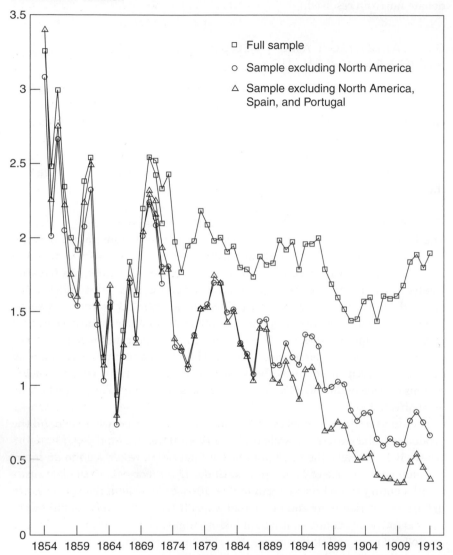

NOTE: Wage data are urban, male, purchasing-power-parity adjusted.
SOURCE: Williamson (1996a, figure 1).

migrants. But the correlation is still very strong. Furthermore, the effect on the labor force was very important, augmenting the New World labor force by almost 37 percent and reducing the Old World labor force by 18 percent (at least among the emigrant countries around the European periphery), much larger than U.S. experience in the 1980s. One estimate suggests that mass migrations explain about 70 percent of the real wage convergence in the late nineteenth century. This estimate, in contrast with the contemporary debate about immigration in the 1980s, which focuses only on immigration into Europe and the United States, includes the total impact on rich receiving countries *and* poor sending countries.

Because the migrants tended to be unskilled, and increasingly so toward the end of the century, they flooded the receiving countries' labor markets at the bottom of the skill ladder. Thus immigration must have lowered unskilled wages relative to those of skilled artisans and educated white-collar workers and relative to land rents. These immigration-induced trends implied increased inequality in rich countries, while emigration-induced trends must have moved in the opposite direction and reduced inequality in poor countries.

So much for plausible assertions. What were the facts?

Establishing the Facts, 1870–1913

How did the typical unskilled worker near the bottom of the distribution do relative to the typical landowner or capitalist near the top, or even relative to the skilled blue-collar worker and educated white-collar employee near the middle? The debate over inequality in the late twentieth century has fixed on wage inequality, but a century earlier, land and landed interests were far more important sources of income, so they need to be added to the inquiry. (I believe this is true throughout the developing world, certainly its poorer parts.) In any case, two kinds of evidence are available to document nineteenth century inequality trends so defined: the ratio of unskilled wages to farm rents per acre, and the ratio of the unskilled wage to GDP per worker hour. Everyone knows that farm land was abundant and cheap in the New World, while scarce and expensive in the Old World. And labor was scarce and expensive in the New World, while abundant and cheap in the Old World. Thus, the ratio of wage rates to farm rents was high in the New World and low in the Old. What everyone *really* wants to know, however, is how the gap evolved over time: Are the trends consistent with the predictions of the globalization and inequality literature? Was there, in Wood's language, relative factor price convergence in the late-nineteenth century, implying rising inequality in rich countries and declining inequality in poor countries? Figure 2 supplies some affirmative answers.

In the New World the ratio of wage rates to farm rents plunged. By 1913 it had fallen in Australia to a quarter of its 1870 level; in Argentina to a fifth of its mid-1880 level; and in the United States to less than half of its 1870 level. In the Old World the reverse occurred, especially where free trade policies were pursued. In Great Britain the ratio in 1910 had increased by a factor of 2.7 over its 1870 level, while the Irish ratio had increased even more, by a factor of 5.5. The Swedish and Danish ratios had both increased by a factor of 2.3. The surge was less pronounced in protectionist countries, increasing by a factor of 1.8 in France, 1.4 in Germany, and not at all in Spain.

FIGURE 2 Ratio of Unskilled Wages to Land Values, 1870–1913 (1911 = 100)

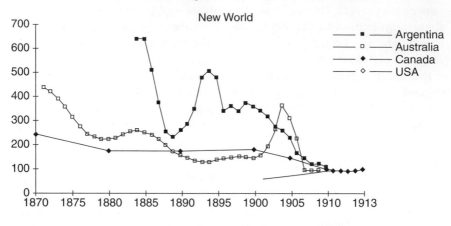

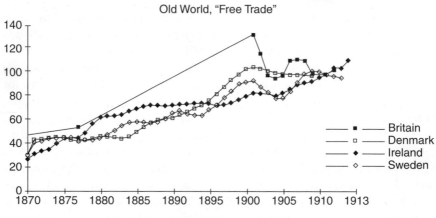

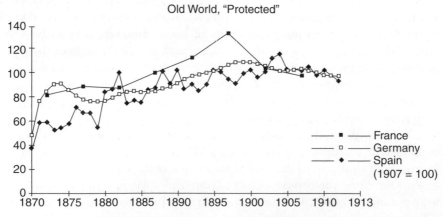

SOURCE: O'Rourke, Taylor, and Williamson (1996, figs. 1, 2, 3)

Because landowners tended to be near the top of the income distribution pyramid, this evidence confirms Hypothesis 1: inequality rose in the rich, labor scarce New World and fell in the poor, labor-abundant Old World. There is also some evidence that globalization mattered: countries that were open to trade absorbed the biggest distributional changes; those that retreated behind tariff walls sustained the smallest distributional changes. . . .

THE IMPACT OF GLOBALIZATION ON INEQUALITY TRENDS, 1870–1913

Theory suggests that globalization can account for this key stylized fact: In an age of unrestricted international migration, poor countries should have the highest emigration rates and rich countries should have the highest immigration rates; in an age of liberal trade policy, poor countries should export labor-intensive products and rich countries should import labor-intensive products. Theory is one thing: fact is another. What evidence on trade and migration in the late nineteenth century supports this (apparently plausible) globalization hypothesis?

I start with trade effects. There was a retreat from trade liberalism after 1880, and the retreat included France, Germany, Italy, Portugal, and Spain. In the absence of globalization forces, poor labor-abundant countries that protect domestic industry should raise the returns to scarce factors (such as land) relative to abundant factors (such as unskilled labor). In the face of globalization forces, the same countries should at least mute the rise in the relative scarcity of unskilled labor and thus stem the fall in inequality. The evidence seems to be roughly consistent with these predictions. That is, the correlation between rising inequality and initial labor scarcity turns out to be better for 1870–90—an environment of shared liberal trade policies—than for 1890–1913—an environment of rising protection on the Continent.

I turn next to the impact of mass migration. As indicated above, the impact of mass migration on labor supplies in sending and receiving countries between 1870 and 1910 ranged from 37 percent for three New World destination countries (Canada at 44 percent absorbing the largest supply of immigrant labor) to –18 percent for six poor European sending countries (Italy at –39 percent losing the largest share of its labor supply). Migration's impact on the receiving country's labor force is also known to be highly correlated with an initial scarcity of labor, although not perfectly. Migration is therefore a prime candidate in accounting for the distribution trends. Figure 3 plots the result: where immigration increased the receiving country's labor supply, inequality rose sharply; where emigration reduced the sending country's labor supply, inequality declined.

Unfortunately it is impossible to decompose globalization effects into trade and migration using this information because the correlation between migration's impact and initial labor scarcity is so high. Yet an effort has been made

FIGURE 3 Inequality Trends vs. Migration's Impact on Labor Force, 1870–1913

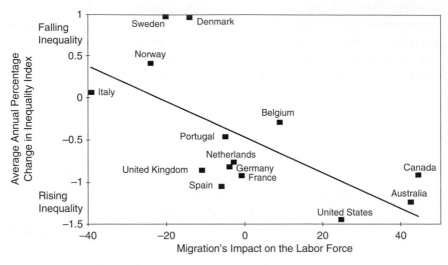

SOURCE: Williamson (1996b).

by constructing a trade-globalization-impact variable as the interaction of initial labor scarcity and "openness." The result is that the impact of migration is still powerful, significant, and of the right sign: when immigration rates were small, inegalitarian trends were weak; when emigration rates were big, egalitarian trends were strong; when countries had to accommodate heavy immigration, inegalitarian trends were strong. In the Old World periphery, where labor was most abundant, the more open economies had more egalitarian trends, just as the Heckscher-Ohlin trade model would have predicted. It appears that the open economy tigers of that time enjoyed benign egalitarian effects, while those among them opting for autarky did not. In the Old World industrial core, this effect was far less powerful. It appears that open economy effects on income distribution were ambiguous among the land-scarce industrial leaders in Europe where the farm sector was relatively small. Heckscher and Ohlin would have predicted this result too. In the labor scarce New World, however, the more open economies also had more egalitarian trends, which is certainly *not* what Heckscher and Ohlin would have predicted. The result is not significant, however.

Overall, I read this evidence as strong support for the impact of mass migration on income distribution and as weak support for the role of trade. This empirical exercise explains about two-thirds of the variance in distributional trends across the late nineteenth century. What forces could possibly account for the remaining third, forces that were also highly correlated with initial labor scarcity and GDP per worker-hour? Late twentieth century critics of the globalization thesis have argued that the answer lies with techno-logical change. Lawrence and Slaughter (1993) contend that a skill-using bias in the United States has driven rising inequality. Wood (1994) counters that it cannot be so because inequality in the United States and the other OECD countries was on the rise just when the slowdown in productivity was in full swing. Whichever view the reader believes, it is important to remember that we are searching for an explanation that can account simultaneously for fall-ing inequality in the South, rising inequality in the North, and some mixture among the newly industrializing countries in the middle. But is there any reason to believe that technological change should be unskilled labor-saving in rich countries and unskilled labor-using in poor countries?

This issue has been explored at length (O'Rourke, Taylor, and Williamson 1996) using the data on the ratio of wages to land rent shown in figure 2. Almost by definition, industrial revolutions embody productivity growth that favors industry. Because industrial output makes little use of farmland, industrialization instead raises the relative demands for labor and capital. Industrial revolutions tend, therefore, to raise wages relative to land rents. According to this prediction, more rapid industrialization in Europe than in the New World should also have raised the wage-rental ratio by more in Europe. Such events should have contributed to a convergence in the prices of factors of production, including a rise in real wages in Europe relative to those in the New World. This prediction would be reinforced if productivity advance in the late nineteenth century New World was labor-saving and land-using, as the above hypothesis suggests and as economic historians generally believe. The prediction would be further reinforced if productivity advance in the Old World was land-saving and labor-using, as economic historians gen-erally believe.

O'Rourke, Taylor, and Williamson's results (1996, Table 4) are striking. The combination of changes in land-labor ratios and capital deepening accounted for about 26 percent of the fall in the wage-rental ratio in the New World, but for none of its rise in the Old World. Commodity price convergence and Heckscher-Ohlin effects accounted for about 30 percent of the fall in the New World wage-rental ratio and for about 23 percent of its rise in the Old World. Advances in productivity, as predicted, were labor-saving in the labor-scarce New World and labor-using in the labor-abundant Old World. Labor-saving technologies appear to have accounted for about 39 percent of the drop in the wage-rental ratio in the New World, while labor-intensive technologies accounted for about 51 percent of its rise in the Old World, powerful techno-logical forces indeed. Globalization accounted for more than half of the ris-ing inequality in rich countries and for a little more than a quarter of the falling inequality in poor ones. Technology accounted for about 40 percent of the rising inequality in rich countries in the forty years before World War I, and about 50 percent of the decline in inequality in poor countries.

FIGURE 4   Initial Real Wage vs. Inequality Trends, 1921–1938

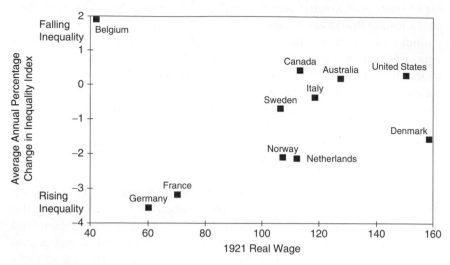

NOTE: The real wage in 1921 relative to an index where the United Kingdom = 100 in 1927.

SOURCE: Williamson (1996b).

ESTABLISHING THE INEQUALITY FACTS, 1921–38

What happened after World War I, when quotas were imposed in immigrating countries, capital markets collapsed, and trade barriers rose?

First, wage differentials between countries widened. Some of the differences were war-related, and some were due to the Depression, but even in the 1920s the trend was clear. Second, the connection between inequality and the forces of globalization was broken (see figure 4). Inequality rose more sharply in poorer countries than in richer countries, where in four cases, it actually declined.

SOME THINGS NEVER CHANGE

At least two events distinguish the late nineteenth century period of globalization from that of the late twentieth century. First, a decline in inequality seems to have been significant and pervasive in the poor, industrial latecomers in the late nineteenth century sample. This move toward equality has not been universally true of the Latin American and East Asian countries recently studied by other researchers. Second, mass migration appears to have had a more important effect than trade on inequality in the late nineteenth century. Except for the United States, and perhaps West Germany, this phenomenon does not seem to have been true of the late twentieth century, although it should be noted that no economist has assessed the impact of emigration on wages and inequality in Turkey, Mexico, the Philippines, or other developing countries in which net outmigration has been significant over the past quarter century or so.

Some things never change, and that fact implies a warning. Globalization and convergence ceased between 1913 and 1950. It appears that rising inequality in rich countries induced by globalization was responsible, at least in part, for the interwar retreat from globalization. The connection between globalization and inequality was also broken between World War I and 1950. Rising inequality in the rich countries stopped exactly when immigration was choked off by quotas, global capital markets collapsed, and the international community retreated behind high trade barriers. Are these interwar correlations spurious? The pre-WWI experience suggests not.

Is there a lesson from this history? Will the world economy soon retreat from its commitment to globalization just as it did almost a century ago?

REFERENCES

Lawrence, Robert Z., and Matthew J. Slaughter. 1993. "International Trade and American Wages in the 1980s: Giant Sucking Sound or Small Hiccup?" *Brookings Papers on Economic Activity, Microeconomics* 2:161–226.

O'Rourke, Kevin H., Alan M. Taylor, and Jeffrey G. Williamson. 1996. "Factor Price Convergence in the Late 19th Century." *International Economic Review* 37(3):499–530.

Williamson, Jeffrey G. 1996a. "Globalization, Convergence and History." *Journal of Economic History* 56(June):277–306.

Williamson, Jeffrey G. 1996b. "Globalization and Inequality, Past and Present." Appendixes 1, 2. Harvard University, Department of Economics, Cambridge, Mass.

Wood, Adrian. 1994. *North-South Trade, Employment, and Inequality: Changing Fortunes in a Skill-Driven World*. Oxford: Clarendon Press.

28

The Political Economy of Trade Policy Reform: Lessons from Developing Countries

RAZEEN SALLY

Developing countries have been laboring to reform their economic systems for up to three decades. The arduous process of moving from import substituting industrialization (ISI) to freer markets and more openness to the world economy has been fraught with economic and political setbacks, causing "reform fatigue" to set in. Razeen Sally documents this growing skepticism with policy reform and considers the reasons for it. His account highlights domestic factors, such as how the gains and pains of economic reform are distributed within countries and how domestic institutions protect property rights and channel benefits and costs to individuals and groups. He argues that labor-abundant countries like China and India have the most promising political economy to support continued global integration. By contrast, resource-abundant countries in Latin America, Africa, the Middle East, Russia, and other parts of the former Soviet Union face a more problematic future. In these countries, interest groups and predatory institutions are geared more toward capturing trade-generated wealth than ensuring that broad swaths of society benefit from globalization.

I. THE GLOBAL CLIMATE FOR EXTERNAL LIBERALISATION

There is less appetite for further liberalisation and associated structural reforms now compared with the heyday of the Washington Consensus in the 1980s and 1990s. Reforms have not been reversed, but their forward momentum has slowed. Governments are more sceptical and defensive about further liberalisation; there has been relatively little in the way of "second-generation" reforms (in domestic trade-related regulations and institutions) to underpin external liberalisation and boost competition. The last two years have seen creeping protectionism (rather than major liberalisation-reversal), e.g. FDI restrictions to protect "national champions" in "strategic" sectors, and export controls on agricultural and other commodities to combat food and fuel inflation. It is a matter of speculation whether protectionism will accelerate in response to global financial crisis, but the chances of that happening are increasingly evident.

Liberalisation slowdown applies to the West, and to most developing-country regions. In the developed world, pervasive agricultural protectionism continues, with an admixture of new protectionism directed against China. The West has no *grand project* for liberalisation in the early twenty-first century to compare with the Reagan and Thatcher reforms in the 1980s, or the EU's Single Market programme in the late 1980s and early 1990s. Eastern-European countries are suffering from "reform fatigue" after their accession to the EU. This is also the state of play in much of Latin America, Africa, south Asia and southeast Asia. It is true of leading developing countries, notably Brazil, Mexico, South Africa and India. All have their real bursts of trade-and-FDI liberalisation behind them. In Russia, liberalisation has been put into reverse gear. This has also happened in other resource-rich countries enjoying a revenue windfall, e.g. Venezuela and Bolivia. Overall, protectionist flare-ups and lack of reform momentum in the West have reinforced liberalisation-slowdown outside the West.

China was the conspicuous exception: liberalisation proceeded apace before and after WTO accession, in what has been the biggest opening of an economy the world has ever seen. However, domestic political conditions for further liberalisation are now more difficult. Market-based reforms have slowed down since about 2006, with a noticeable increase in industrial-policy interventions and FDI restrictions to support favoured national champions, especially in the public sector.

A variety of factors accounts for liberalisation-scepticism today. There is much anxiety about globalisation, despite record growth across the world in the five years ending in 2007. Macroeconomic crises provided windows of opportunity for fast-and-furious liberalisation in the 1980s and 1990s, but that has not happened since the Asian and other financial crises of the late 1990s. Indeed, the latter may have brought about a popular backlash, and certainly induced more caution regarding further liberalisation. Also, further liberalisation entails tackling border and, increasingly, domestic regulatory barriers in politically-sensitive areas such as agriculture and services. Inevitably, this runs up against more powerful interest group opposition than was the case with previous waves of (mainly industrial-goods) liberalisation. Individuals matter too: The new century has not yet brought forth a Cobden, Gladstone, Erhard, Thatcher or Reagan to champion free markets or free trade.

Not least, the climate of ideas has changed, for prevailing weather conditions have become more inclement since the Washington Consensus reached its zenith only a decade ago. There is, now as before, an extreme anti-globalisation critique, a root-and-branch rejection of capitalism, but this is street theatre on the fringe. Of greater political importance is a more mainstream critique that accepts the reality of the market economy and globalisation, but rejects the comprehensive liberalisation associated (perhaps unfairly) with the Washington Consensus.

Critics point to tenuous links between liberalisation, openness, growth and poverty reduction; wider inequalities within and between countries that result from globalisation; the damaging effects of large and sudden trade liberalisation in developing countries; the renewed emphasis on aid to poorer developing countries, without which trade liberalisation will not work; the need for developed-country liberalisation while retaining developing-country protectionism; and the need for more flexible international rules to allow developing-country governments to pursue selective industrial policies, especially to promote infant industries. Lastly, there is the pervasive fear—in the South as much as in the North—of being run over by an unstoppable Chinese export juggernaut.

It is important to confront these arguments head on: to defend liberalisation to date, while accepting that its record is mixed; to make the case for further liberalisation; and to identify the political conditions that might make it succeed. Protectionism and industrial-policy intervention has mostly failed across the developing world: history, not just theory, should be a warning not to go down this route again.

Firstly, in-depth country studies by the OECD, NBER and World Bank, going back to the 1970s and 1980s, suggest strongly that countries with more liberal trade policies have more open economies and grow faster than those with more protectionist policies. These are much more reliable than superficial cross-country regression analyses. That said, even most of the latter point to large gains from trade liberalisation.

Putting together calculations done by the World Bank and Angus Maddison, a snapshot of the developing world in the year 2000 reveals the following. There are about 25 "new-globalising" developing countries (the World Bank's term) with a total population of about 3 billion. Since 1980, this group registered massive increases in their trade-to-GDP ratios and real per-capita incomes, alongside big cuts in levels of tariff protection. In the same period, over 50 "less-globalised" developing countries, with a combined population of about 1.5 billion, saw stagnant trade-to-GDP ratios, a modest increase in real per-capita incomes, alongside relatively modest cuts in average import tariffs. The—overwhelmingly Asian—new globalises have also seen dramatic reductions in poverty and improvements in human-welfare indicators (such as adult literacy, infant mortality, life expectancy and nutritional intake).

Secondly, it is not true that globalisation "excludes" certain developing countries. Rather they support the argument that globalisation provides an enabling environment that some countries have taken advantage of and others have not. Political disorder, macroeconomic instability, insecure property rights, rampant government intervention and high external protection have kept other countries "non-globalised" and thereby retarded growth and development. Most of these countries are cursed with dysfunctional or failed states. None of this is "caused" by globalisation.

Thirdly, NGOs and developing-country governments have been clamouring for one-sided liberalisation in the Doha round. Their interpretation of "development" in the Doha Development Agenda is that it behoves developed countries to liberalise in areas that are protected against labour-intensive, developing-country exports. But developing countries should not reciprocate with their own liberalisation. What these critics fail to say is that developing countries' own protectionist policies harm them even more than developed-country barriers. The World Bank estimates that 80 per cent of the developing-country gain from worldwide agricultural liberalisation would come from developing countries' liberalisation of their highly protected agricultural markets. It is unskilled rural labour—the poorest of the poor—who would gain most since such liberalisation would reduce the anti-agricultural bias in domestic economies.

Fourthly, the historical record is not kind to "hard" industrial policies of the infant-industry variety. Infant-industry success in nineteenth-century USA and Germany is contested. In east Asia, its record is mixed at best in Japan, South Korea and Taiwan; non-existent in free-trade Hong Kong and Singapore; and failed in southeast Asia (e.g. national car policies in Malaysia and Indonesia). In northeast Asia, there is scant evidence to show that protection of infants actually led to higher social rates of return and higher overall productivity growth. Southeast Asia's conspicuous success is in FDI-led electronics exports—a result of drastically lower tariffs and an open door to inward investment. China, like southeast Asia, has grown fast through FDI-led exports, not infant-industry protection. Arguably, other factors—political and macroeconomic stability, competitive exchange rates, private property rights, openness to the world economy, education and infrastructure—were much more important to east-Asian success than "picking winners." Finally, infant-industry protection in Latin America, south Asia and Africa has been a disaster not dissimilar to industrial planning in ex-command economies.

II. TRADE AND FDI LIBERALISATION: RECENT EXPERIENCE AND UNFINISHED BUSINESS

There has been a policy revolution and a strong liberalisation trend in developing countries and countries in transition since the early 1980s. Cross-border trade and capital flows—though not of people—have become freer. There is less discrimination between domestic and international transactions. Domestic prices of tradable goods and services are closer to world prices (though less the case in services than in goods). In terms of measures undertaken, import and export quotas, licenses, state trading monopolies and other non-tariff barriers (NTBs) have been drastically reduced. Tariffs have been simplified and reduced. So have foreign exchange controls, with unified exchange rates and much greater currency convertibility, especially on current account transactions. FDI has been liberalised, with fewer restrictions on entry, ownership, establishment and operation in the domestic economy. And the services sectors have been opened to international competition through FDI liberalisation, privatisation and domestic deregulation. Overall, trade and FDI in manufactured goods has been liberalised most; trade and FDI in services was liberalised later, and to a much lesser extent; and trade liberalisation in agriculture has lagged behind. Lastly, trade and FDI liberalisation has taken place in the context of wide-ranging macro—and microeconomic market-based reforms—roughly the "stabilisation and liberalisation" package of the Washington Consensus, as described by John Williamson.

This still leaves fairly high levels of protection around the world. There are pockets of developed-country protection—agricultural subsidies, peak tariffs and tariff escalation in agriculture and manufactures, anti-dumping (AD) duties, assorted regulatory barriers such as onerous product standards, and high restrictions on the cross-border movement of workers that continue to damage developing-country growth prospects. But developing countries' own protection on almost all these counts is much higher. Average applied tariffs in developing countries are more than double those in developed countries, with much higher bound rates in the WTO. Developing countries have become bigger users of anti-dumping actions than developed countries. Developing countries, with the exception of countries in transition and those that have recently acceded to the WTO, have far fewer multilateral commitments in services than developed countries. There has been a general increase in the use of technical, food-safety and other standards that affect trade, as indicated by the number of measures notified under the WTO's TBT and SPS agreements.

Political Economy and Trade-Policy Reforms

The politics of economic policy reform is as much about distribution as it is about wealth generation. This is true of international politics; it is even truer of domestic politics. Shifts in trade policy—from protection to openness or vice versa—trigger redistribution of gains and losses between regions (especially between rural and urban areas), sectors of the economy (agriculture, industry, services), classes (owners of capital, educated and skilled workers, semi- and unskilled workers), and even between ethnic groups. Such disruption, especially in the short term, can be particularly unsettling in developing countries with political instability, corrupt elites, wide disparities in wealth and influence, meagre safety nets, ethnic divides and generally brittle institutions. Hence trade and other forms of liberalisation take place in a snake pit of messy and sometimes poisonous politics.

What are the determinants of trade-policy reform, especially in the direction of liberalisation? What follows is a simple taxonomy of relevant factors: a) circumstances, especially crises; b) country size; c) interests; d) ideas; e) institutions; f) factor endowments; g) foreign policy and international politics.

A. CIRCUMSTANCES/CRISES. The practical politician, official or businessman knows that choices are dictated by responses to often unanticipated events. In reality, major episodes of economic policy reform have mostly taken place in response to political and/or economic crises. A macroeconomic crisis, with symptoms such as extreme internal or external indebtedness, hyperinflation, a terms-of-trade shock, or a severe payments imbalance leading to a plummeting currency, provides the classic backdrop. Sometimes this is combined with a political crisis, whose most dramatic expression is a change of political system (from authoritarianism or totalitarianism to democracy or vice versa).

An economic crisis, with or without political system-change, is when "normal politics" is suspended, and when a period of "extraordinary politics" can provide a window of opportunity for thoroughgoing reforms (that would not be possible in "normal" political circumstances). Examples are legion: Chile in 1973–74; Mexico in 1986; Brazil and Argentina in the early 1990s; South Africa in the mid-1990s; Sri Lanka in 1977; India in 1991; eastern Europe and the ex-Soviet Union in the early 1990s; Australia and New Zealand in 1983–84.

But the crisis explanation cannot be taken too far. Firstly, a crisis can precipitate swings both ways: sometimes towards liberalisation; sometimes the other way, as happened during the Depression in the 1930s, and, to a lesser extent, in the 1970s after the first oil-price shock. Secondly, different governments act in different ways in response to similar external shocks. Thirdly, a crisis might trigger some reforms, but it is no guarantee of the sustainability of those reforms, nor of further reforms down the line. That is one key difference between east-central Europe and the Baltic states, on the one hand, and Russia and other parts of the ex-Soviet Union, on the other. Lastly, there are counter-examples of gradual, but cumulatively substantial, reforms without a sudden crisis as a triggering mechanism. That is, roughly, the east-Asian record.

Why have some countries sustained reforms while others have not? Why have some gone farther than others? What happens to a reform programme post-crisis, when "normal" political and economic conditions return? These questions demand supplementary explanations.

It may not seem urgent to pursue liberalising reforms in "normal" conditions, especially after so much reform heavy-lifting has been done. But complacency is dangerous. It means that the economy continues to live off reforms accomplished some time ago. Reforms needed to make the economy flexible and adaptable to changing global conditions, and resilient to unanticipated shocks, are neglected. Meanwhile, distortions and rigidities build up. A future crisis is then the trigger for long overdue reforms. These come at a much higher political, economic and social cost than would otherwise be the case.

Depending on a crisis for reform is myopic, and ultimately crazy, policy. It is far better to nurture a culture of permanent, incremental and mutually

reinforcing reforms. But that is terribly difficult in practice. Still, star reformers such as Chile, Australia and New Zealand show that it can be done. All
three have followed up crisis-induced first-generation reforms with deeper
second-generation reforms rolled out over almost two decades. These, however, are small open economies where the reform imperative is stronger than
in medium-sized and large economies.

B. COUNTRY SIZE.   Generally, small countries reliant on the world economy
have liberalised farther and faster than bigger countries. This is the case in
the OECD and the developing world. Ireland, Chile, Australia, New Zealand
and Estonia (among other East-Central European and Baltic countries) stand
out as very strong reformers. So do Hong Kong and Singapore, with long traditions as free-port city-states. Sri Lanka pioneered liberalising reforms in
south Asia, before ethnic conflict compromised economic prospects from
1983. Mauritius and Botswana stand out in Africa.

It is generally believed that the economics and politics of reform in small
countries are easier. Larger countries have more differentiated economies.
They are less reliant on the world economy and have more inward-looking,
protectionist-inclined interests. That translates into more complicated politics. But big countries are not preprogrammed to avoid reforms or do them
sluggishly. China is the most populous country on Earth, but it is the strongest reformer among large developing countries. Others in the latter category—
Brazil, India, Indonesia, South Africa, Nigeria, Egypt, Russia—have mixed or
unfavourable records compared with some smaller countries in their respective regions.

C. INTERESTS.   Mainstream economists, following Adam Smith, tend to rely
on an interest-group explanation of trade politics. Free trade is the optimal
policy in most circumstances (they say), but protection more often is the result,
because organised rent-seeking interests demand protection that politicians
and officials then supply. The benefits of free trade are diffused over the broad
majority of consumers, but its costs bear down disproportionately on minority
producer interests. The latter, not the former, have the incentive to organise for
collective action. In reality, "iron quadrangles" of politicians, bureaucrats,
employers and unions imposed a straightjacket of protection in developing
countries from the 1930s to the 1970s. Mostly this benefited capital-intensive,
unionised, urban manufacturing industries producing for the domestic market, at the expense of agriculture and tradable sectors. India's license raj was its
most notorious incarnation. In many countries, a crisis was used to overcome
interest-group opposition and push through liberalising reforms (as happened
in India in 1991).

But what role do interest groups play after an initial burst of external liberalisation and in post-crisis conditions when "normal" politics returns? Here
the picture differs across countries and regions. In some parts of the world,
protectionist coalitions have halted or slowed down liberalisation. This is the

case with "nomenklatura" coalitions in Russia, Ukraine and other parts of the ex-Soviet Union. Elsewhere, radical opening has triggered major economic shifts in favour of sectors exposed to the world economy. Traditional protectionist interests have been weakened, and countervailing coalitions have emerged. The latter comprise exporters, users of imported inputs, multinationals with global production networks, and cities and regions seeking to be magnets for trade and FDI. These interests lobby for the maintenance and extension of open trade and FDI regimes. This has happened in strong-liberalising countries in east Asia, eastern Europe and Latin America. It happened in Australia and New Zealand from the early 1980s. It is also evident in India after the 1991 reforms.

Now the biggest challenge is to harness open-economy interests to the wagon of further liberalisation, and especially to domestic regulatory reforms. Their stakes in structural, microeconomic reforms are becoming ever clearer. Previous liberalisation has spurred firm-level restructuring, export orientation and overseas expansion. But firms remain hamstrung by high-cost domestic business environments, which they feel puts them at a disadvantage compared to foreign competitors with more salubrious business climates in their home markets. That also translates into defensiveness in trade negotiations. Structural reforms at home would lower business costs, boost the international competitiveness of local firms, make them less resistant to opening domestic markets to foreign competition, and translate into less defensive positions in trade negotiations.

Starting this virtuous cycle begins with reforms at home, not in the WTO or FTAs. In terms of interest-group activity, it implies a new and different political economy to that of hitching exporting interests to tariff concessions in trade negotiations.

D. IDEAS.   It is always difficult to gauge the influence of ideas (or ideology) in policy. But practical observation teaches us that the prevailing climate of ideas, interacting with interests and events, can entrench or sway this-or-that set of policies. A policy consensus on import substitution, state planning and foreign aid was strongly embedded in developing-country governments and international organisations up until the 1970s. This was buttressed by a post-colonial political ideology of mercantilist state-building, and an interventionist consensus in development economics. This set of ideas was overturned by what came to be called the Washington Consensus, which reflected sea changes in political ideology and in development economics. The latter returned to classical and neoclassical foundations, emphasising market-based pricing, "outward orientation", the prevalence of "government failure" over "market failure," not to mention a dose of aid scepticism.

The Washington Consensus ideas took stronger hold in countries where reforms were substantial, especially in ministries of finance, central banks and presidential/prime-ministerial offices. These agencies tend to be the cockpits of policy reform, especially in crisis situations. They have been staffed by technocrat-economists (dubbed "technopols" by John Williamson) committed to Washington Consensus prescriptions. Technopols are much less in evidence and less influential outside macroeconomic policy, especially in line ministries and regulatory agencies which control microeconomic policies.

But now the climate of ideas has changed somewhat, not least in reaction to global financial crisis. This does not yet presage a return to full-blown pre-Washington Consensus thinking. The pendulum, however, is swinging towards more attention to market failure and government intervention, e.g. to ease back on further liberalisation, expand "policy space," promote infant industries, defend "food security" and increase foreign aid. The question is what effect this is having, and is likely to have, on trade policies.

E. INSTITUTIONS.   In the broad sense, institutions are the steel frame of the economy, its "formal rules and informal constraints," according to Douglas North. The legal framework governing property rights and contracts, production and consumption, comes to mind. "Formal rules" comprise bankruptcy laws, competition laws, regulations governing financial markets and corporate governance, and much else besides. "Informal constraints" are (often non-legal) traditions and norms influencing the intersecting worlds of business, government and the law.

Evidently, "institutions" are much broader and more difficult to pin down than "policies"; the two are of course intimately connected. Historically-conditioned institutions, domestic and external, set the scene for government action, interest-group lobbying and the influence of ideas. They are the arena for policy choices and their implementation. Making generalisations about institutional constraints on policy choice, and how this might explain differences in national and regional economic performance over time, is notoriously difficult. To what extent must "good" institutions be in place before "good" policies can take hold and work their magic? Conversely, to what extent are institutions the result, rather than the cause, of policy choices? These are chicken-and-egg questions.

In the narrow sense, institutions are the organisational map of decision making at the junction where politics and public policy meet business and society. On trade policy, this map is much more complicated than it used to be. Trade policy is no longer just about a clutch of border instruments, and the preserve of trade ministries. It is increasingly "trade-related," a matter of non-border regulation reaching deep into the domestic economy and its institutions. That is reflected in more complex multilateral, regional and bilateral trade agreements. This brings in agencies across the range of government and many actors outside government as well. Now the management of trade policy involves the division of labour between the executive, legislature and judiciary; the role of the lead ministry; the participation of other ministries and regulatory agencies on trade and trade-related policies; the WTO mission in Geneva; interagency coordination within government; the involvement of non-governmental actors, such as business and unions, and now including NGOs and think tanks; and the role of donors and international organisations.

Inasmuch as one can make generalisations about institutions and trade policy in developing countries, here are a few. Firstly, it is the more advanced developing countries (in terms of per-capita income and human-welfare indicators) that have liberalised more and plugged themselves better into globalisation than other developing countries. They have lower trade and FDI barriers, higher ratios of trade and FDI to GDP, and better-performing tradable sectors of the economy. They also have stronger institutions in the broad sense: better enforcement of property rights and contracts (i.e. the rule of law), better-functioning judiciaries and public administration, better-regulated financial markets, a stronger competition culture, less corruption and so on. This is the divide that separates Chile and a few other Latin American countries, eastern Europe, the northeast-Asian and southeast-Asian Tigers, and a tiny handful of African countries (Mauritius, Botswana and South Africa), from the rest. Large developing countries such as China, India, Indonesia and Brazil do not fit into this pattern. They still have weak institutions. Institutional improvements have taken place, but these have lagged well behind big policy shifts—not least lower trade and FDI restrictions—and fast-paced global integration.

Writing from the 1990s rightly stresses institutional capacity, within the state and beyond it. This fills in the institutional vacuum in studies on market-based policy reforms in the 1970s and 1980s. But the later literature sometimes goes too far in setting high institutional preconditions for reformist policies to work. The extreme is "institutions come first." The reality is a complex interplay between market-based policies, including trade and FDI liberalisation, and improving domestic institutions. Often policy reforms provide the stimulus for institutional change. As Adam Smith realised over two centuries ago, opening markets to international trade and investment triggers powerful incentives to improve infrastructure, public administration and the rule of law. Then producers and consumers can reap more gains from international commerce. China and Vietnam are shining successes of policy reform. But reforms in both countries, including opening to the world economy, began when institutions were very weak. That is also true of Indonesia in the mid-1960s, and Cambodia and Laos in the 1980s and 1990s.

Secondly, looking at institutions in the narrower organisational sense, strong and sustained trade policy and wider economic policy reforms were driven, more often than not, by powerful presidential or prime-ministerial offices, ministries of finance and central banks, insulated from blocking pressures in other parts of government and outside government. Ministries of finance were particularly important in driving trade liberalisation during crises, often overriding protectionist-inclined ministries of trade and industry.

But, post crises, the former have retreated to their core macroeconomic functions, leaving line ministries and regulatory agencies to handle trade policy with much less oversight.

Thirdly, advanced developing countries have stronger capacity, in terms of qualified, experienced manpower and other resources, for formulating and implementing trade policy, whether done unilaterally or through international negotiations and agreements. China and India are exceptional: they are low-income countries with relatively weak institutions (in the broad sense), but with relatively strong trade-policy capacity.

Fourthly, it is very difficult to make generalisations about the link between political systems and economic policy reforms. Across the developing world, liberalisation has taken place under authoritarian and democratic systems. In the short-to-medium term, authoritarian regimes may find it easier to go further with reforms (China from the early 1990s, Indonesia in the 1980s). But in Russia, increasing authoritarianism under President Putin proceeded alongside partial reform reversal. In the medium-to-long term, a question hangs over authoritarian regimes due to arbitrary and opaque decision-making, and lack of popular legitimacy. That might compromise the durability of policy reforms. In reasonably stable liberal democracies, reforms, however slow and piecemeal, may be more durable due to their sanction in the political marketplace. That is the silver lining for Brazil and India, and perhaps for Indonesia and South Africa.

F. FACTOR ENDOWMENTS.   Explaining the trajectory of policy reforms is not complete without factoring in the relative mix of land (or natural resources), labour and capital in an economy. We know from recent economic history that the star developing-country performers are from east Asia. These countries had different starting positions, but, at a certain stage of development, relative abundance of labour allowed them to break into labour-intensive manufactured exports, which became an engine of growth and in turn aided poverty reduction and human-welfare improvement. Of course this was not inevitable: it depended on the right policies and improving institutions. South Asia, with similar factor endowments, remained stuck on a low-growth, high-poverty path because it did not adopt market-based policies.

Latin American and African countries, on the other hand, are largely land- or resource-abundant and labour-scarce. Absent import-substitution policies, they are better able to exploit comparative advantage in land and resources—as Brazil, Argentina, Chile, Australia and New Zealand have done in agriculture since they liberalised, and as all the latter and many other countries besides have been doing in the present China-driven commodities boom.

Thus a simple story based on an early 21st-century comparative advantage would point to all-around gains from trade: for technologically-advanced and capital-abundant countries in the West; the labour-abundant countries of east and south Asia; and land and resource-abundant countries elsewhere.

But the political economy of factor endowments reveals a different and more problematic story. Arguably, land- and resource-abundant countries are at a structural disadvantage compared with labour-abundant countries. By plugging into global markets for manufacturing, and now labour-intensive services too, the latter seem to be on sustainable growth paths. Labour-intensive exports attract FDI (and the technology and skills that come with it), feed quickly into poverty-reducing, welfare-improving employment, and, more gradually, into better infrastructure and institutions. This creates and strengthens a constellation of interests to support open trade and FDI policies.

On the other hand, land- and resource-abundant countries, given their relatively high price of labour, seem to be crowded out of global manufacturing markets by east-Asian (especially Chinese) competition. This leaves them dependent on cyclical and volatile commodities markets. FDI in resource-abundant countries tends to be capital-intensive and generate big rents in not-so-competitive market segments. Often the result is an FDI enclave, without an employment, technology or wealth spillover to the rest of the economy, but with big profits to distribute among a corrupt local business and political elite.

Thus most research-dependent countries have the interest-group constellation to squander rents from resource booms, but not to spread wealth and improve governance and institutions. A retreat to protectionism, however, would repeat past mistakes and make matters worse. This is the dilemma inherent in the present "China-in-Africa" phenomenon. It is an acute dilemma for Russia, Nigeria, Saudi Arabia and other overwhelmingly resource-abundant countries. But there are notable exceptions to the "resource-curse" rule: Chile has successfully exploited comparative advantage in agriculture and resources (mainly copper) through liberal trade policies, while diversifying the economic base and improving institutions. That is also true of Australia and New Zealand.

G. FOREIGN POLICY AND INTERNATIONAL POLITICS.   Trade policy links down to national economic policies and institutions. But it also links up to foreign policy and international politics. A reasonably stable international political order is the categorical imperative for economic development. Without the global Pax—an orderly framework for international relations—there can be no security for international commerce.

The end of the Cold War and the collapse of the Soviet Union reshaped international politics. It was the catalyst for the twin political and economic transitions in eastern Europe and the former Soviet Union. But it also reverberated elsewhere. It brought on a foreign-policy transformation in India. It looked west to a *rapprochement* and closer relations with the USA, and in the second instance with Europe. It also looked east, first to southeast Asia and then to China. Stronger security relations with the USA and other countries have proceeded in tandem with stronger commercial relations with the same countries. Arguably, India's foreign policy shift is an important factor influencing its belated embrace of the world economy.

China's foreign policy transformation began in the 1980s and accelerated in the 1990s. Its emphasis is on "constructive engagement" with the USA, Europe and emerging developing-country powers. China's "soft power" has been very effective in its east-Asian neighbourhood, although less so with Japan (not to mention Taiwan). Its self-advertised "peaceful rise" is geared to regional political stability and steady integration into the world economy. Trade diplomacy, in the WTO and FTAs, is perhaps the most visible sign of China's foreign-policy transformation.

Russia's trade policy has also followed the swings of its foreign policy. The opening of the economy in the 1990s occurred alongside closer relations with the USA and western Europe. This seemed to be reinforced during President Putin's first term but his second term has seen a distancing of relations with the West, and a more aggressive stance towards Russia's "near abroad," particularly through energy politics. It is part of Russia's assertion of "big-power" status. This is the context for more statist energy policies and ambivalence about further external liberalisation.

Preliminary Summary

In many strong-liberalising countries, an economic crisis, sometimes combined with a political crisis, has led to a big opening of the economy. New open-economy interest-group constellations have emerged to counter traditional protectionist interests. Washington Consensus ideas have spread through technopols (although more influential in macroeconomic than microeconomic policy), leadership focus on growth (much more so in east Asia than in other regions), and pragmatic emulation of successful policies elsewhere. In some democracies, a party-political and wider public consensus, however partial and patchy, has gradually formed around reforms. Gradually improving institutions are better able to support and manage open-market policies, although they remain relatively weak in most developing countries. Shifts in foreign policy have also encouraged external opening and closer relations with major trading partners. Russia is a major exception to these trends, given partial reform reversal.

Labour-abundant countries in east Asia, and now in south Asia, have the most promising political economy to support external liberalisation and global integration—China and India prominent among them. Resource-abundant countries in Latin America, Africa, the Middle East, Russia and other parts of the ex-Soviet Union, have been doing well in the China-driven commodities boom. But their political economy is problematic: their predatory governments and interest groups are geared more to squandering rents than to creating and spreading wealth sustainably.

Multi-track Trade Policy
Another way of cutting into trade-policy reform is to look at it on several levels. Some reforms are carried out unilaterally; others reciprocally through (bilateral, regional, multilateral) trade negotiations, or in agreements with donors. Most developing countries now do trade policy on all these levels concurrently, although the relative balance differs from country to country. What follows is a brief summary of the main features of "multitrack" trade policy in developing countries.

Unilateral Liberalisation
This is the Nike strategy ("Just Do It!"). Governments "liberalise first and negotiate later," as Mart Laar, the former prime minister of Estonia, puts it. In theory, this makes good economic sense. The gain from liberalisation comes from imports, which release domestic resources for more productive uses, including exports, and help to open the door to inward investment. Why, therefore, delay the gain by waiting for cumbersome, bureaucratic trade negotiations to deliver the goods? Unilateral liberalisation can make political sense too, since it can be tailored to local conditions rather than being dictated by "one-size-fits-all" donor conditionality and international trade agreements.

The British led the way with unilateral free trade in the nineteenth century. The first half of the twentieth century witnessed unilateral protectionism by country after country. Since 1945, most developed countries have liberalised reciprocally, through the GATT and bilateral/regional trade agreements. But most developing-country trade and FDI liberalisation has been done unilaterally, not through trade negotiations. The World Bank estimates that two-thirds of developing-country tariff liberalisation since the early 1980s has been done unilaterally. The strongest liberalisers have been unilateral liberalisers: the east-Asian countries, now led by China; Chile and Mexico; the east-European countries; Australia and New Zealand. Nearly all of India's post-1991 liberalisation has been done unilaterally.

China's external liberalisation now matters most, for it is the biggest the world has ever seen, with the biggest spillover effect in Asia. China's opening not only spurred southeast-Asian liberalisation pre-Asian crisis; it probably helped to prevent liberalisation reversal post-Asian crisis. It has also encouraged east-Asian countries to further liberalise at the margin of the post-Asian crisis—for fear of losing trade and FDI to China. Not least, China has probably had a knock-on effect on the Indian opening to the world economy. India has recently accelerated its liberalisation of tariffs, and eased FDI restrictions in some services sectors. This has occurred outside trade negotiations, as was the case with previous Indian trade-and-investment liberalisation since 1991. Would this have happened, or happened as fast, if China had not concentrated minds? Probably not.

That is not to say that China-induced unilateral liberalisation is a total solution. It is unlikely to induce further external liberalisation in the developed world, and least of all in the USA, EU and Japan. In the developing world, its results will inevitably be patchy and messy. Unilateral liberalisation has been more successful in manufacturing than in services and agriculture; it has tackled border barriers much better than non-border regulatory barriers. More generally, unilateral measures do not lock in liberalisation against future backtracking. They do not provide fair, stable and predictable rules for international commerce. Finally, unilateral liberalisation has slowed down across the developing world, now including China.

On its own, therefore, unilateral liberalisation cannot slay protectionist dragons and solve international commercial conflicts. That leaves room for reciprocal negotiations and international agreements, i.e. for the WTO and FTAs.

Multilateral Liberalisation

The rationale for liberalisation through "multilateral reciprocity" is that unilateral liberalisation is politically difficult in the $20^{th}/21^{st}$-century conditions of democratic politics and strong interest-group activity. The GATT/WTO negotiations help to contain protectionist interests and mobilise exporting interests; multilateral agreements provide fair, non-discriminatory rules for all.

Multilateral liberalisation was successful during the GATT when the latter had a relatively slim agenda, club-like decision-making dominated by a handful of developed countries (especially the USA and EU), and the glue of Cold War alliance politics. It has proved spectacularly unsuccessful in the WTO, given its large, unwieldy agenda, chaotic UN-style decision-making in a vastly expanded membership, and without the glue of military alliances after the Cold War. The deadlock in the Doha Round probably shows that future multilateral liberalisation will be elusive, and modest, at best.

Arguably, the best the WTO can hope for is to lock in pre-existing unilateral liberalisation through binding commitments, and gradually improve the functioning of non-discriminatory multilateral rules. That implies scaling back ambitions and expectations. Market-access negotiations (to deliver extra liberalisation) should be more modest and incremental; maybe trade rounds should become a thing of the past. There should be a shift of focus to safeguarding and improving trade rules.

Finally, to get business done, WTO decision-making should fall in line with the political and economic realities outside of Geneva. About 30 countries (counting the EU as one) account for about 90 per cent of international trade and FDI. That includes 20–25 developing countries. They should gather in plurilateral "coalitions of the willing" to make key market-access and rule-making decisions, and correspondingly take on stronger commitments than the rest of the WTO membership. Within this outer core there is an inner core of "big beasts," including China, India and Brazil. They should exercise co-leadership alongside the USA, EU and perhaps Japan (if the latter can get its act together). In other words, the WTO needs "variable geometry" in order to function effectively.

Moving in this direction will be difficult, given the parlous state of the WTO. There is every prospect that multilateral trade rules will be undermined by major players seeking to evade them, with extra pressure coming from proliferating, discriminatory bilateral and regional trade agreements. Weaker multilateral rules will be a much bigger cost for developing countries than the extra multilateral liberalisation forgone as a result of the failure of the Doha Round.

Bilateral and Regional Liberalisation

Negotiations for new preferential trade agreements—overwhelmingly FTAs, but also some customs unions and partial-scope agreements—have occurred at an increased pace since 1999/2000, and even more so since the launch of the Doha Round. Eastern Europe, Africa and Latin America have long been involved in PTA activity. East Asia, which previously relied on non-discriminatory unilateral and multilateral liberalisation, is now playing PTA catch-up, as is south Asia. All the major regional powers—China, India and Japan—are involved in Asian PTAs, as are the USA, EU, Korea, Australia, New Zealand, Hong Kong, other south-Asian countries and the ASEAN countries.

Proponents argue that small clubs of like-minded members can take liberalisation and rules faster, wider and deeper than in the WTO, and act as "building blocks" to further multilateral liberalisation and rule-making. Sceptics say they are "stumbling blocks," diverting attention from the WTO, creating "spaghetti bowls" of discriminatory trade restrictions, and generally favouring powerful players at the expense of the weak.

The reality is mixed. Non-discriminatory unilateral and multilateral liberalisation blunt the damaging effects of discriminatory trade agreements. There is little prospect of the world economy retreating to the warring trade blocs of the 1930s. Strong, "WTO-plus" FTAs can also make sense in certain circumstances but the record in developing-country regions is not encouraging.

With few exceptions, FTAs and customs unions are weak, often falling short of WTO provisions. This is particularly true of South-South PTAs (i.e. between developing countries), but also holds for many North-South PTAs. These tend to be driven by foreign-policy aspirations, but with justifications that are all too often vague, muddled and trivial, having little relevance to commercial realities and the economic nuts and bolts of trade agreements. This can amount to little more than symbolic copycatting of other countries' PTA activity and otherwise empty gesture politics. In such cases economic strategy is conspicuous by its absence. In short, such PTAs are "trade-light."

The predictable results of foreign-policy-driven PTA negotiations light on economic strategy are bitty, quick-fix sectoral deals. Politically sensitive sectors in goods and services are carved out, as are crucial areas where progress in the WTO is elusive (especially disciplines on anti-dumping duties and agricultural subsidies). Little progress is usually made in tackling domestic regulatory barriers (e.g. relating to investment, competition, government procurement, trade facilitation, cross-border labour movement, and food-safety and technical standards). These PTAs hardly go beyond WTO commitments, deliver little, if any, net liberalisation and pro-competitive regulatory reform, and get tied up in knots of restrictive, overlapping rules of origin (ROOs). Especially for developing countries with limited negotiating capacity, resource-intensive PTA negotiations risk diverting political and bureaucratic attention from the WTO and from necessary domestic reforms. Finally, the sway of power politics can result in highly asymmetrical deals, especially when one of the negotiating parties is a major player.

Latin America and Africa have a messy patchwork of weak FTAs that do not liberalise much trade or improve upon WTO rules, but do create complications, especially through trade-restricting rules of origin, and divert attention both from the WTO and from unilateral reforms. This is also the emerging picture of FTAs in east and south Asia.

The Role of Donors

Foreign aid, with conditions attached by the IMF, World Bank and other donors, has clearly played a big part in driving Washington Consensus-type reforms in many developing countries. This has gone way beyond developing countries' (relatively weak) liberalising commitments in the WTO and PTAs. Arguably, unilateral liberalisation has not been truly "unilateral" when it has depended on donor policy preferences and aid with strings attached. The record of IMF stabilisation packages and World Bank structural adjustment packages has been mixed at best, and certainly disappointing compared with optimistic expectations in the 1980s. Often donor-driven reforms have proceeded in stops and starts, with reversals en route. Projected growth and poverty-alleviation effects have not materialised. The politics of aid are even more dubious than its economics. "Conditionality" is empty rhetoric when self-serving interests at both ends of the pipeline ensure that aid continues to flow, even when promised reforms are not delivered. And the perception that Western donors are imposing reforms on otherwise reluctant countries is hardly sustainable: local "ownership" is lacking (to borrow aid jargon), and it invites a backlash and reform-reversal at home.

The bottom line is that countries that have seen strong, sustained, unilateral liberalising reforms are those whose governments have driven reforms ("from below," as it were) rather than having them imposed by donors ("from above"). Aid at its best has smoothed short-term adjustments, as happened with the IMF package to India in 1991, and Japanese aid to Indonesia in the 1980s. The IMF and World Bank have sometimes been useful sources of policy and technical advice. More than anything else, donor conditionality has provided a "good housekeeping seal of approval"—an international signal of reform credibility—for determined home-driven reforms. In these countries (mostly in east Asia and eastern Europe with a few in Latin America), aid has played a marginal role. Where there has been more reliance on aid and donor conditionality—especially in Africa—reforms have a far worse record.

Hence grand aid blueprints, notably the UN Millennium Project and the Africa Commission Report, are questionable. They are not critical to successful trade-policy reforms, and they may be counterproductive. The WTO's "aid-for-trade" initiative, though more modest, should face the same critical questioning.

Preliminary Summary

Developing countries have relied mostly on unilateral liberalisation to open their economies to the world. But unilateral liberalisation has stalled or slowed down and some countries—notably Russia—have seen partial reform reversal. In some countries, trade negotiations have gained the upper hand over unilateral measures, but led to little or no additional liberalisation.

The WTO has been of second-line assistance by providing a framework of multilateral trade rules for unilateral reforms but GATT/WTO commitments have contributed little extra liberalisation in most developing countries. China and other newly-acceded developing countries are exceptions. In China, however, the primary thrust of reforms was domestic and unilateral, coming from national leadership rather than external pressure in trade negotiations.

Developing countries' PTAs are trade-light: they are driven more by foreign policy than commercial strategy; their noodle-bowl discriminatory patchwork causes complications for business and multilateral rules; and they are unlikely to spur regional or global integration. Hence further substantial liberalisation through trade negotiations, whether in the WTO or PTAs, is unlikely. Trade negotiations and resulting agreements are subject to diminishing returns as a vehicle for extra liberalisation, especially on non-border regulatory issues.

Foreign aid has been important in some crisis situations but it has played a marginal role in medium- to long-term trade-policy reforms in countries that have successfully globalised. Generally, aid-induced liberalisation has not really worked: its political economy is dubious. Hence it would be a mistake to rely on aid for further market-based reforms.

Finally, unilateral measures and competitive emulation are likely to be the main vehicle for future trade and FDI liberalisation. Much depends on a Chinese engine. Further unilateral liberalisation in China will probably set imitative reforms in motion, elsewhere in Asia and beyond. A workable post-Doha WTO can help to lock in reforms, but more by strengthening multilateral rules than through market-access negotiations. Much more caution needs to be exercised with PTAs; serious attempts made to minimise the damage from their discriminatory provisions.

What Lessons for Future Reforms?

To recapitulate, the conditions for further liberalisation and associated structural reforms are more difficult today than they were in the heyday of the Washington Consensus. Reform complacency results from a post-crisis environment of buoyant growth and normal interest group politics. There is dissatisfaction with previous reforms in parts of the developing world. Some anti-liberalisation ideas are enjoying a minor revival. This revival might become major in the wake of the global financial crisis. Lastly, the politics of "second-generation" trade-policy reforms is proving to be much more difficult than that of the "first-generation" reforms. The latter involve the reduction and removal of border barriers. This is relatively simple technically and can be done quickly—although politically these measures are rarely easy. The former are all about complex domestic (though trade-related) regulation, such as services regulation, regulation of food-safety and technical standards, intellectual-property protection, public procurement, customs administration and competition rules. These reforms are technically and administratively difficult, and take time to implement. They demand a minimum of capacity across government, especially for implementation and enforcement. Above all, they are politically very sensitive, since they affect entrenched interests that are extremely difficult to dislodge.

Still, there is a strong case for further market-based reforms in general, and for external liberalisation in particular. Reduction of what are still high barriers to trade, foreign investment and the cross-border movement of people holds out the promise of higher growth, and significant poverty reduction and improvements in human welfare. Stalled reforms and reform reversal threaten to deprive hundreds of millions of people of the life-chances they deserve. These are the stakes. . . .

VII

CURRENT PROBLEMS IN INTERNATIONAL POLITICAL ECONOMY

Entering the new millennium, the international economy is ever more global in scope and orientation. In the 1970s, analysts worried that America's economic decline would lead to a new bout of protectionism and economic closure. In the 1980s, scholars trumpeted the Japanese model of state-led economic growth and feared the consequences of the international debt crisis. Today, policy makers and analysts alike are concerned with the consequences of a global market. Although less fearful that the international economy will collapse into a new round of beggar-thy-neighbor policies, analysts and individual citizens today worry more about untrammeled markets degrading the environment, displacing the nation-state as the primary locus of political activity, and undermining the social welfare state, which had been the foundation of the postwar international economic order in the developed world.

As we become increasingly aware of the effects of environmental degradation—both globally, as with ozone depletion, and locally, as with species preservation—pressures build for the imposition of greater governmental regulations to control pollution and manage scarce natural resources. But these pressures have increased at different rates in different countries, creating difficult problems of international policy coordination. Jeffrey A. Frankel (Reading 29) surveys the economics of environmental degradation, examines how efforts to protect the environment affect trade, and explores how countries with different preferences and policies on the environment can best manage their relations and influence environmental quality without damaging trade relations.

As the international political economy becomes more "globalized," many observers predict that nation-states will be forced to relinquish aspects of their social welfare systems in order to remain competitive in international markets. Kenneth F. Scheve and Matthew J. Slaughter (Reading 30) turn this argument on its head. The way to sustain public support for globalization, they argue, is to *expand* the welfare state so that the gains from international trade and foreign investment can be shared more widely. In a similar vein, Dani Rodrik (Reading 31) presents a forward-looking analysis of globalization. He contends that the gains from pushing economic openness further are likely to be small. The real danger, he argues, is of a political backlash against globalization arising from the absence of institutional underpinnings that make open markets politically sustainable.

The worldwide financial crisis that began in the United States in 2008 with the meltdown in the sub-prime mortgage market is the topic of our final selection. Simon Johnson (Reading 32) notes the similarities between this crisis and emerging market crises of the late 1990s and early 2000s. His most provocative argument is that the finance industry has effectively captured the government of the United States—a state of affairs that is more typical of emerging market countries that have experienced crises.

29

Globalization and the Environment

JEFFREY A. FRANKEL

The links between global economic integration and environmental quality are complex, which may partly explain why this is a highly contentious political issue. On one side of the debate are those who contend that globalization produces a regulatory "race to the bottom" wherein nations compete to attract foreign investment and trade by lowering their environmental standards. On the other are those who maintain that globalization promotes economic development which, in turn, leads to better environmental outcomes—a relationship known as the "Environmental Kuznets Curve." Economist Jeffrey A. Frankel examines the evidence for each of these positions and finds qualified support for the latter view. His qualifications reflect institutional considerations. For domestic environmental problems, globalization is beneficial when domestic political institutions are structured to channel growth-induced demands for a better environment into effective regulations. However, global environmental problems like climate change require global institutions to solve the free rider problem.

At the ministerial meeting of the World Trade Organization in Seattle in November 1999, when anti-globalization protesters launched the first of their big demonstrations, some wore turtle costumes. These demonstrators were concerned that international trade in shrimp was harming sea turtles by ensnaring them in nets. They felt that a WTO panel had, in the name of free trade, negated the ability of the United States to protect the turtles, simultaneously undermining the international environment and national sovereignty. Subsequently, anti-globalization protests became common at meetings of multinational organizations.

Perhaps no aspect of globalization worries the critics more than its implications for the environment. The concern is understandable. It is widely (if not universally) accepted that the direct effects of globalization on the economy are positive, as measured by Gross Domestic Product. Concerns rise more with regard to "noneconomic" effects of globalization. Of these, some, such as labor rights, might be considered to be a subject properly of national sovereignty, with each nation bearing the responsibility of deciding to what extent it wishes to protect its own labor force, on the basis of its own values, capabilities, and politics. When we turn to influences on the environment, however, the case for countries sticking their noses into each other's business is stronger. We all share a planet.

Pollution and other forms of environmental degradation are the classic instance of what economists call an externality: the condition under which individuals and firms, and sometimes even individual countries, lack the incentive to restrain their pollution, because under a market system the costs are borne primarily by others. The phrase "tragedy of the commons" was originally coined in the context of a village's shared pasture land, which would inevitably be overgrazed if each farmer were allowed free and unrestricted use. It captures the idea that we will foul our shared air and water supplies and deplete our natural resources unless somehow we are individually faced with the costs of our actions.

A central question for this chapter is whether globalization helps or hurts in achieving the best tradeoff between environmental and economic goals. Do international trade and investment allow countries to achieve more economic growth for any given level of environmental quality? Or do they undermine environmental quality for any given rate of economic growth? Globalization is a complex trend, encompassing many forces and many effects. It would be surprising if all of them were always unfavorable to the environment, or all of them favorable. The highest priority should be to determine ways in which globalization can be successfully harnessed to protect the environment rather than to degrade it.

One point to be emphasized here is that it is an illusion to think that environmental issues could be effectively addressed if each country were insulated against incursions into its national sovereignty at the hands of international trade or the WTO. Increasingly, people living in one country want to protect the air, water, forests, and animals not just in their *own* countries, but also in *other* countries as well. To do so international cooperation is required. National sovereignty is the obstacle to such efforts, not the ally. Multilateral institutions are a potential ally, not the obstacle.

In the course of this chapter, we encounter three ways in which globalization can be a means of environmental improvement. So the author hopes to convince the reader, at any rate. Each has a component that is new.

First is the exercise of *consumer power*. There is the beginning of a worldwide trend toward labeling, codes of corporate conduct, and other ways that environmentally conscious consumers can use their purchasing power to give expression and weight to their wishes. These tools would not exist without international trade. American citizens would have few ways to dissuade Mexican fishermen from using dolphin-unfriendly nets if Americans did not import tuna to begin with. The attraction of labeling is that it suits a decentralized world, where we have both national sovereignty and consumer sovereignty. Nevertheless, labeling cannot be a completely laissez-faire affair. For it to work, there need to be some rules or standards. Otherwise, any producer could inaccurately label its product as environmentally pure, and any country could unfairly put a pejorative label on imports from rival producers. This consideration leads to the second respect in which globalization can be a means of environmental improvement.

International environmental issues require international cooperation, a system in which countries interact under a set of *multilateral rules* determined in multilateral negotiations and monitored by multilateral institutions. This is just as true in the case of environmental objectives, which are increasingly cross-border, as of other objectives. It is true that, in the past, the economic objectives of international trade have been pursued more effectively by the GATT and other multilateral organizations than have environmental objectives. But multilateral institutions can be made a means of environmental protection. This will sound like pie-in-the-sky to the many who have been taken in by the mantra that recent WTO panel decisions have overruled legislative efforts to protect the environment. But the WTO has actually moved importantly in the environmentalists' direction in recent years.

The front lines of multilateral governance currently concern—not illusory alternatives of an all-powerful WTO versus none at all—but rather questions about how reasonably to balance both economic and environmental objectives. One question under debate is whether countries are to be allowed to adopt laws that may be trade-restricting, but that have as their objective influencing other countries' processes and production methods (PPMs), such as their fishermen's use of nets. While the issue is still controversial, the WTO has moved clearly in the direction of answering this question in the affirmative, that is, asserting in panel decisions countries' ability to adopt such laws. The only "catch" is that the measures cannot be unnecessarily unilateral or discriminatory. The environmentalist community has almost entirely failed to notice this major favorable development, because of confusion over the latter qualification. But not only is the qualification what a reasonable person would want, it is secondary to the primary issue of countries' rights under the trading system to implement such laws. By ignoring their victory on the main issue—the legitimacy of addressing PPMs—environmentalists risk losing the opportunity to consolidate it. Some players, particularly poor countries, would love to deny the precedent set in these panel decisions, and to return to a system where other countries cannot restrict trade in pursuit of others.

Third, countries can learn from others' experiences. There has recently accumulated *statistical evidence* on how globalization and growth tend to affect environmental objectives on average, even without multilateral institutions. Looking for patterns in the data across countries in recent decades can help us answer some important questions. Increased international trade turns out to have been beneficial for some environmental measures, such as SO_2 pollution. There is little evidence to support the contrary fear that international competition in practice works to lower environmental standards overall. Rather, globalization can aid the process whereby economic growth enables people to demand higher environmental quality. To be sure, effective government regulation is probably required if this demand is ever to be translated into actual improvement; the environment cannot take care of itself. But the statistical evidence says that high-income countries do indeed eventually tend to use some of their wealth to clean up the environment, on average, for measures such as SO_2 pollution. For the increasingly important category of global environmental externalities, however, such as emission of greenhouse gases, regulation at the national level is not enough. An international agreement is necessary.

These three new reasons to think that globalization can be beneficial for the environment—consumer power, multilateralism, and cross-country statistical evidence—are very different in nature. But in each case what is striking is how little the facts correspond to the suspicions of critics that turning back the clock on globalization would somehow allow them to achieve environmental goals. The rise in globalization, with the attempts at international environmental accord and quasi-judicial oversight, is less a threat to the environment than an ally. It is unfettered national sovereignty that poses the larger threat.

This chapter will try to lay out the key conceptual points concerning the relationship of economic globalization and the environment, and to summarize the available empirical evidence, with an emphasis on what is new. We begin by clarifying some basic issues, such as defining objectives, before going on to consider the impact of globalization.

OBJECTIVES

It is important to begin a consideration of these issues by making clear that both economic income and environmental quality are worthy objectives. Individuals may disagree on the weight that should be placed on one objective or another. But we should not let such disagreements lead to deadlocked political outcomes in which the economy and the environment are both worse off than necessary. Can globalization be made to improve the environment that comes with a given level of income in market-measured terms? Many seem to believe that globalization necessarily makes things worse. If Mexico grows rapidly, is an increase in pollution inevitable? Is it likely, on average? If that growth arises from globalization, rather than from domestic sources, does that make environmental damage more likely? Less likely? Are there policies that can simultaneously promote *both* economic growth and an improved environment? These are the questions of interest.

Two Objectives: GDP and the Environment

An extreme version of environmental activism would argue that we should turn back the clock on industrialization—that it is worth deliberately impoverishing ourselves—if that is what it takes to save the environment. If the human species still consisted of a few million hunter-gatherers, man-made pollution would be close to zero. Thomas Malthus, writing in the early nineteenth century, predicted that geometric growth in population and in the economy would eventually and inevitably run into the natural resource limits of the carrying capacity of the planet. In the 1960s, the Club of Rome picked up where Malthus had left off, warning that environmental disaster was coming soon. Some adherents to this school might favor the deliberate reversal of industrialization—reducing market-measured income below current levels in order to save the environment.

But environmental concerns have become more mainstream since the 1960s. We have all had time to think about it. Most people believe that both a clean environment and economic growth are desirable, that we can have a combination of both, and it is a matter of finding the best tradeoff. Indeed, that is one possible interpretation of the popular phrase "sustainable development."

To evaluate the costs and benefits of globalization with regard to the environment, it is important to be precise conceptually, for example to make the distinction between effects on the environment that come *via* rapid economic growth and those that come *for a given level* of economic output.

We have a single concept, GDP, that attempts to measure the aggregate value of goods and services that are sold in the marketplace, and that does a relatively good job of it. Measurement of environmental quality is much less well advanced. There are many different aspects of the environment that we care about, and it is hard to know how to combine them into a single overall measure. It would be harder still to agree on how to combine such a measure with GDP to get a measure of overall welfare. Proponents of so-called *green GDP accounting* have tried to do exactly that, but so far the enterprise is very incomplete. For the time being, the best we can do is look at a variety of separate measures capturing various aspects of the environment.

A Classification of Environmental Objectives

For the purpose of this chapter, it is useful to array different aspects of the environment according to the extent to which damage is localized around specific sources, as opposed to spilling out over a geographically more extensive area.

The first category of environmental damage is pollution that is *internal* to the household or firm. Perhaps 80 percent (by population) of world exposure to particulates is indoor pollution in poor countries—smoke from indoor cooking fires—which need not involve any externality. There may be a role for dissemination of information regarding long-term health impacts that are not immediately evident. Nevertheless, what households in such countries primarily lack are the economic resources to afford stoves that run on cleaner fuels. In the case of internal pollution, higher incomes directly allow the solution of the problem.

Some other categories of environmental damage pose potential externalities, but could be internalized by assigning property rights. If a company has clear title to a depletable natural resource such as an oil well, it has some incentive to keep some of the oil for the future, rather than pumping it all today. The biggest problems arise when the legal system fails to enforce clear divisions of property rights. Tropical forest land that anyone can enter to chop down trees will be rapidly over-logged. Many poor countries lack the institutional and economic resources to enforce laws protecting such resources. Often corrupt arms of the government themselves collude in the plundering. Another example is the dumping of waste. If someone agreed to be paid to let his land be used as a waste disposal site, voluntarily and without hidden adverse effects, economics says that there would not necessarily be anything wrong with the arrangement. Waste has to go somewhere. But the situation would be different if the government of a poor undemocratic country were to agree to be paid to accept waste that then hurt the environment and health of residents who lacked the information or political clout to participate in the policy decision or to share in the benefits.

A second category, *national externalities*, includes most kinds of air pollution and water pollution, the latter a particularly great health hazard in the third world. The pollution is external to the individual firm or household, and often external to the state or province as well, but most of the damage is felt within the country in question. Intervention by the government is necessary to control such pollution. There is no reason why each national government cannot undertake the necessary regulation on its own, though the adequacy of economic resources to pay the costs of the regulation is again an issue.

A third category is *international externalities*. Increasingly, as we will see, environmental problems cross national boundaries. Acid rain is an example. In these cases, some cooperation among countries is necessary. The strongest examples are purely *global externalities*: chemicals that deplete the stratospheric ozone layer, greenhouse gases that lead to global climate change, and habitat destruction that impairs biological diversity. Individual countries should not expect to be able to do much about global externalities on their own. The distinctions among internal pollution, national externalities, and global externalities will turn out to be important.

The Relationship between Economic Production and the Environment

Scholars often catalog three intermediating variables or channels of influence that can determine the aggregate economic impacts of trade or growth on the environment.

1. The *scale* of economic activity: for physical reasons, more output means more pollution, other things equal. But other things are usually not equal.

2. The *composition* of economic activity: Trade and growth can shift the composition of output, for example, among the agricultural, manufacturing, and service sectors. Because environmental damage per unit of output varies across these sectors, the aggregate can shift.

3. The *techniques* of economic activity: Often the same commodity can be produced through a variety of different techniques, some cleaner than others. Electric power, for example, can be generated by a very wide range of fuels and techniques. To the extent trade or growth involve the adoption of cleaner techniques, pollution per unit of GDP will fall.

The positive effects of international trade and investment on GDP are already moderately well established, both theoretically and empirically. The relationship between GDP and the environment is not quite as well understood, and is certainly less of a constant relationship. The relationship is rarely monotonic: sometimes a country's growth is first bad for the environment and later good. The reason is the three conflicting forces that were just noted. On the one hand, when GDP increases, the greater scale of production leads directly to more pollution and other environmental degradation. On the other hand, there tend to be favorable shifts in the composition of output and in the techniques of production. The question is whether the latter two effects can outweigh the first.

The Environmental Kuznets Curve

A look at data across countries or across time allows some rough generalization as to the usual outcome of these conflicting effects. For some important environmental measures, a U-shaped relationship appears: at relatively low levels of income per capita, growth leads to greater environmental damage, until it levels off at an intermediate level of income, after which further growth leads to improvements in the environment. This empirical relationship is known as the Environmental Kuznets Curve. The label is by analogy with the original Kuznets Curve, which was a U-shaped relationship between average income and inequality. The World Bank (1992) and Grossman and Krueger (1993, 1995) brought to public attention this statistical finding for a cross section of countries. Grossman and Krueger (1995) estimated that SO_2 pollution peaked when a country's income was about \$5,000–\$6,000 per capita (in 1985 dollars). Most developing countries have not yet reached this threshold.

For countries where a long enough time series of data is available, there is also some evidence that the same U-shaped relationship can hold across time. The air in London was far more polluted in the 1950s than it is today. (The infamous "pea soup" fogs were from pollution.) The same pattern has held in Tokyo, Los Angeles, and other cities. A similar pattern holds typically with respect to deforestation in rich countries: the percentage of U.S. land that was forested fell in the eighteenth century and first half of the nineteenth century, but rose in the twentieth century.

The idea behind the Environmental Kuznets Curve is that growth is bad for air and water pollution at the initial stages of industrialization, but later on reduces pollution, as countries become rich enough to pay to clean up their environments. The dominant theoretical explanation is that production technology makes some pollution inevitable, but that demand for environmental quality rises with income. The standard rationale is thus that, at higher levels of income per capita, growth raises the public's demand for environmental quality, which can translate into environmental regulation. Environmental regulation, if effective, then translates into a cleaner environment. It operates largely through the techniques channel, encouraging or requiring the use of cleaner production techniques for given products, although regulation might also have a composition effect: raising the price of polluting goods and services relative to clean ones and thus encouraging consumers to buy more of the latter.

It would be inaccurate to portray the Environmental Kuznets Curve as demonstrating—or even claiming—that if countries promote growth, the environment will eventually take care of itself. Only if pollution is largely confined within the home or within the firm does that Panglossian view necessarily apply. Most pollution, such as SO_2, NO_x, etc., is external to the home or firm. For such externalities, higher income and a popular desire to clean up the environment are not enough. There must also be effective government regulation, which usually requires a democratic system to translate the popular will into action (something that was missing in the Soviet Union, for example), as well as the rule of law and reasonably intelligent mechanisms of regulation. The empirical evidence confirms that the participation of well-functioning democratic governments is an important part of the process. That is at the national level. The requirements for dealing with cross-border externalities are greater still.

Another possible explanation for the pattern of the Environmental Kuznets Curve is that it works naturally via the composition of output. In theory, the pattern could result from the usual stages of economic development: the transition from an agrarian economy to manufacturing, and then from manufacturing to services. Services tend to generate less pollution than heavy manufacturing. This explanation is less likely than the conventional view to require the mechanism of effective government regulation. If the Kuznets Curve in practice resulted solely from this composition effect, however, then high incomes should lead to a better environment even when externalities arise at the international level, which is not the case. No Kuznets Curve has yet appeared for carbon dioxide, for example. Even though emissions per unit of GDP do tend to fall, this is not enough to reduce overall emissions, in the absence of a multilateral effort.

REGULATION

It will help if we clarify one more fundamental set of issues before we turn to the main subject, the role of globalization per se.

It is logical to expect environmental regulation to cost something, to have a negative effect on measured productivity and income per capita. "There is no free lunch," Milton Friedman famously said. Most tangible good things in life cost something, and for many kinds of regulation, if effective, people will readily agree that the cost is worth paying. Cost-benefit tests and cost-minimization strategies are economists' tools for trying to make sure that policies deliver the best environment for a given economic cost, or the lowest economic cost for a given environmental goal. Taxes on energy, for example, particularly on hydrocarbon fuels, are quite an efficient mode of environmental regulation (if the revenue is "recycled" efficiently). Fuel efficiency standards are somewhat less efficient. (Differentiated CAFE standards for vehicles, for example, probably encouraged the birth of the SUV craze.) And crude "command and control" methods are less efficient still. (Government mandates regarding what specific technologies firms must use, for example, deny firms the flexibility to find better ways to achieve a given goal.) Some environmental regulations, when legislated or implemented poorly, can impose very large and unnecessary economic costs on firms, as well as on workers and consumers.

Occasionally there are policy measures that have both environmental and economic benefits. Usually these "win-win" ideas constitute the elimination of some previously existing distortion in public policy. Many countries have historically subsidized the use of coal. The United States subsidizes mining and cattle grazing on federal land, and sometimes logging and oil drilling as well, not to mention water use. Other countries have substantial subsidies for ocean fishing. Elimination of such subsidies would improve the environment and save money at the same time—not just for the federal budget, but for people's real income in the aggregate as well. Admittedly the economists' approach—taxing gasoline or making ranchers pay for grazing rights—is often extremely unpopular politically.

Another idea that would have economic and environmental benefits simultaneously would be to remove all barriers against international trade in environmental equipment and services, such as those involved in renewable energy generation, smokestack scrubbing, or waste treatment facilities. There would again be a double payoff: the growth-enhancing effect of elimination of barriers to exports (in a sector where the United States is likely to be able to develop a comparative advantage), together with the environment-enhancing effect of facilitating imports of the inputs that go into environmental protection. A precedent is the removal of barriers to the imports of fuel-efficient cars from Japan, which was a clear case of simultaneously promoting free trade and clean air.

A different school of thought claims that opportunities for saving money while simultaneously saving the environment are common rather than rare. The *Porter Hypothesis* holds that a tightening of environmental regulation stimulates technological innovation and thereby has positive effects on both the economy and the environment—for example, saving money by saving energy. The analytical rationale for this view is not always made clear. (Is the claim that a change in regulation, regardless in what direction, stimulates innovation, or is there something special about environmental regulation? Is there something special about the energy sector?) Its proponents cite a number of real-world examples where a new environmental initiative turned out to be profitable for a given firm or industry. Such cases surely exist, but there is little reason to think that a link between regulation and productivity growth holds as a matter of generality. The hypothesis is perhaps better understood as making a point regarding "first mover advantage." That is, if the world is in the future to be moving in a particular direction, such as toward more environmentally friendly energy sources, then a country that innovates new products and new technologies of this sort before others do will be in a position to sell the fruits to the latecomers.

EFFECTS OF OPENNESS TO TRADE

The central topic of this chapter is the implications of trade for the environment. Some effects come via economic growth, and some come even for a given level of income. In both cases, the effects can be either beneficial or detrimental. Probably the strongest effects of trade are the first sort, via income. Much like saving and investment, technological progress, and other sources of growth, trade tends to raise income. As we have seen, higher income in turn has an effect on some environmental measures that is initially adverse but, according to the Environmental Kuznets Curve, eventually turns favorable.

What about effects of trade that do not operate via economic growth? They can be classified in three categories: systemwide effects that are adverse, systemwide effects that are beneficial, and effects that vary across countries depending on local "comparative advantage." We consider each in turn.

Race to the Bottom

The "*race to the bottom*" hypothesis is perhaps the strongest basis for fearing that international trade and investment specifically (rather than industrialization generally) will put downward pressure on countries' environmental standards and thus damage the environment across the global system. Leaders of industry, and of the unions whose members are employed in industry, are always concerned about competition from abroad. When domestic regulation raises their costs, they fear that they will lose competitiveness against firms in other countries. They warn of a loss of sales, employment, and investment to foreign competitors. Thus domestic producers often sound the competitiveness alarm as a way of applying political pressure on their governments to minimize the burden of regulation.

To some, the phrase "race to the bottom" connotes that the equilibrium will be a world of little or no regulation. Others emphasize that, in practice, it is not necessarily a matter of globalization leading to environmental standards that literally decline over time, but rather retarding the gradual raising of environmental standards that would otherwise occur. Either way, the concern is that, to the extent that countries are open to international trade and investment, environmental standards will be lower than they would otherwise be. But how important is this in practice? Some economists' research suggests that environmental regulation is not one of the more important determinants of firms' ability to compete internationally. When deciding where to locate, multinational firms seem to pay more attention to such issues as labor costs and market access than to the stringency of local environmental regulation.

Once again, it is important to distinguish (1) the fear that globalization will lead to a race to the bottom in regulatory standards, from (2) fears that the environment will be damaged by the very process of industrialization and economic growth itself. Opening of national economies to international trade and investment could play a role in both cases, but the two possible channels are very different. In the first case, the race to the bottom hypothesis, the claim is that openness undermines environmental standards even for a given path of economic growth. This would be a damning conclusion from the standpoint of globalization, because it would imply that by limiting trade and investment in some way, we might be able to attain a better environment for any given level of GDP. In the second case, the implication would be that openness only affects the environment in the way that investment, or education, or productivity growth, or any other source of growth affects the environment, by moving the economy along the Environmental Kuznets Curve. Trying to restrict trade and investment would be a less attractive strategy in this case, because it would amount to deliberate self-impoverishment.

Gains from Trade

While the possibility that exposure to international competition might have an adverse effect on environmental regulation is familiar, less widely recognized and more surprising is the possibility of effects in the beneficial direction, which we will call the *gains from trade hypothesis*. Trade allows countries to attain more of what they want, which includes environmental goods in addition to market-measured output.

How could openness have a positive effect on environmental quality, once we set aside the possibility of accelerating progress down the beneficial slope of the Environmental Kuznets Curve? A first possibility concerns technological and managerial innovation. Openness encourages ongoing innovation. It then seems possible that openness could encourage innovation beneficial to environmental improvement as well as economic progress. A second possibility is an international ratcheting up of environmental standards. The largest political jurisdiction can set the pace for others. Within the United States, it is called the "California effect." When the largest state sets high standards for auto pollution control equipment, for example, the end result may be similar standards in other states as well. The United States can play the same role globally.

Multinational corporations (MNCs) are often the vehicle for these effects. They tend to bring clean state-of-the-art production techniques from high-standard countries of origin, to host countries where they are not yet known, for several reasons:

> First, many companies find that the efficiency of having a single set of management practices, pollution control technologies, and training programmes geared to a common set of standards outweighs any cost advantage that might be obtained by scaling back on environmental investments at overseas facilities. Second, multinational enterprises often operate on a large scale, and recognise that their visibility makes them especially attractive targets for local enforcement officials. . . . Third, the prospect of liability for failing to meet standards often motivates better environmental performance (Esty and Gentry 1997: 161).

The claim is not that all multinational corporations apply the highest environmental standards when operating in other countries, but rather that the standards tend on average to be higher than if the host country were undertaking the same activity on its own. Corporate codes of conduct, as under the U.N. Global Compact promoted by Kofi Annan, offer a new way that residents of some countries can pursue environmental goals in other countries. Formal international cooperation among governments is another way that interdependence can lead to higher environmental standards rather than lower.

Furthermore, because trade offers consumers the opportunity to consume goods of greater variety, it allows countries to attain higher levels of welfare (for any given level of domestically produced output), which, as before, will raise the demand for environmental quality. Again, if the appropriate institutions are in place, this demand for higher environmental quality will translate into effective regulation and the desired reduction in pollution.

Attempts to Evaluate the Overall Effects of Trade on the Environment

If a set of countries opens up to trade, is it on average likely to have a positive or negative effect on the environment (for a given level of income)? Which tend in practice to dominate, the unfavorable "race to the bottom" effects or the favorable "gains from trade" effects? Econometrics can help answer the question.

Statistically, some measures of environmental quality are positively correlated with the level of trade. . . . But the causality is complex, running in many directions simultaneously. One would not want to claim that trade leads to a cleaner environment, if in reality they are both responding to some other third factor, such as economic growth or democracy.

Eiras and Schaeffer (2001: 4) find: "In countries with an open economy, the average environmental sustainability score is more than 30 percent higher than the scores of countries with moderately open economies, and almost twice as high as those of countries with closed economies." Does this mean that trade is good for the environment? Not necessarily. It might be a result of the Porter hypothesis—environmental regulation stimulates productivity—together with the positive effect of income on trade. Or it might be because democracy leads to higher levels of environmental regulation, and democracy is causally intertwined with income and trade. As noted, democracy raises the demand for environmental regulation. . . . But there remain other possible third factors.

A number of studies have sought to isolate the independent effect of openness. Lucas et al. (1992), study the toxic intensity implied by the composition of manufacturing output in a sample of 80 countries, and find that a high degree of trade-distorting policies increased pollution in rapidly growing countries. The implication is that trade liberalization now is good for the environment. Harbaugh, Levinson, and Wilson (2000) report in passing a beneficial effect of trade on the environment, after controlling for income. Dean (2002) finds a detrimental direct of liberalization for a given level of income, via the terms of trade, though this is outweighed by a beneficial indirect effect via income.

Antweiler, Copeland and Taylor (2001) and Copeland and Taylor (2001, 2003a) represent an extensive body of empirical research explicitly focused on the effects of trade on the environment. They conclude that trade liberalization that raises the scale of economic activity by 1 percent works to raise SO_2 concentrations by .25 to .5 percent via the scale channel, but that the accompanying technique channel reduces concentrations by 1.25 to 1.5 percent, so that the overall effect is beneficial. But none of these studies makes allowance for the problem that trade may be the *result* of other factors rather than the cause. Antweiler et al. point out this potential weakness.

Frankel and Rose (2003) attempt to disentangle the various causal relationships. The study focuses on exogenous variation in trade across countries, attributable to factors such as geographical location. It finds effects on several measures of air pollution (particularly SO_2 and NO_x concentrations), for a given level of income, that are more good than bad. This suggests that the "gains from trade" effects may be at least as powerful as the "race to the bottom" effect. The findings are not so optimistic for other measures of environmental quality, however, particularly emissions of CO_2.

Differential Effects Arising from Comparative Advantage

So far we have only considered effects that could be expected to hold for the average country, to the extent that it is open to international trade and investment. What if the environment improves in some open countries and worsens in others? An oft-expressed concern is that, to the extent that countries are open to international trade and investment, some will specialize in producing dirty products, and export them to other countries. Such countries could be said to exploit a comparative advantage in pollution. The prediction is that the environment will be damaged more in this set of countries, as compared to what would happen without trade. The environment will be *cleaner* in the second set of countries, those that specialize in clean production and instead import the dirty products from the other countries. Leaving aside the possibility of a race to the bottom effect, the worldwide environment on average might even benefit somewhat, just as aggregate output should benefit, because of the gains from trade. But not everyone would approve of such a bargain.

What determines whether a given country is expected to be in the set of economies specializing in clean or dirty environmental production? There are several possible determinants of comparative advantage.

ENDOWMENTS AND COMPARATIVE ADVANTAGE. First, trade patterns could be determined by endowments of capital and labor, as in the standard neoclassical theory of trade, attributed to Heckscher, Ohlin, and Samuelson. Assume manufacturing is more polluting than alternative economic activities, such as services. (If the alternative sector, say agriculture, is instead just as polluting as manufacturing, then trade has no overall implications for the environment.) Since manufacturing is capital intensive, the country with the high capital/labor ratio—say Japan—will specialize in the dirty manufactured goods, while countries with low capital/labor ratios—say China—will specialize in cleaner goods.

For example, Grossman and Krueger predicted that NAFTA might reduce overall pollution in Mexico and raise it in the United States and Canada, because of the composition effect: Mexico has a comparative advantage in agriculture and labor-intensive manufacturing, which are relatively cleaner, versus the northern comparative advantage in more capital intensive sectors. This composition effect runs in the opposite direction from the usual worry, that trade would turn Mexico into a pollution haven as a result of high demand for environmental quality in the United States. That theory is discussed in the next section.

Second, comparative advantage could be determined by endowments of natural resources. A country with abundant hardwood forests will tend to export them if given the opportunity to do so. Here there cannot be much doubt that trade is indeed likely to damage the environment of such countries. True, in theory, if clear property rights can be allocated and enforced, someone will have the proper incentive to conserve these natural resources for the future. In practice, it seldom works this way. Poor miners and farmers cannot be kept out of large tracts of primitive forest. And even if there were clear property rights over the natural resources, private firms would not have the correct incentives to constrain external side effects of logging and mining, such as air and water pollution, soil erosion, loss of species, and so on. Government regulation is called for, but is often stymied by the problems of inadequate resources, at best, and corruption, at worst.

POLLUTION HAVENS. Third, comparative advantage could be deliberately created by differences in environmental regulation itself. This is the pollution haven hypothesis. The motivation for varying levels of regulation could be differences in demand for environmental quality, arising, for example, from differences in income per capita. Or the motivation could be differences in the supply of environmental quality, arising, for example, from differences in population density.

Many object to an "eco dumping" system according to which economic integration results in some countries exporting pollution to others, even if the overall global level of pollution does not rise. They find distasteful the idea that the impersonal market system would deliberately allocate environmental damage to an "underdeveloped" country. A Chief Economist of the World Bank once signed his name to an internal memo with economists' language that read (in the summary sentence of its most inflammatory passage) "Just between you and me, shouldn't the World Bank be encouraging *more* migration of the dirty industries to the LDCs?" After the memo was leaked, public perceptions of the young Larry Summers were damaged for years.

There is some empirical evidence, but not very much, to support the hypothesis that countries that have a particularly high demand for environmental quality—the rich countries—currently specialize in products that can be produced cleanly, and let the poor countries produce and sell the products that require pollution. For the case of SO_2, the evidence appears to be, if anything, that trade leads to a reallocation of pollution from the poor country to the rich country, rather than the other way around. This is consistent with the finding of Antweiler, Copeland and Taylor (2001) that trade has a significantly less favorable effect on SO_2 emissions in rich countries than in poor countries. Their explanation is that rich countries have higher capital/labor ratios, capital-intensive industries are more polluting, and this factor-based pollution-haven effect dominates the income-based pollution-haven effect.

Is the Majority of U.S. Trade and FDI with Low-Standard Countries?

To listen to some American discussion of globalization, one would think that the typical partner in U.S. trade and investment is a poor country with low environmental or labor standards. If so, it would help explain the fear that opening to international trade and investment in general puts downward pressure on U.S. standards. In fact, less than half of U.S. trade and investment takes place with partners who have lower wages and lower incomes than we do. Our most important partners have long been Canada, Japan, and the

European Union (though Mexico has now become important as well). These trading partners often regard the United States as the low-standard country rather than the opposite.

DOES ECONOMIC GLOBALIZATION CONFLICT WITH ENVIRONMENTAL REGULATION?

There is a popular sense that globalization is a powerful force undermining environmental regulation. This can be the case in some circumstances. The "race to the bottom" phenomenon can potentially put downward pressure on the regulatory standards of countries that compete internationally in trade and investment. But, as an argument against globalization, it leaves much out.

First is the point that, for most of us, environmental quality is one goal, but not the only goal. As already noted, we care also about income, and trade is one means of promoting economic growth. The goals often need to be balanced against each other.

Environmental concerns can be an excuse for protectionism. If policymakers give in to protectionist arguments and erect trade barriers, we will enjoy less growth in trade and income. We will not even necessarily end up with a better environment. Import-competing corporations (or their workers), in sectors that may themselves not be particularly friendly to the environment, sometimes seek to erect or retain barriers to imports in the name of environmental protection, when in reality it is their own pocketbooks they are trying to protect. In other words, environmentalism is an excuse for protectionism.

Often, the problem is less sinister, but more complex. To see how the political economy works, let us begin with the point that most policy debates are settled as the outcome of a complicated mix of multiple countervailing arguments and domestic interest groups on both sides. Most of the major viewpoints are in some way represented "at the table" in the federal government decisionmaking process. In the case of environmental measures, there are often representatives of adversely affected industry groups sitting across the table from the environmentalists, and they have an effect on the final political outcome. But when the commodity in question happens to be produced by firms in foreign countries, then that point of view largely disappears from the table around which the decision is made. If the issue is big enough, the State Department may weigh in to explain the potential costs facing foreign countries. But, understandably, the foreigners receive less weight in the policy process than would the identical firms if they were American. The result is that the environmental policies that are adopted on average can discriminate against foreign firms relative to domestic firms, without anyone ever deliberately having supported a measure out of protectionist intent.

One possible example is the strong opposition in Europe to Genetically Modified Organisms (GMOs). A Biosafety Agreement was negotiated in Montreal, January 29, 2000, in which the United States felt it had to agree to label grain shipments that might in part be bio-engineered, and to allow countries to block imports of GMOs. In some ways, these negotiations might serve as a useful model for compromise in other areas. But why have Europeans decided that they want to keep out genetically modified varieties of corn, despite the emergence of little or no scientific evidence against them as of yet, where American consumers are far less agitated? Is it because Europeans are predisposed to have higher standards for environmental issues? Perhaps. An important part of the explanation, however, is that Monsanto and other U.S. technology companies, and U.S. farmers, are the ones who developed the technology and produce the stuff, not European companies or European farmers. Thus it is American producers, not Europeans, who stand to lose from the European squeamishness. European agriculture need not consciously launch a campaign against GMOs. All that the European movement needed was an absence around the table of producers who would be adversely affected by a ban. But the result is to reduce trade, hurt American producers, and benefit European farmers.

Whatever the source of different perceptions across countries, it is important to have a set of internationally agreed rules to govern trade, and if possible a mechanism for settling disputes that arise. That is the role of the WTO. The need for such an institution does not vanish when environmental issues are a part of the dispute. Certainly if one cares at all about trade and growth, then one cannot automatically sign on to each and every campaign seeking to block trade on environmental grounds. But even if one cares solely about the environment, claims need to be evaluated through some sort of neutral process. One can be easily misled; corporations make dubious claims to environmental motivations in, for example, seeking federal support of "Clean Coal" research or ethanol production. Most of the time, there is no substitute for investigating the details and merits of the case in question. One should not presume that an interest group's claims are right just because that group happens to be of one's own nationality. . . .

Environmental Concerns Cross National Borders

Even those who do not care about trade at all should appreciate the need for some international agreements and institutions. The reason is the increasing importance of major sources of environmental damage that cross national borders, and that would do so even if there were no such thing as international trade. Some externalities have long spilled over from each country to its immediate neighbors—such as SO_2 pollution, which is responsible for acid rain, or water pollution, which flows downriver. They can be addressed by negotiations between the two countries involved (e.g., U.S. and Canada). An increasing number of environmental externalities are truly global, however. The best examples are greenhouse gases. A ton of carbon dioxide creates the same global warming potential regardless where in the world it is emitted.

Other good examples of direct global externalities are stratospheric ozone depletion, depletion of ocean fish stocks, and threats to biodiversity.

Even localized environmental damage, such as deforestation, is increasingly seen as a valid object of international concern. A distinction is traditional between trade measures that target specific undesirable products, such as asbestos, and those that target *Processes and Production Methods* (PPMs), such as the use of prison labor in the manufacture of the commodity in question. It is clear that a country concerned about its own health or environment has the right to tax or ban products that it regards as harmful, so long as it does not discriminate against foreign producers. Indeed, such bans are less liable to become a vehicle for surreptitious protectionism than are attempts to pass judgment on other countries' production methods that are unrelated to the physical attributes of the product itself. But is it legitimate for importing countries also to discriminate according to how a given product was produced? Some ask what business is it of others whether the producing country wants to use its own prison labor, or cut down its own forests, or pollute its own environment?

Often an international externality can be easily identified. Forests absorb carbon dioxide (a process called sequestration, or creating carbon sinks), so logging contributes to global climate change. An endangered species may contain a unique genetic element that someday could be useful to international scientists. Desertification can lead to social instability and political conflict, which can in turn produce problems for international security. Thus environmental damage in one country can have indirect effects on others.

But foreign residents increasingly care about localized environmental damage as well, even when they live far away and even when there is no evident link to their interests. The idea of "non-use value" is that many people place value on keeping, for example, a river canyon unspoiled, even if they know they will never see it. While the methodology of estimating the value according to what people say they would pay ("contingent valuation") is fraught with problems, the basic principle of non-use value is now widely accepted. This means that citizens in one country may have a stake in whether another country dams up a gorge, kills its wildlife, or pollutes its air and water.

Reversing Globalization Would Not End the Tension of Regulation vs. Sovereignty

Thus, for an increasingly important set of environmental issues, the idea that individual countries could properly address the issues if left on their own is myth. If countries do not cooperate through multilateral institutions, each will be tempted to free ride on the efforts of others, and little will get done. Globalization and multilateral institutions are not the obstacle—and the appeal of national sovereignty is not an ally—in international efforts to protect the environment. Rather, environmentalists need global agreements and global agencies if they are going to get other countries to do the things they want them to do. It is the appeal of national sovereignty that is the obstacle.

The mistake of blaming all ills on globalization and multilateral institutions such as the WTO has yielded some very strange bedfellows. Environmentally concerned protestors have been treating labor unions and poor countries as comrades in arms, proud of the fact that a disparate set of groups have supposedly been brought together by a shared opposition to globalization. But in fact, some of these groups are on the other side of the environmental issue. U.S. labor unions are strong opponents of the Kyoto Protocol on Global Climate Change. Poor countries tend to be strong opponents of international environmental agreements in general. Both groups cite national sovereignty in support of their positions. It is particularly puzzling that some environmentalists see pro-sovereignty supporters as natural allies, when so many environmental problems in fact need to be addressed by means of multilateral institutions that in fact infringe on national sovereignty.

If labor unions and environmentalists can come together on an issue, that is fine. *But they have to agree on that issue.* They should share something more than an emotional antipathy to some particular multilateral institution: they should want the institution to move in the same direction, not opposite directions. They don't have to get into fine details, if they don't want to. But if, for example, one group thinks that the proper response to globalization is that the multilateral institutions should exercise less invasion of national sovereignty in the pursuit of environmental regulation and the other thinks the institutions should exercise more invasion of national sovereignty in that pursuit, then they are in truth hardly allies.

INTERNATIONAL AGREEMENTS AND INSTITUTIONS

Those who live in the world of international trade negotiations tell those who live in the environmentalist world along the lines that their concerns may be valid, but that they should address them by their own, separate, negotiations, and their own multilateral agencies.

Multilateral Environmental Organizations

The one multilateral organization dedicated to environmental issues in general, the United Nations Environmental Program, is universally considered small and weak, even by the standards of UN agencies. Some may favor beefing it up. Many feel that it is not fixable, that—to begin with—it would have to be based somewhere like Geneva in order to be taken seriously, not in Nairobi as now. On these grounds, some have proposed a new, powerful, multilateral World Environment Organization. Daniel Esty (1994) has proposed that it be called the Global Environmental Organization, providing the appropriate acronym GEO. But the source of the problem is not some accident of bureaucratic design history or geography. The problem, rather, is that there is very little support among the world's governments for a powerful multilateral agency in the area of the environment. They fear infringement on their sovereignty.

One can say that in concentrating their fire on the WTO, environmental activists are adopting a strategy of taking the multilateral trading system hostage. They envy the relative success of the WTO system. They are aware that international environmental treaties, even if successfully negotiated and ratified, may be toothless. The agreements made at Rio de Janeiro in 1992 are an example. The activists would ideally like to adopt trade sanctions as a means of enforcement, as does the WTO itself.

Such proposals do not explain attempts to take globalization hostage more broadly, for example by demonstrations at WTO ministerial meetings. There is nothing in the WTO to block multilateral environmental treaties from adopting penalties against relevant trade with nonmembers. Indeed, the Montreal Protocol on stratospheric ozone depletion has such trade controls, ran into no problems under international trade rules, and is generally considered to have been successful in achieving its goals. Admittedly there is strong resistance in other cases. Most governments do not favor international environmental agreements that are so aggressive as to include trade sanctions. Again, the failure does not mean that globalization and global institutions like the WTO are the problem. More likely it is the other way around: globalization is the ally, and national sovereignty is the obstacle.

Bilateral and Regional FTAs

Regional and bilateral agreements, such as the European Union or the Australia-New Zealand Closer Economic Relationship, have incorporated environmental components more often than have multilateral agreements. Whether because of cultural homogeneity or the small numbers involved, a group consisting of a few neighbors is usually readier to contemplate the sort of "deep integration" required for harmonization of environmental standards than are negotiators in groups with more than 100 diverse members, such as the WTO.

In the public debate over the North American Free Trade Agreement, one of the most prominent concerns of opponents was the pollution that had already accompanied industrialization in northern Mexico, particularly among the *maquilladoras* along the border, which in turn was a result of the ability to trade with the United States. The final agreement departed from previous U.S. trade agreements, or those in most other parts of the world, by taking into account environmental concerns, at least in a small way. The preamble includes environmentally friendly language, such as a stipulation that the NAFTA goals are to be pursued "in a manner consistent with environmental protection and conservation." Chapter 7B allows the member countries to continue adopting sanitary and phyto-sanitary standards. Chapter 9 allows countries to set whatever environmental standards they want, provided only that they do not discriminate or discourage trade unnecessarily.

Nevertheless, environmental groups were unhappy with the subsequent outcome. Proposed side-agreements, for example, to establish a bank to finance environmental clean-up along the border, received a lot of attention during Bill Clinton's presidential campaign and during the subsequent NAFTA ratification campaign. Follow-up after the NAFTA went into effect in 1994, however, was disappointing.

Meanwhile, provisions under Chapter 11, which governs direct investment, have turned out to be important. On the one hand, the text reads "the Parties recognize that it is inappropriate to encourage investment by relaxing domestic health, safety or environmental measures." On the other hand, protection of the rights of investors has confirmed some environmentalists' fears, particularly a case brought by a Canadian company called Metalclad under the dispute settlement mechanism. Under a clause that forbids a signatory from taking measures "tantamount to nationalization or expropriation" of firms from other member countries, Metalclad in August 2000 won a judgment from a NAFTA tribunal against a local Mexican regulators' attempt to close its hazardous waste disposal plant without compensation. The finding that Mexican regulation had denied a foreign firm fair and equitable treatment was potentially an important precedent under the NAFTA. But it would be strange, even from a pro-business viewpoint, if an American or Canadian firm were extensively protected against regulatory "takings" in Mexico when it would not be protected in its country of origin.

The NAFTA experience reinforced environmentalists' concerns with trade agreements. They urged the US government to bring environmental issues inside trade negotiations, for example, forbidding parties in trade agreements from relaxing environmental regulation in order to seek competitive advantage. A preferential trading arrangement negotiated by the United States at the end of the Clinton Administration, the Jordan-U.S. free trade agreement, incorporated such environmental provisions directly in the text, rather than as a side agreement, a precedent that was hoped to establish a "template" or precedent for future agreements. In addition, an Executive Order now requires that the government prepare an "environmental impact statement" whenever negotiating new trade agreements in the future, to guard against possible inadvertent side-effects adverse to the environment. . . .

The WTO and Some Panel Cases

In the postwar period, the vehicle for conducting the multilateral negotiations that succeeded in bringing down trade barriers in many countries was the General Agreement on Tariffs and Trade. An important outcome of the Uruguay Round of negotiations was the replacement of the GATT organization with a real agency, the World Trade Organization, which came into existence in 1995. One reason why the change was important is that the new institution featured a dispute settlement mechanism, whose findings were to be binding on the member countries. Previously, a party that did not like the ruling of a GATT panel could reject it.

Why do so many environmentalists apparently feel that the still-young WTO is a hostile power? Allegations concern lack of democratic accountability and negative effects on the environment. It is difficult to see how these allegations could apply to the process of setting WTO rules themselves. Regarding the alleged lack of democracy, the GATT and WTO are in principle one-country one-vote bodies that make decisions by consensus. Clearly in practice, some countries—particularly the United States—matter far more than others. But consider what it would mean to make this process more democratic. It would presumably mean giving less weight to U.S. views and more to the views, for example, of India, the world's most populous democracy. But, given India's preferences and its aversion to "eco-imperialism," this would clearly mean giving *less* attention in the WTO to environmental goals, not more.

The allegation that the GATT and WTO are hostile to environmental measures could conceivably arise from the core provisions of the GATT, which prohibit a member country from discriminating against the exports of another, in favor of "like products" made either by a third country (that is the Most Favored Nation provision of Article I) or by domestic producers (the national treatment provision of Article III). But Article XX allows for exceptions to the nondiscrimination principle for environmental reasons (among others), provided that the measures in question are not "a means of arbitrary or unjustifiable discrimination" or a "disguised restriction on international trade." Moreover, umbrella clauses allow countries to take actions to protect human, animal or plant life or health, and to conserve exhaustible natural resources.

Under the GATT, there was ambiguity of interpretation as to what was to happen when Article XX conflicted with the nondiscrimination articles. To clarify the matter, language was added to the preamble to the articles agreed to at Marrakech that established the WTO specifying that its objectives were not limited to promoting trade but included also optimal use of the world's resources, sustainable development, and environmental protection. Environmental objectives are also recognized specifically in the WTO agreements dealing with product standards, food safety, intellectual property protection, etc.

The protests are in a sense a puzzle. It would be easy to understand a political campaign in favor of the WTO taking a more aggressive pro-environment stance. But how does one explain the common view in the protest movement that the WTO currently is actively harmful to the environment?

When members of the protest movement identify specifics, they usually mention the rulings of WTO panels under the dispute settlement mechanism.

The panels are quasi-judicial tribunals, whose job is to rule in disputes whether parties are abiding by the rules that they have already agreed to. Like most judicial proceedings, the panels themselves are not intended to be democratic. The rulings to date do not show a pattern of having been dominated by any particular country or interest group. There have been three or four fairly prominent WTO panel rulings that concern the environment in some way. Most within the environmentalist and NGO community have at some point acquired the belief that these rulings told the United States, or other defendant country, that their attempts to protect the environment must be repealed. The mystery is why this impression is so widespread, because it has little basis in fact.

The four WTO cases that will be briefly reviewed here are Canadian asbestos, Venezuelan reformulated gasoline, U.S. hormone-fed beef, and Asian shrimp and turtles. We will also touch on the Mexican tuna-dolphin case. Each of the cases involves an environmental measure that the producer plaintiff alleged to have trade-distorting effects. The complaints were not based, however, on the allegation that the goal of the measure was not valid, or that protectionism was the original motivation of the measure. In most of the cases, the allegation was that discrimination against foreigners was an incidental, and unnecessary, feature of the environmental measure.

CANADIAN ASBESTOS.   One case is considered a clear win for the environmentalists. The WTO Appellate Body in 2001 upheld a French ban on asbestos products, against a challenge by Canada, which had been exporting to France. This ruling made real the WTO claim that its charter gives priority to health, safety, and environmental requirements, in that for such purposes GATT Article XX explicitly allows exceptions to the Most Favored Nation and national treatment rules.

VENEZUELAN REFORMULATED GASOLINE.   In the reformulated gasoline case, Venezuela successfully claimed that U.S. law violated national treatment, i.e., discriminated in favor of domestic producers (with regard to whether refineries were allowed to use individual composition baselines when measuring pollution reduction). The case was unusual in that the intent to discriminate had at the time of passage been made explicit by U.S. administration officials seeking to please a domestic interest group. If the WTO had ruled in the U.S. favor, it would have been saying that it was fine for a country to discriminate needlessly and explicitly against foreign producers so long as the law came under an environmental label. Those who oppose this panel decision provide ready-made ammunition for the viewpoint that environmental activism is a false disguise worn by protectionist interests.

The United States was not blocked in implementing its targets, under the Clean Air Act, as commonly charged. Rather, the offending regulation was easily changed so as to be nondiscriminatory and thus to be permissible under the rules agreed to by members of the WTO. This case sent precisely the right message to the world's governments, that environmental measures should not and need not discriminate against foreign producers.

HORMONE-FED BEEF. What happens if the commodity in question is produced entirely, or almost entirely, by foreign producers, so that it cannot be conclusively demonstrated whether a ban, or other penalty, is or is not discriminatory? The WTO has attempted to maintain the rule that such measures are fine so long as a scientific study has supported the claimed environmental or health benefits of the measure. In the hormone-fed beef case, the WTO ruled against an EU ban on beef raised with growth hormones because the EU conspicuously failed to produce a science-based risk assessment showing that it might be dangerous. It thus resembles the case of the EU moratorium on GMOs.

These are genuinely difficult cases. On the one hand, where popular beliefs regarding a scientific question vary widely, a useful role for a multilateral institution could be to rule on the scientific merits. Or at least a useful role could be, as under the current WTO procedures, to rule on whether the country seeking to impose the regulation has carried out internally a reasonable study of the scientific merits. This logic suggests overruling the EU bans. On the other hand, the world may not be ready for even this mild level of loss of national sovereignty. If a nation's intent is to protect its health or environment, even if the measure has little scientific basis and even if its primary burden would fall on foreign producers, perhaps ensuring that the ban does not unnecessarily discriminate among producing countries is the best that can be done.

Despite the WTO ruling on hormone-fed beef, the Europeans did not cancel the ban. Their strategy, which they justify with the name "precautionary principle," is to continue to study the matter before allowing the product in. The precautionary principle, as the Europeans apply it, says to prohibit new technologies that have not yet been proven safe, even if there is no evidence that they are dangerous. At a minimum, it seems that they should be forced to allow imports of American beef subject to labeling requirements, as in the Montreal agreement on GMOs. Let the consumer decide.

SHRIMP-TURTLE. Perceptions regarding the WTO panel ruling on a dispute about shrimp imports and the protection of sea turtles probably vary more widely than on any other case. The perception among many environmentalists is that the panel ruling struck down a U.S. law to protect sea turtles that are caught in the nets of shrimp fishermen in the Indian Ocean. (The provision was pursuant to the U.S. Endangered Species Act.) In reality, the dispute resembled the gasoline case in the respect that the ban on imports from countries without adequate regulatory regimes in place was unnecessarily selective and restrictive. The WTO panel and appellate body decided that the U.S. application of the law, in a complex variety of ways, was arbitrarily and unjustifiably discriminatory against the four plaintiff countries (Asian shrimp suppliers). The United States had unilaterally and inflexibly banned shrimp imports from countries that did not have in place for all production a specific turtle-protection regime of its own liking, one that mandated Turtle Excluder Devices.

The case could in fact be considered a victory for the environmentalists, in that the WTO panel and the appeals body in 1998 explicitly stated that the United States could pursue the protection of endangered sea turtles against foreign fishermen. The United States subsequently allowed more flexibility in its regulation, and made good-faith efforts to negotiate an agreement with the Asian producers, which is what it should have done in the first place. The WTO panel and appellate body in 2001 found the new U.S. regime to be WTO-compliant. The case set a precedent in clarifying support for the principle that the WTO rules allow countries to pass judgment on other countries' Processes and Production Methods, even if it means using trade controls to do so, provided only that the measures are not unnecessarily discriminatory.

TUNA-DOLPHIN. In an earlier attempt to protect another large flippered sea animal, the United States (under the Marine Mammal Protection Act) had banned imports of tuna from countries that allowed the fishermen to use nets that also caught dolphins. Mexico brought a case before the GATT, as this predated the WTO, and the GATT panel ruled against the U.S. law. Its report was never adopted. The parties instead in effect worked out their differences bilaterally, "out of court." The case could be considered a setback for trade-sensitive environmental measures, at least unilateral ones, but a setback that was to prove temporary. That the GATT ruling in the tuna case did not affirm the right of the United States to use trade bans to protect the dolphins shows how much the environmentalist cause has progressed under the WTO, in the subsequent gasoline, shrimp-turtle, and asbestos cases.

A system for labeling tuna in the US market as either "dolphin safe" or not was later found consistent with the GATT. The American consumer response turned out to be sufficiently great to accomplish the desired purpose. Since 1990, the major companies have sold only the dolphin-safe kind of tuna. The moral is not that the goal of protecting the dolphins was accomplished despite globalization in its GATT incarnation, but rather that *globalization was instrumental in the protection of the dolphins*. The goal could not have been accomplished without international trade, because American citizens would have had no effective way of putting pressure on Mexico. Leaving the U.S. government free to regulate its own fishermen would not have helped.

Multilateral Environmental Agreements

When it comes to global externalities such as endangered species, stratospheric ozone depletion, and global climate change, it is particularly clear that the problem cannot be addressed by a system where each country pursues environmental measures on its own. Multilateral negotiations, agreements, and institutions are required. Furthermore, the point is not simply that global regulatory measures are needed to combat the effects of economic globalization. If countries had industrialized in isolation, without any international trade or investment among them, they would still be emitting greenhouse gases, and we would still need a globally coordinated response.

Multilateral environmental agreements (MEAs), even if they involve trade-restricting measures, are viewed more favorably under the international rules than unilateral environmental measures. Leaving aside the Law of the Sea, the Basel Convention on Hazardous Wastes, and a large number of relatively more minor agreements, three MEAs merit particular mention.

The Convention on International Trade in Endangered Species (CITES) was negotiated in 1973. Although it lacks the teeth that many would like, it was notable as a precedent establishing that MEAs are compatible with the GATT even if they restrict trade. An interesting issue relevant for species protection is whether a plan of using animals to support the economic livelihood of local residents can be a more sustainable form of protection than attempts to leave them untouched altogether.

The Montreal Protocol on Substances that Deplete the Ozone Layer is the most successful example of an MEA, as it has resulted in the phasing out of most use of CFCs (Chlorofluorocarbons) and other ozone-depleting chemicals. The success of this agreement is partly attributable to the enforcement role played by trade penalties: the protocol prohibits trade in controlled substances with countries that do not participate. This created the necessary incentive to push those developing countries that otherwise might have been reluctant into joining. If substantial numbers of countries had nevertheless remained outside the protocol, the trade controls would have also accomplished the second objective—minimizing *leakage*, that is, the migration of production of banned substances to nonparticipating countries. One reason why the protocol succeeded was there were a relatively small number of producers. It also helped that there turned out to be good substitutes for the banned substances, though that was not known until the ban was tried. One might say it also helped establish the principle that PPM-targeted measures were not necessarily incompatible with the GATT: the agreement threatened nonparticipants not only with a ban on trade in ozone-depleting chemicals themselves, but also a potential ban on trade in goods manufactured with such chemicals in the sense that governments were required to determine the feasibility of such a ban. But it never went further than that.

The Kyoto Protocol on Global Climate Change, negotiated in 1997, is the most ambitious attempt at a multilateral environment agreement to date. This is not the place to discuss the Kyoto Protocol at length. The task of addressing Climate Change while satisfying the political constraints of the various factions (particularly, the U.S., EU, and developing countries) was an inherently impossible task. Most economists emphasize that the agreement as it was written at Kyoto would impose large economic costs on the United States and other countries, while making only a minor dent in the problem. The Clinton Administration's interpretation of the protocol insisted on so-called flexibility mechanisms, such as international trading of emission permits, to bring the economic costs down to a modest range. This interpretation was rejected by the Europeans at the Hague in November 2000. Without the flexibility mechanisms, the United States would be out of the protocol, even if the subsequent administration had been more environmentally friendly than it was. (Ironically, now that European and other countries are trying to go ahead without the United States, they are finding that they cannot manage without such trading mechanisms.)

Even most of those who for one reason or another do not believe that Kyoto was a useful step, however, should acknowledge that multilateral agreements will be necessary if the problem of Global Climate Change is to be tackled. The Bush administration has yet to face up to this. The point for present purposes is that a system in which each country insists, based on an appeal to national sovereignty, that it be left to formulate environmental policies on its own, would be a world in which global externalities like greenhouse gas emissions would not be effectively addressed.

SUMMARY OF CONCLUSIONS

The relationship between globalization and the environment is too complex to sum up in a single judgment—whether "good" or "bad." In many respects, global trade and investment operate like other sources of economic growth. They tend to raise income as measured in the marketplace. On the one hand, the higher scale of output can mean more pollution, deforestation, and other kinds of environmental damage. On the other hand, changes in the composition and techniques of economic activity can lower the damage relative to income. Although it is not possible to generalize universally about the net effect of these channels, it is possible to put forward general answers to some major questions.

- A key question is whether openness to international trade undermines national attempts at environmental regulation, through a "race to the bottom" effect. This no doubt happens sometimes. But there is little statistical evidence, across countries, that the unfavorable effects on average outweigh favorable "gains from trade" effects on measures of pollution, such as SO_2 concentrations. If anything, the answer seems to be that favorable effects dominate.
- Perceptions that WTO panel rulings have interfered with the ability of individual countries to pursue environmental goals are poorly informed.

In cases such as Canadian asbestos, Venezuelan gasoline, and Asian shrimp, the rulings have confirmed that countries can enact environmental measures, even if they affect trade and even if they concern others' Processes and Production Methods (PPMs), provided the measures do not unnecessarily discriminate among producer countries.

■ People care both about the environment and the economy. As their real income rises, their demand for environmental quality rises. Under the right conditions, this can translate into environmental progress. The right conditions include democracy, effective regulation, and externalities that are largely confined within national borders and are therefore amenable to national regulation.

■ Increasingly, however, environmental problems do in fact spill across national borders. The strongest examples are pure global externalities such as global climate change and ozone depletion. Economic growth alone will not address such problems, in a system where each country acts individually, due to the free rider problem. International institutions are required. This would be equally true in the absence of international trade. Indeed, trade offers a handle whereby citizens of one country can exercise a role in environmental problems of other countries that they would otherwise not have. Consumer labeling campaigns and corporate codes of conduct are examples.

■ Many aspects of the environment that might have been considered purely domestic matters in the past, or that foreign residents might not even have known about, are increasingly of concern to those living in other countries. This again means that multilateral institutions are needed to address the issues, and expressions of national sovereignty are the obstacle, not the other way around. Indeed, if one broadens the definition of globalization, beyond international trade and investment, to include the globalization of ideas and of NGO activities, then one can see the international environmental movement as itself an example of globalization.

REFERENCES

Antweiler, Werner, Brian Copeland and M. Scott Taylor. 2001. "Is Free Trade Good for the Environment?" *NBER Working Paper* No. 6707. *American Economic Review*, 91, no. 4 (September): 877–908.

Copeland, Brian, and M. Scott Taylor. 2001. "International Trade and the Environment: A Framework for Analysis." *NBER Working Paper* No. 8540, Oct.

———. 2003. *Trade and the Environment: Theory and Evidence*. Princeton: Princeton University Press.

Dean, Judy. 2002. "Does Trade Liberalization Harm the Environment? A New Test." *Canadian Journal of Economics* 35, no. 4 (November): 819–42.

Eiras, Ana, and Brett Schaefer. 2001. "Trade: The Best Way to Protect the Environment." *Backgrounder*, The Heritage Foundation no. 1480, September 27.

Esty, Daniel. 1994. *Greening the GATT: Trade, Environment, and the Future*. Washington, DC: Institute for International Economics.

Esty, Daniel, and Bradford Gentry. 1997. "Foreign Investment, Globalisation, and the Environment." In Tom Jones, ed. *Globalization and the Environment*. Paris: Organization for Economic Cooperation and Development.

Frankel, Jeffrey, and Andrew Rose. 2003. "Is Trade Good or Bad for the Environment? Sorting Out the Causality." RWP03–038, Kennedy School of Government, Harvard University, September. Revised version of NBER Working Paper 9201. Forthcoming, *Review of Economics and Statistics*.

Grossman, Gene, and Alan Krueger. 1993. "Environmental Impacts of a North American Free Trade Agreement." In Peter Garber, ed. *The U.S.-Mexico Free Trade Agreement*. Cambridge: MIT Press.

———. 1995. "Economic Growth and the Environment." *Quarterly Journal of Economics*, 110, no. 2 (May): 353–77.

Harbaugh, William, Arik Levinson, and David Wilson. 2000. "Reexamining the Empirical Evidence for an Environmental Kuznets Curve." *NBER Working Paper* No. 7711, May.

Lucas, Robert E.B., David Wheeler, and Hememala Hettige. 1992. "Economic Development, Environmental Regulation and the International Migration of Toxic Industrial Pollution: 1960–1988." In Patrick Low, ed. *International Trade and the Environment*. World Bank Discussion Papers no. 159. Washington, DC: The World Bank.

World Bank. 1992. *Development and the Environment*, World Development Report.

30

A New Deal for Globalization

KENNETH F. SCHEVE AND MATTHEW J. SLAUGHTER

The United States appears to be on the verge of reversing its long-standing support of economic globalization. On the one hand, public support for globalization is declining; on the other, U.S. foreign economic policy is becoming more protectionist. Kenneth F. Scheve and Matthew J. Slaughter connect these two trends and show they have common cause: policy is becoming more protectionist because, with the incomes of most citizens stagnating or falling, the public is becoming more protectionist. In order to build public support for globalization and thereby avert a full protectionist backlash against globalization, the authors recommend a dramatic expansion of the welfare state—"A New Deal for Globalization." By reforming the tax system, the government can engineer significant income redistribution so that globalization's gains are shared more widely.

WAGES FALLING, PROTECTIONISM RISING

Over the last several years, a striking new feature of the U.S. economy has emerged: real income growth has been extremely skewed, with relatively few high earners doing well while incomes for most workers have stagnated or, in many cases, fallen. Just what mix of forces is behind this trend is not yet clear, but regardless, the numbers are stark. Less than four percent of workers were in educational groups that enjoyed increases in mean real money earnings from 2000 to 2005; mean real money earnings rose for workers with doctorates and professional graduate degrees and fell for all others. In contrast to in earlier decades, today it is not just those at the bottom of the skill ladder who are hurting. Even college graduates and workers with nonprofessional master's degrees saw their mean real money earnings decline. By some measures, inequality in the United States is greater today than at any time since the 1920s.

Advocates of engagement with the world economy are now warning of a protectionist drift in public policy. This drift is commonly blamed on narrow industry concerns or a failure to explain globalization's benefits or the war on terrorism. These explanations miss a more basic point: U.S. policy is becoming more protectionist because the American public is becoming more protectionist, and this shift in attitudes is a result of stagnant or falling incomes. Public support for engagement with the world economy is strongly linked to labor-market performance, and for most workers labor-market performance has been poor.

Given that globalization delivers tremendous benefits to the U.S. economy as a whole, the rise in protectionism brings many economic dangers. To avert them, U.S. policymakers must recognize and then address the fundamental cause of opposition to freer trade and investment. They must also recognize that the two most commonly proposed responses—more investment in education and more trade adjustment assistance for dislocated workers—are nowhere near adequate. Significant payoffs from educational investment will take decades to be realized, and trade adjustment assistance is too small and too narrowly targeted on specific industries to have much effect.

The best way to avert the rise in protectionism is by instituting a New Deal for globalization—one that links engagement with the world economy to a substantial redistribution of income. In the United States, that would mean adopting a fundamentally more progressive federal tax system. The notion of more aggressively redistributing income may sound radical, but ensuring that most American workers are benefiting is the best way of saving globalization from a protectionist backlash.

RISING PROTECTIONISM

U.S. economic policy is becoming more protectionist. First, consider trade. The prospects for congressional renewal of President George W. Bush's trade promotion authority, which is set to expire this summer, are grim. The 109th Congress introduced 27 pieces of anti-China trade legislation; the 110th introduced over a dozen in just its first three months. In late March, the Bush administration levied new tariffs on Chinese exports of high-gloss paper—reversing a 20-year precedent of not accusing nonmarket economies of illegal export subsidies.

Barriers to inward foreign direct investment (FDI) are also rising. In 2005, the Chinese energy company CNOOC tried to purchase U.S.-headquartered Unocal. The subsequent political storm was so intense that CNOOC withdrew its bid. A similar controversy erupted in 2006 over the purchase of operations at six U.S. ports by Dubai-based Dubai Ports World, eventually causing the company to sell the assets. The Committee on Foreign Investments in the United States, which is legally required to review and approve certain foreign acquisitions of U.S. businesses, has raised the duration and complexity of many reviews. Both chambers of the 109th Congress passed bills to tighten CFIUS scrutiny even further; similar legislation has already passed in the current House.

This protectionist drift extends to much of the world. The Doha Development Round of trade negotiations, the centerpiece of global trade liberalization, is years behind schedule and now on the brink of collapse. Key U.S. trading partners are becoming increasingly averse to foreign investment, as expressed both in their rhetoric (recent public pronouncements by the governments of France and Germany) and in their actions (new restrictions in China on foreign retailers).

At first glance, this rise in protectionism may seem puzzling. The economic gains from globalization are immense. In the United States, according to estimates from the Peter G. Peterson Institute for International Economics and others, trade and investment liberalization over the past decades has added between $500 billion and $1 trillion in annual income—between $1,650 and $3,300 a year for every American. A Doha agreement on global free trade in goods and services would generate, according to similar studies, $500 billion a year in additional income in the United States.

International trade and investment have spurred productivity growth, the foundation of rising average living standards. The rate of increase in output per worker hour in the U.S. nonfarm business sector has doubled in the past decade, from an annual average of 1.35 percent between 1973 and 1995 to an annual average of 2.7 percent since 1995. Much of the initial acceleration was related to information technology (IT)—one of the United States' most globally engaged industries, at the forefront of establishing and expanding production networks linked by trade and investment around the globe.

Gains from globalization have been similarly large in the rest of the world. China and India have achieved stupendous rates of productivity growth, lifting hundreds of millions of people out of poverty. Central to this success has been the introduction of market forces, in particular international market forces related to trade and FDI. In Chinese manufacturing, foreign multinational companies account for over half of all exports. And in the Indian IT sector, Indian and foreign multinational firms account for two-thirds of sales.

Freer trade and investment can also enhance other foreign policy goals. The Doha Round was launched shortly after 9/11 because of the view that global poverty is intimately linked to international insecurity and instability. The Doha Round was also intended to remedy the widespread perception that previous rounds of trade negotiations had treated poor nations unfairly by failing to open the very sectors—such as agriculture—whose openness would most likely help the world's poor. Accordingly, it is believed that a successful Doha agreement would enhance the United States' image and promote its interests around the world.

There are three common explanations for why protectionism is on the rise in the United States even though globalization is good for both the U.S. economy and U.S. security interests. None, however, is convincing. The first is that a narrow set of industries, such as agriculture and apparel manufacturing, have been harmed by freer trade and, in response, have lobbied hard to turn lawmakers against liberalization. But the incentives for these industries to oppose globalization have not changed in recent years, and there are also many industries that have benefited from, and thus lobbied for, further liberalization. What is new today is that special-interest protectionists are facing a more receptive audience.

The second explanation is that policymakers and the business community have failed to adequately explain the benefits of freer trade and investment to the public. But in fact, public-opinion data show the opposite: large majorities of Americans acknowledge these broad benefits. If anything, the public seems to understand certain benefits better than ever—for example, that its enjoyment of relatively affordable toys, DVD players, and other products depends on globalization.

Finally, there is the security explanation: that the need to balance economic interests with national security concerns has resulted in a more protectionist stance. This may help explain policy debates on certain issues, such as immigration. But generally, security concerns strengthen rather than weaken the case for further trade and investment liberalization, as long as such liberalization is viewed as fair to the developing world.

THE ROOTS OF PROTECTIONISM

The fundamental explanation is much simpler: policy is becoming more protectionist because the public is becoming more protectionist, and the public is becoming more protectionist because incomes are stagnating or falling. The integration of the world economy has boosted productivity and wealth creation in the United States and much of the rest of the world. But within many countries, and certainly within the United States, the benefits of this integration have been unevenly distributed—and this fact is increasingly being recognized. Individuals are asking themselves, "Is globalization good for me?" and, in a growing number of cases, arriving at the conclusion that it is not.

This account of rising protectionism depends on two key facts. First, there is a strong link between individuals' labor-market interests and their policy opinions about globalization. Second, in the past several years labor-market outcomes have become worse for many more Americans—and globalization is plausibly part of the reason for this poor performance.

Research on polling data shows that opinions about trade, FDI, and immigration are closely correlated to skill and educational levels. Less skilled Americans—who make up the majority of the U.S. labor force—have long led opposition to open borders. Workers with only high school educations are almost twice as likely to support protectionist policies as workers with college educations are.

This divide in opinion according to skill level reflects the impact that less skilled Americans expect market liberalization to have on their earnings. It also reflects their actual poor real and relative earnings performance in recent decades. It is now well established that income inequality across skill levels has been rising since (depending on the measure) the mid- to late 1970s and that the benefits of productivity gains over this time accrued mainly to higher-skilled workers. For example, from 1966 to 2001, the median pretax inflation-adjusted wage and salary income grew just 11 percent—versus 58 percent for incomes in the 90th percentile and 121 percent for those in the 99th percentile. Forces including skill-biased technological change played a major role in these income trends; the related forces of globalization seem to have played a smaller role—but a role nonetheless.

There are two important points about this link between policy opinions and labor-market skills and performance. One is that it does not simply reflect different understandings of the benefits of globalization. Polling data are very clear here: large majorities of Americans acknowledge the many benefits of open borders—lower prices, greater product diversity, a competitive spur to firms—which are also highlighted by academics, policymakers, and the business community. At the same time, they perceive that along with these benefits, open borders have put pressures on worker earnings.

Second, a worker's specific industry does not appear to drive his view of globalization. This is because competition in the domestic labor market extends the pressures of globalization beyond trade- and foreign-investment-exposed industries to the entire economy. If workers in a sector such as automobile manufacturing lose their jobs, they compete for new positions across sectors—and thereby put pressure on pay in the entire economy. What seems to matter most is what kind of worker you are in terms of skill level, rather than what industry you work in.

The protectionist drift also depends on worsening labor-market outcomes over the past several years. By traditional measures, such as employment growth and unemployment rates, the U.S. labor market has been strong of late. Today, with unemployment at 4.5 percent, the United States is at or near full employment. But looking at the number of jobs misses the key change: for several years running, wage and salary growth for all but the very highest earners has been poor, such that U.S. income gains have become extremely skewed.

Of workers in seven educational categories—high school dropout, high school graduate, some college, college graduate, nonprofessional master's, Ph.D., and M.B.A./J.D./M.D.—only those in the last two categories, with doctorates or professional graduate degrees, experienced any growth in mean real money earnings between 2000 and 2005. Workers in these two categories comprised only 3.4 percent of the labor force in 2005, meaning that more than 96 percent of U.S. workers are in educational groups for which average money earnings have fallen. In contrast to in earlier decades, since 2000 even college graduates and those with nonprofessional master's degrees—29 percent of workers in 2005—suffered declines in mean real money earnings.

The astonishing skewness of U.S. income growth is evident in the analysis of other measures as well. The growth in total income reported on tax returns has been extremely concentrated in recent years: the share of national income accounted for by the top one percent of earners reached 21.8 percent in 2005—a level not seen since 1928. In addition to high labor earnings, income growth at the top is being driven by corporate profits, which are at nearly 50-year highs as a share of national income and which accrue mainly to those with high labor earnings. The basic fact is clear: the benefits of strong productivity growth in the past several years have gone largely to a small set of highly skilled, highly compensated workers.

Economists do not yet understand exactly what has caused this skewed pattern of income growth and to what extent globalization itself is implicated, nor do they know how long it will persist. Still, it is plausible that there is a connection. Poor income growth has coincided with the integration into the world economy of China, India, and central and eastern Europe. The IT revolution has meant that certain workers are now facing competition from the overseas outsourcing of jobs in areas such as business services and computer programming. Even if production does not move abroad, increased trade and multinational production can put pressure on incomes by making it easier for firms to substitute foreign workers for domestic ones.

These twin facts—the link between labor-market performance and opinions on globalization and the recent absence of real income growth for so many Americans—explain the recent rise in protectionism. Several polls of U.S. public opinion show an alarming rise in protectionist sentiment over the past several years. For example, an ongoing NBC News/*Wall Street Journal* poll found that from December 1999 to March 2007, the share of respondents stating that trade agreements have hurt the United States increased by 16 percentage points (to 46 percent) while the "helped" share fell by 11 points (to just 28 percent). A 2000 Gallup poll found that 56 percent of respondents saw trade as an opportunity and 36 percent saw it as a threat; by 2005, the percentages had shifted to 44 percent and 49 percent, respectively. The March 2007 NBC News/*Wall Street Journal* poll found negative assessments of open borders even among the highly skilled: only 35 percent of respondents with a college or higher degree said they directly benefited from the global economy.

Given the lack of recent real income growth for most Americans, newfound skepticism about globalization is not without cause. Nor is it without effect: the change in public opinion is the impetus for the protectionist drift in policy. Politicians have an incentive to propose and implement protectionist policies because more citizens want them, and protectionist special interests face an audience of policymakers more receptive to their lobbying efforts than at any time in the last two decades.

INADEQUATE ADJUSTMENTS

Because the protectionist drift reflects the legitimate concerns of a now very large majority of Americans, the policy debate needs fresh thinking. There is reason to worry even if one does not care about social equity. When most workers do not see themselves as benefiting from the related forces of globalization and technology, the resulting protectionist drift may end up eliminating the gains from globalization for everybody. Current ignorance about the exact causes of the skewed income growth is not reason for inaction. Policymakers may not be able to attack the exact source (or sources) and likely would not want to even if they could identify them, because doing so could reduce or even eliminate the aggregate gains from globalization.

Supporters of globalization face a stark choice: shore up support for an open global system by ensuring that a majority of workers benefit from it or accept that further liberalization is no longer sustainable. Given the aggregate benefits of open borders, the preferable option is clear.

Current policy discussions addressing the distributional consequences of globalization typically focus on the main U.S. government program for addressing the labor-market pressures of globalization—Trade Adjustment Assistance (TAA)—and on investing more in education. These ideas will help but are inadequate for the problem at hand.

The problem with TAA is that it incorrectly presumes that the key issue is transitions across jobs for workers in trade-exposed industries. Established in the Trade Act of 1974 (with a related component connected to the North American Free Trade Agreement), the program aids groups of workers in certain industries who can credibly claim that increased imports have destroyed their jobs or have reduced their work hours and wages. TAA-certified workers can access supports including training, extended unemployment benefits while in full-time training, and job-search and relocation allowances.

In short, TAA is inappropriately designed to address the protectionist drift. The labor-market concern driving this drift is not confined to the problem of how to reemploy particular workers in particular sectors facing import competition. Because the pressures of globalization are spread economy-wide via domestic labor-market competition, there is concern about income and job security among workers employed in all sectors. . . .

The idea behind investing in education is that higher-skilled workers generally earn more and are more likely to directly benefit from economic openness. The problem with this approach, however, is that upgrading skills is a process that takes generations—its effects will come far too late to address today's opposition to globalization. It took 60 years for the United States to boost the share of college graduates in the labor force from six percent (where it was at the end of World War II) to about 33 percent (where it is today). And that required major government programs, such as the GI Bill, and profound socioeconomic changes, such as increased female labor-force participation.

If the United States today undertook the goal of boosting its college-graduate share of the workforce to 50 percent, the graduation of that median American worker would, if the rate of past efforts are any indication, not come until about 2047. And even this far-off date might be too optimistic. In the past generation, the rate of increase in the educational attainment of U.S. natives has slowed from its 1960s and 1970s pace, in part because college-completion rates have stalled. Rising income inequality may itself be playing a role here. Since 1988, 74 percent of American students at the 146 top U.S. colleges have come from the highest socioeconomic quartile, compared with just 3 percent from the lowest quartile. Moreover, even college graduates and holders of nonprofessional master's degrees have experienced falling mean real money earnings since 2000. If this trend continues, even completing college will not assuage the concerns behind rising protectionism.

GLOBALIZATION AND REDISTRIBUTION

Given the limitations of these two reforms and the need to provide a political foundation for engagement with the world economy, the time has come for a New Deal for globalization—one that links trade and investment liberalization to a significant income redistribution that serves to share globalization's gains more widely. Recall that $500 billion is a common estimate of the annual income gain the United States enjoys today from earlier decades of trade and investment liberalization and also of the additional annual income it would enjoy as a result [of] global free trade in goods and services. These aggregate gains, past and prospective, are immense and therefore immensely important to secure. But the imbalance in recent income growth suggests that the number of Americans not directly sharing in these aggregate gains may now be very large.

Truly expanding the political support for open borders requires a radical change in fiscal policy. This does not, however, mean making the personal income tax more progressive, as is often suggested. U.S. taxation of personal income is already quite progressive. Instead, policymakers should remember that workers do not pay only income taxes; they also pay the FICA (Federal Insurance Contributions Act) payroll tax for social insurance. This tax offers the best way to redistribute income.

The payroll tax contains a Social Security portion and a Medicare portion, each of which is paid half by the worker and half by the employer. The overall payroll tax is a flat tax of 15.3 percent on the first $94,200 of gross income for every worker, with an ongoing 2.9 percent flat tax for the Medicare portion beyond that. Because it is a flat-rate tax on a (largely) capped base, it is a regressive tax—that is, it tends to reinforce rather than offset pretax inequality. At $760 billion in 2005, the regressive payroll tax was nearly as big as the progressive income tax ($1.1 trillion). Because it is large and regressive, the payroll tax is an obvious candidate for meaningful income redistribution linked to globalization.

A New Deal for globalization would combine further trade and investment liberalization with eliminating the full payroll tax for all workers earning below the national median. In 2005, the median total money earnings of all workers was $32,140, and there were about 67 million workers at or below this level. Assuming a mean labor income for this group of about $25,000, these 67 million workers would receive a tax cut of about $3,800 each. Because the economic burden of this tax falls largely on workers, this tax cut would be a direct gain in after-tax real income for them. With a total price tag of about $256 billion, the proposal could be paid for by raising the cap of $94,200, raising payroll tax rates (for progressivity, rates could escalate as they do with the income tax), or some combination of the two. This is, of course, only an outline of the needed policy reform, and there would be many implementation details to address. For example, rather than a single on-off point for this tax cut, a phase-in of it (like with the earned-income tax credit) would avoid incentive-distorting jumps in effective tax rates.

This may sound like a radical proposal. But keep in mind the figure of $500 billion: the annual U.S. income gain from trade and investment liberalization to date and the additional U.S. gain a successful Doha Round could deliver. Redistribution on this scale may be required to overcome the labor-market concerns driving the protectionist drift. Determining the right scale and structure of redistribution requires a thoughtful national discussion among all stakeholders. Policymakers must also consider how exactly to link such redistribution to further liberalization. But this should not obscure the essential idea: to be politically viable, efforts for further trade and investment liberalization will need to be explicitly linked to fundamental fiscal reform aimed at distributing globalization's aggregate gains more broadly.

SAVING GLOBALIZATION

Averting a protectionist backlash is in the economic and security interests of the United States. Globalization has generated—and can continue to generate—substantial benefits for the United States and the rest of the world. But realizing those broad benefits will require addressing the legitimate concerns of U.S. voters by instituting a New Deal for globalization.

In many ways, today's protectionist drift is similar to the challenges faced by the architect of the original New Deal. In August 1934, President Franklin Roosevelt declared:

> Those who would measure confidence in this country in the future must look first to the average citizen. . . .
>
> This Government intends no injury to honest business. The processes we follow in seeking social justice do not, in adding to general prosperity, take from one and give to another. In this modern world, the spreading out of opportunity ought not to consist of robbing Peter to pay Paul. In other words, we are concerned with more than mere subtraction and addition. We are concerned with multiplication also—multiplication of wealth through cooperative action, wealth in which all can share.

Today, such multiplication will depend on striking a delicate balance—between allowing globally engaged companies to continue to generate large overall gains for the United States and using well-targeted fiscal mechanisms to spread the gains more widely.

Would addressing concerns about income distribution make voters more likely to support open borders? The public-opinion data suggest that the answer is yes. Americans consistently say that they would be more inclined to back trade and investment liberalization if it were linked to more support for those hurt in the process. The policy experience of other countries confirms this point: there is greater support for engagement with the world economy in countries that spend more on programs for dislocated workers.

U.S. policymakers face a clear choice. They can lead the nation down the dangerous path of creeping protectionism. Or they can build a stable foundation for U.S. engagement with the world economy by sharing the gains widely. A New Deal for globalization can ensure that globalization survives.

31

How to Save Globalization from Its Cheerleaders

DANI RODRIK

In this selection, Dani Rodrik presents a forward-looking analysis of the prospects for globalization in light of current stresses and problems. He contends that the gains from pushing for greater economic openness are likely to be small; indeed, problems like financial crises, rising inequality, and social unrest have little to do with inadequate openness. The larger concern, he argues, is the possibility of protectionist backlash on the order of the 1930s retreat from world markets. Rather than prying markets open even more, policy makers should work to make globalization more politically sustainable. This will require a new institutional framework that facilitates compromises between globalization and national sovereignty. Paradoxically, the path to saving globalization is to provide nations with the "policy space" to pursue their individual national objectives.

I. INTRODUCTION

When future economic historians write their textbooks, they will no doubt marvel at the miraculous turn the world economy took after 1950. Over the long stretch of history, neither the Industrial Revolution nor the subsequent economic catch-up of the United States and other "western offshoots" looks as impressive (Figure 1). The period since 1950 has witnessed more rapid economic growth than any other period before, with only the classical gold standard era between 1870 and 1913 coming close. Even more striking, there has been a quantum jump in the growth rate of the most rapidly growing countries since 1950. Prior to 1950, growth superstars experienced growth rates that barely surpassed 2 percent per annum (in per capita terms) over long stretches. Compare this with the post-1950 growth champions: Japan, South Korea, and China; each grew at 6–8 percent per annum during 1950–73, 1973–90, and 1990–2005, respectively. Even allowing for the shorter time slices, this indicates that the world economy became a much more enabling environment for economic growth after 1950. Clearly, the architects of this new world economic system got something right.

Going forward, there can be few things more important than to maintain a global economic environment that is as enabling in the future as it has been in the recent past. This requires that we interpret the reasons behind the post-1950 boom appropriately. A simple "it's all due to globalization" view

FIGURE 1 The Expanding Growth Frontier

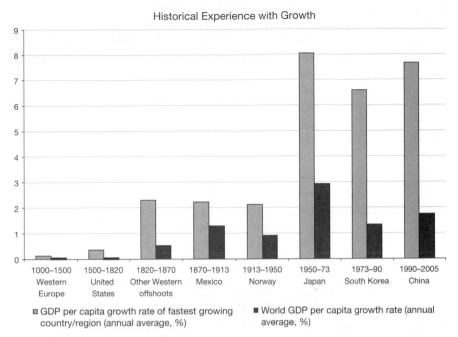

Historical Experience with Growth

1000–1500	1500–1820	1820–1870	1870–1913	1913–1950	1950–73	1973–90	1990–2005
Western Europe	United States	Other Western offshoots	Mexico	Norway	Japan	South Korea	China

☐ GDP per capita growth rate of fastest growing country/region (annual average, %)

■ World GDP per capita growth rate (annual average, %)

receives little support from Figure 1. It is significant that the world economy experienced a more significant boost during 1950–73 than it did during either the post-1990 period of gung-ho globalization or the transition period between 1973–90. Second, and perhaps even more tellingly, the countries that did best under each one of these periods were hardly poster children for open markets and laissez-faire economics. These countries combined orthodoxy on some (mostly macroeconomic) policy fronts with a good bit of heterodoxy on others (especially in microeconomic policies). Japan, South Korea, and China each played by very different rules than those enunciated by the guardians of orthodox globalization—multilateral institutions such as the World Bank, IMF, and GATT/WTO and by Western-based academics.

In this paper I present a forward-looking evaluation of globalization. I accept as my premise that globalization, in some appropriate form, is a major engine of economic growth (as Figure 1 amply demonstrates). However, I will argue that several paradoxical features require us to rethink its rules. First, as I already indicated, globalization's chief beneficiaries are not necessarily those with the most open economic policies. Second, globalization has come with frequent financial crises and considerable amounts of instability, which are both costly and in principle avoidable. Third, globalization remains unpopular among large segments of the people it is supposed to benefit (especially in rich countries).

It is not that these features have gone unnoticed in the recurrent debate on globalization. In fact, we can talk of a new conventional wisdom that has begun to emerge within multilateral institutions and among Northern academics. This new orthodoxy emphasizes that reaping the benefits of trade and financial globalization requires better domestic institutions, essentially improved safety nets in rich countries, and improved governance in the poor countries. With these institutions in place (or in construction), it remains safe and appropriate to pursue a strategy of "more of the same, but better" to continue to open markets in trade and finance, while strengthening institutions. Enhanced trade adjustment assistance (and perhaps more progressive taxation) in the advanced countries, the Doha trade agenda, IMF surveillance over exchange rate policies, the World Bank's governance agenda, "aid-for-trade," and international financial codes and standards are some of the visible markers of this approach.

This strategy is predicated on the presumption that insufficiently open markets continue to pose an important constraint on the world economy. Its proponents' concerns therefore center on the question: what institutional reforms are needed at home and internationally to render further market opening politically acceptable and sustainable?

Is this presumption really valid? I shall argue here that lack of openness is (no longer) the binding constraint for the global economy. I will provide a range of evidence on trade and capital flows that indicates that the obstacles faced by developing countries do not originate from inadequate access to markets abroad or to foreign capital. The gains to be reaped by further liberalization of markets are meager for poor and rich countries alike.

This leads me to an alternative approach to globalization, one that focuses on enhancing policy space rather than market access. Such a strategy would focus on devising the rules of the game to better manage the interface between national regulatory and social regimes. A good argument can be made that it is lack of policy space—and not lack of market access—which is (or likely to become soon) the real binding constraint on a prosperous global economy. This argument can be buttressed by current evidence from rich and poor countries along with reference to historical experience with the previous wave of globalization.

What do we mean by policy space and can we really create it without running into the slippery slope of creeping protectionism? By the end of the paper, I hope I will have given the reader some reason to believe that an alternative conception of globalization—one that is more likely to maintain an enabling global environment than the path we are on currently—is worth thinking about and potentially workable.

II. THE PARADOXES OF GLOBALIZATION AS WE KNOW IT

In 2001 the World Bank published a volume entitled Globalization, Growth, and Poverty: Building an Inclusive World Economy. In it, the Bank identified four countries as star globalizers—countries that had greatly increased their integration with the world economy and at the same time had grown rapidly and made progress with poverty reduction. The countries were China, India, Vietnam, and Uganda. With the possible exception of Uganda, these still constitute Exhibit A of the case for globalization's benefits.

However, as Table 1 shows, these countries' policies can hardly be described as being of the free-trade type. In fact, by standard measures, such as the height of import tariffs and prevalence of non-tariff barriers, India, China, and Vietnam were among the most heavily protected countries in the early 1990s. China and Vietnam were not even members of the WTO and therefore could engage in policies—such as trade subsidies and quantitative restrictions—that are unavailable to other countries. In each one of these cases, whatever trade liberalization took place happened with a significant delay after the onset of economic growth. For example, China significantly reduced its trade barriers in the mid-1990s and beyond, but this came after at least fifteen years of rapid growth.

It is true of course that these countries greatly increased their volumes of trade and inward foreign investment, but that is precisely the paradox. They did so despite—and in fact because of—their heterodox strategies. Simply put, countries that have benefited the most from globalization are those that did not play by the rules.

By contrast, Latin America, which tried harder than any other part of the world to live by the orthodox rules, experienced on the whole a dismal performance since the early 1990s. This occurred despite the boost provided by the natural bounce-back from the debt crisis of the 1980s. Here the paradox is not just that Latin America did worse than Asia, it is also that Latin America did worse than its pre-1980s performance (Figure 2). Let's recall that the

TABLE 1 Trade Policies in the World Bank's Star "Globalizers" of the 1990s

	Growth rate	Average tariffs (early to mid-'90s)	NTBs?	WTO member? (early to mid-'90s)
China	7.1	31.2	yes	no
Vietnam	5.6	30–50	yes	no
India	3.3	50.5	yes	yes
Uganda	3.0	14.4		yes

NOTE: List of star globalizers taken from World Bank, *Globalization, Growth, and Poverty: Building an Inclusive World Economy*, 2001.

FIGURE 2 Comparative Growth Rates

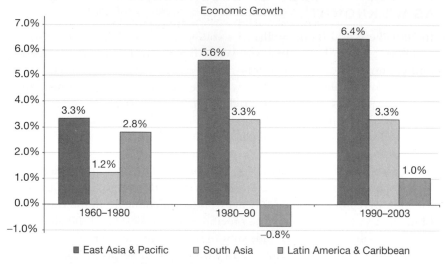

Economic Growth

East Asia & Pacific   South Asia   Latin America & Caribbean

pre-1980s were the era of import substitution, protectionism, and macroeconomic populism. That the region did better with these discredited policies than it has under open-market policies is a fact that is quite hard to digest within the conventional paradigm.

Let us now turn to international finance. Here the paradox is that financial globalization, which was supposed to enable developing countries to augment their savings, raise their investment levels, and grow more rapidly, has in fact done little of any of it. Such is the absence of evidence of these direct benefits that the new wave of research on financial globalization focuses on a search for its "indirect" benefits. Neither has financial globalization enhanced risk-sharing and consumption smoothing for developing nations; if anything, the evidence points in the reverse direction. Instead, one noticeable consequence of financial globalization has been a series of costly financial crashes—in Mexico, Thailand, Indonesia, South Korea, Russia, Argentina, Turkey, and many other countries. This has forced developing nations to accumulate huge amounts of foreign reserves in order to purchase self-insurance against the fickleness of financial-market sentiment. As Figure 3 shows, reserves in developing countries (measured in months of imports) now stand at 3–4 times the levels observed in the advanced countries. In view of the low yields and high social opportunity cost of these reserves, the costs of this strategy amount to almost 1 percent of GDP in developing nations annually.

The world economy has avoided similar financial crises in recent years. This indicates that developing nations have become more resilient to financial turbulence. That is due, in no small part, to the mountains of liquidity that developing nations now sit on. It is also due to the fact that many emerging

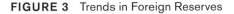

FIGURE 3 Trends in Foreign Reserves

Foreign Reserves (excluding gold) in Months of Imports
Industrial and Non-oil Developing Countries

markets are now running trade surpluses—i.e., lending money to the rest of the world. In other words, in order to protect themselves from the whiplash of financial crises, developing countries have been forced not only to shun its benefits, but to make transfers to rich countries on top!

The third paradox is that globalization remains restricted in precisely those areas where further relaxation of barriers would yield the greatest economic benefits. Barriers on labor mobility in particular are inordinately higher than they are anywhere else. It is easy to show that even minor reductions in labor-market barriers would generate gains that are vastly larger than those from the conventional areas under negotiation in the WTO and elsewhere. Consider for example a temporary South-to-North labor mobility scheme that would expand the industrialized countries' labor force by about three percent (0.03). (The existing share of immigrants and of foreign-born in advanced country labor markets is about ten percent on average.) Let's use, as our estimate of the earnings gap, the figure $17,500, . . . the earning premium for a Mexican worker in the United States. Given a Northern labor force of around half billion (0.5), the net gains generated for nationals of poor countries would amount to $262.5 billion per annum (0.5 × 0.03 × 17,500). By contrast, current estimates of the gains to developing countries from the completion of the Doha Round do not exceed $30 billion. The disparity between these two numbers reflects the fact that poor countries already have fairly good access to rich country markets where goods are concerned, but are virtually shut out from Northern labor markets (with only a few exceptions).

Many tears have been shed about the recent demise of the Doha Round. Meanwhile multilateral negotiations on reducing barriers to labor mobility are not even on the agenda. A recent proposal in the United States Senate to institute a temporary guest worker program was eventually killed, alongside the proposed immigration reform.

Finally, lest one think that globalization has produced paradoxical outcomes just for developing countries, it is worth pointing out that globalization remains quite unpopular in most advanced countries. A recent Financial Times poll reports that individuals in the United States and other rich countries who believe globalization is a positive force are greatly outnumbered (by a factor of between 2 to 3) by those who think it is a negative force. The same poll reports that "large majorities of people in the US and in Europe want higher taxation for the rich and even pay caps for corporate executives to counter what they believe are unjustified rewards and the negative effects of globalization" (Financial Times, July 22, 2007). This is only the most recent of a long series of polls that show globalization's benefits are either not filtering down, or if they are, not being adequately appreciated.

It has become harder over the years to ascribe such views to sheer ignorance and the search for easy culprits. It is remarkable that many outspoken and prominent boosters of globalization such as Paul Krugman, Lary Summers, and Alan Blinder have recently acknowledged that globalization is contributing to inequality and insecurity. . . . The search is on for tax and adjustment policies that would respond to the middle-class malaise that is widely felt to endanger the sustainability of globalization.

III. THE NEW CONVENTIONAL WISDOM

In response to the developments I have just reviewed, a new conventional wisdom has been emerging during the last few years. The main contours of this emergent consensus can be described as follows:

- Globalization is indeed contributing to rising inequality, stagnant median wages, and the growing sense of insecurity in the advanced economies, even if it is still unclear as to what extent globalization is the dominant influence. This is in sharp contrast to the views expressed by most establishment economists during the "trade and wages" debate of two decades ago, in which blame was ascribed to skill-biased technological change rather than to globalization, but the rise of China and of global outsourcing has made those earlier views untenable.
- Trade and financial openness are unlikely to lead to economic growth on their own, and may occasionally even backfire, in the absence of a wide range of complementary institutional and governance reforms. This is in sharp contrast to the views expressed in the literature on trade

and growth of some 10–15 years ago, in which the assertion was that trade liberalization in particular has an unconditional and strong effect on economic growth on its own—even absent other reforms. Once again, the evidence has rendered the older views untenable.

■ Therefore, globalization requires a range of institutional complements in both rich and poor countries in order to deliver its benefits in full and remain sustainable. In the advanced countries of the North, the complementary measures relate in large part to improved social safety nets and enhanced adjustment assistance. In the developing countries, the requisite institutional reforms range all the way from anti-corruption to labor market and financial market reforms.

This new conventional wisdom finds expression in a multipronged effort to deepen globalization in its current form. One element is the completion of the Doha "development" round, with its focus on agricultural liberalization. At present, the Doha process seems dead on its tracks due to a combination of unwillingness of the rich countries to offer substantial cuts in agricultural supports and market access as well as the reticence of developing nations to offer low enough bindings on their own tariffs. Another element is the promotion of "cautious" capital account opening in developing countries, by a coalition of the IMF and financial interests in the developing countries themselves. A third flank is the governance agenda of the multilateral institutions, focusing on anticorruption at the World Bank and financial regulation and supervision at the IMF. A fourth is the ongoing discussion in the U.S. and other advanced countries on a menu of proposals to take the "pain" out of globalization: increased progressivity in taxation, enhanced adjustment assistance, portability of health insurance, and wage insurance to cover part of the income losses due to dislocation.

Many of these efforts are useful in their own right, of course. Essentially we can conceive of this strategy as the answer to the following question: what institutional reforms are needed at home and internationally to render further market opening politically acceptable and sustainable? The maintained hypothesis behind it is that the greatest bang for the global reform buck lies in pushing for increased openness and market access, while ensuring that the adverse consequences of openness are taken care of.

In the next section, I will question the validity of this view, and suggest that the binding constraint on maintaining a healthy global economy lies elsewhere.

IV. HOW CONSTRAINING ON ECONOMIC GROWTH ARE THE REMAINING BARRIERS TO INTERNATIONAL ECONOMIC INTEGRATION?

Under certain conditions, economic integration can be a powerful force for economic convergence, and it can promote rapid economic growth in poorer regions. The historical experience of the United States is telling in this regard. The U.S. experienced economic convergence within its own national economy, but did so only after a truly common and integrated set of product, capital, and labor markets were established nationally. What the U.S. experience shows is that achieving integration of this kind is not just a matter of eliminating barriers to interstate commerce (which are prohibited in the constitution itself). National economic convergence entailed a lot more: the elimination (through a civil war) of divergent social institutions in the South, the establishment of a truly free labor market with no interstate restrictions, the creation of the Federal Reserve system, a national financial regulator and lender-of-last resort, a national system of fiscal transfers, a Federal legal system, and a Supreme Court to prevent individual states from re-imposing restrictions. Put simply, a national market required a national polity. It was only then that the transaction costs associated with jurisdictional and legal discontinuities across state lines eroded sufficiently to permit economic convergence.

The European Union today presents another interesting case, since it displays the significant growing pains associated with efforts to create seamless integration. The EU is currently engaged in a process of legal, institutional, political integration that is somewhat similar to the process that took the United States some two centuries. Some key markers in this process are the vast supranational regulatory apparatus that is in construction (the acquis communautaire is more than 90,000 pages in length and growing by the day); the European Court of Justice (which has the power to strike down national laws and regulations); an almost Europe-wide monetary system (which eliminates monetary autonomy and restricts fiscal policy); the various cohesion and structural funds aimed at pulling up lagging regions; and of course full labor mobility within the union. Even with all this, convergence within the EU is far from complete, and remains a stop-and-go process.

In the absence of the legal and political integration of the type that the U.S. has already achieved and the EU is attempting to construct, transaction costs condemn the global economy to a patchwork of national economies. This is the model of "shallow integration" in contrast to the US/EU models of "deep integration" (the terms have been coined by Robert Lawrence). In a world of shallow integration, the prospects for convergence are doomed to remain incomplete. Capital flows are hindered by sovereign risk and the absence of international financial regulation and bankruptcy procedures. Financial panics and crashes are rendered more likely by the absence of a true international lender-of-last resort. Labor can flow in very small quantities, and often only illegally. Differences in national regulatory, legal, and currency regimes also impose severe transaction costs on international trade. . . . Net capital flows end up being too small, and often go in the "wrong" direction—that is, from poor to rich nations. Trade flows similarly remain too small, compared to intranational trade, and national borders exert a significant depressing effect on trade even in the absence of import duties or other government-imposed barriers. Many of the paradoxical syndromes of globalization that I discussed above are a direct consequence of this incompleteness.

What is the implication of all this for developing countries? The vast majority of countries do not face the realistic option of full economic integration with their rich trade partners; legal and political integration à la the EU or U.S. model is not on offer, and even if it were, national sovereignty is perceived to be too valuable for many to give up. They need to recognize, therefore, that they are living in a second-best world, in which international economic integration remains incomplete due to the transaction costs I just discussed. Living in a second-best world requires second-best strategies; if markets cannot solve your problems of labor surplus and capital shortage (because the former is not free to leave and the latter comes only in small quantities), you need roundabout policies. You may need to postpone import liberalization in order to protect employment for a while. You may need to subsidize your tradables to achieve more rapid structural change. In fact, you may need a whole range of industrial policies in order to build technological and productive capacity at home.

This line of reasoning helps us understand why some countries that sharply lowered their barriers to trade and capital flows are still waiting for the rewards, while others who have been much more cautious have done so much better. Consider for example the contrast between El Salvador and Vietnam. Both countries returned to peace and political stability after a long period of civil war. Vietnam started its reforms in the late 1980s, while El Salvador's reforms came in the early 1990s. El Salvador quickly eliminated all quantitative barriers to imports, slashed tariffs, established convertibility on the capital account, and dollarized its economy. It became an open economy in both trade and financial senses of the term. It also became the recipient of large amounts of remittances from its expatriates in the United States. Vietnam, meanwhile, followed a Chinese-style reform, based on gradual external liberalization, pragmatism, and a concerted effort to diversify the economy through public encouragement and investment where needed. Vietnam did not rush into the WTO, and has only just become a member. Looking at these policies wearing a conventional lens, it would be hard to see how El Salvador's policies could have been improved. Yet private investment and growth remained lackluster in El Salvador. Meanwhile Vietnam achieved phenomenal success in terms of both growth and poverty reduction.

These examples can be multiplied many times over. Perhaps the most notable development failure of the last fifteen years is Mexico. This is a country that has free and preferential access to the U.S. market for its exports, can send several millions of its citizens across the border as workers, receives huge volumes of direct investment and is totally plugged into U.S. production chains, and for which the U.S. Treasury has acted as a lender of last resort. It is hard to imagine a case where globalization gets any better. Yet even though trade and investment flows have expanded rapidly, the results have been underwhelming, to say the least, where it matters—in economic growth, employment, poverty reduction, and real wage growth. NAFTA, it turns out, is another instance of shallow integration.

The standard response when cases like El Salvador and Mexico are brought out is to point out, in line with the new conventional wisdom I summarized previously, that these countries did not undertake the complementary reforms needed to make globalization work. What specific reforms are in question depends on who is talking and when, but the usual line is that both countries need more judicial and (in the case of Mexico especially) "structural" reform. However, this is hardly a satisfactory response in light of the fact that success-ful countries that did not open themselves up as fully to international trade and finance had, if anything, even worse institutional preconditions. It is dif-ficult to argue that Vietnam or China—two authoritarian socialist economies with extensive state ownership and widespread corruption—had the institu-tional prerequisites which Mexico and El Salvador lacked. This standard riposte reflects once again the habit of using first-best reasoning when cir-cumstances demand second-best thinking. It is of course trivially true, but largely besides the fact, that if Mexico and El Salvador had first-world institu-tions, they would be as rich as the advanced countries. Successful growth strategies are based on making the best of what you have, not on wishing you had what you lack.

Given successive rounds of multilateral trade liberalization and the exten-sive unilateral liberalization that developing countries have already under-taken, the shallow integration model has already run into strong diminishing returns. This is one reason why Doha has stalled. There are simply not enough gains to get people excited. . . . By 2015, developing countries stand to reap gains on the order of one percent of GDP, while developed country gains are substantially smaller. At this point, further global trade liberalization is hardly a force for economic convergence. . . .

If the realistic gains from further trade liberalization are small, what about international finance? Once again, we can imagine a world where international capital flows make a significant contribution to fostering devel-opment in the poorer countries of the world—that would be a world of "deep integration." That is very far from the world we inhabit presently, with the various transaction costs imposed by fragmented sovereignty. Our world is one where countries that rely more on external capital markets grow less rap-idly. That is the astonishing finding of a recent paper by Prasad et al. (2007).

The bottom line of this paper is . . . countries do not do that well when they attract capital from abroad. The authors show that this is a robust result, and likely has to do with various imperfections in credit and product markets which are aggravated in the presence of capital inflows. . . . This is another reminder that a proper evaluation of the prospective benefits from further liberalization requires second-best thinking.

In sum, the likely gains from further liberalization in goods and capital markets are small, as long as the world remains politically fragmented and transaction costs emanating from jurisdictional discontinuities prevent "deep" economic integration.

V. SAVING GLOBALIZATION FROM ITS CHEERLEADERS: THE NEED FOR POLICY SPACE

Strong diminishing returns may have set in on the prevailing liberalization agenda, but the losses from a real retreat from today's globalization would be catastrophic. A collapse towards protectionism and bilateralism à la 1930s can never be ruled out—it has happened before—and would be bad news for poor and rich nations alike. Therefore, we ought to place a high premium on policies that make such a retreat less likely—even if they run contrary (in the short run at least) to a market-opening agenda.

In order to maintain globalization in some version of its current form, we need to diagnose well the problems that confront it. These problems do not arise, as I argued in the previous section, from liberalization not having gone far enough—unless, that is, we are ready to envisage deep integration as a feasible option. They originate instead from something that is closer to the opposite, namely the clash between the liberalization agenda and the weakness of the institutional underpinnings that make open markets functional and politically sustainable. Once we put the problem this way, the challenge becomes not "how do we liberalize further," but "how do we create the *policy space* for nations to handle the problems that openness creates." The policy space in question would allow:

—*Rich nations* to address issues of social insurance and concerns about the labor, environmental, and health consequences of trade; and
—*Poor nations* to position themselves better for globalization through economic restructuring and diversification.

In this section I will make a case for such policy space by showing that globalization's constraints do bite where legitimate economic and social ends are concerned in these two sets of countries—and will bite even more if we continue to pursue a market-opening agenda.

I begin with the advanced countries. Consider the following dilemmas that our present arrangements pose.

▪ *Labor standards:*
Domestic labor laws protect workers from being displaced through "unfair" employment practices at home, such as the hiring of child labor or the employment of workers under hazardous conditions. WTO rules do not make room for similar protections when displacement

occurs through trade but why should trade be allowed to contravene an established domestic norm?

▪ *Environmental, health and safety standards:*
If European citizens want to apply a higher precautionary standard than other countries, should trade rules prevent them from doing so because this has an effect on trade?

▪ *Regulatory "takings":*
Why should foreign firms in the U.S. receive greater protection from policy changes that affect their profits than domestic firms (as NAFTA and bilateral investment treaties (BITs) may require)?

▪ *Redistributive provision of social insurance:*
If taxation of capital and skilled professionals has historically helped fund social insurance programs and generate equity, should their international mobility be allowed to undercut this "social compact"?

▪ *Currency policies and "unfair trade":*
WTO rules recognize the concept of "unfair trade" in cases of explicit subsidization of exports and allow importing countries to respond through countervailing duties. Should countries that undervalue their currencies, and hence subsidize their exports in non-fiscal ways, be allowed to get away with it?

▪ *Trade versus technological change:*
Domestically, R&D and technological progress are highly regulated (*cf.* the stem cell controversies). Why should trade, which is analogous to technological change, be left unregulated as a rule?

These are all difficult questions, without clear-cut answers. They will likely increase in salience with the explosive growth in off-shore provision of services. The appropriate locus for their discussion and resolution is most likely the national polity, given the wide variety of standards and norms that prevail across the globe. If so, countries will need the policy space with which they can act on their deliberations.

Sometimes dilemmas of the kinds illustrated above are pooh-poohed by economists as instances of self-interested pleading on the part of lobbies adversely affected by imports. However, there is a variety of evidence that points to more than narrow self-interest being at work in rich countries. For example, when Alan Krueger (1996) examined where the support for a Congressional bill aimed against child labor was coming from, he found that the support was strongest not in districts with a concentration of low-skilled labor, but in well-to-do districts with preponderantly skilled labor. People were against child labor not because it meant more competition, but because they felt it was wrong. Similarly, recent research by Hiscox and Smyth (2006) documents significant willingness-to-pay by U.S. consumers for improved labor standards in developing nations. Also, in our analysis of attitudes to trade in a large cross-section of countries, Anna Maria Mayda and I found that individuals with negative attitudes towards trade and globalization were motivated only partly by labor-market concerns and pocket-book issues (Mayda and Rodrik, 2005); values and norms mattered too. In particular, we found that individuals with high levels of attachment to their neighborhood and immediate community were more likely to have negative views on trade.

When economists talk about comparative advantage and gains from trade, they typically ignore whether trade opportunities involve exchanges that most people would consider unacceptable if they took place at home. It is immaterial whether the gains from trade are created, say, by a company shutting down its factory at home and setting up a new one abroad using child labor, but the archetypal person on the street reacts differently to trade-induced changes in distribution than to technology-induced changes (i.e., to technological progress). Both increase the size of the economic pie, while often causing large income transfer, but a redistribution that takes place because home firms are undercut by competitors who employ deplorable labor practices, use production methods that are harmful to the environment, or enjoy government support is procedurally different than one that takes place because an innovator has come up with a better product through hard work or ingenuity. Trade and technological progress can have very different implications for procedural fairness. This is a point that most people instinctively grasp, but economists often miss. (Notice that even in the case of technology, we have significant restrictions on what is allowable—*cf.* human-subject review requirements—and wide-ranging debates about the acceptability of things like stem-cell research.)

So globalization is a hot button issue in the advanced countries not just because it hits some people in their pocket book; it is controversial because it raises difficult questions about whether its outcomes are "right" or "fair." That is why addressing the globalization backlash purely through compensation and income transfers is likely to fall short. Globalization also needs new rules that are more consistent with prevailing conceptions of procedural fairness.

Turning to developing countries, where do the constraints bite? As I have already argued, successful development strategies often require second-best and therefore unorthodox policies. Current thinking has moved considerably away from a standardized Washington Consensus-style approach to a diagnostic strategy which focuses on each country's own binding constraints. Differences in the nature of these constraints shape the appropriate economic strategies. For example, investment-constrained economies respond differently to capital inflows than saving-constrained economies, and need to have a different policy stance vis-à-vis the capital account. Moreover, as the examples of East Asian countries show, desirable policy reforms often take heterodox form because they try to make the best of pre-existing institutional capabilities and configurations. In China, non-standard policies such as dual-track pricing, township-and-village enterprises (TVEs), and special economic zones (SEZs) provided effective price incentives, some security of property rights, and outward orientation—but did so in highly unusual ways. Successful heterodoxy is a reflection of the need to overcome second-best complications. Trying to apply uniform best-practice rules or harmonizing policy differences away does not serve the needs of developing and transitional economies. The need to maintain "space" for developmental policies is now recognized even by ardent supporters of free trade (Wolf, 2007).

Some of the key areas where globalization's constraints bite for developing nations are the following:

- *The trade regime:* WTO agreements on subsidies, trade-related investment measures (TRIMs), and intellectual property rights (TRIPs) entail a considerable narrowing of space for the conduct of "industrial policies," and preclude the adoption of strategies that worked well for growth superstars such as South Korea, Taiwan, and China. While determined governments can find ways around these restrictions, developed countries are demanding further tightening of restrictions in these and other areas. One reason developing countries such as India and Brazil have lost interest in Doha is that they are being pushed to significantly lower their own tariff bindings. Bilateral and regional trade agreements, especially those negotiated with the U.S., often contain clauses on intellectual property rights and investment that go significantly beyond what is in the WTO.
- *The international financial regime:* The promulgation of international financial codes and standards follows a "best-practice" approach that is overly concerned with financial stability and the need to make economies resilient to capital flows, even when the promotion of such capital flows may not be a priority. These arrangements narrow the scope for traditional development banking and rule out credit market interventions (such as credit subsidies or directed credit) in support of industrialization. The preference of the IMF for central bank independence and free floating crowds out the use of the exchange rate as a developmental policy instrument. Currency undervaluation has been a potent tool for promoting growth in Asian and other countries. The recent adoption by the IMF of enhanced surveillance guidelines on exchange-rate policies will make such strategies more difficult.

Once again, these are all areas where there are difficult trade-offs to consider. Currency undervaluation and subsidization policies may be good for developing nations, but they do impose political and economic costs on advanced countries, as I discussed previously. The point is not that there is an obvious right or wrong in each of these areas. My argument is that we need to recognize these frictions and focus our efforts on devising rules that can manage them, instead of proceeding with a market-opening agenda as if they were of little consequence.

Here the lessons of history are invaluable. Economic historians agree that the earlier wave of globalization (1815–1913) collapsed because of the inability of the international system to cope with the tensions created by the expansion of global finance and trade. Harold James (2001) cites inherent instabilities in global finance, a growing social and political backlash, and the overloading of institutions that manage globalization as the leading contenders to explain the downfall of this earlier globalization. These problems are remarkably similar to those we face today. They all have their origin in the tug-of-war between markets that are straining to become truly global and their mechanisms of governance which remain largely national and parochial.

Jeffry Frieden's (2006) account of the interwar period explains how the tug-of-war was eventually resolved:

> The ensuing backlash [against globalization] had some predictable properties. Supporters of the classical order had argued that *giving priority to international economic ties required downplaying such concerns as social reform, nation building, and national assertion.* In the new environment, some of those newly empowered responded that if the choice was between social reform and international economic integration, they would choose social reform—thus leading to the Communists' option of radical autarky. If the choice was between national assertion and global economic integration, another set of mass movements chose nation-building—thus leading to fascist autarky in Europe and economic nationalism in the developing world. (Emphasis added.)

In other words, national purpose reasserted itself in one form or another over the demands of international economic integration. Because the upholders of the international economic regime were blind to the conflict, the process was messy and the resulting outcomes (communism and fascism) were less than ideal.

That is the real danger our globalization faces today. The risk is that the pursuit of a more perfect globalization—more openness—endangers our imperfect, but still remarkable globalization by intensifying the conflicts that the system inevitably generates.

VI. CAN POLICY SPACE BE ENHANCED WITHOUT DOING MORE DAMAGE THAN GOOD?

The question posed in this section's title lies at the heart of the matter. The conventional view is that there is a slippery slope whereby even the slightest relaxation of international disciplines spawns further demands for protection—to the point that the system of free trade and finance eventually unravels. This view sometimes finds expression in the "bicycle theory" of international trade, which states that maintaining an open economic regime requires constant efforts to liberalize. In this line of reasoning, policy space is a rec-ipe for mischief. National polities cannot be trusted to work out reasonable internal compromises among competing domestic political forces with vary-ing views on globalization. They need to have a straitjacket imposed from the outside.

Yet there is little evidence that favors the slippery slope hypothesis in our contemporary political economy. The political balance in most countries, including developing countries, has tilted sharply in recent decades towards groups that favor links with the global economy. Notable departures from free trade, such as the Multi-Fiber Arrangement (MFA) and the voluntary export restrictions (VERs) of the 1980s, did not spawn increasing protection. In fact, they were removed once they had served their primary purpose of increasing the comfort level of rich country citizens. There are also some provisions of the GATT/WTO regime that are highly open to protectionist abuse, but these have had only limited impact on trade. The anti-dumping (AD) provisions of trade law are particularly notable in this respect, since they provide easy access to protection in circumstances where the economic case for protection is weak or non-existent. While countries do make use of AD provisions, it is hard to argue that the world economy has greatly suffered as a result. In retrospect, what is striking is not that AD provisions are used, but that they are used so infrequently in light of the flexibility of the rules, and that it has caused so little damage. Indeed, we could argue that AD strat-egies have made the trade regime more resilient by providing a safety valve for protectionist pressures. These pressures might have had more damaging consequences otherwise, if they had to make their way outside international rules rather than within them.

That is precisely the principle behind the "policy space" approach: negoti-ated opt-outs, with internationally agreed procedural constraints, are better than disorganized, unilateral opt-outs. It is better for the rules to recognize that sometimes countries need their own maneuvering room than to leave such a possibility outside the scope of the rules.

An even better illustration of this principle at work is the WTO's Agree-ment on Safeguards (Art. XIX). The Safeguards Agreement allows countries to re-impose tariffs or quantitative restrictions under certain circumstances and for a limited time period, when countries experience a surge in imports of specific products and when such imports are determined to "cause or threaten to cause serious injury" to an industry at home. Aside from being temporary, the restrictions in question must be applied on a most-favored nation (MFN) basis, i.e., non-selectively, and affected exporters must receive compensation.

While the principle behind Safeguards is clear, the restrictions currently placed on it make less sense. Why limit the application of the clause to instances of injury to producers, for example, or require that it be triggered only by a surge in imports? It could be that the "injury" in question is a conflict with deeply-held values at home (say in the case of imports made using child labor or imposing environmental costs). Such injury could well be triggered by new information rather than by an import surge per se—consumers at home may discover unsavory facts about labor practices abroad or there may be new scientific information about safety or harm to the environment. In these instances, applying safeguard action on an MFN basis will not necessarily make sense (child labor may be a problem in Vietnam but not in Mauritius). Requiring compensation may not be appropriate either. In effect, the Agreement vests too many of the residual rights on trade interests and too few on the broader interests at stake.

We can envisage broadening the Safeguards Agreement to a wider set of circumstances in which the legitimacy of trade is at issue, subject to institutional and procedural prerequisites that minimize the risk of protectionist capture (and in particular the empowering of interests who would be harmed by trade restrictions). We can also imagine a similar "development box" provision, to facilitate the pursuit of developmental policies that may conflict with existing rules (e.g., subsidies). In effect, rich and poor nations would then be in the game of exchanging policy space instead of market access. Negotiators would be tasked not with maximizing the flow of trade and investment, but with designing rules that managed the interface among different regulatory environments. . . .

A broadened safeguard agreement—call it an agreement on social and developmental safeguards—would enable countries to opt out from their international obligations under specified circumstances. The process for obtaining such an exemption would be a domestic one, as in the case of AD and safeguards currently, but it would be subject to multilateral review to ensure procedural requirements are met. Any interested party would be allowed to seek an exemption or opt-out. One requirement would be for the plaintiff to make a compelling case that the international economic transactions in question are in conflict with a widely shared social or developmental norm at home. For example, an NGO may try to make the case that goods imported using child labor violate domestic views about what is an acceptable economic transaction or a consumer body may want to ban imports of certain goods from a country because of safety concerns.

A second procedural requirement would be to ensure that producer and other groups who have a stake in the international exchanges in question are able to present their case as well. In particular, the investigative body would be required to seek the views of those groups who would be adversely affected by the exemption. This is to ensure that the antiprotection views are given full hearing. One of the most important problems with AD and Safeguard proceedings at present is the lack of such a requirement. This prevents the full story from coming out and creates a protectionist bias in the system. When there is a truly widely-held norm or principle at stake, it would be difficult for the pro-trade groups to mount an effective defense. It is hard to imagine that a business lobby representing importers would defend free trade when it involves, for example, slave labor or exceptionally harsh and exploitative working conditions. However, in other instances, there are real trade-offs to consider, and a well-designed set of procedures—whether administrative or judicial—would help bring out the relevant considerations on all sides.

Finally, the ultimate decision would rest with a semiautonomous government body that would consider the testimony given and determine (a) whether there is sufficiently broad support for the exercise of some kind of opt-out; and (b) what the best remedies are in cases where the answer to (a) is affirmative. The decision would be subject to periodic review to ensure that protection does not become permanent. It would also be open to review in a multilateral setting (say the WTO) to ensure that multilaterally-agreed procedural requirements have been met.

A main advantage of the proposed scheme is that it forces deliberation and debate at the national level on the nature of the international economy, the economic gains it generates, and the circumstances under which domestic practices and needs come into conflict with it. This differs from the traditional, technocratic manner in which international governance is approached. It may seem overly messy and idealistic. But it has the virtue of bringing democracy to bear on these questions, and as such it has the potential to enhance the legitimacy of the global economy.

VII. CONCLUDING REMARKS

We can summarize the main arguments of this paper by using Figure 4, which underscores the mutual incompatibility of deep integration, national sovereignty, and democracy. I have argued that deep economic integration—a truly "flat" world economy to use Thomas Friedman's evocative phrase—is rendered infeasible by the fragmented nature of political sovereignty around the globe. Jurisdictional discontinuities impose transaction costs on international trade and finance that remain in place even when conventional barriers in the form of import duties and financial restrictions are removed.

Of course, deep integration could still be attainable if national sovereigns were to restrict their actions only to those that are fully compatible with its requirements. This is the "golden straitjacket" option depicted in Figure 4. Its real-world counterpart was the classical gold standard era of the 19th century. This is a model that rules out democracy, since it requires that political authorities be unresponsive to national policy imperatives and domestic needs. It is not a coincidence that the gold standard collapsed following the expansion of mass franchise and spread of democracy in the major industrial powers. Facing the conflicting needs of employment creation and parity with gold, a democratic Britain made its choice in favor of the former and went off gold in 1931.

FIGURE 4   The Political Trilemma of the World Economy: Pick Two, Any Two

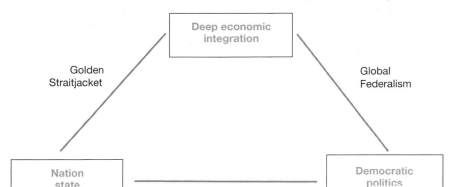

Bretton Woods Compromise

We could also theoretically combine democracy with deep integration by eroding national sovereignty and carrying democratic politics to the global level. This is the "global federalism" model in Figure 4. It corresponds to the U.S. or EU model writ large, on a global scale. Needless to say, this outcome does not seem practical anytime soon.

The only alternative we have left, therefore, is the Bretton Woods compromise, named after the golden era of 1950–1973 in which the world economy achieved unprecedented economic growth under a shallow model of economic integration. I have argued in this paper that our main challenge at the moment is to re-create this compromise, by designing a global architecture that is sensitive to the needs of countries—rich and poor alike—for policy space. This requires us to move away from a market-opening mindset, and to recognize that what nations need to do in order to maintain social peace and spur economic development in our second-best global economy often conflicts with the free movement of goods, services and capital. The only way to save globalization is to not push it too hard.

REFERENCES

Frieden, Jeffry. 2006. "Will Global Capitalism Fall Again?," Presentation for BRUEGEL's Essay and Lecture Series, Brussels, June.

Hiscox, Michael J., and Nicholas F. B. Smyth. 2006. "Is There Consumer Demand for Improved Labor Standards? Evidence from Field Experiments in Social Labeling," Department of Government, Harvard University.

James, Harold. 2001. "The End of Globalization: Lessons from the Great Depression," Harvard University Press, Cambridge: MA.

Krueger, Alan B. 1996. "Observations on International Labor Standards and Trade," NBER Working Paper W5632, June.

Mayda, Anna Maria, and Dani Rodrik. 2005. "Why Are Some Individuals (and Countries) More Protectionist than Others?" *European Economic Review*, August.

Prasad, Eswar, Raghuram Rajan, and Arvind Subramanian. 2007. "Foreign Capital and Economic Growth," Brookings Papers on Economic Activity 1, March.

Wolf, Martin. 2007. "The Growth of Nations," *Financial Times*, July 21.

World Bank. 2005. "Economic Growth in the 1990s: Learning from a Decade of Reform," Washington, DC: World Bank.

32

The Quiet Coup

SIMON JOHNSON

MIT professor Simon Johnson knows of what he speaks when he says there are important similarities between the global financial meltdown of 2008–2009—which emanated from the United States—and earlier financial crises in developing countries. As former chief economist at the International Monetary Fund, he had many opportunities to observe the characteristics of crisis economies. The most striking similarity reflects a domestic-societal logic: In the United States, just as in many emerging markets, the financial industry has effectively captured the government. Johnson argues that the "financial oligarchy" in the United States played a central role in reducing regulatory oversight in the run-up to the crisis. Then, after the inevitable collapse, this powerful interest group lobbied strongly for bailouts and against the needed regulatory reforms. This pattern of politics, Johnson argues, is very typical of "banana republics."

One thing you learn rather quickly when working at the International Monetary Fund is that no one is ever very happy to see you. Typically, your "clients" come in only after private capital has abandoned them, after regional trading-bloc partners have been unable to throw a strong enough lifeline, after last-ditch attempts to borrow from powerful friends like China or the European Union have fallen through. You're never at the top of anyone's dance card.

The reason, of course, is that the IMF specializes in telling its clients what they don't want to hear. I should know; I pressed painful changes on many foreign officials during my time there as chief economist in 2007 and 2008. And I felt the effects of IMF pressure, at least indirectly, when I worked with governments in Eastern Europe as they struggled after 1989, and with the private sector in Asia and Latin America during the crises of the late 1990s and early 2000s. Over that time, from every vantage point, I saw firsthand the steady flow of officials—from Ukraine, Russia, Thailand, Indonesia, South Korea, and elsewhere—trudging to the fund when circumstances were dire and all else had failed.

Every crisis is different, of course. Ukraine faced hyperinflation in 1994; Russia desperately needed help when its short-term-debt rollover scheme exploded in the summer of 1998; the Indonesian rupiah plunged in 1997, nearly leveling the corporate economy; that same year, South Korea's 30-year economic miracle ground to a halt when foreign banks suddenly refused to extend new credit.

But I must tell you, to IMF officials, all of these crises looked depressingly similar. Each country, of course, needed a loan, but more than that, each needed to make big changes so that the loan could really work. Almost always, countries in crisis need to learn to live within their means after a period of excess—exports must be increased, and imports cut—and the goal is to do this without the most horrible of recessions. Naturally, the fund's economists spend time figuring out the policies—budget, money supply, and the like—that make sense in this context. Yet the economic solution is seldom very hard to work out.

No, the real concern of the fund's senior staff, and the biggest obstacle to recovery, is almost invariably the politics of countries in crisis.

Typically, these countries are in a desperate economic situation for one simple reason—the powerful elites within them overreached in good times and took too many risks. Emerging-market governments and their private-sector allies commonly form a tight-knit—and, most of the time, genteel—oligarchy, running the country rather like a profit-seeking company in which they are the controlling shareholders. When a country like Indonesia or South Korea or Russia grows, so do the ambitions of its captains of industry. As masters of their mini-universe, these people make some investments that clearly benefit the broader economy, but they also start making bigger and riskier bets. They reckon—correctly, in most cases—that their political connections will allow them to push onto the government any substantial problems that arise.

In Russia, for instance, the private sector is now in serious trouble because, over the past five years or so, it borrowed at least $490 billion from global banks and investors on the assumption that the country's energy sector could support a permanent increase in consumption throughout the economy. As Russia's oligarchs spent this capital, acquiring other companies and embarking on ambitious investment plans that generated jobs, their importance to the political elite increased. Growing political support meant better access to lucrative contracts, tax breaks, and subsidies. And foreign investors could not have been more pleased; all other things being equal, they prefer to lend money to people who have the implicit backing of their national governments, even if that backing gives off the faint whiff of corruption.

But inevitably, emerging-market oligarchs get carried away; they waste money and build massive business empires on a mountain of debt. Local banks, sometimes pressured by the government, become too willing to extend credit to the elite and to those who depend on them. Overborrowing always ends badly, whether for an individual, a company, or a country. Sooner or later, credit conditions become tighter and no one will lend you money on anything close to affordable terms.

The downward spiral that follows is remarkably steep. Enormous companies teeter on the brink of default, and the local banks that have lent to them collapse. Yesterday's "public-private partnerships" are relabeled "crony capitalism." With credit unavailable, economic paralysis ensues, and conditions just get worse and worse. The government is forced to draw down its foreign-currency reserves to pay for imports, service debt, and cover private losses. But these reserves will eventually run out. If the country cannot right itself before that happens, it will default on its sovereign debt and become an economic pariah. The government, in its race to stop the bleeding, will typically need to wipe out some of the national champions—now hemorrhaging cash—and usually restructure a banking system that's gone badly out of balance. It will, in other words, need to squeeze at least some of its oligarchs.

Squeezing the oligarchs, though, is seldom the strategy of choice among emerging-market governments. Quite the contrary: at the outset of the crisis, the oligarchs are usually among the first to get extra help from the government, such as preferential access to foreign currency, or maybe a nice tax break, or—here's a classic Kremlin bailout technique—the assumption of private debt obligations by the government. Under duress, generosity toward old friends takes many innovative forms. Meanwhile, needing to squeeze *someone*, most emerging-market governments look first to ordinary working folk—at least until the riots grow too large.

Eventually, as the oligarchs in Putin's Russia now realize, some within the elite have to lose out before recovery can begin. It's a game of musical chairs: there just aren't enough currency reserves to take care of everyone, and the government cannot afford to take over private-sector debt completely.

So the IMF staff looks into the eyes of the minister of finance and decides whether the government is serious yet. The fund will give even a country like Russia a loan eventually, but first it wants to make sure Prime Minister Putin is ready, willing, and able to be tough on some of his friends. If he is not ready to throw former pals to the wolves, the fund can wait. And when he is ready, the fund is happy to make helpful suggestions—particularly with regard to wresting control of the banking system from the hands of the most incompetent and avaricious "entrepreneurs."

Of course, Putin's ex-friends will fight back. They'll mobilize allies, work the system, and put pressure on other parts of the government to get additional subsidies. In extreme cases, they'll even try subversion—including calling up their contacts in the American foreign-policy establishment, as the Ukrainians did with some success in the late 1990s.

Many IMF programs "go off track" (a euphemism) precisely because the government can't stay tough on erstwhile cronies, and the consequences are massive inflation or other disasters. A program "goes back on track" once the government prevails or powerful oligarchs sort out among themselves who will govern—and thus win or lose—under the IMF-supported plan. The real fight in

Thailand and Indonesia in 1997 was about which powerful families would lose their banks. In Thailand, it was handled relatively smoothly. In Indonesia, it led to the fall of President Suharto and economic chaos.

From long years of experience, the IMF staff knows its program will succeed—stabilizing the economy and enabling growth—only if at least some of the powerful oligarchs who did so much to create the underlying problems take a hit. This is the problem of all emerging markets.

BECOMING A BANANA REPUBLIC

In its depth and suddenness, the U.S. economic and financial crisis is shockingly reminiscent of moments we have recently seen in emerging markets (and only in emerging markets): South Korea (1997), Malaysia (1998), Russia and Argentina (time and again). In each of those cases, global investors, afraid that the country or its financial sector wouldn't be able to pay off mountainous debt, suddenly stopped lending. And in each case, that fear became self-fulfilling, as banks that couldn't roll over their debt did, in fact, become unable to pay. This is precisely what drove Lehman Brothers into bankruptcy on September 15, causing all sources of funding to the U.S. financial sector to dry up overnight. Just as in emerging-market crises, the weakness in the banking system has quickly rippled out into the rest of the economy, causing a severe economic contraction and hardship for millions of people.

But there's a deeper and more disturbing similarity: elite business interests—financiers, in the case of the U.S.—played a central role in creating the crisis, making ever-larger gambles, with the implicit backing of the government, until the inevitable collapse. More alarming, they are now using their influence to prevent precisely the sorts of reforms that are needed, and fast, to pull the economy out of its nosedive. The government seems helpless, or unwilling, to act against them.

Top investment bankers and government officials like to lay the blame for the current crisis on the lowering of U.S. interest rates after the dotcom bust or, even better—in a "buck stops somewhere else" sort of way—on the flow of savings out of China. Some on the right like to complain about Fannie Mae or Freddie Mac, or even about longer-standing efforts to promote broader home-ownership. And, of course, it is axiomatic to everyone that the regulators responsible for "safety and soundness" were fast asleep at the wheel.

But these various policies—lightweight regulation, cheap money, the unwritten Chinese-American economic alliance, the promotion of homeownership—had something in common. Even though some are traditionally associated with Democrats and some with Republicans, they *all* benefited the financial sector. Policy changes that might have forestalled the crisis but would have limited the financial sector's profits—such as Brooksley Born's now-famous attempts to regulate credit-default swaps at the Commodity Futures Trading Commission, in 1998—were ignored or swept aside.

The financial industry has not always enjoyed such favored treatment. But for the past 25 years or so, finance has boomed, becoming ever more powerful. The boom began with the Reagan years, and it only gained strength with the deregulatory policies of the Clinton and George W. Bush administrations. Several other factors helped fuel the financial industry's ascent. Paul Volcker's monetary policy in the 1980s, and the increased volatility in interest rates that accompanied it, made bond trading much more lucrative. The invention of securitization, interest-rate swaps, and credit-default swaps greatly increased the volume of transactions that bankers could make money on. And an aging and increasingly wealthy population invested more and more money in securities, helped by the invention of the IRA and the 401(k) plan. Together, these developments vastly increased the profit opportunities in financial services.

Not surprisingly, Wall Street ran with these opportunities. From 1973 to 1985, the financial sector never earned more than 16 percent of domestic corporate profits. In 1986, that figure reached 19 percent. In the 1990s, it oscillated between 21 percent and 30 percent, higher than it had ever been in the postwar period. This decade, it reached 41 percent. Pay rose just as dramatically. From 1948 to 1982, average compensation in the financial sector ranged between 99 percent and 108 percent of the average for all domestic private industries. From 1983, it shot upward, reaching 181 percent in 2007.

The great wealth that the financial sector created and concentrated gave bankers enormous political weight—a weight not seen in the U.S. since the era of J.P. Morgan (the man). In that period, the banking panic of 1907 could be stopped only by coordination among private-sector bankers: no government entity was able to offer an effective response. But that first age of banking oligarchs came to an end with the passage of significant banking regulation in response to the Great Depression; the reemergence of an American financial oligarchy is quite recent.

THE WALL STREET–WASHINGTON CORRIDOR

Of course, the U.S. is unique. And just as we have the world's most advanced economy, military, and technology, we also have its most advanced oligarchy.

In a primitive political system, power is transmitted through violence, or the threat of violence: military coups, private militias, and so on. In a less primitive system more typical of emerging markets, power is transmitted via money: bribes, kickbacks, and offshore bank accounts. Although lobbying and campaign contributions certainly play major roles in the American political system, old-fashioned corruption—envelopes stuffed with $100 bills—is probably a sideshow today, Jack Abramoff notwithstanding.

Instead, the American financial industry gained political power by amassing a kind of cultural capital—a belief system. Once, perhaps, what was good for General Motors was good for the country. Over the past decade, the attitude took hold that what was good for Wall Street was good for the country. The banking-and-securities industry has become one of the top contributors to political campaigns, but at the peak of its influence, it did not have to buy favors the way, for example, the tobacco companies or military contractors might have to. Instead, it benefited from the fact that Washington insiders already believed that large financial institutions and free-flowing capital markets were crucial to America's position in the world.

One channel of influence was, of course, the flow of individuals between Wall Street and Washington. Robert Rubin, once the co-chairman of Goldman Sachs, served in Washington as Treasury secretary under Clinton, and later became chairman of Citigroup's executive committee. Henry Paulson, CEO of Goldman Sachs during the long boom, became Treasury secretary under George W. Bush. John Snow, Paulson's predecessor, left to become chairman of Cerberus Capital Management, a large private-equity firm that also counts Dan Quayle among its executives. Alan Greenspan, after leaving the Federal Reserve, became a consultant to Pimco, perhaps the biggest player in international bond markets.

These personal connections were multiplied many times over at the lower levels of the past three presidential administrations, strengthening the ties between Washington and Wall Street. It has become something of a tradition for Goldman Sachs employees to go into public service after they leave the firm. The flow of Goldman alumni—including Jon Corzine, now the governor of New Jersey, along with Rubin and Paulson—not only placed people with Wall Street's worldview in the halls of power; it also helped create an image of Goldman (inside the Beltway, at least) as an institution that was itself almost a form of public service.

Wall Street is a very seductive place, imbued with an air of power. Its executives truly believe that they control the levers that make the world go round. A civil servant from Washington invited into their conference rooms, even if just for a meeting, could be forgiven for falling under their sway. Throughout my time at the IMF, I was struck by the easy access of leading financiers to the highest U.S. government officials, and the interweaving of the two career tracks. I vividly remember a meeting in early 2008—attended by top policy makers from a handful of rich countries—at which the chair casually proclaimed, to the room's general approval, that the best preparation for becoming a central-bank governor was to work first as an investment banker.

A whole generation of policy makers has been mesmerized by Wall Street, always and utterly convinced that whatever the banks said was true. Alan Greenspan's pronouncements in favor of unregulated financial markets are well known. Yet Greenspan was hardly alone. This is what Ben Bernanke, the man who succeeded him, said in 2006: "The management of market risk and credit risk has become increasingly sophisticated. . . . Banking organizations of all sizes have made substantial strides over the past two decades in their ability to measure and manage risks."

Of course, this was mostly an illusion. Regulators, legislators, and academics almost all assumed that the managers of these banks knew what they were doing. In retrospect, they didn't. AIG's Financial Products division, for instance, made $2.5 billion in pretax profits in 2005, largely by selling underpriced insurance on complex, poorly understood securities. Often described as "picking up nickels in front of a steamroller," this strategy is profitable in ordinary years, and catastrophic in bad ones. As of last fall, AIG had outstanding insurance on more than $400 billion in securities. To date, the U.S. government, in an effort to rescue the company, has committed about $180 billion in investments and loans to cover losses that AIG's sophisticated risk modeling had said were virtually impossible.

Wall Street's seductive power extended even (or especially) to finance and economics professors, historically confined to the cramped offices of universities and the pursuit of Nobel Prizes. As mathematical finance became more and more essential to practical finance, professors increasingly took positions as consultants or partners at financial institutions. Myron Scholes and Robert Merton, Nobel laureates both, were perhaps the most famous; they took board seats at the hedge fund Long-Term Capital Management in 1994, before the fund famously flamed out at the end of the decade. But many others beat similar paths. This migration gave the stamp of academic legitimacy (and the intimidating aura of intellectual rigor) to the burgeoning world of high finance.

As more and more of the rich made their money in finance, the cult of finance seeped into the culture at large. Works like *Barbarians at the Gate, Wall Street,* and *Bonfire of the Vanities*—all intended as cautionary tales— served only to increase Wall Street's mystique. Michael Lewis noted in *Portfolio* last year that when he wrote *Liar's Poker,* an insider's account of the financial industry, in 1989, he had hoped the book might provoke outrage at Wall Street's hubris and excess. Instead, he found himself "knee-deep in letters from students at Ohio State who wanted to know if I had any other secrets to share. . . . They'd read my book as a how-to manual." Even Wall Street's criminals, like Michael Milken and Ivan Boesky, became larger than life. In a society that celebrates the idea of making money, it was easy to infer that the interests of the financial sector were the same as the interests of the country—and that the winners in the financial sector knew better what was good for America than did the career civil servants in Washington. Faith in free financial markets grew into conventional wisdom—trumpeted on the editorial pages of *The Wall Street Journal* and on the floor of Congress.

From this confluence of campaign finance, personal connections, and ideology there flowed, in just the past decade, a river of deregulatory policies that is, in hindsight, astonishing:

- insistence on free movement of capital across borders;
- the repeal of Depression-era regulations separating commercial and investment banking;
- a congressional ban on the regulation of credit-default swaps;
- major increases in the amount of leverage allowed to investment banks;
- a light (dare I say *invisible?*) hand at the Securities and Exchange Commission in its regulatory enforcement;
- an international agreement to allow banks to measure their own riskiness;
- and an intentional failure to update regulations so as to keep up with the tremendous pace of financial innovation.

The mood that accompanied these measures in Washington seemed to swing between nonchalance and outright celebration: finance unleashed, it was thought, would continue to propel the economy to greater heights.

AMERICA'S OLIGARCHS AND THE FINANCIAL CRISIS

The oligarchy and the government policies that aided it did not alone cause the financial crisis that exploded last year. Many other factors contributed, including excessive borrowing by households and lax lending standards out on the fringes of the financial world. But major commercial and investment banks—and the hedge funds that ran alongside them—were the big beneficiaries of the twin housing and equity-market bubbles of this decade, their profits fed by an ever-increasing volume of transactions founded on a relatively small base of actual physical assets. Each time a loan was sold, packaged, securitized, and resold, banks took their transaction fees, and the hedge funds buying those securities reaped ever-larger fees as their holdings grew.

Because everyone was getting richer, and the health of the national economy depended so heavily on growth in real estate and finance, no one in Washington had any incentive to question what was going on. Instead, Fed Chairman Greenspan and President Bush insisted metronomically that the economy was fundamentally sound and that the tremendous growth in complex securities and credit-default swaps was evidence of a healthy economy where risk was distributed safely.

In the summer of 2007, signs of strain started appearing. The boom had produced so much debt that even a small economic stumble could cause major problems, and rising delinquencies in subprime mortgages proved the stumbling block. Ever since, the financial sector and the federal government have been behaving exactly the way one would expect them to, in light of past emerging-market crises.

By now, the princes of the financial world have of course been stripped naked as leaders and strategists—at least in the eyes of most Americans. But as the months have rolled by, financial elites have continued to assume that their position as the economy's favored children is safe, despite the wreckage they have caused.

Stanley O'Neal, the CEO of Merrill Lynch, pushed his firm heavily into the mortgage-backed-securities market at its peak in 2005 and 2006; in October 2007, he acknowledged, "The bottom line is, we—I—got it wrong by being overexposed to subprime, and we suffered as a result of impaired liquidity in that market. No one is more disappointed than I am in that result." O'Neal took home a $14 million bonus in 2006; in 2007, he walked away from Merrill with a severance package worth $162 million, although it is presumably worth much less today.

In October, John Thain, Merrill Lynch's final CEO, reportedly lobbied his board of directors for a bonus of $30 million or more, eventually reducing his demand to $10 million in December; he withdrew the request, under a firestorm of protest, only after it was leaked to *The Wall Street Journal*. Merrill Lynch as a whole was no better: it moved its bonus payments, $4 billion in total, forward to December, presumably to avoid the possibility that they would be reduced by Bank of America, which would own Merrill beginning on January 1. Wall Street paid out $18 billion in year-end bonuses last year to its New York City employees, after the government disbursed $243 billion in emergency assistance to the financial sector.

In a financial panic, the government must respond with both speed and overwhelming force. The root problem is uncertainty—in our case, uncertainty about whether the major banks have sufficient assets to cover their liabilities. Half measures combined with wishful thinking and a wait-and-see attitude cannot overcome this uncertainty. And the longer the response takes, the longer the uncertainty will stymie the flow of credit, sap consumer confidence, and cripple the economy—ultimately making the problem much harder to solve. Yet the principal characteristics of the government's response to the financial crisis have been delay, lack of transparency, and an unwillingness to upset the financial sector.

The response so far is perhaps best described as "policy by deal": when a major financial institution gets into trouble, the Treasury Department and the Federal Reserve engineer a bailout over the weekend and announce on Monday that everything is fine. In March 2008, Bear Stearns was sold to JP Morgan Chase in what looked to many like a gift to JP Morgan. (Jamie Dimon, JP Morgan's CEO, sits on the board of directors of the Federal Reserve Bank of New York, which, along with the Treasury Department, brokered the deal.) In September, we saw the sale of Merrill Lynch to Bank of America, the first bailout of AIG, and the takeover and immediate sale of Washington Mutual to JP Morgan—all of which were brokered by the government. In October, nine large banks were recapitalized on the same day behind closed doors in Washington. This, in turn, was followed by additional bailouts for Citigroup, AIG, Bank of America, Citigroup (again), and AIG (again).

Some of these deals may have been reasonable responses to the immediate situation. But it was never clear (and still isn't) what combination of interests was being served, and how. Treasury and the Fed did not act according to any publicly articulated principles, but just worked out a transaction and claimed it was the best that could be done under the circumstances. This was late-night, backroom dealing, pure and simple.

Throughout the crisis, the government has taken extreme care not to upset the interests of the financial institutions, or to question the basic outlines of the system that got us here. In September 2008, Henry Paulson asked Congress for $700 billion to buy toxic assets from banks, with no strings attached and no judicial review of his purchase decisions. Many observers suspected that the purpose was to overpay for those assets and thereby take the problem off the banks' hands—indeed, that is the only way that buying toxic assets would have helped anything. Perhaps because there was no way to make such a blatant subsidy politically acceptable, that plan was shelved.

Instead, the money was used to recapitalize banks, buying shares in them on terms that were grossly favorable to the banks themselves. As the crisis has deepened and financial institutions have needed more help, the government has gotten more and more creative in figuring out ways to provide banks with subsidies that are too complex for the general public to understand. The first AIG bailout, which was on relatively good terms for the taxpayer, was supplemented by three further bailouts whose terms were more AIG-friendly. The second Citigroup bailout and the Bank of America bailout included complex asset guarantees that provided the banks with insurance at below-market rates. The third Citigroup bailout, in late February, converted government-owned preferred stock to common stock at a price significantly higher than the market price—a subsidy that probably even most *Wall Street Journal* readers would miss on first reading. And the convertible preferred shares that the Treasury will buy under the new Financial Stability Plan give the conversion option (and thus the upside) to the banks, not the government.

This latest plan—which is likely to provide cheap loans to hedge funds and others so that they can buy distressed bank assets at relatively high prices—has been heavily influenced by the financial sector, and Treasury has made no secret of that. As Neel Kashkari, a senior Treasury official under both Henry Paulson and Tim Geithner (and a Goldman alum) told Congress in March, "We had received inbound unsolicited proposals from people in the private sector saying, 'We have capital on the sidelines; we want to go after [distressed bank] assets.'" And the plan lets them do just that: "By marrying government capital—taxpayer capital—with private-sector capital and providing financing, you can enable those investors to then go after those assets at a price that makes sense for the investors and at a price that makes sense for the banks." Kashkari didn't mention anything about what makes sense for the third group involved: the taxpayers.

Even leaving aside fairness to taxpayers, the government's velvet-glove approach with the banks is deeply troubling, for one simple reason: it is inadequate to change the behavior of a financial sector accustomed to doing business on its own terms, at a time when that behavior *must* change. As an unnamed senior bank official said to *The New York Times* last fall, "It doesn't matter how much Hank Paulson gives us, no one is going to lend a nickel until the economy turns." But there's the rub: the economy can't recover until the banks are healthy and willing to lend.

THE WAY OUT

Looking just at the financial crisis (and leaving aside some problems of the larger economy), we face at least two major, interrelated problems. The first is a desperately ill banking sector that threatens to choke off any incipient recovery that the fiscal stimulus might generate. The second is a political balance of power that gives the financial sector a veto over public policy, even as that sector loses popular support.

Big banks, it seems, have only gained political strength since the crisis began. And this is not surprising. With the financial system so fragile, the damage that a major bank failure could cause—Lehman was small relative to Citigroup or Bank of America—is much greater than it would be during ordinary times. The banks have been exploiting this fear as they wring favorable deals out of Washington. Bank of America obtained its second bailout package (in January) after warning the government that it might not be able to go through with the acquisition of Merrill Lynch, a prospect that Treasury did not want to consider.

The challenges the United States faces are familiar territory to the people at the IMF. If you hid the name of the country and just showed them the numbers, there is no doubt what old IMF hands would say: nationalize troubled banks and break them up as necessary.

In some ways, of course, the government has already taken control of the banking system. It has essentially guaranteed the liabilities of the biggest banks, and it is their only plausible source of capital today. Meanwhile, the Federal Reserve has taken on a major role in providing credit to the economy— the function that the private banking sector is supposed to be performing, but isn't. Yet there are limits to what the Fed can do on its own; consumers and businesses are still dependent on banks that lack the balance sheets and the incentives to make the loans the economy needs, and the government has no real control over who runs the banks, or over what they do.

At the root of the banks' problems are the large losses they have undoubtedly taken on their securities and loan portfolios. But they don't want to recognize the full extent of their losses, because that would likely expose them as insolvent. So they talk down the problem, and ask for handouts that aren't enough to make them healthy (again, they can't reveal the size of the handouts that would be necessary for that), but are enough to keep them upright a little longer. This behavior is corrosive: unhealthy banks either don't lend (hoarding money to shore up reserves) or they make desperate gambles on high-risk loans and investments that could pay off big, but probably won't pay off at all. In either case, the economy suffers further, and as it does, bank assets themselves continue to deteriorate—creating a highly destructive vicious cycle.

To break this cycle, the government must force the banks to acknowledge the scale of their problems. As the IMF understands (and as the U.S. government itself has insisted to multiple emerging-market countries in the past), the most direct way to do this is nationalization. Instead, Treasury is trying to negotiate bailouts bank by bank, and behaving as if the banks hold all the cards—contorting the terms of each deal to minimize government ownership while forswearing government influence over bank strategy or operations. Under these conditions, cleaning up bank balance sheets is impossible.

Nationalization would not imply permanent state ownership. The IMF's advice would be, essentially: scale up the standard Federal Deposit Insurance Corporation process. An FDIC "intervention" is basically a government-managed bankruptcy procedure for banks. It would allow the government to wipe out bank shareholders, replace failed management, clean up the balance sheets, and then sell the banks back to the private sector. The main advantage is immediate recognition of the problem so that it can be solved before it grows worse.

The government needs to inspect the balance sheets and identify the banks that cannot survive a severe recession. These banks should face a choice: write down your assets to their true value and raise private capital within 30 days, or be taken over by the government. The government would write down the toxic assets of banks taken into receivership—recognizing reality—and transfer those assets to a separate government entity, which would attempt to salvage whatever value is possible for the taxpayer (as the Resolution Trust Corporation did after the savings-and-loan debacle of the 1980s). The rump banks—cleansed and able to lend safely, and hence trusted again by other lenders and investors—could then be sold off.

Cleaning up the megabanks will be complex. And it will be expensive for the taxpayer; according to the latest IMF numbers, the cleanup of the banking system would probably cost close to $1.5 trillion (or 10 percent of our GDP) in the long term. But only decisive government action—exposing the full extent of the financial rot and restoring some set of banks to publicly verifiable health—can cure the financial sector as a whole.

This may seem like strong medicine. But in fact, while necessary, it is insufficient. The second problem the U.S. faces—the power of the oligarchy—is just as important as the immediate crisis of lending. And the advice from the IMF on this front would again be simple: break the oligarchy.

Oversize institutions disproportionately influence public policy; the major banks we have today draw much of their power from being too big to fail.

Nationalization and re-privatization would not change that; while the replacement of the bank executives who got us into this crisis would be just and sensible, ultimately, the swapping-out of one set of powerful managers for another would change only the names of the oligarchs.

Ideally, big banks should be sold in medium-size pieces, divided regionally or by type of business. Where this proves impractical—since we'll want to sell the banks quickly—they could be sold whole, but with the requirement of being broken up within a short time. Banks that remain in private hands should also be subject to size limitations.

This may seem like a crude and arbitrary step, but it is the best way to limit the power of individual institutions in a sector that is essential to the economy as a whole. Of course, some people will complain about the "efficiency costs" of a more fragmented banking system, and these costs are real. But so are the costs when a bank that is too big to fail—a financial weapon of mass self-destruction—explodes. Anything that is too big to fail is too big to exist.

To ensure systematic bank breakup, and to prevent the eventual reemergence of dangerous behemoths, we also need to overhaul our antitrust legislation. Laws put in place more than 100 years ago to combat industrial monopolies were not designed to address the problem we now face. The problem in the financial sector today is not that a given firm might have enough market share to influence prices; it is that one firm or a small set of interconnected firms, by failing, can bring down the economy. The Obama administration's fiscal stimulus evokes FDR, but what we need to imitate here is Teddy Roosevelt's trust-busting.

Caps on executive compensation, while redolent of populism, might help restore the political balance of power and deter the emergence of a new oligarchy. Wall Street's main attraction—to the people who work there and to the government officials who were only too happy to bask in its reflected glory—has been the astounding amount of money that could be made. Limiting that money would reduce the allure of the financial sector and make it more like any other industry.

Still, outright pay caps are clumsy, especially in the long run. And most money is now made in largely unregulated private hedge funds and private-equity firms, so lowering pay would be complicated. Regulation and taxation should be part of the solution. Over time, though, the largest part may involve more transparency and competition, which would bring financial-industry fees down. To those who say this would drive financial activities to other countries, we can now safely say: fine.

TWO PATHS

To paraphrase Joseph Schumpeter, the early-20th-century economist, everyone has elites; the important thing is to change them from time to time. If the U.S. were just another country, coming to the IMF with hat in hand, I might be fairly optimistic about its future. Most of the emerging-market crises that

I've mentioned ended relatively quickly, and gave way, for the most part, to relatively strong recoveries. But this, alas, brings us to the limit of the analogy between the U.S. and emerging markets.

Emerging-market countries have only a precarious hold on wealth, and are weaklings globally. When they get into trouble, they quite literally run out of money—or at least out of foreign currency, without which they cannot survive. They *must* make difficult decisions; ultimately, aggressive action is baked into the cake. But the U.S., of course, is the world's most powerful nation, rich beyond measure, and blessed with the exorbitant privilege of paying its foreign debts in its own currency, which it can print. As a result, it could very well stumble along for years—as Japan did during its lost decade—never summoning the courage to do what it needs to do, and never really recovering. A clean break with the past—involving the takeover and cleanup of major banks—hardly looks like a sure thing right now. Certainly no one at the IMF can force it.

In my view, the U.S. faces two plausible scenarios. The first involves complicated bank-by-bank deals and a continual drumbeat of (repeated) bailouts, like the ones we saw in February with Citigroup and AIG. The administration will try to muddle through, and confusion will reign.

Boris Fyodorov, the late finance minister of Russia, struggled for much of the past 20 years against oligarchs, corruption, and abuse of authority in all its forms. He liked to say that confusion and chaos were very much in the interests of the powerful—letting them take things, legally and illegally, with impunity. When inflation is high, who can say what a piece of property is really worth? When the credit system is supported by byzantine government arrangements and backroom deals, how do you know that you aren't being fleeced?

Our future could be one in which continued tumult feeds the looting of the financial system, and we talk more and more about exactly how our oligarchs became bandits and how the economy just can't seem to get into gear.

The second scenario begins more bleakly, and might end that way too. But it does provide at least some hope that we'll be shaken out of our torpor. It goes like this: the global economy continues to deteriorate, the banking system in east-central Europe collapses, and—because eastern Europe's banks are mostly owned by western European banks—justifiable fears of government insolvency spread throughout the Continent. Creditors take further hits and confidence falls further. The Asian economies that export manufactured goods are devastated, and the commodity producers in Latin America and Africa are not much better off. A dramatic worsening of the global environment forces the U.S. economy, already staggering, down onto both knees. The baseline growth rates used in the administration's current budget are increasingly seen as unrealistic, and the rosy "stress scenario" that the U.S. Treasury is currently using to evaluate banks' balance sheets becomes a source of great embarrassment.

Under this kind of pressure, and faced with the prospect of a national and global collapse, minds may become more concentrated.

The conventional wisdom among the elite is still that the current slump "cannot be as bad as the Great Depression." This view is wrong. What we face now could, in fact, be worse than the Great Depression—because the world is now so much more interconnected and because the banking sector is now so big. We face a synchronized downturn in almost all countries, a weakening of confidence among individuals and firms, and major problems for government finances. If our leadership wakes up to the potential consequences, we may yet see dramatic action on the banking system and a breaking of the old elite. Let us hope it is not then too late.

ACKNOWLEDGMENTS

It is in violation of the law to reproduce these selections by any means whatsoever without the written permission of the copyright holder.

Daron Acemoglu: "Root Causes," *Finance and Development*, Vol. 40, No. 2, June 2003, pp. 27–30. Copyright © 2003 by the International Monetary Fund. Reprinted by permission of the International Monetary Fund.

James E. Alt and Michael Gilligan: "The Political Economy of Trading States: Factor Specificity, Collective Action Problems and Domestic Political Solutions," *The Journal of Political Philosophy*, Vol. 2, No. 2, 1994, pp. 165–66, 168–88. Copyright © 1994 Blackwell Publishing Ltd. Reproduced with permission of Blackwell Publishing Ltd.

Michael A. Bailey, Judith Goldstein, and Barry R. Weingast: "The Institutional Roots of American Trade Policy: Politics, Coalitions, and International Trade," *World Politics*, Vol. 49, No. 3, April 1997, pp. 309–338. © 1997 The Johns Hopkins University Press. Reprinted with the permission of Cambridge University Press.

J. Lawrence Broz: "The Domestic Politics of International Monetary Order: The Gold Standard," *Contested Social Orders and International Politics*, edited by David Skidmore, pp. 53–84. Copyright © 1997 by Vanderbilt University Press. Reprinted with permission.

Richard E. Caves: "The Multinational Enterprise as an Economic Organization," *Multinational Enterprise and Economic Analysis, 2nd Edition*, pp. 1–5, 7–9, 11–21, 23. © Cambridge University Press 1996. Reprinted with the permission of Cambridge University Press.

Benjamin J. Cohen: "The Triad and the Unholy Trinity: Lessons for the Pacific Region," Richard Higgott, Richard Leaver, and John Ravenhill, eds., *Pacific Economic Relations in the 1990s: Cooperation or Conflict?*, pp. 133–139, 146–149, 152–155. © Australian Fulbright Commission, 1993. Reprinted by permission of the publisher, Allen & Unwin Pty Ltd, www.allenandunwin.com.

Cletus C. Coughlin: Excerpted from "The Controversy Over Free Trade: The Gap Between Economists and the General Public," Federal Reserve Bank of St. Louis *Review*, January/February 2002, Vol. 84, Issue 1, pp. 1–21. http://research.stlouisfed.org/publications/review/02/01/1-22Coughlin.pdf. Reprinted with permission.

Alan V. Deardorff and Robert M. Stern: "What You Should Know About Globalization and the World Trade Organization," *Review of International Economics*, Vol. 10, No. 3, 2002, pp. 404–18, 421. Copyright © 2002 Blackwell Publishing Ltd. Reproduced with permission of Blackwell Publishing Ltd.

David Dollar: "Globalization, Poverty, and Inequality since 1980," *The World Bank Research Observer*, Vol. 20, No. 2, 2005. Copyright © 2005 by The World Bank. Reprinted by permission of Oxford University Press.

584 ▪ Acknowledgments

Daniel Drezner: "Globalization and Policy Convergence," *International Studies Review*, Vol. 3, No. 1, 2001, pp. 53–78. Copyright © 2001 International Studies Association. Reproduced with permission of Blackwell Publishing Ltd.

Barry Eichengreen: "Hegemonic Stability Theories of the International Monetary System," Cooper, Richard N., ed. *Can Nations Agree? Issues in International Economic Cooperation*. Pp. 255–287. © 1989, the Brookings Institution. Reprinted with permission.

"The Political Economy of the Smoot-Hawley Tariff," *Research in Economic History*, Vol. 12 (1989), pp. 1–43. © Emerald Group Publishing. Reprinted by permission of the publisher.

Zachary Elkins, Andrew T. Guzman, and Beth A. Simmons: "Competing for Capital: The Diffusion of Bilateral Investment Treaties 1960–2000," *International Organization*, Vol. 60, Issue 4, 2006, pp. 811–846. Copyright © 2006 The IO Foundation and Cambridge University Press. Reprinted with the permission of Cambridge University Press.

Jeffrey A. Frankel: "Globalization of the Economy," Nye, Joseph S. Jr. and John D. Donahue, eds., *Governance in a Globalizing World*, pp. 45–71. © 2000, Visions of Governance for the 21st Century. Reprinted with permission of the Brookings Institution.

"The Environment and Economic Globalization," from *Globalization: What's New?*, ed. Weinstein. Copyright © 2005 Council on Foreign Relations. Reprinted with permission of Columbia University Press.

Richard B. Freeman: "Are Your Wages Set In Beijing?" *Journal of Economic Perspectives*, Vol. 9, No. 3, Summer 1995, pp. 15–32. © 1995 American Economic Association. Reprinted with permission.

Jeffry A. Frieden: "Globalization and Exchange Rate Policy," *The Future of Globalization: Explorations in Light of Recent Turbulence*, ed. Ernesto Zedillo, pp. 344–357. © 2008 Jeffry A. Frieden. Reprinted by permission of Routledge, an imprint of the Taylor & Francis Group.

"International Investment and Colonial Control: A New Interpretation," *International Organization*, 48:4 (Autumn, 1994), pp. 559–593. © 1994 by the World Peace Foundation and the Massachusetts Institute of Technology. Reprinted by permission of MIT Press.

Matthew Gabel: "Divided Opinion, Common Currency: The Political Economy of Public Support EMU," *The Political Economy of European Monetary Unification*, edited by Barry Eichengreen and Jeffry A. Frieden, pp. 49–50, 54–62, 64–72. Copyright © 2001 by Westview Press. Reprinted by permission of Westview Press, a member of Perseus Books Group.

Peter Alexis Gourevitch: "International Trade, Domestic Coalitions and Liberty: Comparative Responses to the Crisis of 1873–1896," *The Journal of Interdisciplin-*

ary History, 8:2 (Autumn, 1977), pp. 281–313. © 1977 by the Massachusetts Institute of Technology and the editors of The Journal of Interdisciplinary History. Reprinted by permission of MIT Press.

Simon Johnson: "The Quiet Coup." Copyright 2009 The Atlantic Media Co., as first published in *The Atlantic* Magazine, May 2009. Distributed by Tribune Media Services. Reprinted with permission.

Stephen D. Krasner: "State Power and the Structure of International Trade," *World Politics*, Vol. 28, No. 3, April 1976, pp. 317–343. © 1976 The Johns Hopkins University Press. Reprinted with the permission of Cambridge University Press.

David Lake: "British and American Hegemony Compared: Lessons for the Current Era of Decline," *History, the White House and the Kremlin: Statesmen as Historians*, edited by Michael Fry, pp. 106–122. © Michael Fry, 1991. Reprinted by kind permission of the author and Continuum International Publishing Group.

Dani Rodrik: "How To Save Globalization From Its Cheerleaders," *Journal of International Trade & Diplomacy*, Vol. 1, No. 2, Fall 2007, pp. 1–33. Reprinted with permission.

Ronald Rogowski: From *Commerce and Coalitions*, pp. 3–13, 16–20. © 1989 Princeton University Press, 1990 paperback edition. Reprinted by permission of Princeton University Press.

Razeen Sally: "The Political Economy of Trade Policy Reform: Lessons from Developing Countries," *Journal of International Trade & Diplomacy*, Vol. 2, No. 2, Winter 2008, pp. 55–61, 66–92. Reprinted with permission.

Kenneth F. Scheve and Matthew J. Slaughter: "A New Deal for Globalization," *Foreign Affairs*, Vol. 86, No. 4, July/August 2007, pp. 34–47. Reprinted by permission of *Foreign Affairs*. Copyright 2007 by the Council on Foreign Relations, Inc. www.ForeignAffairs.com.

Sergio L. Schmukler: "Financial Globalization: Gain and Pain for Developing Countries," from Federal Reserve Bank of Atlanta *Economic Review*, 2nd Quarter 2004, pp. 39–66. Reprinted by permission of the author.

Cheryl Schonhardt-Bailey: "Introduction" from *Free Trade: The Repeal of the Corn Laws*. © Thoemmes Press 1996. Reprinted by kind permission of Continuum International Publishing Group.

Kenneth L. Sokoloff and Stanley L. Engerman: "History Lessons: Institutions, Factors Endowments, and Paths of Development in the New World," *Journal of Economic Perspectives*, Vol. 14, No. 3, Summer 2000, pp. 217–232. © 2000 American Economic Association. Reprinted with permission.

Shah M. Tarzi: "Third World Governments and Multinational Corporations: Dynamics of Host's Bargaining Power," *International Relations*, Vol. 10, No. 3,

237–249 (1991). Copyright © 1991, Sage Publications. Reprinted by permission of Sage.

Jeffrey G. Williamson: Used with permission of World Bank, from "Globalization and Inequality, Past and Present," *The World Bank Research Observer*, Vol. 12, No. 2, August 1997, pp. 117–135, © 1997 The International Bank for Reconstruction and Development; permission conveyed through Copyright Clearance Center, Inc.